The Shemitta Sensation

A Deeper Look into the Jewish Sabbatical Year

Written by:
Rabbi Binyamin Zimmerman

HES ER
Hebrew/English Source Based Educational Resources

MIZRACHI
WORLD MOVEMENT
MIZRACHI PRESS

The Shemitta Sensation
A Deeper Look into the Jewish Sabbatical Year

ISBN 978-1-7377617-0-9, Softcover

Written By:	Rabbi Binyamin Zimmerman
Editor:	Meira Mintz
Copy Editing:	Sherry Zimmerman, Rabbi Jonathan Ziring
Technical Assistance:	Noam Hayman, Yehuda Karol
Graphics and Typesetting:	Shulamit Meir
Cover Design:	Ayala Zagori, Shulamit Meir
Graphic Picture Design:	Ayala Zagori

Please send questions and correspondence to Binyamin Zimmerman
ravbinyamin@mizrachi.org

First Printing: Jerusalem, Israel 2021
Mizrachi Press

Dedicated in Loving Memory of
Aryeh Leib ben HaRav Yehoshua (Larry) Westreich

The reader of this book will undoubtedly be struck by the dedication and perseverance necessary to properly fulfill the dictates of shemitta. Unlike most societal norms we are acquainted with, *shemitta* does not seem to benefit the land-owner, as it mandates the complete sacrifice of his crop for others. It seems remarkable, even supernatural, that Jewish farmers have been willing to make that sacrifice. Indeed, it is a testament to the deep connection between the Jewish People and the Land of Israel, which has enabled us to overcome the challenges of *mitzvah* observance throughout history and in current times.

It is thus fitting that this important work be dedicated in memory of a person who embodied the connection between the Jewish People and their land. Larry Westreich (Aryeh Leib ben HaRav Yehoshua), lived in the diaspora, but spent significant time in Eretz Yisrael and extended substantial support to its inhabitants. He developed connections with many Israeli organizations, ranging from critical medical-care organizations, to Yeshivot and Torah centers, to the lone soldiers of the Israeli Defense Force. He believed deeply in the sacredness of the Land of Israel, especially the Old City of Jerusalem, and he expended much time and resources to enable proper honor to the Kotel and surrounding areas.

The pinnacle of Larry's altruism was demonstrated each and every Shabbat he spent in Israel, as he would make his way back to his hotel from the Kotel. Every week, he would invite complete strangers – students studying in Israel, soldiers, or poor people on the street – to enjoy a lavish meal, without regard for cost or quantity. To his mind, the more the better. In this regard, he reflected the generosity of the farmer during *shemitta*, who opens his doors to the inhabitants of the land.

We are confident that Larry, the epitome of generosity, would have greatly enjoyed studying the concepts we will explore in this book, which reflect his character and worldview. May his memory be in an inspiration, providing a model of the courage necessary to implement the lessons of *shemitta*.

The Westreich Family

יוסף צבי רימון

ראש הישיבה ורב המרכז האקדמי לב
רבה של אלון שבות דרום

מכתב ברכה לספר שמיטה

שמחתי מאוד לראות חלקים מספרו של הרב בנימין צימרמן שליט"א על השמיטה. כפי שניתן לראות
בספר, לרב צימרמן שליטה בדברי חז"ל, ראשונים ואחרונים, יכולת העמקה וניתוח, ויכולת לסדר את
הדברים בצורה יפה.

ספר השמיטה של הרב צימרמן נותן מבט עמוק על השמיטה, העובר גם על פרשיות השמיטה בתורה, וגם
על ההשפעה הרחבה של השמיטה. השפעת השמיטה גם על עולמנו הרוחני וגם על עולמנו החברתי.

שמיטה זו מצווה מרגשת במיוחד. אלפי שנים לא היינו בארץ ישראל, ולא זכינו לקיום את מצוות השמיטה.
השמיטה, מסמלת אפוא שלב נוסף בתהליך גאולתנו. גם בעניין זה נגע הרב צימרמן בספרו, וחיבר בין
השמיטה ובין הגאולה ההולכת ומתגלה לנגד עינינו.

גם הפן הכלכלי בשמיטה, בשמיטת הכספים ובצדקה, מקבל התייחסות רצינית בספרו של הרב צימרמן,
ומאפשר לראות כיצד הכלכלה היהודית נותנת מענה לצדדים חשובים כל כך, גם במציאות המודרנית.

הרב צימרמן הוא תלמיד חכם וירא שמים, ובע"ה שיזכה להוציא ספרים נוספים, להמשיך ללמוד וללמד,
להגדיל תורה ולהאדירה.

ברכת ה' עליכם,

MIZRACHI
WORLD MOVEMENT

It is a great honor for us at Mizrachi to partner with Rabbi Binyamin Zimmerman in this wonderful publication, The Shemitta Sensation: A Deeper Look Into the Jewish Sabbatical Year.

Rabbi Zimmerman is the Head of Mizrachi's Semicha program and a senior member of our leadership and educational teams driving our many leadership programs. He combines the twin qualities of outstanding scholarship as an erudite תלמיד חכם with being deeply caring and compassionate towards his many talmidim. It is, therefore, a privilege for us to partner further with Rav Binyamin in this important and timely publication as part of the Mizrachi Press. The aim of Mizrachi Press is the dissemination of the unique ideology of תורת ארץ ישראל. The centrality of the land of Israel is clear in תורה שבעל פה and תורה שבכתב and is a central axis around which Torah Judaism revolves. The Shemitta year in general, and this publication in particular, is a sterling example of this.

Of the many gifts that the Jewish people has given the world, one of the remarkable ones is the concept of שבת – both the weekly Sabbath as well as the Sabbatical year. The Torah consistently uses the word שבת to describe both the seventh day and the seventh year, Shemitta, and both are considered a שבת להשם, a time designated to G-d and heavenly pursuits. What the Shabbat is to the individual Jew so is the Shemitta year to Jewish society in the Land of Israel. Both are designed to remind us that we are so much more than what we are able to produce for our material benefit and individual and collective sustenance. The frenetic urgency of results and output inevitably associated with industry and productivity must be tempered with spiritual meaning and ethical values. The weekly Sabbath and Sabbatical year are the times for resetting our spiritual compass, giving primacy to cherished relationships and reconnecting with our core values: a time of perspective and wholeness.

These and many other themes are explored deeply and broadly throughout this unique book. It is indeed a sensation combining analysis of the underlying philosophies and values at the heart of the extraordinary Shemitta year and its vision in how it can transform the lives of an entire society, serving as a source of inspiration to the world.

Yasher Kochacha, Rav Binyamin.

With friendship,

Rabbi Doron Perez
Executive Chairman
Ellul 5781

Acknowledgments

For the past two thousand years, few Jews have enjoyed the opportunity of *shemitta* observance. We live in a special time, as the Jewish population in the Land of Israel continues to grow and the *mitzvot hateluyot ba'aretz*, the agricultural *mitzvot* unique to Israel, play a more significant role in our lives. *Mitzvot* that Jews in the past could only dream of fulfilling have become central to our religious experience. The chance to write about this topic is thus a precious opportunity.

Ever since I made *aliya*, I have been enthralled by *shemitta*. The more I learned about it, the more I connected to it. The unhappy reactions of all too many who weren't excited about *shemitta* – and were quite vocal about it – rubbed me the wrong way. Would others share my *shemitta* excitement if they had the opportunity to learn more about it? I searched for comprehensive English-language works on the more profound messages of *shemitta*, but I failed to find any.

The idea of writing such a work to fill the need seemed important, but the endeavor appeared to be a formidable challenge that I lacked the time and wherewithal to complete. Seven years ago, Rabbi Reuven Zeigler suggested a more realistic plan. He proposed writing a series for Yeshivat Har Etzion's Virtual Beit Midrash on the "Philosophy of *Shemitta*," in advance of the 5775 (2014-2015) *shemitta* year, which would cover thirty lessons on the topic. Although less comprehensive than I had initially envisioned, he correctly noted that it would ensure I would be committed to writing about the topic throughout the year and that it would serve as the basis for a more comprehensive work on the topic. I thank Rabbi Zeigler for his advice, and he along with Rav Ezra Bick for the opportunity to write that series, which demanded the initial research necessary for developing many of the ideas in this book.

With the publication of the "Philosophy of *Shemitta*" series, the seven-year hourglass started ticking. My initial plan to find some spare time over the last year and a half to write this book didn't consider several factors – chiefly among them, Covid-19. Lockdowns are not particularly conducive to quiet learning and writing time. More than once, it seemed that this book would have to wait another seven years.

This finished product results from tremendous *siyata dishmaya* (divine assistance), coupled with angelic human beings who assisted in too many ways to count. Besides my wife and immediate family, who graciously provided the opportunities for researching and writing, many others were indispensable to the effort.

My mother personally reviewed some sections and proofread almost the entire book. Her editorial skills are evident throughout. I cannot thank her enough for everything she does for me, my family, and so many others.

Meira Mintz is an exceptional editor who has done wonders for the clarity of this work. I thank her for her willingness to take on the project, her speed, and her professional editing. Her dedication to the project certainly made it possible, and her writing acumen ensured a far more readable and concise finished product.

Headed by Shulamit Meir, the graphics team has gone above and beyond to make this book aesthetically pleasing. I am particularly grateful to Shulamit for putting everything together and to Ayala Zagori for developing most of the pictures used to represent different aspects of *shemitta*.

Rabbi Jonathan Ziring provided erudite comments from his wealth of knowledge on the first and third sections of the book. Additionally, I thank Yehuda Karol and Noam Hayman for their editing and technical assistance. Thank you to Levi Solomyak for his essential input for the chapter on *Hakhel*. Many others, too many to count, assisted throughout.

I had the privilege to learn *Hilchot Shemitta* with many *Rabbanim* over the years. At times, I was able to find a *chevruta* (study partner) to learn the material. Last *shemitta,* I learned many of the subjects with Rabbi Yonatan Snowbell. This year I enjoyed a special zoom *chevruta* with Marc Zeffren. Both of them contributed significantly to my understanding of the ideas presented, and for that I am very grateful.

Additionally, I benefited from the wealth of written materials on *shemitta*. Special mention must be made of Rav Yosef Zvi Rimon's *Shemitta: Halacha MiMekora,* and conversations with Rav Rimon helped clarify many issues. I thank Rav Rimon for his time and his written blessings for the book.

I owe a debt of gratitude to all my *Rabbanim* who guided my learning in general and who increased my understanding of *shemitta* and so many other topics. Their imprint is found on every page of the book (other than the errors that may appear, which are exclusively mine).

Joe Westreich, the chairman of the board of H.E.S.B.E.R. (Hebrew English Source Based Educational Resources), has been an indispensable friend and confidante throughout this project. He donated and raised funds necessary to publish this book, as well as our student book in the "From the Source" series. He donated in memory of his father, Larry Westreich (Aryeh Leib ben HaRav Yehoshua), who loved *Eretz Yisrael* with his entire being. May the book be a tribute to his memory.

It is a privilege to work for World Mizrachi and partner with them in printing this book. Rav Doron Perez revitalized this extremely significant organization and has helped it play an ever-increasing role in transforming Jewish society across the globe. Rav Doron and the entire staff have made me feel at home in the organization, providing a wonderful atmosphere for using my skills to impact the Jewish world positively. I am proud to be part of their incredible team. Mizrachi Press has made its mission to assist in publishing material that expresses *Torat Eretz Yisrael,* and I hope that this book will contribute towards that goal.

* * *

The publication of this book provides me with the opportunity to express gratitude to many individuals who have assisted me and my family for many years.

It is not possible to properly thank my parents, Saul and Sherry Zimmerman, for everything they have given me throughout my life. They spare nothing to help their children, and I am grateful to have them as parents.

My in-laws, Rabbi Danny and Tova Rhein, are role models for me and so many others. They are supportive of all our endeavors and cherish opportunities to contribute to Torah education. Thank you to my mother-in-law for editing *The Shemitta Experience,* a book for young adults that presents a sampling of the ideas in the current work.

Special thanks to my siblings and siblings-in-law for their love and support.

My children, Shoshana Beracha, Yisroel Dov, Ayelet Ahuva, Aharon Arye, Moshe Yair, Adi Shira, and Sarah Hodaya, have all contributed significantly to this book. First and foremost, they have sacrificed time that could have been spent with their father when he was working on this book. Additionally, their ideas and the time we learn together contributed in many ways to the final product.

V'at alit al kulana – My wife, Alisa, is my partner in life and my best friend. She has made this entire project possible, taking on extra responsibilities to enable me to work on this book. Without her encouragement and excitement, I would never have made it to the finish line. She is the mover behind this and many other initiatives in our lives, and any success I may achieve is in her credit.

Finally, but most profoundly, I am grateful to Hashem for the opportunity to complete this work and offer it to the community. This is only a tiny part of the tremendous gratitude we owe Hashem for everything we have as a family and as a people, and words are inadequate to express my gratitude. I can simply conclude in appreciation for the fact ששמת חלקי מיושבי בית המדרש.

Binyamin Zimmerman

כ"ח מנחם אב, תשפ"א

Table of Contents

Table of Contents

Table of Contents

Table of Contents

The Gift of the *Shemitta* Challenge

A *Shevi'it* Overview

Shemitta Excitement?

Shemitta, the sabbatical year, is once again soon upon us. With immense gratitude to the Almighty, we introduce this work on *machshevet ha-shemitta*, the philosophy of the *shemitta* year.

We live in a privileged generation, in which we are not only afforded the opportunity to write about this topic, but to practice the *halachot* as well. After almost two thousand years of exile, *Eretz Yisrael* (the Land of Israel) is now home to more than forty percent of the Jewish People. The nation's return to the Land brought with it an agricultural rebirth. In place of the "sackcloth and ashes" of Palestine, famously described by Mark Twain (Innocents Abroad, 1867), Israel is now the world's leader in agricultural development and innovation.

The *midrash* (*Sifrei, Re'eh* 80) refers to living in the Land as "equal to all other *mitzvot*." This Land is like no other. It is the Land that Hashem chose as His Land. He entered into a covenant with our forefathers to give the Land to their children, and He commanded us to acquire, live in, and develop the Land. Cultivating the Land agriculturally not only fulfills this extremely significant *mitzvah*, but is an ideal way of connecting to the Land.

The return to the Land and its agricultural advancement presents both opportunities and challenges. *Eretz Yisrael* is not only the homeland of the Jewish People; it is home to a series of unique *mitzvot*, referred to as *mitzvot ha-teluyot ba-aretz*, agricultural commandments whose observance is limited to the Land. Generations of Diaspora Jews longed not only to return to the Land, but also to fulfill its *mitzvot*. Although there has always been a small Jewish presence in Israel even after the exile and dispersion, most Jews had little agricultural involvement in the Land, and *mitzvot* like *shemitta* were not relevant[1]. *Eretz Yisrael*

The agricultural rebirth that began when the Jewish people returned to their land brought new questions. We had longed for this opportunity for centuries, but were we ready to face the challenges of fulfilling the *mitzvot ha-teluyot ba-aretz*? Fledgling Jewish settlements with limited resources and lacking storehouses were faced with dire questions. Would they survive the *shemitta* year or the years that followed if they were to observe its *halachot*? Is it worth living in the Land if one cannot keep its *mitzvot* properly? Is it appropriate to find

---

1   Interestingly, although Rav Yosef Karo, the author of the *Shulchan Aruch* lived in *Eretz Yisrael*, he did not discuss the *halachot* of *shemitta* there. A practical explanation is that he limited the discussion in the Shulchan Aruch to *halachot* that were mentioned in the Tur (see Magen Avraham 156), but one sees from his Teshuvot (Avkat Rochel 24) that the primary halachic debate of his day was the status of non-Jewish produce grown on gentile land during Shevi'it. Seemingly, as Jews weren't farming the Land at the time, and he only discussed practical *halachot* that were in practice in his day. The halachot of Jews refraining from planting were much less applicable.

a *halachic* means to circumvent *shemitta*'s requirements for the greater goal of living in the Land and living off it?

The Torah (*Vayikra* 26:34) indicates that *shemitta* observance ensures successful settlement in the Land. Although its observance is fraught with challenges for the farmer, they are what generate its opportunities. Should this be considered in our practical considerations? It is often difficult for a non-farmer to appreciate the gravity of these questions. Different communities have responded and continue to respond to these questions in different ways.

Farmers and gardeners are the primary observers of many of the *halachot* of *shemitta*, followed by the Land's residents, who are directly impacted by its ramifications on their produce. But the *mitzvot ha-teluyot ba-aretz* are commandments that present a social vision. They are the framework for a uniquely charitable society, ensuring shared resources while maintaining the dignity of the needy. Chief among these *mitzvot* is *shemitta*. Although it occurs only once in seven years, its messages are present far beyond, and its lesson applies to Jews wherever they live. *Shemitta*'s arrival allows us to practice and study its vision, and thereby to connect to the Land and its *mitzvot*.

Will the Real *Shemitta* Please Stand Up?

As we will learn in this book, *Shemitta* calls for a break, a timeout from our normal routine, every seven years. Every fifty years *Yovel* goes even further, calling for a restart of the national economy and the social structure of society. *Shemitta*, which is practiced in our day and age, has much to teach us even as we live in a non-agricultural society. The messages of *shemitta* and the vision it projects are multifaceted, and at times even subject to dispute.

Some focus their attention on *shemitta*'s goal of connecting our nation to the Land of Israel; others highlight its economic vision or its unparalleled focus on *chessed*. Some see it as a reminder that everyone requires a much-needed physical rest, while others focus on *shemitta*'s ability to rejuvenate the soul and body. More recently, others have embraced *shemitta* by highlighting other themes, seeing it as a necessary call for increasing ecological awareness and fortifying social justice initiatives.

Which one is it? Is it perhaps all these themes? Only by studying the subject and by dedicating ample time to prepare for *shemitta*'s momentous arrival will we begin this significant year with proper excitement that will hopefully radiate throughout and will only increase as we continually advance its message.

This work aims to foster understanding and appreciation of the *halachot* of *shemitta* and its messages. This is not a practical *halachic* work, although it will deal with several *halachic* issues to understand its nature and uncover its philosophical underpinnings.

Excitement or Dread

Shemitta is a topic that brings mixed emotions. Even those who have lived in Israel their whole lives must jog their memories every seven years to remember how to observe *shemitta* properly, let alone how to appreciate it. Like all *mitzvot* that apply infrequently, there is an element of excitement in fulfilling these *mitzvot*.

Mitzvot that are performed only once a year are typically accompanied by the joyous recitation of a special blessing, *Shehecheyanu*, recognizing God as the source of all blessing and thanking Him for enabling us to partake in this special time. By that token, logically, the system of *mitzvot* associated with *shemitta*, occurring only once in seven years, should certainly call for the recitation of the *Shehecheyanu* blessing. Yet no *Shehecheyanu* is recited over *shemitta*.

There are many *halachic* considerations to justify this omission.[2] However, what is more alarming than this question is the all-too-prevalent lack of excitement regarding the arrival of the *shemitta* year. For many, *shemitta's* arrival brings tension, even dread. Although we will attempt to gain a deeper understanding of why this is true, we will begin by emphasizing that the greatest way to deeply appreciate *shemitta*, and perhaps to even get excited about it, is through knowledge and preparation. Greater understanding about the year and its purpose and greater efforts to prepare for its arrival will hopefully generate greater appreciation and longing.

The *Shemitta* Renaissance

Fortunately, there seems to be a growing population whose excitement for the *shemitta* year is palpable. This cycle's pre-*shemitta* bears witness to almost every (if not every) Jewish city in the Land of Israel formulating a *shemitta* plan to ensure that the gardens of their city will remain beautiful while fully maintaining the laws of *shemitta*. This is a clear indication of the deep connection that Israel's residents have to the Land of Israel, irrespective of their level of religious observance. It is also a reflection of greater overall knowledge. Municipalities have become aware that with proper preparation leading up to the *shemitta* year, they can bring their gardens to a level at which they can be maintained appropriately within the confines of the laws of *shemitta*, and they are often committed to the endeavor.

In general, we have witnessed a great degree of excitement associated with *shemitta* in recent years. *Shemitta* observance has become more widespread, and many have invested in learning about its messages and connecting to its vision. If one goes to a supermarket in Israel immediately after Rosh Hashana of *shemitta*, he will undoubtedly find lines of individuals anxiously waiting to buy produce with *kedushat shevi'it*, *shemitta* sanctity. This is an expression of the aspects of *tosefet shevi'it* and *hachana le-shevi'it* that we will discuss.

The two elements we have noted, knowledge and preparation, are the keys to appreciating

---

2 Some explain that the *beracha* is not recited for technical reasons; the experience of *shemitta* is primarily associated with the land and the produce growing in the fields, rather than with man, and therefore no *bracha* is recited. However, Rav Shlomo Zalman Auerbach maintained that we do not omit *Shehecheyanu* because it does not deserve a *beracha*, but rather because it already has one; the *shemitta* year always begins on Rosh Hashana (see *Rosh Hashana* 2a), which has a *Shehecheyanu* of its own. According to this approach, one should intend during the recitation of *Shehechiyanu* on Rosh Hashana of the seventh year that he is presently ushering in the *shemitta* year (See *Ashrei HaIsh Moadim* 14:3).

shemitta and inculcating its messages, while also connecting to its vision. In fact, we will see that *shemitta* is deeply connected to Har Sinai, the original source of our nation's knowledge, and preparation for *shemitta* is an essential aspect of its *halachot*.

When one recognizes that *shemitta* is a gift that accords significance and even legitimacy to our sojourning in our land, the excitement is often tangible. This does not mean, of course, that even the most excited *shemitta* observers do not experience moments, even extended periods, of challenge associated with *shemitta* observance. However, they appreciate the *mitzvot* and message, such that their excitement for *shemitta* knows no bounds.

Hopefully, the more we learn about *shemitta*, the greater our excitement will be.

Shemitta Amid a Pandemic

Writing this book during a pandemic has given new meaning to *shemitta* and its message. Covid-19 had various impacts on the world. First and foremost, it began a period of illness for many, and at times, even worse. Secondly, besides the medical impact, it forced many people into lockdowns. Much of the regular economic activity came to a halt or a slowdown, and many were faced with the questions of what to do with one's "free time", and can society really afford to halt economic activity for an extended period of time? The lockdowns certainly gave many people some time for much needed rest. For some, it was very welcome (at least at the beginning); for others, it was far from appreciated. For a time, the world came to a stop, businesses shut down, and "nonessential workers" rarely left their houses. For most, cessation from normalcy was not productive, but there were some side benefits.

Covid-19 and *shemitta* are very different, but perhaps it is now more possible to imagine a *shemitta* built into the calendar every seven years. With proper preparation, one can maximize the period. Instead of a coronavirus-rest full of shutdowns and lockdowns, we can use *shemitta* to achieve the positive elements of rest without its negative effects.

It is not the contemporary reality of *shemitta* that makes its observance difficult; it is the modern world that makes its message necessary. Our goal in this book is to explain why.

This Book

This book is for anyone interested in devoting time to deepening their understanding of this important year. *Shemitta* is a multifaceted year that calls for unique treatment in many areas, ranging from the Land and its produce to the entire financial system. It is easy to lose one's footing. We hope that the graphics and color-coding in this work will make it easier to understand.

Color coding

We recognize that understanding the nature of *shemitta* or other *halachic* topics requires appreciating the ideas from their sources. *Mitzvot* like *shemitta*, which are discussed throughout the Torah and its themes and *halachot* explicated throughout the Mishna and Talmud, require an appreciation of the source of each source. For this reason sources are color-coded according to time period to enable appreciating which sources are rooted in *Torah She-biichtav* (the written Torah), *Torah Sheb'al Peh* (the oral Torah) ,and later sources.

מקור בתורה שבכתב (תנ"ך) Sources from the Written Torah

מקור משנה Sources from the Mishna

מקור גמרא Sources from Gemara

מקור ממפרשי התלמוד הראשונים, ופסקי השלחן ערוך Sources From The *Rishonim* (Early Commentaries on the *Gemara*) and the Rulings of the Shulchan Aruch

מקור ממפרשי השלחן ערוך ומהאחרונים Sources From the Commentaries on the Shulchan Aruch and the Later Commentators

מקור מפוסקי זמנינו Sources From the Contemporary Poskim (*Halachic* Decisors)

When quoting non-rabbinic sources, they will be presented in a non-color text box:

מקור לא רבני Non Rabbinic source

Graphics

Additionally, graphics are interspersed throughout the book to enhance the understanding of certain topics. Hopefully, the graphics and the color-coding together will enable a deeper appreciation of *shemitta* and its ideas.

Section 1

The *Parashiyot* of *Shevi'it* –
The Torah's Presentation of its *Mitzvot* and its Message(s)

Chapter 1

What is *Shemitta*?

A Basic Overview

The term *shemitta* generally refers to unique sets of agricultural and financial *halachot* that apply every seven years in *Eretz Yisrael*, the Land of Israel. Much like the seventh day of the week, Shabbat, is a day of rest. The Land is given a rest every seven years. During this year, landowners limit their agricultural activity, and the produce of the year has a special status.

Although the seventh year is often referred to as *shemitta*, when we study the *pesukim*, we find that it is only one of the names the Torah uses to refer to this multifaceted year. Understanding these different names will help clarify the *halachot* and goals of the *shemitta* year.

In the agricultural realm, we refer to two distinct aspects of the seventh year: *shabbat ha-aretz*, which focuses on the Land's rest, and *shemittat karka'ot*, which focuses on the unique *halachot* of the seventh year's produce.

Shabbat Ha-Aretz

The Torah's name for the *halachot* requiring that the land rest, thus limiting agricultural activity.

Shemittat Karka'ot

The Torah's reference to the seventh year as a year of release and relinquishing. Landowners renounce ownership of the produce grown in their fields. All seventh year produce has a sanctified status.

In addition to the agricultural *shemitta*, there is a financial *shemitta* that takes effect in the final moment of the seventh year. At that moment, creditors relinquish collection rights to virtually all of their outstanding loans. We refer to this aspect of the seventh year as *shemittat kesafim* (financial *shemitta*).

Shemittat Kesafim

This is a reference to the *halachot* regarding release of loans at the conclusion of the seventh year.

While these three terms for the seventh year reflect different aspects of the year, they combine to establish the overall uniqueness of the seventh year.

Due to the multidimensional nature of the year, throughout this work, we will primarily refer to the seventh year by the Hebrew word which precisely means that: שביעית / *shevi'it* (the seventh year). This term combines all three elements and unites them into a unified whole:

Basics of Agricultural *Halachot*

We can identify four distinct phases in the process that begins with preparing land for planting until its produce reaches one's refrigerator:

❶	**❷**	**❸**	**❹**
The Land Before Planting	**The Land During the Growing Season**	**The Vegetation and Crops While Growing (on trees or in the ground)**	**The Produce After it is Harvested**

The first two stages focus on the land and are therefore subject to the *halachot* of *shabbat ha-aretz*.

The second two stages focus on the produce and are therefore entail *shemittat karka'ot*.

Shabbat Ha-Aretz- Halachot of the Land Before and During Growth

The Torah requires that the Land and its inhabitants rest, demanding limited agricultural intervention throughout the year. We will see those certain agricultural activities - including planting and pruning (and possibly some others) – are essentially entirely prohibited the entire year. Other activities that foster growth are permitted when performed to maintain previous growth and prevent loss.

During this year of rest, the farmer enjoys a year to focus on the areas of life that are commonly overlooked during the often grueling routine of six years of agricultural development.

Shemittat Karka'ot- Halachot of the Produce

שְׁמִטַּת קַרְקָעוֹת

The produce of *Eretz Yisrael* enjoys a special status in all years, but the *shemitta* year elevates the crops and produce to a unique level. *Shemitta* produce enjoys a special sanctity known as *kedushat shevi'it*, the sanctity of the seventh-year produce. Any produce with this sanctity is treated uniquely both while growing and after it is harvested.

Produce while Growing in the Ground

All produce with *kedushat shevi'it* is to be declared ownerless (*hefker*) by its owner. Everyone enjoys equal access to the crop. In other words, one can enter another person's field and take some delicious fruit from their trees (we will discuss some of the specifics later on.)

During the seventh year, produce is not harvested in its usual manner, and only harvesting for one's short-term needs is permitted.

On the most superficial level, the classic rules of ownership are put to rest for the year. For a full year, large fields of food-producing vegetation are no longer status symbols. The owner releases his property rights to his produce and invites all those in need to enter the field and partake of its bounty as equal owners (though the land itself remains the owner's). Even the charitable wealthy individuals are no longer givers of charity, as all share equal ownership in the Land's yield.

Produce after the Harvest

Produce retains *kedushat shevi'it* after its harvest. Ordinarily, the overwhelming majority of produce that fields yield is sold for profit, and it is used for multiple purposes other than food (such as medicines, cosmetics, fuel etc.). During *shevi'it*, however, the Torah instructs that the goal of the produce is "*le-ochla*" – it must be consumed through its usual manner of consumption. This means that the produce is no longer a merchandisable commodity, but rather a food intended to be shared by all members of the population. It cannot be wasted or exported. These *halachot* further require special treatment of the produce and unique means of discarding unconsumed produce.

These *halachot* have a most significant impact on the consumer. For a full year, no produce is regular, and none is treated as it is under ordinary circumstances.

A quick perusal of these *halachot* is sufficient to make clear that *shevi'it* entails a challenging reality for those who are more financially fortunate and a year of opportunities for those in need. Some might even wonder if it is genuinely possible for society, especially an agricultural one, to continue to operate while resting from agricultural and economic development every seven years.

After learning about *shevi'it*, the answer will hopefully be an ecstatic yes. It is certainly physically possible to do so; in fact, on a values level, we will begin to wonder if it is really possible not to?

These *halachot* herald a "refocus and restart" every seven years and ensure that society functions economically and socially as the Torah envisions. The challenges of *shemitta* give us opportunities for growth that would be unimaginable otherwise.

With that in mind, let us begin our journey.

Why *Shevi'it* Isn't Fully Appreciated and What Can Be Done to Change That

The Torah's various descriptions of *shevi'it* highlight the centrality of the religious experience it brings, one that is fundamental to Judaism. While it only comes every seven years, it is an essential means of transforming our overall outlook on several crucial issues. *Shevi'it* raises existential questions regarding the purpose of humanity, the economy, the role of wealth, the definition of ownership, and the reality of God's hand in our daily sustenance.

While highlighting the pivotal role *shevi'it* plays in Jewish thought and practice, the Torah does not obscure the challenges posed by *shevi'it*. Thus, one who fails to appreciate the *halachot* of *shevi'it* and identify with its messages, will not be excited about *shevi'it*, and may instead feel dread. There are several culprits responsible for the lack of understanding and appreciation of *shevi'it*:

Lack of Study/ Incomplete Approach to its Study

The first culprit is the lack of study. Although our fixed calendar ensures that the arrival of *shevi'it* is no surprise, many people feel as though *shevi'it* somehow jumps on them unexpectedly, without giving them time to prepare. There are so many *halachot* involved, and just keeping track of them all is complicated.

Even those who study may miss crucial aspects. Much of the *halachic* instruction associated with *shevi'it* is in the form of overviews and summaries delineating dos and don'ts (often focusing on the don'ts). Not surpisingly, this often instills fear of this once-in-seven-years experience. As long as even the direct messages of *shevi'it* remain hidden from the public, it should not be surprising that *shevi'it* appears as a burden in people's eyes, rather than the bearer of an ideological message.

Admittedly, the fact that the Torah does not present the different aspects of *shevi'it* in one place makes study of the topic complex. However, it also makes it more enriching. *Shevi'it* carries with it more than one message, and the Torah wants us to appreciate each aspect on its own, instead of swallowing the entire experience whole. Only adequate study can uncover the various dimensions of *shevi'it* and unlock the different educational lessons that it imparts.

No quick-fix overview can attempt to do what the Torah shied away from doing: presenting *shevi'it* through an elevator pitch that summarizes all its *halachot* and goals. Studying it as the Torah intended may not allow us to master it quickly, but it will hopefully help us appreciate its inner messages.

To a certain degree, the first culprit in the lack of appreciation for the *mitzvot* of *shevi'it* has diminished over time, as great books dealing with the *halachot* of *shevi'it* are currently available. However, many of the Enlish works on the subject do not typically focus on the philosophical underpinnings of the *mitzvah*. In this book, we will approach *shevi'it* with a focus on its message, examining how the sources are reflected in current practice.

Highlighting Certain Elements of the Year

Another culprit for the lack of appreciation for *shevi'it* lies in the tendency to focus on only one aspect of this multifaceted year. Lack of understanding the unified message of *shevi'it* contributes to a fragmented view, inhibiting appreciation of its broader vision.

Some contemporary works choose to highlight certain aspects of *shevi'it* that are often overlooked, presenting them as the fundamental objectives of *shevi'it*. Indeed, at times it seems that *shevi'it* has become the educational tool for imparting many progressive ideas in modern society – ranging from social justice to ecology, environmentalism, renewable energy, and much more.

There is no doubt that contemporary society embraces ideals that overlap with *shevi'it*. Nevertheless, one would be hard-pressed to declare with integrity that they are the year's primary goals. If *shevi'it* were synonymous with the common usage of these ideals, it would not be limited to once every seven years in the Land of Israel. Moreover, if these modern understandings of the ideals were identical with *shevi'it*, they would call for something as radical as *shevi'it*, but rarely do they call for anything remotely similar.

The most effective way to understand *shevi'it* is to follow the Torah's lead, analyzing each *parasha* independently, and then trying to piece the broader puzzle together. Thus will provide a nuance and complete picture of the Torah's vision for *shevi'it*.

Chapter 2

A Brief Overview of the
Parashiyot of *Shevi'it*

Shevi'it appears explicitly in five different *parashiyot* in the Torah. Each *parasha* highlights an additional element of the year and, as mentioned, often refers to it by only one of its names. *Parashat Behar*, which includes the longest description of the year, divides its discussion of *shevi'it* into two separate sections, bringing the number to six. Additionally, Rabbi Akiva asserts that an additional *parasha* refers to *shevi'it*, so that there are a total of seven discussions of *shevi'it* in the Torah.

These seven *parashiyot*, an appropriate number for our topic, are the key to uncovering *shevi'it*'s goals and lessons. The central lessons will emerge by studying the two primary units that discuss *shevi'it*, especially by noting the different elements highlighted in each. We now turn to to those treatments in *Parashat Mishpatim* and *Parashat Behar*.

Parashat Mishpatim: The Social Aspects
....

Shevi'it is first mentioned in *Parashat Mishpatim*. In one *pasuk*, the Torah describes the normal working of the Land for six years and the changes the seventh year brings with it:

וְשֵׁשׁ שָׁנִים תִּזְרַע אֶת אַרְצֶךָ וְאָסַפְתָּ אֶת תְּבוּאָתָהּ: וְהַשְּׁבִיעִת תִּשְׁמְטֶנָּה וּנְטַשְׁתָּהּ וְאָכְלוּ אֶבְיֹנֵי עַמֶּךָ וְיִתְרָם תֹּאכַל חַיַּת הַשָּׂדֶה כֵּן תַּעֲשֶׂה לְכַרְמְךָ לְזֵיתֶךָ: שֵׁשֶׁת יָמִים תַּעֲשֶׂה מַעֲשֶׂיךָ וּבַיּוֹם הַשְּׁבִיעִי תִּשְׁבֹּת לְמַעַן יָנוּחַ שׁוֹרְךָ וַחֲמֹרֶךָ וְיִנָּפֵשׁ בֶּן אֲמָתְךָ וְהַגֵּר:

And six years you shall sow your Land and shall harvest its fruits. But [in] the seventh (*shevi'it*), you shall release it (*tishmetenna*) and let it lie fallow (*u-ntashtah*); and the poor of your nation will eat, and what they leave over the beasts of the field shall eat. So you shall do with your vineyard and with your olive grove. Six days you shall do your work, and on the seventh day you shall rest (*tishbot*), in order that your ox and your donkey may rest, and that your bondman and the stranger may be refreshed. (*Shemot* 23:10-12)

The Torah introduces us to the seventh year by referring to it by the name we have chosen to describe it – *shevi'it*, the seventh year. The Torah then indicates that this is a year of "shemitta," as it requires that during this year, "תִּשְׁמְטֶנָּה וּנְטַשְׁתָּהּ, *tishmetenna u-ntashtah*." These two words are of fundamental importance, but they are not easily translated. The standard explanation is that they mean to "release it and let it lie fallow," but that is only one understanding, and even that is inadequate and unclear.

Note that in these *pesukim*, the Torah makes no mention of *shevi'it*-observance being limited to the Land of Israel, possibly implying that at least some of its aspects, including its goals and messages, are applicable and relevant throughout the world.

The Torah also seems to provide an explicit goal and purpose for the year: וְאָכְלוּ אֶבְיֹנֵי עַמֶּךָ

, "and the poor of your nation shall eat." During this year, the needy have greater access to food, and even the animals are afforded greater eating opportunities. This underscores *shevi'it*'s role as providing a message of social concern for the poor and helpless.

Immediately after describing the seventh year, the Torah mentions the laws of the weekly Shabbat in the next *pasuk*. The juxtaposition seems to equate to some degree the similar systems of six and seven – six units of work followed by a seventh period of cessation. Only the units of time vary; *shevi'it* is a system of years, while Shabbat is a system of days. This parallel, although not explicit in the *pesukim*, leads us to consider whether the seventh year has a Shabbat element as well. Interestingly, even Shabbat here appears with a message of social concern, with the goal of providing a time of rest for one's workers and animals.

The concise description of the seventh year in *Parashat Mishpatim* leaves us with a lack of clarity regarding its *halachot*. Nevertheless, at least one element of its message is clear: This is a year of release, *shemitta*, which carries a social vision of increased access to food for the poor and animals.

Parashat Behar: Shabbat of the Land

Parashat Behar provides a much lengthier and detailed description of the seventh year. The *parasha* introduces *shevi'it* as having been taught on Har Sinai (Mount Sinai). This is significant, as the entire Book of *Vayikra* up to this point was taught in the *Ohel Mo'ed*, the Tent of Meeting. Rashi famously asks, מָה עִנְיַן שְׁמִטָּה אֵצֶל הַר סִינַי? "What does the sabbatical year have to do with Mount Sinai?" which has become a colloquialism for introducing off-the-topic discussions. Indeed, many commentators wonder about the connection between Sinai and *shemitta*. It seems that the opening *pasuk* of *Parashat Behar* sets the stage for a year with underlying religious significance, much like the Har Sinai experience. The ensuing description seems to reinforce that perception.

וַיְדַבֵּר ה' אֶל מֹשֶׁה בְּהַר סִינַי לֵאמֹר: דַּבֵּר אֶל בְּנֵי יִשְׂרָאֵל וְאָמַרְתָּ אֲלֵהֶם כִּי תָבֹאוּ אֶל הָאָרֶץ אֲשֶׁר אֲנִי נֹתֵן לָכֶם וְשָׁבְתָה הָאָרֶץ שַׁבָּת לַה': שֵׁשׁ שָׁנִים תִּזְרַע שָׂדֶךָ וְשֵׁשׁ שָׁנִים תִּזְמֹר כַּרְמֶךָ וְאָסַפְתָּ אֶת תְּבוּאָתָהּ: וּבַשָּׁנָה הַשְּׁבִיעִת שַׁבַּת שַׁבָּתוֹן יִהְיֶה לָאָרֶץ שַׁבָּת לַה' שָׂדְךָ לֹא תִזְרָע וְכַרְמְךָ לֹא תִזְמֹר: אֵת סְפִיחַ קְצִירְךָ לֹא תִקְצוֹר וְאֶת עִנְּבֵי נְזִירֶךָ לֹא תִבְצֹר שְׁנַת שַׁבָּתוֹן יִהְיֶה לָאָרֶץ: וְהָיְתָה שַׁבַּת הָאָרֶץ לָכֶם לְאָכְלָה לְךָ וּלְעַבְדְּךָ וְלַאֲמָתֶךָ וְלִשְׂכִירְךָ וּלְתוֹשָׁבְךָ הַגָּרִים עִמָּךְ: וְלִבְהֶמְתְּךָ וְלַחַיָּה אֲשֶׁר בְּאַרְצֶךָ תִּהְיֶה כָל תְּבוּאָתָהּ לֶאֱכֹל:

God spoke to Moshe on Mount Sinai, saying: Speak to *Bnei Yisrael* and say to them: When you come to the Land which I shall give you, the Land shall rest (*ve-shaveta ha-aretz*) a sabbath to God. Six years you may sow your field and six years you may prune your vineyard and gather in the produce. But in the seventh year, the Land shall have a sabbath of complete rest (*shabbat shabbaton*), a sabbath to God; you shall not sow your field nor prune your vineyard. You shall not reap the after-growth of your harvest, nor gather the grapes of your untrimmed vines; it shall be a year of complete rest (*shenat shabbaton*) for the Land. But the sabbath of the Land (*shabbat ha-aretz*) shall be for all of you to eat – for you, and for your servant, and for your maid, and for your hired servant and for the residents by your side that sojourn with you. And for your cattle and for the beasts that are in your Land, shall all the produce of it be for food. (*Vayikra* 25:1-7)

These *pesukim* make no mention of the word *shemitta*. Instead, they repeatedly refer to the year as "Shabbat." This is no longer simply an association between the laws of the seventh year and the seventh day; the Torah here names the year *shabbat ha-aretz*, sabbath of the Land. Just as the world that God created has its Shabbat every seventh day after six days of work, the Land that God gives the Jewish People has its rest every seventh year after six years of work. Indeed, the root ת.ב.ש., *sh.b.t*, appears in these *pesukim*– you guessed it –seven times!

It is clear from the *pesukim* in this passage that the unique *halachot* of the seventh year apply only in the Land of Israel. The Torah is also explicit that this is a year of agricultural rest, delineating four agricultural labors prohibited during the seventh year (*zeria*, planting, *zemira*, pruning, *ketzira*, harvesting grains, *betzira*, harvesting grapes; other acts are the subject of debate and are discussed in Section III).

The Torah goes on to discuss the laws of *yovel*, the Jubilee year, which occurs after seven cycles of *shevi'it*. The *pesukim* then provide what appears to be a reasoning for all of the *halachot* of *shevi'it* in *Parashat Behar*:

וְהָאָרֶץ לֹא תִמָּכֵר לִצְמִתֻת כִּי לִי הָאָרֶץ כִּי גֵרִים וְתוֹשָׁבִים אַתֶּם עִמָּדִי: וּבְכֹל אֶרֶץ אֲחֻזַּתְכֶם גְּאֻלָּה תִּתְּנוּ לָאָרֶץ:

And the Land shall not be sold for eternity, for the Land is Mine, for you are strangers and sojourners with Me. (*Vayikra* 25:23).

This description seems to underscore that *shevi'it* and *yovel* are periods that remind us of Hashem's control of the Land; our "ownership" is mere squatter's rights. This seems to further the theme that *shevi'it* is a spiritual time that entails developing a relationship with God through a period of rest – a *shabbat la-Hashem*.

To sum up, the Torah's two primary mentions of *shevi'it* refer to the year by different names and highlight various aspects of the year:

Parashat Mishpatim	**Parashat Behar**
שְׁמִטַּת קַרְקָעוֹת	שַׁבַּת הָאָרֶץ
Focus on the social aspects of shevi'it	Focus on the Shabbat of the Land, the Land's rest

While these emphases are in no way contradictory, the Torah clearly has reasons for the divergent themes, as we will see.

The Dual Nature of Each Mention

Although these two *parashiyot* portray two different descriptions of the year, it is important to note that each *parasha* makes reference to the aspect highlighted in the other description. As we saw, *Parashat Mishpatim* mentions the weekly Shabbat immediately after discussing *shevi'it*, and although *Parashat Behar* focuses on a period of spiritual rest, it does not omit the social benefits of such a rest, as the Torah describes the produce of the year as being designated for consumption by all elements of society (*Vayikra* 25:6-7).

The overlap of the messages indicates that these two models of the seventh year are intertwined. The different focuses unite to create a multifaceted yet unified message. Similarly, although the other relevant *parashiyot* seem to champion either the social or religious elements, they invest significant effort in explicating both messages. After we study these *parashiyot* in greater detail, we will consider what messages the Torah wanted to convey by separating the distinct elements of *shevi'it* into different *parashiyot* with distinctive titles and complimentary messages.

We will provide a short overview of the rest of the *parashiyot* discussing *shevi'it* in the order in which they appear in the Torah.

Parasha 3-Parashat Ki Tisa- The Questionable Mention

As we have seen, there are two primary *parashiyot* that deal with agricultural *shevi'it*. According to Rabbi Akiva, however, agricultural *shevi'it* is mentioned in a third *parasha* as well. In *Parashat Ki Tisa*, after the episode of the *Egel HaZahav*, the golden calf, the Torah states:

> שֵׁשֶׁת יָמִים תַּעֲבֹד וּבַיּוֹם הַשְּׁבִיעִי תִּשְׁבֹּת בֶּחָרִישׁ וּבַקָּצִיר תִּשְׁבֹּת:
>
> Six days you shall work, but on the seventh day you shall rest; in plowing and in harvesting you shall rest. (*Shemot* 34:21)

The first part of the *pasuk* states that as opposed to the six days of work, one must rest on the seventh day of the week. This straightforward repetition of the principle of Shabbat is followed by three ambiguous words: בֶּחָרִישׁ וּבַקָּצִיר תִּשְׁבֹּת, "in plowing and harvesting you shall rest."

Given that the weekly Shabbat requires rest from all *melacha* – all creative, transformative activity – there is no need to specify that it is necessary to rest from plowing and harvesting. The demand of *tishbot*, "rest," should be unqualified. What are we supposed to learn from these words referring to resting from plowing and harvesting?

The Talmud cites a dispute between Rabbi Akiva and Rabbi Yishmael regarding the proper interpretation of this *pasuk*. Rabbi Yishma'el explains that the Torah is qualifying the type of harvesting prohibited on Shabbat; Rabbi Akiva, in contrast, teaches that the Torah is instructing us about a different Shabbat – the *shabbat* of the Land.

> דְּתַנְיָא בֶּחָרִישׁ וּבַקָּצִיר תִּשְׁבֹּת רַבִּי עֲקִיבָא אוֹמֵר אֵינוֹ צָרִיךְ לוֹמַר חָרִישׁ וְקָצִיר שֶׁל שְׁבִיעִית שֶׁהֲרֵי כְּבָר נֶאֱמַר

> שָׂדְךָ לֹא תִזְרָע וְגוֹ' אֶלָּא חָרִישׁ שֶׁל עֶרֶב שְׁבִיעִית הַנִּכְנָס לִשְׁבִיעִית וְקָצִיר שֶׁל שְׁבִיעִית הַיּוֹצֵא לְמוֹצָאֵי שְׁבִיעִית.
>
> "In plowing and in harvesting, you shall rest" – Rabbi Akiva says: There is no need to be told to desist from plowing or reaping in the seventh year, for it is already stated: "You shall not sow your field..." [It can be taken] only [to prohibit] plowing in the pre-sabbatical year [which may cause agricultural benefits] extending into the seventh year, and [likewise] to the harvesting of the seventh year's crops that mature in the post-sabbatical year. (TB *Rosh Hashana* 9a)

According to Rabbi Akiva, not only does this *pasuk* refer to *shevi'it*, as opposed to Shabbat, but it also teaches us several important details regarding *shevi'it*. First, it suggests that besides the four agricultural activities explicitly mentioned in *Parashat Behar*, plowing is also prohibited during *shevi'it* (at the very least due to the positive commandment requiring resting from plowing). Second, Rabbi Akiva understands that this *pasuk* expands *shevi'it*'s impact by referring to *tosefet shevi'it*, the period before and after *shevi'it* that carries with it unique agricultural halachot.

Additionally, the verb "*tishbot*" in this context, in a *pasuk* that initially seems to refer to the weekly Shabbat, reinforces the Shabbat element of the year. Beyond the similarity to *Parashat Behar*, the active form of the verb "*tishbot*" seems to require an active type of rest. Thus, Rabbi Akiva understands it as a reference to expanding *shevi'it* rest beyond the seventh year through *tosefet shevi'it*.

Parasha 4- Continuation of *Parashat Behar*- *Shemitta* as Part of the *Yovel* Cycle

After the *pesukim* in *Parashat Behar* highlighting the seventh year as the year of *shabbat ha-aretz*, the Torah continues its description of *shevi'it* with a discussion of *yovel*, the Jubilee year. The Torah states that the courts must count seven such cycles of seven years, after which they sanctify the fiftieth year as *yovel*.

After delineating the unique *halachot* of *yovel*, the Torah addresses a question that is likely to haunt an individual before the *shemitta* year: "What shall we eat?!" (This is a particularly pressing question in the forty-eighth year of the cycle, the year preceeding *shemitta* that is followed by *yovel*, as there will be two consecutive years in which there will be no planting.[3]) The Torah guarantees a divine blessing in the sixth year that will supply the needs of the sixth, seventh, and eighth years. This is followed by many *halachot* regarding the sale of property and the proper care and concern for the unfortunate members of society. The Torah mentions the prohibition of selling one's field in perpetuity, as the Land belongs to God:

> וְכִי תֹאמְרוּ מַה נֹּאכַל בַּשָּׁנָה הַשְּׁבִיעִת הֵן לֹא נִזְרָע וְלֹא נֶאֱסֹף אֶת תְּבוּאָתֵנוּ: וְצִוִּיתִי אֶת בִּרְכָתִי לָכֶם בַּשָּׁנָה הַשִּׁשִּׁית וְעָשָׂת אֶת הַתְּבוּאָה לִשְׁלֹשׁ הַשָּׁנִים: וּזְרַעְתֶּם אֵת הַשָּׁנָה הַשְּׁמִינִת וַאֲכַלְתֶּם מִן הַתְּבוּאָה יָשָׁן עַד הַשָּׁנָה

---

3   See the discussion in the Sifra (ad loc.) if the blessing for three years of produce was only applicable when Shemitta was followed by *yovel*, or every *shemitta* year. Throughout this work we accept the common understanding that it is applicable every *shemitta* year.

הַתְּבוּאָתֵנוּ עַד בּוֹא תְּבוּאָתָהּ תֹּאכְלוּ יָשָׁן: וְהָאָרֶץ לֹא תִמָּכֵר לִצְמִתֻת כִּי לִי הָאָרֶץ כִּי גֵרִים וְתוֹשָׁבִים אַתֶּם עִמָּדִי:

And if you say, "What shall we eat in the seventh year? We shall neither plant nor gather our produce!" I will send you my blessing in the sixth year and the Land shall yield produce for the three years. While you plant during the eighth year, you shall eat from the old crop; until the ninth year, until its harvest comes in, you shall eat from the old crop. And the Land shall not be sold permanently, for the Land belongs to Me, for you are strangers and [temporary] residents with Me. (*Vayikra* 25:20-23)

This *parasha* highlights the divine blessing and reliance upon Hashem that *shevi'it* brings. Without *emuna* (faith), *shevi'it* might be unbearable; with *emuna*, it is an unparalleled opportunity to connect with God in His Land, approaching life in a new way. This *parasha* illustrates some economic and philosophical necessities of life in the Land and ensures that we are mindful of the the Land of Israel's true Owner.

Parasha 5-Parashat Bechukotai-
The Necessity of *Shevi'it* Observance

The importance of the observance of *shevi'it* is highlighted in *Parashat Bechukotai*. The *parasha* discusses the blessings awarded to the nation when they follow God's *mitzvot*, followed by the *tochacha*, the rebuke, delineating the horrible punitive measures that will befall the nation if they violate God's will.

In the section of the blessings, we are told that adhering to God's will ensures that the people will live safely in the Land:

אִם בְּחֻקֹּתַי תֵּלֵכוּ וְאֶת מִצְוֹתַי תִּשְׁמְרוּ וַעֲשִׂיתֶם אֹתָם: וְנָתַתִּי גִשְׁמֵיכֶם בְּעִתָּם וְנָתְנָה הָאָרֶץ יְבוּלָהּ וְעֵץ הַשָּׂדֶה יִתֵּן פִּרְיוֹ: וְהִשִּׂיג לָכֶם דַּיִשׁ אֶת בָּצִיר וּבָצִיר יַשִּׂיג אֶת זָרַע וַאֲכַלְתֶּם לַחְמְכֶם לָשֹׂבַע וִישַׁבְתֶּם לָבֶטַח בְּאַרְצְכֶם: וְנָתַתִּי שָׁלוֹם בָּאָרֶץ וּשְׁכַבְתֶּם וְאֵין מַחֲרִיד וְהִשְׁבַּתִּי חַיָּה רָעָה מִן הָאָרֶץ וְחֶרֶב לֹא תַעֲבֹר בְּאַרְצְכֶם:

If you follow my statutes and observe my commandments... I will give your rains in their time, the Land will yield its produce ... and you will live in security in your Land. And I will grant peace in the Land, and you will lie down with no one to frighten [you] ... (*Vayikra* 26:3-6)

The converse is mentioned in the ensuing verses of the *tochacha*. Violation of God's will result in punishment. At first, it seems like the punishments are a result of general disobedience leading to abrogation of the covenant, as the *pesukim* state:

וְאִם לֹא תִשְׁמְעוּ לִי וְלֹא תַעֲשׂוּ אֶת כָּל הַמִּצְוֹת הָאֵלֶּה: וְאִם בְּחֻקֹּתַי תִּמְאָסוּ וְאִם אֶת מִשְׁפָּטַי תִּגְעַל נַפְשְׁכֶם לְבִלְתִּי עֲשׂוֹת אֶת כָּל מִצְוֹתַי לְהַפְרְכֶם אֶת בְּרִיתִי:

But if you do not obey Me and do not observe all these commandments, if you reject My laws, and disregard My rule, so that you do not observe all My commandments and you break my covenant... (14-15)

However, in the continuation of the *pesukim*, after detailing the starvation, plagues, and exile that will befall the nation, the Torah indicates what is accomplished by exiling the Jewish People and allowing the Land to lay in desolation:

וְאֶתְכֶם אֱזָרֶה בַגּוֹיִם וַהֲרִיקֹתִי אַחֲרֵיכֶם חָרֶב וְהָיְתָה אַרְצְכֶם שְׁמָמָה וְעָרֵיכֶם יִהְיוּ חָרְבָּה: אָז תִּרְצֶה הָאָרֶץ אֶת
שַׁבְּתֹתֶיהָ כֹּל יְמֵי הָשַּׁמָּה וְאַתֶּם בְּאֶרֶץ אֹיְבֵיכֶם אָז תִּשְׁבַּת הָאָרֶץ וְהִרְצָת אֶת שַׁבְּתֹתֶיהָ: כָּל יְמֵי הָשַּׁמָּה תִּשְׁבֹּת
אֵת אֲשֶׁר לֹא שָׁבְתָה בְּשַׁבְּתֹתֵיכֶם בְּשִׁבְתְּכֶם עָלֶיהָ:

I will scatter you among the nations and will unsheathe the sword to pursue you. Your Land will be desolate and your cities in ruins. The Land (*ha-aretz*) shall then be appeased for its Sabbaths, while it is desolate and you are in the Land of your enemies; the Land shall rest and have appeasement for its Sabbaths. All the days of its desolation it shall be at rest, according to the rest that it did not enjoy while you dwelt in it. (33-35)

While the *tochacha* is not explicit that the punishments are a direct result of nonobservance of *shevi'it*, it is clear that the Land must be "appeased" for all the *shabbatot ha-aretz* (sabbaths of the Land) that were not properly fulfilled. Just as *shabbat ha-aretz* involves leaving the Land uncultivated, the exile of the Jews from the Land and its desolation will bring about the necessary rest that was ignored during Israel's sojourn on the Land. The severity of punishment is linked to the nonobservance of *shevi'it*.

The relationship between *shevi'it* and the punishments of the *tochacha* may also be gleaned from the recurrence of the number seven in the description of the punishments:

וְאִם עַד אֵלֶּה לֹא תִשְׁמְעוּ לִי וְיָסַפְתִּי לְיַסְּרָה אֶתְכֶם שֶׁבַע עַל חַטֹּאתֵיכֶם: וְאִם תֵּלְכוּ עִמִּי קֶרִי וְלֹא תֹאבוּ לִשְׁמֹעַ
לִי וְיָסַפְתִּי עֲלֵיכֶם מַכָּה שֶׁבַע כְּחַטֹּאתֵיכֶם: ...וְהִכֵּיתִי אֶתְכֶם גַּם אָנִי שֶׁבַע עַל חַטֹּאתֵיכֶם: ...וְיִסַּרְתִּי אֶתְכֶם אַף
אָנִי שֶׁבַע עַל חַטֹּאתֵיכֶם:

And if you will not listen to Me, I will chastise you sevenfold for your transgressions. And if you walk with me with indifference and will not hearken to Me, I will strike you sevenfold according to your transgressions. … I will also strike you/afflict you sevenfold for your transgressions. (*Vayikra* 26:18,21,24,28)

We see from this *parasha* that *shevi'it* is not merely an assortment of positive and negative commandments; it is almost as if it is the ticket to secure dwelling in the Land of Israel. If the nation fails to leave their Land fallow in the seventh year, God promises that the Land will remain fallow for many years, as Israel will be in exile and incapable of cultivation and planting.

In fact, with almost the exact same words, the concluding chapter of *Tanach* tells us that non-observance of *shemitta* in fact caused a lengthening of the exile:

וַיֶּגֶל הַשְּׁאֵרִית מִן הַחֶרֶב אֶל בָּבֶל וַיִּהְיוּ לוֹ וּלְבָנָיו לַעֲבָדִים עַד מְלֹךְ מַלְכוּת פָּרָס: לְמַלֹּאות דְּבַר ה' בְּפִי יִרְמְיָהוּ
עַד רָצְתָה הָאָרֶץ אֶת שַׁבְּתוֹתֶיהָ כָּל יְמֵי הָשַּׁמָּה שָׁבָתָה לְמַלֹּאות שִׁבְעִים שָׁנָה:

And those who had escaped from the sword were taken by King Nevuchadnetzar into exile to Babylon, and they became servants to him and his sons until the kingdom of Persia came to power. To fulfill the word of God through Yirmiyahu – until the Land of Israel finally enjoyed its sabbath rests; all the days it lay desolate, it kept the sabbath, to complete seventy years. (II *Divrei Ha-Yamim* 36:20-21)

These *pesukim* in the Torah would seem to be the basis for the *mishna's* statement:

גָּלוּת בָּא לָעוֹלָם עַל עוֹבְדֵי עֲבוֹדָה זָרָה וְעַל גִּלּוּי עֲרָיוֹת וְעַל שְׁפִיכַת דָּמִים וְעַל הַשְׁמָטַת הָאָרֶץ

> Exile comes to the world on account of idol-worshippers, illicit relations, bloodshed, and [nonobservance of] *shemitta* of the Land. (*Avot* 5:9)

Parashat Bechukkotai informs us of the ramifications for *shevi'it* violations and indicate its importance. Violation results in exile and dispersion; in contrast, observance of the Shabbat of the Land results in secure living in the Land.

While these *parashiyot* highlight *shevi'it*'s agricultural *halachot* and the ramifications for its nonobservance, the two last mentions of *shevi'it* focus on two other elements – financial *shevi'it* and *Hakhel*.

Parasha 6- Parashat Re'eh-Shemittat Kesafim

In *Parashat Re'eh*, the Torah declares that at the conclusion of the seventh year, creditors release the collection rights for outstanding loans. This financial *shemitta* is referred to in *halachic* literature as *shemittat kesafim*, the release of monetary funds (i.e., debts).

> מִקֵּץ שֶׁבַע שָׁנִים תַּעֲשֶׂה שְׁמִטָּה: וְזֶה דְּבַר הַשְּׁמִטָּה שָׁמוֹט כָּל בַּעַל מַשֵּׁה יָדוֹ אֲשֶׁר יַשֶּׁה בְּרֵעֵהוּ לֹא יִגֹּשׂ אֶת
> רֵעֵהוּ וְאֶת אָחִיו כִּי קָרָא שְׁמִטָּה לַה': אֶת הַנָּכְרִי תִּגֹּשׂ וַאֲשֶׁר יִהְיֶה לְךָ אֶת אָחִיךָ תַּשְׁמֵט יָדֶךָ:

At the end of seven years you shall make a release (*shemitta*). And this is the manner of the release; release (*shamot*) the hand of every creditor from what he lent his friend; he shall not exact from his friend or his brother, because the time of release for God has arrived. From a foreigner you may exact, but whatever of yours is by your brother your hand shall release (*tashmeit*). (*Devarim* 15:1-3)

This *parasha* is the most significant description of the "shemitta" element of the year, as the root ש.מ.ט, sh.m.t., is repeated a number of times. It is here that the Torah teaches at length the parameters of the *mitzvah* of *tzedaka* and its relationship to the financial *shemitta*.

Parasha 7-Parashat Vayelech-
The *Hakhel* Conclusion to a Transformational Year

The final mention of the *shemitta* year in the Torah appears in *Parashat Vayelech*, adding an additional spiritual component to this already-fascinating period:

> וַיְצַו מֹשֶׁה אוֹתָם לֵאמֹר מִקֵּץ שֶׁבַע שָׁנִים בְּמֹעֵד שְׁנַת הַשְּׁמִטָּה בְּחַג הַסֻּכּוֹת: בְּבוֹא כָל יִשְׂרָאֵל לֵרָאוֹת אֶת פְּנֵי
> ה' אֱ-לֹהֶיךָ בַּמָּקוֹם אֲשֶׁר יִבְחָר תִּקְרָא אֶת הַתּוֹרָה הַזֹּאת נֶגֶד כָּל יִשְׂרָאֵל בְּאָזְנֵיהֶם: הַקְהֵל אֶת הָעָם הָאֲנָשִׁים
> וְהַנָּשִׁים וְהַטַּף וְגֵרְךָ אֲשֶׁר בִּשְׁעָרֶיךָ לְמַעַן יִשְׁמְעוּ וּלְמַעַן יִלְמְדוּ וְיָרְאוּ אֶת ה' אֱ-לֹהֵיכֶם וְשָׁמְרוּ לַעֲשׂוֹת אֶת כָּל
> דִּבְרֵי הַתּוֹרָה הַזֹּאת: וּבְנֵיהֶם אֲשֶׁר לֹא יָדְעוּ יִשְׁמְעוּ וְלָמְדוּ לְיִרְאָה אֶת ה' אֱ-לֹהֵיכֶם כָּל הַיָּמִים אֲשֶׁר אַתֶּם חַיִּים
> עַל הָאֲדָמָה אֲשֶׁר אַתֶּם עֹבְרִים אֶת הַיַּרְדֵּן שָׁמָּה לְרִשְׁתָּהּ:

And Moshe commanded them, saying: At the end of every seven years, at the time of the year of release (*ha-shemitta*), on the festival of Sukkot. When all Israel comes to see the presence of the Lord your God in the place that He will choose, read this Torah before all of Israel to their ears. Assemble the entire nation, men, women, and children, and the strangers who dwell within your gates, in order that they hear and in order that they learn to fear God their God and keep the words of this Torah. And their children, who do not know, will listen and will learn to fear the Lord your God, all the days that you live upon the Land which you are crossing the Jordan to inherit. (*Devarim* 31:10-13)

This *mitzvah*, known as *Hakhel*, is performed every seven years on the Sukkot immediately following the *shemitta* year (see Rashi, Ramban ad loc.). After experiencing a year of agricultural limitation during the seventh year, culminating in the canceling of loans in the final moments of the year, and before the planting season of the eighth year begins after Sukkot, all the Jews gather together for a spiritual experience that includes the reading of the Torah by the king in the presence of every Jew.

The spiritual supplement to the seventh year indicates that this period is not only one with agricultural *halachot*, the canceling of loans, and economic refocusing. It is supposed to bring about a grand spiritual reawakening.

"And the name is..."

The seven *parashiyot* of the seventh-year leave much to be understood, but clarify one fundamental point: The seventh year is a truly fascinating period, and no real explanation can focus its attention on only one of the numerous aspects it incorporates.

The root "shemitta" is only found in three *parashiyot*: the requirement of *tishmatenah* in *Parashat Mishpatim*, the release of the rights to collect loans at the conclusion of the seventh year, and the description of the year when presenting the experience of *Hakhel* on Sukkot following the seventh year.

In all three of the passages explicitly dealing with the agricultural laws of the land during the seventh year, there is no mention of a "*shemitta*." The root appears only in the phrase "*tishmetenna u-ntashta*" in *Parashat Mishpatim*, and, as noted above, these terms are difficult to translate. Some of the commentators, in fact, explain that *tishmetenna* is a reference to *shemittat kesafim*, as the word *shemitta* refers to the release of loans in that context. Even if we explain *tishmetenna* as connected to the agricultural component, it would be difficult to name the entire year of agricultural *halachot* with this term.

Alongside the year's distinction as a *shemitta* year, the seventh year is a year of *shabbat*, but not just any *Shabbat* – *shabbat ha-aretz*. While the description of *shemittat kesafim* in *Parashat Re'eh* uses the root of *shemitta* six times, indicating the term's centrality in that context, *Parashat Behar* refers to the sabbatical year as *shabbat* seven times. People might not look forward to a year of releasing their hold on the Land, a year in which they are limited in what they can do to further cultivate their fields, but if one recognizes that the seventh year is a year of *shabbat ha-aretz*, one might view the year in a different light. Although the weekly Shabbat limits what we can do, anyone who recognizes the beauty of Shabbat acknowledges that the restrictions are nothing more than a prescription for a meaningful experience. A recurring theme in this work will be that any understanding of the sabbatical year must embrace its character as *shabbat ha-aretz*.

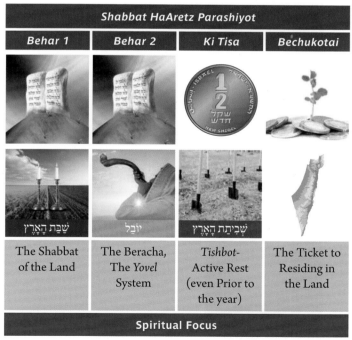

While each *parasha* highlights its unique elements, the Torah intertwines the messages for a multifaceted description of this monumental year.

A Deeper Look at the *Parashiyot*- One by One

We have seen that the Torah discusses *shevi'it* in seven different contexts, at each point focusing on distinct elements of the year. We will divide our deeper analysis of the pesukim into these seven contexts (although two appear in the same *Parasha*) and attempt to assign a unique theme to each one of them:

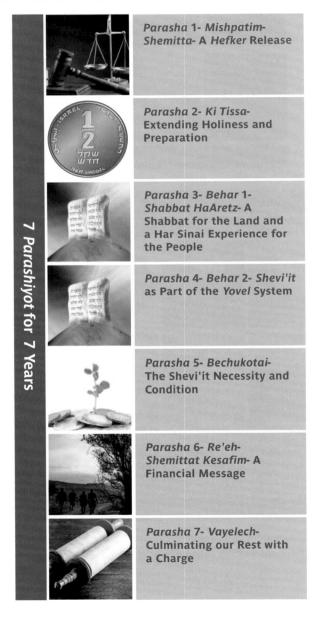

7 Parashiyot for 7 Years

Parasha 1- Mishpatim-
Shemitta- A Hefker Release

Parasha 2- Ki Tissa-
Extending Holiness and
Preparation

Parasha 3- Behar 1-
Shabbat HaAretz- A
Shabbat for the Land and
a Har Sinai Experience for
the People

Parasha 4- Behar 2- Shevi'it
as Part of the Yovel System

Parasha 5- Bechukotai-
The Shevi'it Necessity and
Condition

Parasha 6- Re'eh-
Shemittat Kesafim- A
Financial Message

Parasha 7- Vayelech-
Culminating our Rest with
a Charge

Parasha 1: Shevi'it in Parashat Mishpatim

The majority of *Parashat Mishpatim* (*Shemot* 21-24) records the laws of damages and other interpersonal interactions. At the *parasha's* end, it discusses the covenant made at the time of the giving of the Torah. It is in this *parasha* that the Torah introduces the uniqueness of the seventh year. What does *shevi'it* have in common within this context?

The answer to this question will revolutionize our conception of interpersonal relationships and the fundamental aspects of the covenant at Sinai. In the middle of *Parashat Mishpatim*, the Torah states:

> וְשֵׁשׁ שָׁנִים תִּזְרַע אֶת אַרְצֶךָ וְאָסַפְתָּ אֶת תְּבוּאָתָהּ: וְהַשְּׁבִיעִת תִּשְׁמְטֶנָּה וּנְטַשְׁתָּהּ וְאָכְלוּ אֶבְיֹנֵי עַמֶּךָ וְיִתְרָם תֹּאכַל חַיַּת הַשָּׂדֶה כֵּן תַּעֲשֶׂה לְכַרְמְךָ לְזֵיתֶךָ:

And six years you shall sow your land (*artzecha*) and shall harvest its fruits. But [in] the seventh (*shevi'it*), you shall release it (*tishmetenna*) and let it lie fallow (*u-ntashtah*), and the poor of your nation will eat, and what they leave over the beasts of the field shall eat. So you shall do with your vineyard and with your olive grove. (*Shemot* 23:10-11)

This description is followed by a *pasuk* discussing the weekly Shabbat:

> שֵׁשֶׁת יָמִים תַּעֲשֶׂה מַעֲשֶׂיךָ וּבַיֹּום הַשְּׁבִיעִי תִּשְׁבֹּת לְמַעַן יָנוּחַ שׁוֹרְךָ וַחֲמֹרֶךָ וְיִנָּפֵשׁ בֶּן אֲמָתְךָ וְהַגֵּר:

Six days you shall do your work, and on the seventh day you shall rest (*tishbot*), so that your ox and your donkey shall repose, and your maidservant's son and the stranger shall be refreshed (*ve-yinafesh*). (23:12)

In our overview of the *pesukim*, we noted that in this *parasha*, the seventh year is not known by any appellation other than its ordinal number – "*shevi'it*." Nevertheless, this *parasha* introduces us to the seventh year as a year of "*tishmetenna u-ntashtah*," the root of which is sh.m.t, the root of the word *shemitta*. Although we translated this phrase as "you shall release it and let it lie fallow," its meaning is the subject of great dispute, as we will see.

Immediately after introducing the sabbatical year, the Torah describes Shabbat. Both involve a system of six and seven – six units of work followed by the seventh unit of ceasing. Only the units of time vary – years versus days.[4]

The Context of *Parashat Mishpatim*

The context of these *pesukim* is significant, as the Torah chose to introduce *shemitta* here, though its central exploration is elsewhere.

---

4   Interestingly, the Torah describe both *shevi'it* and Shabbat in *Parashat Mishpatim* with the verb forms of the nominative terms for these periods: *tishmetenna* gives us *shemitta*, and *tishbot* gives us Shabbat. Although the word *tishbot* regarding Shabbat is reminiscent of how *shevi'it* is described in *Parashat Behar*, the root sh.b.t. does not appear in the verb form in that context, as it does here.

The Overall Context

Parashat Mishpatim, particularly its first three chapters (*Shemot* 21-23), contains primarily civil laws, rather than ritual laws. This unit is sandwiched in between two narratives of the giving of the Torah on Mount Sinai. The preceding portion, *Parashat Yitro*, contains a detailed account of the giving of the Torah, the incredible display of God's greatness at the Revelation at Sinai, in which God gives the Torah and the Jews receive it (ibid. 19-20). At the conclusion of *Parashat Yitro*, a number of ritual laws are mentioned, and then the Torah begins to detail the civil laws of *Parashat Mishpatim*. Immediately after these chapters, the Torah returns (ibid. 24) to the depiction of the Giving of the Torah, including the Jewish People's declaration of acceptance, "*Naaseh ve-nishma*," "We will do and we will listen" (ibid. 24:7).

Why are the civil laws presented in the midst of the description of the giving of the Torah? Why do they deserve such a central position in the Torah?

Parashat Yitro	Parashat Mishpatim	The End of *Parashat Mishpatim*
The Torah describes receiving the commandments on Har Sinai	The Torah juxtaposes the Sinai experience with numerous interpersonal social *mitzvot*, primarily revolving around civil law	The Torah returns to the discussion of Har Sinai, detailing the covenant between the Jewish People and Hashem.

The Torah itself appears to draw a connection between the laws in this *parasha* and the events of the Revelation at Sinai, introducing them with the phrase, "וְאֵלֶּה הַמִּשְׁפָּטִים," "And these are the civil law precepts." The fact that the *parasha* begins with the conjunction "and" (the letter *vav*) indicates that these civil laws somehow follow from the previous unit describing the Har Sinai experience.

The Ramban (see commentary *Shemot* 21:1, 20:22) explains that the laws of *Parashat Mishpatim* are included in the middle of the Sinai revelation because they were taught at that juncture.[5] But this merely strengthens the question. What is the connection between the laws of damages and the Revelation at Sinai?

Furthermore, it is in this context that the Torah introduces *shevi'it*, with its social message of "*ve'achlu evyonei amecha*," "and the poor of your nation shall eat." The mitzvot that surround *shemitta* in *Parashat* Mishpatim are:

---

5   Other commentators, such as Rashi and Abarbanel, understand that the covenant described in chapter 24 was actually a prelude to the revelation described in chapter 19. They invoke the principle that the Torah does not necessarily follow strict chronological order (*ein mukdam u-me'uchar ba-Torah*), but rather follows a thematic, educationally-driven order. According to the understanding of these commentators, *Parashat Mishpatim* was not taught as part of the Sinai experience. Nevertheless, the Torah's thematic placement of these laws as if they were taught at this juncture clearly illustrates a connection between the two.

1. The laws of proper judgment in the courts
2. Proper treatment of the *ger* (the stranger/convert)
3. *Shevi'it* and the need for *shemitta*, releasing one's hold on their fields
4. The weekly Shabbat as a time of physical and spiritual rest
5. The Festivals as a time to connect to Hashem in the *Mikdash*.

What is the connection between the *mitzvah* of *shevi'it*, *Parashat Mishpatim*, and Sinai?

These questions highlight the need to understand the relationship between religious experience and civil law. They illustrate an overall relationship between the social and the religious elements of many *mitzvot*, and *shevi'it* in particular.

A number of commentaries (see Shemot 21:1) explain that the fact that the *mishpatim* are placed in the middle of the Har Sini description is testament to the centrality of *mishpat*, justice. This incorporates not only civil law, but also how God's statutes and laws play themselves out in society. The *mishpatim*, which comprise the basis of the Jewish legal system, are the means of translating the will of God into the everyday situations that arise. The judge, basing his decisions on the *mishpatim*, expresses God's will as taught by the Torah.

Rav Yitzchak Berkowitz[6] explains that the term "*mishpatim*" refers to laws whose reasoning affects their application. Unlike a *chok*, which is an absolute rule, a *mishpat* is the exact opposite. The reasoning behind a *mishpat* is its very definition. Thus, the same act may be considered a *mitzvah* in one case and a sin in another. Being kind and considerate of others requires understanding whom one is dealing with – what they need and how one can help.

In short, a *mishpat* is a principle, while a *chok* is a rule. It is insufficient to learn the *mishpatim* or even to memorize them. Since they are principles, one must develop an understanding of the *ta'am* (reason) of each law, the principle behind it by which every individual must live. Knowledge of the laws alone is insufficient; one must learn how to apply them and how to make judgment calls, and in the process to be sensitized and transformed by the appreciation of the Godly principles of justice in society.

Social and civil laws are not merely practical necessities for effective governing. They are divine daily expressions of the Sinai experience. Therefore, no place is more fitting practically or thematically for *Parashat Mishpatim*. These laws are part and parcel of the daily reenactment of the Sinai experience.

This understanding of *mishpatim* in general and their placement as part of the Har Sinai experience has clear implications for *shevi'it*. *Shevi'it*'s connection to Sinai is made apparent in the longer description in *Parashat Behar*, as the Torah introduces the ritual aspects of *shemitta* observance as the archetypical system of *mitzvot* taught at Sinai. However, *Parashat Mishpatim* introduces *shevi'it*'s social aspects within the context of the central role of *mishpatim* in the Torah. In this *parasha*, the Torah describes *shevi'it* as a time when owners relinquish their field's yield, sharing their crop with the poor and even the animals.

---

6   Heard on a recording.

Parashat Mishpatim indicates that beyond the importance of these *mitzvot* taught as part of the Har Sinai experience, they are not merely rules; they are principles whose reasoning must be understood to be performed properly. *Shevi'it*'s social release is one of the "Har Sinai principles" central to our tradition and essential for our mindset, not only practice.

The Specific Context

As noted above, the *mitzvah* of *shevi'it* immediately follows several laws regarding righteous judgments, culminating with the laws of proper treatment of the stranger:

וְגֵר לֹא תִלְחָץ וְאַתֶּם יְדַעְתֶּם אֶת נֶפֶשׁ הַגֵּר כִּי גֵרִים הֱיִיתֶם בְּאֶרֶץ מִצְרָיִם:

And you shall not oppress a stranger, for you know the feelings of the stranger, since you were strangers in the land of Egypt. (*Shemot* 23:9)

Some commentaries explain that *shevi'it* follows the Torah's emphasis on maintaining justice as a matter of cause and effect. For instance, Alshich explains that the reward for a society in which justice prevails is agricultural success. The Or Ha-Chayim explains that *shevi'it* immediately follows the laws of proper treatment of the stranger because observing *Shevi'it* prevents exile and the need to live as a stranger in the lands of others (as noted in *Vayikra* 26).

Rav Yonatan Snowbell[7] suggests an additional explanation for the connection between *shevi'it* and the stranger. During the *shemitta* year, one feels like a stranger in one's own land, realizing that the land is not really his property, as that term is commonly understood. Since the *shevi'it* year enables all to feel what it means to be a stranger, it reminds us of the level of concern we must always exhibit to those who feel out of place.

Rav Hirsch (commentary on *Shemot* 23:9) explains that this *pasuk* demanding proper treatment of the stranger refers back to a verse in the previous chapter: "You shall not wrong a stranger or oppress him, for you were strangers in the land of Egypt" (ibid. 22:20). There, the Torah requires equality before the law as the foundation of a Jewish society. The true test of society's lovingkindness, Rav Hirsch writes, is reflected in its treatment of foreigners, as it is "an accurate indication of the extent to which justice and humanity prevail in the state."

Rav Hirsch continues to explain that the various *mitzvot* in *Parashat Mishpatim*, including *shevi'it*, are only outlined broadly. Despite the singular nature of each *mitzvah*, the Torah groups them all together due to their common feature:

> They nurture in the nation the spirit of equality and humanity. For these laws are intended to instill in the people the awareness that they, too, should regard themselves as merely strangers and sojourners in God's land and on God's earth; hence, they should not exaggerate the importance of material property — an exaggeration which always creates legal inequality and harshness in human relationships. Observance of these laws will guide the people to a proper and heightened appreciation of all the moral and spiritual values that make man truly human, and that are the basis for the

---

7   In conversation.

equality of all men under the law and for mutual love between man and his fellow man.

Shabbat of the years, i.e., *shemitta*, and Shabbat of the days, the Festivals... are all presented here in broad outlines from this one point of view.

Thus, at the end of *Parashat Mishpatim*, which includes the fundamentals of social law, the Torah shows us the importance of these laws (although *shemitta*, Shabbat, etc. are generally considered "religious" institutions) for social life. What is more, these laws are the true soul of social life; they are a never-failing source from which the social existence of the nation can draw nourishment and abiding vitality for its spirit and life-force. Only by dint of these laws will there emerge from the nation's inner essence a national life based on justice and humanity. Without these laws, countries strive in vain — and always clumsily — to base such a national life on all sorts of superficial statutes and state institutions.

Rav Hirsch deals with the larger question of why *shemitta* and the holidays are included in *Parashat Mishpatim*, which deals with social laws. His answer is essentially that through this context, the Torah indicates that the perspective of separation of church and state – that is, differentiating between ritual *mitzvot* and interpersonal instructions for the benefit of society – is often flawed. The two not only overlap, but often interact and intertwine.

Rav Hirsch's comments reinforce that *Parashat Mishpatim* is a *parasha* that underscores the Torah's plan for a society of lovingkindness. It is the heart of the Sinaitic covenant, ensuring a spiritual community pervaded by social concern and interpersonal virtues. *Shevi'it* is one of the quintessential expressions of a society built on bridging the spiritual and interpersonal.

The Six Years and the Seventh

The Torah introduces the special *halachot* of the seventh year by contrasting them with the previous six years:

וְשֵׁשׁ שָׁנִים תִּזְרַע אֶת אַרְצֶךָ וְאָסַפְתָּ אֶת תְּבוּאָתָהּ:

And six years you shall sow your land and shall harvest its fruits. (*Shemot* 23:10)

The Torah introduces Shabbat with a similar introduction, mentioning six years of creative activity followed by the seventh, a period of rest:

שֵׁשֶׁת יָמִים תַּעֲשֶׂה מַעֲשֶׂיךָ וּבַיּוֹם הַשְּׁבִיעִי תִּשְׁבֹּת:

Six days you shall do your work, and on the seventh day you shall rest. (ibid. 23:12)

The Torah indicates that the seventh period of rest is an aberration to the overall goals of the six years, during which we are to plant and develop the land. Unlike the common practice in antiquity, when most fields were left fallow every other year, the Alshich (Shemot 23:10-11) understands that theTorah calls for working the land six years straight, without the need for crop leaving the land fallow for any of the years. Only in the seventh year does the entire nation simultaneously rest their fields. Logic might dictate that it would be more sensible for every individual to leave one-seventh of his fields fallow every year, but the Torah requires a more revolutionary mold. Every individual puts the land to rest every seven years, without fail. The Torah indicates that divine assistance will ensure that working the land consistently for six years will not dilute its resources.[8]

The Alshich (ibid.) notes that resting during the seventh year is not necessary due to the depleted land's need for a break because it is incapable of growing.[9] Rather, the land rests for a greater purpose –to enable all that *Shevi'it* has to offer.

The Rashbam (*Shemot* 23:10-11) adds that the Torah contrasts the six years with the seventh, because in all other years, one is not permitted to declare their produce *hefker* (ownerless). The laws of *shevi'it* are not an ideal that can be applied to all years; rather, they are specific requirements only for the seventh year.

Furthermore, the *Da'at Zekenim* (*Shemot* 23:10-11) cites a tradition that the Torah's description of six years of working the land is an actual obligation specifically in the Land of Israel:

> Even if one only has a small scorched piece of land in his garden, he must work it every day.

The *Da'at Zekenim* reasons that the *mitzvah* to work one's land during the six years applies specifically to the Land of Israel so that there will be more gifts given to the *Kohanim* and *Levi'im*. One might alternatively suggest that the *mitzvah* to continuously develop and build up the land of Israel is due to the *mitzvah* of *yishuv Eretz Yisrael*, settling and cultivating the land of Israel.

The Torah's emphasis on the six years of planting and developing *Eretz Yisrael* makes it more difficult to understand why we must leave the land fallow during the seventh year. If it is not necessary for replenishing the land's nutrients, why is it done? The Torah seems to present two contradictory messages. For six years we must cultivate, illustrating an ideal of self-sufficiency and advancing the beauty and bounty of the Land of Israel. In the seventh, however, we halt, as the goal of developing the land is put aside for the sake of a larger ideal.

The Torah clearly does not want *shevi'it* rest to undo the six years of land enhancement. It does not desire the Land of Israel to become destitute and unbeautiful. Instead, as we maintain the current beauty of the land, our focus shifts to retaining religious ideals and avoiding escapades in personal conquest and agricultural wealth-building. *Shevi'it* allows us to recognize the ultimate purpose of our activities in the field and that one's success is part of a larger, unified national objective rather than a personal attempt to build up one's fortune.

Against this backdrop, we can appreciate Alshich's (ibid.) comments regarding the

---

8   It is worth noting that unlike the Alshich's explanation, it is clear from discussions in the third chapter of Bava Batra that fields were left fallow at points, and there was also crop rotation practiced.

9   The notion that the ground is still sufficiently fertile for things to grow seems to emerge from the *pesukim* discussing *sefiach*, i.e., produce that grows without being planted. Clearly some produce can grow in the land even if it isn't planted, surely if it were planted more would grow.

necessary ingredients for allowing one to miraculously plant for six years straight without depleting the land's resources:

> Whereas in other countries, the earth needs to recover after each year and cannot be worked six years in succession, Israelites in their land can work the same soil six years in a row without fear of famine, as famines are the penalty for social injustice. In fact, in the seventh year, the same soil will produce a crop without it having been worked at all. Even in that year, the soil does not need to recuperate from having produced harvests for six years consecutively. Your poor will have food to eat, and there will be leftovers for the beasts of the field.

Alshich points out that adhering to the values of *shevi'it* and its social messages enables the land to be fruitful. Maintaining perspective and refraining from planting during *shevi'it* allows the land to be more productive during the other six years.

In a similar vein, the *midrash* (*Yalkut Shimoni Mishpatim* 333 s.v. *sheish*) explains that when the nation observes the *halachot* of *shevi'it*, the laws are necessary only once in seven years. When the nation fails in its *shevi'it* observance, however, they must observe four *shemittot* in seven years, as the land will not bear fruit yearly, but will instead require allowing the land to rest so it is cultivatable only every other year.

Chizkuni (*Shemot* 23:10) and Ibn Ezra (*Shemot* 23:10) note that the mention of the six years here serves another purpose as well. One might think that due to the seventh year, one may rest assured that the poor have been taken care of. The verse therefore states that one should not rely on *shevi'it* alone, even though it affords a powerful means of helping the poor; there are charitable requirements attached to the fields throughout the rest of the *shemitta* cycle.

The Reinvigorating Shabbat

Beyond the divine blessing built into a seven-year cycle including *shevi'it* observance, *shevi'it* provides an opportunity for human rest much more than the land's rest. The farmer is given the opportunity to regain his physical strength. The Alshich (*Shemot* 23:12) notes that the laws of *shevi'it* are followed in the Torah by those of Shabbat, described as a day of physical rest for the animals and a day of *"va-yinafash"* for the male and female servants. The Alshich notes that this term is the *Talmudic* source for the idea of a *neshama yetera*, an expanded soul on Shabbat (TB *Beitza* 16a). He explains that the term *vayinafash* used here in the context of *shevi'it*, indicates that one gains a *neshama yetera* on *shevi'it* as well, and must take advantage of it:

> Should you think that the legislation is designed to give man a year's vacation, this is not so. Just as it had been decreed to abstain from work every Shabbat, as a reminder of the fact that God imbued the Shabbat with sanctity already at the time of creation, so the seventh-year legislation is also rooted in similar considerations. Both on the Shabbat and during the seventh year, a person acquires an additional spiritual dimension, similar to the *neshama yetera*.
> The aspect of physical rest mentioned here applies only to "your ox and your donkey."

> Humans, even your non-Jewish slaves, must fulfill part of the Torah precepts, so they are to benefit from *ve-yinafesh*, this additional soul. There is no need to mention again the fact that this concept applies in an even greater measure to the Jew.

Similarly, Rav Hirsch (ad loc.) describes how Shabbat and *shevi'it* share the similar goal of enabling the people to recognize the Creator. This is why the Torah juxtaposes the two *mitzvot*:

> Just as the Shabbat year of the land establishes the nation's standing in its land, the Shabbat day establishes man's standing in the world. By observing the Shabbat, man acknowledges God as the Creator and Master of the world and of himself. On the seventh day, man refrains from exercising his own mastery over any of God's creations and humbly subordinates himself and his world to the Creator. While he observes the Shabbat, the Shabbat teaches him to respect every other creature alongside himself, as all are equal before God and all are His children.
>
> This dismantling of man's mastery over all creatures is one of the objectives of the Shabbat, the day on which man pays homage to God, so that rest should come to the working animals and beasts of burden, and so that the son of your handmaid and the stranger in your midst shall "return to themselves" (*yinafesh*), become conscious of their own human dignity, and recognize that their purpose in life is their very own.
>
> From "in order that your ox and your donkey shall repose," the *Mechilta* derives that a person has a special obligation toward his animals: Not only must one leave one's animals at rest on the Shabbat, but one must also turn them out and allow them to graze undisturbed.

We have seen that understanding the context of *Parashat Mishpatim* within the Har Sinai experience and *shevi'it*'s mention alongside the laws of proper judgment and proper treatment of strangers illustrates its social messages and the importance of applying its reasoning while observing its *halachot*. Furthermore, we learned that the Torah's contrast between the six years of planting and the seventh year of release indicates the importance of developing Israel's land throughout the six years. It also illustrates the miraculous blessings that Hashem provides for Israel throughout the six years. The resting on *shevi'it* provides an opportunity for *va-yinafash*, soul rest, just like the resting on Shabbat.

The primary *mitzvah* of *shevi'it* in *Parashat Mishpatim* highlights *shevi'it*'s social messages: "You shall release it (*tishmetenna*) and let it lie fallow (*u-ntashtah*)." We will now take a deeper look at this commandment.

Tishmetenna U-ntashtah –
Relinquishing Ownership of Produce

The primary obligation during *shevi'it* as described in *Parashat Mishpatim* is the call of *tishmetenna u-ntashtah*:

וְשֵׁשׁ שָׁנִים תִּזְרַע אֶת אַרְצֶךָ וְאָסַפְתָּ אֶת תְּבוּאָתָהּ: וְהַשְּׁבִיעִת תִּשְׁמְטֶנָּה וּנְטַשְׁתָּהּ וְאָכְלוּ אֶבְיֹנֵי עַמֶּךָ וְיִתְרָם
תֹּאכַל חַיַּת הַשָּׂדֶה כֵּן תַּעֲשֶׂה לְכַרְמְךָ לְזֵיתֶךָ:

And six years you shall sow your land and shall harvest its fruits. But [in] the seventh (*shevi'it*), you shall release it (*tishmetenna*) and let it lie *fallow* (*u-ntashtah*), and the poor of your nation will eat, and what they leave over the beasts of the field shall eat. So you shall do with your vineyard and with your olive grove. (*Shemot* 23:10-11)

The Torah distinguishes the seventh year as a year of *tishmetenna u-ntashtah*, as opposed to the preceding six years, which are periods of sowing and harvesting. The Torah indicates that following this instruction allows "the poor of your nation" to eat (and what they leave over will be food for animals). *Shevi'it* is a year during which the landowners and the underprivileged enjoy and benefit from the produce and crops equally.

Financial or Agricultural?

The precise meaning of the words *tishmetenna u-ntashtah*, however, remains elusive. It is especially important to define them properly, as the root of *tishmetenna* – sh.m.t. – is the source of the word *shemitta*, which we use to describe the entire year. As we have noted, the lengthy description of the agricultural *halachot* of *shevi'it* in *Parashat Behar* never uses the term *shemitta*, instead focusing on the idea of *shabbat ha-aretz*. In fact, we might question if there is an idea of an agricultural "*shemitta*" altogether. Perhaps that is a term that is appropriate only for *shemittat kesafim*, the remission of loans during *shevi'it*, while the agricultural *halachot* reflect the element of *shabbat ha-aretz*.

Is the appearance of the directive *tishmetenna* an indication that agricultural *shemitta* does indeed exist? Or is *tishmetenna* an earlier iteration of the financial *shemitta* described at great length in *Parashat Re'eh*?

The Understanding of Ibn Ezra and Seforno

The Ibn Ezra and Seforno explain that the term *tishmetenna* is a reference to the financial release of loans, *shemittat kesafim*, while *u-ntashta* is a reference to agricultural obligations during *shevi'it*. Ibn Ezra (short commentary) states explicitly:

Tishmetenna is a reference to the release of loans, while **u-ntashtah** refers to letting the land lie fallow, "as if it is not his."

Similarly, the Seforno explains:

Tishmetenna — this refers to the release of debts… **U-ntashtah** — abandon it so that the poor of your people may eat. Through the release of the soil, the poor will also be able to eat.

Both commentaries seemingly view *Parashat Re'eh's* repetition of the term *shemitta* in the financial context as indicative of the term *shemitta's* sole meaning as a requirement to release loans. They would appear to maintain that there is really no concept of agricultural *shemitta*, as the seventh year is a year of agricultural rest (*shabbat*) and abandonment (*u-ntashta*), not agricultural release (*shemitta*).

Although these commentaries distinguish between the terms associated with the financial and agricultural elements of the seventh year, they understand that the *pasuk* in *Parashat Mishptaim* juxtaposes the monetary relinquishment of the seventh year (*tishmatenna*) with the agricultural obligations to leave the land fallow (*u-ntashtah*). The Torah tells us that *shevi'it* is marked by two intertwined components that together respond to social concerns: *shabbat ha-aretz*, the agricultural aspects of the year, and *shemittat kesafim*, the financial aspects associated with remitting debts.

The Common Understanding of *Tishmetenna*

Most commentaries understand that the term *tishmetenna* refers to the agricultural laws of *shevii't*, rather than the monetary laws.[10] Several commentaries concur that *tishmetenna* is a requirement to perform an act of *shemitta* on one's land, although they differ as to what exactly this entails.

Some explain that *tishmetenna* and *u-ntashtah* refer to different agricultural elements of *shemitta*: *Tishmetenna* focuses on the ground, while *u-ntashtah* focuses on the produce. For example, Targum Yonatan explains that *tishmetenna* bans working the field, and *u-ntashtah* requires that one declare the fruits *hefker* (ownerless).

Others explain the verse as referring to two obligations regarding the field. Rashi (in his second explanation, based on one opinion in *Mo'ed Katan* 3a) states:

> **Tishmetenna** — [release] from real work, such as plowing and sowing. **U-ntashtah** — and abandon it from fertilizing and hoeing.

Rashi understands *tishmetenna* as a positive requirement to release one's hold on the land by refraining from the explicit agricultural prohibitions mentioned in *Parashat Behar* and *Parashat Ki Tisa* (sowing and plowing). *U-ntashtah* adds that one must additionally refrain from other agricultural acts that are not mentioned explicitly in the Torah.

The Ramban takes issue with the explanations of Rashi and the Ibn Ezra, noting that neither of their explanations is in line with the Sages' understanding of the *pesukim*. He explains that the requirement of *tishmetenna u-ntashtah* is a contrast to the activity during the previous six years. The Torah states that during the six years, one plants and harvests the crops. Thus:

> On the seventh year, *tishmetenna* — you must not sow your land; *u-ntashtah* — you must not gather in what grows on its own. Instead, you are to leave it so that the poor

---

10 According to those who see *tishmetenna* as a reference to agricultural *shevi'it*, the Torah clearly connects the agricultural and financial elements of the year. Although the financial *shemitta* occurs in one split second at the year's conclusion, agricultural *shemitta* applies throughout the seventh year for vegetables and even continues into the eighth year for fruits.

> of your people and the beasts of the field may eat the fruits of the tree and the produce of the vineyard.

The Ramban concurs that the two terms refer to the land and the fruits, respectively, limiting the landowner's hold on "his" property.

The Ramban's explanation is unique in that he views this *pasuk* as lacking any legal novelties that we would not have known from *Parashat Behar*. There, the Torah states that the seventh year is a year of *shabbat ha-aretz*, during which one is restricted from sowing the land and normal harvesting. (The rest, as the Alshich notes, is far more than a vacation from physical exertion. The individual is endowed with a *neshama yeteira*, a heightened soul, during this year. Rest allows one to tap into that soul by merging the physical and spiritual. [See chapter 11 for a lengthier discussion of this *neshama yeteira*.])According to the Ramban, the novelty of *Parashat Mishpatim* is not the legal requirement, but rather how we look at it.

Parashat Mishpatim focuses on the social aspects of equality that *shevi'it* provides, declaring the result of one's *shemitta* as, "and the poor of your nation shall eat." The *shemitta (tishmetenna)* requirement ensures that one releases himself from his standard relationship with their fields and what grows in it. This release entitles everyone to eat from the produce, and all are given time to rest from their backbreaking work. Thus, while the agricultural laws are more commonly descibred in the Torah as *shabbat ha-aretz*, focusing on the rest of the land, there is an element of *shemitta* that is relevant as well.

Perhaps the Torah is indicating that the land's rest is an outgrowth of the individual's willingness to release his hold on what he feels is his property. By doing so, he allows the land and himself to rest, thereby connecting to the opportunities that *shevi'it* has to offer.

Shemitta- Release Your Hold on the Produce as It Grows on "Your" Land

The *Mechilta* (*deRebbi Yishmael- Mishpatim Parasha* 20, 18) offers another understanding of the term *tishmetenna u-ntashtah* that views the phrase as a reference to **how** one is to relinquish his hold over the agricultural produce in the field. This understanding is accepted by the Rambam, who may be the primary influence in terming the seventh year "*shemitta*."

The Rambam explains that the requirement to declare all produce growing in one's field as *hefker* (ownerless) is learned from the phrase *tishmetanna u-ntashtah*:

> והמצוה הקל"ד היא שצונו להפקיר כל מה שתצמיח הארץ בשנת השמיטה והפקיר צמחי אדמתינו כלם
> לכל אדם. והוא אמרו ית' (משפטי' כג) והשביעית תשמטנה ונטשתה וכו'....
>
> The 134th *mitzvah* is that we are commanded to disown everything that the land produces during the *shemitta* year, to release everything that grows on our property for the use of any living creature. The source of this commandment is God's statement, "But in the seventh, *tishmetenna u-ntashtah*." (*Sefer Ha-Mitzvot, Aseh* 134)

In his *Mishneh Torah*, the Rambam expands upon the requirements of declaring one's produce *hefker* as an act of *shemitta* (using the term from the *pasuk*), explaining what violating it means:

> It is a positive commandment to divest oneself from everything that the land produces in the *shemitta* year ... Anyone who locks his vineyard or fences off his field in the *shemitta* year has nullified a positive commandment. This also holds true if he gathers all his produce into his home. Instead, he should leave everything ownerless. Thus, everyone has equal rights in every place, as the verse states: "And the poor of your nation will eat." One may bring a small amount into one's home, just as one brings from ownerless property, e.g., five jugs of oil, fifteen jugs of wine. (*Hilchot Shemitta* 2:4)

The Rambam explains that any act of locking one's vineyard or actively preventing others from taking possession of one's fruits is a violation of this *mitzvah*. Whereas *Parashat Behar* describes the requirement that one refrain from normal harvesting of his produce throughout the year, this *pasuk* in *Parashat Mishpatim* tells us one primary reason for doing so. One must release his hold on his property, engage in *shemitta*, and release himself from his usual mindset regarding his produce.

This requirement of rendering the produce *hefker* is central to the identity of the *shemitta* year. The *Sefer Ha-Chinuch* (*mitzvah* 84) points out that this requirement is what earns the year its appellation. The Rambam's explanation of *tishmetenna* won out. Indeed, he terms the section of the *Mishneh Torah* dealing with the *halachot* of the seventh year *Hilchot Shemitta V'Yovel*, the laws of *shemitta* and *yovel*. This accepted term for the seventh year not only refers to the year, but underscores its nature.

Understanding *tishmetenna* as a reference to relinquishing one's rights to the fields' produce adds a new element that is not explicit in *Parashat Behar*. There, the focus is how to treat the land; here, the focus is how the owner must act with his produce.

As we have previously noted, there are four distinct phases involving the land and its produce during the seventh year:

❶	❷	❸	❹
The Land Before Planting	**The Land During the Growing Season**	**The Vegetation and Crops While Growing (on trees or in the ground)**	**The Produce After it is Harvested**

The commentaries who identify *tishmetenna* as a reference to refraining from agricultural activities see it as a reference to the first two phases. The Rambam, however, identifies *tishmetenna* as a reference to the third stage. As the produce is ready to be picked, one can imagine that the landowner who has toiled would want to harvest it, feed himself and family, and sell the rest of the crop as a return on investment and hopefully a little profit. Indeed, this is how the Torah describes the appropriate practice for the first six years. But in the seventh year, the Torah teaches that one must put that practice to rest. One performs "*shemitta*," releasing his hold on their produce and simultaneously releasing his hold on his field. He opens up the gates that generally restrict outsiders from traversing his property, replacing them with a giant sign: "These fruits are *hefker*, ownerless. Come one, come all, and partake!" The fact that the Torah introduces these laws with such a challenging concept, which for the Rambam defines the year's essence, points to the central role of this idea for *shevi'it*.

The Lessons of *Tishmetenna*

In section III, we will discuss at greater length the various rationales for this act of *shemitta*, but some of them are readily apparent. The Torah explicitly states a social benefit: "And the poor of your nation will eat." The "owner" of the fruit no longer has any advantages over the poor, as all equally benefit from the produce.

This result is significant, but the owner's act of releasing is also significant, impacting his perspective and character. Spiritually, relinquishing one's hold on the land allows the owner to "remember that the land that brings forth its fruits yearly does not bring forth fruits through its own powers, but because there is a master over the land and over the land's owners..." (*Sefer Ha-Chinuch, mitzvah* 84). Through this recognition, one also fortifies his *bitachon* (trust) in God, as he realizes, in the absence of "his" fields, his survival and success are dependent upon the Almighty alone. Rabbeinu Bachayei (*Vayikra* 25) adds that since the purpose of the *shemitta* year is to realize God's mastery over the land, one releases the hold on the land "in order to allow man to contemplate in his heart that God is the true owner and Master."

The *Shem Mi-Shmuel* (*Vayikra* 25) notes that the *shemitta* year is the ideal time for one to acknowledge God's true control and ownership by relinquishing one's hold on the land. The Kli Yakar (ibid.) states that the primary reason for relinquishing ownership is in order to recognize God's possession, but once one is already doing so, it is proper that it then be abandoned so that the poor can benefit from it.

Concluding Thoughts on *Parashat Mishpatim*

We noted that *Parashat Mishpatim* is the Torah's introduction to the year of *shevi'it*. It notes a social benefit of "and the poor of your nation will eat" and requires an act of *tishmetenna u-ntashtah*. Although some commentaries understand *tishmetenna* as a reference to loan remittance at the conclusion of the seventh year, most commentaries identify this act of *shemitta* as a fundamental element of the agricultural elements of *shevi'it*. For some, it refers to refraining from standard agricultural practices in the field, but the Rambam sees it as the call to release one's hold on his produce as it grows in the field.

The root *sh.m.t.*, release, seems to lie at the heart of the year, which proclaims a need to release and relinquish. The Torah chose to discuss the other elements of the year in different *parashiyot*, but made it clear in *Parashat Mishpatim*: This is a year of release, and through that prism take a look at its other *parashiyot*.

Chapter 4

Parasha 2: *Shemitta* in *Ki Tisa* – Extending Holiness

Chronologically, the second *parasha* that may discuss the seventh year is *Parashat Ki Tisa*, although, as noted above, its mention is not explicit. After describing the *teshuva* following the nation's remorse after the episode of the golden calf, the Torah details a list of *mitzvot* that closely resembles those that appear in *Parashat Mishpatim*:

> שֵׁשֶׁת יָמִים תַּעֲבֹד וּבַיּוֹם הַשְּׁבִיעִי תִּשְׁבֹּת בֶּחָרִישׁ וּבַקָּצִיר תִּשְׁבֹּת:
>
> Six days you shall work, but on the seventh day, you shall rest [*tishbot*]; in plowing and in harvesting, you shall rest. (*Shemot* 34:21)

The glaring difficulty in the *pasuk* is that the requirement of resting from performing *melacha* (labor) on the weekly Shabbat does not require resting only from the two activities explicitly mentioned in the *pasuk* – plowing and harvesting. After all, there are thirty-nine prohibited *melachot* on Shabbat. Why are only these two singled out?

The Rashbam explains that these acts are simply the most common:

> If these important labors are prohibited, although they are necessary for humankind, then other labors are certainly forbidden!

Similarly, Ibn Ezra explains that these *melachot* are singled out for their importance, as man's sustenance is dependent on them. In his shorter commentary, Ibn Ezra adds that these *melachot* are time sensitive. Even if there is a lot of rain, if one has not plowed properly, one cannot plant. Thus, an explicit prohibition of these two indicates that all others are certainly proscribed.

Alshich (ad loc.) offers a novel explanation for why Shabbat is discussed in *Parashat Ki Tisa* at all, which further explains why the *pasuk* specifically emphasizes the need to abstain from plowing and harvesting on Shabbat.

> The guiding principle is that through the *mitzvot* that are mentioned [here], man is supposed to recognize God's creation of the world... Perhaps you will say that the weekly Shabbat provides a remembrance of God's creation, and that alone should suffice. Therefore, the Torah spells out that for six days a man works... indicating that Shabbat represents the conclusion of this renewal of the creative process, and accordingly also assumes a national significance for Israel, in addition to the universal one. Yet, while Shabbat observance indicates that one has faith in God's creation of the world, it does not prove such a belief [as it was not directly witnessed]. Therefore, there is a weakening of one's resolve to strictly observe Shabbat by refraining from working for one's sustenance, specifically when the plowing and harvesting times arrive, as it is difficult for the farmer to interrupt his work when time is of the essence. Therefore, Shabbat here is mentioned alongside Pesach and the *mitzvot* of the firstborn, as the fact that Pesach was witnessed firsthand explicitly reminds the Jew of the world order that was created anew, strengthening his resolve to observe Shabbat

carefully, in spite of what may appear to be a significant inconvenience. This, then, is why we have the laws of Shabbat interposed between the laws of Pesach and Shavuot.

For the Alshich, two of the most challenging *melachot* to refrain from on Shabbat are plowing and harvesting, as they must be done at very specific times. The Torah juxtaposes Shabbat and the Festivals to illustrate that if one finds it difficult to maintain his resolve to observe the Shabbat, as no individual witnessed the world's creation, he should remember the fFestivals, which commemorate miraculous events witnessed by the Jewish people. The farmer should thereby harness his trust in God and his willingness to accept His word.

Rabbi Akiva and Rabbi Yishmael

These commentators explain the *pasuk* as referring to the weekly Shabbat, providing an explanation for its placement and the reason it mentions these two *melachot* specifically. In the Talmud, Rabbi Akiva and Rabbi Yishmael both maintain that the *pasuk* intends to teach us something beyond its simple meaning.

The (anonymous) *mishna* in *Shevi'it* (1:4) and Rabbi Akiva (*Rosh Hashana* 9a; *Mo'ed Katan* 3b) maintain that this *pasuk* does not refer only to the weekday Shabbat, but rather teaches something about *shevi'it* as well:

> דְּתַנְיָא בֶּחָרִישׁ וּבַקָּצִיר תִּשְׁבּוֹת רַבִּי עֲקִיבָא אוֹמֵר אֵינוֹ צָרִיךְ לוֹמַר חָרִישׁ וְקָצִיר שֶׁל שְׁבִיעִית שֶׁהֲרֵי כְּבָר נֶאֱמַר שָׂדְךָ לֹא תִזְרָע וְגוֹ' אֶלָּא חָרִישׁ שֶׁל עֶרֶב שְׁבִיעִית הַנִּכְנָס לִשְׁבִיעִית וְקָצִיר שֶׁל שְׁבִיעִית הַיּוֹצֵא לְמוֹצָאֵי שְׁבִיעִית:
>
> "In plowing and in harvest you shall rest" – Rabbi Akiva says: There is no need to be told to desist from plowing or harvesting in the sabbatical year, for it is already stated [elsewhere]: "You shall not sow your field," etc. [It can be taken] only [to prohibit] plowing in the pre-sabbatical year [which may cause agricultural benefits] extending into the sabbatical year, and [likewise] to the harvest of the sabbatical year's [fruit] crops which mature in the post-sabbatical year.(TB *Rosh Hashana* 9a)

As Rashi explains in his commentary on the *pasuk*, Rabbi Akiva maintains that although the first part of the *pasuk* refers to the weekly Shabbat, the second part of the *pasuk* makes an entirely different point. According to Rabbi Akiva, the *pasuk* is referring to another form of Shabbat when the *melachot* of plowing and harvesting are prohibited. This refers to *tosefet shevi'it*, the time added on to the year of *shevi'it* at its beginning and end. Plowing before *shevi'it* is sometimes prohibited; similarly, harvesting fruits in the usual manner is restricted even after the *shevi'it* year ends.

According to Rabbi Akiva, the Talmud adds, not only does this *pasuk* teach that one must add on to *shevi'it*, but it serves as the model for *tosefet kedusha*, adding on a period before and after all other sanctified periods, such as Shabbat and Festivals.

Rabbi Yishmael disagrees with Rabbi Akiva's interpretation, explaining the *pasuk* as referring specifically to the weekly Shabbat, while teaching an important limitation:

> רַבִּי יִשְׁמָעֵאל אוֹמֵר מָה חָרִישׁ רְשׁוּת אַף קָצִיר רְשׁוּת יָצָא קָצִיר הָעוֹמֶר שֶׁהוּא מִצְוָה:
>
> Rabbi Yishmael says: [It is purely a Shabbat law]; just as the plowing [forbidden on Shabbat] is optional plowing, so is the harvesting optional harvesting. This comes

to exclude the harvesting [of the new barley] for the *omer*, which is a religious duty.

Rabbi Yishmael understands that the Torah here equates the prohibition of plowing with that of harvesting. There is no explicit *mitzvah* anywhere in the Torah to plow, but there is an explicit *mitzvah* to harvest barley for the *omer* offering on the night of the sixteenth of Nissan. The fact that the Torah equates these two prohibitions on Shabbat indicates that only non-*mitzvah* harvesting is prohibited, just as only non-*mitzvah* plowing (i.e., all plowing) is prohibited. *Mitzva*-harvesting is permitted on Shabbat.

Is *Shemitta* Missing?

What is it that leads Rabbi Akiva to interpret the *pasuk* in *Parashat Ki Tisa* as a reference to *shevi'it*? Although the mention of the *melachot* of plowing and harvesting does demand an explanation, Rabbi Akiva's reading – introducing the concept of *tosefet shevi'it* into a *pasuk* that is about the weekly Shabbat – seems like quite a stretch. In truth, a careful comparison of the *pesukim* in *Parashat Ki Tisa* with those in *Parashat Mishpatim* lends support to Rabbi Akiva' reading.

As we have discussed, *Parashat Mishpatim* describes various social laws and concludes with a list of *mitzvot*, followed by a description of the Sinaitic covenant. *Parashat Ki Tisa* describes the tragic episode of the golden calf and its harmful ramifications on the relationship between Hashem and His people. After Moshe Rabbeinu's successful pleading on behalf of the Jewish People, Hashem reestablishes the covenant with them. The list of *mitzvot* initially discussed in *Parashat Mishpatim* (*Shemot* 23:10-19) is then essentially repeated in *Parashat Ki Tisa* (ibid. 34:18-26), restating the covenant in the wake of the sin of the golden calf.

There is only one *mitzvah* from the first list that is absent from the second – *shevi'it*! Rav Hirsch offers one possible explanation:

Above, at the conclusion of the fundamentals of social law, the *mitzvot* of Shabbat and *shevi'it* are mentioned first because the Torah wants to first mention the *mitzvot's* relation to the principles of equality and brotherhood, on which all these laws are based. Shabbat and *shevi'it* continuously proclaim that God is the sole owner of the land and of the universe; it follows naturally that all citizens and all people are equal before the Law. Here, as the covenant is renewed, the same concepts are mentioned, but primarily with regard to their contrast to heathenism. Here, the point of departure is the Exodus from Egypt, the great act that demonstrates God's immanence, and in this connection, the Torah also mentions the *mitzvah* of Shabbat…

The earth will submit only to that work of yours which is done in the service of God. By not working on Shabbat, you express the significance of your work as an act of homage to God… [The mention of resting from plowing and harvesting serves to indicate that] you shall give expression to your homage and to the subservience of your world to God even in the case of work on which your livelihood depends…

Whereas above, in connection with the civil laws, the *mitzvah* of *shevi'it* precedes the *mitzvot* of Shabbat and the Festivals, here it is not mentioned at all, because here the Torah emphasizes the relationship of the Jew to God, not the relationship of the Jewish state to God.

Rav Hirsch reasons that *shevi'it* serves as a lesson in equality and brotherhood, which is an important aspect of recognizing God's relationship to the Jewish state, a topic fitting for *Mishpatim*, but it is understandably absent from *Ki Tisa*, which focuses on the Exodus and one's personal connection to God.

Rabbi Akiva, however, explains that, in fact, *shevi'it* is not absent. Instead, it is alluded to in the *pasuk* about Shabbat[11]. Rabbi Akiva sees the lists of mitzvoth in Mishpatim and Ki Tissa as completely parallel, but the hidden mention of *shevi'it* in the guise of Shabbat informs us of the concept of *Tosefet Shevi'it* in particular, and the power of expanding *kedusha*.

Tosefet Shevi'it

Understanding *tosefet shevi'it* and the concept of *tosefet kedusha* in general will help us appreciate its connection to *shevi'it*.

What is *Tosefet Shevi'it*?

Tosefet Shevi'it extends the uniqueness and holiness of the seventh year into the preceding and following year. Chronologically, it is the first element of *shevi'it* that one confronts and the last component of *shemitta* that one experiences.[12]

Tosefet shevi'it means that some laws of *shevi'it* apply even before the seventh year begins. The Mishna (*Shevi'it* 2:6) and the Gemara (*Mo'ed Katan* 2b-3b) state that the Biblical prohibition of plowing before *shemitta* – as derived either from our *pasuk* or from oral tradition – lasts only thirty days. The Rabbis, however, extended the prohibition to an even longer period. Essentially, plowing is prohibited from the point at which it is no longer performed for the benefit of the sixth year's crop, but rather as preparation for planting in the seventh year. The *mishna* distinguishes between grain fields, regarding which the prohibition begins on Pesach of the sixth year, and orchards, regarding which it begins only from the festival of Shavuot.

The reason for the distinctions regarding the permissibility of plowing for different forms of fields relates to the goal of the plowing. Plowing is sometimes a means of softening the earth for the purposes of later planting (which should not be done in the seventh year), and it is sometimes done to maintain existing trees, ensuring their continued growth. As the Rambam explains:

> It is a law conveyed to Moshe at Sinai that it is forbidden to work the land in the last thirty days of the sixth year, just before the sabbatical year, as in doing so one is preparing [the land] for the seventh year. (*Hilchot Shemitta* 3,1)

Essentially, the *tosefet shevi'it* period requires one to contemplate whether his actions in

---

11   In reference to Rav Hirsch's explanation, it is possible that Rabbi Akiva views *shevi'it* as serving a personal role as well, and therefore fitting for the post-golden calf covenant.

12   For this reason, it is not surprising that Mishna *Shevi'it* opens with a description of *tosefet shevi'it*, as that is essentially how *shevi'it* begins.

the field at the end of the sixth year are necessary for what is already growing or serve as preparation for the growth of the seventh year.[13]

A Deeper Look at the Debate Between Rabbi Akiva and Rabbi Yishmael

A deeper look at Rabbi Akiva and Rabbi Yishmael's opinions reveals a great deal about *shevi'it* and the idea of a sanctified year in general. As we saw, Rabbi Akiva understands the *pasuk* as referring to the concept of *tosefet shevi'it* and, by extension, the idea of adding on to the *kedusha* of all sanctified periods. Although Rabbi Yishmael interprets the *pasuk* differently – as teaching that it is permissible to perform the *omer*-harvest on Shabbat – the Talmud explains that he too accepts the general principle that one must extend periods of *kedusha*, but based on a different source:

> וְרַבִּי יִשְׁמָעֵאל מוֹסִיפִין מֵחוֹל עַל קֹדֶשׁ מְנָא לֵיהּ נָפְקָא לֵיהּ מִדְּתַנְיָא וְעִנִּיתֶם אֶת נַפְשׁוֹתֵיכֶם בְּתִשְׁעָה יָכוֹל בְּתִשְׁעָה תַּלְמוּד לוֹמַר בָּעֶרֶב אִי בָּעֶרֶב יָכוֹל מִשֶּׁתֶּחְשַׁךְ תַּלְמוּד לוֹמַר בְּתִשְׁעָה הָא כֵּיצַד מַתְחִיל וּמִתְעַנֶּה מִבְּעוֹד יוֹם מְלַמֵּד שֶׁמּוֹסִיפִין מֵחוֹל עַל קֹדֶשׁ:

> If so, from where does Rabbi Yishmael derive [this principle of] extending a sacred time period by adding from the profane? He derives it from that which is taught in a *baraita*: The verse states [in reference to Yom Kippur]: "And you shall afflict your souls on the ninth of the month in the evening" (*Vayikra* 23:32). One might have thought that one must fast the entire day on the ninth of the month. Therefore, the verse states: "In the evening." If Yom Kippur begins in the evening, one might have thought that one need only begin to fast from when it is dark [after nightfall, when the tenth day of the month begins]. Therefore, the verse states: "On the ninth." How so? One begins to fast on the ninth of the month while it is still day. This teaches that one extends a sacred time period by adding at the beginning from the profane to the sacred. (TB *Rosh Hashana* 9a-b)

Thus, although Rabbi Akiva and Rabbi Yishmael disagree as to whether the concluding words of the verse in *Ki Tisa* are discussing *shevi'it* or Shabbat, they agree that there is a concept of *tosefet Shabbat* and *tosefet Yom Tov*. They simply disagree regarding the source of that concept. Importantly, Rabbi Yishmael does not derive the concept of *tosefet shevi'it* from the *pasuk* about Yom Kippur. Rather, in his view, that law is a *Halacha L'Moshe MiSinai*, and oral tradition that is not based on a verse or derivation.

The source of the idea of *tosefet shevi'it* is not a mere detail. The idea that one can extend *kedusha* from a sanctified period is a novel concept, and its source may have important implications. After all, it is not intuitive that we can extend *kedusha* beyond the time established on our calendar for it.

Why does Rabbi Akiva choose to find a cryptic source alluding to *tosefet shevi'it* in the last three words of a *pasuk* about Shabbat, instead of attributing the *halacha* to a Mosaic

---

13 In addition to the restrictions on plowing the field in the sixth year when done in order to prepare the land for planting the following year, there are additional restrictions on planting near the end of the seventh year that exist independently of *tosefet shevi'it* (see Section III).

tradition, as Rabbi Yishmael does? This is especially surprising given that most of the *halachot* of *tosefet shevi'it* are derived from oral tradition. Moreover, if the *pasuk* intends to speak about the seventh year, rather than the seventh day, why not mention it explicitly?

It seems that Rabbi Akiva maintains that the Torah wanted to teach us this concept of *tosefet kedusha* specifically by camouflaging the idea of *tosefet shevi'it* in a *pasuk* about Shabbat. Both Shabbat and *shevi'it* represent sanctified times that provide us with the opportunity to add sanctity on our own.

The *pesukim* in *Parashat Ki Tisa* (34:11-24) emphasize that when we fulfill the Torah properly, we will not be susceptible to the attempts of our enemies to conquer our land. The placement of the source of *tosefet shevi'it* in this context evidently indicates that a fundamental aspect of the covenant and our secure right to success in the land is in the way we approach its *kedusha*. It is insufficient to just focus our observance of the spiritual potential of *shevi'it* (which is expressed elsewhere in regard to the seventh year itself), but we seek to expand that *kedusha* through *tosefet shevi'it*. As we will see, *tosefet shevi'it* not only involves certain *halachot* that precede and follow the actual *shemitta* year; it also serves as a source for preparing to accept *kedusha*, longing for it, and ensuring its impression lasts.

In contrast to Rabbi Akiva, Rabbi Yishmael maintains that the source of *tosefet kedushat zeman* is the idea of *tosefet Yom Kippur*. Rav Moshe Luria (*Avnei Shoham*, p. 233) explains that the concept is learned from Yom Kippur – as opposed to Shabbat, the source of the idea of refraining from *melacha* during designated periods – because the primary aspect of *tosefet kedusha* is not the additional prohibitions, but rather the human desire to extent sanctity. In kabbalistic terms, this is termed "אִתְעָרוּתָא דְלְתַתָּא, awakening from below." Extending the period of sanctity creates a period of additional prohibition, but that is merely a reflection of the desire to extend the holiness into the mundane time that precedes and follows it. Additionally, the timing of Yom Kippur depends on the court's sanctification of the month, whereas the timing of Shabbat is not dependent on human determination. Therefore, Rabbi Yishmael observes, *tosefet Yom Kippur* is the template for human initiative in extending holiness, and *tosefet Shabbat* is derived from it.

Additionally, the example of Yom Kippur teaches that the manner in which one can actively increase *kedusha* is by broadening the time period for purification from sin, peacemaking, and eschewing grudges and resentment. In the process, one understands that those aspects of purification and making peace are the essential ingredients for adding *kedusha* throughout one's life. These attributes of Yom Kippur make it a fitting source for deriving *tosefet kedusha* for all holy days.

Unlike Rabbi Yishmael who sees Yom Kippur as the model for *tosefet kedusha*, Rabbi Akiva learns all forms of *tosefet kedusha* from *shevi'it*. It is possible that Rabbi Akiva views *shevi'it* as a more appropriate source for these concepts, as *shevi'it* encompasses these aspects of Yom Kippur and offers additional lessons. Rabbi Akiva's understanding of the *pesukim* indicates that the limitations of *tosefet shevi'it* should not be viewed from the vantage point of its restrictions, but rather its prescriptions – the desire, and perhaps *mitzvah*, of *mosifin mei-chol al ha-kodesh*, extending the *shevi'it* experience. The focus of this period is on dedicating time to the goals of *shevi'it* even prior to its advent. For this reason, *tosefet shevi'it* serves as the archetype for extending the holy time into the mundane, spreading the sanctity of Shabbat Festivalsinto the mundane days around them.

Tosefet Shevi'it and Tosefet Kedusha

Tosefet shevi'it serves as the model for *tosefet Shabbat* and is the source for several *halachot*. For instance, the Rema (*Darchei Moshe*, OC 261:1) cites the Maharach Or Zarua (185), who says that the period of *tosefet Shabbat* should parallel the period of *tosefet shevi'it*. Just as the extension of *shevi'it* is one month, a twelfth of the entire *shevi'it* period, *tosefet Shabbat* should be two halachic hours long – one twelfth the length of the Shabbat day itself.

Despite the similarities between *tosefet shevi'it* and other *kedusha*-extensions, however, there are also significant differences between them. As we have seen, *tosefet shevi'it* requires that one refrain from any plowing during the sixth year that primarily benefits the ground during the seventh year. *Tosefet Shabbat*, in contrast, does not restrict performing *melachot* on *erev Shabbat* that continue to create benefit on Shabbat itself. Thus, regarding most *melachot*, as long as the act is performed before the onset of Shabbat, one can set up an apparatus that enables the *melacha* to continue into Shabbat.[14]

In addition, while *tosefet Shabbat* requires a minimal addition onto Shabbat, one may, on his own initiative, extend Shabbat for longer. No such concept applies to *tosefet shevi'it*.

Another distinction is location. *Tosefet Shabbat* applies wherever one may be. It is therefore classified as a *chovat gavra*, a personal obligation incumbent upon each individual. *Tosefet shevi'it*, on the other hand, is restricted to the area of the world in which *shevi'it* applies. Since the sabbatical year is only applicable in the Land of Israel due to its holiness, the extension of the *kedusha* of that year is only applicable in the Land of Israel, as one can only extend *kedusha* that already exists.

The Chatam Sofer (*Rosh Hashana* 9a) provides a rationale for the distinctions between *tosefet Shabbat* and *tosefet shevi'it* based on their respective focuses and natures. The focus of weekly Shabbat is the individual and his rest. Therefore, as long as the individual does not perform *melacha* on Shabbat itself, there are no restrictions (at least biblically) on what one does prior to the onset of Shabbat, even if one will benefit directly from the *melacha* on Shabbat itself. In the case of *shevi'it*, however, the focus is not upon the individual, but on the land; it is *shabbat ha-aretz*, and the land must take part in the resting. Therefore, any *melacha* performed before *shevi'it* that will directly affect growth during *shevi'it* may be subject to restriction.

On a weekly basis, we take a rest from our physically creative activities, with the goal of a

---

14   The *Mechilta De-Rabbi Yishma'el* (*Vayakhel* 1) expounds that according to Rabbi Akiva, the final phrase of *Shemot* 35:3, "You shall not kindle a fire in all your dwellings on the Shabbat day," indicates that only on Shabbat itself is it forbidden to kindle a fire. The *Meshech Chochma* (*Shemot* 23) explains that one might have thought that according to Rabbi Akiva, *tosefet Shabbat* and *tosefet shevi'it* are one and the same, since he understands that *tosefet shevi'it* is the source for *tosefet Shabbat*. Rabbi Akiva therefore requires a verse stating that the prohibition of *melacha* begins only on the Shabbat day itself, and not beforehand. Even according to Rabbi Akiva, there are significant differences between *tosefet shevi'it* and *tosefet Shabbat*.

restful body able to focus on other forms of creativity – furthering one's relationship with God, His Torah, and one's family and community. One is given the opportunity through *tosefet* Shabbat to extend this *kedusha* into Friday and Saturday evening, extending this period of refocusing and rest. During *shevi'it*, however, the year of rest calls for a more complete makeover. Besides the individual's rest, the land and society's rest enable a new outlook on the world we live in, leading us to question whether it is progressing positively. *Tosefet shevi'it* requires thinking about the land's rest prior to the seventh year as well. This requires restricting some agricultural activity beforehand and enables us to begin focusing on *shevi'it* and the purpose of the year even before it begins.

The Difficult Concept of *Tosefet Kedusha*

The particulars of *tosefet shevi'it* are less significant in our day and age, as they no longer apply after the destruction of the *Mikdash*. However, since it is the source of the concept of *tosefet kedusha* (at least according to Rabbi Akiva), the concept deserves our attention.

As we have seen, the laws of *tosefet shevi'it* serve as a model for transforming mundane periods of time (*chol*) into holy ones (*kodesh*). This concept, however, leads to a number of questions. The very idea of "adding" to *kedusha* seems to be problematic, as the Torah instructs us not to add or subtract from the 613 *mitzvot* of the Torah:

> לֹא תֹסִפוּ עַל הַדָּבָר אֲשֶׁר אָנֹכִי מְצַוֶּה אֶתְכֶם וְלֹא תִגְרְעוּ מִמֶּנּוּ לִשְׁמֹר אֶת מִצְוֹת ה' אֱ-לֹהֵיכֶם אֲשֶׁר אָנֹכִי מְצַוֶּה אֶתְכֶם:

Neither add (*tosifu*) to the matter which I command you, nor diminish from it, to observe the commandments of the Lord your God which I command you. (*Devarim* 4:2)

This *mitzvah* is repeated later, indicating its severity:

> אֵת כָּל הַדָּבָר אֲשֶׁר אָנֹכִי מְצַוֶּה אֶתְכֶם אֹתוֹ תִשְׁמְרוּ לַעֲשׂוֹת לֹא תֹסֵף עָלָיו וְלֹא תִגְרַע מִמֶּנּוּ:

As everything I command you, so you must be careful to do it. You shall neither (*tosef*) add to it, nor diminish from it. (Ibid. 13:1)

It is not difficult to comprehend why this prohibition of adding onto the Torah is so significant. After all, who is mortal man to modify God's law? Understanding the Torah as the word of God necessarily precludes giving mankind the prerogative to alter it as he wishes. But where does the idea of *tosefet kedusha* fit in?

The difficulty is even more pronounced when we consider the application of the concept of *tosefet kedusha* to *shevi'it* and Shabbat. The seventh day of the week is sacred because *Hashem* rested on that day:

> וַיְכֻלּוּ הַשָּׁמַיִם וְהָאָרֶץ וְכָל צְבָאָם: וַיְכַל אֱ-לֹהִים בַּיּוֹם הַשְּׁבִיעִי מְלַאכְתּוֹ אֲשֶׁר עָשָׂה וַיִּשְׁבֹּת בַּיּוֹם הַשְּׁבִיעִי מִכָּל מְלַאכְתּוֹ אֲשֶׁר עָשָׂה: וַיְבָרֶךְ אֱ-לֹהִים אֶת יוֹם הַשְּׁבִיעִי וַיְקַדֵּשׁ אֹתוֹ כִּי בוֹ שָׁבַת מִכָּל מְלַאכְתּוֹ אֲשֶׁר בָּרָא אֱ-לֹהִים לַעֲשׂוֹת:

Now the heavens and the earth were completed and all their hosts. And God completed on the seventh day His work that He did, and He ceased on the seventh day fall His work that He did. And God blessed the seventh day and He sanctified it, for thereon He ceased all His work that God had created to do. (*Bereishit* 2:1-3)

Similarly, He sanctifies the seventh year due to the special uniqueness of this period. Unlike the Festivals, which are determined by the Jewish courts and sanctified by the Jewish People, the *kedusha* of Shabbat and *shevi'it* are invested by God Himself.[15] *Chazal* (TB *Pesachim* 117a) tell us that the *kedusha* of Shabbat is "*kevia ve-kaima*" – it's *kedusha* is established as applying to the seventh day. Similarly, the *kedusha* of *shevi'it* is predetermined by God. How is it possible to add on to a time that is determined by God Himself?!

It is for these two reasons that the idea of *tosefet shevi'it* could not have been invented by the Sages, and the basic halacha exists only by virtue of an explicit source in the Torah. The thought of independently altering or "improving" Shabbat or *shevi'it* would be blasphemous, were it not for the fact that the Torah explicitly instructs us to do so. The *pesukim*, "In plowing and in harvesting, you shall rest" (*Shemot* 34:21, according to Rabbi Akiva) and, "On the ninth of the month in the evening" (*Vayikra* 23:32, according to Rabbi Yishmael) indicate that expanding holy periods is exactly what God wants. It is man's prerogative to decide how much time to actively sanctify and add, but G-d deputized man to do so. Humans are able to add *kedusha* in this world.

Kedushat Zeman

The concept of extending the sanctified period beyond the strict barriers of the unchanging seventh day or year encapsulates within it several prime lessons regarding our overall outlook about *kedusha* as a whole.

The concept of *kedushat makom*, sanctity of a particular location, is relatively easy for us to understand. Humans have embraced physical structures from the very beginning of time (see *Bereishit* 4:22 and ch. 11), and it is not difficult for us to comprehend the idea that a building could encapsulate spiritual presence. The land of Israel is a uniquely holy place, and holiness expresses itself in structures such as the temporary *Mishkan* and the later permanent structure of the *Beit Ha-Mikdash* in Jerusalem..

The concept of *kedushat zeman*, the sanctity of time, is often more difficult to understand, as time cannot be seen. Had the Torah not introduced us to the concept of *kedushat zeman* in the context of Shabbat (as cited above), the idea of distinguishing among different periods would probably have been foreign to us. Shabbat demonstrates that time can be qualitatively different at various points. More than quality time, it is "qualitative time." Specific periods are qualitatively holier than others.

Interestingly, *Kedushat zeman* seems to take precedence over the more intuitive *kedushat makom*, as Shabbat observance overrides the construction of the *Mishkan*. It is almost as if

---

15   The Talmud (*Rosh Hashana* 25b) derives from *Vayikra* 23:4 that the court determines the Jewish calendar by the power vested in them by God. The *gemara* (*Beitza* 17a) refers to this distinction between Shabbat and the Festivals in its explanation of the difference in the blessings of "*kedushat ha-yom*" recited on the respective days. On Shabbat, we acknowledge that God is "*mekadesh ha-Shabbat*." He alone sanctifies Shabbat. On the Festivals, in contrast, we state that God is "*mekadesh et Yisrael ve-et ha-zemanim*." He sanctifies the Jewish People, who in turn sanctify the Festivals.

Hashem explicitly taught that despite the strong desire to create a place for G-d's presence to rest in the world through the *Mishkan,* it cannot come at the expense of the sanctified time of Shabbat.

The third form of sanctity is not rooted in time or place but in humanity. Holiness in our world can only be grasped through this third form of *kedusha,* which binds these two concepts – *kedushat ha-adam,* the sanctity of humankind. Humanity's uniqueness amongst all of G-d's creations is explicit in the Torah. G-d's creation of man is described as:

וַיִּיצֶר ה' אֱ-לֹהִים אֶת הָאָדָם עָפָר מִן הָאֲדָמָה וַיִּפַּח בְּאַפָּיו נִשְׁמַת חַיִּים וַיְהִי הָאָדָם לְנֶפֶשׁ חַיָּה:

And the Lord God formed man of dust from the ground, and He breathed into his nostrils the soul of life, and man became a living soul. (*Bereishit* 2:7)

In the process of creating man, God gives him a divine image and imparts within him the capability of small-scale creation (see *Nefesh Ha-Chayim* 1:1-4). Among man's charges are to take an active part in producing *kedusha* in partnership with God.

Bessides the innate uniqueness of all of humanity, the Jewish nation is granted a special holy status. God sanctifies the Jewish people at Sinai as "a kingdom of priests and a holy nation" (*Shemot* 19:6).

Interstingly, in all three areas where innate holiness exists, the Torah commands us to expand on that holiness. Although we are a holy nation, God commands us, "*Kedoshim tihyu,*" "You shall be holy" (*Vayikra* 19:2). Similarly, with regard to *kedushat makom,* God commands man to take an active role in bringing that *kedusha* by building the *Mishkan* and the *Mikdash*: "Make for me a sanctuary, and I will dwell among you" (*Shemot* 25:8). Most importantly for our purposes, although God sanctified certain times at the dawn of creation, He nevertheless instructs: "Remember the Sabbath day *lekadsho,* to sanctify it" (*Shemot* 20:8). Shabbat, despite its innate *kedusha,* is first in the list of days mentioned in *Vayikra* 23 of times designated as "*mikra kodesh,*" periods which must be "declared holy" by the Jewish People.

In short, God consecrates, but He leaves man to sanctify and endows him with the power and the charge to do so. Man cannot sanctify beyond the confines of the framework of holiness that God provides, but man is bidden to bring the *kedusha* to life and extend it wherever and whenever empowered to do so.

Three Forms of *Kedusha*	קדושת האדם Sanctity of Humans	קדושת מקום Sanctity of Place	קדושת זמן Sanctity of Time
The Innate Kedusha	*Hashem* endowed our nation with kedusha: ואתם תהיו לי ממלכת כהנים וגוי קדוש	Hashem endowed the land of Israel with innate kedusha, as the *mishna* states: ארץ ישראל מקודשת מכל הארצות	Hashem endowed Shabbat with kedusha from the dawn of time: ויקדש אותו
The Charge to Enhance that Innate Kedusha	*Hashem* Commands קדושים תהיו – to sanctify ourselves even more	*Hashem* commands us to build a *Mikdash* and enhance that kedusha ועשו לי מקדש ושכנתי בתוכם	*Hashem* commands us זכור את יום השבת לקדשו, to enhance that kedusha through the way we observe Shabbat

This is the backdrop for the concept of *tosefet kedushat zeman*, calling upon mankind to not only recognize the qualitatively consecrated time, but to actively sanctify it.[16]

The Message of *Tosefet Kedusha*

The *mitzvah* of *tosefet kedushat zeman* refers specifically to the periods before and after Shabbat and *shevi'it*, the mundane time that can be made holy, but the message of *tosefet* also tells us how to sanctify the consecrated period during Shabbat and *shevi'it* themselves. It demands we recognize *kedusha*, harness it, and even extend it. Teaching the concepts of *tosefet kedusha* through the medium of Shabbat is understandable as it is the prooftext that innate *kedusha* can be extended. Shabbat's mention at the beginning of the list of *Mikraei Kodesh* (in *Vayikra* 23) illustrates this. Shabbat's position serves as the model for both recognizing and enhancing *kedusha* in time. Similarly, the seventh year, also referred to as a *shabbat la-Hashem*, serves as the model for recognizing, enhancing, and extending *kedusha*. Thus, Rabbi Akiva sees it as the model for *tosefet kedushat zeman*, inspiring mankind to take an active role in *kedusha*. Besides adding on a period before Shabbat and *shevi'it* which begin some of its *halachot* early, the Jewish People are meant to extend Shabbat's influence throughout the week and *shevi'it*'s influence throughout the other six years.

---

16 These three aspects of Kedusha and their implications will be discussed again at the beginning of Section III.

The Illustrative Role

First and foremost, *tosefet Shabbat* serves an illustrative role, demonstrating that we anticipate Shabbat rather than merely doing the minimum required. The *Bnei Yissaschar* (*Shabbat, Ma'amar* 2) explains that *tosefet Shabbat* demonstrates that we love and cherish *mitzvot*. We show our desire to magnify *mitzvot* and fulfill them beyond what is required; these commands are not a burden, but appreciated gifts of *kedusha*. We want more. We want to connect to spirituality by sanctifying unconsecrated time.

Similarly, the *Chafetz Chayim* (*Bereishit* 2:3) notes that the only day of the week that is blessed is Shabbat, while the other days of the week, set aside for work, are included in the curse to Adam: "By the sweat of your brow you will eat bread" (*Bereishit* 3:19). One who adds on to Shabbat expands the day of blessing at the expense of the days of hard labor.

Additionally, the more one takes hold of *kedusha* and the more one adds on to God's precious Shabbat, with all the difficulty involved, the more one displays recognition that God is the source of one's blessing. The story is told that the Sanzer Rebbe took issue with his Chasidim, who requested of the local city administration to move the market day from Friday to Thursday so that they would be able to serve all of their customers before the onset of Shabbat. The Sanzer Rebbe remarked:

> A Jew is standing in the market with his merchandise and in front of him there is a long line of eager buyers. But the Jew is unimpressed. He packs up his goods early, so that he has enough time to go to the *mikveh* in honor of Shabbat and take a nap so he will be rested in honor of Shabbat. If you knew how much happiness you bring to God, you would never have petitioned the city administration to move the market-day. (*Shalosh Sarigim*)

The Partnership Role

Tosefet zeman accomplishes more than this, however. By accepting Shabbat early, we not only express our love of Shabbat, our desire for more, and our ability to sanctify the unconsecrated. Fundamentally, we express our control over time and our ability to merge the physical and the spiritual realms:

> *Tosefet Shabbat* is not holy in its own right, but it is a means of spreading and extending the *kedusha* of Shabbat into the days of the week. (*Eretz Ha-Tzvi*, vol. II, p. 93)

The *Bnei Yissaschar* writes that one who adds on to Shabbat is fulfilling the directive of "imitatio dei," imitating God (*Devarim* 28:9). Just as God initially sanctifies Shabbat, man does the same. To a certain degree, the man who sanctifies the mundane time by extending Shabbat creates qualitative time, just as God did.

The *Bnei Yissaschar* takes this idea one step further. Essentially, the day of Shabbat itself is *kevia ve-kaima*; it exists whether we like it or not, whether we are ready or not. But the Torah instructs us "לַעֲשׂוֹת אֶת הַשַּׁבָּת," "to make Shabbat" (*Shemot* 31:16). Man should be the one to actively sanctify Shabbat; he should not wait for God to do so.

The *Or Ha-Chayim* (*Shemot* 31:16) explains that the seventh day is set in stone, but it is man who is the one who actually "makes" the Shabbat:

The words "la-asot et ha-Shabbat" are designed to counter the prevailing perception that the Shabbat is a day on which one is passive and restful, treating it as a day to indulge one's laziness. The basic purpose of the Shabbat is not to provide physical rest for the body, but to actively fulfill the various *mitzvot* associated with the Shabbat. The wording [of *la-asot et ha-Shabbat*] may also allude to what we have learned: that one must add from the weekday to Shabbat. We do not commence the Shabbat only at sundown; we add a period prior to sundown in order to demonstrate how welcome Shabbat is to us... Similarly, one does not conclude Shabbat immediately... but adds time to demonstrate that one does not want to rid himself of Shabbat as one would do with a burden... God expresses His willingness to dignify the extra hours or minutes the Jews add to the Shabbat of their own volition with the name "Shabbat." In turn... this period before Shabbat man actually transforms and makes into Shabbat.

The *Sefat Emet* (Yom Kippur 5641) also provides a deeper look into the nature of *tosefet Shabbat*, viewing it as personal responsibility to expand *kedushat zeman* and other forms of *kedusha* as well. God originally consecrated the holy days themselves, but it is difficult for man to truly connect with them, as they are *mei'ein olam ha-ba*, a taste of the world to come. The *kedusha* that man imparts to the day, in contrast, is *kedusha* from this world, and man can therefore truly connect to it.[17]

A Contrast to *Tosefet Kedushat Makom*

While the weekly Shabbat allows for an appreciation of extending *kedushat zeman*, *Shevi'it* is not only a manifestation of *kedushat zeman*, but *kedushat makom* – the Land of Israel. The *Shem Mi-Shmuel* (*Vayetzei* 5682) notes that just as the seventh day is the Shabbat of time, the Land of Israel is Shabbat of place.

Interestingly, the concept of *tosefet kedusha* is also applicable to *kedushat makom*. Although the Land of Israel is the sanctified land, containing ten varying levels of holiness (*Mishna Kelim*, ch. 1), there is a means of extending both the *kedusha* of Jerusalem as well as the *kedusha* of the entire land. The Torah tells us (Devarim 11:24, see also *Yehoshua* 1:3) that although there are borders to the Land that Hashem gives us, every place that we conquer will become part of our Land. However, there is one caveat to this extended *kedusha*: According to Tosafot (Gittin 8a s.v. *Kibbush*) the *kedusha* of the Land of Israel can only be extended after the initial *kedusha* is complete. First, the Land of Israel and Jerusalem must be fully in control and sanctified, and then one can expand the borders and extend that holiness. This is the nature of *tosefet kedushat makom*.

Tosefet kedushat zeman is different than the *tosefet kedushat makom* of the Land of Israel. *Tosefet kedushat zeman* always begins **before** the consecrated time has begun. There is an effort to extend completed holiness by initating it before the *kedusha* comes from above. It reflects the awakening of the Jew who strives to increase *kedusha* and transform the mundane into a holy period that has not yet begun.

---

17   A similar idea is found in writings of Breslover Hasidic thinkers, who explain that *tosefet Shabbat* enables man to impart the *kedusha* of Shabbat to the week, a window of opportunity for extending *kedusha* to all aspects of man's existence.

We may understand the discrepancy between the two types of adding *kedusha* based on an element that applies uniquely to *tosefet kedushat zeman* – the element of *hachana*, preparation.

The period of preparation prior to a sanctified time is at the very least a practical necessity. During the consecrated period, one is restricted; one must therefore make sure that everything is ready in advance. However, there is a second element of *hachana* – the feeling of intensity that accompanies the preparations for a long-awaited event, of wanting to actively contribute as much as possible to make that event special.

This is part of the Rav Kook's message in his introduction to his work *Shabbat Ha-Aretz*. One who understands the *kedushat zeman* of Shabbat and *shevi'it* recognizes that they specifically lend themselves to *tosefet kedusha*. Their essence is taking a needed break from the harrying mundane work and physically creative enterprise throughout the six units of work, for a long-awaited respite that enables one to spiritually rejuvenate and contemplate direction and focus. The more holiness one adds to the week, the more one is empowered to refocus and to enable the perspective of Shabbat to permeate the rest of the week. The extra time after Shabbat and *shevi'it* allows one to extend holiness into the mundane period that follows. The addition beforehand, at a time when holiness is not yet apparent, teaches us to actively prepare to maximize the period of *kedushat zeman*. A real rendezvous with holiness requires precautionary steps to ensure one is ready for the challenges and restrictions and can transition into an appreciable change in mindset.

Chapter 5

Parasha 3: *Behar* 1: Shabbat Ha-Aretz and Mount Sinai

The longest description of *shevi'it* and its *mitzvot* appears in *Parashat Behar*. The first seven *pesukim* of the *parasha* define the nature of the year and its various agricultural *halachot*:

וַיְדַבֵּר ה' אֶל מֹשֶׁה בְּהַר סִינַי לֵאמֹר: דַּבֵּר אֶל בְּנֵי יִשְׂרָאֵל וְאָמַרְתָּ אֲלֵהֶם כִּי תָבֹאוּ אֶל הָאָרֶץ אֲשֶׁר אֲנִי נֹתֵן לָכֶם וְשָׁבְתָה הָאָרֶץ שַׁבָּת לַה':שֵׁשׁ שָׁנִים תִּזְרַע שָׂדֶךָ וְשֵׁשׁ שָׁנִים תִּזְמֹר כַּרְמֶךָ וְאָסַפְתָּ אֶת תְּבוּאָתָהּ:וּבַשָּׁנָה הַשְּׁבִיעִת שַׁבַּת שַׁבָּתוֹן יִהְיֶה לָאָרֶץ שַׁבָּת לַה' שָׂדֶךָ לֹא תִזְרַע וְכַרְמֶךָ לֹא תִזְמֹר: אֵת סְפִיחַ קְצִירְךָ לֹא תִקְצוֹר וְאֶת עִנְּבֵי נְזִירֶךָ לֹא תִבְצֹר שְׁנַת שַׁבָּתוֹן יִהְיֶה לָאָרֶץ: וְהָיְתָה שַׁבַּת הָאָרֶץ לָכֶם לְאָכְלָה לְךָ וּלְעַבְדְּךָ וְלַאֲמָתֶךָ וְלִשְׂכִירְךָ וּלְתוֹשָׁבְךָ הַגָּרִים עִמָּךְ: וְלִבְהֶמְתְּךָ וְלַחַיָּה אֲשֶׁר בְּאַרְצֶךָ תִּהְיֶה כָל תְּבוּאָתָהּ לֶאֱכֹל:

And Hashem spoke to Moshe at Har Sinai saying: When you come to the land which I shall give you, the land shall rest (*ve-shaveta ha-aretz*) a Shabbat to the Lord. Six years you may sow your field and six years you may prune your vineyard and gather in the produce. But in the seventh year the land shall have a shabbat of complete rest (*shabbat shabbaton*), a shabbat to God; you shall not sow your field nor prune your vineyard. You shall not reap the after-growth of your harvest nor gather the grapes of your untrimmed vines; it shall be a year of complete rest (*shenat shabbaton*) for the land. But the shabbat of the land (*shabbat ha-aretz*) shall be for all of you to eat, for you, and for your servant and for your maid, and for your hired servant and for the residents by your side that sojourn with you. And for your cattle, and for the beasts that are in your land, shall all the produce of it be for food. (*Vayikra 25:1-7*)

As we have noted, *Parashat Behar* refers to the seventh year as *shabbat ha-aretz*, using the root *sh.b.t.* seven times. Although *Parashat Mishpatim* mentions that the seventh year is a year of *tishmatenna*, *Parashat Behar* describes the year as a *shabbat* for the land and for man.

Given that the term *shemitta* does not appear in this passage in *Parashat Behar*, why do the commentaries and *midrashim* refer to the seventh year as *shemitta* even in this context? Evidently, these commentaries understood that the Torah's reference to the seventh year in *Parashat Mishpatim* as a year of "*tishmatenna*" defines the nature of the year. The year is a *shemitta* year, during which one releases his hold on their land and crops, and at the conclusion of which one releases loans. *Parashat Behar* continues where *Mishpatim* left off, describing how *shemitta* can be accomplished agriculturally through *shabbat ha-aretz*.

Indeed, in his comment on the first *pasuk* of *Parashat Behar*, Rashi refers to the agricultural *halachot* of shevi'it as *shemittat karka'ot*, a term recognizing the preeminence of *Parashat Mishpatim*'s description of *shevi'it*. Although it is a year of *shevita*, as described in *Parashat Behar*, it is defined as a year of *shemitta*, as per *Parashat Mishpatim*.

The Ramban goes one step further, explaining that the general principle of "*tishmatenna u-ntashtah*," "you shall release and lie fallow," is described in *Mishpatim*, while *Behar* includes the details of how this is achieved. *Shemitta* is achieved through *shevita*. One who rests can begin to let go of what he thinks he possesses and embrace the land and *shemitta*'s value system.

We will see, however, that the Torah's designation of *shevi'it* as "*shabbat ha-aretz*" in this context does have implications and reflects the goals of the seventh year.

Shabbat Ha-Aretz Basics:
The Halachot of Working the Land

Before confronting the underlying messages of the *pesukim*, since *Parashat* Behar covers most of shevi'it's agricultural halachot, we'll provide a broad overview of the halachot that appear in the pesukim. (In Section III of this work, we will elaborate on these agricultural *halachot* and their deeper meanings).

The *pesukim* indicate that shevi'it applies only in *Eretz Yisrael* – "the land which I shall give you" – and takes place every seven years as a Shabbat of the land.

As noted earlier, the *pesukim* further identify four stages relating to the land and its growth:

❶	❷	❸	❹
The Land Before Planting	**The Land During the Growing Season**	**The Vegetation and Crops While Growing (on trees or in the ground)**	**The Produce After it is Harvested**

The first two stages focus on the land and reflect the "*shabbat ha-aretz*" elements of *shevi'it*. The final two stages focus on the produce and reflect the "*shemitta*" elements of the year.

The *pesukim* in *Behar* make clear that there is one *mitzvat asei* (positive commandment) that relates to the first two stages, as well as four *mitzvot lo ta'aseh* (negative commandments), which iterate specific actions one must refrain from during *shevi'it*:

שַׁבָּת הָאָרֶץ

וּבַשָּׁנָה הַשְּׁבִיעִת שַׁבַּת שַׁבָּתוֹן יִהְיֶה לָאָרֶץ שַׁבָּת לַה' שָׂדְךָ לֹא תִזְרָע וְכַרְמְךָ לֹא תִזְמֹר: אֵת סְפִיחַ קְצִירְךָ לֹא תִקְצוֹר וְאֶת עִנְּבֵי נְזִירֶךָ לֹא תִבְצֹר שְׁנַת שַׁבָּתוֹן יִהְיֶה לָאָרֶץ:

But in the seventh year the land shall have a shabbat of complete rest (shabbat shabbaton), a shabbat to God; you shall not sow your field nor prune your vineyard. You shall not reap the after-growth of your harvest nor gather the grapes of your untrimmed vines; it shall be a year of complete rest (*shenat shabbaton*) for the land. (*Vayikra* 25:4-5)

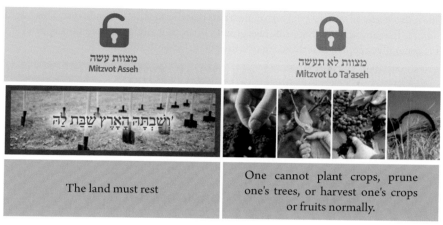

מצוות עשה Mitzvot Asseh	מצוות לא תעשה Mitzvot Lo Ta'aseh
The land must rest	One cannot plant crops, prune one's trees, or harvest one's crops or fruits normally.

Of the four prohibited acts, to apply to grain in a field – זריעה (planting new crops) and קצירה (harvesting the grain or vegetables in the normal manner) – and two are similar actions that relate to trees or vineyards – זמירה (pruning, cutting the branches of a tree in a manner that will be best for fruit growth) and בצירה (harvesting the fruit in the normal manner). We refer to these prohibited acts as *melachot* (a term familiar from *Hilchot Shabbat*).

זריעה and זמירה are prohibited during the first stages of *shabbat ha-aretz*, when no work is done to the land; קצירה and בצירה are prohibited during the second stages of *shemitta*, when the crops that grow are not treated normally.

What is the status of other agricultural activities that promote growth, such as watering trees, cutting weeds, and the like, which are not mentioned in the *pesukim*?

The Torah introduces all the agricultural halachot of shevi'it with a general mitzvat asseh that it repeatedly mentions in other forms:

דַּבֵּר אֶל בְּנֵי יִשְׂרָאֵל וְאָמַרְתָּ אֲלֵהֶם כִּי תָבֹאוּ אֶל הָאָרֶץ אֲשֶׁר אֲנִי נֹתֵן לָכֶם וְשָׁבְתָה הָאָרֶץ שַׁבָּת לַה':

When you come to the land which I shall give you, the land shall rest (*ve-shaveta ha-aretz*) a Shabbat to the Lord. (*Vayikra* 25:2)

The *mitzvat asei* of "וְשָׁבְתָה הָאָרֶץ שַׁבָּת לַה'" instructs that the land itself should rest. This might indicate that any activity that promotes growth of crops is not permitted during *shevi'it*[18]. It is generally accepted that there are two tiers of *melachot* during *shevi'it*:

Melachot Min Ha-Torah	Additional Melachot (Mi-DeRabbanan)
The actions that are explicitly mentioned in the Torah, which are Biblically prohibited under all conditions.	The actions that are not explicitly mentioned but are prohibited Rabbinically, and therefore may be performed during *shevi'it* under certain conditions.

Harvesting- For Consumption Only

As we have seen, there are two prohibitions relating to harvesting crops during *shevi'it* – *ketzira* (harvesting grain and vegetables) and *betzira* (harvesting grapes and other fruits). One might think that the reason it is prohibited to harvest the crops is that they are not supposed to be eaten, but that can't be the case. The *pesukim* tell us (verses 6-7) that the crops are *hefker*, in order to permit the poor to take from them, and it is explicitly stated that those crops are intended לאכלה, to be eaten. The *Torat Kohanim* explains only certain harvesting is prohibited:

לֹא תִקְצֹר כְּדֶרֶךְ הַקוֹצְרִים, לֹא תִבְצֹר כְּדֶרֶךְ הַבּוֹצְרִים

Do not harvest grain the way a professional harvests grain, and to not harvest grapes the way a professional harvests grape. (*Torat Kohanim Vayikra* 25)

שֶׁלֹּא כְּדֶרֶךְ הַבּוֹצְרִים   בְּצִירָה   שֶׁלֹּא כְּדֶרֶךְ הַקוֹצְרִים   קְצִירָה

The Rambam explains that one is not allowed to harvest the fruits in the normal manner in which they are usually harvested:

...שֶׁלֹּא יִקְצֹר כְּדֶרֶךְ שֶׁקּוֹצֵר בְּכָל שָׁנָה... אֶלָּא קוֹצֵר מְעַט מְעַט וְחוֹבֵט וְאוֹכֵל:

...He should not harvest the way that he harvests every other year... but rather should harvest small quantities, beat the grain (to separate the chaff) and eat it. (*Hilchot Shemitta* 4:1)

Since the purpose of this harvest is purely to provide food, one needs much less than for commerce, and the harvest is therefore performed differently. Rashi provides the basic rationale for this law:

---

18   In Section III we will discuss if additional forms of cultivating the land are prohibited Biblically due to this requirement of the land resting, or rabbinically required.

אַף עַל פִּי שֶׁאֲסַרְתִּים עָלֶיךָ, לֹא בַּאֲכִילָה וְלֹא בַּהֲנָאָה אֲסַרְתִּים, אֶלָּא שֶׁלֹּא תִּנְהוֹג בָּהֶם כְּבַעַל הַבַּיִת, אֶלָּא הַכֹּל
יִהְיוּ שָׁוִים בָּה, אַתָּה וּשְׂכִירְךָ וְתוֹשָׁבְךָ:

Even though I have prohibited them to you, I have not prohibited them from consumption or benefit. Rather, **you should not act with them as though you were the owner; instead, everyone should have equal access to them** – you, your hired worker, and those who live among you. (Rashi *Vayikra* 25:6)

In other words, this is a year when one stops treating "his fruit" as a business commodity, but instead shares it with everyone else. This is the *shemitta* element – declaring our fruit *hefker*, ownerless, and releasing our hold on it.

שְׁמִטָּה

Rav Hirsch (*Shemot* 23:10-11) explains some of the significant lessons of one's act of declaring his crops ownerless, explaining how releasing one's hold on their property rights can reshape society's outlook both for those who have more and those who have less:

For six years you shall sow your land and treat it as your own property, but in the seventh year *tishmatenna*, literally, you shall let the ground slip from your hand. You must neither plow it nor sow it. *U-ntashta* – you must abandon whatever grows upon it; leave it alone; do not treat it as your own. The poor among your people, who at all other times are dependent on your good will, may now enjoy the produce of your land, without first having to ask your permission. And whatever they leave over shall be left for the beasts of the field…

By observing the *mitzvah* of *shemitta* an entire nation proclaims before the world that its land belongs to God, and that He is the land's one, sole true Master. In the seventh year, the nation refrains from exercising its rights of ownership and humbly returns its land to the Lord of all the earth. By doing so, the people acknowledge that they are *geirim ve-toshavim*, strangers and sojourners on their own land, dwelling on it only be grace of the Owner. Then the arrogance that causes men, secure on their own land, to become callous and harsh in dwelling with those without property, melts away, yielding place to love and kindness toward the stranger and the poor. Even the wild animals, as God's creatures, are considered endowed with rights on God's earth, on which all are to dwell together.

Kedushat Shevi'it

Shevi'it not only impacts the way we treat the Land of Israel and its crops while they are growing, but also has a lasting impression on the produce that develops during the year.

The Torah refers to the *shemitta* and *yovel* years as קֹדֶשׁ, holy:

(כִּי יוֹבֵל הִוא קֹדֶשׁ תִּהְיֶה לָכֶם מִן הַשָּׂדֶה תֹּאכְלוּ אֶת תְּבוּאָתָהּ:)

For it is the *yovel* year; it shall be santified for you; you will eat its produce from the field. (*Vayikra* 25:12)

The *Yerushalmi* (*Shevi'it* 4:7) derives from the Torah's terminology that not only is the year holy, but any produce that grows in it is holy as well:

יוֹבֵל הִיא - מָה הִיא קוֹדֶשׁ אַף תְּבוּאָתָהּ קוֹדֶשׁ:

Just as *yovel* is sanctified, so too its grain [i.e., crops and produce that grow during it] are sanctified.

All produce of the *shemitta* year is treated with special sanctity, referred to as קְדֻשַּׁת שְׁבִיעִית, *kedushat shevi'it*. The Torah states that as an expression of this sanctity, the food is designated *le-ochla*, to be eaten in a special manner:

וְהָיְתָה שַׁבַּת הָאָרֶץ לָכֶם לְאָכְלָה לְךָ וּלְעַבְדְּךָ וְלַאֲמָתֶךָ וְלִשְׂכִירְךָ וּלְתוֹשָׁבְךָ הַגָּרִים עִמָּךְ:

And the [produce grown during the] resting of the land shall be for you to eat (le-ochla), for you, and for your servant and maidservant, and hired servant, and resident who live with you. (*Vayikra* 25:6)

Although crops are usually eaten, farmers generally do not eat all the produce they grow. The majority is generally sold, and some is used for non-food related purposes. Therefore, *Chazal* explain that the unique term לְאָכְלָה teaches several *halachot* regarding *shevi'it* produce:

לְאָכְלָה וְלֹא לְהֶפְסֵד	לְאָכְלָה וְלֹא לִסְחוֹרָה
For eating and not for wasting	For eating and not for business

Addtionally, some understand that there is an actual *mitzvah* to eat *shevi'it* produce (see Section III). The produce of *shevi'it* is not a commodity that one can treat as one pleases. The produce is meant to be eaten in special sanctity. Since no individual can eat so much produce alone, and since he cannot sell it either, the owner declares it *hefker*, renouncing his ownership and share his crops with all the poor of the land.[19]

The Lesson of *Kedushat Shevi'it*

In his introduction to *Shabbat Ha-Aretz*, Rav Kook explains that these *halachot* transform many of the ills of society:

There is no desecration of sanctity expressed by strict claims of private property regarding anything that grows during this seventh year; the endless desire of wealth, which is stimulated by business and trade, will be forgotten, as *shemitta* food is "le-ochla ve-lo le-sechora," for eating and not for business trade. *Ayin tova*, a beneficent eye

---

19   Other *halachot* are learned from the *pesukim* as well. For instance, from the word בְּאַרְצֶךָ we learn that one shouldn't export any *shevi'it* produce outside of *Eretz Yisrael*.

[and point of view [and deep appreciation will rest on all with the blessing of God in the fruit of the land, "le-ochla ve-lo le-hefsed," for eating and not for loss. Mankind will return to their healthy nature in a manner in which they will not need healing for sicknesses, which mostly come on account of harming one's balance in life while distancing oneself from the pure spiritual nature of man, "le-ochla ve-lo le-melugma ve-lo le-refua ve-lo la-assot mimenah afiktevizing, for eating and not for making medicines or for use as bandages. A holy and elevated spirit will be poured out on all of life: "It will be a year of complete rest for the land- A Sabbath of the Lord" (*Vayikra* 25:4-5).

The specifics of these *halachot*, as well as their themes and goals, will be discussed in Section III.

Mah Inyan Shemitta Etzel Har Sinai?

The name of the *parasha*, *Behar*, derives from the first *pasuk*. Prior to introducing the laws of *shevi'it*, the Torah indicates where these laws were taught: "God spoke to Moshe *be-Har Sinai* (Mt. Sinai)."

וַיְדַבֵּר ה' אֶל מֹשֶׁה בְּהַר סִינַי לֵאמֹר: דַּבֵּר אֶל בְּנֵי יִשְׂרָאֵל וְאָמַרְתָּ אֲלֵהֶם כִּי תָבֹאוּ אֶל הָאָרֶץ אֲשֶׁר אֲנִי נֹתֵן לָכֶם וְשָׁבְתָה הָאָרֶץ שַׁבָּת לַה':...

And Hashem spoke to Moshe in Har Sinai saying: When you come to the land which I shall give you, the land shall rest (*ve-shaveta ha-aretz*) a *shabbat* to Hashem... (*Vayikra* 25:1-2)

The *midrashim* and commentaries find this introduction striking. Rashi, citing a *midrash* (*Torat Kohanim* Behar 1:1), asks the question in a manner that has become an idiom used to refer to off-topic discussions:

בְּהַר סִינַי- מָה עִנְיַן שְׁמִטָּה אֵצֶל הַר סִינַי?

"What does the sabbatical year have to do with Mount Sinai?" (Rashi, *Vayikra* 25,1)

Rashi elaborates on his question: "Were not all the laws taught at Sinai?" Why here are we told specifically that the laws of *shevi'it* were conveyed there?

This question is strengthened when understood on the backdrop of the rest of *Sefer Vayikra*. At the beginning of the *sefer*, the Torah describes where the *halachot* of *Sefer Vayikra* were taught:

וַיִּקְרָא אֶל מֹשֶׁה וַיְדַבֵּר ה' אֵלָיו מֵאֹהֶל מוֹעֵד לֵאמֹר:

And He called out to Moshe, and Hashem spoke to him from the *Ohel Mo'ed* (Tent of Meeting), saying. (*Vayikra* 1:1)

All of the *mitzvot* recorded in *Sefer Vayikra* – until *Parashat Behar* – were taught in the *Ohel Mo'ed*. Yet *Parashat Behar*, beginning with the laws of *shevi'it*, and the rest of the book were taught on Har Sinai. The concluding *pasuk* of *Sefer Vayikra* reminds us that *Vayikra's* last two *parashiyot* were taught on Har Sinai:

אֵלֶּה הַמִּצְוֹת אֲשֶׁר צִוָּה ה' אֶת מֹשֶׁה אֶל בְּנֵי יִשְׂרָאֵל בְּהַר סִינָי:

These are the *mitzvot* that Hashem commanded to Moshe for *Bnei Yisrael* on Mount Sinai. (*Vayikra* 27:34)

The Rashbam writes that the fact that the Torah explicitly points out that the last two *parashiyot* in the Torah were conveyed on Mount Sinai indicates that these laws were taught before the beginning of *Sefer Vayikra*, which was taught after the erection of the *Mishkan*.

According to this understanding of the *pesukim*, there is no particular connection between *shevi'it* and Har Sinai. The introduction to *Parashat Behar* simply informs us that the Torah presents the end of *Sefer Vayikra* in non-chronological order.

Rabbi Yoni Grossman explains what the Torah might be teaching us by doing so. *Sefer Vayikra* primarily discusses the laws of *korbanot* (sacrifices), the *Mishkan*, and the *Kohanim*, three elements whose holiness is restricted to specific individuals and a very specific location. By informing us that the conclusion of *Sefer Vayikra* was taught a Har Sinai, the Torah indicates that God's message is applicable throughout the world; it is not limited to specific places or people.[20]

Rashi, however, cites the midrashic answer:

... אֶלָּא מַה שְׁמִטָּה נֶאֶמְרוּ כְּלָלוֹתֶיהָ וּפְרָטוֹתֶיהָ וְדִקְדּוּקֶיהָ מִסִּינַי אַף כֻּלָּן נֶאֶמְרוּ כְּלָלוֹתֵיהֶן וְדִקְדּוּקֵיהֶן מִסִּינַי,

[It teaches us that] just as the generalities, specifics, and details of the sabbatical year were taught at Sinai, so generalities and details of all the commandments were taught at Sinai.

The agricultural laws of *shevi'it* are not mentioned as being taught in the Plains of Moav (at the end of the forty-year journey in the desert, as recorded in *Sefer Devarim*). Therefore, informing us that they were initially taught in full detail at Har Sinai indicates that **all** laws were taught in detail at Har Sinai, even if they were later repeated at the Plains of Moav.

The Ramban (ad loc.) adds that the *Torat Kohanim* cited in Rashi can be understood literally: The laws of *shevi'it* observance conveyed in *Parashat Behar* are the *peratim*, the specfics, of the general *mitzvah* of *shevi'it* taught in *Parashat Mishpatim*, in the midst of the Har Sinai experience. There the Torah describes the *kelal*, the broad *mitzvah* of *shevi'it* – "tishmatenna u-ntashtah." *Parashat Behar* then goes on to describe the details by providing an in-depth description of agricultural *shevi'it*. The Torah indicates that just as *shevi'it*'s general *halachot* and specifics were taught at Sinai, the same is true of all other *mitzvot*.

---

20   See   https://www.etzion.org.il/en/tanakh/torah/sefer-vayikra/parashat-bechukotai/shemitta-and-covenant-bechukotai where he states: "Here the discussion concerns the sanctity of place and necessitates specific conduct. There may be a specific place where God causes His presence to be manifest, but by the same token 'the whole earth is mine.' Through these laws, every tiller of the land must realize that the entire world belongs to God and that by His will alone it is given to man to work it and to derive sustenance. When the nation as a whole desists from working the land every seventh year, it indicates God's ownership of the whole earth, and not only the place of the Temple where His presence is manifest."

The Importance of the *Kelal* and *Peratim*

Both Rashi and the Ramban understand *shevi'it* is an example that illustrates that the *kelal* (general, broad picture) and *peratim* (details) of all *mitzvot* were taught at Har Sinai. All elements of *mitzvot* were taught at Har Sinai.The Torah's illustrating that both generalities and specifics were taught at Har Sinai seems to indicate that both are essential for a complete appreciation of the Torah. Many identify with the overall outlook of Torah, but find the particulars to be difficult to comprehend, or even distressing. They understand the big picture but find the details challenging. If God wants me to perform a *mitzvah*, is the precision with which it is commanded really part of His will?

On the other hand, others have no problem mechanically following the details and specifics of Jewish law, but are unwilling to stop to gain a broader appreciation of what the Torah intends to inculcate through the *mitzvot*.

To this, the Torah responds in the context of *shevi'it* that both are necessary. The Torah has broad principles that lie behind all the specific details, but the broad picture is not enough. Only through careful attention to the details can one truly achieve the Torah's general goals. As our understanding of the world grows, we recognize that God created a world of intense depth and meticulous accuracy. This applies to His Torah as well, as the Zohar teaches "God looked into the Torah and created the world" (Zohar *Toladot* 134), using the Torah as the blueprint of Creation.

Rav Avraham Yitzchak HaKohein Kook (*Orot Ha-Torah* 3:8) cites the *Kuzari* (1:68-9) that just as we recognize the greatness and vastness of God's creation, we must recognize the beauty in His precision and exactness. He cites the verse in *Tehillim* (92:6): "How great are your actions, God!" He adds that one must also say: How precise — to the smallest detail — are your actions, God!

> In the same manner in which we are overcome with wonder at the great luminaries, the wondrous expanses filling the amazing universe, and the powerful natural forces, so too, we are overcome with wonderment when looking at the depth of precision in all aspects of creation, in the details seen in the limbs of the smallest creatures, etc. And through this complete analysis of the two extremes [the big picture and the small detail], the image of reality will become full in one's heart.

Rav Kook goes on to say that just as one can become enamored with the broad picture and the details of the natural world, the same is true with Torah. One should make sure to see the big picture alongside the exacting details of righteousness and spiritual wisdom. He references a Talmudic passage (*Menachot* 29b) that depicts Rabbi Akiva deriving mountains of laws from every jot and tittle of the Torah. Torah greatness requires the whole scene – the big picture of the forest and the detailed aspects of the trees.

This is reminiscent of passage at the end of *Megilla* (31a), which states: "Any place in which you find the greatness of God there you find His humility," proving this from various verses. This idea is repeated throughout *Tanach*, demonstrating that God applies the same precision with which He creates the solar system to caring for the orphan and the widow. This passage was often quoted by Rav Yehuda Amital who writes:

It seems that the Torah was concerned with the possibility that people would observe the general principles but not the details. People are sometimes prepared to accept the general principles of the Torah, but when it comes to the smaller details, whose relation to the overall idea is not immediately apparent, they have difficulty in fulfilling them. The general principles of Judaism are easy enough to "sell," but the details present much greater difficulty.

Let us take, for example, the laws of Shabbat. The idea of one day of rest from work every week is accepted and practiced today worldwide, but if it also entails a prohibition of switching on lights, etc., the whole package becomes less attractive. Rav Kook writes that the reason for secularization in his generation was not contempt for the ideals of the Torah, but rather that people were not prepared to live up to the detailed daily demands of the law.

Rav Amital continues to explain that the opposite perspective, losing sight of the forest for the trees, is also a major flaw:

On the other hand, the reverse phenomenon also exists. There are people who are so engrossed in the details that they lose sight of the general principles. Today, the search for extra stringencies and the desire to set up new "boundaries around the Torah" has sometimes led people to ignore the goals of the *mitzvot*. The Torah thus wished to stress the importance of both the general principles and the nitty-gritty details.

Shemitta and Har Sinai

Although the *midrash* explains that the Torah is teaching a crucial lesson by noting that both the broad outlines and details of *shevi'it* were taught at Har Sinai, it does not draw a direct connection between Har Sinai and those laws specifically. *Shevi'it* is chosen for illustrative purposes – to emphasize the importance of both the trees and the forest, so to speak, and to demonstrate that all *mitzvot* were originally conveyed at Har Sinai.

In other words, the response to the question, "*Ma inyan shemitta etzel Har Sinai*" appears to be: "You are correct. There is no essential connection." Others note reasons for *shevi'it* to be the vehicle for teaching this message.

Rav Hirsch makes reference to the context of *Parashat Behar*, explaining the connection between *shevi'it* and the previous chapter in the Torah, which concludes *Parashat Emor* – the episode of the blasphemer.

The concluding verses of the preceding chapter teach us that God is the source of all justice; the personality of God is the basis for all the laws governing the rights of men and pertaining to the things men mark out as their property. The present chapter deals with the narrower sphere of agrarian law, and it teaches us that the Land of Israel and every man of Israel and his property are owned by God alone; and on the basis of this legal principle, it develops a code of agrarian, personal, and property law. *Shemitta* and *yovel*, the redemption of land, houses and servants, the laws of usury — these are all logical outgrowths of one legal principle: Israel and its land belong to God, Who has the sole legitimate claim to them.

Rav Hirsch notes that in the episode of the blasphemer, Moshe had to consult God to find out the penalty for the crime. Therefore, the Torah stresses that the *mitzvot* of *shemitta*, although not applicable until the Jewish People inhabit the land of Israel, was taught with all its principles and specifics at Sinai. All *mitzvot* other than blasphemy were taught in this manner. It was only in reference to blasphemy that the Torah left the matter as a general principle, without teaching its details until history made it necessary. (Evidently, the Torah did not want to raise the possibility that such a grave offense would occur.)

According to Rav Hirsch, *shemitta's* connection to Sinai is only that its lacks immediate relevance when the Torah was given, allowing it to serve as a model indicating that the general principles and specifics of all *mitzvot* were taught at Sinai.

Other commentaries explain that the lesson of the *midrash* is, in fact, very pertinent to *shevi'it*, and that the connection of Har Sinai to *shevi'it* goes beyond what is explicitly mentioned in the *midrash*. Some explain that *shevi'it* is an essential component of our covenant with Hashem at Sinai, which is a precondition of our residing in the Land of Israel. Ibn Ezra (ad loc.), for instance, explains that the Torah discusses *shemitta* and *yovel* in *Behar* and then blessings and curses in *Bechukkotai*, to indicate that our covenant at Sinai includes the observance of *shemitta* as a precondition for remaining in the Land of Israel. The *midrash* (Mechilta, Yitro 3) cites Rabbi Yishmael's view that only once the Jewish People accepted *shemitta* and *yovel*, along with the blessings and curses associated with their fulfillment, was God willing to give the Torah to them. Without *shevi'it*, there is no Sinai- covenant.

But this simply leads us to another question. What is it about *shemitta* that is so connected to Sinai and so central to the Sinaitic covenant?

Rav Amital elsewhere explains why *shemitta* was specifically chosen as the topic to teach the significance of the general principles as well as the details. He notes that a basic reason already appears in the Talmud:

> אָמַר הקב"ה לְיִשְׂרָאֵל זִרְעוּ שֵׁשׁ וְהִשְׁמִיטוּ שֶׁבַע כְּדֵי שֶׁתֵּדְעוּ שֶׁהָאָרֶץ שֶׁלִּי הִיא:
>
> God said to Israel: Plant for six years and let it lie fallow the seventh, so that you will know that the land is Mine. (TB *Sanhedrin* 39a)

Rashi there (s.v. *kedei*) explains:

> So that your heart will not grow haughty with the prosperity of your land, leading you to forget the yoke of His Kingship.

The Talmudic passage explicates an idea that is essentially expressed in the Torah itself:

> הָאָרֶץ לֹא תִמָּכֵר לִצְמִתֻת כִּי לִי הָאָרֶץ כִּי גֵרִים וְתוֹשָׁבִים אַתֶּם עִמָּדִי:
>
> And the land shall not be sold for eternity, for the land is Mine, for you are strangers and sojourners with Me. (*Vayikra* 25:23)

The Torah indicates that *shevi'it* teaches us that even if one works the land and it yields fruit, he must always recall that he is not its owner; it belongs to God.

If this is the goal of *shevi'it*, then it is easy to identify the connection between its specific laws and this general principle. The Torah forbids us to sow, reap, prune, etc., in order that we remember that we are not the real owners of the land. Every detail comes to teach the same lesson: that only God decides what will happen to the land, because the land is in fact His and not ours.

Thus, it is understandable why the Torah chooses the laws of *shevi'it* as the opportunity to teach us that we are obligated to observe not only the general principles but also the details. *Shevi'it* is one of the very few *mitzvot* regarding which the function of every detail is understood. Therefore, the Torah tells us that just as in the case of the *mitzvah* of *shemitta* we understand that all the details contribute to the overall *mitzvah*, we must recognize the importance of both aspects of all the other *mitzvot* as well, even though sometimes the connection between them is less clear to us.

An Indication of Importance

A number of commentators explain that teaching *shevi'it* at Har Sinai is an indication of the pivotal role it plays among *mitzvoth* Rav Shlomo Yosef Zevin explains that it is because *shevi'it's* message is so broad – containing *bein adam la-Makom, ben adam la-chavero,* and *bein adam le-atzmo* elements (see Section II, the Torah singled out that it was taught at Sinai.

This idea is expressed by the *Ketav Sofer* (*Behar*) as well, who notes that *shevi'it* encompasses such fundamental lessons that it is only appropriate that it be taught at Har Sinai. It represents the pillars of all aspects of Jewish ideals: faith, humility, kindness.

He quotes his father, the *Chatam Sofer*, who describes the central role of *shevi'it* in providing lessons of *emuna* and *bitachon*:

> …*Shemitta* makes visible to the eyes of all that the Torah is from heaven and Moshe did not proclaim it of his own accord, for how would it have been possible for him to promise, "It shall produce the crop of the three years," which is unnatural? Rather, the Torah surely is from Heaven.

The *Ketav Sofer* himself adds that *shevi'it* also teaches one humility, which is a pillar of the Torah, as reflected in the humble mountaintop on which God chose to give it. *Shevi'it* therefore serves as a lesson for all aspects of the Torah, which also require much humility. In his next piece, the *Ketav Sofer* goes even further:

> "What does the sabbatical year have to do with Mount Sinai…?" It is indisputable that the Torah was given at Mount Sinai. Why, then, did He specify here "at Mount Sinai"? **Since this *mitzvah* is the basis and foundation of all commandments**, He writes here that it was proclaimed from Sinai and inclusive of all commandments.

Additionally, Abarbanel (*Behar* II) notes that *shemitta* helps one realize that man's days on earth are numbered; many individuals only have 50 years of active life after their first 20 years of youth:

> While the farmer relies on God to provide his needs, he is free to occupy himself with other matters, possibly even extremely important matters that one doesn't normally

have the proper time to contemplate.

... It is appropriate that wholesome people be more concerned with loss of their time than with loss of all possessions and money that they have, for the days of one's years and one's life are the path in which one walks to attain his perfection, ... It therefore is appropriate that one not waste his time... In order that one always keep this in mind, divine wisdom saw fit to awaken him through its *mitzvot* to the brevity of his days and the limited number of his years. ... Indeed, for this very reason, He gave us the commands of *shemitta* and of *yovel*, for in the *shemitta* [cycle] there are six years of cultivating the land and in the seventh year is comprehensive rest, which serves to awaken and imply that the span of one's life is seventy years...

According to Abarbanel, the *mitzvah* allows man to realize that life is too short to focus on merely attaining wealth, especially in that it will not remain after death.

With this in mind, returning to the original question, "What does *shemitta* have to do with Har Sinai?" the answer is – everything!

For both practical and fundamental reasons, *shemitta* affords an opportunity for the Jew to reconnect with Har Sinai and its lessons of learning Torah and re-experiencing the revolutionary event of the Sinai experience, which is so central to our identity. *Shemitta* affords an opportunity to reconnect to Torah learning by forcing people to rest from their normal activities. The awe-inspiring experience of *shevi'it* also ensures this study will be undertaken humbly, which is essential (as the *Ketav Sofer* notes).

One might also add an additional fundamental connection between the Torah of Sinai and the sabbatical year.

The unifying elements of *shevi'it* break down class barriers and allow people to unite "as one man with one heart," as happened at Sinai (Rashi *Shemot* 19:2). Moreover, the *mitzvah* of *Hakhel* – a reenactment of the Sinai experience – is observed on the Sukkot after the *shemitta* year, serving as a fitting culmination.[21]

The *Mitzvah* of Preparing for *Shevi'it* – Ensuring a Sinaitic *Shabbat Ha-Aretz* Experience

One might offer an additional insight into the relationship between the seventh year and Har Sinai. Interestingly, the midrash cited in Rashi questions "*Mah inyan shemitta etzel Har Sinai*"), what is the relationship between *shemitta* and Har Sinai; however, the Torah specifically mentioned *shevi'it's* connection to Har Sinai in *Parashat Behar* where no mention of *shemitta* appears. As noted, *Behar* repeatedly refers to *shevi'it* as *Shabbat ha-aretz*, where the land rests a "*shabbat la-Hashem*. Maybe the Torah specifically focused on the seventh year's relationship to Har Sinai in the context of the year's identity as Shabbat

---

21 By referring to the seventh year as shabbat ha-aretz and connecting it to Har Sinai, the Torah seems to be conveying that to make the sabbatical year spiritually uplifting and meaningful, one must reconnect both individually and collectively to Sinai. Shabbat ha-aretz is another opportunity for a Har Sinai experience, provided that we prepare properly.

to teach us the necessity of experiencing *shevi'it* through aspects that are shared by Shabbat and Har Sinai.

One connection between the weekly Shabbat and Har Sinai is that both the Revelation at Sinai and the weekly Shabbat require significant preparation. Possibly the Torah wants to teach us that for *Shabbat Ha-Aretz* to be transformative and meaningful, it requires extensive preparation throughout the preceding six years.

Preparing for Har Sinai

The preparation for Sinai began long, long before the giving of the Torah. In fact, the Sages tell us that from the dawn of Creation, God made the existence of the world conditional upon the ultimate acceptance of the Torah at Sinai by the Jewish People:

> דְּאָמַר רֵישׁ לָקִישׁ, מַאי דִּכְתִיב: "וַיְהִי עֶרֶב וַיְהִי בֹקֶר יוֹם הַשִּׁשִּׁי", ה' יְתֵירָה לָמָּה לִי? מְלַמֵּד שֶׁהִתְנָה הַקָּדוֹשׁ
> בָּרוּךְ הוּא עִם מַעֲשֵׂה בְרֵאשִׁית וְאָמַר לָהֶם: אִם יִשְׂרָאֵל מְקַבְּלִים הַתּוֹרָה אַתֶּם מִתְקַיְּימִין, וְאִם לָאו אֲנִי מַחֲזִיר
> אֶתְכֶם לְתוֹהוּ וָבוֹהוּ.

> Reish Lakish said: Why does the verse state, "And it was the evening and it was the morning, the sixth day" (*Bereishit* 1:31)? Why is the definite article necessary [indicating a specific sixth day]? This teaches that God made a condition with the creations and said to them: If Yisrael accepts the Torah [on the sixth day of Sivan], you will continue to exist; and if not, I will return you to void and nothingness. They [the works of creation] were all suspended until "the sixth day," referring to the sixth day of Sivan, which was destined for the Giving of the Torah (TB *Shabbat* 88a).

The need for preparation before *Matan Torah* is indicated by the fact that the people arrived at Sinai six days before the revelation (*Shemot* 19:1), and Moshe was commanded to separate from the rest of the nation prior to *Ma'amad Har Sinai*. The Talmud (*Yoma* 3b) quotes Reish Lakish's explanation that Moshe's separation from the people indicates that one cannot prepare for a spiritual experience without at least six days of separation. This is the source for the High Priest's yearly preparation before entering the Holy of Holies on Yom Kippur, separating from his wife and others for seven days:

> A *baraita* was taught in accordance with the opinion of Reish Lakish that sequestering is derived from Sinai: Moshe ascended in the cloud, and was covered in the cloud, and was sanctified in the cloud, in order to receive the Torah for the Jewish people in sanctity, as it is stated: "And the glory of God abode upon Mt. Sinai and the cloud covered him six days, and He called to Moshe on the seventh day from the midst of the cloud" (*Shemot* 24:16). (TB *Yoma* 3b)

Furthermore, the Torah was not given immediately after the Exodus from Egypt, but rather only fifty days later. Much like *yovel*, described in the continuation of *Parashat Behar*, the Har Sinai experience involved seven periods (weeks) of seven (days) before arriving at the fiftieth. This period was dedicated to the necessary prepration for a meaningful Har Sinai experience.

Parashat Behar comes on the heals of *Parashat Emor*, the preceding *parasha*. There we are introduced to the the seven weeks of *sefirat ha-omer* (*Vayikra* 23:15-22). Although the Torah does not explicitly state that Shavuot commemorates the giving of the Torah, but rather describes it as the Festival that celebrates the wheat harvest, *Chazal* tell us that Shavuot commemorates the Revelation at Sinai. Thus, the *Sefer Ha-Chinuch* (*mitzvah* 306) explains that the purpose of counting the days and weeks between Pesach and Shavuot is to express the yearing and desire for receiving the Torah:

> The simple explanation is that the essence of the Jewish People is the Torah, and because of the Torah, the heaven, earth, and Israel were created, as the verse states, "If not for My covenant [of Torah] day and night, I would not have appointed the laws of heaven and earth" (*Yirmiyahu* 33:25). [Torah] is the foundation and the reason that we were redeemed and left Egypt – in order to receive the Torah at Sinai and to keep it ...
> Since the acceptance of the Torah was the goal of our redemption and serves as the foundation of the Jewish people, and through it we achieved our greatness, we were commanded to count from the day after [the first day of] Pesach until the day that the Torah was given. This manifests our great desire for that awesome day which our hearts yearn for just as a servant yearns for shade. We count constantly – when will the day come that we yearn for, the day that we left slavery? Because counting [towards a certain date] shows a person that all his desire and longing is to reach that time.

Taking this idea one step further, *sefirat ha-omer* not only expresses excitement, but also charts the path for daily preparation for a yearly Har Sinai experience. *Parashat Emor* teaches us that spiritually uplifting opportunities like Shavuot only achieve their purpose if one prepares for them in advance.[22]

The Ramban (*Vayikra* 23:36) notes that Shavuot, the holiday of the giving of the Torah, is always referred to as *Atzeret* in Rabbinic literature, a term usually used for the final day of an extended festival such as Pesach and Sukkot, coming after *chol ha-mo'ed*, the intermediate days during which certain types of labor are allowed. Thus, the period of *sefirat ha-omer* is akin to *chol ha-moed*, as Shavuot is the culmination of the Exodus. The *Sefer Chinuch* states that Pesach is merely a prelude to receiving the Torah, and the counting expresses the eager anticipation of the newly freed Jews to receive the Torah, affirming the overwhelming importance of Torah in Jewish life.

Rabbi Joseph B. Soloveitchik develops this theme at length in an essay entitled "Sacred and Profane." He argues that time consciousness is a prerequisite for freedom. After explaining

---

22 Interestingly, the Torah describes Shavuot as a day celebrating the wheat harvest and connects it to the agricultural gifts to the poor, without mentioning Shavuot's connection to Har Sinai and its commemoration of the receiving of the Torah. In contrast, the Torah specifically connects *shabbat ha-aretz* to Har Sinai. It is almost as if the Torah presents *shevi'it* and Shavuot in the exact opposite fashion, connecting *shevi'it* to Sinai and Shavuot to agriculture! One explanation for this may be that certain aspects of unqiue periods are readily apparent, while others are not. Shavuot's commemoration of the Har Sinai experience is known to any student of Torah history, but its celebration of the beautiful agricultural system of Torah life in *Eretz Yisrael* is less appreciated. Similarly, *shevi'it's* agricultural goals are already elucidated in broad strokes in *Parashat Mishpatim*, but its connection to Har Sinai is less apparent and needs to be stressed.

Additionally, the Torah may be emphasizing that Shavuot is only really a celebration of the Har Sinai experience if one prepares himself for that and ensures it is celebrated with that in mind.

the lack of time-consciousness among slaves, including the Jews before the Exodus, he writes (p. 16):

> When the Jews were delivered from the Egyptian oppression and Moses rose to undertake the almost impossible task of metamorphosing a tribe of slaves into a nation of priests, he was told by God that the path leading from the holiday of Pesach to Shavuot, from initial liberation to consummate freedom, leads through the medium of time. The commandment of *sefira* was entrusted to the Jew; the wondrous test of counting forty-nine successive days was put to him. These forty-nine days must be whole. If one day is missed, the act of numeration is invalidated.

If a slave is capable of appreciating each day – of grasping its meaning and worth, of weaving every thread of time into a glorious fabric, quantitatively stretching over the period of seven weeks but qualitatively forming the warp and woof of centuries of change – he has achieved freedom and is eligible for Torah. Rav Michael Rosensweig adds:

> On this basis, many of the peculiar and seemingly incongruous facets of *sefirat ha-omer* can be justified. The very act of counting acquires significance and requires a *beracha* in as much as it represents a process whose aim is to sensitize man to this indispensable religious dimension of time-consciousness. If we identify *sefirat ha-omer* with time-awareness, then our act of counting is more than a simple marking of time between *Pesach* and *Shavuot*... rather, *sefirat ha-omer* becomes a means of effecting an important psychological and religious transformation, which is most effectively achieved by verbal articulation and daily expression. The Ramban's allusion, an analogy to the concept of *chol ha-moed*, is particularly apt inasmuch as *sefirat ha-omer* constitutes an essential period of transition between the slave mentality of the immediate post-*Pesach* era and the time-conscious mindset of true freedom that is a prerequisite for receiving the Torah on *Shavuot*. ("Reflections on *Sefirat Ha-Omer*, http://www.torahweb.org/torah/1999/moadim/rros_sefira.html)

However, it is not just consciousness of time that is critical; that must be paired with an understanding of the purpose of that time. Thus, the Torah instructs:

רַק הִשָּׁמֶר לְךָ וּשְׁמֹר נַפְשְׁךָ מְאֹד פֶּן תִּשְׁכַּח אֶת הַדְּבָרִים אֲשֶׁר רָאוּ עֵינֶיךָ וּפֶן יָסוּרוּ מִלְּבָבְךָ כֹּל יְמֵי חַיֶּיךָ
וְהוֹדַעְתָּם לְבָנֶיךָ וְלִבְנֵי בָנֶיךָ:

> Only beware for yourself and greatly beware for your soul, lest you forget the things that your eyes have seen and lest you remove them from your heart all the days of your life, and make them known to your children and your children's children. (*Devarim* 4:9)

The Ramban understands that there is a daily requirement to remember *Ma'amad Har Sinai*. Just as preparation was necessary before the giving of the Torah on Har Sinai, it is necessary before we re-accept the Torah on Shavuot or at any other time, as reflected in the yearly *sefirat ha-omer*. This ensures that the miraculous experience of revelation will not be forgotten.

Weekly Shabbat Preparation

The Talmud uses the weekly Shabbat as the prime example of something that requires preparation as a functional necessity:

מִי שֶׁטָּרַח בְּעֶרֶב שַׁבָּת יֹאכַל בְּשַׁבָּת, מִי שֶׁלֹּא טָרַח בְּעֶרֶב שַׁבָּת מֵהֵיכָן יֹאכַל בַּשַּׁבָּת?

On who has toiled before Shabbat will have what to eat on Shabbat; one who has not toiled before Shabbat, from what will he eat on Shabbat? (*Avoda Zara* 3a)

However, preparing for Shabbat seems to have something more to it, as there is an independent requirement to prepare for Shabbat. The Rambam summarizes the four basic obligations of Shabbat, *Zachor, Shamor, Kavod* and *Oneg*:

אַרְבָּעָה דְּבָרִים נֶאֶמְרוּ בַּשַּׁבָּת שְׁנַיִם מִן הַתּוֹרָה וּשְׁנַיִם מִדִּבְרֵי סוֹפְרִים וְהֵן מְפֹרָשִׁין עַל יְדֵי הַנְּבִיאִים, שֶׁבַּתּוֹרָה זָכוֹר וְשָׁמוֹר, וְשֶׁנִּתְפָּרְשׁוּ עַל יְדֵי הַנְּבִיאִים כָּבוֹד וְעֹנֶג שֶׁנֶּאֱמַר (יְשַׁעְיָהוּ נ"ח) וְקָרָאתָ לַשַּׁבָּת עֹנֶג וְלִקְדוֹשׁ ה' מְכֻבָּד..

There are four [dimensions] to the [observance of] the Sabbath: two originating in the Torah, and two originating in the words of our Sages, which are given exposition by the Prophets. In the Torah are the commandments "Remember (*Zachor*)" and "Observe (*Shamor*)."

Those given exposition by the Prophets are honor (*kavod*) and pleasure (*oneg*), as the *pasuk* (*Yeshayahu* 58:13) states: "And you shall call the Sabbath a delight, sanctified unto God and honored." (Rambam, *Hilchot Shabbat* 30:1)

The Vilna Gaon (O.C. 529) explains the distinction between the latter two: *oneg* involves enjoying Shabbat itself, while *kavod* involves preparing for it. in other words, it is a *mitzvah* to prepare for Shabbat.

Furthermore, The Talmud tells us that the principle of *"mitzvah bo yoter mi-be-shlucho,"* "it is preferable that one do the *mitzvah* himself rather than rely on an agent," applies to Shabbat preparation (*Kiddushin* 41a). If the point of Shabbat preperation were results, there would be no need for personal involvement. Yet the Talmud (Shabbat 119a) and *Shulchan Aruch* (O.C. 250:1) tell us that even one who has many attendants must be personally involved in at least one element of Shabbat preparation. Preparation for Shabbat is a *mitzvah*, and possibly even a goal in its own right.

The first two elements of Shabbat explicit in the Torah, *Zachor* and *Shamor*, both point in this direction. The Ramban (*Shemot* 20:8) notes that the *mitzvah* of *Zachor* not only means to remember Shabbat, but to anticipate it – to count the days of the week in reference to Shabbat. Chizkuni (*Devarim* 4) and others point out that *Shamor* similarly not only means safeguarding the Shabbat by refraining from labor on that day. One guards that which is precious. *Shamor* requires one to anxiously await Shabbat. But the week prior to Shabbat is not only a period of longing, but a period of preparation. The Talmud (*Beitza* 16a) records how Shammai and Hillel each prepared for Shabbat from the beginning of the week until the end, in fulfillment of *Zachor*.

Even the intense preparations on *erev* Shabbat are not entirely pragmatic. When the Torah describes the Jewish People's first Shabbat in the desert, it describes the need for preparation and the gathering of a double portion of manna:

> וְהָיָה בַּיּוֹם הַשִּׁשִּׁי וְהֵכִינוּ אֵת אֲשֶׁר יָבִיאוּ וְהָיָה מִשְׁנֶה עַל אֲשֶׁר יִלְקְטוּ יוֹם יוֹם:
>
> But on the sixth day, when they prepare what they have brought in, it shall [prove to be] double the amount they gather each day. (*Shemot* 16:5)

Seforno (ad loc.) notes that this description of *"ve-heichinu"* is a *mitzvah* to prepare for Shabbat zealously:

> The Torah states "They shall prepare" to awaken one to be zealous in [preparing to] delight on Shabbat with tasty foods and express this on *erev Shabbat*.

The *Shulchan Aruch* (OC 250) cites this pasuk as a source that one should wake up early on Friday morning to prepare for Shabbat. The *Sefer Chasidim* (149) explains the seriousness with which one must perform this *mitzvah*:

> One must be zealous in preparing Shabbat needs with speed and alacrity. If one were to hear that the queen is coming and will be staying in his home or the bride and her entourage are arriving at his house, what would one do? He would be extremely happy at the arrival of such illustrious individuals to partake of his hospitality... He would personally take part in the preparations, even if he has thousands of servants. [So too] who do we have more significant than Shabbat, bride and queen, who is called "delight," one must personally prepare...

Personal involvement in the preparation is nothing less than an indication of one's recognition of the arrival of the Shabbat queen, the privilege and opportunity.

Rabbi Soloveitchik (*On Repentance*, pp. 88-89 fn.), eloquently expresses the lost feeling of anticipation for the Shabbat Queen, what he saw as the primary emotion on *erev Shabbat* in his youth:

> Allow me, please, to make a "private confession" concerning a matter that has caused me such loss of sleep. I am not so very old, yet I remember a time when ninety percent of world Jewry were observant and the secularists were a small minority at the fringes of the camp. I still remember – it was not so long ago – when Jews were still close to G-d and lived in an atmosphere pervaded with holiness. But, today, what do we see? The profane and the secular are in control wherever we turn. Even in those neighborhoods made up predominantly of religious Jews one can no longer talk of the "sanctity of the Sabbath day." True, there are Jews in America who observe the Sabbath. The label "Sabbath observer" has come to be used as a title of honor in our circles, just like "HaRav HaGaon" – neither really indicates anything and both testify to the lowly state of our generation. **But it is not for the Sabbath that my heart aches; it is for *erev Shabbat*, "the eve of the Sabbath."** There are Sabbath-observing Jews in America, **but there are not *erev Shabbat*** Jews who go out to greet the Sabbath with beating hearts and pulsating souls. There are many who observe the precepts with their hands, with their feet and/or with their mouths – but there are few, indeed, who truly know the meaning of service of the heart!

The *mitzvah* of *ve-heichinu*, "They shall prepare," is nothing less than the call to become this *erev Shabbat* Jew, whose longing for Shabbat permeates the entire week and who is so overcome by the feeling of *kedusha* that his eyes are on Shabbat throughout the week. Throughout the day on Friday, after waking up early to prepare, the longing continuously increases along with the preparation, until reaching its pinnacle moments before Shabbat begins.

The Talmud (*Bava Kama* 32a) states that if one runs in haste in a public domain and accidentally causes damage, he is liable, unless it is on *erev Shabbat* close to sunset, as one is permitted to run at that time. The Talmud then details an early practice of *Kabbalat Shabbat*, going out to greet the Shabbos Queen, citing the practices of two scholars. Rabbi Chanina ran outside to greet Shabbat, while Rabbi Yannai would clothe himself with his *tzitzit* and rise to invite the Queen to his house. Both would greet the Shabbat bride verbally, "בּוֹאִי כַלָּה בּוֹאִי כַלָּה," "Come bride, Come bride" (as later repurposed in *Lecha Dodi*).

The Maharsha explains these practices, noting that the repetition of the words, "Come, bride" is indicative of the two stages of marriage – betrothal and consummation. Friday is the period of betrothal, a time of loving anticipation and desire to be unified. Only after this betrothal can there be a marriage in which the couple lives together.

Rav Hutner, in an essay recorded in *Pachad Yitzchak*, expresses the deeper meaning of this by pointing out that the preparation on *erev Shabbat* accords it independent significance:

> Friday has its own source of holiness. In fact, to some extent, the holiness of Friday opens the door to the possibility of Shabbat, in effect serving as an impetus for Shabbat to arrive. There is an explicit verse to this effect…: "See that God gave you the Shabbat; therefore, He gives you on the sixth day enough bread for two days." (*Shemot* 16:29)
>
> The verse explicitly states that the proof of the gift of Shabbat is Friday. This shows that the preparation for Shabbat that takes place on Friday represents the intrinsic holiness of Friday… The meaning of betrothal is that there is a level of commitment that obligates the man to complete the process of marriage… (*Pachad Yitzchak*, Shabbat)

As Rav Hutner explains, *erev Shabbat* is not only a time of preparation, but of creation. Shabbat does not come without a day of preparation, a day with an intrinsic holiness, a time devoted to opening the world to a certain truth, allowing the arrival of Shabbat to embody that truth. The *erev Shabbat* Jew that Rav Soloveitchik discusses appreciates this and expresses it with every fiber of their being.

This idea that betrothal can be more potent and powerful than marriage itself is expressed by Rav Kook, who focuses on the longing that betrothal represents:

> Even though after marriage they are closer to each other than during the stage of betrothal, there is a special element in betrothal, as it expresses an elevated element of cleaving to God… It turns out that it exists forever, as the verse states: "And I will betroth you forever." (*Siddur Olat Re'iya*, p. 35)

The longing of *erev Shabbat* is a necessary prerequisite for a meaningful "marriage" and union with God on Shabbat itself. By the same token, one can appreciate how the period of *sefirat Ha-omer*, dedicated to counting up and preparing for a yearly re-experience of Har Sinai, is a period of betrothal awaiting the communion on Shavuot. One who prepares gets in touch with his inner longing, expressing the desire for a meaningful marriage experience and sanctifying the period with its own holiness.

Shabbat Ha-aretz: Preparation and Lasting Message

Shabbat is the prime example of *kedushat zeman,* sanctity of time, and Har Sinai was the first experience of *kedushat makom,* a sanctified location. The concept of *shabbat ha-aretz* merges both forms of *kedusha* – time and place. The opportunities it provides are endless, but like the experience of accepting the Torah and Shabbat, they may only be realized with adequate preparation.

> Rav Tzaddok of Lublin (*Kedushat Shabbat* 1) explains that the six days of *melacha* (labor) are a preparation for the seventh of *menucha* (repose), and the same holds true for *shabbat ha-aretz.* **Just** as one prepares for Shabbat throughout the week, throughout the six years, one is supposed to prepare for the upcoming *shabbat ha-aretz.* Rav Tzaddok (*Peri Tzaddik, Behar*) notes that the Torah introduces the sabbatical year by first mentioning the six years. This indicates that: Corresponding to the intent [towards the seventh year] that one has in one's work over the six years will be the holiness of *shemitta.*

He further connects the *mitzvah* upon the courts to count each sabbatical year leading up to *yovel* to the *mitzvah* of *sefirat ha-omer,* counting towards Sinai.

> The court counts every year, as the closer one gets to *shemitta,* the greater is the recognition that the land belongs to God. Similarly, every week there is greater recognition... So too, in relation to eating, the *shemitta* fruits have sanctity just like eating on Shabbat. Counting throughout the fifty years of *yovel* is an act of preparation, and the level of preparation, specifically in regard to the years that immediately precede *shemitta,* will determine its power.

Similarly, the *Tiferet Shlomo* (*Parashat Behar*) states:

> "And you shall sanctify" [in reference to *yovel*] indicates preparing and inaugurating — meaning: prepare yourselves through your righteous actions for the fiftieth year, which is *yovel,* during which "each one will return"... which is the language of repentance and returning to God...

This period of preparation that is so essential to *shevi'it* also helps explain why *shevi'it* serves as the source for *tosefet kedushat zeman,* expanding holiness of time (see our discussion of *Parashat Mishpatim*). One who appreciates the anticipatory, preparatory period prior to the onset of Shabbat/*shabbat ha-aretz* has a strong desire to extend that time into the period of sanctified preparation.

As a general rule, just about anything meaningful in life must involve preparation. Nevertheless, the Torah goes out of its way to note the importance of preparation specifically in the context of the unforgettable experience at Har Sinai; in order for it to be fully meaningful, it requires various forms of preparation. Regarding the weekly Shabbat as well, preparation adds new dimensions that elevate *erev Shabbat*. The Torah's mention of *shabbat ha-aretz* in conjunction with Har Sinai underscores this lesson as well. For *shevi'it's* message to be powerful, it requires spiritual preparation.

Yet another answer to the question, "What does *shabbat ha-aretz* have to do with Har Sinai?" is that in order to be appreciated as a full Sinai experience, one must prepare for *shevi'it*. Sufficient preparation might actually enable an extended Har Sinai experience throughout the entire seventh year.

For those who are reading this book before *shevi'it*, maximizing whatever time is left prior to *shevi'it* is a worthwhile investment. For those who are introduced to these ideas after *shevi'it* begins, these concepts might be disheartening. Nevertheless, *shevi'it* continues. The more we prepare to maximize the experience, the more memorable and unforgettable it will be (and, of course, there is ample time to prepare for the next *shevi'it*, six years hence).

Kabbalat Shabbat (Ha-Aretz)

The comparison between *erev Shabbat* and *erev shevi'it*, the concluding period of the sixth year, is not at all arbitrary. The *midrash* (*Mechilta De-Rabbi Yishamel, Yitro*) notes that just as there was a blessing of a double portion of *manna* from Heaven prior to the weekly Shabbat in the desert, the Torah promises an added blessing during the sixth year; that year's produce will suffice for three years – the sixth, seventh, and eighth – until the post-*shevi'it* crops are grown). The *Zohar* (*Behar* 110b) equates these two blessings. The sixth day and sixth year are both rewarded for the Shabbat that follows, even before their Shabbat observance is apparent.

Similarly, *shabbat ha-aretz*, like the weekly Shabbat, requires thought-out preparation to ensure adequate food supply and ease of maintaining one's garden and trees. At the same time, the connection between *shevi'it* and Shabbat indicates that a different type of preparation is necessary as well – a spiritual type.

All the power of *erev Shabbat* reaches its zenith in the moments prior to Shabbat. The wedding day is about to arrive, and the final moments of longing and preparation are powerful. The Kabbalists of Tzefat introduced *Kabbalat Shabbat*, composed of chapters of *Tehillim* and the *piyut Lecha Dodi*, to help focus one's energies as the Shabbat Queen enters the world. The custom of reciting *Shir Ha-Shirim* (Song of Songs) before Shabbat, which describes the love between Hashem and His nation, is a further expression of tapping in to this period of pre-Shabbat excitement.

It is not surprising that the *tefillot* of *Kabbalat Shabbat*, escorting in the Shabbat Queen, are also *tefillot* of longing for something greater – for the reunion of the groom and the bride relationship with God with the arrival of *Mashiach* and the rebuilding of Jerusalem. Those awaiting Shabbat in Tzfat also awaited all that Shabbat symbolizes. Thus, *Lecha Dodi* expresses a vivid description of longing for Yerushalayim as well.

Although the prepration throughout the week and Friday serves a utilitarian role as well, the *tefillot* of *Kabbalat Shabbat* actually cut short one's physical preparation, in order to focus on spiritual build-up and anticipation. After all, that is the deeper goal of the preparation period. As Rav Kook explains, what Shabbat is for the individual, *shabbat ha-aretz* is for the entire nation. The land observing this Shabbat deserves a greeting, just as an individual greets Shabbat.

This idea hits home with the powerful story of the Ponevizher Rav's expressing his support to the religious pioneers of *Kibbutz Shaalavim*. In the fledgling State of Israel, a number of religious *kibbutzim* sprang into existence, some right before the *shemitta* year of 1951. The *kibbutzim* had little time to practically prepare for survival during *shemitta*, and they were faced with the decision of whether to rely on the *heter mechira* or to observe *shevi'it* completely. The Ponevezher Rav wanted to show his support to those who decided to observe *shevi'it* according to the rulings of the Chazon Ish, which did not accept the *heter mechira*. He spent an *erev Shabbat* in *kibbutz Shaalviim* during *shevi'it* and simultaneously expressed his love for Shabbat and *Shabbat Ha-Aretz*. He greeted everyone he saw with the greeting, "*A gutten erev Shabbos*," and then he went to every tree that was resting on the Shabbat of the Land and said, "*A gutten Shabbos Eretz Yisrael!*"

A custom that is currently not commonly observed but will hopefully grow in popularity and gain greater traction is *Kabbalat Shabbat Ha-Aretz*. On Erev Rosh Hashana – a busy day during all years, but certainly before *shevi'it* – one puts aside his utilitarian preparations and gathers with others by a field that will observe *shabbat ha-aretz*. There, one has the opportunity to say, "*A gutten erev Shabbos Eretz Yisrael*," to feel the spiritual power as the zenith of six years of preparation and betrothal, awaiting those final moments until the marriage begins. The *tefilla* of *Lecha Dodi*, calling for the rebuilding of Yerushalayim and the *Mikdash*, is very appropriate. The Shabbat in time merges with the sanctity of space for a rendezvous with eternity with Hashem's sanctified nation.

Chapter 6

Parasha 4: Behar II- Shevi'it through the Eyes of Yovel

As we have seen, the first seven *pesukim* of *Parashat Behar* elucidate the seventh year's character as *shabbat ha-aretz* and describe the various agricultural *halachot* of the seventh year. The Torah distinguishes this section by concluding it as a *parasha setuma*, requiring a break in the middle of the line before the next section. The following section begins by discussing *yovel*, the fiftieth year following seven complete *shemitta* cycles:

וְסָפַרְתָּ לְךָ שֶׁבַע שַׁבְּתֹת שָׁנִים שֶׁבַע שָׁנִים שֶׁבַע פְּעָמִים וְהָיוּ לְךָ יְמֵי שֶׁבַע שַׁבְּתֹת הַשָּׁנִים תֵּשַׁע וְאַרְבָּעִים שָׁנָה: וְהַעֲבַרְתָּ שׁוֹפַר תְּרוּעָה בַּחֹדֶשׁ הַשְּׁבִעִי בֶּעָשׂוֹר לַחֹדֶשׁ בְּיוֹם הַכִּפֻּרִים תַּעֲבִירוּ שׁוֹפָר בְּכָל אַרְצְכֶם: וְקִדַּשְׁתֶּם אֵת שְׁנַת הַחֲמִשִּׁים שָׁנָה וּקְרָאתֶם דְּרוֹר בָּאָרֶץ לְכָל יֹשְׁבֶיהָ יוֹבֵל הִוא תִּהְיֶה לָכֶם וְשַׁבְתֶּם אִישׁ אֶל אֲחֻזָּתוֹ וְאִישׁ אֶל מִשְׁפַּחְתּוֹ תָּשֻׁבוּ: יוֹבֵל הִוא שְׁנַת הַחֲמִשִּׁים שָׁנָה תִּהְיֶה לָכֶם לֹא תִזְרָעוּ וְלֹא תִקְצְרוּ אֶת סְפִיחֶיהָ וְלֹא תִבְצְרוּ אֶת נְזִרֶיהָ: כִּי יוֹבֵל הִוא קֹדֶשׁ תִּהְיֶה לָכֶם מִן הַשָּׂדֶה תֹּאכְלוּ אֶת תְּבוּאָתָהּ: בִּשְׁנַת הַיּוֹבֵל הַזֹּאת תָּשֻׁבוּ אִישׁ אֶל אֲחֻזָּתוֹ:

And you shall count for yourself seven sabbaths of years, seven years seven times over, and the seven sabbaths of years shall number for you forty-nine years. And you shall sound a blast on the shofar in the seventh month on the tenth of the month; on Yom Kippur shall you sound the shofar throughout your land. And you shall sanctify the fiftieth year, and you shall proclaim liberty (*deror*) in the land for all its inhabitants. It shall be a *yovel* for you, and each man shall return to his estate, and each man shall be returned to his family. The fiftieth year shall be for you a *yovel*; you shall neither sow nor harvest that which grows by itself in the field or in the vineyard. For it is the *yovel*, it shall be holy to you; you shall eat the produce of the field. In this year of *yovel*, each man shall return to his estate. (*Vayikra* 25: 8-13)

The court counts seven *shemitta* cycles, seven sets of seven years, followed by the *yovel*, a sanctified year that incorporates the agricultural *halachot* of the seventh year but goes further. *Yovel* is heralded with *shofar* blasts and completely transforms society, as ancestral lands that have been sold are returned to their initial owners and all servants are set free. This is a national "reset" far more radical than what happens every seven years, delineating a socio-economic ideal. The laws of *yovel* and their impact on the financial system are a topic on their own, irrespective of *yovel*'s relationship to *shevi'it*, and they will be discussed at length in chapter 11.

Immediately after its discussion of *yovel*, the Torah describes the laws of *ona'ah*, exploitation and overcharging. The Torah indicates that there is a prohibition to permanently sell one's ancestral land in *Eretz Yisrael*. Therefore, any sale of land is essentially simply renting for up to fifty years, and this should be reflected in the price of the "sale." After reinforcing and repeating the prohibition of *ona'ah*, the Torah promises that adherence to these laws and *mitzvot* in general ensures that the people will be satiated from the land's produce and live securely in the land:

וְכִי תִמְכְּרוּ מִמְכָּר לַעֲמִיתֶךָ אוֹ קָנֹה מִיַּד עֲמִיתֶךָ אַל תּוֹנוּ אִישׁ אֶת אָחִיו: בְּמִסְפַּר שָׁנִים אַחַר הַיּוֹבֵל תִּקְנֶה מֵאֵת עֲמִיתֶךָ בְּמִסְפַּר שְׁנֵי תְבוּאֹת יִמְכָּר לָךְ: לְפִי רֹב הַשָּׁנִים תַּרְבֶּה מִקְנָתוֹ וּלְפִי מְעֹט הַשָּׁנִים תַּמְעִיט מִקְנָתוֹ כִּי מִסְפַּר תְּבוּאֹת הוּא מֹכֵר לָךְ: וְלֹא תוֹנוּ אִישׁ אֶת עֲמִיתוֹ וְיָרֵאתָ מֵאֱ-לֹהֶיךָ כִּי אֲנִי ה' אֱ-לֹהֵיכֶם: וַעֲשִׂיתֶם אֶת חֻקֹּתַי וְאֶת מִשְׁפָּטַי תִּשְׁמְרוּ וַעֲשִׂיתֶם אֹתָם וִישַׁבְתֶּם עַל הָאָרֶץ לָבֶטַח: וְנָתְנָה הָאָרֶץ פִּרְיָהּ וַאֲכַלְתֶּם לָשֹׂבַע וִישַׁבְתֶּם לָבֶטַח עָלֶיהָ:

When you sell property to your neighbor, or buy any from your neighbor, you shall not exploit one another. In buying from your neighbor, you shall deduct only for the number of years since the *yovel*; and in selling to you, he shall charge you only for the remaining crop years. The more such years, the higher the price you will pay; the fewer such years, the lower the price; for what he is selling you is a number of harvests. Do not exploit one another, but fear your God; for I *Hashem* am your God. You shall observe My laws and faithfully keep My rules, that you may live upon the land in security. The land shall yield its fruit and you shall eat your fill, and you shall live upon it in security. (*Vayikra* 24:14-19)

Charging a price that would be appropriate when selling a field permanently constitutes overcharging and is the model for a general prohibition of overcharging in all business situations. The *mitzvah* of *ona'ah*, prohibiting overcharging and underpaying, is a call to be scrupulously forthcoming in business, especially when dealing with the underprivileged members of society always, not only once in a *yovel*.

The Question

Interestingly, in the course of its discussion of *yovel*, the Torah mentions a question regarding *shevi'it* observance as a whole, earning it the distinction of being the fourth passage in the Torah that discusses *shevi'it*.

The Torah presents a question that the nation is likely to ask regarding *shevi'it* that should seemingly have been mentioned in the earlier section dealing with the laws of *shevi'it*:

וְכִי תֹאמְרוּ מַה נֹּאכַל בַּשָּׁנָה הַשְּׁבִיעִת הֵן לֹא נִזְרָע וְלֹא נֶאֱסֹף אֶת תְּבוּאָתֵנוּ:

And if you should say, "What shall we eat in the seventh year? We will not sow, and we will not gather in our produce!" (*Vayikra* 25:20)

In response, the Torah promises a special boon:

וְצִוִּיתִי אֶת בִּרְכָתִי לָכֶם בַּשָּׁנָה הַשִּׁשִּׁית וְעָשָׂת אֶת הַתְּבוּאָה לִשְׁלֹשׁ הַשָּׁנִים: וּזְרַעְתֶּם אֵת הַשָּׁנָה הַשְּׁמִינִת וַאֲכַלְתֶּם מִן הַתְּבוּאָה יָשָׁן עַד הַשָּׁנָה הַתְּשִׁיעִת עַד בּוֹא תְּבוּאָתָהּ תֹּאכְלוּ יָשָׁן:

I will send you such a blessing in the sixth year that the land will yield enough for three years. While you plant during the eighth year, you will eat from the old crop and will continue to eat from it until the harvest of the ninth year comes in. (*Ibid*. 21-22)

The Netziv (*Ha'amek Davar* 25:20) points out that the fact that the Torah addresses the questions of an "average individual" regarding how he will support his family during the challenging *shevi'it* years indicates that this *mitzvah* and its message are not only for the most pious individuals who never question, but is rather a *mitzvah* for all. *Shevi'it* is an economic move that takes God's role into account.

One possible reason that this question presented only in the context of *yovel*, instead of in the earlier discussion of *shevi'it* where it seems to belong, is that the answer to this question makes clear that God's role in the economy is a necessary element of the economic framework of *shevi'it* and *yovel*. *Shevi'it* and *yovel* have no place in most economics textbooks. The full socio-economic model that the Torah calls for embraces God's role in all aspects of life and creates a society that is not limited by the laws of economics. When God is in the picture, economic goals can best ensure fairness; one may expect the unexpected based on values and commitment, not only the luck of the draw.

The *parasha* of *yovel* and *shevi'it* concludes with *pesukim* that might express the most explicit rationale for the entire framework. The Torah returns to the prohibition of selling land permanently:

וְהָאָרֶץ לֹא תִמָּכֵר לִצְמִתֻת כִּי לִי הָאָרֶץ כִּי גֵרִים וְתוֹשָׁבִים אַתֶּם עִמָּדִי: וּבְכֹל אֶרֶץ אֲחֻזַּתְכֶם גְּאֻלָּה תִּתְּנוּ לָאָרֶץ:

For the land must not be sold for eternity, for the land is Mine; you are but strangers and residents with Me. Throughout the land that you hold, you must provide redemption for the land. (*Vayikra* 25:23-24)

The Torah's rationale for the limitations on sales provides deeper insight into *shevi'it* and *yovel* as well. One cannot sell land for eternity because the land belongs to God and because of the direct outgrowth of that point – "You are but strangers and residents with me." When *yovel* arrives all land reverts back to its original ancestral owners. In *Eretz Yisrael*, the Torah teaches us that one's possession over land is not an indication of true ownership, as the land belongs solely to Hashem. Furthermore, even the "owners" whose land is returned to them must recognize that they are but strangers and residents on the land. Hashem maintains sole proprietorship over the land and allows the nation to reside in the land while observing His laws for it. Recognizing the uniqueness of the land and God's title to it, and therefore observing its laws, is the ticket to securely residing in the land, and ultimately redemption.

Understanding the Question and Answer

The Torah describes the question of "what shall we eat" in the context of *yovel*, and doesn't state explicitly at what point this question is asked. This raises several questions.

- Is the question asked in anticipation of *shevi'it*, or is it asked only once every fifty years when *yovel* arrives?

- Why are the questioners only concerned with what they will eat in the seventh year (since planting will not resume until the eighth year, logically, their stored food is more likely to last through the seventh year than the eighth!)?

- Additionally, why does the Torah present this as a question asked by the people and responded to by Hashem? Couldn't the Torah just stated that there is no need to worry about food as there will be a divine blessing? Is the blessing of the crops of the sixth year only a response to the question? What would have happened if no one asked this question all together?

Some of these issues are subject to dispute. Rashi, for example, interprets the *pesukim* as expressing a general promise during every *shevi'it* cycle, while the Ramban understands it to be a reference specifically to instance in which *yovel* follows *shevi'it*. Additionally, some commentaries discuss whether the blessing will be felt through increased food yield or produce that is more satiating.

Several commentaries probe the fundamental question underlying many of the issues here: How does this back and forth relate to the general concept of *bitachon*, total reliance on God? One approach espoused by Rav Zusha (cited by his brother, the *Noam Elimelech*) is that God's blessing exists at all times for those who fulfill the word of God, and there is therefore no true need for a special blessing during the sixth year. However, if God is questioned, the blessing dissipates on its own, as the blessing is reserved for those who trust unwaveringly in Hashem. Thus, once one questions God, God must reinstitute the blessing. In essence, there is no need for a new, unique *shevi'it* blessing, as Hashem is always providing behind the scenes, but Hashem's concern for the people observing *shevi'it* recognizes that they might question Hashem. The renewed blessing should hopefully allow the nation to acknowledge God's financial blessing throughout the other years as well.

The Alter of Navordok, Rav Yosef Yoizel Horowitz, who was known for his legendary trust in and reliance on God under all circumstances, champions an even more radical understanding. In a lengthy piece, he begins by questioning God's motivation in commanding a challenging *mitzvah* like *shevi'it*:

> And what of the iron laws of economy? Did the Creator, blessed be He, fail to consult with them before commanding such a sabbatical, to which all economic experimentation is opposed?

After questioning the placement and juxtaposition of this *pasuk*, he wonders regarding the timing of the question:

> We ought to be even more surprised by the question itself: When would one ask [this]? Before the sixth year he has [food to eat] and the time to fulfill the *mitzvah* has not yet come, so that he is not pressed to ask, "What shall we eat in the seventh year?" Then, when the time to fulfill the *mitzvah* comes in the seventh year, one will already see with his [own] eyes the blessing of the three years, so that he no longer has occasion to ask!

The Alter answers these questions with a radically novel interpretation of the *pasuk*, explaining that the question is not asked in the sixth or even in the seventh year:

> ...but specifically in the first year, for human nature is to gaze and look far ahead and worry today about several years [hence]. If it occurs to him, then, that a while later he will need some critical thing, he already becomes frightened of arriving at tomorrow empty-handed, and due to his preoccupation with the thought that he may not attain all that he will need tomorrow, he begins hoarding today for tomorrow, even cutting back on the today's needs for tomorrow.

One cannot enjoy today if he is worried about tomorrow. This worry pervades the six years of work and prevents one from absorbing the *shemitta* message.

> In effect, there is here a great trap of worries about tomorrow, which is liable to entirely disrupt the objective of the law of *shemitta*, for its purpose is to teach one wisdom, so that one knows that the land belongs to God, and so that even when one occupies himself with his field during the six years, he not say, "My strength and the power of my hand made me this wealth," but knows instead that it is "Neither by wealth nor by strength, but by my spirit,' says God." The Torah forbids even "the after-growth of your harvest," such that he is forbidden to benefit even from past efforts, so that he remember the forty years when Israel ate manna in the wilderness...

A person's worries may translate into hoarding, causing him to lose sight of the *mitzvah* of *shevi'it*, whose main objective it to teach the trait of faith and to expand conviction and trust in the assistance of God. One who fails to absorb this message of *shevi'it* existentially cannot earnestly fulfill its laws physically, both because he is missing the *mitzvah's* point and because his lack of faith will not enable him to withstand the *shevi'it* challenge.

> The Torah therefore writes, "and you will eat to satiety, and live upon it securely," such that one might explain that the idea of the verse is not only to promise, but also to admonish—that is, I command you to eat to satiety and not to cut back at all, for the Torah anticipates one's thoughts. At the beginning of the first year, one might already harbor worries about tomorrow due to the law of *shemitta*, which he would want to fulfill, and he surely would adopt the course of hoarding. The Torah therefore admonished firmly, "and you will eat to satiety"—that one not implement the stratagem of hoarding and not cut back today in anticipation of what is to come— "and live upon it securely"—with no worries about tomorrow due to observance of the law of *shemitta*.
>
> This is the reason for juxtaposition of the question of, "And if you should say, 'What shall we eat in the seventh year?'" and the warning not to hoard—if it is so, what shall we eat? Are worries about tomorrow not a logical consideration? If we do not hoard today, with what shall we sustain our needs tomorrow? To this the verse responds, "I will send you such a blessing," for the preparatory work is not up to you, but up to Me: I Myself will assign my blessing in the sixth year for the three years. You, meanwhile, will not prepare at all, because your preparations are the curse of hoarding and cutting back and the petty calculations of poverty. Instead, I shall prepare for you through blessing: "The land will yield enough for three years," i.e., the very growth will be blessed, in that enough for three years will sprout from the planting of one, and you will have no need to resort to the practice of hoarding. Instead, have faith in God, and you will witness a blessing.

The Alter of Navordok understands *shevi'it's* blessing as a general directive on life. The Torah instructs an individual to trust in God and to express that *bitachon* by not constantly limiting oneself throughout the six years to ensure they have what to survive on in the seventh.

This radical interpretation has at least two sets of direct implications. First, one who trusts in God does not need to hoard throughout other years, but can and should enjoy the blessings they were given to him without worrying about the future. Second, *shevi'it's* goal is to impress upon us that the economic laws that so often dictate our mindset and decisions are deficient. They fail to recognize God's blessing and His defining role in who will succeed.

Can We Rely on the Blessing? Must We?

Some have pointed to this blessing as a reason to raise concern regarding what is known as *keren ha-shevi'it,* a fund that helps support *shevi'it*-observing farmers. Isn't providing human financial support to such farmers a contradiction to the divine blessing, which should be sufficient to live in prosperity? However, the prevalent understanding is that the divine blessing supporting *shevi'it* observers can come in many forms. The money donated to the farmers is part and parcel of the blessing, as the providers are Hashem's agents, sharing in His commitment to *shevi'it* observers.

There is also a discussion if the blessing applies in our day and age, when *shevi'it* is only Rabbinically mandated according to most opinions. Some (see *Sema* C.M. 67,2) maintain that *shevi'it* was Biblically ordained and the unique blessing was applicable only during the period when the majority of the nation lived in the Land according to tribal affiliation. The *Chazon Ish* (18,4), however, understood that the blessing still applies, but it requires that one do his utmost to be a funnel for the blessing to be achieved in what appears to be natural ways.

For our purposes, the blessing is another reminder that God's role in the economy is paramount and that the ideal Jewish outlook on economy and society must factor in God's blessing for those who observe His commandments. This blessing not only allows us to see God's interaction in our world through our business ventures, but also should enable us to be resilient and maintain our convictions and values even when doing so is difficult.

Similarly, Rav Yitzchak Breuer (*Nachaliel*) opines that the entire question is not really a question:

> *Shemitta* is a festive demonstration against the iron laws of the economy! These laws do not rule; rather, reality is determined by the "to-do" list of the Creator, blessed be He, and the "to-do" list of man. The economy too is purposeful and submits to the supreme value of the entirety of creation: becoming one with the Creator, blessed be He, until His name becomes one just as He is one.

Although an individual might be tempted to ask what there will be to eat when observing *shevi'it,* the entire premise of the question is wrong. Economic experience is relative; the only ironclad laws are those of God. One farmer might have food to eat without planting, while another farmer who works hard will have his crop consumed by locusts. *Shevi'it* reminds us to see God's role in the economy. Rav Breuer advises us to keep *shevi'it* in mind throughout the other six years of work, just like we are cognizant of Shabbat throughout the six-day workweek:

The law of *shemitta* is to be the foundational law of the national economy of the nation of the Torah, perpetually influencing all six years of endeavor, just as Shabbat perpetually influences the six days of endeavor. The entire Jewish economy is to be an economy of *shemitta*, and then, if the physical and intellectual investments have been properly made, accepting the law of *shemitta* as one that is unbreakable, then the Creator, blessed be He, promises to bestow the same blessing that He, blessed be He, bestows on the Shabbat day. You are to sanctify the six years of endeavor with the blessing of *shemitta*! For six years you are to work, but you are neither to work to live nor live to work. Rather, work for six years in order to live the seventh year, the year of *shemitta*...

Feeling the Blessing

It is apparent from the blessing promised to those who observe *shevi'it* that *shevi'it* observance was not meant to be simple. For good reason, *Chazal* refer to *shevi'it*-observers as "*gibborei ko'ach*," exemplifiers of immeasurable strength for standing up to the challenges that *shevi'it* presents. On the other hand, if farmers were to be convinced that *shevi'it* does, in fact, provide blessing – not only time off from toil in the field, but also financial sustenance and even success – many would embrace it and even seek to expand it beyond the agricultural realm.

Books have been written collecting some of the miraculous blessings *shevi'it* observers have experienced. While these blessings do not discount the challenges that *shevi'it*-observing farmers face, for some farmers, even not fully observant ones, the blessings are so commonplace that they almost take them into account. In our day, minimal government assistance and organizational backing makes *shevi'it* observance more tenable, but during the period of the founding of the State, the only way for most *shevi'it* observers to survive was through openly miraculous blessings. The following astounding testimony about Moshav Komemiyut, one of the few religious moshavim in Israel in 1950, beautifully illustrates this point:

I was among the original founders of the Komemiyut agricultural settlement in southern Israel.

Our second year, Fall 1950-Summer 1951, coincided with the *shemitta* sabbatical year, when the Torah forbids agricultural work.

We were among the few settlements in Israel then who observed the sabbatical laws. We refrained from working the land, concentrating instead on building, completing much of our permanent housing that year. Our *moshav* gradually developed and expanded, families moved in, and by the end of the year, we were eighty people.

As the sabbatical year drew to a close, we prepared to renew our farming. We needed seed to grow crops, but could only use wheat from the sixth year preceding *shemitta*, for the seventh year's produce is forbidden. We visited the agricultural settlements in the area, seeking good quality seed from previous years, but found none.

All we could find was old seed in a shed at Kibbutz Gat. No farmer in his right mind would consider using such poor seed for planting. The kibbutzniks burst into laughter when we told them we were actually interested in this infested grain that had been rotting for a few years in a dark, murky corner...

We consulted with our Rabbi Mendelson, who encouraged us. "Use it. The Almighty who causes wheat to sprout from good seed will bless your inferior seed as well."

Having no alternative, we loaded the old, infested seed and returned to Komemiyut. The *shemitta* laws forbade us to turn over the soil until after Rosh Hashana, the beginning of the eighth year, so we didn't actually sow the seed until November, two or three months after the other farmers completed their planting.That year, the rains were late in coming. The farmers from all the kibbutzim and moshavim desperately waited for the first rain, but the heavens were unresponsive.Finally it rained. When? The day after we completed planting our thousand dunam of wheat fields with those wormy seeds, the rains poured down on the parched earth.

We were nervous in anticipation, but we strengthened our faith and trust in God. And it didn't take long time for the hand of the Almighty to be revealed.

The wheat fields planted during the seventh year, months before the first rain, sprouted small, weak crops. At the same time, our fields, sowed with the old, infested seed long after the appropriate season, were covered with an unusually large and healthy yield.

The story spread quickly. Farmers from all over our region came to see the "Komemiyut miracle" with their own eyes.[23]

---

23   Thanks to Rav Eli Ozarowski who shortened this excerpt from http://www.jewish-holiday. com/farmshmittah.html; an expanded story can be found at http://www.arachimusa.org/Index. asp?ArticleID=634&CategoryID=280&Page=1]

Chapter 7

Parasha 5: Bechukotai- Our Ticket to the Land

The Importance of *Shevi'it* Observance

The way in which the Torah portrays *shevi'it* in its first three *parashiyot* indicates that it is a year with a unique set of agricultural laws, financial implications, an economic vision, and a spiritual dimension. It is clear that *shevi'it* is important, but there is no reason to believe that violating the various *mitzvot* that accompany it, whether positive and negative, should incur any out-of-the-ordinary punishments. With all its importance, the fact that no severe punishment is mentioned would seem to indicate that the *mitzvot* of *shevi'it* should be treated like all other *mitzvot*.

Ordinarily, we do not assign "grades" to *mitzvot* or determine the relative importance of various *mitzvot*. This is seemingly the lesson of the *mishna* in *Avot*:

> וֶהֱוֵי זָהִיר בְּמִצְוָה קַלָּה כְּבַחֲמוּרָה שֶׁאֵין אַתָּה יוֹדֵעַ מַתַּן שְׂכָרָן שֶׁל מִצְוֹת.
> One should be cautious with a light mitzvah just as with a weighty one, for one does not know the reward for *mitzvot*. (Avot 2:1)

At the same time, the Torah does give some means of determining preference among *mitzvot* when necessary. The Talmud (*Yoma* 83a) details the order of prohibited foods that may be fed to one whose life is in danger, with the guiding principle being that the lighter a food's prohibition, the first it is to be used. For this reason, the Rambam, in his commentary on the *mishna* cited above, explains that as much as we take all *mitzvot* seriously, there are gradations regarding their importance:

> Regarding all the negative precepts, we know from their punishments which of them is more severe and which less so, there being eight levels...
> Regarding the positive precepts, however, [God] did not explicitly state the reward for each of them, so that we may know which are grave and which are less so. Rather, He commanded us to observe this one and that one, without informing us which one's reward is greater...
> Even though the value of one *mitzvah* in relation to another was never stated explicitly, there is a way to evaluate the matter. That is, any positive precept regarding which you find that its violation carries a grave punishment, you know that its fulfillment brings great reward...

The Rambam states that negative commandments are judged by the severity of punishment one incurs for their violations, and one can weigh the relative importance of positive *mitzvot* by viewing the punishment for one's failure to fulfill them. For instance, the importance of the positive *mitzvot* of Shabbat is apparent from the capital punishment and excision given to Shabbat violators.

Based on these sources in the Talmud and the Rambam, we would be hard-pressed to categorize either the positive or negative *mitzvot* of *shevi'it* as being overly significant. *Shevi'it* observance involves a host of positive and negative *mitzvot*, but the most severe punishment for a person's violation would be *malkot* (lashes), the punishment common for most negative commandments. Individual *shevi'it* violators would be taken to task and punished, but seemingly with standard punishment.

A Challenge with Consequences

The Torah is clearly aware that observing both the agricultural and monetary aspects of *shevi'it* is difficult, yet it does not tolerate *shevi'it* negligence. The Torah explicitly mentions the fear that will grip lenders due to *shemittat kesafim*, remittance of loans at the conclusion of *shevi'it*:

> הִשָּׁמֶר לְךָ פֶּן יִהְיֶה דָבָר עִם לְבָבְךָ בְלִיַּעַל לֵאמֹר קָרְבָה שְׁנַת הַשֶּׁבַע שְׁנַת הַשְּׁמִטָּה וְרָעָה עֵינְךָ בְּאָחִיךָ הָאֶבְיוֹן וְלֹא תִתֵּן לוֹ וְקָרָא עָלֶיךָ אֶל ה' וְהָיָה בְךָ חֵטְא:
>
> Beware that there be not an unworthy [*beliya'al*] thought in your heart, saying, "The seventh year, the year of release, is at hand;" and your eye be evil against your needy brother, and you give him nothing; and he cry unto God against you, and it be reckoned to you a sin. (*Devarim* 15:9)

These fears of lending money are understandable, as *shemittat kesafim* will prevent enforcible collection of any outstanding loans, but the Torah nevertheless prohibits refraining from lending. The Torah even refers to these thoughts as *"beliya'al,"* meaning *"beli ol,"* signifying complete removal of the yoke of divine kingship. The term *beliya'al* is found elsewhere in the Torah only with regard to idol worship! But what is so unacceptable about the natural fear that one's interest-free loan will not be repaid?[24]

As we have seen, regarding agricultural *shemitta*, the Torah foresees the question that would be nagging those observing *shemitta* as they wonder what they will be able to eat, assuring the questioners with a promised blessing:

> וְכִי תֹאמְרוּ מַה נֹּאכַל בַּשָּׁנָה הַשְּׁבִיעִת הֵן לֹא נִזְרָע וְלֹא נֶאֱסֹף אֶת תְּבוּאָתֵנוּ: כא) וְצִוִּיתִי אֶת בִּרְכָתִי לָכֶם בַּשָּׁנָה הַשִּׁשִּׁית וְעָשָׂת אֶת הַתְּבוּאָה לִשְׁלֹשׁ הַשָּׁנִים: וּזְרַעְתֶּם אֵת הַשָּׁנָה הַשְּׁמִינִת וַאֲכַלְתֶּם מִן הַתְּבוּאָה יָשָׁן עַד הַשָּׁנָה הַתְּשִׁיעִת עַד בּוֹא תְּבוּאָתָהּ תֹּאכְלוּ יָשָׁן:
>
> And if you should say, "What shall we eat in the seventh year? We will not sow, and we will not gather in our produce!" I will send you such a blessing in the sixth year that the land will yield enough for three years. While you plant during the eighth year, you will eat from the old crop and will continue to eat from it until the harvest of the ninth year comes in. (*Vayikra* 25:20-22)

The Torah recognizes that *shevi'it* poses a challenge to the farmer, and therefore assures him of just reward.[25] One might even suggest that the fact that its observance is so trying might

---

24   History seems to indicate that the Torah's concern indeed came to pass; lenders refused to lend money before the time of *shemittat kesafim*. It was for this reason that Hillel found it necessary to enact the *prozbul* (*Mishna Shevi'it* 10:3), handing over these debts to the court so they could ultimately be collected. (See Section IV regarding *shemittat kesafim* and *prozbul*.)

25   It is interesting to note that both of these descriptions of the difficulty involved in the observance of *shevi'it* are

be a mitigating factor and a possible reason to lessen the punishment for nonobservance.[26]

The Curses of *Parashat Bechukotai*

This brings us to *Parashat Bechukotai*. While we might have had ideas about getting off lightly for personally violating *shevi'it*, here the Torah sets us straight. It discusses the blessings that are awarded to the nation when they follow God's *mitzvot*, followed by the *tochacha*, the rebuke, which delineates the horrible punitive measures that will befall the nation if they violate God's will.

In the section of the blessings, we are told that adhering to God's will ensures that the people will live safely in the Land:

אִם בְּחֻקֹּתַי תֵּלֵכוּ וְאֶת מִצְוֹתַי תִּשְׁמְרוּ וַעֲשִׂיתֶם אֹתָם: וְנָתַתִּי גִשְׁמֵיכֶם בְּעִתָּם וְנָתְנָה הָאָרֶץ יְבוּלָהּ וְעֵץ הַשָּׂדֶה יִתֵּן פִּרְיוֹ: ...וִישַׁבְתֶּם לָבֶטַח בְּאַרְצְכֶם: וְנָתַתִּי שָׁלוֹם בָּאָרֶץ וּשְׁכַבְתֶּם וְאֵין מַחֲרִיד ....:

If you follow my statutes and observe my commandments. I will give your rains in their time, the land will yield its produce ... and you will live in security in your land. And I will grant peace in the land, and you will lie down with no one to frighten [you] ... (*Vayikra* 26:3-6)

The converse is mentioned in the ensuing *pesukim* of the *tochacha*; violation of God's will result in punishment. At first it seems as though the punishments are a result of general disobedience leading to abrogation of the covenant, as the verses state:

וְאִם לֹא תִשְׁמְעוּ לִי וְלֹא תַעֲשׂוּ אֵת כָּל הַמִּצְוֹת הָאֵלֶּה: וְאִם בְּחֻקֹּתַי תִּמְאָסוּ וְאִם אֶת מִשְׁפָּטַי תִּגְעַל נַפְשְׁכֶם לְבִלְתִּי עֲשׂוֹת אֶת כָּל מִצְוֹתַי לְהַפְרְכֶם אֶת בְּרִיתִי:

But if you do not obey Me and do not observe all these commandments. If you reject My laws, and spurn My rule, so that you do not observe all My commandments and you break my covenant... (Ibid. 14-15)

However, in the continuation of the *pesukim*, after detailing the starvation, plagues, and exile that will befall the nation, the Torah teaches that all these punishments come for a particular purpose:

וְאֶתְכֶם אֱזָרֶה בַגּוֹיִם וַהֲרִיקֹתִי אַחֲרֵיכֶם חָרֶב וְהָיְתָה אַרְצְכֶם שְׁמָמָה וְעָרֵיכֶם יִהְיוּ חָרְבָּה: אָז תִּרְצֶה הָאָרֶץ אֶת שַׁבְּתֹתֶיהָ כֹּל יְמֵי הָשַׁמָּה וְאַתֶּם בְּאֶרֶץ אֹיְבֵיכֶם אָז תִּשְׁבַּת הָאָרֶץ וְהִרְצָת אֶת שַׁבְּתֹתֶיהָ: כָּל יְמֵי הָשַׁמָּה תִּשְׁבֹּת

---

not found in the primary description of these *mitzvot*. The Torah seems to conclude its discussion of the laws of *shevi'it* in *Vayikra* 25:7, and it then begins discussing the *mitzvot* of *yovel*. Yet, thirteen verses later, it returns to the question that is bound to be on the minds of many: "What shall we eat"? Similarly, in *Parashat Re'eh*, after seemingly concluding the description of the *mitzvah* of *shemittat kesafim* and discussing the more general *mitzvah* of giving charity, the Torah returns to the topic, criticizing the illegitimate thought that might enter one's mind before the loan remittance at the conclusion of the seventh year.

In both contexts, the *mitzvah* is described independently; the difficulty involved is addressed as an afterthought, embedded in the description of the similar but different *mitzvah* that follows each discussion. The reason for this presentation may be that only after having the time to digest *shevi'it*'s revolutionary agricultural and financial ideas is one able to formulate the difficulty associated with the *mitzvah*.

26   Although one might wonder why the Torah would demand something so challenging, the question might be the answer. Since these *mitzvot* come from God, the all-powerful and omniscient Creator, there certainly must be a significant reason for them, despite their difficulty. If God calls for something so challenging, the stakes of what it has to offer must be quite high. In fact, *shevi'it*'s benefits are a direct result of its challenging nature. (See Section II)

אֵת אֲשֶׁר לֹא שָׁבְתָה בְּשַׁבְּתֹתֵיכֶם בְּשִׁבְתְּכֶם עָלֶיהָ:

I will scatter you among the nations and will unsheathe the sword to pursue you. Your land will be desolate and your cities in ruins. The land [ha-aretz] shall then be appeased for its Sabbaths while it is desolate and you are in the land of your enemies; the land shall rest and have appeasement for its Sabbaths. All the days of its desolation it shall be at rest, according to the rest that it did not enjoy while you dwelt in it. (ibid. 33-35)

Here the sabbatical year is given special mention, as if its violation is the cause for all the punishments detailed in the *tochacha*! Although it is not explicit that the punishments are a direct result of nonobservance of *shevi'it*, it is clear that the land will need to be "appeased" for all the *shabbatot ha-aretz* that were not properly fulfilled. Just as *shabbat ha-aretz* involves leaving the land uncultivated, the exile of the Jews from the land and its desolation will bring about the necessary rest that was ignored during Israel's sojourn on the land. The severity of punishment is linked to the nonobservance of *shevi'it*.

The relationship between *shevi'it* and the punishments of the *tochacha* may also be gleaned from the recurrence of the number seven in the description of the punishments:

And if you will not listen to Me, I will chastise you sevenfold for your transgressions. And if you walk with me with indifference and will not hearken to Me, I will strike you sevenfold according to your transgressions.
I will also strike you sevenfold for your transgressions. (24, 28)

Additionally, Rabbanit Sharon Rimon[27] points out that "Aside from the fact that the introduction and conclusion of the subject of exile focus on the land, the subject of the land, its desolation and its sabbaths are repeated several times in these verses.

- The word "land" appears seven times (six times in the above verses and once in verse 42, "And I will remember the land").

- The root *sh-m-m* (desolation) recurs seven times in these verses (six times in verses 31-35 and again in verse 43).

- The root *sh-b-t* (*shabbat*, sabbath) likewise appears seven times (six times in verses 31-35 and then again in verse 43).

This description seems to portray *shevi'it* as far more than a multifaceted year with various *mitzvot*, but almost as if it is the ticket to secure dwelling in the Land of Israel. If the nation fails to leave their land fallow in the seventh year, God promises that the land will remain fallow for many years, as Israel will be in exile and incapable of cultivation and planting.

In a frightening manner, with almost the same words, the concluding chapter of *Tanach* tells us that this came to be; the nonobservance of *shevi'it* caused a lengthening of the exile:

וַיֶּגֶל הַשְּׁאֵרִית מִן הַחֶרֶב אֶל בָּבֶל וַיִּהְיוּ לוֹ וּלְבָנָיו לַעֲבָדִים עַד מְלֹךְ מַלְכוּת פָּרָס: לְמַלֹּאות דְּבַר ה' בְּפִי יִרְמְיָהוּ

---

27   See Rabbanit Sharon Rimon, Behar | Exile, Desolation and Lying Fallow | Etzion.org.il

עַד רָצְתָה הָאָרֶץ אֶת שַׁבְּתוֹתֶיהָ כָּל יְמֵי הָשַׁמָּה שָׁבָתָה לְמַלֹּאות שִׁבְעִים שָׁנָה:

And Those who had escaped from the sword were taken by King Nevuchadnetzar into exile to Babylon, and they became servants to him and his sons until the kingdom of Persia came to power. The Land of Israel finally enjoyed Sabbath rests. All the days it lay desolate, it kept the Sabbath, to complete seventy years, in fulfillment of the word of God. (*II Divrei Ha-Yamim* 36:20-21)

These *pesukim* in the Torah seem to be the basis for the *mishna's* statement:

גָּלוּת בָּא לָעוֹלָם עַל עוֹבְדֵי עֲבוֹדָה זָרָה וְעַל גִּלּוּי עֲרָיוֹת וְעַל שְׁפִיכַת דָּמִים וְעַל הַשְׁמָטַת הָאָרֶץ:

Exile comes to the world on account of idol-worshippers, illicit relations, bloodshed, and [nonobservance of] *shemitta* of the land. (Avot 5,9)

Without *Parashat Bechukotai*, we would have little reason to believe that violating *shemitta* would be the cause of exile and dispersion, or any stringent punishment for that matter, yet the Torah here states very clear that *shevi'it* observance is required to live in the land securely, or at all. But why?

The Abarbanel's Understanding

The Abarbanel explains that the placement of the *tochacha* in *Parashat Bechukotai* immediately after the discussion of *shemitta* and *yovel* in *Parashat Behar* indicates that the blessings and curses in *Parashat Bechukotai* are linked to observance of *shevi'it* and the other *mitzvot hateluyot ba-aretz*.

The Abarbanel notes that the challenging nature of certain *mitzvot* leads us to question their feasibility, and one is liable to "opt" for the "financially secure" alternative, although it involves *mitzvah* violations. The Torah here directly challenges that narrative, indicating that what one might view as sacrifice is in fact the ticket to success. Since the ultimate decision of success and failure lies with God, adhering His word is the only sure way for success –and the opposite is true as well. The Torah explicitly links the punishments with lack of *shevi'it* observance; desolation will come on account of thinking that failure to observe *shevi'it* will actually be a catalyst for growth.

The Shabbat Connection

Others see the description of the desolation brought on account of lack of *shevi'it* observance as an indication of *shevi'it's* centrality in our right to live in the Land. Evidently, there is some deeper significance to this set of *mitzvot*. Although violating them is not punishable with capital punishment in human court or even excision in the Heavenly Court, violation of *shevi'it* by the nation precipitates exile and destruction.

We might be inclined to attribute the significance of *shevi'it* observance to the Shabbat element of the year. Shabbat is a *mitzvah* of fundamental importance, as indicated by the severity of the punishment for one who performs prohibited *melacha* (labor) on it (as per the Rambam's means of determining *mitzvah*-severity). However, despite the connection between *shevi'it* and Shabbat, there is good reason to believe that the severity of Shabbat desecration is due to elements that are not shared with *shevi'it*. The Rambam explains why nonobservance of Shabbat results in one being treated like an idolater:

> [The observance of] Shabbat and [the prohibition against] worshiping false deities are each equivalent to [the observance] of all the *mitzvot* of the Torah. And Shabbat is the eternal sign between the Holy One, blessed be He, and us. For this reason, whoever transgresses the other *mitzvot* is considered to be one of the wicked of Israel, but a person who violates the Shabbat is considered as an idolater.…(*Rambam, Hilchot Shabbat* 30:15)

The weekly Shabbat reminds us of and even serves to testify to God's creation of the world *ex nihilo*. Although *shabbat ha-aretz* is indeed referred to as *shabbat*, its importance is not as readily apparent. Furthermore, *shevi'it* observance is specifically connected in the verses in *Bechukotai* to the Land of Israel, something that does not seem to be the focus of Shabbat.

On the other hand, just as secular Zionist poet Ahad Ha'am (Asher Ginsburg's) notably said about the weekly Shabbat that "more than the Jews have safeguarded Shabbat, the Shabbat has safeguarded the Jews," *Parashat Bechukotai* make it clear that safeguarding the Shabbat of the land is what safeguards and ensures a thriving Jewish presence in the Land of Israel. The question is why. What is the secret of *shevi'it's* significance and its connection to the land?

The Connection Between Man and the Land- In Israel and Beyond

In order to take the first steps towards answering this question, we must note the broader issue of the impact that man's actions have on the land. As we will see, it is not only in regard to the observance of *shevi'it* that the Torah connects observance to the right to dwell in the Land of Israel.

At the dawn of time, as man was created, there was a relationship between man and the ground. After all, man was a composite of the dust of the earth and a divine soul, as his name would testify: *Adam*, man, is derived from the word *adama*.

> וַיִּיצֶר ה' אֱ-לֹהִים אֶת הָאָדָם עָפָר מִן הָאֲדָמָה וַיִּפַּח בְּאַפָּיו נִשְׁמַת חַיִּים וַיְהִי הָאָדָם לְנֶפֶשׁ חַיָּה: וַיִּטַּע ה' אֱ-לֹהִים גַּן בְּעֵדֶן מִקֶּדֶם וַיָּשֶׂם שָׁם אֶת הָאָדָם אֲשֶׁר יָצָר:
>
> And the Lord God formed the man (*Adam*) of the dust of the earth (*adama*) and breathed into his nostrils the breath of life; and the man became a living soul. And the Lord God planted a garden eastward in Eden; and there he put the man whom He had formed. (*Bereishit* 2:7-8)

The *midrash* (*Tanchuma* Tzav 14) points out that the relationship of Adam to *adama* is inherent in man's name:

> Why from earth? For man was created from earth, and he is called Adam because he comes from earth (*adama*).

This relationship between man and the ground is similarly reflected in the punishment and curse placed on Adam and the *adama* after Adam's sin of eating from the *Eitz Ha-Da'at* (Tree of Knowledge):

וּלְאָדָם אָמַר כִּי שָׁמַעְתָּ לְקוֹל אִשְׁתֶּךָ וַתֹּאכַל מִן הָעֵץ אֲשֶׁר צִוִּיתִיךָ לֵאמֹר לֹא תֹאכַל מִמֶּנּוּ אֲרוּרָה הָאֲדָמָה בַּעֲבוּרֶךָ בְּעִצָּבוֹן תֹּאכֲלֶנָּה כֹּל יְמֵי חַיֶּיךָ: וְקוֹץ וְדַרְדַּר תַּצְמִיחַ לָךְ וְאָכַלְתָּ אֶת עֵשֶׂב הַשָּׂדֶה: בְּזֵעַת אַפֶּיךָ תֹּאכַל לֶחֶם עַד שׁוּבְךָ אֶל הָאֲדָמָה כִּי מִמֶּנָּה לֻקָּחְתָּ כִּי עָפָר אַתָּה וְאֶל עָפָר תָּשׁוּב:

And to Adam He said: "Because you listened to the voice of your wife and you ate from the tree about which I commanded you, saying, Do not eat from it. – Cursed be the ground (*adama*) because of you; by your toil you shall eat of it all the days of your life. Thorns and thistles shall it sprout for you, but your food shall be grass of the field. By the sweat of your brow shall you get bread to eat until you return to the ground from which you were taken. For dust you are and to dust you shall return." (*Bereishit* 3:17-19)

Although it was Adam who sinned, it was the ground that was cursed. This interrelationship of man's actions to the state of the *adama* continues to haunt the next generation as well, as seen from Kayin's punishment after killing his brother Hevel:

וַיֹּאמֶר מֶה עָשִׂיתָ קוֹל דְּמֵי אָחִיךָ צֹעֲקִים אֵלַי מִן הָאֲדָמָה: וְעַתָּה אָרוּר אָתָּה מִן הָאֲדָמָה אֲשֶׁר פָּצְתָה אֶת פִּיהָ לָקַחַת אֶת דְּמֵי אָחִיךָ מִיָּדֶךָ: כִּי תַעֲבֹד אֶת הָאֲדָמָה לֹא תֹסֵף תֵּת כֹּחָהּ לָךְ נָע וָנָד תִּהְיֶה בָאָרֶץ:

Then He said, "What have you done? Your brother's blood cries out to me from the ground (*adama*). Therefore you shall be more cursed than the ground which opened up its mouth to receive your brother's blood from your hand. If you till the ground, it shall no longer yield its strength to you. You shall become a ceaseless wanderer on the earth." (*Bereishit* 4:10-12)

At this point, Kayin is cursed more than the *adama*, and the growing abilities of the field are further compromised.

Upon deeper analysis, it is clear that there is another element in both Adam's and Kayin's curses that is also very relevant to the curses in *Parashat Bechukotai*. Adam's actions result in his exile, as he is sent out of the Garden of Eden. Kayin's actions also result in banishment, as he is to become a ceaseless wanderer on the earth. This is similar to exile from the Land of Israel and the land being "cursed" by laying fallow due to nonobservance of *shemitta*. In both *Bereishit* and *Bechukotai*, it is clear that to be given the rights to one's *adama*, one must act appropriately.

The connection between *Adam* and *adama* continues to express itself in numerous places in the Torah. It lies at the heart of the destruction of the earth at the time of the flood, as man's sins result in mankind being almost completely annihilated and removed from the earth:

וַיַּרְא ה' כִּי רַבָּה רָעַת הָאָדָם בָּאָרֶץ... וַיִּנָּחֶם ה'... כִּי עָשָׂה אֶת הָאָדָם בָּאָרֶץ:... וַיֹּאמֶר ה' אֶמְחֶה אֶת הָאָדָם אֲשֶׁר בָּרָאתִי מֵעַל פְּנֵי הָאֲדָמָה:... וְנֹחַ מָצָא חֵן בְּעֵינֵי ה':

And God saw that the wickedness of man was great in the land (*ha-aretz*)... And God repented for having made man in the land... And God said: "I shall wipe out man whom I have created from the ground (*ha-adama*)..." But Noach found favor in God's eyes. (*Bereishit* 6:5-8)

It is notable that although God initially sees the wickedness of man in the "*eretz*," he decides to wipe man off the face of the *"adama."* These terms are similar, but there may be an important difference in their implications, as we will see below.

Importantly, after Noach emerges from the destruction of the flood and brings an offering, God forges a covenant with man that seems to sever the relationship between man's actions and the state of the ground:

> וַיֵּצֵא נֹחַ וּבָנָיו וְאִשְׁתּוֹ וּנְשֵׁי בָנָיו אִתּוֹ... ... וַיֹּאמֶר ה' אֶל לִבּוֹ לֹא אֹסִף לְקַלֵּל עוֹד אֶת הָאֲדָמָה בַּעֲבוּר הָאָדָם כִּי
> יֵצֶר לֵב הָאָדָם רַע מִנְּעֻרָיו וְלֹא אֹסִף עוֹד לְהַכּוֹת אֶת כָּל חַי כַּאֲשֶׁר עָשִׂיתִי:
>
> Noach came out, together with his sons, his wife... Hashem said to himself: "Never again will I curse the ground because of man, since the inclinations of man's mind are evil from his youth; nor will I ever destroy every living being as I have done." (8:18-21)

Here the Torah seems to explicitly release the ground from culpability for man's actions. Why, then, does *Parashat Bechukotai* seems to reinstate such a connection, specifically regarding *shevi'it* observance?

In order to understand what changed, we must first understand the nature of the relationship between *"adam"* and *"adama."*

The Name "Adam"

At first glance, the name *"Adam,"* emphasizing the earthly aspect of man's existence, might be viewed as a bit derogatory, as it seems to overlook the other aspect of man's character – the divine breath of life. It essentially seems to convey that although man has a divine soul, when all is said and done, he is not much more than a piece of dirt. Referring to man as *"adam"* might not only indicate his source, but express man's inability to overcome his earthly nature.

On the other hand, although man's physical form as well as his spirit are divinely created, it is the breathing of the divine into man that makes him the crown of creation. Rav Hirsch (*Bereishit* 2:7) explains that this, in fact, is what distinguishes man from other creations:

> What is it that sets man apart from the animal? The living individuality of the animal depends on earthly matter; like its body, so its soul too, was taken from the earth. Not so man. In the creation of man, only the inert material was taken from the earth; only **when God breathed into him the breath of life did he become a living individual.** Herein lies the ability and immortality of man... Thus man is composed of two elements that are completely different from each other. One of these was taken from the earth. But man does not belong to the earth; rather, the earth — as its name, *adama*, implies — has been given to man to rule. So too, man's body, which is dust of the ground, is subject to man's control...

The Maharal views the matter differently. Referring to man as *"Adam"* does not relegate him to a base, physical existence. Rather, the link to *adama* focuses on the power of activating one's potential, as the value of the dirt of the earth lies solely in its potential for production. This indicates that a human's true value lies not in where he is at present, but in where he can be:

> A name indicates that which is exclusive and special to a creature; that which expresses what makes man unique. And that is why man is called "*Adam*" on account of his [being created from] dust of the "*adama*." And now we must ask: are not other creatures as well made from the *adama*?... But [in truth] man is more connected to *adama*, as the ground is special in that it signifies potential that can be brought out and activated through plants, trees, and everything else that can potentially be brought forth from the land. Similarly, man is all potential, which achieves completion when activated; and therefore, the name which is appropriate for man is that which is shared by the *adama*, as it is reminiscent of the power of activating the potential in man and the ground. (*Tiferet Yisrael* 3)

From What Dirt?

The potential that "*Adam*" possesses might depend on which dirt was used to form man.

It is clear from the *pesukim* that Adam was not created from the dust of the Garden of Eden, as he was placed there only afterward. When Adam sins, the *pesukim* tell us that his fate will be that he will eventually return to the *adama* from which he was created. The precise location of this dust is debated in the *midrash*, as cited by Rashi:

> עָפָר מִן הָאֲדָמָה - צָבַר עֲפָרוֹ מִכֹּל הָאֲדָמָה מֵאַרְבַּע רוּחוֹת, שֶׁכֹּל מָקוֹם שֶׁיָּמוּת שָׁם תְּהֵא קוֹלַטְתּוֹ לִקְבוּרָה.
>
> דָּבָר אַחֵר - נָטַל עֲפָרוֹ מִמָּקוֹם שֶׁנֶּאֱמַר בּוֹ (שמות כ כא) מִזְבַּח אֲדָמָה תַּעֲשֶׂה לִּי, אָמֹר הַלְוַאי תִּהְיֶה לוֹ כַּפָּרָה וְיוּכַל לַעֲמֹד:
>
> **Dust from the *adama*:** He gathered his [Adam's] dust from the four corners of the globe, so that in whatever place he might die, the ground would absorb him in burial. An alternative explanation: God took his dust from the place of which it is said, "You shall make an altar of *adama* for me" (*Shemot* 20:21). He said: "I wish that he may achieve atonement so that he can survive." (Rashi *Bereishit* 2:7)

The first opinion views man as a collection of dust from all over the world, while the second opinion focuses on man's unique nature due to his being created from the dust of the place where the great altar will be built on Mount Moriah. Man's origin from the dust of the altar will ensure he will always be able to achieve atonement for his actions.

The second opinion seems to echo the notion of man's potential. In fact, if Adam's name reminds us of the sanctified physical dirt that is his source, then his name actually possesses an added spiritual element.

Rav Yosef Dov HaLevi Soloveitchik (*Majesty and Humility*) points out that there is a certain dichotomy in man, indicating that both of these opinions are simultaneously true:

> Man was created of cosmic dust. God gathered the dust, of which man was fashioned from all parts of the earth, indeed, from all the uncharted lanes of creation. Man belongs everywhere. He is no stranger to any part of the universe.... Man is cosmic through his intellectual involvement. His intellectual curiosity is of cosmic, universal dimensions. He wants to know, not only about the things that are close to him, as, for example, the flowering bush in his backyard, but also things far removed from him,

things and events millions of light years away....

Let us examine the other interpretation of the verse in Genesis: Man was created from the dust of a single spot. Man is committed to one locus. The creator assigned him a single spot he calls home. Man is not cosmic; he is here-minded. He is a rooted being, not cosmopolitan but provincial, a villager who belongs to the soil that fed him as a child and to the little world into which he was born.

Rav Soloveitchik explores these two views in the way man searches for God. Significantly, he emphasizes that one need not choose which one is correct, as there is merit to both. Man is both cosmic, connected to the world, and origin-centered, rooted in a specific place and a specific message. Rashi doesn't choose one of the two opinions in the *midrash*, as both reflect a particular aspect of man.

The fact that *"Adam"* is connected to the *adama* of the whole world allows us to explain how man's actions impact his surroundings. He is derived from the physical world, from the dust of the ground, and through his divine soul, he is awarded the potential to transform physicality into a merged spiritual existence. Failure to live up to this calling taints one's surroundings. If *"Adam"* doesn't elevate himself and activate his potential, he contaminates the *adama* that was the raw material for his growth.

This natural relationship begins at the dawn of time. Adam is sent from the Garden of Eden, Kayin is relegated to wandering, and the world is flooded and destroyed at the time of Noach. As man fails to rise to his potential, he takes the *adama* and everything with it down. After the Flood, when Noach builds an altar and offers sacrifices — according to tradition, on the very spot where man was created —God promises that He will no longer punish the *adama* on account of man's actions.

Rav Hirsch (*Bereishit* 8:21) explains that initially:

God impeded the development of the *adama*, and he did so for man's benefit and for his moral and spiritual salvation; thus it was in the days of Adam, Kayin, and so on. Henceforth, God will no longer curtail the power of the earth; He will not limit its fertility in order to educate mankind.

Thus, when the generation of the Dispersion built their tower — which, according to tradition, was an attempt to wage war with God in Heaven — they were not destroyed along with the land, but were rather dispersed throughout the four corners of the earth, all the areas where the dust of their creation was derived from.

The notion that man was created from the dust of the place of the altar is similarly attributed great significance. As much as his Godly spirit distinguishes man, the uniqueness of man lies in his ability to sanctify the physical as well. Recognition of the spiritual potential of the physical world is man's calling. The fact that the human body housing the soul is physical indicates that it too was created in a form worthy of God, and man's duty is to sanctify the physical, including his body. There is no better place to indicate such a mission than the site of the altar. It is there that Heaven meets earth, as man sacrifices physical objects towards a spiritual goal. Man might be connected to the *adama* throughout the world, but his mission is to elevate the physical to the sanctified dirt of the altar.

The Special Dirt: From *Adama* to *Eretz*

A few years after God disperses humanity and the seventy nations are sent throughout the world, God commands one man to leave all he has and knows and to go to the land (*eretz*) that God will show him. Here we see that there is a certain level of significance to a certain type of land and earth.

Although the *adama* will not be cursed due to the actions of Adam, man's actions will still have a clear impact on his surroundings. In most of the world in the post-Flood era, the *adama* will no longer be cursed. However, a special *eretz*, the land housing the unique dirt of the altar, is only beginning to show its importance. The mutual interdependence of the land and the nation chosen to receive it as a divine gift will be crucial.

The *adama* that responds in kind to every act of man at the dawn of time would not be able to survive if divine providence continued to make its success and even existence dependent on the acts of man. But at the same time, God chooses Avraham, a man who has chosen Him,[28] and in the process chooses one land to serve as the model for the interconnection of the physical world with the spiritual behavior of man. All the world will see the descendants of this person and will understand the nature of divine providence, which, by rights, should have affected the whole world.

Avraham's Dual Connection to the Land

This would seem to be explicit in the command to Avraham to leave his homeland:

וַיֹּאמֶר ה' אֶל אַבְרָם לֶךְ לְךָ מֵאַרְצְךָ וּמִמּוֹלַדְתְּךָ וּמִבֵּית אָבִיךָ אֶל הָאָרֶץ אֲשֶׁר אַרְאֶךָּ: וְאֶעֶשְׂךָ לְגוֹי גָּדוֹל וַאֲבָרֶכְךָ
וַאֲגַדְּלָה שְׁמֶךָ וֶהְיֵה בְּרָכָה: וַאֲבָרְכָה מְבָרֲכֶיךָ וּמְקַלֶּלְךָ אָאֹר וְנִבְרְכוּ בְךָ כֹּל מִשְׁפְּחֹת הָאֲדָמָה:

And God said to Avram: "Go forth from your land and from your birthplace and from your father's house, to the land [*ha-aretz*] that I will show you. And I will make you into a great nation, and I will bless you, and I will aggrandize your name, and [you shall] be a blessing. And I will bless those who bless you, and the one who curses you I will curse, and all the families of the earth [*adama*] shall be blessed in you." (*Bereishit* 12:1-3)

Avram is given an *eretz* that will serve as the educational forefront for the people in all four corners of the *adama*.

Why is this land chosen to be the model? The Kli Yakar explains that it is due to the unique *afar min ha-adama* that comes from the site of the altar, which lies at its center. The Kli Yakar explains that God could not initially reveal the place He wanted Avraham to go to, because Avraham could not appreciate it properly outside of the Land. Only after experiencing the unique soul that one attains in the Land of Israel can one truly recognize how the Land is uniquely suited to the development of oneself.

"*Lech*" – Go; "*lecha*" – to yourself.... To the land that I will show you... To the place of the origin of Man's body and soul. ... for as long as you are outside the land, you

---

28   See our discussion regarding Avraham's chosenenss at http://vbm-torah.org/archive/chavero2/26chavero.htm.

cannot appreciate the identity of your soul, whose source is from Mount Moriah, nor appreciate even your physical self, which also was formed from the dust of the mount... Therefore, it is worth your leaving all you know behind to go and cleave to that holy place... (*Kli Yakar, Bereishit* 12:1)

The Land of Israel is the extension of Mount Moriah, the same place where Avraham would later be sent with the same words, "*Lech lecha,*" for the binding of his son to the altar – the site that is the origin and life-force of man.

Elsewhere (*Bereishit* 13:17), the Kli Yakar continues his train of thought, beautifully describing the dual nature of the Land of Israel as a physical wonderland and a spiritual storehouse. He notes the varying descriptions of Avraham's future in the land. At first, Avraham is told:

וַיקֹוָק אָמַר אֶל אַבְרָם אַחֲרֵי הִפָּרֶד לוֹט מֵעַמּוֹ שָׂא נָא עֵינֶיךָ וּרְאֵה מִן הַמָּקוֹם אֲשֶׁר אַתָּה שָׁם צָפֹנָה וָנֶגְבָּה וָקֵדְמָה וָיָמָּה: כִּי אֶת כָּל הָאָרֶץ אֲשֶׁר אַתָּה רֹאֶה לְךָ אֶתְּנֶנָּה וּלְזַרְעֲךָ עַד עוֹלָם: וְשַׂמְתִּי אֶת זַרְעֲךָ כַּעֲפַר הָאָרֶץ אֲשֶׁר אִם יוּכַל אִישׁ לִמְנוֹת אֶת עֲפַר הָאָרֶץ גַּם זַרְעֲךָ יִמָּנֶה:

And God said to Avram after Lot had parted from him: "Now raise your eyes and see, from the place where you are, northward and southward and eastward and westward. For all the land which you see I will give to you and to your seed forever. And I will make your seed like the dust of the land (*afar ha-aretz*), so that if a man will be able to count the dust of the land, so will your seed be counted." (*Bereishit* 13:14-16)

Avraham is promised all the land that he can see, which will be given to him and his descendants, as they will be more numerous than the dust of the earth. In the following verse, however, Avraham is told:

קוּם הִתְהַלֵּךְ בָּאָרֶץ לְאָרְכָּהּ וּלְרָחְבָּהּ כִּי לְךָ אֶתְּנֶנָּה:

"Go walk the land, to its length and to its breadth, for I will give it to you." (*Bereishit* 13:17)

From this statement, it seems that Avraham's acquisition of the Land of Israel requires walking its length and breadth; the only promise is that he will be given the land, not his descendants.

The Kli Yakar explains that there are actually two acquisitions of the Land of Israel, as it is both a physically beautiful land and an extension of the spiritual potential of Mount Moriah. The two acquisitions, he explains, have different rules.

The spiritual advantage is acquired merely by seeing, by looking at Mt. Moriah, the site from which all universes, spiritual and physical, were created. He who looks at the Place is immediately clothed in a spirit of purity and holiness, ennobled by the Presence of God. This phenomenon was enshrined for eternity in the *mitzvah* of the pilgrimage to the Temple on the holidays of Pesach, Shavuot and Sukkot.

The physical blessings promised to Avram were to be acquired only by physical occupation of the Land, by getting up and walking the entire Land, its length and breadth. And this physical acquisition will not be forever and unconditional, as is the first, spiritual one; so verse 15 says, "For all the land which you see I will give to you

> and to your seed forever," but verse 17 says, "Go walk the land, for I will give it to you," but it does not say "forever."

Avraham's children will always have the capability of recognizing that inner spiritual plane that is so central to the Land of Israel. In the process, they will become as numerous as the dust of the land. This dust is not the physical dust of *afar min ha-adama*, but rather the dust with a spiritual character – *afar ha-aretz*, as the pasuk describes. If the whole world, both of mankind and the entire earth, could not live upon the plane of divine providence, at least one nation in one land could.

The Link between the Nation's Actions and the Land of Israel

The *eretz* is significant because it is the land of the special *afar min ha-adama*, the warehouse of the transcendent potential that enables mankind to spiritualize the physical world. For that reason, throughout *Sefer Devarim*, this term *adama* reappears alongside *eretz*.[29] In chapter 28 of *Devarim*, the chapter that details the second *tochacha* in the Torah, both terms appear side by side. The impact of man's obedience or disobedience towards God will affect the Jewish People's right to reside on the *adama* that will be given to them as their special *eretz*.

Throughout the rest of the world, the bond of the physical *adama* to the actions of man has been severed. The earth will no longer be cursed on account of man. However, the unique bond of the Jewish People to the Land of Israel is very much dependent on the Jews' actions. This principle forms the basis of the second paragraph of the *Shema*, recited twice daily:

וְהָיָה אִם שָׁמֹעַ תִּשְׁמְעוּ אֶל מִצְוֹתַי אֲשֶׁר אָנֹכִי מְצַוֶּה אֶתְכֶם הַיּוֹם ... וְנָתַתִּי מְטַר אַרְצְכֶם בְּעִתּוֹ ... וְאָסַפְתָּ דְגָנֶךָ וְתִירֹשְׁךָ וְיִצְהָרֶךָ: ...הִשָּׁמְרוּ לָכֶם פֶּן יִפְתֶּה לְבַבְכֶם וְסַרְתֶּם וַעֲבַדְתֶּם אֱלֹהִים אֲחֵרִים וְהִשְׁתַּחֲוִיתֶם לָהֶם: וְחָרָה אַף ה' בָּכֶם וְעָצַר אֶת הַשָּׁמַיִם וְלֹא יִהְיֶה מָטָר וְהָאֲדָמָה לֹא תִתֵּן אֶת יְבוּלָהּ וַאֲבַדְתֶּם מְהֵרָה מֵעַל הָאָרֶץ הַטֹּבָה אֲשֶׁר ה' נֹתֵן לָכֶם:

If you follow the commandments that I enjoin upon you this day ... I will give rain for your land in season...you shall gather in your new grain, wine and oil.... Take care not to be lured away to serve other gods and bow to them For God's anger will flare up and He will hold back the heavens and there will be no rain and the ground (*adama*) will not yield its produce; and you will soon perish from the good land (*aretz*) that God is assigning to you." (*Devarim* 11:13-17)

The Ramban (*Vayikra* 18:25) explains that the Land of Israel requires a certain level of spiritual commitment due to the fact that it is God's Land. Lack of fulfillment of *mitzvot* will result in dispersion and exile. Yet even the *mitzvot* that one fulfills in exile, according to the Ramban, pale in comparison to those very same *mitzvot* when performed in the

---

29　The word "*adama*," which is so prominent in *Sefer Bereishit*, is almost completely absent from the rest of the Torah, appearing intermittently in *Sefer Shemot*, only twice in *Sefer Vayikra*, and a few times in *Sefer Bamidbar*. Instead, the term used is "*eretz*" (or "*aretz*", depending on the syntax). The Land of Israel is often referred to as "*ha-aretz*," the Land, due to its special and unique nature. No further description is necessary. In *Sefer Devarim* – also known as "*Mishneh Torah*" due to its repetition of certain important principles of the Torah – the Land of Israel is referred to in both ways: *ha-aretz* as well as *ha-adama* (see also *Shemot* 20:12).

Holy Land:

> God is the God of all powers outside the Land of Israel, but in the Land of Israel He is the "direct" God of the Land which is the "heritage of God"...The Land is thus not like other lands; it does not sustain sinners... And so the verse states: "And the land has been conquered *before God* and before His people" (*I Divrei Ha-Yamim* 22:18). Based on this concept, the Sages state in Sifrei, "And so even though I exile you from the Land, make yourselves distinguished through my commandments, so that when you return to the Land they will not be new to you"... For in fact, the primary obligation of *all* of the commandments is for those who reside in the Land of God... This is the meaning of the Sages' statement that dwelling in the Land of Israel is equal in importance to observing all the commandments of the Torah. For living in the Land of Israel leads almost automatically to a more complete fulfillment of all the laws of the Torah.

In fact, the spiritual component of the Land of Israel requires that its mistreatment be expressed physically in the land itself.

With this background, we can begin to understand the tremendous punishments described in *Parashat Bechukotai* to be inflicted on the nation and the land due to failure to fulfill *shabbat ha-aretz*. The Jews' right to the *eretz* depends on their behavior, and the greatest expression of recognizing the spiritual character of the physical land of Israel is through *shevi'it* and its *mitzvot*.

Shevi'it Fulfillment's Implications for our Rights to the Land

The Effects of Man's Actions on the Land

As we have seen, the Torah repeats in numerous contexts that only a life of listening to the call of God will lead to successful living in the Land of Israel. This is the lesson detailed in the *Shema*, which dictates that man's actions will affect the *adama,* the ground God promised our forefather Avraham. It is repeated elsewhere as well; the result of the performance of certain iniquities is the contamination of the land and being spit out from it. One such instance involves the defiling of a Jewish girl:

אַל תְּחַלֵּל אֶת בִּתְּךָ לְהַזְנוֹתָהּ וְלֹא תִזְנֶה הָאָרֶץ וּמָלְאָה הָאָרֶץ זִמָּה:

> Do not profane your daughter by causing her to act unfaithfully, so that the land not act unfaithfully and the land not be filled with lewdness. (*Vayikra* 19:29)

Rav Hirsch (ad loc.) explains the Torah's warning that sinful human action affects the agricultural output of the Land of Israel:

> The Earth, as a planet, has its place in the cosmos, but the Earth's surface, which bears its fruit, is called *adama*, and the *adama* is wedded to man, "*adam.*" If man betrays his moral duty, then the land too will betray man. If man is careless with the choice fruit of his world, viz. the seed of man, the land too will withhold or spoil its fruit.

Although the message that man's actions will affect how he lives in the Land of Israel is oft-repeated, there is a special distinction in how it is presented in *Parashat Bechukotai*. The shocking description in *Bechukotai* depicts a series of extreme steps taken in regards to the Land on account of the sins of its Jewish inhabitants. It is not only that man's actions will result in a lack of rain, defiling of the land, and expulsion. Rather, at every stage, man will be struck, and the land will become more and more vulnerable and impoverished. The various stages of the curses culminate with the connection to *shemitta*. The land will be left desolate, as if there were an extended *shevi'it*:

וְאֶתְכֶם אֱזָרֶה בַגּוֹיִם וַהֲרִיקֹתִי אַחֲרֵיכֶם חָרֶב וְהָיְתָה אַרְצְכֶם שְׁמָמָה וְעָרֵיכֶם יִהְיוּ חָרְבָּה: אָז תִּרְצֶה הָאָרֶץ אֶת שַׁבְּתֹתֶיהָ כֹּל יְמֵי הֳשַׁמָּה וְאַתֶּם בְּאֶרֶץ אֹיְבֵיכֶם אָז תִּשְׁבַּת הָאָרֶץ וְהִרְצָת אֶת שַׁבְּתֹתֶיהָ: כָּל יְמֵי הָשַּׁמָּה תִּשְׁבֹּת אֵת אֲשֶׁר לֹא שָׁבְתָה בְּשַׁבְּתֹתֵיכֶם בְּשִׁבְתְּכֶם עָלֶיהָ:

I will scatter you among the nations and will unsheathe the sword to pursue you. Your land will be desolate and your cities in ruins. The land (*ha-aretz*) shall then be appeased for its Sabbaths while it is desolate and you are in the land of your enemies; the land shall rest and have appeasement for its Sabbaths. All the days of its desolation it shall be at rest, according to the rest that it did not enjoy while you dwelt in it. (*Vayikra* 26:33-35)

Although we understand that the Land of Israel is affected by man's actions, why is there such severity with regard to failure to observe *shevi'it* proplery? There are various factors that contribute to this particular connection.

The Message of the Shabbat of the Land
We have noted that *shevi'it* is referred to by different terms in the Torah. In both *Parashat Behar* and *Parashat Bechukotai, shevi'it* is referred to as *shabbat ha-aretz*. Shabbat marks the culmination of creation as God rests, indicating that the world had achieved its purpose. Essentially, Shabbat attributes spiritual significance to the physical world and gives it purpose and direction. For this reason, Rav Hirsch (*Bereishit* 2:1) points out that one of the messages of the weekly Shabbat is the spiritual purpose in the creation of the physical world. Shabbat is the crown of the world:

There is no gulf between physical nature and the moral world of man. The Shabbat was placed in the very midst of the natural world, as its goal and crowning perfection. The purpose of the earth is to be *adama*, the ground and realm of *Adam*, who, created in the image of God, is to rule over the earth according to His Will. The *adama* is wedded to *Adam*, as a woman is wedded to a man. The land blooms and rejoices with the moral blossoming of man; the land withers and mourns at the moral degeneration of its inhabitants. This truth, which runs like a thread throughout *Tanach*, is rooted here, in the Shabbat narrative. With man's Shabbat, God completes creation; teaching about man's Shabbat is the final touch that Gods put on all His work.

The character of Shabbat is also expressed in *shevi'it*, especially when referred to as *shabbat ha-aretz*. *Shevi'it* is not only a *shabbat* of the Land, but it is also a *shabbat* of *Hashem*, a distinction shared only with the weekly Shabbat. Like Shabbat, *shevi'it* teaches us how to merge the physical with the spiritual.

What Shabbat is to the world, *shabbat ha-aretz* is to the land. The *shabbat* of the *eretz* ensures that the Jewish People do not forget that their physical acquisition of the Land of Israel must be accompanied by the recognition of the spiritual purpose behind the Land. In the terms we have developed, *shevi'it* constitutes recognition that the Land of Israel is composed not only of *afar min ha-adama*, dust from the ground, but is a unique *afar ha-aretz*, reserved for the nation that carries the banner of bridging man's physicality and spirituality. The Land of Israel has its center upon Mount Moriah, the origin of the dust of man's body and the core of man's unique spirit – the place where heaven meets earth.

The Natural Aspect of the *Shemitta* of the Land

Although the concept of *shabbat ha-aretz* helps us understand the role of *shevi'it* in merging the physical and the spiritual, the connection between the *mitzvot* of *shemitta* and the inheritance of the Land is no less important. The deep-seated connection between *shevi'it* and inheriting the Land is apparent from the way in which the Torah introduces the *mitzvah* in *Parashat Behar*.

> שֵׁשׁ שָׁנִים תִּזְרַע שָׂדֶךָ וְשֵׁשׁ שָׁנִים תִּזְמֹר כַּרְמֶךָ וְאָסַפְתָּ אֶת תְּבוּאָתָהּ:
>
> ...When you come to the land which I shall give you, the land shall rest a Sabbath to God. Six years you may sow your field and six years you may prune your vineyard and gather in the produce. But in the seventh year the land shall have a Sabbath of complete rest, a Sabbath to God; you shall not sow your field nor prune your vineyard. (*Vayikra* 25:2-4)

The presentation here seems to be out of order. The opening *pasuk* mentions resting, and only then does the Torah mention that one plants for six years. Rav Shlomo Yosef Zevin explains:

> There is a difference between the Land of Israel and lands outside it with reference to the relationship between *mitzvot* and holiness. In lands outside Israel, holiness comes through the power of the *mitzvot*. The things that exist in the world do not contain any holiness, but through the fulfillment of the *mitzvot* involving these things, they become sanctified and improved... The opposite is true for the Land of Israel, as the *mitzvot* specific to the land come through the force of its holiness. "'For the land is Mine' — the holiness of the land belongs to me" (*Gittin* 47a)... It is the actual sanctity of the Land that brings about the obligations of those *mitzvot* that are dependent on the land. From this we may see that the power of *shemitta* is fixed firmly in the land, as a *mitzvah* that is dependent on the Land of Israel.

After expanding on the inherent connection between the Land of Israel and its *mitzvot*, Rav Zevin continues:

> *Shemitta* has deep roots in the essence and nature of the Land and its holiness. "When you come to the land which I shall give you," there already exists in this land through its resting in the year of *shemitta* when you arrive — "the land shall rest a Sabbath to God." This rest, in practical terms, comes after six years of work... In the seventh year, there becomes manifest in practice that which was latent in it from the beginning of its holiness.

Since *shemitta* observance is so naturally manifested in the character of the Land, it is not difficult to understand that nonobservance results in exile.

The Status of *Shevi'it* and *Yovel* in Our Day
If *shemitta* is naturally manifested in the Land given to the descendants of Avraham, it is also understandable that the relationship between the nation and the Land as expressed through *shevi'it* continues to have implications in our day.

We noted that *shevi'it* appears in *Parashat Behar* immediately prior to a discussion of the *mitzvah* of *yovel*, the jubilee year, which is observed after counting seven cycles of *shemitta*. *Yovel* shares the agricultural laws of *shevi'it*, but includes other *halachot* as well, including the freeing of all servants: "Proclaim liberty throughout all the land unto all the inhabitants thereof." (*Vayikra* 25:10)

The Talmud (*Arachin* 32b) cites a *baraita* that teaches a very important *halacha* based on these words: *Yovel* applies only when a majority of inhabitants resides in their land according to their ancestral settlings, as indicted by the words "all the inhabitants." (This will be discussed in greater detail in section III).

Although there is a dispute as to the exact meaning of this phrase and its implications, this is one of the significanct sources behind the opionion that *shevi'it* observance in our day is only rabbinically mandated. This would seem to be the opinion of Rav Yosef Karo (*Beit Yosef*, YD 331), who explains that the Rambam ruled accordingly (although in his *Kesef Mishneh*, *Hilkhot Shemitta* 9:1, 10:9, he seems to understand the Rambam's view to be that *shevi'it* is biblically required). This view is accepted by the primary contemporary halachic authorities who have dealt with the question since the re-emergence of *shevi'it* as a pressing halachic issue in the late nineteenth century (*Chazon Ish* 3:8; Rav Kook, Introduction to *Shabbat HaAretz*; Rav Ovadya Yosef, *Yabia Omer* 10:37). These authorities maintain that although the requirement of the Land of Israel being inhabited by all Jews does not pertain to other *mitzvot ha-teluyot ba-aretz*, since *shevi'it* is connected to *yovel*, that requirement applies to *shevi'it* as well.

Why does this requirement pertain to *yovel* and *shevi'it*?
One possible explanation is that other *mitzvot* specific to *Eretz Yisrael* are primarily focused on agriculture, and the holiness of the land is therefore the critical factor. *Yovel*, in contrast, includes an agricultural component as well as a social one. The laws of *yovel* allow those who suffered economically and were consequently forced to sell their property or themselves to regain that which they lost. People who lost their property and their freedom are able to rebuild their lives. This aspect of *yovel* is not rooted in the soil, but rather in an ethical, social, and economic ideal to which the Jewish people should aspire.

The ethical sensitivities that inspire these laws always apply. However, *yovel* and its laws are binding only when the vision of *yovel* can be realized. When some of the tribes are no longer in *Eretz Yisrael*, the nation can no longer function as an organic whole, and the vision of "liberty throughout all the land unto all the inhabitants thereof" is no longer attainable. The socio-ethical component cannot be achieved, and *yovel* as a complex idea cannot be implemented. Put simply, the agricultural component cannot be applied independently of the social component. Therefore, there is no *yovel* when freedom for all the land's inhabitants cannot be fulfilled.

According to the ruling that *shevi'it* is observed only rabbinically due to the lack of sufficient Jewish inhabitants in the Land of Israel, the implications of the *pesukim* in *Bechukotai* recorded above are even more astounding. To a certain degree, the destruction of the Land and the exile of its inhabitants is not only significant insofar as the punishment is concerned. It has implications for the future applicability of *shevi'it*! Once the Jews as a people are expelled from the land due to their actions, the *mitzvot* of *shevi'it* and *yovel* cease to be obligatory. The land loses a *mitzvah* integral to its character and deeply implanted in its nature. Why would that be?

Behar and Bechukotai: A Shared Message

The relationship between *Parashiot Behar* and *Bechukotai* goes far beyond their juxtaposition. As we have noted, the Torah connects the horrifying results depicted in *Bechukotai* to the failure to properly observe the *shabbat ha-aretz* described in *Behar*. The Torah goes out of its way to teach us that both were taught on Har Sinai (*Vayikra* 25:1, 26:46, 27:34) and constantly repeats the number seven in both contexts. Further, there are parallel *pesukim* in the two *parashiot* (compare 25:18-19 and 26:3-5, and the *beracha* regarding *shemitta*, 25:20-22).[30]

Evidently, *shevi'it* and *yovel* provide the "glasses" that allow for life in *Eretz Yisrael* with a recognition of it being the land of *Hashem* (25:23). They describe a religious ideal of human faith reciprocated by divine providence, containing a promise of a relationship between *Hashem* and Yisrael, and they are therefore the context for attaining the *berachot* of the covenant.

These parallels focus on the *berachot* (blessings) bestowed upon the nation in the Land of Israel when they fulfill the will of God. The ensuing *tochacha* details the unfortunate results of the opposite reality, when the Jewish people fail to uphold their part of the bargain. Interestingly, this punishment is not instantaneous; the verses detail a five-step process, with incremental levels of punishment. God does not merely punish the nation with expulsion at the first sight of iniquity; there is a progression. The first four stages are essentially calls to improve before the fifth stage – the destruction of the *Beit Ha-Mikdash* and exile:

- The first stage involves illnesses and losing sovereignty to one's enemies. There is still a harvest and planted crops grow, but the nation does not benefit from them; the enemies eat the agricultural harvest. The nation becomes impoverished, but does not begin to die.

- The second stage (26:9) is characterized by a drought and famine. Planting is futile, but what has already grown is available for harvest.

- The third phase denotes another sevenfold punishment, including death by

---

30   Rav Yair Kahn (http://vbm-torah.org/archive/parsha71/32-71Behar.htm) beautifully illustrates some of the parallels and reasons.

beasts (26:22). One might suggest that this refers to the beasts who were not able to enjoy the produce that was supposed to be left for them during the year of *shevi'it*.

- The fourth phase introduces the avenging sword (26:6), with war and bloodshed.

All of these stages appear in the Torah in one paragraph. The Torah begins a new paragraph for the fifth and final stage. In this stage, the famine is so fierce that parents devour the flesh of their own children; the cities are laid waste and the Temple is destroyed. The people are sent into exile and the land becomes desolate due to nonobservance of *shabbat ha-aretz*.

Evidently, this fifth stage is a disaster that God wants to avoid at all costs. He therefore sends four stages of divine messages, informing us that our behavior will not only result in personal punishment, but will affect the land as well. When the message is not received and the nation continues with its inappropriate behavior on the land, the only option left for God is the fifth stage – expulsion, desolation, and destruction.

A careful reading of the verses reveals another message as well. As much as the first four stages are warnings, once the fifth stage arrives, it is too late for repentance. Although there is a mention of some measure of confession and repentance (26:40), the results of the people's stubbornness are unavoidable; it is too late to turn back the destruction.[31]

While the Torah consistently links the bounty of *Eretz Yisrael* with the behavior of its Jewish inhabitants, it is only regarding *shevi'it* that the Torah presents a step-by-step description that illustrates the stages of punishment, including the effects of the nation's misbehavior on the land. Perhaps *shevi'it* is chosen to convey this lesson due to its Shabbat aspect, which merges the physical and the spiritual and is illustrative of the inherent connection between *shevi'it* and the Land. *Shevi'it* is a *mitzvah* whose very existence is dependent on the nation inhabiting the land and settling it according to the tribes. Therefore, it is only proper to illustrate the nation's forced exile through the imagery of *shevi'it*.

Thus, the Torah clearly states that the nonobservance of *shabbat ha-aretz* is the cause of the land's desolation; due to the nation's sins, the land will finally rest. This is more than just a depiction of what would and ultimately did happen to the people and the land. As noted above, it is the cause of modern-day *shevi'it* observance's status as only rabbinic in nature.

Defining *Ritzui*
The *pesukim* describe the period of desolation as "*ritzui*" for the unobserved *shabbatot ha-aretz*: "אז תרצה הארץ את שבתותיה" (*Vayikra* 26:34).

The Chizkuni (ad loc.) presents three possible explanations for this term: compensation, expiation, or reconciliation. Nine *pesukim* later, when the Torah describes the people's recognition of their culpability for this sorry situation, the Chizkuni embraces the third

---

31   In the context of *Hashem*'s promise to redeem the Jewish People from Egypt, there are five "languages of redemption" (*Shemot* 6:1-8). The description here of five stages of destruction seems to be the undoing of each of those stages of redemption.

explanation:

> There will be reconciliation between the people and their God. They will be penitent, admitting that they had only suffered due to their disloyalty to God and their negative attitude towards his Torah.

According to the Chizkuni, the people must learn the historical lesson and recognize that expulsion is caused by nonobservance of *shevi'it*. Only this will bring about reconciliation with God.

Rav Hirsch (26:34) explains sin as a debt to be paid off:

> As soon as the sinner attains true insight, he is happy that his past sin has been converted into a debt, for this gives him the possibility of redressing the wrong. He finds solace and satisfaction in the debt of the sin, and from then onward his whole focus is to satisfy the claim upon him.
>
> All the years of desolation are regarded as Shabbat years... The Sabbaths of the land that were not kept by us are converted into a debt which we must pay. This debt demands repayment, and we are expected to satisfy this demand. The debt is settled by the desolation of the land during the years of exile. The land rejoices in the Sabbath-desolation of the period of our exile, and satisfies the demand of the *shabbatot ha-aretz* that were neglected by us.

Similarly, the Netziv (*Ha'amek Davar. Vayikra* 26:35) notes that the *shevita* (rest) of the land when the Jews are in exile is much greater than what the *mitzvot* of *shevi'it* call for. During *shevi'it*, one may not plant, but there is still growth; during the exile, the land is totally desolate.

The Message behind the Expulsion and Desolation

While the Land of Israel is connected to the people and the people's sins demand payment through the land, we must still consider what message is supposed to be gleaned from the land's desolation. One understanding among the commentaries is that *shevi'it* observance sends a message to the people and the world. When *shevi'it* is not properly observed, that message is conveyed through the desolation of the land.

Several commentators use the vivid descriptions of the desolation that will befall the Land as proof that God has left it, with the ensuing hunger and destruction befalling the inhabitants serving as a sharp contrast to the once-beautiful state of the land. The Ibn Ezra (referring to *Eicha* 2:15) points out that the nations who once praised the beauty of the Holy Land will be disgusted by its current state. The nation's failure to recognize that the land belongs to God requires that God display His ownership through destruction.

Others add that the level of desolation of the once-beautiful land will serve as a proof to the people and the world that only divine retribution for sin could be responsible for such a magnitude of destruction. In a similar vein, Rav Hirsch (ibid.) explains that proper dwelling in the land expresses God's kingship to the world; when the nation fails to fulfill this mission through their settlement of the land, the message must be proclaimed through their exile and the continued desolation:

Just as *shemitta* and *yovel* are supposed to express homage to God in the life of the country and to give light amidst the nations even faraway, so too, the desolation of the Land of Israel expresses homage to God. God warns of it in advance, and He carries out the decree which He ordained long ago. The desolation of the land continues throughout all the hundreds of years of our exile, until this very day. The desolation is a large exclamation mark in God's book of history, attesting that the land is God's and that He expects his Torah to be observed in the land.

The land must play its intended role in exhibiting God's control over the world. If it cannot do so in the ideal state of the Jewish people's prosperity living in the Land and observing *mitzvot*, it must do so through the ravages of desolation following their expulsion.

Thus, the expulsion and subsequent desolation indicate to the people (and possibly the world) Who, in fact, is the legitimate owner of the land. They enable the land to display its Godly message on its own, when the people do not do their part.

While not discounting the severity of this punishment, some commentators approach the destruction and desolation from a different angle, in a positive light, viewing it as ultimately a blessing in disguise. (This approach will be discussed in Section II Theme 6, the Return to the Land.)

Chapter 8

Parasha 6: Parashat Re'eh - שְׁמִטַּת כְּסָפִים / Financial *Shemitta*

In addition to the Torah's descriptions of the various aspects of agricultural *shevi'it*, the Torah discusses financial *shemitta* in *Parashat Re'eh*. It is in this context that the Torah primarily uses the root *sh.m.t.*, repeatedly referring to "*shemitta*" – a total of six times.

Although *shemittat kesafim* takes place at the conclusion of the seventh year, the Torah explicitly relates it to the entire seventh year:

> מִקֵּץ שֶׁבַע שָׁנִים תַּעֲשֶׂה שְׁמִטָּה: וְזֶה דְּבַר הַשְּׁמִטָּה שָׁמוֹט כָּל בַּעַל מַשֵּׁה יָדוֹ אֲשֶׁר יַשֶּׁה בְּרֵעֵהוּ לֹא יִגֹּשׂ אֶת
> רֵעֵהוּ וְאֶת אָחִיו כִּי קָרָא שְׁמִטָּה לַה': כִּי יִהְיֶה בְךָ אֶבְיוֹן מֵאַחַד אַחֶיךָ בְּאַחַד שְׁעָרֶיךָ בְּאַרְצְךָ אֲשֶׁר ה' אֱ-לֹהֶיךָ
> נֹתֵן לָךְ לֹא תְאַמֵּץ אֶת לְבָבְךָ וְלֹא תִקְפֹּץ אֶת יָדְךָ מֵאָחִיךָ הָאֶבְיוֹן: כִּי פָתֹחַ תִּפְתַּח אֶת יָדְךָ לוֹ וְהַעֲבֵט תַּעֲבִיטֶנּוּ
> דֵּי מַחְסֹרוֹ אֲשֶׁר יֶחְסַר לוֹ: הִשָּׁמֶר לְךָ פֶּן יִהְיֶה דָבָר עִם לְבָבְךָ בְלִיַּעַל לֵאמֹר קָרְבָה שְׁנַת הַשֶּׁבַע שְׁנַת הַשְּׁמִטָּה
> וְרָעָה עֵינְךָ בְּאָחִיךָ הָאֶבְיוֹן וְלֹא תִתֵּן לוֹ וְקָרָא עָלֶיךָ אֶל ה' וְהָיָה בְךָ חֵטְא: נָתוֹן תִּתֵּן לוֹ וְלֹא יֵרַע לְבָבְךָ בְּתִתְּךָ לוֹ
> כִּי בִּגְלַל הַדָּבָר הַזֶּה יְבָרֶכְךָ ה' אֱ-לֹהֶיךָ בְּכָל מַעֲשֶׂךָ וּבְכֹל מִשְׁלַח יָדֶךָ: כִּי לֹא יֶחְדַּל אֶבְיוֹן מִקֶּרֶב הָאָרֶץ עַל כֵּן
> אָנֹכִי מְצַוְּךָ לֵאמֹר פָּתֹחַ תִּפְתַּח אֶת יָדְךָ לְאָחִיךָ לַעֲנִיֶּךָ וּלְאֶבְיֹנְךָ בְּאַרְצֶךָ:

> At the end of seven years you shall perform a release (*shemitta*). And this is the substance of the release: that every creditor release his hand from that which he has lent to his friend. He shall not exact from his friend or from his brother, because he will have declared the time of the release for the Lord … When there is a destitute person among you, any of your brothers, in one of your settlements in your land that the Lord, your God, is giving to you, you shall not harden your heart and you shall not shut your hand against your destitute brother. Rather, you shall generously open your hand to him, and extend to him any credit necessary for providing that which he lacks. Beware lest there be a lawless thought in your heart saying, "The seventh year, the year of remission, is approaching," and you treat your destitute brother with miserliness and refuse to give to him. You shall surely give to him, and let your heart not feel bad when you give to him, because for this the Lord, your God, will bless you in all of your deeds and in all of your endeavors. (*Devarim* 15:1,7–10)

The nature of *shemittat kesafim* and its relationship to the agricultural elements of *shemittat karka'ot* and *shabbat ha-aretz* deserve their own discussion, as it relates to a broader financial outlook espoused by the Torah. For this reason, an entire subsection of Section IV is devoted to *shemittat kesafim* and its broader implications. For now, we will simply clarify some basics regarding the institution and its *halachot*.

After introducing the concept of *shemittat kesafim*, loan remittance, at the conclusion of *shevi'it*, and describing a *mitzvat asei* requiring release of outstanding loans and a *mitzvat lo ta'aseh* forbidding forceful collection of loans, the Torah details the general *mitzvot* of *tzedaka*. It is almost as if the institution of loans and *shemittat kesafim* are the necessary context for the Torah's conception of *tzedaka*.

Immediately after, the Torah prohibits withholding new loans simply because the *shemitta* year is about to arrive and it will be difficult to compel payment of the loan if the borrower does not pay it back.

Shemittat kesafim essentially involves two types of *mitzvot*:

Mitzvah 1	Mitzvah 2
Continue to lend people money interest-free, even though *shemitta* will arrive soon.	At the conclusion of the seventh year, you must perform *shemitta* (a *mitzvat asei* to release the loan), and you cannot request repayment (a *mitzvat lo ta'aseh*)

To appreciate the significance of *shemittat kesafim*, we must consider why the Torah seems to prefer giving interest-free loans over *tzedaka*.

There are significant benefits to providing loans rather than providing charity:

- **From the giver's (lender's) standpoint**: The lender can give more money, knowing that it will eventually be returned, and everyone can help each other when they are in need.

- **From the recipient's (borrower's) standpoint**: The recipient maintains his dignity, not feeling like someone who needs charity.

But what happens if the recipient cannot pay back the loan? He might try to secure other loans to pay back the first, leading to a situation of extreme debt.

Those in this challenging position often find it impossible to start fresh. A loan, as opposed to a donation, gives the needy individual dignity, but now that he is in debt, how can he get out of it?

This is where the Torah commands *shemittat kesafim*, allowing for a fresh restart for those in need.

There is an unfortunate misunderstanding that *shemitta* cancels all loans completely, but the *mishnayot* indicate otherwise

הַמַּחֲזִיר חוֹב בַּשְּׁבִיעִית יֹאמַר לוֹ מְשַׁמֵּט אֲנִי אָמַר לוֹ אַף עַל פִּי כֵן יְקַבֵּל מִמֶּנּוּ שֶׁנֶּאֱמַר (דְּבָרִים טו) "וְזֶה דְּבַר הַשְּׁמִטָּה."

[If a borrower wishes to] return a loan after the sabbatical year, [the lender] should say to him, "I release the obligation." If the borrower replies, "Nevertheless [I wish to repay it]," then the lender should accept the repayment, as it states, "this is the word of the release" (*Devarim* 15:2). (*Mishna Shevi'it* 10:8)

If a borrower wants to pay back the loan after *shemitta*, the lender must declare, "*Shamot*," "I release the obligation," but after doing so, if the borrower wants to pay back, the lender should accept the money.

The next *mishna* goes further, explaining that it is praiseworthy to pay back the loan after *shemitta*:

הַמַּחֲזִיר חוֹב בַּשְּׁבִיעִית, רוּחַ חֲכָמִים נוֹחָה מִמֶּנּוּ.

One who repays a debt after the sabbatical year – the Sages are pleased with him. (ibid. 10:9)

As Rav Kook explains, the loan isn't cancelled; the Torah simply gives the borrower who can't pay back his loans a chance to start again.

> At the end of each sabbatical-year cycle, the repayment of every previously contracted debt remains only as a moral obligation; payment of the debt is left to the discretion of the one who incurred it. Because of the trust that the Torah places in him, the debtor, instead of feeling weighed down by his debt burden, feels morally uplifted. Repaying the debt of his own free will now be a matter of personal honor for him. (*Ein Aya, Peah*)

The actual *halacha* of *shemitta* is that the lender cannot **demand** the loan anymore, but the borrower still has a moral obligation to pay. He will hopefully do so when he can, but he should not feel weighed down by the debt. What a wonderful *mitzvah*!

Shemittat Kesafim's Universal Application and Beauty

Shemitta kesafim is the one aspect of *shevi'it* that applies equally in *Eretz Yisrael* and outside of it. Although the agriculture and the land in *chutz la-aretz* is not holy, one must make sure that he uses his money in a holy manner, no matter where he is.

We conclude with Rav Sha'ul Yisraeli's powerful perspective regarding the beauty of *shemittat kesafim*:

> With this *mitzvah*, whatever sum of money could have accumulated due to economic and manufacturing success, thus creating deep economic and class differences, cannot remain in place for long. First, the Torah prohibits keeping money inert like some unmovable rock if someone is in need of it at any time; you bear an ongoing obligation to lend it to him, and this loan must be made gratis. The Torah, after all, prohibited interest with the full force of law and with quite a number of admonitions to the borrower, the creditor, and the witnesses. Yet the Torah did not make do with that. In addition to *shemitta* of the land and renouncing ownership of produce comes the *mitzvah* of relinquishing debts, by which all debts not collected by the end of the *shemitta* year expire and cease to be subject to collection.
>
> Imagine: A person toils and travails until he has gathered some given amount. The Torah has already warned against fraud, deception, withholding a hired worker's wages, and the like. It has already required honest business dealings, a conscientious "yes" and a conscientious "no." The money that has nevertheless accumulated in a person's possession is thus his own money, achieved conscientiously and with much effort—and now you require him to lend it to his fellow gratis! He does this wholeheartedly; he does not demand any part of the profits that this money may bring his fellow. There is just one thought that gnaws at his heart, just one thing that he would assure himself: that he will in fact be returned his money—his money, without any sort of profits – that his fellow not profit from his toils and travails and give back

nothing. Our natural course of thought would tend to side with him entirely. Yet the Torah does not think thus. It would be "contemptible" for such a thought to cross your mind. It demands geniality and kindheartedness of you when the loan is given, despite your knowledge that it is to be lost!

One who walks in the way of the Torah, who observes this *mitzvah* once admonished severely regarding it—no less than regarding any other *mitzvah*—will perform a whole social revolution that quietly and peacefully, in one fell swoop, voids the economic and social disparities that have occupied human society since time immemorial. With the conclusion of the *shemitta* year, the whole nation's course of work and creativity begins anew, in a state in which all people have virtually the same means at their disposal.

Chapter 9

Parasha 7: Parashat Vayelech-Concluding a Year with the Everlasting Lessons of Har Sinai

The final *parasha* discussing *shevi'it* is one of the final *parashiyot* of the Torah. Near its conclusion, as the Torah describes the transmission of the Torah from Moshe Rabbeinu to his student Yehoshua and the elders, the Torah details an event known as *Hakhel*, which is performed once every seven years. The Torah explicitly indicates that *Hakhel* is performed "at the time of the *shemitta* year on the Festival of Sukkot" (*Devarim* 31:10), which *Chazal* explain refers to the Sukkot at the beginning of the eighth year, immediately following the conclusion of *shevi'it*.

> וַיְצַו מֹשֶׁה אוֹתָם לֵאמֹר מִקֵּץ שֶׁבַע שָׁנִים בְּמֹעֵד שְׁנַת הַשְּׁמִטָּה בְּחַג הַסֻּכּוֹת: בְּבוֹא כָל יִשְׂרָאֵל לֵרָאוֹת אֶת פְּנֵי ה' אֱלֹהֶיךָ בַּמָּקוֹם אֲשֶׁר יִבְחָר תִּקְרָא אֶת הַתּוֹרָה הַזֹּאת נֶגֶד כָּל יִשְׂרָאֵל בְּאָזְנֵיהֶם: הַקְהֵל אֶת הָעָם הָאֲנָשִׁים וְהַנָּשִׁים וְהַטַּף וְגֵרְךָ אֲשֶׁר בִּשְׁעָרֶיךָ לְמַעַן יִשְׁמְעוּ וּלְמַעַן יִלְמְדוּ וְיָרְאוּ אֶת ה' אֱלֹהֵיכֶם וְשָׁמְרוּ לַעֲשׂוֹת אֶת כָּל דִּבְרֵי הַתּוֹרָה הַזֹּאת: וּבְנֵיהֶם אֲשֶׁר לֹא יָדְעוּ יִשְׁמְעוּ וְלָמְדוּ לְיִרְאָה אֶת ה' אֱלֹהֵיכֶם כָּל הַיָּמִים אֲשֶׁר אַתֶּם חַיִּים עַל הָאֲדָמָה אֲשֶׁר אַתֶּם עֹבְרִים אֶת הַיַּרְדֵּן שָׁמָּה לְרִשְׁתָּהּ:
>
> Moshe commanded them, saying, "At the end of [every] seven years, at the time of the shemitta year, on the Sukkot festival, When all Israel comes to be seen near the presence of *Hashem*, your God, in the place that He will choose, you shall read this Torah before all Israel, to their ears. Assemble the nation, the men and the women and the children and the strangers who are within your gates, so that they hear and so that they learn to fear *Hashem*, your God, and take care to fulfill all the words of this Torah. And their children who do not know will listen and will learn to revere *Hashem*, your God, all the days that you live on the land that you are crossing the Jordan to inherit. (*Devarim* 31:10-13)

The *pesukim* describe that all members of the nation – men, women, children, and converts – take part in this event at the *Mikdash*. The Torah sets very high goals for *Hakhel*, explaining that it is a learning and listening experience for all, aimed at inculcating awe and fear of God in the people.

After a year of limited agricultural activity culminating in the cancellation of loans, before the planting season of the eighth year begins after Sukkot, all the Jews gather for a spiritually recharge that the *gemara* explains features the king's reading of the Torah in the presence of every last Jew (see *Sota* ch. 7). This spiritual culmination of the *shemitta* experience clearly indicates that the year is not only an occasion for certain agricultural practices, cancelling loans, and economic refocusing, but one that is supposed to bring about a spiritual reawakening.

The Rambam defines the event as one that is essential for every member of the nation:

> מִצְוַת עֲשֵׂה לְהַקְהִיל כָּל יִשְׂרָאֵל אֲנָשִׁים וְנָשִׁים וְטַף בְּכָל מוֹצָאֵי שְׁמִטָּה בַּעֲלוֹתָם לָרֶגֶל וְלִקְרוֹת בְּאָזְנֵיהֶם מִן הַתּוֹרָה פָּרָשִׁיּוֹת שֶׁהֵן מְזָרְזוֹת אוֹתָן בְּמִצְוֹת וּמְחַזְּקוֹת יְדֵיהֶם בְּדַת הָאֱמֶת.

> It is a biblical positive command to assemble all Israelites, men, women, and children after the close of every sabbatical year, when they go up to make the pilgrimage, and recite to them sections from the Torah which will urge them to perform the precepts and encourage them to cling to the true religion. (*Hilchot Chagiga* 3:1)

The Torah tells us that the goal of *Hakhel* is to be a learning and spiritually uplifting experience.

The Rambam is more explicit in how it achieves this. He describes it as something important for new converts to Judaism as well as scholars, as it reconnects us to a cataclysmic event in our nation:

> וְגֵרִים שֶׁאֵינָן מַכִּירִין חַיָּבִין לְהָכִין לְבָּם וּלְהַקְשִׁיב אָזְנָם לִשְׁמֹעַ בְּאֵימָה וְיִרְאָה וְגִילָה בִּרְעָדָה כְּיוֹם שֶׁנִּתְּנָה בּוֹ בְּסִינַי. אֲפִלּוּ חֲכָמִים גְּדוֹלִים שֶׁיּוֹדְעִים כָּל הַתּוֹרָה כֻּלָּהּ חַיָּבִין לִשְׁמֹעַ בְּכַוָּנָה גְּדוֹלָה יְתֵרָה. וּמִי שֶׁאֵינוֹ יָכוֹל לִשְׁמֹעַ מְכַוֵּן לִבּוֹ לִקְרִיאָה זוֹ שֶׁלֹּא קְבָעָהּ הַכָּתוּב אֶלָּא לְחַזֵּק דַּת הָאֱמֶת וְיִרְאֶה עַצְמוֹ כְּאִלּוּ עַתָּה נִצְטַוָּה בָּהּ וּמִפִּי הַגְּבוּרָה שׁוֹמְעָהּ. שֶׁהַמֶּלֶךְ שָׁלִיחַ הוּא לְהַשְׁמִיעַ דִּבְרֵי הָאֵ-ל:

> Proselytes who did not know Hebrew were required to direct their hearts **and listen with utmost awe and reverence, as on the day the Torah was given at Sinai.** Even great scholars who knew the entire Torah were required to listen with utmost attention. If there was a person who could not hear, he had to direct his heart to this reading, **which Scripture has instituted only for the purpose of strengthening the true faith. Each had to regard himself as if he had been charged with the Torah now for the first time, and as though he had heard it from the mouth of God, for the king was an ambassador proclaiming the words of God.** (ibid. 3:6)

The Rambam defines the *mitzvah* as a reenactment of *ma'amad Har Sinai*, in which the entire nation comes together to accept the Torah again.

If *shemitta* has a spiritual agenda (such as an opportunity to study Torah, as we will see), it is only fitting to perform *Hakhel* as it ends, before people go back to working the land and have less time to focus on spiritual endeavors. This last mention of *shevi'it* seems to add another dimension to the relationship between *shevi'it* and Har Sinai. After presenting *shevi'it* in *Parashat Mishpatim* in the middle of the Har Sinai experience and connecting it to Har Sinai in *Parashat Behar*, it is not surprising that the Torah indicates this year should be concluded with a re-experiencing of Har Sinai. One might even conjecture that after a year of living a life similar to that of the Jews in the desert, sustained by divine blessing rather than physical toil, the Jews are once again capable of re-experiencing Har Sinai.

This event serves not only the culmination of *shevi'it*, but the means of the nation taking the lessons of *shevi'it* with them as they return to the normal routine after Sukkot. As Israel's rainy season is about to begin and farmers will once again begin planting and working the land, the Torah wants to ensure that *shevi'it* leaves a lasting impression. *Hakhel* is its means of doing so.

The goals of *Hakhel* are varied and will be discussed at length in Section IV.

Chapter 10

Yovel- The Fiftieth Year

While each and every *shevi'it* is significant, the Torah also presents *shevi'it* within a broader framework that leads to the *yovel* year. In our analysis of *Parashat Behar*, we saw that after discussing the laws of *shevi'it*, the Torah describes the occurrence of *yovel* every seven *shevi'it* cycles:

וְסָפַרְתָּ לְךָ שֶׁבַע שַׁבְּתֹת שָׁנִים שֶׁבַע שָׁנִים שֶׁבַע פְּעָמִים וְהָיוּ לְךָ יְמֵי שֶׁבַע שַׁבְּתֹת הַשָּׁנִים תֵּשַׁע וְאַרְבָּעִים שָׁנָה:

And you shall count for yourself seven sabbaths of years, seven years seven times over, and the seven sabbaths of years shall number for you forty-nine years. (*Vayikra* 25:8)

We noted that certain aspects of *shevi'it* are only mentioned in the context of *yovel*, such as the promise of a blessing in the sixth year to all those who abide by the laws of *shevi'it*. However, although the fiftieth year has much in common with the seventh, it goes further. It is heralded with shofar blasts and completely transforms society. Ancestral lands that have been sold are returned to their initial owners, and all servants are set free. If every seven years *shevi'it* calls for a time out from our normal routine, Yovel heralds a more radical national "reset", delineating a socioeconomic ideal.

Thus, *shevi'it* years are essentially part of a larger process, helping the nation appreciate and inculcate *yovel*'s lessons:

וְהַעֲבַרְתָּ שׁוֹפַר תְּרוּעָה בַּחֹדֶשׁ הַשְּׁבִעִי בֶּעָשׂוֹר לַחֹדֶשׁ בְּיוֹם הַכִּפֻּרִים תַּעֲבִירוּ שׁוֹפָר בְּכָל אַרְצְכֶם: וְקִדַּשְׁתֶּם אֵת שְׁנַת הַחֲמִשִּׁים שָׁנָה וּקְרָאתֶם דְּרוֹר בָּאָרֶץ לְכָל יֹשְׁבֶיהָ יוֹבֵל הִוא תִּהְיֶה לָכֶם וְשַׁבְתֶּם אִישׁ אֶל אֲחֻזָּתוֹ וְאִישׁ אֶל מִשְׁפַּחְתּוֹ תָּשֻׁבוּ: יוֹבֵל הִוא שְׁנַת הַחֲמִשִּׁים שָׁנָה תִּהְיֶה לָכֶם לֹא תִזְרָעוּ וְלֹא תִקְצְרוּ אֶת סְפִיחֶיהָ וְלֹא תִבְצְרוּ אֶת נְזִרֶיהָ: כִּי יוֹבֵל הִוא קֹדֶשׁ תִּהְיֶה לָכֶם מִן הַשָּׂדֶה תֹּאכְלוּ אֶת תְּבוּאָתָהּ: בִּשְׁנַת הַיּוֹבֵל הַזֹּאת תָּשֻׁבוּ אִישׁ אֶל אֲחֻזָּתוֹ:

And you shall sound a blast on the *shofar* in the seventh month on the tenth of the month; on Yom Kippur shall you sound the shofar throughout your land. And you shall sanctify the fiftieth year, and you shall proclaim liberty (*deror*) in the land for all its inhabitants. It shall be a *yovel* for you, and each man shall return to his estate, and each man shall be returned to his family. The fiftieth year shall be for you a *yovel*; you shall neither sow nor harvest that which grows by itself in the field or in the vineyard. For it is the *yovel*, it shall be holy to you; you shall eat the produce of the field. In this year of *yovel*, each man shall return to his estate. (*Vayikra* 25:9-13)

The blowing of the shofar, freeing servants, and restoring lands are all significant acts of *yovel*, but all those actions seem to last a moment, not a year. What else is so unique about this year? Additionally, the Torah refers to *yovel* as a year of *deror*, liberty, for **all** the inhabitants of the land (a statement prominently displayed on America's Liberty Bell) – but the return of ancestral lands and servants will clearly not affect everyone. How does *yovel* proclaim a message of freedom to all the inhabitants of the land?

The Need for Counting

Understanding the count up to yovel might help reveal part of its uniqueness. Yovel doesn't just happen every fifty years, but the Torah requires counting up to this year. *Beit Din* (the Jewish court) counts each of the seven *shevi'it* cycles, as well as the 49 individual years followed by the sanctified fiftieth year of *yovel*. This model of counting seven sets of seven followed by a sanctified fiftieth is not unique to *yovel*. The *mitzvah* of counting the *omer* for 49 days after Pesach in order to arrive at the festival of *Shavuot* presents the same model.

The Maharal and others explain that counting seven and sanctifying the eigth is representative of the symbolism in each. Seven, the number of the days of the week, is the number of nature, while eight goes beyond nature. Therefore, *berit milah*, the covenant of circumcision, is performed on the eighth day. Similarly, the fiftieth unit, following seven periods of the natural cycle of seven, allows one to move beyond mundane limitations.

However, there are differences between the counts. *Torat Kohanim* notes that the Torah tells us to count the *omer* in the plural ("*u-sefartem*," *Vayikra* 23:15), as it is performed by all of the individuals of the Jewish People, but the command to count towards *yovel* is in the singular ("*u-sefarta*," *Vayikra* 25:8), as it is a *mitzvah* performed by the court. Rav Hirsch explains:

> By counting the *omer*, the individual... pays homage to God and acknowledges Him as Creator and King. On this basis, man strives seven times toward moral freedom, rendering himself worthy of receiving the Torah (on the fiftieth).
>
> By counting the sabbatical and jubilee years, the nation signals that the seven sabbatical cycles recognize God as the owner of its land. On this basis, it strives seven times toward internal political freedom, rendering itself worthy of the rebirth of the state in the jubilee year.

A Fifty-Year Reset

The Jewish nation is forged upon leaving Egypt, as the Israelites are freed from bondage and became servants of God. Fifty days later they receive the Torah on Sinai and are given a religious direction. After arriving in the Land of Israel and conquering it, the territory is divided according to tribes and families.

Thus, there are three pillars of the Jewish nation:

- The pillar of faith recognizes God as the One who took the nation out of Egypt (as stated in the first of the Ten Commandments).

- The second pillar is the social-theological construct, "For the Israelites are My servants" (*Vayikra* 25:55) – not servants to others.

- The third pillar has religious and economic elements: dividing the land by tribes.

Rav Meir Tzvi Gruzman (*Kara Shemitta*) notes that fifty years is a sufficient period for many nations to lose sight of three primary details of their character. If the nation continues on a path of self-destruction, it is liable to lose all aspects of its unique heritage. Thus, fifty years is enough time for various societal changes to eat away at the pillars of Jewish belief.

Time comes with comfort for some and economic turmoil for others. *Yovel* is a return to one's roots every fifty years, during which the Torah calls for a return to the basics on the national, religious, societal, and economic levels. Fields are returned, servants are freed, and the realization that " the land is Mine," that God is the owner of the land, is made apparent to all. This allows for the creation of a nation reinvigorated and renewed by understanding its roots.

Since *yovel's* messages go beyond the particular actions that occur during it, its proclamation frees the entire nation, not only the servants and those who have sold their land. It is a year of sanctity that can elevate everyone to a higher level through its social, economic, and religious messages.

The message of *yovel* is clearly not supposed to be viewed as a momentary or even a one-year lesson. *Yovel* teaches that the fields are not merely economic holdings, but a *nachala*, an inheritance expressing a deeply-rooted familial and tribal connection to the land (see Rav Nevenzahl's *Sichot Le-Sefer Vayikra, Parashat Behar*). The original *nachlaot* were provided to the tribes and their families when the Jewish nation entered the land, and they return every *yovel* to the descendants of the original owners. Since the land's ownership remains in the hands of the family's of the original "owners" ordained by God, the returning of the land is a constant reminder of who really owns the land, Hashem. All others might possess the land, but they are "strangers and sojourners with Me [God]".

As we have seen, *Chazal* derived from the Torah's reference to the freedom proclaimed "for all its inhabitants" that *yovel* applies only when all of the Jewish People is settled by tribe in *Eretz Yisrael*. The message of *yovel* is too broad to be limited to a small part of the nation. For this reason, *yovel* has not been in practice since the period of the Second Temple.

The Three Aspects of *Yovel*

Thus, *yovel* has three focuses. First is the *shofar* blast on *Yom Kippur* of the *yovel* year which acts as a proclamation of liberty. Additionally, we will see that it may also tie in with the Rosh Hashana theme of coronation of God, recognizing the land as His.

The second aspect of the *yovel* year, freeing slaves, focuses on the social issue. Rav Lichtenstein notes:

> Its message is revolutionary both from a philosophical point of view and certainly in its practical implementation. To some extent this represents an act of erasing the gaps which have been created in the past and a new beginning. There is an aspiration towards social justice, towards a closing of gaps and equality. Until the *yovel* it appears that "he shall serve him forever" — the radical gap and difference between slave and master — will prevail eternally. Then the *yovel* year comes around and declares, "And

you shall return each man to his estate and each to his family." There is economic and social restoration.

The third primary aspect of *yovel* affects the social sphere but also gets to the physical and economic infrastructure of social reform through the return of ancestral lands.

The *yovel* year thus spreads its influence in three main areas: the religious sphere, the social sphere, and the physical-economic sphere. Each of them is indispensable, as Rav Lichtenstein notes:

> When we translate this *halacha* into more general terms, it means that we are obligated to internalize most profoundly the realization that there can be no "shofar blast" — no coronation of God — without "freeing of slaves" and "returning of fields," without an awareness of social justice and of economic development and reform. Conversely, there can be no social justice nor real equality in the absence of a consciousness of man's "Divine image" and of Divine Kingship. There can be no possession of land if there is not at the same time sufficient concern for people living upon it. The strengthening of the people must go hand in hand with the redemption of the land. We are speaking here of spheres which must be intertwined, with each nourishing and being nourished by the other. Neglect of one area means neglect of the entire framework.

Yom Kippur of *Yovel*

An important element of *yovel* is the unique date of its commencement. One would expect that the *yovel* year, much like the seven *shevi'it* cycles that precede it, would begin on Rosh Hashana, the first of Tishrei. However, the Torah clearly tells us that the laws of *yovel* go into effect on the tenth of that month, on the holy day of Yom Kippur. The *shofar* is ordinarily associated with Rosh Hashana, and the unique prayers of that day are arranged around it, but when it comes to *yovel*, the *shofar* blast proclaiming a return of man to his estate and to his family is sounded on Yom Kippur and accompanied by the *tefillot* generally associated with Rosh Hashana (see *Rambam Hilchot Shemitta Ve-Yovel* 10). Why?

The Rambam (ibid. 10:14) explains that the period before Rosh Hashana was a sort of limbo period:

> From Rosh Hashana until Yom Kippur, servants were not sent to their homes nor were they subjugated to their masters, and fields did not return to their owners. Rather, the servants would eat, drink and celebrate, with crowns upon their heads. When Yom Kippur came, the court would sound the *shofar*, the servants were sent to their houses, and the fields returned to their owners.

Rav Aharon Lichtenstein[32] notes that the Yom Kippur of the *yovel* year is multifaceted, as it is both the day of *teshuva* that characterizes Yom Kippur of any year as well as a special Yom Kippur that serves as a Rosh Hashana of sorts. On this Yom Kippur, the blowing of the *shofar* totally transforms the reality with which all are familiar.

---

32   See https://torah.etzion.org.il/en/shiur-01-difference-between-shemitta-and-yovel.

It was a Yom Kippur representing economic revolution, social rehabilitation, a reorganization of the status quo... *Teshuva*, often translated repentance, is literally return. It is the primary aspect of Yom Kippur every year and *yovel* as well: "The personal dimension of *teshuva* is thus combined and intertwined with a process on both a public and personal level: "You (plural) shall return each man to his estate" — it is a process of simultaneously returning and being returned. Each aspect nourishes and is nourished by the other. The outward strengthening combines with soul-searching, and the entire day — through this combination and intertwining — overflows with national and spiritual majesty and power.

The Unique Shofar of *Yovel*

Chazal compare the *shofar* blasts of Rosh Hashana to those of Yom Kippur of *yovel* (*Rosh Hashana* 33b), but also not (Mishna *Rosh Hashana* 3:5) a number of differences between them.

One explanation for the distinctions might be the nature of the *mitzvah* of *shofar* for each respective time. Most *Rishonim* maintain that on Rosh Hashana, there is a *mitzvah* to hear the shofar (as the *beracha* on the *shofar* attests: "*le-shmo'a kol shofar*"). The *shofar* is both a call to *teshuva* and a device of *tefilla*, a means of bringing the prayers of the nation to God. In contrast, the Rambam notes that the *mitzvah* of shofar during *yovel* is a *mitzvah* to **blow** and is incumbent upon every individual, and its purpose is very different:

> It is well-known that this *shofar* blowing for *yovel* is only to publicize the emancipation and is part of the proclamation mandated by the verse, "And you shall proclaim liberty in the land." It is not like the *shofar* blowing of Rosh Hashana, which is "a remembrance before God," while this is to designate the freeing of servants... (*Sefer Ha-Mitzvot*, positive command 137)

If the *shofar* blowing is all about notifying the public, why is it a *mitzvah* incumbent on individuals? The *Sefer Ha-Chinuch* answers this question by explaining the difficulty involved in freeing one's servants:

> As for the root purposes of the precept, it is known that the sound of the *shofar* arouses the heart of human beings, whether to peace or to war. The matter of releasing a servant who has served his master a great amount of time is very difficult in the eyes of his master. Therefore, to inspire the heart of people about the matter, encourage their spirit, and adjure them about the *mitzvah*, the *shofar* is sounded, so that they will realize that this is something standard throughout the land and that all must do so. For this reason, we are all commanded regarding this *mitzvah*; there is nothing that will so encourage the heart of human beings as something done by everyone, as the saying of the wise man goes: "The suffering of many is consolation." (*Sefer Ha-Chinuch, mitzvah* 331)

The *shofar* empowers each individual with the message of freedom and awakens all to the power of the period. It allows for the social message to become a reality for everyone and allows all masters to realize their limitations and present a global message of freedom and real allegiance to God, that which prevents people from owning others or taking their land in perpetuity.

The message of the *Sefer Ha-Chinuch* is extremely pertinent. Peer pressure is a powerful motivator. People can manage to bear difficulty when they recognize others are in the same boat. Moreover, the *shofar* echoes in every ear, so all may recognize the social disruption others may experience. *Yovel* is not only a national experience; it makes people realize how they are affected by their surroundings, and they would do well to choose surroundings that are positive (a message oft-repeated by the Rambam).

Additionally, the *Sefer Ha-Chinuch* continues, the *shofar* sends a message to the servant himself:

> Moreover, the servant himself will also be aroused to go out, like all the servants, from the possession of his master whom he loves, and as a result the precept will be fulfilled that all should return to the domain of the Master and Ruler of all.

Yovel frees those servants who decided to stay with their masters after completing their six years of indentured servitude. They convinced themselves that they were not capable of taking care of themselves, that they needed the protection and special treatment that the Torah requires masters to give to the Hebrew servant. Now, as they are propelled into their own realm, they will have to deal with the difficulties of society. The Torah tells them that they can break free. If they recognize their true Master, they can also build homes of their own and become productive members of society.

The Blowing of the Courts and Individuals

The Torah mentions the blowing of the *shofar* twice (*Vayikra* 25:6), first in the singular (*"ve-avarta shofar"*) and then in the plural (*"ta'aviru shofar"*). Based on what we have seen above, the singular tense is a requirement that the act be done by the court, on behalf of the unified nation, while the plural is a call for each individual to perform the act. Indeed, the Talmud (*Rosh Hashana* 9b, codified by the Rambam, ibid. 10:10) rules that there is a double obligation; first the court blows the *shofar*, and then each individual.

The *Minchat Chinuch* (331) argues that this is superfluous. He maintains that the courts have no specific obligation above others; rather, the ruling teaches us that the court must blow (even though it is not involved in the freeing of servants or the return of agricultural lands), but not before individuals do.

Based on what we have seen, however, we may suggest a reason for the courts blowing and then each individual. The entire discourse of the nation must be altered to leave room for a new outlook and enable the social revolution *yovel* calls for. The courts blow the *shofar* first to recognize and proclaim the communal message, but specifically due to the societal message, every individual must blow the *shofar* personally and take part in the proclamation. This transforms the atmosphere and paves the way for the true revolutionary steps of *yovel*.

On the individual plane as well, the servant who has decided to remain in servitude must realize that he has one master, and that is God. But this individual responsibility is not merely for one who serves a human master. Most individuals lose their own decision-making abilities in certain situations and are "enslaved" to certain people or realities. The *shofar* is a call for liberty, a call to realize that servitude to anyone other than the Only One is useless. In fact, there is no better day for such an approach than Yom Kippur, the day upon which we wipe away our sins and return to God.

The Yom Kippur of *yovel* includes aspects of both Yom Kippur and Rosh Hashana. While both are days of *teshuva*, they differ in approach. On Rosh Hashana, no individual sins are mentioned; rather, the focus is upon identifying one's true self. Rosh Hashana is the anniversary of the creation of the world, and one recreates his or her world by identifying who he or she is and wants to be. Through the *shofar*, man exhales the "breath of God" that was blown into him on this very day. If the *shofar* is to be maximized, one must connect it to a commitment to the coronation of God. On *yovel*, the *shofar* of Rosh Hashana combines with the repentance of Yom Kippur, allowing individual, communal, and national recognition of true identity, rootedness, and recognition of the mastery of God.

Rav Hirsch (*Vayikra* 25:9) writes that this is apparent in the two sounds that are emitted from the *shofar*, the staccato *terua* and the unwavering *tekia*:

> This call is sounded in the Name of God by the Great Court, which represents the nation as a whole; it is then continued by every one of the people and spreads throughout the land. For it is a call from God into the midst of the country. It calls everyone and everything to the Master of all. Its purpose is to release the shackles of social bondage, in which everything is bound, *terua*. And it restores everything to pristine social conditions, *tekia*.

The Meaning of "Yovel"

Why is the fiftieth year referred to as *yovel*? The word is usually translated as "jubilee," which is arrived at based on the *shoresh* y-j, v-b, l-l, but it has a broader meaning.Rashi notes that *yovel* is also the term for a horn, a synonym for *shofar*. In fact, the description of the Revelation at Har Sinai refers to both a *shofar* and *yovel*: "When the *yovel* sounds long, they may ascend the mountain." (*Shemot* 19:13)

Ibn Ezra acknowledges that Rashi's explanation follows that of *Chazal*; in their view, a *yovel* is a horn of an animal of the sheep family. Ibn Ezra himself, however, suggests that *yovel* means "sending away".

The Ramban takes issue with Rashi's understanding, particularly because it does not fit all three appearances of *yovel* in the verses (*Vayikra* 25:10-12). If *yovel* means a *shofar*, how are we to understand the verse, "For it is *yovel*; it shall be holy for you" (25:12)? Furthermore, *yovel* specifically refers to a ram's horn, which is the preferred *shofar* for Rosh Hashana, as it recalls the Binding of Yitzchak. This is not necessary for the Yom Kippur of *yovel*. The Ramban therefore rejects Rashi's understanding and explains along the lines of Ibn Ezra:

> In my opinion, it is not the sounding of the *shofar*, but rather the liberty that marks *yovel*... "It is *yovel*" during which everyone will be restored..." (Ramban *Vayikra* 25:10-11)

The Ramban notes that the word *"yuval"* means "will be brought" (cf. *Yeshayahu* 18:7(, and other *pesukim* prove that the root refers to bringing. The Ramban notes that the word for the produce of one's crop is *"yevul"*; it is what one brings home from the field. *Yovel* is supposed to serve as a homecoming, when every man is "brought" home to his property.

The Abarbanel suggests that *shevi'it* and *yovel* remind us of God's two great acts on behalf of the Jewish People:

> 1) Physical creation of a world of perfection, which is recognized through *Shabbat* and *shemitta*, the sabbath of the land. *Shabbat* is the culmination of creation, and *shemitta* recognizes it through the land.
> 2) The second great gift, which is the essence of the *yovel* year, is God's granting the Torah, key to spiritual perfection, to His people. Just as seven periods of seven preceded the Giving of the Torah, seven periods of seven lead to *yovel*.
> The *shofar* is not related to Creation, but to the experience at Sinai, where the people were commanded to sanctify themselves, just as they are commanded to sanctify the fiftieth year.
> *Yovel* does not refer to a *shofar* per se, but to the specific *shofar* sounded at the Giving of the Torah and its unique role.

Our focus on our material lives can easily get out of proportion, and we therefore need to stop normal farming and economic life in order to refocus energy and ensure we're on track. However, once every fifty years, at least once in an average lifetime, we must allow for society to return to its beginnings, to a nation founded in the desert and unified by the word of God and the Sinai experience.[33] This is symbolized by the blowing of the *shofar*, the *yovel*.

Why do the verses reiterate three times that the year is one of *"yovel"*? The Abarbanel explains that each *"yovel"* refers to a different aspect of the year: release of servants, agricultural restrictions, and joint partaking of the produce. All three relate back to Sinai, when there was no servitude, no working or even treading upon the mountain, and no private property.

Deror

In order to properly understand the message of *yovel*, we must also explore the meaning of the word דְּרוֹר, *deror*, often translated as freedom or liberty, which appears almost exclusively in the context of *yovel*.[34] The Torah refers to the slaves going free after their six years of servitude in both *Shemot* (21:2) and *Devarim* (15:12), but the root that is

---

33 In a similar vein, the *Meshech Chochma* (ad loc.) explains that the restrictions on one's field and the need to renounce ownership of the produce lessen the reluctance to return the land to its ancestral owners.

34 The term is used as an adjective in *Shemot* 30:23, where it modifies myrrh ("מר דרור"), but as a noun only in the context of *yovel*.

used in those contexts is *chofesh*. Why in the context of *yovel* are we to "declare *deror*" (*Vayikra* 25:10) and not *chofesh*, the word more commonly associated with liberation from servitude (Shemot 25:2)?

The Ramban understands *deror* to refer to freedom of movement, the freedom to settle wherever one sees fit. Although the precise meaning of the word is elusive, Nechama Leibowitz (Studies in the Weekly *Parasha, Behar*) points out that it is clear that it encapsulates more than physical freedom. *Deror* connotes the positive aspects of freedom and liberty, while *chofesh* refers to release from the yoke of servitude. Only during *yovel*, when the entire nation is freed and receives liberty and independence, is this term appropriate. As the Torah states twice in the *parasha*:

כִּי לִי בְנֵי יִשְׂרָאֵל עֲבָדִים עֲבָדַי הֵם אֲשֶׁר הוֹצֵאתִי אוֹתָם מֵאֶרֶץ מִצְרָיִם אֲנִי ה' אֱ-לֹהֵיכֶם:

For the Israelites are my servants; they are my servants, whom I brought forth out of the land of Egypt. (*Vayikra* 25:55, cf. 25:42)

Chazal explain this *pasuk*:

כִּי לִי בְנֵי יִשְׂרָאֵל עֲבָדִים - עַבְדִי הֵם, וְלֹא עֲבָדִים לַעֲבָדִים.

"For the Israelites are my servants" and not servants to [human] servants.

Could servitude to God really bring about *deror*, liberty? With a better understanding of the concept of liberty it will become clear that servitude is actually a necessary component.

We find a clear delineation in the Torah between two models of "freedom/ liberty", one referred to as *chofesh* and the other as *deror*. Secular thinkers from the time of Kant have already noted that the words "liberty" and "freedom" are often used interchangablly for two very different, often contradictory expressions of freedom. A Jewish thinker, Isaiah Berlin, elaborated on these two forms of liberty and termed them "negative liberty" and "positive liberty".

"Negative liberty" refers to the absence of constraints, be they barriers or human interference of any kind. "Positive liberty", however, requires the presence of something, as it involves the ability to act in a manner with the control necessary to fulfill one's fundamental purpose in life. This often requires the presence of self-mastery, self-determination, or self-realization.

In other words, Negative liberty is defined as freedom *from*–the freedom from any restraint on one's actions. Positive liberty is defined as freedom *to*–the freedom to achieve what one really wants to achieve. In Berlin's words, positive liberty requires one to ask "What, or who, is the source of control or interference that can determine someone to do, or be, this rather than that?"

In a common example, one driving in an area that has no street signs requiring them to stop might feel free, but if they are in the area trying to purchase an illegal substance they are addicted to, they are far from free. While negative liberty might convince them that they are in the driver's seat, positive liberty would view them as far from free, as they are in fact being driven by addiction.

The Torah clearly wants us to be not only free from obstruction, but given the free will to really make the decisions that underlie our purpose in life. If *yetziat Mitzrayim*, the exodus from Egypt, set us free from obstruction, only Shavuot, the giving of the Torah provided us with positive liberty, a path in life and the tools to follow it properly. This idea of true freedom requiring a path and purpose is expressed vividly by the Mishna which declares who is truly free:

אָמַר רַבִּי יְהוֹשֻׁעַ בֶּן לֵוִי....שֶׁאֵין לְךָ בֶּן חוֹרִין אֶלָּא מִי שֶׁעוֹסֵק בְּתַלְמוּד תּוֹרָה

Rabbi Yehoshua ben Levi said: There is no free man other than one who is involved in Torah study." (Avot 6:2)

Although the Torah may be perceived as a list of laws that binds man, placing restriction and responsibility upon him, it is actually liberating. Understanding that Torah comes from God, our Creator, whose laws allow us to be in control and live life the way it is meant to be, is an essential part of freedom.

This is why servitude to Hashem as opposed to human "servants" is a necessary ingredient of freedom, as it precludes subjugation to anything else. The *deror* of *yovel* is the freedom to serve Hashem instead of man. From this perspective, the connection of *yovel* to the *shofar* blast of Sinai is also understandable, as it recognizes that freedom is truly achived through the Giving of the Torah. A similar idea about freedom from external human subjugation as liberating is expressed by Rabbi Joseph B. Soloveitchik:

A very eminent psychiatrist once said to me: Had I the authority to do so, I would eliminate the prayer recited on the High Holy Day that begins with the words, "Cast Thy fear," as fear is the major cause of the mental illnesses that beset mankind. In order to preserve one's mental health one should be free of fears, and so there is certainly no reason why one should ever pray for fear. (On Repentance, p. 223)

Rav Soloveitchik counters that fear of God is actually the most liberating of emotions:

Though I am not a psychiatrist, what he said helped me to understand the true nature of that prayer which was ordained by the Sages of Israel. And that is what I told that psychiatrist: Everyone seems to be beset with fears of all kinds. Some are afraid that they will not be able to succeed in their careers, others fear losing their wealth or status or that they will fail to attain sufficient prominence. Many people are afraid of sickness and bodily weakness. In generations past, fear of leprosy engulfed the world; today people live in fear of cancerous growth. Many people do not go to see a doctor even when they have pains lest he diagnose "the disease." Man is plagued constantly by all sorts of lesser fears. I am not a psychiatrist, but I do know that one major source of fear can wipe out all of these lesser fears. What fear can overtake man, thereby uprooting all other fears, such as that of failure, of poverty, of old age, of rejection or of disease? Only the fear of the Lord! That is the reason behind the expression in the High Holy Day prayer, "Cast Thy fear, O Lord our God, upon all Thy handiwork and Thine awe upon all that Thou hast created." We pray that this great fear will free us from those other ones which lurk everywhere, upsetting our lives. (*On Repentance*, pp. 223-224)

Deror refers to this paradox. The ultimate freedom and liberation is the recognition that one is responsible only to God, and with this positive liberty can make life meaningful and purposeful[35].

A Year of Return

The freedom granted by *yovel* is further expressed in its being a year of return. The root ב.ש., *sh.v.*, return, appears repeatedly in the *pesukim*:

> ... יוֹבֵל הִוא תִּהְיֶה לָכֶם וְשַׁבְתֶּם אִישׁ אֶל אֲחֻזָּתוֹ וְאִישׁ אֶל מִשְׁפַּחְתּוֹ תָּשֻׁבוּ: ... בִּשְׁנַת הַיּוֹבֵל הַזֹּאת תָּשֻׁבוּ
> אִישׁ אֶל אֲחֻזָּתוֹ:

> And each man shall return to his estate, and each man shall be returned to his family...
> In this year of *yovel*, each man shall return to his estate. (*Vayikra* 25:10, 13)

Rav Lichtenstein points out that the goal is not simply a year of return to one's point of departure, but a return that elevates the individual:

> Like the process of *teshuva* on Yom Kippur — 'Return us, O God, to You and we shall return; renew our days as of old' — the "return" and *teshuva* of the *yovel* year, too, are a return not just to the "days of old" of Adam, as the Midrash interprets it, but also a renewal which is built on the past. Not a cycle but rather a spiral.

Yovel and *Shevi'it*

Although *yovel* shares many agricultural laws with *shevi'it*, the *halachot* of these two years are not entirely the same. The Rambam rules:

> The law of letting the land rest for the *yovel* year is the same, in all respects, as the law for the *shemitta* year: Whatever agricultural work is forbidden in the *shemitta* year is forbidden also in the *yovel* year, and whatever is permitted in the *shemitta* year is permitted also in the *yovel* year. Whatever labor incurs a penalty of flogging in the *shemitta* year incurs the same penalty in the *yovel* year. Similarly, the laws governing the consumption, sale, and removal of the produce in the *yovel* year are the same as the laws of the *shemitta* year in all respects.
>
> The seventh [year] is greater than the *yovel* year in that the seventh cancels debts, while *yovel* does not. The *yovel* year is greater than the seventh in that *yovel* emancipates indentured servants and restores land to its original owner... The *yovel* year releases the land at its beginning, while the seventh cancels debts only at its end, as we have explained. (*Hilchot Shemitta Ve-Yovel* 10:15-16)

Rav Aharon Lichtenstein notes that there is reason to believe that even the agricultural *mitzvot* share only a general resemblance; the particulars of the *halachot* of *shevi'it* and *yovel* are actually different.

---

35 For this reason, when the prophet Yirmiyahu describes the punishment of one who does not grant the liberty of *yovel*, he uses the term *deror*: "לֹא שְׁמַעְתֶּם אֵלַי לִקְרֹא דְרוֹר אִישׁ לְאָחִיו" (*Yirmiyahu* 34:17). Those who deny freedom are punished with the unleashing of the sword and pestilence. Either one surrenders physical "freedom" and gains God as a protector, or one chooses to be "free" and ends up losing everything, from wealth to one's life.

Indeed, the *Minchat Chinuch* (335:1) notes two differences between *shevi'it* and *yovel* in the framework of agricultural prohibitions. He claims that the elements of the agricultural restrictions related to letting the land remain fallow – which, according to some, prohibit a non-Jew from working a Jew's land – may only apply during *shevi'it*, not during *yovel*. A second distinction accepted by the Rambam (although apparently not by the *Sefer Ha-Chinuch*) is that while agricultural work is proscribed by both negative and positive commands during *shevi'it*, *yovel* entails only a positive commandment. Additionally, during *yovel* all the agricultural prohibitions are grouped into one *mitzvah*, while during *shevi'it* different negative commandments pertain to fields and orchards.

Despite the distinctions between them, the similarities between the agricultural elements of *shevi'it* and *yovel* are clear, and the relationship between *shevi'it* and *yovel* has further implications. For example, there is a Talmudic dispute (*Nedarim* 61a and elsewhere) as to whether the *yovel* year is counted in the *shevi'it* cycle – that is, whether the fiftieth year is the first year counting toward the next *shemitta* or is essentially a year "zero."

The primary distinction between the laws of *shemitta* and *yovel* may be a direct outgrowth of their diverse forms of *kedusha*. The seventh year is *shabbat ha-aretz*, and much like Shabbat, its *kedusha* is rooted in stone. *Yovel*, in contrast, must be consecrated. The people, through the court, must actively sanctify the fiftieth year, as the *pasuk* explicitly states (*Vayikra* 25:10): "וקדשתם," "And you shall sanctify."[36]

The notion that *yovel* must be actively consecrated by the court has ramifications for the three main *mitzvot* related to *yovel*: the blowing of the shofar, the freeing of slaves, and the returning of ancestral lands:

> Our Sages taught: "'It is *yovel*' — even though the lands were not returned and the shofar was not sounded. Can it be *yovel* even if the slaves were not freed? [Yes, and] for this reason it says "it [is *yovel*]," according to R. Yehuda. R. Yosei says: "It is *yovel*" – even though the land was not returned to its owners, and even though the slaves were not freed. Can it be a *yovel* even if the shofar was not sounded? [Yes, and] for this reason it says "it [is *yovel*]..."
> R. Chiya bar Abba said in the name of R. Yochanan: These are the opinions of R. Yehuda and R. Yosei, but according to the Sages, all three are necessary conditions. (TB *Rosh Hashana* 9b)

The law follows the opinion of the Sages, as codified by the Rambam:

> Three things are crucial to a *yovel* year: the sounding of the shofar, the freeing of slaves, and the returning of fields to their owners. (*Hilchot Shemitta Ve-Yovel* 10:13)

This idea is very powerful. Not only does *yovel* require active counting of the years and *shemitta* cycles by the courts, but the existence of *yovel* altogether is predicated upon the fulfillment of its *mitzvot*. This notion is taken one step further by the Meshech Chochma (*Vayikra* 25:2), based on *Torat Kohanim*:

---

36   *Sefer Ha-Terumot* (45:4, cited by the *Ba'al Ha-Ma'or*) maintains that there is an obligation to sanctify the year of *shevi'it*, just as the year of *yovel* is sanctified by the court. This is based on the assumption that *yovel* and *shevi'it* constitute a single unit, with each dependent upon the other.

> The holiness of Shabbat is different from that of the Festivals; Shabbat is fixed and constant, whereas the Festivals are sanctified by Israel, and it is in their power to hasten or delay the festival times ... Likewise, the holiness of the *shemitta* is different from that of the *yovel*. All that applies to the *shemitta* applies also to the *yovel* year, but in the *yovel* if the *shofar* was not sounded, or if the slaves were not freed, or if land was not returned to its original owners, then plowing and sowing are permitted; it is not considered a *yovel* at all, as is explicitly stated, and the Rambam rules accordingly. This is not so in the case of *shemitta*, which has the character of a "royal holiday" and comes about by itself.

Unlike *shevi'it*, *yovel* does not apply if it is not observed properly. *Yovel's* sanctity is akin to the *kedusha* of *Yom Tov*, requiring the input of the court and the people in order for it to apply. The nation must rise to the occasion and actively sanctify the period. Thus, the *pasuk* states, "If there will be a *yovel*" (*Bamidbar* 36:4) – its existence is not a given.

In a similar vein, Rav Chayim of Brisk explains that the sanctity of *yovel* applies precisely through the counting of "seven years seven times over." Rav Aharon Lichtenstein explains:

> The constant and devoted action of counting the years, of preparation and readying, of paving the way towards the fiftieth year — that is precisely what sanctifies it; that is what determines the character and halachic status of the fiftieth year as a "*yovel* year." There is no fiftieth year without forty-nine years of work and effort and sacrifice!

Thus, *yovel* is not simply a *shemitta* that occurs less often. It is rather a period that must be created and sanctified by man to ensure that its lessons are conveyed. For this reason, it applies only when the majority (or all) of the Jewish people are settled in their land by tribe. *Yovel* can reform and renew society, but only when it is complete.

Once in a *Yovel*

The phrase "once in a *yovel*" is the Jewish equivalent of "once in a blue moon." *Yovel* is infrequent, but it influences an entire half-century. It ensures that *shevi'it's* seven-year restructuring has lasting effects.

Every seven years, the nation in the land of Israel puts agricultural competition aside and gives equal access to everyone's fields. Society as a whole recognizes the existence of God and the benefits of honesty, faith (*emuna*), and trust (*bitachon*). *Shevi'it* should not be seen as an economic aberration. Rather, it inculcates a message about the proper model for society in every year: Adherence to God's law thus helps, rather than hurts, the individual. Yet *shevi'it's* septennial message is prelude to the much larger message of *yovel*, which completely resets the economy.

Indeed, the fact that the Torah commands that we count the years toward *yovel* indicates that there should be a constant longing for *yovel*, as its economic and social messages are supposed to be perennially in one's mind. The Chatam Sofer (*Vayikra* 25:8) notes that the Torah states not only that we must count forty-nine years, but seven cycles of seven. He quotes his teacher, Rabbi Pinechas Horowitz, who explains the verse, "and the days of the seven sabbaths of years shall be for you forty-nine years," as an obligation to count each day, much like counting the *omer*. Just as we long to arrive at the Giving of the Torah on Shavuot after Pesach, the counting of the *shevi'it* years recognizes the need for *yovel* and the longing for its message.

For forty-nine years, the Jew is involved in business, but the message of *shemitta* and *yovel* must guide his actions. Although society might take on a deeply-rooted capitalist attitude during these intermediate years, it must maintain its bearings and conduct its commerce with an understanding of the societal and economic messages of *shevi'it* and *yovel* (see Section II theme 7).

In a similar vein, the Kli Yakar and Abarbanel (*Vayikra* 25) both note that the semi-centennial occurrence of *yovel* relates to a period that spans the average working lifetime, demanding that one not be self-centered. *Yovel* is to serve as a constant focus and an urgent reminder of the greater purpose in one's existence. *Shevi'it* and *yovel* allow man's dealings throughout the year to be driven towards the goals and messages that *shevi'it* and *yovel* present.

Rav Kook on *Yovel*

In his introduction to his work *Shabbat Ha-Aretz,* Rav Kook poetically describes the power of *shevi'it*, which allows us to take a necessary time out from the vicissitudes of life in order to reveal the spiritual goals of the nation and to renew the link between one's physical existence and one's spiritual goals. He notes that *yovel* goes one step further:

> [*Yovel* is] strong enough to correct the deviations and the turpitude of the past and to restore the conditions of life of the nation to the original state of its tender infancy...

The timing of Yom Kippur is appropriate for the shofar blast heralding *yovel*:

> The supreme spirit of total forgiveness that pervades every individual on the Day of Atonement rises here through the sanctity of the *yovel* in its collective aspect, while the nation, imbued with the spirit of forbearance and repentance, endeavors to rectify the distortions of the past.

Through the seven cycles of seven years, social ills arise that demand rectification:

> [Individuals] allowed themselves to become servants, forgetting their own sublime value and that the "ear that heard declare on Mount Sinai: 'For the Israelites are my servants' — not servants to servants, yet they chose to acquire a master for themselves" (Rashi, *Shemot* 21:6). They recover their personal respect and liberty through the life-stream of sanctity that emanates from the supreme source from which the nations draws the light of her soul, and liberty is proclaimed throughout the land.

In addition, *yovel* mandates the restoration of property:

> To compensate for the unbalanced state of the landed property, the result of physical and spiritual weakness caused by man's sins, which sap his strength and cause him to forfeit the inheritance of his forefathers — to right this imbalance comes *yovel*, which harmonizes with the pristine moral standard of the nation, bringing this basic real property to those who had been weighted down with the burden of life which

distorted their values. In this year of *yovel*, each man shall return to his estate.

Rav Kook sees the societal norms that develop over the forty-nine years as a synonym for "deviations and turpitude" that must be rectified. They dim the radiance of the nation's soul. Shabbat accomplishes a respite for the individual and *shevi'it* (*shabbat ha-aretz*) for the nation, and *yovel* proclaims liberty and engenders a spirit of forbearance and repentance to allow the rectification of the distortions of the past.

Praise for the *Shevi'it-Yovel* Economic Model

The social and economic messages of *yovel* and *shevi'it* are not lost on some prominent economic thinkers, including non-Jews, who are amazed by the laws and convinced that they present an economic model that could only be devised by God.

Although we know that the Torah is God's wisdom and does not need any human support, it is nevertheless interesting to see how some Christian political thinkers are quick to point out its benefits. For instance, political economist and economic philosopher Henry George (1839-1897) points out the Torah's radical deviation from the economic models known in the past, calling for a redeemed, socially concerned, and value-based economy.

Interestingly, George authored the book *Progress and Poverty* in 1879, which sold millions of copies (a tremendous feat for any book, certainly one about economics). It outsold every other book in the 1890's other than the Bible, the book he based his economic outlook on. Having lived through poverty, he studied the nature of the beast and was initially confounded as to how poverty continues despite economic progress. He identified the source of the problem in land value, as progress increases the price of land, and those with control of land continue to grow their wealth while others are driven into poverty.

He noted that the Bible already understood this self-perpetuating problem and solved it through the institution of yovel. There would never be an upper echelon in society which would gain control of all the land and shared resources, as yovel would ensure every fifty years land would return to its original owners. In the absence of a contemporary equivalent of yovel, he devise a single tax system on land (and other natural resources), which he felt would be the most effective model for continual progress without poverty. His works initiated a new school of thought, Georgism, which he hoped to implement through political office, which was rendered impossible due to his untimely death.

The basis for *Progress and Poverty* is George's lecture turned essay, *Moses*, which he delivered a year earlier. He notes how *shevi'it* marks a strong contrast to the capitalist regimes with which he was familiar, presenting a moral outlook on the economy that could potentially solve many of the ills of inequality. He focuses on the social messages that emerge from the Torah's economic system of *mitzvot ha-teluyot ba-aretz*.

George notes that the Jewish People begin as a pastoral family surrounded by Egypt, a society built upon slavery, disregard for humanity, and wealth-mongering. One would thus expect a tremendous amount of Egyptian influence on Judaism – but the influence does not bring the Torah to mimic Egyptian culture, but rather to do the opposite:

It is not remarkable, therefore, that the ancient Hebrew institutions show in so many points the influence of Egyptian ideas and customs. What is remarkable is the dissimilarity. To the unreflecting, nothing may seem more natural than that a people, in turning their backs upon a land where they had been long oppressed, should discard its ideas and institutions. But the student of history, the observer of politics, knows that nothing is more unnatural. Habits of thought are even more tyrannous than habits of the body. They make for the masses of people a mental atmosphere out of which they can no more rise than out of the physical atmosphere...

In general, societies that rebel against tyranny end up creating an even more oppressive system, but not Judaism:

The striking differences between Egyptian and Hebrew polity are not of form, but of essence. The tendency of the one is to subordination and oppression; of the other to individual freedom. Strangest of recorded births! From out of the strongest and most splendid despotism of antiquity comes the freest republic.

George notes that the ability of the Jewish People to form a society so dissimilar to that of Egypt is rooted in Moses' great leadership and his ability to see to it that the Jewish economy would be the mirror image of Egypt, the emphasis reversed, recognizing a:

God of the market place as well as of the temple; a God whose judgments wait not another world for execution, but whose immutable decrees will, in this life, give happiness to the people that heed them and bring misery upon the people that forget them.

George praises the Jewish commonwealth and economy by recognizing among others the laws of Shabbat, *shabbat ha-aretz*, and *yovel* in preventing unhindered slavery and the rich from monopolizing the land:

It was a commonwealth based upon the individual – a commonwealth whose ideal it was that every man should sit under his own vine and fig tree, with none to vex him or make him afraid. It was a commonwealth in which none should be condemned to ceaseless toil; in which, for even the bond slave, there should be hope; and in which, for even the beast of burden, there should be rest... It is not the protection of property, but the protection of humanity, that is the aim of the Mosaic code. Its sanctions are not directed to securing the strong in heaping up wealth as much as to preventing the weak from being crowded to the wall. At every point it interposes its barriers to the selfish greed that, if left unchecked, will surely differentiate men into landlord and serf, capitalist and working person, millionaire and tramp, ruler and ruled. Its Sabbath day and Sabbath year secure, even to the lowliest, rest and leisure. With the blast of the Jubilee trumpets the slave goes free, the debt that cannot be paid is cancelled, and a re-division of the land secures again to the poorest their fair share in the bounty of the common Creator...

While Henry George is mesmerized by the teachings of Moses and his success in directing a mass of slaves from tyrannical Egypt to build an economically just society, students of Torah recognize that this is not Moshe's doing as a statesman, but rather as a messenger of God. Moshe Rabbeinu is called the "servant of God" (*Devarim* 34:5), as his success is a direct outgrowth of his role in being God's agent. As great a leader as Moshe is, it is not his statesmanship which creates a just society and economy, as much as his commitment to teaching God's word to a people prone to wondering why they had left the land of Egypt. God's teachings are the basis for the just and moral socioeconomic model the Torah advocates, not only Moshe's leadership.

The laws of Shabbat, *shabbat ha-aretz*, and *yovel*, as well as the society of justice and redeemed economy that they create, are only possible with God at the helm. The goal of these periods is to take a step back, reconnect with God's role of mastery, and study the ideal society and economy that can be created by those who recognize God's role. As Rav Breuer (*Nachaliel*) concludes:

> The sabbath of the land is its return to the Creator, blessed be He, its shedding of the form of nature and donning of the garments of creation, for the land's rest is also the Jew's rest. It is an entire year of freedom from the bonds of physical and of intellectual aspiration, in which the visionary ego gazes upon all of nature and the whole expanse of the broad world—and they are all of creation—and in it he sees himself, with all his smallness. Out of his liberty, the highest level of all of creation, comes self-recognition of all of creation. For an entire year he studies Torah, the Torah of man and the Torah of creation, with a clear mind and loving heart, and for an entire year he occupies himself with commandments and through them performs acts of kindness for all of creation. There is no tragedy in his view of the entire world, because he enjoys the radiance of the Divine Presence…

Yovel and *Ona'ah*-
The Prohibition of Distressing Others

A further indication of *yovel's* impact on society throughout all years can be seen from its connection to the laws of *ona'ah*. Immediately after its discussion of *yovel*, the Torah describes the laws of *ona'ah*, exploitation and overcharging. The basis for the law is that since there is a prohibition to permanently sell one's ancestral land in *Eretz Yisrael*, any sale of land is essentially simply renting for up to fifty years, and this should be reflected in the price of the "sale". Any attempt to overcharge violates the laws of *ona'ah*:

וְכִי תִמְכְּרוּ מִמְכָּר לַעֲמִיתֶךָ אוֹ קָנֹה מִיַּד עֲמִיתֶךָ אַל תּוֹנוּ אִישׁ אֶת אָחִיו: בְּמִסְפַּר שָׁנִים אַחַר הַיּוֹבֵל תִּקְנֶה מֵאֵת עֲמִיתֶךָ בְּמִסְפַּר שְׁנֵי תְבוּאֹת יִמְכָּר לָךְ: לְפִי רֹב הַשָּׁנִים תַּרְבֶּה מִקְנָתוֹ וּלְפִי מְעֹט הַשָּׁנִים תַּמְעִיט מִקְנָתוֹ כִּי מִסְפַּר תְּבוּאֹת הוּא מֹכֵר לָךְ: וְלֹא תוֹנוּ אִישׁ אֶת עֲמִיתוֹ וְיָרֵאתָ מֵאֱלֹהֶיךָ כִּי אֲנִי ה' אֱ-לֹהֵיכֶם: וַעֲשִׂיתֶם אֶת חֻקֹּתַי וְאֶת מִשְׁפָּטַי תִּשְׁמְרוּ וַעֲשִׂיתֶם אֹתָם וִישַׁבְתֶּם עַל הָאָרֶץ לָבֶטַח: וְנָתְנָה הָאָרֶץ פִּרְיָהּ וַאֲכַלְתֶּם לָשֹׂבַע וִישַׁבְתֶּם לָבֶטַח עָלֶיהָ:

When you sell property to your neighbor, or buy any from your neighbor, you shall not exploit one another. In buying from your neighbor, you shall deduct only for the number of years since the *yovel*; and in selling to you, he shall charge you only for the remaining crop years. The more such years, the higher the price you will pay; the fewer such years, the lower the price; for what he is selling you is a number of harvests. Do not exploit one another, but fear your God; for I *Hashem* am your God. You shall observe My laws and faithfully keep My rules, that you may live upon the land in security. The land shall yield its fruit and you shall eat your fill, and you shall live upon it in security. (*Vayikra* 24:14-19)

The laws of *ona'a* apply at all times and in all commercial contexts, yet the Torah specifically teaches them in the context of *yovel*. Charging a price that would be appropriate when selling a field permanently constitutes overcharging[37] and is the model for a general prohibition of overcharging in all business situations. Evidently, the Torah wants to indicate that *shevi'it* and *yovel*, which play such a fundamental role in exhibiting the Torah's recipe for a just and value-based society, are part of a more extensive set of laws that ensure fairness and concern for the weaker sectors at all times. Additionally, the religious nature of yovel merges with economic laws that ensure just social interaction. These and other laws create a society whose constant and pervasive economic outlook is in line with the values of a "*shevi'it* and *yovel* nation", informing every part of society.

Two Forms of *Ona'ah*

The Torah proscribes *ona'ah* twice in the course of the *yovel* passage (*Vayikra* 25:14, 17). *Chazal* explain that the first mention, in the context of charging appropriate prices for one's *nachala*, refers to ona'ah in the realm of commerce (*ona'at mammon*).

A few *pesukim* later, the Torah repeats the prohibition of "*lo tonu*," this time adding that one must fear God. *Chazal* understood the repetition of this prohibition as establishing a second form of *ona'ah*, beyond monetary exploitation:

The Torah states: "No one of you shall wrong his comrade" — this verse refers to *ona'at devarim*, verbal abuse. (*Bava Metzia* 58b)

Thus,*Chazal* explain, the Torah taught us two forms of prohibited *ona'a* – one financial (*ona'at mammon*) and one verbal (*ona'at devarim*).

The Torah's teaching two forms of *ona'ah* by the same terminology *lo tonu*, and in the context of yovel seems to express an underlying theme. Besides being a further indication of a theme we have seen throughout, the economic sphere is integrally connected to overall interpersonal laws, there is clearly an underlying foundation to both forms of *ona'ah*. The *Sefer Ha-Chinuch* describes *ona'ah* as taking advantage of another's weakness:

The Torah commands us not to cause grief to another Jew by way of speech — i.e., not to say to another Jew something that might pain him or aggrieve him when he is

---

37 The laws of *ona'ah* require buyers and sellers of property to factor the number of years left until *yovel* when determining the price for a piece of land, as the property will be reverting to its original owner at *yovel*. Essentially, the property must be rented, not sold. *Ona'ah* calls upon consumers and merchants to buy and sell fairly, without demanding inordinately low or high prices for merchandise. *Chazal* defined *ona'at mammon* as overcharging or underpaying by more than one sixth of market value. A sale may even be revoked when the price differs drastically from the market value of the object.

incapable of defending himself. (*Sefer Ha-Chinuch, mitzvah* 338)

Similarly, Rav S.R. Hirsch explains *ona'a* as "the exploitation of the weakness of man, in order to cheat him," a definition that leaves room for two diverse types, commercial and personal:

> In commerce, *ona'a* is the exploitation of the other party's ignorance, in order to cheat him… It includes any reduction in quantity or quality of the object… or any kind of fraud…
>
> Whoever verbally abuses his fellow violates this prohibition… In particular, the prohibition of *ona'at devarim* includes wronging another by words when their evil intent is apparent only to God; hence, the verse stresses "And you shall fear your God"…
>
> *Ona'at devarim* and *ona'at mammon* have this in common: In both cases, one exploits another's weakness, his ignorance of the merchandise or his personal sensitivity. (Rav Hirsch, *Vayikra* 25:14, 17)

Nechama Leibowitz explains that the reason why people behave in this disdainful manner is "the sense of superiority experienced by the one who lectures to his fellow man or preaches to a person in distress" (*Iyunim, Vayikra*, p. 550). However, weakness manifests itself in many different areas. *Ona'a* can take the form of overcharging those unknowledgeable in business, committing practical jokes against merchants, using nicknames, or in many other ways.[38]

Fear of God

Ona'at devarim is unique in the tremendous scope of cases included in the prohibition. The prohibition of verbal abuse is not limited to outright defamation or other forms of clearly harmful speech, but also includes a broad array of cases that do not seem so terrible on the surface. Any form of causing pain with words is included in the prohibition, and the examples extend beyond the expected.

After listing the numerous forms of *ona'at devarim*, including cases in which one feigns interest in buying a product he or she cannot afford or has no interest in, the Talmud comments again on the Torah's mention of *yirat Elokim* in the context of *ona'at devarim*:

> For the matter depends on a person's intent, and concerning matters which depend on a person's true intent, the Torah says, "And you shall fear your God."

Rashi explains:

> "For the matter depends on a person's intent" — This is why it says "And you shall fear your God"… For one's good nature or bad nature is not discernible, but in the heart of the one performing the action. Are his motives pure or crooked? He may say, "I only acted for the good; I thought that you had produce to sell," or "I honestly intended to buy this product."

---

38   The Torah goes beyond warning us about mistreating those who are in a position that prevents them from defending themselves. In a number of places, it specifies certain underprivileged individuals who require special treatment with extraordinary care so as not to hurt their feelings. In fact, the Torah requires that we go out of our way to show them compassion.

While both forms of *ona'a* involve exploitation of a weaker party, the added clause, "And you shall fear your God," serves to highlight the distinction between monetary exploitation, which is detectable, and the kind that can be covered up. *Ona'at devarim* includes circumstances in which one's verbal abuse is hidden and undetectable to others, which is why it is necessary for the Torah to remind the potential perpetrator to fear God, who knows every individual's intentions. A special dose of fear of God is necessary in order to overcome the urge to hurt another, given that one's negative intentions can often be concealed. A cover-up is a sign of erasing God from the picture. This is similar to misleading others in the context of selling land before *yovel*, as if one doesn't recognize that God's ownership of the land supersedes that of any human.

In addition to indicating that *ona'at devarim* is more severe than *ona'at mammon*, the Talmud states that God provides an immediate and direct response to victims of *ona'ah*, even when all other avenues of prayer to God are closed. Thus, before speaking, one must think one step ahead and consider in advance whether his or her remarks could cause another person any pain. One should certainly realize that feigning innocence when using words or body language to hurt another only makes one more deserving of severe punishment.

Personal development is determined not only by one's interactions with others, but by one's behavior *bein adam le-atzmo*, the type of individual one becomes inside. What type of person would one be if he or she is constantly searching for avenues to maliciously malign others while hiding behind a guise of good intentions? The punishment for mistreating others is so severe because one who does so expresses a lack of understanding of all of the messages we have outlined.

The Torah's choice of teaching these two forms of *ona'ah* in the context of yovel might point to some other lessons as well. *Yovel* teaches us the temporariness of property. One's acquisition of another's rightful land can last no more than fifty years. This understanding should hopefully lead one to think twice before engaging in dishonest business tactics:

> When one realizes that his ownership of the land will eventually be terminated, he will refrain from stealing and cheating. (*Melechet Machshevet*, quoted by Nechama Leibowitz)

Yovel also reinforces the concept of *nachala*. Land is much more than real estate. Beyond its financial value it connects one to their agricultural heritage in the land of Israel. Understanding the deeper value of one's possesions is a value that clearly reveals itself through many aspects of *shevi'it* and *yovel*.

Notably, specifically in the context of yovel the Torah iterates the importance of *yirat Elokim*. Rav Hirsch explains it's connection to here:

> "And you shall fear your God" is the direct result of *shemitta* and *yovel*, as regards the communal life of the people of the land. These laws introduce the name of God into all of commercial life and bring the thought continually to mind that all people live and work together on the soil of God, in the land of God, where God is the master of all property; as tribute, He demands that His rule be implemented in every phase of life.

One of shevi'it's primary messages is that God is concerned with the marketplace as well as the synagogue:

> God watches over all of communal life, for God does not dwell only in the sanctuary. Rather, He dwells in the midst of the people and blesses its commerce. However, God bestows His blessing only if commerce brings prosperity and happiness to all, only if one does not wrong and aggrieve the other and one does not abuse the position which he has attained to cheat the other. God bestows His blessing only if the truth of all truths, that He is our God, is realized in every phase of our lives, both as individuals and as a nation.

Indeed, the next *pesukim* (25:18-19) state that if the Jewish people follow the will of God, we will live securely upon the land. The recognition of the conceptual basis of *shevi'it* and *yovel* – the need to treat others with dignity and to create a spiritual society in all aspects – ensures the security of the Jewish way of life in the Jewish land. Particularly in the Land of Israel, economic and interpersonal perfection is necessary.

On a practical level, connecting the requirement to conduct oneself ethically in business with the requirement to watch one's words constitutes an added lesson about keeping one's priorities straight when involved in speech connected to money-making. People in the midst of competition often find themselves saying things they shouldn't have[39]. On a broader level, *ona'ah* reminds us that we must always interact with others with fear of God, ensuring a fair and just economy, and a caring and peaceful society. This is part of *yovel's* heritage even in our day and age.

Yovel for Us

The *gemara* (*Erachin* 32b) explains that *yovel* no longer applies, as a majority of Jews no longer live in their ancestral lands in *Eretz Yisrael*. Most opinions rule that for the same reason, *shevi'it* – which the Torah inextricably links to *yovel* – is not a Biblical requirement in our day. Nevertheless, *shevi'it* is Rabbinically mandated, as its once-in-seven-years lessons are essential for our settlement in the land, and its application is less dependent on the ideal realities that make *yovel* applicable.

While *yovel* no longer applies, the interpersonal laws the Torah teaches in the context of *yovel* certainly do. *Yovel* impresses upon us the necessity of *yirat Elokim* and religious awareness in all aspects of our interactions with others. Refraining from overcharging and other forms of economic exploitation, as well as careful speech aimed at ensuring one doesn't hurt another verbally, are all part of *yovel's* overall imprint. A society with God at the helm, both economically and interpersonally, is a caring and just society – the type of society that we must strive to achieve.

In the next section, we will aim to analyze the various themes that can be culled from *shevi'it* and *yovel*.

---

39   There might be a halachic explanation for this interconnection as well. The Ohr Ha-Chayim writes that even though *ein ona'a le-karkaot*, andy case of *ona'a* that does not fit the technical definition of *ona'at mammon* — such as overcharging on real estate — still falls into the category of *onaat devarim*. Essentially, the two types of *ona'ah* are linked; if one tries to outsmart the system and overcharge on items in such a way that the sale will not be revoked, the use of sweet talk will ensure that the act will be a violation of the more severe *ona'at devarim*.

Section 2

Seven Themes for Seven Years

Chapter 11

An Introduction to *Shevi'it's* Varied Themes

Now that we have seen how *shevi'it* is presented in the *pesukim*, it should be apparent that it is impossible to summarize the goals of *shevi'it* in a concise adage. The more we delve into this intriguing year, the more it is evident that *shevi'it* encompasses many of the Torah's lessons, as reflected in its connection to Har Sinai.

In order to capture as much of its essence as possible, we will divide the themes of *shevi'it* (appropriately) into seven. Through our analysis of these themes, we will be in a better position to organize the various components of *shevi'it* into a beautiful and wholesome vision.

The Contradictions

One of the main reasons for dividing *shevi'it* into varied themes is that the different *parashot* we have studied present the year with different names and from different perspectives.

Parashat Mishpatim emphasizes the social aspect of *shevi'it*, presenting it as a year in which there is equal access to the produce of the fields for the poor and the owners: "And the poor of your nation will eat" (*Shemot* 23:11). The command, "*tishmetenna u-ntashtah*," usually translated "release it and let it lie fallow" (ibid.), is the first appearance of the root *sh.m.t.*, but the precise meaning of the term is subject to dispute.

In *Parashat Behar*, the other primary portion dealing with agricultural *shevi'it*, the year is referred to seven times by the term *shabbat*; it is termed *shabbat ha-aretz* (*Vayikra* 25:6) and *shabbat la-Hashem* (25:2). The focus is on this sabbatical period for the land itself, suggesting a set of ritual obligations rather than the expression of a social message.

In the following *parasha*, *Parashat Bechukotai*, *shabbat ha-aretz* is integrally connected to the land itself. It is the terminology used by the Torah to describe the exile that will be the lot of the nation if it fails to observe the *mitzvot*. *Shevi'it* is presented as the ultimate sign of the intertwined destinies of the nation and the land.

Additionally, *shevi'it* appears in the Torah in a number of other contexts. In the continuation of *Parashat Behar*, the laws of *yovel* are taught. Beyond its agricultural obligations, which are identical to those of *shevi'it*, servants are freed and all lands return to their ancestral owners. This is an extreme social message coupled with a completely new outlook on the economy and the balance of wealth in society. Alongside *yovel*, the *halachot* of *ona'ah* (exploitation) are taught – another financial message relating to the economy and proper business practices. In the context of *yovel*, the Torah also informs us of the blessing promised to *shevi'it* observers and seems to provide a general rationale for the inability to sell the land permanently: "For the land is mine, for you are strangers and sojourners with me" (*Vayikra* 25:23). Indeed, this explanation may provide a rationale for *shevi'it* and *yovel* as a whole.

The financial element of *shevi'it* appears again in *Parashat Re'eh*, which discusses *shemittat kesafim*, the release of the right to debt collection in the final moment of the *shevi'it* year. Again, this indicates that *shevi'it* bears a financial message, guiding the nation to the formation of a redeemed economy.

Finally, in *Parashat Vayelech*, the Torah's presents the once-every-seven-years *mitzvah* of *Hakhel*, performed in the wake of the year of *shevi'it*. Evidently, *shevi'it* is supposed to enable a spiritual reawakening, among its other messages.

Is *shevi'it* a year with an interpersonal social agenda, a year of an economic utopia, or a year of spiritual solitude? Which of these diverse messages is meant to be the guiding principle of the year?

A deeper look at *shevi'it* indicates that there is no need to choose. *Shevi'it* carries a multifaceted message, with each facet significant in its own right, and all of those aspects combining to form a bigger picture.

The Multifaceted Nature of *Shevi'it*

In fact, *shevi'it*'s varied messages are a tribute to its importance and indicate its significance. As we present an array of comments regarding the nature of *shevi'it* and its ideas, we will focus on seven themes that underscore many aspects of *shevi'it*. After analyzing each theme independently, we will notice how these various aspects combine for a much broader, interconnected message. In Section III, we will also see many of these themes brought to life through the various agricultural *halachot* of *shevi'it*.

Rav Shaul Yisraeli (*Shemitta L'Orech HaDorot*) and others note that it is clear that *shevi'it* encompasses all four elements of *mitzvot*.

- The Torah explicitly *mentions shevi'it's* social purpose in providing for the poor. Interpersonal *mitzvot* (*bein adam le-chavero*) are uniquely focused on achieving results, requiring that one actually benefit others.

- Additionally, *shevi'it* conveys a religious message for improving one's relationship with God like other *mitzvot bein adam la-Makom*. In ritual obligations, the intent is critical. The primary focus of these *mitzvot* is furthering one's relationship with Hashem by fulfilling His will.

- Thirdly, *shevi'it* includes a *bein adam le-atzmo* (character-building) element as well. *Mitzvot bein adam le-atzmo* are *mitzvot* whose primary purpose is to impact those who perform them by shaping one's personality to inculcate God-like behavior and attitudes. Deed is not necessarily reflective of character; a person with many severe character faults may still do good deeds. These *mitzvot* involve emulating God not merely by performing positive acts, but by undergoing an internal change and developing one's character in the process.

- Furthermore, as we have seen, *shevi'it* also illustrates the relationship between the Jew and his land (*bein adam le-artzo*). Identifying *Shevi'it*'s impact on our connection to nature in general and *Eretz Yisrael*, in particular, is a further reflection of *shevi'it*'s multifaceted lessons.

These four aspects of *shevi'it* help us appreciate the Torah's multifaceted presentation of *shevi'it's* mitzvot and nature. *shevi'it* affects every facet of one's interaction with the world around them. Additionally, *shevi'it* also allows us to understand the nature of the Torah's view on rest and sabbaticals in general. What is to be gained from a time out? *Shevi'it* also enables us to take a broader look at the Torah's outlook on the ideal economy and how to ensure development and progress in a manner that benefits all and not just the richest and powerful? Lastly, to appreciate our contemporary observance of *shevi'it,* we need to view it against the backdrop of our recent return to our land and the reemergence of *shevi'it* after years of the nation's exile and the land's desolation.

An attempt to appreciate these various aspects of *shevi'it* raises a question. Should we just blanketly accept and perform the Torah's mitzvot without seeking their underlying themes, or alongside a commitment to their observance, seek out their rationale?

The Enterprise of *Ta'amei Ha-Mitzvot*

Broadly speaking, rationalizing *mitzvot* may be inadvisable, as doing so implies a certain level of presumptuousness, tantamount to a human claiming the capability to determine the divine reason behind a *mitzvah* instituted by the omniscient Creator. As human beings, we recognize that we understand only a tiny portion of what there is to know about the physical world, notwithstanding our scientific advancements. How, then, can we possibly hope to understand the world of the spirit?

Nevertheless, commentators throughout the generations sought to explicate *ta'amei ha-mitzvot,* often translated as the reason or rationale behind the commandments. However, it seems that the goal of looking for a *ta'am* for a *mitzvah* is not to discover *why* it should be observed. First of all, we can never fully grasp a *mitzvah's* purpose; second, we fulfill *mitzvot* because God commanded us to do so, and for no other reason. Instead, our goal in searching for a *ta'am* is to appreciate the *mitzvah* better and understand some of the messages it conveys. In fact, *ta'am* is also the Hebrew word for taste. *Ta'amei ha-mitzvot* are essentially taste enhancers, as they enable us to savor and appreciate the commandments.

The various flavorings of the *ta'amei ha-mitzvot* presented should in no way be viewed as exclusive, especially in the context of *shevi'it.* After all, the Torah itself provides such a broad, varied perspective on *shemitta* that we cannot doubt that there are many "flavors" to relish here.

The Rambam's Rationales

To illustrate some of the various flavors involved in *shevi'it* observance, let's take a look at a dispute amongst the Rishonim searching for *shevi'it's* underlying themes. This discussion begins with the Rambam's explanations, found in the third section of his *Moreh Ha-Nevuchim,* which discusses *ta'amei ha-mitzvot.* There, the Rambam offers two reasons for the *mitzvot* of *shevi'it:*

> With regard to all the commandments that we have enumerated in *Hilchot Shemitta Ve-Yovel,* some of them are meant to lead to compassion and promoting the well-being of all men, as the Torah states: "That the poor of your people may eat" (*Shemot* 23:11)... and are meant to make the earth more fertile and stronger through letting

> it lie fallow. Some are inspired by compassion for the slaves and the poor – that is to say the release of money and the release of slaves. Others are designed to redress the inequities of income and the economy. Since the land cannot be estranged from its owners, it is impossible to sell it for eternity... A man's property remains for him and his heirs. (*Moreh Nevuchim* 3:39)

The Rambam identifies two aspects of *shevi'it*: one social, benefiting the poor, and the other agronomical, benefitting the farmland.

Since ancient times, there has been recognition that excessive planting of the same crops year after year is detrimental to the land. It was common practice for many to plant in their fields only every other year, as yearly planning would deplete the ground of its nutrients. The exact parameters of the agricultural benefits involved involve many factors. Still, the Rambam's second rationale is that allowing the land to "rest" for a year will enable it to produce greater yields in the future.

Several commentators take issue with this second reason. Is *shevi'it* really an agriculturally beneficial *mitzvah*? If so, why would it carry such dire consequences for non-fulfillment? Additionally, if the land is weakened by excessive planting, the sixth year's crop should be from when the land is weakest, yet the Torah promises it will increase three-fold?

Others ask more fundamental questions as well, underscoring the uniqueness of *shevi'it* requirements. If *shevi'it's* goal is to ensure that the agricultural land will be fertile, at least in the Land of Israel where there is a *mitzvah* of beautifying the land, why would the Torah require that all land be left fallow during the same year? This would obviously cause a period of tremendous deprivation, if not for our reliance on a divine blessing. The Torah could have easily prohibited planting any field for seven years straight, achieving the agricultural objective of selective cultivation without requiring *shemitta* for the whole country simultaneously. This would ensure that the land would continue to be fertile with little impact on overall production (especially if one has many fields).

From the fact that the Torah requires *shemitta* rather than crop rotation, it is clear that even if there are agricultural benefits to *shevi'it*, its message is much broader. The commentators who take issue with the Rambam focus on other elements that mark *shevi'it* as unique and significant.

Rav Yitzchak Arama: Spiritual Focus

Rav Yitzchak Arama (*Akeidat Yitzchak, Behar* 69) is adamantly opposed to explaining utilitarian crop rotation as the underlying theme of such an essential set of *mitzvot*. He focuses on the fact that disregarding *shevi'it's* laws results in a host of punishments, including national exile, arguing that it is impossible to believe that the purpose of such a *mitzvah* is for the agricultural aim of crop rotation, which will ensure the fertility of the land. If so, nonobservance would result in poor crops rather than such a harsh punishment! He presents an alternative reason:

> It seems, therefore, that the *shemitta* legislation is designed to alert us to the important truth that ownership of the land is an asset for our development towards our national

and individual spiritual goals only when such ownership is used in the way the Torah wishes it to be used.

Just as the week, with six working days plus one Shabbat, testifies to the fact that there is one Creator… *shemitta* reminds us that ownership rests with God and that we have to fulfill His commandments. Once one accepts the creation ex nihilo, it follows that the Creator is entitled to be the lawgiver. The Torah spells out that the purpose of *shemitta* is "for God" and that our function in taking advantage of the land is basically "to eat it," to fulfill our physical needs, not… our greed…

The requirement in that year to release all monetary debts is a further clear indication that material wealth must never be allowed to become an end in and of itself. The *yovel*… is a reminder to man that just as he has to return to the earth at the end of his life, so the idea of rejuvenation of the land, restoring it to its original ownership, keeps alive the idea that we ourselves are not on this earth permanently.

Rav Arama provides an explanation that unifies the theme behind the agricultural *shemitta* of the land, the financial *shemitta* of canceled loans, and the elements of *yovel* mentioned immediately after *shevi'it*, which apply after the conclusion of seven *shevi'it* cycles. In his view, the purpose of all of these elements is to make sure that man does not become overly involved in the material world, but instead views the material world as a means to a spiritual end.

Abarbanel: The Land's Expression

The Abarbanel, in his commentary on *Avot* (*Nachalat Avot* 5:11), takes issue with Rav Arama's explanation. The ideas presented in *Akeidat Yitzchak* are generally correct; one must not become overly entrenched in the physicality of the world, and a period of Shabbat, both of the week and the years, allows people to remove themselves from an endless pursuit of materialism. Nevertheless, the Abarbanel claims that this cannot be the reasoning behind *shevi'it*. Although Shabbat and *shevi'it* allow for a greater realization of the purpose of existence, any rationale for *shevi'it* must explain why it is specifically violating *shevi'it* that leads to exile from *Eretz Yisrael*.

The Abarbanel provides a fascinating alternative understanding, rooted in a more profound appreciation of the broad connection between the principles of faith expressed through the *mitzvot ha-teluyot ba-aretz* and those expressed through observing the Shabbat:

However, the truth of the matter is that the Land of Israel has within it a wonderful uniqueness and an excellent capacity for receiving the divine spark, and the supreme supervision of Divine Providence is focused in that land, unparalleled in any other land. The Sages, teaching of the greatness of the land itself, noted that God created Adam specifically from a holy place, the site of the Temple. Similarly, when He chooses Avraham, He commands him, "Go from your land…to the land that I shall show you," indicating that by virtue of being a servant of God … he must relocate himself to the place of perfection. It thus follows that this land is, by nature and by its relationship to the transcendent, chosen from among all other lands… indicating that the land itself is sacred independently of the nation dwelling in it, for which

reason most of the *mitzvot* are linked to the land, as they are part of its cultivation...
Hence, He (may He be blessed) chose and desired the Land of Israel from among all
other lands, just as the Israelite nation was chosen from among all other nations... The
Holy one, blessed is He, therefore desires that just as the entire nation commemorates
His act of creation by resting on the seventh day, affirming... the creation and
inception of the world, the chosen land [also] attests to this by being left uncultivated
in the seventh year. He thus gives the reason for the *mitzvah* of *shemitta* as, "the land
shall have a complete rest, a rest for God," meaning that the *shemitta* of the land is to
be similar to the sacred Shabbat of Israel and that this rest alludes and attests to the
Shabbat of Creation as a Shabbat for God, as He rested on it from all His labor. It is as
if this land, by virtue of its holiness and despite being unable to speak, corroborates
fundamentally that which the Israelite nation confirms with its *Shabbatot*, with the
land's testimony given in the unit of time most discernible with regard to it, i.e. a year,
due to the new produce that comes forth from it.

The Abarbanel explains the punishment for Shevi'it's nonobservance in this vein:

He thus concludes the passage describing this matter, "And the land shall not be
sold permanently, for the land is Mine, for you are sojourners and settlers with me,
and throughout the land of your heritage, you shall give the land redemption," thus
explaining that the land is not given to them on an absolute basis, because in any
event the land and that which is in it belong to God. They thus will be unable to
sell it permanently or oppress others in its cultivation, because they are sojourners
and settlers within it, and God is the master of the land. It is therefore appropriate
that they act within it as He desires and give it redemption, for if they fail to do so,
exile will come upon them, for the owner (may He be blessed) will expel them from
His land. This, then, is the meaning of, "Then the land shall enjoy its *Shabbatot*": for
the chosen land had been abused by the Children of Israel, when they withheld its
shemitta from it ... and due to all this, it is stated in the *mishna* that [violation of] the
land's *shemitta* is among those things that bring about exile.

The novelty in the Abarbanel is in the emphasis he lays upon the land as an independent
force in the *shevi'it* process.

Kli Yakar: Symbol of Faith

The Kli Yakar (*Vayikra* 25:2) quotes the earlier discussion but disagrees with the
Abarbanel. If *shevi'it*'s message is identical to that of Shabbat, what can *shevi'it* teach us
each septennial that Shabbat cannot teach us weekly? Therefore, he states:

The purpose of this *mitzvah* is to imbue Israel with the quality of faith and trust in
God, for the Holy One, blessed is He, was concerned that when they came to the land,
they would occupy themselves with agriculture, as is the natural order of things, and
when their hands produced much, they would forget God and abandon their trust
in Him, thinking that their strength and the power of their hand had made them this
wealth, that the world progresses according to its natural order; they would think that
it were their land and they its exclusive owners. God therefore wholly removes them

from the natural order of things, for it is the way of the nations in six years to have two years of planting and one year fallow, so as not to deplete its resources. Yet the Holy One, blessed is He, says, "Six years shall you plant your field"—every year—and I promise you to augment its energy so that it is not depleted. Further, there is a miracle within this miracle. Normally, when one plants for six years, even if in the sixth year its strength is not depleted, at the very least it will not increase its strength. Yet God said that in the sixth year, on the contrary, he would give it so much more strength... so much that the same crop will suffice for three years, which certainly is the greatest and most manifest miracle of all. Through all these proofs that I have demonstrated to you, know that the earth is mine. Let your eyes thus be raised to God...

The Kli Yakar explains that the lack of fulfillment of *shevi'it* represents a fundamental absence of faith, and therefore incurs expulsion from the land.

Embracing Numerous Themes

While each commentary suggests a certain underlying theme for all of the *halachot* of *shevi'it* and note difficulties with the themes championed by others, there is no reason to limit our understanding to any particular focus. Why not accept all the rationales, just without viewing them as exclusive? The seven *parashiyot* of *shevi'it* combine to present a multidimensional year – with not only one theme, but a minimum of seven!

In fact, if we try to identify which of the four types of *mitzvot* enumerated above most accurately represents *shevi'it*'s various themes, we would be hard-pressed to put our finger on any particular one.

The Rambam's first understanding focuses on the *bein adam le-chavero* aspect by noting the charitable aspects of *shemitta*, described in *Parashat Mishpatim*. He includes the *bein adam le-atzmo* focus as well, by explicating the character traits this *mitzvah* seeks to develop: "compassion and promoting the well-being of all men."

Rav Arama, explaining why *shevi'it* nonobservance results in exile, characterizes the year as a break from the endless pursuit of material gain, with a sabbatical opportunity to refocus on that which is truly important. His emphasis on the spiritual perspective one can gain is further noted by the Kli Yekar, who also offers a *bein adam la-Makom* rationale, noting how *shevi'it* observance represents the height of faith.

The Abarbanel's explanation displays a dual focus; he accentuates the shared message of Shabbat and *shevi'it*, but he also speaks of the unique nature of the Land of Israel as expressed through *shevi'it*. He characterizes the land's holiness as independent of the Jewish People; their failure to utilize the land to embody its message results in expulsion. His focus is clearly *bein adam le-artzo*.

Just as the Torah does not choose only one message, but rather presents *shevi'it* broadly, the various explanations need not be mutually exclusive. *Shevi'it* contains numerous lessons and guides us in all four areas of our existence. It provides guidance in all four fundamental dimensions of our existence: spiritual relations, *bein adam la-Makom*; interpersonal relations, *bein adam le-chavero*; character development, *bein adam le-*

atzmo; and our relationship to the land, *bein adam le-artzo.* Elaborating upon the *ta'amei ha-mitzvah* will enhance the flavors of this "tasty" *mitzvah.* We will divide *shevi'it* into seven themes that underscore the unique nature of its rest, all four *mitzvah* aspects it embodies, its connection to *Eretz Yisrael,* and its implications for the Torah's guidelines for a redeemed economy.

7 Themes for 7 Years

Theme 1: *Shevita* and Shabbat
A Year of Rest for Man and the Land

בֵּין אָדָם לַמָּקוֹם

Theme 2: *Bein Adam La-Makom*
A Year to Enhance One's Relationship to Hashem through *Emuna* and *Bitachon,* as "*Giborei Ko'ach.*"

בֵּין אָדָם לַחֲבֵרוֹ

Theme 3: *Bein Adam La-Chavero*
"And the Poor of Your Nation Will Eat": The Interpersonal Benefits of *Shevi'it*

בֵּין אָדָם לְעַצְמוֹ

Theme 4: *Bein Adam Le-Atzmo*
A Year to Build Character

בֵּין אָדָם לְארצוֹ

Theme 5: *Bein Adam Le-Artzo*
A Year to Connect to Our Land

Theme 6: Return to *Eretz Yisrael* and its Mitzvot:
Eretz Yisrael's Agricultural Rebirth Upon the Jews' Return

Theme 7: A Successful Spiritual Economy:
The Torah's System for Social Justice

Chapter 12

Theme 1: *Shevita* and Shabbat- A Year of Rest for Man and the Land

We have seen more than once that what we refer to as the *shemitta* year is at the very least also a year of *shabbat ha-aretz*, and that might even be its primary identity. This aspect of the year is repeated seven times in the beginning of *Parashat Behar* and is the focus of *shevi'it* observance being our license to reside in the land in *Parashat Bechukotai*. What is it that makes this year a year of Shabbat of the land? On the simplest level, it is a year of *shevita*, rest.

The root .ת.ב.ש, *sh.v.t.*, brings us back to the first Shabbat, where Hashem rested from creating the world. Much like the weekly Shabbat, there is no doubt that *shevi'it* requires an understanding of the role of *shevita*, personal and agricultural rest. The mere requirement of a weekly and septennial break is antithetical to modern-day thinking, but it is clearly something the Torah wants us to contemplate and put into practice. The question is: What goals does this rest hope to achieve?

While rest is often associated with refraining from something, rest can also be a constructive act with several positive benefits. Appreciating the role of rest in the weekly Shabbat will help us understand how it applies in the context of *shevi'it* as well.

Not too long ago, a five-day workweek was unheard of. The idea of refraining from work on Shabbat was novel. Struggling immigrant Jews in America faced heart-wrenching decisions weekly, as observing Shabbat meant there would be no job to return to on Sunday. Even in contemporary society, many face similar dilemmas in the winter, when Shabbat begins earlier on Friday (although, at least on paper, laws are more protective of religious needs).

Shabbat ha-aretz multiplies this resting from work considerably. Far beyond resting for a twenty-five-hour period, one rests for an entire year. For a farmer, this means a year without production. In fact, another meaning of the word *shevita* in Modern Hebrew is a strike. It almost seems as if one is "striking" from performing agricultural work for an entire year! How is that possible? How many people can fathom not working for a whole year?

Keep in mind that in the past, the majority of the workforce was involved in agriculture and farm production, while in our day and age *Shabbat ha-aretz* directly impacts only the two percent of the Israeli population that works in agriculture. Imagine a year with no farm production. Could the Jewish nation possibly support itself financially?

The Power of Rest

The Torah promises divine blessings for *shevi'it* observers, including a blessing during the sixth year (and the weekly Shabbat's blessing for the six days of the week), which assures at a minimum basic food sustenance during the years directly affected by *shevi'it*. When an entire nation takes that break at once, our "hidden partner" in the business and economy promises to pick up the slack.

Moreover, although a year of resting from normal production might seem like financial suicide in the short run, there is good reason to believe that it might actually herald economic benefits. In what might seem paradoxical, rest often ensures a refreshing look at one's activities and thus breeds success.

We live in an age where "rest" is often denigrated: "You snooze, you lose." Studies show that a quarter of office workers never leave their desks except for lunch. After all, the more time people spend doing, the more they achieve. But is that really true?

Can you think of life without weekends, summer breaks, and holidays? If we had that kind of life, would we really be more successful at achieving our academic, financial, or personal goals?

Studies have shown that people are most effective when taking breaks in the middle of their work or study. Summer vacations and shorter workweeks actually increase productivity. There are business people who have gone even further, closing their businesses for a year to rethink and re-explore – not because they had no work to do, but because they had an overabundance of it. They felt they were losing themselves in their work and were growing out of touch with their creative and spiritual selves. By taking a year off, they gave themselves many years of success, finding themselves again in the process.

Thus, taking a year off from farming may not be as financially unproductive as one might think. In an article in *Psychology Today*, author Nir Ayal explains the basic science behind breaks. The prefrontal cortex (PFC), responsible for logical thinking and executive functioning, is the thinking part of the brain. The PFC plays a central role in all thinking work, including goal-oriented activity that requires concentration. It also enables one to use willpower to avoid temptation. Understandably, giving your PFC a break allows you to keep to your goals and be more productive:

> When we work, our prefrontal cortex makes every effort to help us execute our goals. But for a challenging task that requires our sustained attention, research shows briefly taking our minds off the goal can renew and strengthen motivation later on.[40]

In other words, a little *shevita* actually increases our motivation, especially for long-term goals.

In addition, "movement breaks" are medicine for the body and soul, reducing the health dangers of long stretches of work at a desk and increasing health and productivity. Studies show that breaks also prevent "decision fatigue." When the mind is tired, people tend to procrastinate and make simplistic decisions that require the least work.

A recent study by the World Health Organization attributes hundreds of thousands of deaths a year to long working hours.[41] Besides the danger involved, psychology professor

---

40   psychologytoday.com/intl/blog/changepower/201704/how-do-work-breaks-help-your-brain-5-surprising-answers

41   sciencedirect.com/science/article/pii/S0160412021002208.

Alejandro Lleras's analysis indicates that prolonged attention to a single task actually hinders performance:

> We propose that deactivating and reactivating your goals allows you to stay focused ... From a practical standpoint, our research suggests that, when faced with long tasks (such as studying before a final exam or doing your taxes), it is best to impose brief breaks on yourself. Brief mental breaks will actually help you stay focused on your task!

These studies seem to indicate that Hashem created the human mind and body in such a manner that they are more healthy and productive when they rest. Rest **allows us to replace stress and exhaustion with productivity and creativity while engaged in our goals.**

Science writer Ferris Jabr summarizes the benefits of breaks an article in *Scientific American*:

> Downtime replenishes the brain's stores of attention and motivation, encourages productivity and creativity, and is essential to both achieve our highest levels of performance and simply form stable memories in everyday life ... Moments of respite may even be necessary to keep one's moral compass in working order and maintain a sense of self.[42]

In other words, physical and mental fatigue can mitigate our ability to make ethical decisions because we're too exhausted to remember who we are and what we value.

Over the course of 2020-2021, when the world was forced to take a rest due to the Covid-19 pandemic, the environment has been given some rest time. Satellite pictures of pollution levels before and after Covid-19 aren't even comparable. In the words of Dr. Stuart Pimm of Duke University:

> [This global pandemic] is giving us this quite extraordinary insight into just how much of a mess we humans are making of our beautiful planet. This is giving us an opportunity to magically see how much better it can be.[43]

What all these studies seem to be uncovering might be a small aspect of the beauty of our Shabbat and *shabbat ha-aretz* – a little time off to recharge our batteries and return to greater productivity. The Torah promises that the *shevita* of the *shevi'it* year will provide untold benefits to society and individuals. It is a year to deactivate to enable a much more powerful reactivation at the year's end. Maybe our difficulty understanding its need is another proof of its necessity.

From Sabbath to Sabbatical to Sabbath of the Land

But it is not only the break from one's routine that can be so important and effective; it is also the question of what one opts to do with their time.

---

42   scientificamerican.com/article/mental-downtime/

43   https://www.independent.co.uk/climate-change/news/coronavirus-lockdown-pollution-earth-day-climate-change-india-italy-us-a9477801.html

The weekly Shabbat marks the day that Hashem rested when creating the world, and it is the day that we rest from our physically creative pursuits. It is a time when we disconnect from the world around us in order to connect to bigger things – to Hashem, our family, and our community. Essentially, it is a time to do the things that our weekly routine makes difficult. Besides the leisure time, one who observes Shabbat gets to disconnect from the routine that prevents connecting to broader goals. Imagine if one could do that for an entire year!

The concept of a sabbatical, standardized in academia and some other fields, is that if we give individuals a year off to think and pursue their intellectual and other interests and dreams, they will actually be more productive. The term is a direct derivative of the rest of *shabbat ha-aretz* once every seven years, which allows for an inspiring, purposeful, and creative rest time.

But does it work beyond the field of academia?

Designer Stefan Sagmeister (known for creating album covers for famous musicians) suggests that it does. Every seven years, he closes his business down while he and his staff take a year's sabbatical. In his TED talk, he explains that his decision to take a year off to focus on personal projects was initially done to shake off staleness, but he says it actually was better financially:

> Financially, seen over the long term, it was actually successful. Because of the improved quality, we could ask for higher prices.[44]

While the sabbatical has not been embraced universally, the concept of a weekend "Shabbat" has been embraced by most countries. The seven-day workweek has been replaced by a five or six-day one, as people realize that life is not simply a race to the finish line. We can live life rather than race through it. The realization has begun to set in that time is a currency worth more than money. Many would opt for a job with lower pay but more leisure time.

Not everyone could immediately think of a project to devote oneself to for a sabbatical year. But *shevi'it* calls for a sabbatical that impacts all of agricultural society simultaneously. Since no one is working the land, the entire agrarian society moves from focusing on the crops and land to concentrating on individuals and relationships. A once-in-seven-year opportunity to give one's PFC a much-needed restart, reconnecting with long-term goals, reinforcing who one is and what they stand for, and ensuring that ethical concerns will guide decision-making.

Maximizing Society's Sabbatical

Besides the mindfulness that comes with a year that is not driven by strict deadlines or dependent on the weather or society-imposed norms, the year of rest gives the inner soul the chance to come back to life. On the simplest level, *shevi'it* guides us to take a break

---

44   https://www.ted.com/talks/stefan_sagmeister_the_power_of_time_off?language=en. Winston Chen, a computer executive, followed this advice. During that year, he took up a hobby that became the multi-million dollar company VoiceDream. In Chen's words, "The secret to success is a sabbatical in the arctic islands."

from the physical and enjoy the spiritual. The *Yerushalmi* explains that Shabbat provides ideal time for Torah study:

לֹא נִתְּנוּ שַׁבָּתוֹת וְיָמִים טוֹבִים אֶלָּא לִלְמֹד בָּהֶם תּוֹרָה.

Shabbatot and holidays were only given in order to learn Torah.
(*Yerushalmi*, Shabbat 15:3)

As we noted, *shevi'it* is integrally connected to Har Sinai. Like Shabbat, the yearly break from farming provides the opportunity for a year to reengage with Har Sinai and learn Torah. In modern-day Israel, there are a number of yearlong learning programs for farmers who let their land rest for the entire year of *shevi'it*. They describe it as a wonderful opportunity and recommend it to others.

For those who aren't involved in agriculture, connecting to the concepts of *shevi'it* rest often involves some rethinking. Rabbi Jeremy Bernstein describes how *shevi'it* should be viewed as a solution for contemporary society, rather than a problem:

> What if we looked at *shemitta* not as a problem, but as a solution, and then considered what problems it's meant to solve? In that light, *shemitta* becomes a political statement of social and environmental import, raising deep questions about the nature of a healthy and sustainable life, for individuals, society and the land.
> For instance, currently only academics have a sabbatical year. Why? Our "affluent" society actually decreases leisure and family time, as more people not only choose to work to fulfill what they want to be, but feel compelled to work in order to afford what society says they should have. Consumerism necessitates "producerism" to keep both supply and demand high. Yet as *shemitta* hints, people are indeed like the land, in ways that are more obvious in the modern world: For both, when overwork leads to exhaustion, we engineer continued "vitality" not with true renewal, but with chemicals.
> But just as silence is an integral part of speech, punctuated periods of fallowness are crucial for guaranteeing continued fertility. There's no reason why only an intellectual elite should benefit from a year of learning, reflection, and regeneration. The original sabbatical was for farmers, not physicists…
> The sabbatical principle, dictating periods of enforced restraint, rededication and redistribution, presents a compelling alternative to business as usual. Limiting the share that production and consumption have in our lives will create the space for higher pursuits. The economy must not be an engine that runs of itself, disengaged from social and environmental concerns, but a conscious expression of our spiritual and moral values. Wealth, both money and land, are not personal property to be accumulated, but divine abundance channeled through us to be shared for the benefit of all. (Dr. Jeremy Bernstein, "Stop the Machine! The Sabbatical Year Principle," *The Jerusalem Report*, May 21, 2001, p. 35) [45]

The article suggests that all of society engage in sabbaticals, using the *shevi'it* model to transform society.

---

45 The article can be found at https://www.myjewishlearning.com/article/stop-the-machine-the-sabbatical-year-principle/.

Rest During Shabbat and *Shevi'it*

Thus far, we have seen how *shevi'it's* call for *shevita* allows for a refocusing on priorities and numerous other benefits. But beyond the broad benefits of rest, the rest of Shabbat and *shevi'it* are outgrowths of a sanctified period of time.

The notion that Shabbat is a time for *shevita* is inherent in it, as that is the act the Torah attributes to Hashem during the very first Shabbat at the time of the creation of the world:

וַיְכַל אֱ-לֹהִים בַּיּוֹם הַשְּׁבִיעִי מְלַאכְתּוֹ אֲשֶׁר עָשָׂה וַיִּשְׁבֹּת בַּיּוֹם הַשְּׁבִיעִי מִכָּל מְלַאכְתּוֹ אֲשֶׁר עָשָׂה: וַיְבָרֶךְ
אֱ-לֹהִים אֶת יוֹם הַשְּׁבִיעִי וַיְקַדֵּשׁ אֹתוֹ כִּי בוֹ **שָׁבַת** מִכָּל מְלַאכְתּוֹ אֲשֶׁר בָּרָא אֱ-לֹהִים לַעֲשׂוֹת:

God completed on the seventh day the labor that He did, and He **rested** on the seventh day from all the labor that He did. And God blessed the seventh day and sanctified it, for on it He **rested** from all of the labor that God created to do. (*Bereishit* 2:2-3).

In this passage, the verb used to describe Hashem's rest is *va-yishbot*. In the first mention of the *Aseret Ha-Dibrot* in *Parashat Yitro*, the Torah uses the term *va-yanach*:

כִּי שֵׁשֶׁת יָמִים עָשָׂה ה' אֶת הַשָּׁמַיִם וְאֶת הָאָרֶץ אֶת הַיָּם וְאֶת כָּל אֲשֶׁר בָּם וַיָּנַח בַּיּוֹם הַשְּׁבִיעִי עַל כֵּן בֵּרַךְ ה'
אֶת יוֹם הַשַּׁבָּת וַיְקַדְּשֵׁהוּ:

For in six days God created the heavens and the earth, the seas and everything in them, and He **rested** on the seventh day; thus, God blessed the seventh day and sanctified it. (*Shemot* 20:11)

In two contexts in the Torah, the Torah provides a reason for Shabbat that similarly relates to rest. The first appears in the context of *shevi'it*:

שֵׁשׁ שָׁנִים תִּזְרַע אֶת אַרְצֶךָ וְאָסַפְתָּ אֶת תְּבוּאָתָהּ: וְהַשְּׁבִיעִת תִּשְׁמְטֶנָּה וּנְטַשְׁתָּהּ וְאָכְלוּ אֶבְיֹנֵי עַמֶּךָ וְיִתְרָם
תֹּאכַל חַיַּת הַשָּׂדֶה כֵּן תַּעֲשֶׂה לְכַרְמְךָ לְזֵיתֶךָ: שֵׁשֶׁת יָמִים תַּעֲשֶׂה מַעֲשֶׂיךָ וּבַיּוֹם הַשְּׁבִיעִי תִּשְׁבֹּת לְמַעַן יָנוּחַ
שׁוֹרְךָ וַחֲמֹרֶךָ וְיִנָּפֵשׁ בֶּן אֲמָתְךָ וְהַגֵּר:

And six years you shall sow your land and shall harvest its fruits. But [in] the seventh, you shall release it and let it lie fallow (*tishmetenna u-ntashtah*), and the poor of your nation will eat, and what they leave over the beasts of the field shall eat. So you shall do with your vineyard and with your olive grove. Six days you shall do your work, and on the seventh day you shall rest (*tishbot*) **in order that your ox and your donkey shall repose (*yanuach*), and your maidservant's son and the stranger shall be refreshed (*ve-yinafesh*).** (*Shemot* 23:10-12)

The goal of Shabbat, these *pesukim* tell us, is "*le-ma'an yanu'ach*" – to enable rest.

This theme is repeated in *Parashat Va-Etchanan* in the second recording of the *Aseret Ha-Dibrot* (the Ten Commandments). The Torah discusses Shabbat and explains part of its rationale as "לְמַעַן יָנוּחַ", "עַבְדְּךָ וַאֲמָתְךָ כָּמוֹךָ...וְזָכַרְתָּ כִּי עֶבֶד הָיִיתָ בְּאֶרֶץ מִצְרַיִם", "so that your servant and maidservant will rest like you... Remember that you were a slave in the land of Egypt" (*Devarim* 5:12-14).[46]

---

46 Interestingly, even this idea of rest is presented with social benefits. Rabbi Avigdor Miller (*Rav Avigdor Miller Speaks*) notes that Hashem not only rested and not only wants us to rest, but also wants our animals to rest:

Resting on the same day Hashem rested when He created the world seems to be much more significant than merely gaining the benefits of a day for mindfulness and a lighter workload and giving ourselves and our workers some time off from work.

In his masterpiece The Sabbath, Rav Aryeh Kaplan notes that the concept of Shabbat as a day of rest is usually associated with a day off from work for the weary worker, and is thereby perceived as unessential for one who isn't tired. But while a day of rest is important, the centrality the Torah attributes to Shabbat indicates that there must be more to it:

> The Commandment calls Shabbos, "*Shabbat la-Hashem,* "a Sabbath unto the Lord" (*Shemot* 20:8-11). Exactly what does this mean?
> The Commandment also tells us that our Sabbath is supposed to symbolize God's rest on the seventh day of creation. Why is this important enough to be mentioned in the Commandment?

This idea of "*shabbat la-Hashem*" is shared by both Shabbat and *shabbat ha-aretz*. Evidently, this *shevita* reflects a level of significance far beyond the practical benefits that the time off offers.

Emulating God

It is clear that the time of Shabbat is qualitatively different than other times. The Torah describes Hashem's sanctification and consecration of the seventh day. Each week's Shabbat enjoys a *kedusha,* sanctity that is an outgrowth of Hashem's original resting on that day.

Rashi provides some insight into the mindset that should accompany one which rests from his work as Shabbat arrives:

> כְּשֶׁתָּבֹא שַׁבָּת יְהֵא בְעֵינֶיךָ כְּאִלּוּ מְלַאכְתְּךָ עֲשׂוּיָה, שֶׁלֹּא תְּהַרְהֵר אַחַר מְלָאכָה
>
> When Shabbat arrives, you should feel as if all of your *melacha* has been completed and there is no need to think about your affairs. (Rashi, *Shemot* 20:9)

The Torah describes God's creation of the world as *melacha,* a word often mistranslated as work; the omnipotent and incorporeal God obviously does not "labor" at anything, and He also needs no "rest." In reality, *melacha* refers to creating and transforming in the physical realm. That is what God did while Creating the world, and that is what we refrain from on Shabbat. Our rest from *melacha* on Shabbat involves recognizing that on that day, we need not advance the world. Instead, we focus on what already exists. In this way, we imitate God, whose rest entailed ceasing to create and no longer interfering in the world. As Rav Aryeh Kaplan notes:

Hashem told us about himself so that we can emulate Him. The same way that Hashem was וַיָּנַפַשׁ , the Torah uses that term by the lower social classes as well, וְיִנָּפֵשׁ בֶּן אֲמָתְךָ וְהַגֵּר ... Shabbos teaches us that Hashem desires kindliness. Since the principle involved here is Hashem's kindliness, "Ve-zacharta ki eved hayita be-Eretz Mitzrayim" — on Shabbos we must remember that we were once slaves too. Therefore, we have to learn sympathy for the downtrodden; a Jew has the softest heart — we are rachmanim bnei rachmanim, the compassionate descendants of the compassionate. Shabbos teaches us a model of kindliness, ki chafetz chessed Hu — Hashem desires kindliness. Don't waste the opportunity; think of that great lesson on Shabbos.

During the six days of Creation, G-d asserted His mastery over the universe by actively changing it. On the Sabbath, He "rested" by no longer asserting this mastery. We emulate G-d by relinquishing our mastery over the world on the Sabbath.

A *melacha* is an act that demonstrates man's mastery due to his intelligence and skill, while rest on Shabbat entails refraining from exhibiting mastery over the world:

We must leave nature untouched. We must not demonstrate our mastery over nature, nor change it in any way. We must not intervene in the natural process. Any change or interference, no matter how trivial or small, is a violation of this rest.

On Shabbat, therefore, we not only refrain from physically tiring labors, but any "symbols of man's dominance over nature," even if they involve no difficulty at all. Since we emulate G-d's rest through our Shabbat, even the most trivial act of interference with creation may be considered *melacha* and a violation of Shabbat.

On the Seventh Day, G-d added this dimension of tranquility and harmony to the world. It was no longer in a process of change, and therefore was able to partake of G-d's serenity. As such, it became holy and blessed...The Sabbath thus brought about an integral harmony between G-d and His world. Rather than continuing to change the universe, G-d brought it into harmony with Himself.

Furthermore, God's rest on Shabbat was indicative that the world had reached a milestone. It had a purpose. Before one renews his efforts to partner with God and advance the world during the next six days of *melacha*, one should focus on what is right in the world. As Rav Yitzchak Berkovits notes:

On Shabbat we need to be able to feel the *menucha* in the Creation. *Menucha* means appreciating how life all works out, that everything is just right... We commemorate God's resting on Shabbat because that manifests that Creation is complete and perfect. Shabbat is the totality; it's the whole picture. The *menucha* of Shabbat is taking ourselves out of the world that is full of details that are difficult to understand, and putting ourselves in the totality of Creation – and realizing that it is perfect. Ultimately everything works out. The *menucha* of Shabbat is to be at peace with God, with His actions. We don't understand the answers as details, but we understand the big picture. We understand that it all fits in. Then we can relax our concerns for the issues that are troubling us, knowing that everything will work out, and enjoy the *menucha* of Shabbat. (The Jerusalem Kollel, *Bereishit* 1:31)

The *menucha* of Shabbat is the *menucha* of recognizing purposeful existence to the world. This theme adequately recognizes both Hashem's Creation of a world with purpose, as well as a world of Divine providence, recognizing Hashem's guiding hand in our everyday existence.

These ideas regarding *menucha* are reflected in certain other elements of the day. Shabbat is a day to focus on the good in the world, develop a deeper relationship with family, and provide for society as a whole - an outlook that the purpose of the world is not only to work in order to earn a living in this world, but to live a life of purpose with eternal meaning.

The Rest of *Shabbat HaAretz*

Just as the weekly Shabbat involves a tranquil outlook on the world, recognizing the need to focus on the bigger picture rather than seek out the details that can be advanced, *shevi'it* is also a *shabbat la-Hashem*. In this case, however, that phrase cannot mean that we are emulating *Hashem's* rest, as in the case of Shabbat, although it does similarly entail refraining from *melacha* and taking a break from reflecting one's mastery over the Land of Israel.

The commentaries discuss the Torah's use of the identical terminology of "*shabbat la-Hashem* with regard to both Shabbat and *shabbat ha-aretz*. Rashi (*Vayikra* 25:2) focuses on the importance of intent; both periods should be observed *li-shmah*, with pure and exclusive focus. The Ramban (ad loc.) wonders why a similar level of *li-shmah* is not demanded for other festivals and sanctified periods. The Ramban quotes mystical sources that note that both these periods testify to fundamental truths, including the divine act of creation and the promise of *Olam Ha-Ba* (the World to Come). He explains the severe punishments applied to violations of these *mitzvot* are due to their expressing fundamental tenets of our existence.

Rav Michael Rosensweig[47] elaborates on the different explanations and offers his own:

> Perhaps we should properly conclude that the Torah's unusual formulation determines that this requirement of absolute *lishmah* precisely distinguishes both Shabbat and *shemitah* from other *mitzvot*!... Shared or dual motivations are specifically rejected in these contexts for the same reason that the two *Shabbatot* are linked in the Torah, probably as sanctioning frameworks, with the creative *melachah* norm that they bound. Both *Shabbat bereishit* and *Shabbat ha-aretz* assert Hashem's absolute temporal and geographic sovereignty. For this reason, they constitute not only regular *mizvot*, but tenets of *Yahadut* as reflected in their elevated halachic status. The creative enterprise, *melachah*, is only religiously viable and certainly only spiritually meaningful when takes place in a context that unequivocally projects absolute Divine sovereignty. Only explicit acknowledgement of that awareness and an unambiguous assertion of this theme justifies, sanctions, and, then even sanctifies and elevates human effort. [48]

Both Shabbat and *shabbat ha-aretz* are "*la-Hashem*" in that they are unequivocal testimonies to divine sovereignty of the world as a whole and to *Eretz Yisrael* as Hashem's sanctified land. This intent is essential for advancing the world and the land at other times.

The Shabbat Element of *Shabbat Ha-Aretz*

The similar themes of Shabbat and *shevi'it* are so apparent that *Chazal* even entertain the possibility that there would be no need for the weekly Shabbat during the entire year of

---

47   http://www.torahweb.org/torah/2015/parsha/rros_behar.html

48   Rav Rosensweig further notes that the *Yerushalmi* (*Kilayim* 8:1) rules that the Torah's descirpiton of working the land for six years prior to resting on the seventh is an added *mitzvaht aseh* for the violation of *shemittah*: "One who does not properly acknowledge Hashem's sovereignty over the land, as reflected by his abuse of *shemittah* laws, implicitly surrenders his license to produce and create on the land at all times."

shabbat ha-aretz. Although that possibility is swiftly rejected, it is indicative of a deeper connection, at the very least in purpose, between the two.

As we have seen, what Shabbat is to the world, *shabbat ha-aretz* is to *Eretz Yisrael.* The Shabbat of the land is there to ensure that the Jewish People do not forget the spiritual elements of their land.

Moreover, the numerical aspect is also significant. The *Midrash Aggada (Behar* 25:6) notes that every number seven is significant in the eyes of God: Chanoch (who the Torah describes as "walking with G-d" (Bereishit 5: 22) was the seventh generation of humanity, Moshe Rabbeinu was the seventh generation from Avraham, Shabbat is the seventh day of the week, *shevi'it* is the seventh year, and after seven periods of seven, there is the *yovel* year, just as the Giving of the Torah occurs seven weeks after leaving Egypt.

The Ramban adds an eschatological element: The Sages describe the world as being extant for six millennia, followed by the seventh millennium – that of complete Shabbat and redemption. *Shevi'it* is a reminder of this upcoming reality.

Rav Aharon Lichtenstein summarizes this idea as follows[49]:

> *Sefer Ha-chinnuch* (84) emphasizes the point that, like Shabbat, the sabbatical year indicates God's creation of the world and negates the notion that the world had always existed. In his commentary to the Torah (*Vayikra* 25:2), the Ramban broadens this perspective. He sees the sabbatical year as a reminder and testimony not only to Creation itself, which is more the function of Shabbat, but also to what follows from it – or as he develops the idea at the beginning of the book of *Bereishit* (2:3), the nature of historical development in general. The Sabbath of *shemitta* parallels God's Sabbath and the seventh millennium … At issue here is not only the Creation, but also the continued existence of the world, and to a certain degree the nature of its existence.

Similarly, Rav Hirsch poignantly expresses the goals Shabbat and *shevi'it* share in recognizing God as the Creator of the universe and advancing a social goal:

> Just as the Shabbat year of the land establishes the nation's standing in its country, the Shabbat day establishes man's standing in the world. By observing the Shabbat, man acknowledges God as the Creator and Master of the world and of himself. On the seventh day, man refrains for exercising his own mastery over any of God's creations and humbly subordinates himself and his world to the Creator. While he observes the Shabbat, the Shabbat teaches him to respect every other creature alongside himself, as all are equal before God, and all are His children.
>
> This dismantling of man's mastery over all creatures is one of the objectives of the Shabbat, the day on which man pays homage to God, so that rest should come to the working animals and beasts of burden, and so that the son of your handmaid and the stranger in your midst shall "return to themselves," become conscious of their own human dignity, and recognize that their purpose in life is their very own.

---

49 See Rav Aharon Lichtenstein's article https://www.etzion.org.il/en/halakha/yoreh-deah/eretz-yisrael/conceptual-foundations-shemitta, where the quotes in this section are taken from.

Rav Ben-Tziyon Meir Chai Uzziel, former Sephardic Chief Rabbi of Israel, explains that to understand *shevi'it*, one must take a broad outlook on all its aspects, which indicates the following:

> The sabbatical year and the sabbatical day are connected and rooted in the same principle, each one completing the picture provided by the other one. Through its rest and holiness, the Shabbat day testifies regarding the Creator and Ruler of the world; the *shemitta* year, testifies regarding the King of the world, who created the world with kindness and compassion, as everything belongs to Him and we are fed by his goodness and compassion. All His creations on this world are opportunities for an eternal existence, as our tables are, in fact, His table, where we are His guests in order to prepare ourselves for the ultimate Shabbat while in the hallway to the World to Come. (*Michmannei Uziel*)

Shevi'it achieves these goals by imparting truths regarding God's relationship with the world and inculcating values and morals that affect one's personality. Not only does the land rest, but man rests from expressing his ownership over the land, as he renounces his proprietary rights to the produce that grows during the sabbatical year and learns more about the nature of ownership and possession. In the process, man recognizes God's mastery over the world. As the Chizkuni explains (*Vayikra* 25:2), *shevi'it* is is a *shabbat la-Hashem* because it is "a sign that the land is Mine, that it rests for the sake of My name."

Rav Aharon Lichtenstein, echoing earlier thinkers like Rav Yitzchak Arama (cited earlier), states:

> *Shemitta* detaches man from his material property and from that almost crazy idea that overcomes him the other six years of the sabbatical cycle, namely, that he must hold for dear life to his property and possessions. During the sabbatical year, we are inculcated with the idea of yielding and waiver, of detachment from the world of money and property. The *Chinnuch* noted this point and added to it the idea of *bitachon*, trust in God. During the *shemitta* year there is a sharpening of the sense of man's dependence on God, which stands at the heart of religious consciousness and experience.

Similarly, Seforno explains that the Shabbat element of *shevi'it* indicates how to spend this year. The aforementioned Yerushalmi (*Shabbat* 15:3) states, "The days of Shabbat and Festivals were only given to them to be used for Torah study." Seforno writes:

> The whole year one should be completely free of cultivation of the soil, ready to serve God, as is the case with the Shabbat of Creation... The purpose is to learn and to teach, to observe and to do. So too, all those who work on the land, when they rest in that year, should be inspired to seek God... (Seforno, *Vayikra* 25:3)

A year off from one's toil enables one to focus on that which is essential in life, preventing one from being overly entrenched in the marketplace and the endless pursuit of wealth, on the one hand, and enabling man to spend the year engaged in Torah study, on the other hand.

The efficacy of such a period of rest to reconsider one's priorities and focus on one's character is one of the all-too-necessary aspects of *Shevi'it* for contemporary society.

Va-Yinafash – Connecting to the *Neshama Yetera*

As we discussed, the Torah describes the obligation to rest on Shabbat in the context of the command of *shevi'it* in *Parashat Mishpatim* (*Shemot* 23:12). The Alshich notes that the Torah deliberately distinguishes between the term used to describe the animals' rest on Shabbat, *yanuach*, and the term used to describe humans (*va-yinafash*). While animals get a vacation, human rest should connect one with their soul, their *nefesh*. The Alshich explains that this terminology is indicative of the *neshama yetera*, the expanded soul one attains every Shabbat:

> The aspect of physical rest mentioned here applies only to "your ox and your donkey." Humans, even your non-Jewish slaves, must fulfill part of the Torah precepts, so they are to benefit from *va-yinafesh*, the additional soul. There is no need to mention again the fact that this concept applies in an even greater measure to the Jew.

Rav Hirsch describes how Shabbat and *shevi'it* share similar goals of allowing the people to recognize the Creator.

> Just as the Shabbat year of the land establishes the nation's standing in its land, the Shabbat day establishes man's standing in the world. By observing the Shabbat, man acknowledges God as the Creator and Master of the world and of himself. On the seventh day, man refrains for exercising his own mastery over any of God's creations and humbly subordinates himself and his world to the Creator. While he observes the Shabbat, the Shabbat teaches him to respect every other creature alongside himself, as all are equal before God, and all are His children.

Rav Hirsch adds that the term *va-yinafash* describes the goal of this rest:

> This dismantling of man's mastery over all creatures is one of the objectives of the Shabbat, the day on which man pays homage to God, so that rest should come to the working animals and beasts of burden, and so that the son of your handmaid and the stranger in your midst shall "return to themselves" (*ya-yinafash*), become conscious of their own human dignity, and recognize that their purpose in life is their very own. From "in order that your ox and your donkey shall repose," the *Mechilta* derives that a person has a special obligation toward his animals: not only must one leave one's animals at rest on the Shabbat, but one must also turn them out and allow them to graze undisturbed.

The term *va-yinafash*, in which the word *nefesh*, soul, is used as a verb, is found elsewhere in the Torah as well. In *Parashat Ki Tissa*, the Torah describes the covenant between Hashem and the Jewish nation regarding Shabbat:

וְשָׁמְרוּ בְנֵי יִשְׂרָאֵל אֶת הַשַּׁבָּת לַעֲשׂוֹת אֶת הַשַּׁבָּת לְדֹרֹתָם בְּרִית עוֹלָם: בֵּינִי וּבֵין בְּנֵי יִשְׂרָאֵל אוֹת הִוא לְעֹלָם כִּי שֵׁשֶׁת יָמִים עָשָׂה ה' אֶת הַשָּׁמַיִם וְאֶת הָאָרֶץ וּבַיּוֹם הַשְּׁבִיעִי שָׁבַת וַיִּנָּפַשׁ:

And *Bnei Yisrael* should observe the Shabbat, to make the Shabbat for generations, an eternal covenant. Between Me and *Bnei Yisrael* it is an eternal sign that in six days Hashem made the heavens and the earth, and on the seventh day He rested *va-yinafash*. (*Shemot* 31:16-17)

How can we say that Hashem "returned to Himself" or was "re-souled"? Rav Hirsch explains that this refers to Hashem resting and withdrawing from creation. The *Ketav VeHakabbala*, however, explains that *va-yinafash* is a reference to the world itself. After six days of creation, the creative energy rested. On the seventh day, everything created during the six days of creative activity was equipped with a *nefesh*, an abstract life force of a nature appropriate for it:

> Pay heed. Seeing that this seventh day was singled out at the time of creation, i.e. that the whole creation achieved its perfection on that day and was guaranteed eternal existence, this day has become special for us, the Jewish People. On that day more than on any other, we are apt to achieve our own spiritual potential. Our own "eternity" is bound up and dependent on that day and how we observe it.[50]

Thus, the unique term *va-yinfash* is indicative of the special power in Shabbat and its broader influence on the world at large.

An Added Soul

The Talmud (*Beitza* 16a) learns from this terminology the concept of the *neshama yetera*, an expanded soul afforded to the Jew during the weekly Shabbat:

נְשָׁמָה יְתֵירָה נוֹתֵן הַקָּדוֹשׁ בָּרוּךְ הוּא בָּאָדָם עֶרֶב שַׁבָּת וּלְמוֹצָאֵי שַׁבָּת נוֹטְלִין אוֹתָהּ הֵימֶנּוּ שֶׁנֶּאֱמַר שָׁבַת וַיִּנָּפַשׁ
כֵּיוָן שֶׁשָּׁבַת וַוי אָבְדָה נֶפֶשׁ:

The Holy One, Blessed be He, gives man an additional *neshama* on the eve of Shabbat, and at the end of Shabbat He takes it back, as it says (*Shemot* 31:17): "*shavat va-yinafash*" — once *Shabbat* ends, woe (*vai*) to the spirit (*nefesh*) that is lost.

On Shabbat, there is some sort of internal refreshment and even restoration that affects the inner part of one's personality.

But what is the nature and purpose of this expanded soul? Moreover, the terminology of the Talmud is a little confusing. On the one hand, it calls the additional soul a "*neshama*", yet it cites a *pasuk* that references the *nefesh*.

In fact, although both *nefesh* and *neshama* are terms for the soul, the fact that they are often used in different contexts indicates that they are not completely interchangeable. Both terms initially appear at the beginning of *Bereishit* in the context of the creation of man, but they are used differently:

וַיִּיצֶר ה' א-לֹהִים אֶת הָאָדָם עָפָר מִן הָאֲדָמָה וַיִּפַּח בְּאַפָּיו נִשְׁמַת חַיִּים וַיְהִי הָאָדָם לְנֶפֶשׁ חַיָּה:

God formed man out of the dust of the ground, and blew into his nostrils a breath of life (*nishmat chayim*). Man [thus] became a living creature (*nefesh chaya*). (*Bereishit*

---

50   Alshich takes this a step further and explains that the world's creation was not complete until Shabbat, as it did not
     yet have a "soul." The infusion of sanctity from Shabbat gave the universe a soul, which gives it purpose and allows
     it to continually exist.

2:7).

God blows into man a *nishmat chayim*, and he becomes a *nefesh chaya* (a term also used for animals). Based on these verses, the Kabbala teaches that the human soul, which is what differentiates humanity from the rest of the animal kingdom, actually consists of three parts.

Nefesh refers to the "animal soul" that man has contained in his blood: as the Torah says, "The spirit (*nefesh*) of the flesh is in the blood" (*Vayikra* 17:11). Since man shares many biochemical life processes with the animal kingdom, this soul is represented by the term *nefesh*. Man might have a unique *nefesh*, but the entire animal kingdom possesses some version of it.

The *neshama*, however, is unique to man; it comes directly from God's innermost Essence, His "breath." Whereas the rest of creation derived from God's speech, man's soul was derived specifically from G-d's Essence. The intermediate soul is referred to as *ruach*, the emotional part of the soul.[51]

Each one of the three elements of the soul is located in a different part of the human body. The *nefesh* resides in the blood and is therefore housed in the *kaved*, the liver. The *ruach*, the emotional part of the soul, is found in the *lev*, the heart. And the *neshama*, the pure breath of Hashem's essence, the purest part of one's soul, is housed in the *moa'ch*, the brain. These three aspects of the soul are often collectively referred to as NaRaN (*Nefesh-Ruach-Neshama*).

The three aspects of the soul interact, and the relative influence of each on every individual determines which is in charge. The ideal balance is that the *neshama* sets the lead, followed by the *ruach*, the emotional response, and influencing the *nefesh* and the physical body.[52]

The description of Shabbat as a period of *va-yinafash* underscores the unique role the soul plays on Shabbat and the expanded soul of the day. The difficulty, however, is that the term *va-yinafash* should logically be a reference to an expanded *nefesh*, rather than an expanded *neshama*. This distinction is not just semantics; it lies at the heart of the dispute among the commentators as to the nature of this expanded soul. Is it primarily a physical endowment, more suited for the term *nefesh*, or a spiritual one, more appropriate for the term *neshama*?

---

51   Rav Aryeh Kaplan (The Hadbook of Jewish Thought, Volume II) summarizes the three elements of man's soul as follows:

    The word *neshama* is a cognate of *nesheema*, which means literally "breath." *Ruach* means "wind." *Nefesh* comes from the root *nafash*, meaning "rest," as in the verse, "On the seventh day, [God] ceased work and rested (*nafash*)" (Shemot 31:17).

    God's exhaling a soul can be compared to a glassblower forming a vessel. The breath (*neshama*) first leaves his lips, travels as a wind (*ruach*) and finally comes to rest (*nefesh*) in the vessel. Of these three levels of the soul, *neshama* is therefore the highest and closes to God, while *nefesh* is that aspect of the soul residing in the body. *Ruach* stands between the two, binding man to his spiritual Source. It is for this reason that Divine Inspiration is called *Ruach HaKodesh* in Hebrew.

52   The *sefarim* refer to this interaction as an expression of מֶלֶךְ; the soul is the king of the individual, as it is guided by מוֹחַ-לֵב-כָּבֵד. On the other hand, when one's physical desires, *nefesh*, are in the driver's seat and the control of the soul is backwards, the כָּבֵד-לֵב-מוֹחַ control leads to כֶּלֶם, destruction.

Rashi (*Beitza* 16) focuses on the heightened physical elements of one's soul on Shabbat. He explains that the *neshama yetera* provides "*rochav lev* (a heightened consciousness), *menucha* (repose), *simcha* (joy), and tranquility, including the ability to eat more and not find that one's soul is disgusted by it".

In *Shitta Mekubbetzet* (*Beitza* 16), Rav Betzalel Ashkenazi explains the concept differently, noting that the added soul on Shabbat is actually a spiritual addition, "a Godly abundance and additional intelligence to be able to occupy oneself in Torah and consider the acts of God."

The *Shela* (*Masechet Sukkah Perek Ner Mitzvah*) takes issue with the understanding that the *neshama yetera* simply allows man to eat more, disputing the idea that it is rooted in the physical (although he does not mention Rashi specifically).

Several commentaries attempt to explain that Rashi really agrees that the expanded soul is a spiritual addition. Nevertheless, the simple understanding of Rashi that one's physical capabilities are expanded by the *neshama yetera* would seem to be supported by some other opinions, such as Rabbeinu Chananel (*Ta'anit* 28a) and the *Da'at Zekeinim* (*Shemot* 16:22).

In truth, a careful reading of Rashi's comments would indicate that there is an element of both a *Nefesh* and a *neshama* in this Shabbat addition, i.e., a physical component and a spiritual one. Our goal is to merge these two elements.[53] Indeed, Rashi (*Shemot* 31:17) himself (as well as Ibn Ezra) qualifies that the physical rest referred to by the term *nofesh* includes a spiritual element as well:

כְּתַרְגּוּמוֹ וְנָח, וְכָל לְשׁוֹן נֹפֶשׁ הוּא לְשׁוֹן נֶפֶשׁ, שֶׁמֵּשִׁיב נַפְשׁוֹ וּנְשִׁימָתוֹ בְּהַרְגִּיעוֹ מִטֹּרַח הַמְּלָאכָה;

Now every expression of *nofesh* (rest) is an expression of *nefesh*, for one regains one's soul and one's breath when one rests from the toil of work. (Rashi, *Shemot* 31:17)

An expanded soul (*nefesh*) enabling a heightened physical attentiveness empowers a spiritual focus of one's *neshama*. Rav Hirsch explains that this term *va-yinafash* is ideal, because *nefesh* denotes the individuality of the personality:

Therefore, *nafash* means: to withdraw into one's own personality, the opposite of outwardly directed activity. By extension, it also means: To rest after exertion, literally, "to return to oneself."

Additionally, as Rav Chanan Porat explains (*Me'at Min Ha'Or, Bereishit*), *nefesh* is a reference not only to resting from physical exertion but also to spiritual rest, which involves dreaming about achieving the purpose of existence.

The final stanza of the powerful Shabbat song *Kah Echsof*, composed by Rav Aharon the Great of Karlin, discusses the inner sublimity that one experiences on Shabbat and makes

---

53   This understanding also is fitting for the explanations of a number of commentaries on the Torah who deal with the question of how the term *vayinafash* in the *pasuk*, which seems to be a reference to God, can also be viewed as a reference to man's nature on Shabbat. They explain the term *vayinafash* as used in the Torah in reference to God as simultaneously a reference to some form of resting, which is obviously unnecessary for Hashem, and at the same time, descriptive of a heightened Shabbat soul.

reference to all three areas of one's soul. He calls Shabbat the "pleasantness of *neshamot*, the delight of *ruchot*, and the Eden of the *nefashot*."

Resting on Shabbat and setting aside daily activities allows one to find oneself, to dream about inner spiritual longings, and to recognize the deeper meaning and spiritual purpose of all of physical existence, while in possession of an expanded *nefesh, ruach* and *neshama*, as only Shabbat can provide.

The *Neshama Yetera* of *Shabbat Ha-Aretz*

There is good reason to believe that every Jew in Israel is privileged to be blessed with a similar "expanded soul" throughout the entire year of *shabbat ha-aretz*

As we noted above, the context of the Torah's reference to *"va-yinafash"* on Shabbat is a *pasuk* that immediately follows the command of *shevi'it* in *Parashat Mishpatim* (*Shemot* 23:12). Alshich understands this as a reference to the *neshama yetera* not only of Shabbat, but of *shemitta* as well:

> Should you think that the legislation is designed to give man a year's vacation, this is not so. Just as it had been decreed to abstain from work every Shabbat as a reminder of the fact that God imbued the Shabbat with sanctity already at the time of Creation, so the seventh-year legislation is also rooted in similar considerations, i.e., that both on the Shabbat and during the seventh year a person acquires an additional spiritual dimension, *neshama yetera*.

The *Sefat Emet* mentions this idea in at least three places (*Vayikra*, pp. 200, 203; *Bereishit*, p. 148), vividly describing the *neshama yetera* that accompanies the individual through the entire year of *shevi'it*. He explains that in general, the physical existence of the world has an inner spiritual power that goes beyond the limitations of the physical realm. Both the Land of Israel and Shabbat are referred to as *nachala*, which generally refers to an area with very definitive boundaries. *Eretz Yisrael* is the *nachala* without real limitation in the dimension of space, while Shabbat is its counterpart in the dimension of time. For man to appreciate this inner quality, however, he needs the proper tool, the *neshama yetera*. The residents of the Land of Israel are endowed with a special *neshama* and a unique *ruach* (*Yeshayahu* 42:5). These enable one to rise above society's materialism and recognize their inner power to merge the physical and the spiritual and sanctify their existence even beyond the period of Shabbat.

This is this unique opportunity that the *neshama yetera* of *shevi'it* provides through an entire year of *shabbat ha-aretz*. The fact that *shemitta* provides a *neshama yetera* for the Jew for an entire year allows its impact to be life-altering rather than temporary. Rav Kook (Introduction, *Shabbat Ha-Aretz*) makes reference to the question of how a septennial escape from routine will be sufficient to impact society every year:

> In this year, the divine character of the nation will be revealed in its complete glory, in its Godly, spiritual, core. This illumination, which comes once every seven years, will carry an afterglow of divine ideals that will gradually shape our ethical characters, with a slow refining of our souls in a way that will continue to deepen and control

> their place in life, until the outlook on life which stems from it will become more and more entrenched in our actions; until a more extended, significant period will come, which will succeed in not only raising up individuals, and not even the entire generation, but all the generations of the nation.

Rav Kook continues by describing this ideal as a central aspect of *yovel*, which is not only supposed to impact one generation, but the entire metaphysical stature of the nation as a whole, vertically as well as horizontally.

Rav Kook's Perspective

In his introduction to *Shabbat Ha-Aretz*, Rav Kook explores the role of *shemitta* in transforming Jewish life in Israel on a fundamental plane. Rav Kook does not deny the practical role that *shevi'it* can play in helping refocus one's energies, but he notes that as thinking Jews, we must try to look more deeply:

> What makes the Jewish nation special is that it looks at all of life through the illuminating lens of holiness. With all its life force, it recognizes that life is worthwhile only if it is infused with the Divine, and life lacking the Divine is worthless...
> The potential of the nation, the Divine good which is embedded in it... cannot be actualized within mundane life. Such life, with its constant chaos, hides the spiritual glory of the Divine soul... The urgency of developing and enhancing life needs to be actualized by taking a break and getting a rest from the chaos of normal life.

After this introduction, Rav Kook identifies how both Shabbat and *shevi'it* allow for an escape from the mundane:

> *Shemitta* accomplishes for the nation what Shabbat accomplishes for the individual. This nation has a special need... Periodically, it needs to have the Divine light within it revealed in all its splendor.
> This light must not be suppressed by daily mundane life – with all its toil and worries, anger and competition – so that the purity of its collective soul can be revealed within it...

Rav Kook speaks in similar terms as Seforno, but his focus is not only on the ability to spend time learning Torah, but on reconnecting to the purpose of a nation tasked with the challenge of merging the physical and the spiritual.

Rav Kook describes the natural good of the world and the Jewish nation that often finds difficulty expressing itself, and even finding itself, amidst the secular realities of existence:

> This national treasure (*segula*) that is imprinted deep within us, the image of a world that is good, upright, and godly – aligned with peace, justice, grace, and courage, all filled with a pervasive divine perspective that rests in the spirit of the people – cannot be actualized within a way of life that is purely businesslike. Such a life, full of frenetic action, veils the glory of the divine soul, and the soul's clear light is blocked from shining through the overpowering mundane reality. The impulsive push toward growth and self-realization needs space to come to fruition, by stopping the routine and awakening, while shaking off the wildness of daily life.

Shabbat serves the role of creating the medium for every individual to take one day a week off his weekly routine and to invest it with spirituality:

> The individual is able to shake off the secular mundane routine of life frequently once a week, for "when Shabbat comes, repose comes" (Rashi, *Bereishit* 2:2). The soul begins to be freed from its harsh chains, as "God has given you rest from your sorrow and trouble, and from the hard service that you were made to serve" (*Yeshayahu* 14:3), and [the soul] seeks more elevated pathways of spiritual desires, consonant with is nature spiritual core... [Shabbat is] a holy day, on which the innate inclination of the people for a godly life emerges in each individual, as a sign for the nation that it possesses a treasure (*segula*) in its soul, and has a need and an ability to rejoice in God, in the pleasure of the divine.

Rav Kook writes that this concept is reflected in the idea of the *neshama yetera,* the extra soul granted on Shabbat. The *"segula"* is in the soul of the nation and its ability to rejoice through the spiritual. This is concentrated and gathered into the spiritual point of the *neshama yetera,* which dwells within each and every individual. With this in mind, Rav Kook explains his initial comment: That which Shabbat does for the individual, *shemitta* does for the collective nation:

> The same effect which Shabbat brings about upon the individual, *shemitta* brings about upon the nation as a whole. There is a special need for this nation, in which the Godly creative force is deeply implanted in its essence, in a distinct manner, to periodically reveal its Godly light with its full illuminating intensity, in a manner in which the secular and mundane climate of society, with all its toil, anxiety, anger and competition, won't entirely suffocate the creative force of the nation; but it will be able to reveal [through *shemitta*] the pure collective soul [of the nation] as it truly is.

Rav Kook continues by describing the tension of recognizing one's inner spiritual core amidst involvement in the day-to-day pressure of the marketplace. The challenges that face one involved in the mundane aspects of existence can also rob him of his morality and connection to his spiritual core, if he is not given a system of checks and balances.

> The once-a-week individual Shabbat and the once-every-seven-years national *shevi'it* are built into the fabric of time, to allow the nation the reprieve that will enable it to appreciate its core and learn how to exhibit the moral teachings of the Torah in a mundane reality that militates against it. The land and its spiritual character must express itself in the merging of the physical and spiritual, not with the corruption of either or both.

For this reason, *shevi'it* is referred to as *shabbat ha-aretz,* and much like the weekly Shabbat, it is a *shabbat la-Hashem.*

In Rav Kook's conceptualization of *shabbat ha-aretz* is not only an opportunity for the nation to engage its spiritual core; it also has specific applicability to the land. As we have mentioned, the Land of Israel is not only the homeland of the Jewish People, but it is also where the nation is supposed to establish a government that serves as the foundation for God's throne in the world. *Shevi'it* is necessary for both the nation and the land:

The *segula* of the land and the *segula* of the nation complement each other. Just as the nation is unique in its aptitude to reach spiritual heights from the depths of its everyday life, so too, the land, God's land, prepares the nation who dwells in it as an everlasting inheritance, which comes with a covenant and an oath, with faith in the eternity of Israel, founded upon Godly nature, which is immovably infused in this glorious land, married to the nation which God chose as His *segula*. The soul of the nation and the land together act to bring about the foundation of their existence; they demand their purpose: to actualize their potential and holy longings in this sabbatical year.

This is a mutual relationship, in which each needs the other:

The nation impacts upon the land with its soul-force, while the arm of God is revealed through its spiritual influence; and that land, too, impacts upon the people, refining their character in line with the desire for a complete spiritual life, which is inherent in their makeup.

Rav Kook describes the atmosphere that this unique reality of the *shemitta* year brings:

A year of quiet and serenity, during which there are no tyrants or taskmasters: "he shall not exact from his friend or his brother, because the time of release for God has arrived" (*Devarim* 15:2). A year of equality and relaxation, of expansion of the soul in the expanse of the upright of God who sustains the living with kindness. There is no individual private property, nor are there exclusive rights rigorously guarded; rather the Godly peace pervades all that possesses a soul...

Rav Kook goes on to explain how the laws of *shemitta* enable this reality, something we will keenly feel as we analyze the *halachot* in section III.

The End, Beginning, or Middle?

The outlook we have presented allows us to view Shabbat and *shevi'it* as both launching points and destinations. Rav Aharon Lichtenstein notes that the sabbatical element of *shevi'it* can be expressed on two different planes, just as Shabbat can be seen as the beginning of the week or as its culmination:

Shabbat serves the weekdays, while the days of the week also lead up to Shabbat (in the sense of "a taste of the world-to-come" and "a day that will be all Sabbath and rest in life everlasting"). In *Bereishit*, the *Rishonim* dispute the meaning of *"shevita,"* rest. On the one hand, *shevita* denotes resting today with the intention of returning to work tomorrow – a sort of recess. According to this, the *shevita* of Shabbat is necessary to enhance the next days' work...
The two understandings of *Shabbat* are reflected in this disagreement. And perhaps we can see these two aspects alluded to in the two rationales: "And God ended" (*va-yekhal*), which sets *Shabbat* as the pinnacle of creation. "And He rested" (*va-yishbot*), a temporary recess."

Rav Lichtenstein continues by explaining how the parallelism between Shabbat and *shemitta* carries through all these aspects:

> There is a dialectical relationship between Shabbat and the weekdays; Shabbat enhances the mundane weekdays, refreshes man, and recharges his batteries, but, on the other hand, weekday activity is performed for the sake of those Divine spiritual values which Shabbat symbolizes and represents. This dialectical relationship applies to the sabbatical year as well. On the one hand, the sabbatical year allows repose, a year of solemn rest. On the other hand, the *shemitta* year parallels the seventh millennium, God's rest. It is not an introduction to the six years that will follow in the next cycle, but rather a year toward whose values of spiritual awakening and uplifting man must always stride…
>
> Regarding the rest and repose of Shabbat, we find a parallel in *shemitta*: what we may not do, from what we are liberated, over what we must elevate ourselves. But what aspect of *shemitta* parallels the positive content of Shabbat? What do we do; with what do we occupy ourselves; on what plane do we act? Here there is a certain halachic vacuum.

Rav Lichtenstein continues that this is the meaning of Rav Kook's statement that the same effect which Shabbat has on the individual, *shemitta* has on the nation as a whole, as it allows "its Divine light to reveal itself in its full splendor, so that the mundane life of society with its burdens and worries not extinguish it … so that the purity of its soul in its entirety be able to reveal itself within it." Based on this, Rav Lichtenstein concludes:

> If we accept this transition from the individual to the collective, we can view *shemitta* as attempting to create an ideal society. In the society of the *shemitta* year, equality reigns, produce has no owners, there is no employer and no employee, but rather all share the same status. Such a society acquires new and revolutionary qualities that can change the nature of that society, at least during the *shemitta* period.

The *shemitta* year should be seen, then, not only as a rest stop along the way to the years that will follow, but also as an existence of a different nature within a society that is headed as a whole toward the actualization of a grand and exalted moral idea.

This Shabbat element of shemitta gives it its quality as a year that can transform society and refocus energies on what is really the ultimate goal. With that in mind, there is good reason to believe that many of the ways in which we fall short of the vision that Rav Kook had for the nation upon its return to the land may be rooted in our lack of connection to the observance of the Shabbat elements of *shevi'it*.

Summary
The first theme of *shevi'it* relates to it being a year of rest. We noted the various benefits of rest from one's routine and workload, and we emphasized that Shabbat rest goes far beyond. It emulates Hashem's rest from the creation of the world and reflects an ability to refrain from expressing mastery and to take in the tranquil beauty and purpose of God's world. It reflects recognition of God's total mastery over Creation and *Eretz Yisrael*. The rest for humans is far more than the physical rest enjoyed by animals, as it entails *va-yinafash*, a heightened soul indicative of a *neshama yetera* one possesses for an entire year of *shabbat ha-aretz*.

Chapter 13

Theme 2: *Bein Adam LaMakom*: A Year to Enhance One's Relationship to Hashem through *Emuna* and *Bitachon*, as *Giborei Ko'ach*

Many of the elements of *shevi'it* that we already discussed clearly reflect *shevi'it*'s role in deepening one's relationship with Hashem. That is certainly a central element of *shevi'it*'s place as a *shabbat la-Hashem*, as we discussed regarding the first theme. However, there are additional elements that become readily apparent through many sources.

For the Land is Mine: A Lesson of *Emuna*

The Talmud presents a rationale for *shevi'it* based on a *pasuk* in *Parashat Behar*:

וְהָאָרֶץ לֹא תִמָּכֵר לִצְמִתֻת כִּי לִי הָאָרֶץ כִּי גֵרִים וְתוֹשָׁבִים אַתֶּם עִמָּדִי:

The land shall not be sold permanently, for the land in mine, for you are strangers and residents with Me. (*Vayikra* 25:23)

אָמַר הקב"ה לְיִשְׂרָאֵל זִרְעוּ שֵׁשׁ וְהַשְׁמִיטוּ שֶׁבַע כְּדֵי שֶׁתֵּדְעוּ שֶׁהָאָרֶץ שֶׁלִּי הִיא.

God said to Israel: Plant for six years and let it lie fallow the seventh, so that you will know that the land is Mine. (*Sanhedrin* 39a)

A number of commentators interpret this passage as defining *shevi'it* as a year that will allow one to properly recognize God's hand in one's prosperity. Thus, Rashi explains:

So that your heart will not grow haughty with the prosperity of your land, leading you to forget the yoke of his kingship. (Rashi, *Sanhedrin* 39a, s.v. *Kedei*)

Shevi'it teaches us that even if one works the land and makes it yield fruit, he must always recall that he is not its owner; it belongs to God. In other words, the Gemara seems *shevi'it*'s central motif involves ingraining *emuna* (faith) into the nation.

Emuna, of course, is not a septennial message; rather, it should transform one's outlook and behavior throughout the other years as well, enabling one to recognize God's place in Creation and in the continued existence and sustenance of the world. The *Sefer Ha-Chinuch* explains that imparting *emuna* is the basis of *shevi'it*:

At the root of this precept lies the purpose of establishing in our heart and setting in our thoughts a firm conception of the doctrine that the world was brought into being as a new entity, *ex nihilo*: "For in six days God made the heavens and the earth," and on the seventh day, when He created nothing, He himself is described as "resting." Thus, it serves to remove, uproot, and extirpate from our thinking any concept of the world's timelessness and eternity, in which those who deny the Torah believe. Such a belief would destroy every corner of the Torah and demolish every wall; therefore, the obligation was imposed on us to spend our entire time, day by day, year by year, counting six and resting on the seventh… so that it not depart from our mind…

For this reason, God commanded us to leave free and ownerless all that the land yields this year, so that a man will remember that the land that grows produce for him every year does not do so by its own power and ability, for both the land and its lord have a Master over them, and when He so desires it, He commands him to leave his produce ownerless. (*Sefer Ha-Chinuch, mitzvah 84*)

Rav Shaul Yisraeli adds that this is the primary message of "*ki li ha-aretz*, "the land is mine," as *shevi'it* makes it clear to all that it is God's land and testifies that even if man possesses land, the true master and controller of its growth, is God, its Creator:

The demand that private property be voided this year has no justification and can have no validity without the explanation "for all the earth is mine" (*Shemot* 19:5). The earth is not ours; neither is the power to produce: "The earth and all in it belong to God, civilization and those dwelling therein" (*Tehillim* 24:1). We are His and have given of what is His. One who fulfills this *mitzvah* returns ownership to Him who gave it to him. He thus proclaims his recognition of the mastery and sovereignty of the Master of the World, in theory and in practice. Only one who wholly believes can have the strength to fulfill this *mitzvah* in its entirety. This is his test! (*Shemitta Through the Ages*)

Many commentaries explain that it is for this very reason that *shevi'it* is referred to as a *shabbat*. Just as Shabbat testifies to God's creation, so does *shemitta* (Mizrahi, *Vayikra* 25:2; see Abarbanel cited in Theme 1). Some explain (Malbim, *Vayikra* 25:4) that just as man and his animals rest every Shabbat, the land should have stopped growing on Shabbat. Nevertheless, to maintain the natural order, the *shabbat* of the land was moved to the seventh year, when for an entire year, the land has its Shabbat rest.

Similarly, several Midrashic sources explain the severe punishments for *shevi'it* violations are due to *shevi'it* representing *emuna*. Violating *shevi'it* is akin to denying God. The Torat Kohanim states:

"אָז תִּרְצֶה הָאָרֶץ אֶת שַׁבְּתֹתֶיהָ" אֲנִי אָמַרְתִּי לָכֶם שָׁתְהוּ זוֹרְעִים שֵׁשׁ וּמַשְׁמְטִים לִי אֶחָת, בִּשְׁבִיל שֶׁתֵּדְעוּ שֶׁהָאָרֶץ שֶׁלִּי הִיא וְאַתֶּם לֹא עֲשִׂיתֶם כֵּן, אֶלָּא עָמְדוּ וְגָלוּ מִמֶּנָּה וְהִיא תִּשְׁמֵט מֵאֵילֶיהָ כֹּל שְׁמִיטִים שֶׁהִיא חַיֶּבֶת לִי:

I told you to sow for six years and let it rest for me for one year, to impress upon you that the land is mine. But you failed to do so. Get up and be exiled therefrom, and the soil will earn the rest due to it on account of all the Sabbatical years that it owes me! (*Torat Kohanim, Bechukotai* 2, 7)

Similarly, in the *Midrash Aggada*:

וְכָל כָּךְ לְמָה, לְפִי שֶׁהוּא כוֹפֵר בָּעִקָּר, שֶׁהֲרֵי אָמַר הַקָּדוֹשׁ בָּרוּךְ הוּא כִּי לִי (כָּל) הָאָרֶץ (וַיִּקְרָא כ"ה כ"ג), זַרְעוּ שֵׁשׁ וְהַשְׁמִיטוּ שֶׁבַע, כְּדֵי שֶׁתֵּדְעוּ כִּי הָאָרֶץ שֶׁלִּי:

Why so much [emphasis on the failure to observe *shevi'it*]? Because one [who fails to observe this] denies the essential One, for the Holy One, blessed is He, said, "For the land is Mine" (*Vayikra* 25:23): plant six [years] and relinquish in the seventh so that you know that the land is Mine. (*Midrash Aggada (Buber), Parashat Bechukotai* 26:43)

One who doesn't observe *shevi'it* is like one who denies God, as its observance is a testament to the recognition of God's role in all prosperity, especially that of the Holy Land. Indeed the *pesukim* themselves, stressing *"For the Land is Mine"*, indicate the year's opportunity for deepening one's connection with God.

Shevi'it and *Bitachon*

The opportunities that *shevi'it* provides to deepen one's relationship with God are manifold. The opinions cited above focus on the element of *emuna*, often translated as faith or belief in God, but more properly defined as steadfast knowledge and an unwavering commitment to God.[54] Yet, *emuna* alone, despite its importance, is insufficient. *Emuna* is the untested knowledge and recognition of God, but *shevi'it* also entails a very practical test of whether one will rise to the occasion under the challenging circumstances that *shevi'it* presents. This entails a different concept, known as *bitachon*.

The *Chazon Ish* distinguishes between *emuna* and *bitachon*:

> *Emuna* and *bitachon* are one and the same; however, *emuna* is the general approach of a believing person, and *bitachon* is one's personal practical approach, with *emuna* being the theory and *bitachon* being the practice. It is easy to trust at times when the need to trust doesn't play an important part in one's decisions; but it is much more difficult to have trust at times when it is indeed called for. It is easy to speak of trust when it is just in theory and not in practice; at times like that, a person is just enjoying beautiful and pleasurable dreams; as time goes on, he fools himself and others into thinking that he indeed possesses greater trust in God than his peers, when the reality is that he is using this attribute to make his dreams of an unknown future more pleasant. (*Emuna U-Vitachon*)

In other words, *emuna* is the philosophy and *bitachon* is the practice. The Chazon Ish continues by stating that the real test of one's relationship with God occurs when challenging situations arise that demand reliance on God; then, one must either rise to the occasion or come up with excuses in the process.

The connection between *shevi'it* and *bitachon* emerges explicitly from the *pesukim* in *Parashat Behar*, which refer to dwelling securely in the Land of Israel as a consequence of fulfilling its *mitzvot*:

> וַעֲשִׂיתֶם אֶת חֻקֹּתַי וְאֶת מִשְׁפָּטַי תִּשְׁמְרוּ וַעֲשִׂיתֶם אֹתָם וִישַׁבְתֶּם עַל הָאָרֶץ לָבֶטַח: וְנָתְנָה הָאָרֶץ פִּרְיָהּ וַאֲכַלְתֶּם
> לָשֹׂבַע וִישַׁבְתֶּם לָבֶטַח עָלֶיהָ:
>
> You shall perform my statutes, keep my ordinances and perform them; then you will live on the land securely (*la-vetach*). And the land will then yield its fruit and you will eat to satiety, and live upon it securely (*la-vetach*). (*Vayikra* 25:18-19)

---

54   See http://vbm-torah.org/archive/chavero3/29chavero.htm, where we analyze the intent and meaning of the term *emuna*.

The word *la-vetach* means "securely," but it shares its root with the word *bitachon*, trust and reliance on God, feeling secure due to the knowledge of His control. In fact, in the following verse, after discussing the fear one might have regarding what he will have to eat, the Torah goes out of its way to invoke *bitachon* through the blessing promised during the sixth year:

> וְכִי תֹאמְרוּ מַה נֹּאכַל בַּשָּׁנָה הַשְּׁבִיעִת הֵן לֹא נִזְרָע וְלֹא נֶאֱסֹף אֶת תְּבוּאָתֵנוּ: וְצִוִּיתִי אֶת בִּרְכָתִי לָכֶם בַּשָּׁנָה
> הַשִּׁשִּׁית וְעָשָׂת אֶת הַתְּבוּאָה לִשְׁלֹשׁ הַשָּׁנִים:

And if you should say, "What will we eat in the seventh year? We will not sow, and we will not gather in our produce!" I will command my blessing for you in the sixth year, and it will yield produce for three years. (Ibid. 20-21)

The trust that God will provide for one's needs even if one does not plant or cultivate his field is a prime expression of *bitachon*. The Torah – which so often calls for man to do his utmost and actively seek to improve his lot rather than rely on Divine promise – seems to diverge from its standard message as it calls upon man to refrain from worrying about what he will eat during *shevi'it*.

The *Sefer Ha-Chinuch* points out that this lesson in *bitachon* is one of *shevi'it*'s fundamental lessons:

> Yet another useful benefit to be found in this is that man increases *bitachon* in God. For any man who finds it in his heart to give and leave free, ownerless for all the world, all the produce grown by his lands and the inheritance of his fathers for one whole year, he and his family become trained in this for all their lives; then neither the quality of miserliness nor a lessening of *bitachon* in God will ever seize hold of him. (Sefer Ha-Chinuch, *mitzvah* 84)

By refraining from planting for a year, one recognizes the need to depend on God. However, the goal is not simply to rely on God when in a foxhole and in times of difficulty. One should come to recognize at all times that God is the provider.

Rav Tzvi Hirsch Kalischer (*Sefer Ha-Berit, Behar*) presents a number of rationales for *shevi'it*, one of which is very much connected to this ideal:

> It teaches us to have confidence in the Almighty, for the eyes of God are on us from the beginning of the year until the end of it. And this is the meaning of "Blessed is the man who puts his trust in God." If we desist from work, God will invoke a blessing for him for those three years. Cursed will be one who places no trust in God. He will be brought to selling his goods and eventually to selling himself to a stranger… In this way, he will accustom himself to trusting in God and believing in His providential care over every detail, since the steps of man are established firmly by God.

Shevi'it not only teaches *emuna*, but gives one the opportunity to put it into practice, indicating that its importance lies in imparting the dual essential truths of *emuna* and *bitachon*. One should emerge from *shevi'it* with a fortified understanding of God's place in the world, both in theory and in practice.

The *Meshech Chochma* (*Vayikra* 25:2) writes that the recognition of God's *hashgacha* is a major element in *shemitta*. Indeed, God's providing three years' worth of produce in the sixth year would be reason enough for the *mitzvot* of *shevi'it*, as it indicates that the Jewish People live miraculously, expressing God's providence over the entire world.

The Netziv (*Ha'amek Davar, Shemot* 34:23) goes one step further, noting that *shevi'it* is what enables the realization of the distinction between God's *hashgacha* (providence) in the Land of Israel and His providence in the Diaspora. Only in the Land of Israel can one live such a supernatural existence:

> During the seventh year, God's amazing providence on behalf of the Jewish People is apparent to all. In the other years of the harvest, the distinction between providence in the Land of Israel and other countries is not clear; however, during the seventh year, an entire year without harvesting, it would be impossible for other nations of the world to survive. It is only God who lets them prosper.

Shevi'it is indicative of the special providence that is unique to the Jewish nation in the Land of Israel. Recognizing this reality allows for greater *bitachon* for those residing in the land of Israel.

Relying on Divine Providence

In order to better appreciate *shevi'it*'s influence on our *bitachon*, we need a working definition of the term. What exactly does *bitachon* call for? Does trust in God require the conviction that performing *mitzvot* will always result in easily recognizable divine goodwill? Or does *bitachon* call for a different perspective?

A central reason for the confusion regarding the proper definition of *bitachon* is rooted in what seem to be conflicting messages regarding the proper balance of *bitachon* and *hishtadlut* (active attempts to improve one's lot). On the one hand, the Talmud (*Pesachim* 64b) seems to state that it is improper, if not forbidden, to rely on miracles, yet throughout *Tanach* we find constant recognition of the need to trust in God. Although the exact parameters of *bitachon* are beyond our purview, two basic approaches are worth noting.

One understanding of *bitachon* defines the terms as the certainty that God stands at one's side and has the power to assist him. Some interpreted the words of Rabbeinu Bachya ben Asher (a disciple of the Rashba) as insinuating such an approach:

> The matter of *bitachon* in God was explained by the saintly Rabbeinu Yonah to mean that a person ought to accept wholeheartedly that everything is within the power of Heaven. God can overrule the laws of nature and change a person's fortune, and though a situation may appear to be hopeless, divine intervention can change that reality in an instant. God's salvation is close at hand, for He is omnipotent. Even if a sword rests on a person's neck, he should not imagine that salvation is impossible...
> (*Kad Ha-Kemach, Bitachon*, s.v. *Inyan*)

A more explicit understanding of *bitachon* as advocating an "all will work out for the best" approach appears in Rabbeinu Bachya ibn Pakuda's *Chovot Ha-levavot*, who defines the essence of *bitachon* as:

the peace of mind of the one who trusts, that the one upon whom he relies [whether God or man] will do the best and the most appropriate for him in the matter... The main definition of *bitachon* is that one's heart should believe that the one relied upon will fulfill what he has promised and do good on his behalf, not out of obligation but out of kindness and mercy. (*Sha'ar Ha-bittachon*, chap. 1)

The *Chazon Ish*, however, categorically rejects those who expand the understanding of *bitachon* to include the conviction that God will always assist to bring about the good desired outcome:

...An old error has become rooted in the hearts of many concerning the concept of *bitachon*. *Bitachon*... has come to mean that a person is obligated to believe that whenever he is presented with two possible outcomes, one good and one not, then certainly it will turn out for the good. And if he has doubts and fears the worst, this constitutes a lack of trust. (*Emuna U-vitachon*, beginning of chapter 2)

The *Chazon Ish* continues by criticizing this approach and offering another:

This view of *bitachon* is incorrect, for as long as the future outcome has not been clarified through prophecy, the outcome has not been decided, for who can truly know God's judgments and providence? Rather, *bitachon* means realizing that there are no coincidences in the world, and that whatever happens under the sun is a function of God's decree.[55]

No matter which understanding of *bitachon* we adopt, it surely refers to recognizing divine providence. God is in the picture, and all that happens comes from God. One must undoubtedly rely on Him at all times, especially when the Torah tells us to do so.

What is especially interesting is that according to the *Chazon Ish*'s understanding of *bitachon*, the observance of *shevi'it* calls for something that is not usually required. Beyond the confidence that whatever outcome happens due to the challenging observance is ordained by God, man is instructed not to worry about what he will have to eat, as God **will certainly** take care of him. This reflects the initial approach to *bitachon* that the *Chazon Ish* generally rejects. Financially, economically, and practically, *shevi'it* defies rational reasoning, but farmers and citizens are nevertheless asked to forgo logical business practices for a year. This testifies to one's reliance on God and one's conviction that there

---

55 The *Kad Ha-kemach*, as well, continues by offering an additional element of *bitachon*:
    Also included in the matter of trust is that a person must surrender his soul to God, and should constantly occupy his thoughts with this matter: If brigands should come to kill him or to force him to abrogate the Torah, he should prefer to give up his life rather than go against the Torah. Concerning this, David said, "To You, God, I shall offer up my soul" (*Tehillim* 25:1), and it further states, "My God, in You I have trusted, let me not be disgraced" (ibid. 2). One who gives up his life under such circumstances has performed an act of bittachon.
    As Rav Lichtenstein points out, the two approaches to bitachon have completely different meanings. The second approach is far less popular as it implies a demand much more than a promise: "It does not attempt to scatter the clouds of misfortune, try to raise expectations, or strive to whitewash a dark future. It does not claim that "It will all work out for the best," either individually or nationally. On the contrary, it expresses a steadfast commitment— even if the outcome will be bad, we will remain reliant on and connected to God. We will remain faithful until the end and shall not exchange our trust in God for dependence on man. This approach does not claim that God will remain at our side; rather, it asks us to remain at His side" (*Bitachon: Trust in God*).

is *hashgacha*, Divine providence.

The unique level of *bitachon* necessary for *shevi'it* observance is expressed powerfully by Rav Berel Wein, who explains why *shevi'it* serves as a test:

> The difficulty inherent in the observance of the *mitzvah* of *shemitta* is apparent to all. The Torah itself addresses the issue by saying that one should not be deterred from *shemitta* observance by the obvious impracticality of the *mitzvah*. Thus, *shemitta*, unlike many other *mitzvot*, becomes a test of belief and faith. The Torah, which otherwise adamantly dictates a practical approach to life, here demands a leap of faith and an abandonment of the everyday practicalities of living.

After comparing *shevi'it* observance to *akeidat Yitzchak*, the Binding of Yitzchak, Rabbi Wein writes:

> This correlation between the *akeida* and *shemitta* can help us understand why it is the *mitzvah* of *shemitta*, over and above any other *mitzvah*, that was chosen to represent the divinity of Torah from Sinai. For to all of us today, Sinai is a matter of faith. It is a belief that our ancestors were not liars, that their transmission of the Torah and its values was correct in form and in interpretation, and that the standards of behavior outlined in the Torah are of an eternal nature. For many in the Jewish world, that is a tall order of belief to demand. The modern world is long on narcissistic pleasure and short on faith and sacrifice. But without faith, without a feeling of the spiritual and supernatural, life is a very scary place and experience.[56]

Shevi'it's call for embracing *bitachon* through an extreme divergence from the normal mode of living might be a necessary upheaval. Without *shevi'it*, many people might develop the perspective that nature takes its course and God's Hand is, at most, behind the scenes, rarely openly expressing itself. One without *bitachon* often finds it challenging to avoid agonizing over everything. His entire existence is fraught with constant worry.

Thus, as Rav Yisraeli writes, the Torah addresses the natural concern that one will not have enough to eat with a unique promise:

> In addition to the generosity that this *mitzvah* demands of one, there is the need for a tremendous measure of faith in God's day-to-day providence... There is here a promise that providence will manifest itself in a way that is not natural, as the commentators have explained well... A blessing that comes especially in this year is not by any means to be understood as natural; this is a manifest display of providence. Nonetheless, in order to merit this heavenly blessing, it is necessary to be strong and first to become full of the trait of fearless faith that the blessing will indeed be sent in this year... (*Shemitta* Through the Ages)

Rav Yisraeli reiterates that *shevi'it* is not a problem, but a test of faith:

> We thus learn that any planning, even if pursued within the guidelines of *Halacha*, that takes advantage of agricultural experience and scientific accomplishment to "solve," as it were, the "problem" of *shemitta* stands in opposition to that very *mitzvah*,

---

56   http://www.torah.org/learning/rabbiwein/5760/behar.html

its objective, and its spirit. *Shemitta* is not a "problem" given to us to surmount obliquely. The Holy One, Blessed is He, does not treat His creatures despotically, and His aim is not to burden Israel needlessly. It is an invaluable test, the test of faith and of conviction. Simultaneously, it is a tool of supreme providence that serves to bring about its indubitable manifestation in our world. All the artfulness, all the plans made to reduce or void the practical difficulties that the *mitzvah* puts before a man of Israel, brings to naught the principle aim of this *mitzvah*—and this is not the will of the Torah. This is the aspect of the *mitzvah* between man and God. (ibid.)

Shevi'it observance imparts *emuna* and *bitachon* through its extreme nature; it is a test of faith. The difficulty of observing *shevi'it* is an integral part of its message. It is a trial year, a year of *nisayon*.

The purpose of a *nisayon* is not for God to test man, as God knows man's capabilities. Rather, it is an opportunity for man to raise his banner (*nes*) and witness his capabilities. Will he observe the *mitzvot*, or will he forgo the opportunities and look for loopholes to circumvent obligations? Individuals are enabled to raise a new banner and achieve things they never realized they were capable of doing.

Giborei Ko'ach

Shevi'it's role in imparting *emuna* and *bitachon* in God to the Jewish People is clear. What is especially interesting is that the *mitzvot* of *shevi'it* achieve these lofty spiritual messages through a system that is very demanding and highly challenging. The Sages were well aware of the challenges involved in *shevi'it* observance, characterizing those who observe *shevi'it* without complaint as "*giborei ko'ach*," "mighty in strength," based on a *pasuk* in *Tehillim*:

בָּרְכוּ ה' מַלְאָכָיו גִּבֹּרֵי כֹחַ עֹשֵׂי דְבָרוֹ לִשְׁמֹעַ בְּקוֹל דְּבָרוֹ:

Bless God, you angels of His, you mighty in strength (*gibborei ko'ach*), who fulfill His word, hearkening to the sound of His word. (*Tehillim* 103:20)

The Midrash explains why *shevi'it* requires such *gevura*:

"גִּבֹּרֵי כֹחַ עֹשֵׂי דְבָרוֹ" בַּמֶּה הַכָּתוּב מְדַבֵּר א"ר יִצְחָק בְּשׁוֹמְרֵי שְׁבִיעִית הַכָּתוּב מְדַבֵּר, בַּנֹּהַג שֶׁבָּעוֹלָם אָדָם עוֹשֶׂה מִצְוָה לְיוֹם א' לְשַׁבָּת אֶחָת לְחֹדֶשׁ א' שֶׁמָּא לִשְׁאָר יְמוֹת הַשָּׁנָה וְדִין חַמֵּי חַקְלָה בְּיֵרָה כַּרְמֵיהּ בַּיָרָה וְיָהֲבֵי אַרְנוֹנָא וְשָׁתֵּיק יֵשׁ לָךְ גִּבּוֹר גָּדוֹל מִזֶּה?

"The mighty in strength who fulfill His word" –To whom does the verse refer? Rabbi Yitzchak said: To those who are willing to observe the sabbatical year. In the way of the world, a man may be willing to observe a commandment for a day, a week, a month, but is he capable of doing so for an entire year? But throughout this year, this person sees his field fallow, his vineyard fallow; this mighty man sees his field declared ownerless, his fences broken down, but he pays his taxes without saying a word. Can you conceive a person mightier than he? (*Vayikra Rabba* 1:1)

Observing *shevi'it* requires angelic patience and strength of character for an extended period. The *midrash* extols the virtue of silence displayed by one who may not necessarily comprehend the need to allow his field to lay fallow but who nevertheless abides by the *mitzvot* of *shevi'it*.

The *midrash* goes on to quote Rav Huna's view that the verse in *Tehillim* refers to the Jewish People's angelic declaration at Mount Sinai, "*Na'aseh ve-nishma*," "We will do and we will listen" (*Shemot* 24:7). The Talmud explains that both the angels and the people put these two terms – *asiya* (doing, fulfilling, acting) and *shemia* (listening, hearing, hearkening) – in that order:

בְּשָׁעָה שֶׁהִקְדִּימוּ יִשְׂרָאֵל "נַעֲשֶׂה" לְ"נִשְׁמָע" יָצְתָה בַּת קוֹל וְאָמְרָה לָהֶן: מִי גִּלָּה לְבָנַי רָז זֶה שֶׁמַּלְאֲכֵי הַשָּׁרֵת מִשְׁתַּמְּשִׁין בּוֹ? דִּכְתִיב: "בָּרְכוּ ה' מַלְאָכָיו גִּבֹּרֵי כֹחַ עֹשֵׂי דְבָרוֹ לִשְׁמֹעַ בְּקוֹל דְּבָרוֹ" – בְּרֵישָׁא "עֹשֵׂי", וַהֲדַר "לִשְׁמֹעַ".

When the Jewish People [at Sinai] gave precedence to "We will do" (*na'aseh*) over "we will listen" (*nishma*), a Heavenly voice went out and said: "Who has taught them this [heavenly] secret that the angels use, as it is stated: 'Bless God, you angels of His, you mighty in strength, who fulfill His word, hearkening to the sound of His word.' At first they do, and then they listen." (*Shabbat* 88b)

As we have seen, there is a deep connection between *shevi'it* and Sinai. Therefore, the title *giborei ko'ach* fits both those who rise to the occasion of *shevi'it* observance and those who accept the Torah. Additionally, the Gemara might be illustrating that *shevi'it* observance essentially involves *na'aseh v'nishma*. The powerful declaration of the nation at Sinai that "we will do and we will hear" indicates that they are willing to fulfill God's commandments (do) even before they understand their logic (hear). A *shevi'it* observer who can't fully understand the logic behind leaving all of Israel's fields fallow every seven years, yet does his duty

Gevura and *Ko'ach*

Although the terms *gevura* (might) and *ko'ach* (strength) are often used interchangeably, they are distinct attributes. In fact, in the morning liturgy, we recite two different blessings associated with these qualities, one for each: "אוֹזֵר יִשְׂרָאֵל בִּגְבוּרָה," "Who girds Yisrael with *gevura*," and, " הַנּוֹתֵן לַיָּעֵף כֹּחַ," "Who gives the faint *ko'ach*."

Rav Joseph B. Soloveitchik distinguishes between these two terms. *Ko'ach*, he explains, is the power to move forward and conquer. This notion is readily understandable to modern man, who is used to viewing the conqueror as the victor, but this trait can also be found in animals. The *mishna* provides a different explanation for identifying a *gibor*:

אֵיזֶהוּ גְּבּוֹר? הַכּוֹבֵשׁ אֶת יִצְרוֹ.

Who is a *gibor*? One who conquers his desire. (*Avot* 4:1)

This desire, *yetzer*, represents the natural urges that one possesses. The *gibor* expresses his *gevura* by being able to overcome these urges and conquer his innate desires. *Gevura* consists primarily of the capacity to withdraw, to overcome oneself, to purge or to purify one's existence. For a more lofty cause, the *gibor* can hold back and stop. Thus, Rav Soloveitchik writes that *gevura* may more accurately be rendered as "heroism."

Rav Soloveitchik adds that this is the defining element of the Torah's view of heroic action.

The title *"gibbor"* does not go to the strongest, but rather to one driven by a calling, with the inner strength to live within self-imposed limits:

> This Jewish concept of heroism is so significant because it doesn't only express itself in a moment of victory, but throughout one's life.
>
> It is perhaps the central motif in our existential experience. It pervades the human mind steadily, and imparts to man a strange feeling of tranquility. The heroic person, according to our view, does not succumb to frenzy or excitement. Biblical heroism is not ecstatic but rather contemplative; not loud but hushed; not dramatic or spectacular but mute. The individual, instead of undertaking heroic action sporadically, lives constantly as a hero. (*Catharsis,* p. 42)

In a similar manner, Rav Soloveitchik defines *ko'ach* as power, a physical force shared by man and beast, and *gevura* as something found only among humans:

> The hero is not the one who is physically strong, but the one possessed of the quality of heroism… Heroism means to fight even when the chances of victory are slim, when reason advises capitulation because logically the battle seems lost. Heroism implies doing the paradoxical, the absurd. (*The Rav Speaks,* p. 102)

Rising to the occasion, defying logic and chance, is heroism, and Rabbi Soloveitchik identifies this heroism as the defining characteristic of a Jew. Rav Soloveitchik goes on to describe the heroic aspects of Jewish existence in the modern world, which includes primarily the ability to observe *mitzvot.* Doing so often involves overcoming one's natural, instinctive driving force to act rashly, choosing to act heroically instead.

Based upon this definition, *gevura* is the ability to express true heroism, along with the power to ignore insults. This entails a lifelong pursuit of the composure to answer to a higher calling.

This understanding of *gevura* is undoubtedly relevant for the *shevi'it* observer's heroic behavior. The real heroes are the farmers who withstand the daily challenge of watching their fields under-produce for an entire year, those who have the inner conviction to be able to rely on God with the *emuna* and *bitachon* that *shevi'it* requires and boosts. *Shevi'it* reshapes one's perspective on God's role in the world and one's everyday sustenance, while allowing one to work on himself until he can relinquish his feelings of ownership and abide by the will of God.[57]

The *Ko'ach* Element

The ability to heroically accept the challenges of *shevi'it* without complaint requires *ko'ach* as well. In a different essay, Rabbi Soloveitchik makes reference to the *pasuk* in *Yeshayahu:*

---

57   It is also understandable why our Sages extol as *gibborim* those who are silent in the face of verbal attack, who hear and listen rather than act and respond:
   Those who are humiliated, but do not humiliate; who hear their disgrace, but do not reply; who act out of love and rejoice amidst suffering – of them, Scripture says (*Shofetim* 5:31): "But those who love Him are like the sun rising in its might." (*Shabbat* 88b)
   The ability to be silent and continue to do what is incumbent upon him is the mark of a true *gibor.*

וְקוֹיֵ ה' יַחֲלִיפוּ כֹחַ יַעֲלוּ אֵבֶר כַּנְּשָׁרִים יָרוּצוּ וְלֹא יִיגָעוּ יֵלְכוּ וְלֹא יִיעָפוּ:

But they that wait for God shall renew their strength; they shall mount up with wings as eagles; they shall run and not be weary; they shall walk and not be faint. (*Yeshayahu* 40: 31)

A connection to God enables one to renew one's *ko'ach*, strength, by preventing him from being weary or faint. Rav Soloveitchik distinguishes between these two terms. *Ayefut*, faintness, grows out of failure and unsuccessful effort. *Yegia*, weariness, in contrast, is the result of seeing the blessing in one's work, which brings one to contentment. It involves the recognition of having succeeded at being fruitful and creative.

יְגִיעַ כַּפֶּיךָ כִּי תֹאכֵל אַשְׁרֶיךָ וְטוֹב לָךְ:

When you eat the weariness of your hands, you shall be happy and it will be well with you. (*Tehillim* 128:2)

Although weary, one sees blessing in his actions and is content with his accomplishments.

Each of these moods- faintness and weariness- are dangerous. Faintness may bring about feelings of despair and hopelessness, while weariness might grow into self-satisfaction and self-righteousness. The blessing described in the verses in *Yeshayahu* states that those who wait for God will be girded with the *ko'ach* to prevent the negative effects of either mindset. They will be successful, yet they will not become intoxicated by their achievements. They will recognize that they must continue their efforts, which are endless, but at those points when they experience setbacks and difficulties, they will not allow faintness, despair, or frustration to overcome them.

Ko'ach is the strength that pushes one forward against adversity or complacency. The *giborim* are able to withstand the intellectual challenge of *shevi'it*, but they need *ko'ach* to absorb *shevi'it*'s values. These dual values express themselves in formidable times, enabling one to summon the power to weather the challenges. However, they are required after succeeding as well, lest one feel overly proud of one's *shevi'it* accomplishments. In the midst of contentedness, there is a danger of losing sight of the values of this lifelong struggle for *gevura*. One of *shevi'it*'s gifts is a lifelong ability to balance *ko'ach* and *gevura*, one of the necessary tenets of Torah observance, and the terms appropriately distinguishing our nation which accepted the Torah while declaring *na'aseh v'nishma*.

The Power of These Messages

It is not surprising that the financially revolutionary concepts of *shevi'it* and *yovel* have convinced some individuals of the Torah's veracity. The founder and Chairman of the Board of IDT Corp., In his 2006 book, I'm Not the Boss, I Just Work Here, Howard Jonas relates how these messages personally transformed his life. He describes his search for meaning in existence, which he began to find through reading the Torah. Many of the laws inspired him, as he writes, but one, in particular, transformed him and convinced him to transform his life:

But there was one law that blew me away and made me into an observant Jew. At the age of 17, this one law literally made me change my life, simply because, once I discovered it, I had to concede that the Bible was the work of Divine genius.

Once every 50 years, in what is known as the *Yovel* (jubilee) year, all farmland (that is, the means of production in an agrarian society) must revert to its original owner's family. This meant that no matter how destitute or without hope a person might be, once every 50 years -- at least once in the average lifetime -- that person would have the means of production, the opportunity to rise to any level, placed back in his own hands. It took over 3,000 years for ideas like that to resurface in the form of the Homestead Act (which, in 1862, allowed anyone to claim land as theirs if they had worked it or lived there for at least five years), the GI Bill (which, beginning in 1944, provided education and training for millions of veterans) and, of course, public education (which provides free education to all children).

But this biblical law of the jubilee year guaranteed opportunity to every member of society. It wasn't just a redistribution of wealth, because gold, art, houses, even palatial residences in walled cities didn't revert. It was the *opportunity* that the land represented for independence, self-sufficiency and self-betterment that was redistributed. Prices of such land were always calculated taking this 50-year cycle into account.

In this jubilee year, the ram's horn would be sounded and liberty would be proclaimed to all the inhabitants of the land therein. Do you know where these inspiring words are inscribed today? On the Liberty Bell in Philadelphia. Makes you think, huh?

It sure made me think. When I discovered these biblical laws, I was simply astonished. What a perfect compromise between pure *laissez faire* economics and wealth redistribution strategies, which just lead to a welfare-state cycle of dependence.

But who was it who had thought of all this? Could it be Divine wisdom? Or maybe, to be more precise, a Divine decree? (*I'm Not the Boss, I Just Work Here*)

The powerful message of *emuna* and *bitachon* that emerges from *shemitta* and *yovel* should not only impact the farmer, but anyone who reads the Torah. Anyone who ponders these laws can distinctly recognize that they were not the invention of humans. Only God could be capable of ordaining such laws; clearly, then, there is good reason for them.

Sanctifying Time

Another *bein adam la-Makom* element of *shevi'it* relates to the element of *kedushat zeman*, the sanctification of time. As we saw in Theme 1, *shevi'it* provides the opportunity for a rest and recess from the harrying world we live in, in which man races against the clock. But in addition to the element of setting aside a year of *shabbat*, *shevi'it* acknowledges that rest time must be dedicated to a higher purpose, and not simply to vacation and physical rest.

The concept of rest for the sake of taking it easy just to be lazy, while often championed in our day and age, is generally antithetical to the Torah. Under normal circumstances, the Torah champions work and accomplishment. Whenever the Torah mentions a *mitzvah* of Shabbat, either regarding the weekly Shabbat or *shevi'it*, the Torah always precedes the *mitzvah* with a description of the preceding work: "Six days you shall labor," "Six years you shall plant," etc. The *midrash* views the work of the other six days as an obligation:

> In the same way that Israel was commanded concerning the Shabbat, so in the same way were they commanded regarding performing work [for the six days]. (*Mechilta de-Rabbi Shimon bar Yochai, Shemot* 23)

The *mishna* (*Avot* 1:10) teaches, "Love work," and *Avot De-Rabbi Natan* explains why:

> מְלַמֵּד שֶׁיְּהֵא אָדָם אוֹהֵב אֶת הַמְּלָאכָה וְאַל יִהְיֶה [אָדָם] שׂוֹנֵא אֶת הַמְּלָאכָה שֶׁכְּשֵׁם שֶׁהַתּוֹרָה נִתְּנָה בַּבְּרִית כָּךְ הַמְּלָאכָה נִתְּנָה בַּבְּרִית שֶׁנֶּאֱמַר שֵׁשֶׁת יָמִים תַּעֲבֹד וְעָשִׂיתָ כָּל מְלַאכְתֶּךָ וְיוֹם הַשְּׁבִיעִי שַׁבָּת לַה' א-לֹהֶיךָ
>
> It teaches us that a man should love work, for just as the Torah was bestowed with a covenant, so too work was bestowed with a covenant, as it is written: "Six days shall you … do all your labor, and on the seventh shall be a Sabbath for Lord your God." (*Avot De-Rabbi Natan* 1:11)

Furthermore, the *mishna* decries those who waste their time:

> רַבִּי חֲנִינָא בֶן חֲכִינַאי אוֹמֵר, הַנֵּעוֹר בַּלַּיְלָה וְהַמְהַלֵּךְ בַּדֶּרֶךְ יְחִידִי וְהַמְפַנֶּה לִבּוֹ לְבַטָּלָה, הֲרֵי זֶה מִתְחַיֵּב בְּנַפְשׁוֹ:
>
> Rabbi Chanina the son of Chachinai would say: One who stays awake at night or travels alone on the road and turns his heart to idleness, has forfeited his life. (*Avot* 3:4)

The *mishna's* harsh language, whether it is to be taken literally or not, is a clear indication of the Jewish outlook on the work ethic and proper use of time.

If so, how can one take a full year off?

Shevi'it teaches us that besides the devastation of wasted time, there is also a problem with occupying one's time with work, work, work in a manner that will cause one to lose sight of the purpose of his toil and of existence altogether.

The Abarbanel notes that time is man's most important commodity, and wasting it is therefore nothing short of destructive behavior:

> It is appropriate that wholesome people be more concerned with loss of their time than with loss of all possessions and money that they have, for the days of one's life form the path on which one walks to attain his perfection … In order that one always keep this in mind, divine wisdom saw fit to awaken him through its *mitzvot* to the brevity of his days and his limited lifespan.
>
> Thus, the Torah states that the Creator created His world in seven days, so that one who is alive may take note that the days of his years total seventy years; therefore, he must not spend them in vain, but performing deeds which the Creator has mandated. Then, on the seventh day, he may rest and repose in the spiritual world.
>
> There also are many sevens in the Torah that serve as a reminder of this … all for the purpose of reminding us that the days of our years total seventy years...
>
> Indeed, for this very reason, He (may He be blessed) issued the commandments of *shemitta* and *yovel*, for in the *shemitta* [cycle], there are six years of cultivating the land, and the seventh year is one of comprehensive rest, which serves to awaken us and inculcate that the span of one's years totals seventy. For fifty years after childhood,

he is a powerful man, owner of the land; accordingly, he plants his field and prunes his vineyard and gathers his produce. However, in the seventh year, which alludes to the final decade of his life, it is not appropriate that he work any longer, for he has reached his limit; whether he resides in the domain of old age or in that of the grave. Thus, "the land shall have a complete rest" and "a rest for God," because then the soul adheres to its Creator and abandons physical pursuits. Indeed, the purpose of the law of *shemitta* is that one may recall that the days of his life are numbered...

Time for the Important Things in Life

The *mitzvot* of *shevi'it* directly impact the farmer's life and livelihood by restricting what he can do in the field. While every limiting aspect has a unique purpose and message, there also seems to be a liberating element of all of the *mitzvot* together. When the farmer relies on God to provide for his needs, he is free to occupy himself with other matters—possibly even critical matters that are often overlooked. This rest allows time to focus on what is important in life.

As we saw in our discussion of Theme 1, *shevi'it* provides an opportunity to transfer our focus from physical, corporeal concerns, preventing the darkness of materialism from pervading. Furthermore, *shevi'it* offers the opportunity to reconnect with Sinai and renew one's dedication to Torah learning. We saw above the midrashic analogy between *shevi'it* observance and the *"na'aseh ve-nishma"* declaration. *Shevi'it* is a year of returning to the Mount Sinai experience, culminating with *Hakhel*, a reenactment of the communal acceptance of the Torah.

The Seforno explains that the Shabbat element of *shevi'it* further indicates how one should spend this year:

The whole year one should be completely free of cultivation of the soil, ready to serve God, as is the case with the Shabbat of Creation… The purpose is to learn and to teach, to observe and to do. So too, all those who work on the land, when they rest in that year, should be inspired to seek God … (Seforno, *Vayikra* 25:3)

Similarly, Rav Tzvi Hirsch Kalischer identifies resting from work for spiritual gain as part of the rationale for *shevi'it*:

Yet another reason: In order that they should not always be preoccupied with working the soil to provide for their material needs. For in this one year, they will be completely free. The liberation from the yoke of work gives them the opportunity to study Torah and wisdom. The unlettered will be occupied with crafts and building and supplying these needs in the Land of Israel. Those endowed with special skills will invent new methods in this free time for the benefit of the world. Whoever is endowed with the knowledge of the Torah will occupy himself with Torah and the fear of God, for in this lies the true happiness.

Summary

While the farmer is faced with the challenges of shevi'it's agricultural limitations, he is afforded the opportunity to grow in *emuna* and *bitachon*, a wonderful opportunity for strengthening one's relationship *bein adam la-Makom*. The challenges one endures throughout the year help one employ both *ko'ach* and *gevura*. *A proper balance* entitles shevi'it observers to be crowned as *gibborei ko'ach*, heroes mighty in strength, the ideal appellation applied to the Jewish nation when declaring *na'aseh v'nishma* at Har Sinai. Every seven years, the free time afforded to the farmer is used for a year of spiritual focus, dedicated to Torah learning, a year of Har Sinai.

While non-farmers lack the intense trials of the agricultural sector, they experience some of the challenges as consumers and, at times, as garden owners. What one purchases during the year, how one tends to one's garden are decisions that underscore the opportunities of all to rise in their own way to the calling of *gibborei ko'ach*[58].

---

58   These issues will be discussed in later chapters.

Chapter 14

Theme 3: *Bein Adam LaChavero* - "And the Poor of Your Nation Will Eat": The Interpersonal Benefits of *Shevi'it*

We have seen that the *bein adam la-Makom* aspects of *shevi'it* are primarily rooted in the presentation of *shevi'it* that appears in *Parashat Behar*, where *shevi'it* is characterized as a year of *shabbat la-Hashem*. While these elements are pivotal to *shevi'it* and play a primary role in the various agricultural *mitzvot* of the year, the description in *Parashat Mishpatim* is far different. Rather than focusing on a year dedicated to God, that description highlights the social and interpersonal aspects of *sheviit*, highlighting another dimension of the year's message.

Independent of *Parashat Mishpatim*'s description of the social aspects of agricultural *shevi'it*, at least two other *parashiyot* also focus on interpersonal aspects of this year: the financial *shemitta* involving the canceling of loans at the end of the year discussed in *Parashat Re'eh*, as well as the freeing of slaves and returning of land described in *Parashat Behar* in the context of *yovel*, after seven series of *shevi'it* cycles. Other interpersonal messages are detectable in the other passages as well. As we will see, *shevi'it*'s interpersonal message is so extreme that it only makes sense if divinely ordained.

A Radical Form of Charity

When *shevi'it* is introduced for the first time in *Parashat Mishpatim*, the Torah is very explicit that those who stand to gain are the poor:

> וְהַשְּׁבִיעִת תִּשְׁמְטֶנָּה וּנְטַשְׁתָּהּ וְאָכְלוּ אֶבְיֹנֵי עַמֶּךָ וְיִתְרָם תֹּאכַל חַיַּת הַשָּׂדֶה כֵּן תַּעֲשֶׂה לְכַרְמְךָ לְזֵיתֶךָ:
>
> But [in] the seventh you shall release it (*tishmetenna*) and let it lie fallow (*u-ntashtah*), **and the poor of your nation will eat**, and what they leave over the beasts of the field shall eat. So you shall do with your vineyard and with your olive grove. (*Shemot* 23:10-11)

"*Tishmetenna*" requires owners of the field to relinquish their hold and possession over the produce growing in their fields, essentially abandoning ownership of all they own. The poor are then free to partake of all produce growing in the land.

The benefits to the poor, so explicit in the *pasuk*, are highlighted by the Rambam, who mentions the compassion to the needy as the first reason for *shevi'it*. However, it is essential to point out that the benefit to the poor from *shemitta* far surpasses the right to eat the produce. The concept of charity and gifts to the poor lies at the heart of the Jewish mission; the Torah tells us that Avraham educated his progeny with the ideals of "*tzedaka u-mishpat*" (*Bereishit* 18:19). However, the kindness involved in the laws of *shevi'it* far exceeds any standard form of *tzedaka*.

The *midrash* notes several merciful elements of the sabbatical year:

> How much compassion is there in the acts of *shemitta*! First, [compassion] upon the land, in order that the land may rest for one year, and find water and sun, in order that it be strong for the following year. Second, compassion upon the owners of the field, who are spared a year of hard work in the field. Third, compassion upon the animals, who are freed from their work. Fourth, compassion upon all mankind, as even the servant and maidservant and every worker cannot be refused to eat from one's produce, and they become like him [the owner]. Fifth, compassion upon the animals, who can eat whatever they want from one's field. Sixth, compassion upon Jews whose loans cannot be forcibly collected in that year. (*Pitaron Torah*, *Behar*-p. 96)

The *midrash* describes the laws of *shevi'it* as being rooted in compassion – enabling man and animal to be free from working the field and giving equal produce access to owners, workers, and animals. This form of *tzedaka* goes well beyond routine charitable giving, as the farmer shares ownership with those who don't have any land at all. As the *midrash* puts it, "they become like him."

Shevi'it's unique form of "giving" allows for a host of interpersonal messages, affecting the outlook of the farmer and the perspective of the recipient and in the process unifying an often-splintered nation and providing a remedy for the unequal distribution of wealth.

An Equalizing Factor

The *pesukim* explicitly state there should be no distinction between the property owner and others, who have equal rights to the fields' produce. In fact, the *pesukim* in *Mishpatim* (unlike those in *Behar*) seem to suggest that the owners have no rights to the produce at all, as they only mention that "the poor of your nation will eat, and what they leave over the beasts of the field shall eat." The landowners bear no special privilege in comparison to those who lack territory. It seems according to *Parashat Mishpatim* that the poor are the sole owners of the produce, and they, as opposed to the landowners, enjoy exclusive rights to them. Although *Chazal* note that a deeper appreciation of the *pesukim* indicates that all individuals share equal rights in the produce, the Torah's formulation certainly emphasizes that the poor benefit in place of the actual owners.

Not only does *shevi'it* function as a charitable *mitzvah*, but it does so in a way that educates the attitude one should display to the less fortunate. One doesn't "give" to the poor, as all take equally. The Torah equalizes the perspectives of the haves and have-nots.

A number of the *halachot* that apply to landowners reinforce this perspective, including some that appear in *Parashat Behar*. For instance, one is not allowed to harvest one's crop as he usually would. The Torah states:

> אֶת סְפִיחַ קְצִירְךָ לֹא תִקְצוֹר וְאֶת עִנְּבֵי נְזִירֶךָ לֹא תִבְצֹר שְׁנַת שַׁבָּתוֹן יִהְיֶה לָאָרֶץ:
>
> You shall not reap the after-growth of your harvest nor gather the grapes of your untrimmed vines; it shall be a year of complete rest for the land. (*Vayikra* 25:5)

This *pasuk* cannot be interpreted as an outright restriction on harvesting altogether, as the Torah explicitly states that the *shevi'it* produce is to be eaten. Rashi cites *Chazal's* explanation:

> "You shall not reap" as if to hold onto it, as you would with other produce; rather, it must be abandoned for all to take. (Rashi, *Vayikra* 25:5)

Rashi explains that the Torah informs us that the owner cannot express his ownership over the produce during *shevi'it* by reaping it for his family or commercial purposes. During the *shemitta* year, his job is to abandon it and recognize that all have equal access to that which grows.

An equal right to the agricultural yield acts as a tremendous equalizing factor, precipitating unparalleled unity. The social castes and societal standings often used to characterize individuals and separate them based on earnings and property become meaningless and insignificant for an entire year. The wealthy landowner does not give, but rather shares, possessing no more rights than others. All take; no one gives.

The Right to Receive

Besides teaching us the importance of sharing, *shevi'it* also educates us regarding our perspective on receiving from others on at least two levels.

First, it addresses the proud pauper who does not want to take from others. Several *pesukim* praise individual enterprise, such as: "When you eat the weariness of your hands, you shall be happy, and it will be well with you" (*Tehillim* 128:2); and "He who hates gifts, shall live" (*Mishlei* 15:27). Those in need often don't want to receive from others. *Shevi'it* allows the individual in need to recognize that, at times, taking from another's property doesn't involve "receiving" from them, as God declares all to be equal properties in the fields' yield.

Additionally, the Torah wants even the wealthy landowners who may own thousands of acres, to recognize that they eat during *shevi'it* by the same rights as the poor, landless paupers. Everyone receives from God. Wealthy individuals who recognize that even they are not completely self-sufficient can begin to appreciate that everyone has what to gain and receive from other members of society.

Rav Tzvi Hirsch Kalischer notes this equalizing factor as one of *shevi'it's* primary motivations:

> It teaches us further that the rich should not lord it over the poor. Accordingly, the Torah ordains that all should be equal during the seventh year; both the rich and the poor have equal access to the gardens and fields to eat their full. (*Sefer Ha-Berit, Behar*)

The *Sefat Emet* adds that this allows for the unity that underscores the Har Sinai experience:

> The *mitzvah* of *shemitta* allows for the achievement of unity, in which the hands of the wealthy and needy are equal. This is why *shemitta* is taught at Sinai, as through

shemitta, unity — the attribute of the acceptance of the Torah — is awakened by the Jewish people's singular Torah. (*Sefat Emet, Behar*)

Rav Zevin explains this giving attitude:

Shemitta advocates such a kind of relationship with one's fellow man to the extent that every single living being, man and beast included, is equal in the right to make use of the food. No other nation has ever reached such a high plane, and even we cannot find this in any other *mitzvah.* (*Shemitta , Sinai* 5719)

Eradicating Poverty

The benefits to society go far beyond the lessons that the needy and the wealthy can glean from *shevi'it*. Rav Chayim David Ha-Levi, former Chief Rabbi of Tel Aviv, explains how *shevi'it,* along with other agricultural *mitzvot* that benefit the poor, actually seek to eradicate poverty as much as possible:

In general, the law of *shemitta* is inherently linked to numerous other *mitzvot* that were designated to give to the Jewish nation and to its state financial stability, by ensuring the stability of the poorer members of society... Suppose for whatever reason a poor man lost hold of his land. In that case, he is able to sustain himself by collecting the agricultural gifts of the poor, including gleaning, forgotten sheaves, the corner of the field and the poor man's tithe, and also through the *mitzvah* of *tzedaka*... If he needs a loan, he can get a free loan... And in the seventh year, the poor man is freed from any financial worries, as he can take any vegetation growing for the benefit of his family. And if he failed to repay all his debts, the end of the *shemitta* year comes and does so for him... And if even this doesn't work and he must sell his land — and in the worst case, he sells himself as a slave — the *yovel* year comes and frees all slaves and returns all land to its ancestral holders. At that point, everyone can begin their financial life anew. (*Mekor Chayim*, ch. 5, *Shemittat Kesafim*)

Rav Shaul Yisraeli illustrates that the various economic aspects of *shevi'it* seek not only to give pride to the poor "recipient," but also to alleviate his financial instability and provide him with the ability to start again:

Let us now turn our attention to this *mitzvah* in its full scope and comprehensiveness. First, the social aspect of the *mitzvah* stands out. That the lands rests entails putting to rest private proprietary rights to all fruits of this year... If, during the six years of labor, class-based disparities have come about and taken root, they are null and void for this year. The master has no more right than the servant, the native no more than the sojourner; even the social disparities that generally develop with economic classes dissipate, as it were, for this year; moreover, they are muted going forward.

Rav Yisraeli adds that *shevi'it*'s economic interpersonal message affects both the rich and poor's attitudes to wealth. The *mitzvah* to lend money ensures that deep economic and class differences won't remain in place for long:

Firstly, the Torah prohibits keeping money inert like some unmovable rock if someone is in need of it at any time; you bear an ongoing obligation to lend it to him, and this loan must be made gratis. The Torah, after all, prohibits interest with the full force of law and with quite a number of admonitions to the borrower, the creditor, and the witnesses. Yet the Torah does not make do with that; in addition to *shemitta* of the land and renouncing ownership of produce comes the *mitzvah* of relinquishing debts, by which all debts not collected by the end of the *shemitta* year expire and cease to be subject to collection.

He goes on to explain how extreme this *mitzvah* is, especially in light of all the *mitzvot* mandating honesty in business:

The money which has accumulated in a person's possession is thus his own money, and he has achieved it conscientiously and with much effort — and now you require him to lend it to his fellow gratis! He does this wholeheartedly; he does not demand any part of the profit that this money may bring his fellow. There is just one thought that gnaws at his heart, just one thing that he would assure himself: that he will in fact be returned his money — his own money, without any sort of profit. He merely seeks that his fellow not profit from his toils and travails and give back nothing. Our natural course of thought would tend to side with him entirely. Yet the Torah does not think thusly: it would be "contemptible" for such a thought to cross one's mind. It demands geniality and kindheartedness of you when the loan is given, despite your knowledge that it is to be lost.

With this in mind, it is understandable how *shevi'it* presents the recipe for a financial revolution:

One who walks in the way of the Torah, who observes this *mitzvah* once admonished severely regarding it — no less than regarding any other *mitzvah* — will effect a complete social revolution that quietly and peacefully, in one fell swoop, voids the economic and social disparities that have occupied human society since time immemorial. With the conclusion of the *shemitta* year, the whole nation's course of work and creativity begins anew, in a state where all people have virtually the same means at their disposal.

Rav Yisraeli concludes that the *mitzvah* of *yovel* once every fifty years seals this interpersonal economic message:

And if this is still not enough, since the tool that is the *mitzvah* of relinquishing debt can be implemented for cash in hand but not for money invested in real estate, where conspicuous disparities remain between the one who has succeeded in concentrating land under his ownership and the other who has been compelled to sell his, the *mitzvah* of *yovel* comes, and every person returns to his inheritance and family. All transactions that might have concentrated land under the ownership of a few while another social stratum grows impoverished are null and void; every person again stands upon the inheritance of his fathers, ready to turn a new page. (*Shemitta through the Generations*,)

Based on Rav Yisraeli's analysis, one might contend that *shevi'it* should be the rule rather than a septennial exception. The *Tzeror Ha-Mor*, however, offers a fascinating insight explaining why *shevi'it's* breakdown of social standing is encouraged only once every seven years, and not all the time:

> The subject matter of *shemitta* and *yovel* is one that is permeated by profound secrets deeply shrouded in mystery... including the existence of a material world and how the Torah's laws enable the world to function successfully. Strange as it may seem, the material world cannot endure unless there are both wealthy and poor people that live on it. By legislating the laws of *shemitta* and *yovel*, God endeavors to minimize the gross discrepancy between the lives of the poor and the wealthy on this earth.

He adduces proof that there will always be some more well-off than others from the *pesukim* themselves: "both for you and your servant" (*Vayikra* 25:7); "and the poor of your nation will eat" (*Shemot* 23:11). The objective of the legislation is not to equalize everyone's wealth completely, as the need for some with more and others with less is built into nature. At the very least, some will always possess economic dominance over others:

> Furthermore, we know that the lives of the poor are fraught with anguish and that they suffer all kinds of misery... As a result of the rich man's feeling constantly at ease, he is apt to forget the troubles faced by the poor and needy.
> By decreeing that landowners cannot conduct business as usual during the *shemitta* and *yovel* years, the Torah ensures that they will become aware of how the needy feel all the time... [Specifically when *yovel* follows *shemitta*,] even the wealthy person will have to turn his eyes heavenward asking what is he going to eat in the following year, when all his sources of income have been inactive for two years running... He will realize that this is a question that the poor need to ask every day of every year, as their eyes are always turned heavenward, for they have no one else to turn to. (*Tzeror Ha-Mor, Vayikra* 25)

If there must be a distinction between those who have and those who don't, *shevi'it* ensures that those who have focus on their responsibility rather than their privilege while empathizing with the have-nots.

Rav Yitzchak Breuer's Perspective

Rav Yitzchak Breuer notes that the unique impact of the Ten Commandments governing Jewish religious responsibility parallels the natural world created through God's Ten Utterances (see *Avot* 5). In the Land of Israel, there is no tension between religious observance and nature, and these ideas merge together:

> The nation of meta-history in the land of metaphysics, the nation of *Bereishit* in the land of *Bereishit*, the nation of the Ten Commandments in the land of the Ten Utterances, the nation of the Torah in the land of the Torah, with no contradiction between the nation's natural laws and its Torah.
> Throughout the world, there is Shabbat on the seventh day, but in the land there is an additional Shabbat during the seventh year, to help recognize the need for the Ten

Commandments and religious life to govern one's attitude and approach to the Ten Utterances and nature.

The creation created at *Bereishit* is purposeful, and the Ten Utterances, like the Ten Commandments, are purposeful as well. Between the Ten Utterances and the Ten Commandments stands the *shabbat* of Hashem, stand the laws of nature, with the purpose of giving man dominion over the handiwork of Hashem and letting him choose between good and ill. Albeit the choice of this nation in this land is limited, the metaphysics of the land does not tolerate metahistorical rebellion by the nation, and it richly rewards its metahistorical faith, and the laws of nature swiftly execute the metaphysical verdict, whether of merit or of its opposite—"It shall be if you listen ..."

Rav Breuer poetically notes the beautiful messages of the *shevi'it* year, which enable the Ten Commandments of Sinai to develop the Ten Utterances:

And how much more so if he merits to see the land in its seventh year, its sabbatical year! From all the lands of the world rises the smoke of blood and tears; they clamor with the uproar of jealousy of bread. There is no rest, no repose, no rejuvenation. Yet here the Land of Israel rests its repose, yet here the Land of Israel—the land of creation—is as a nursing infant, lying in the arms of its Creator, blessed is He.

The Jewish man does not alone have a *shabbat*. The Jewish land too has its own *shabbat*! Every seventh day is the rest of the Jewish man. Every seventh year is the rest of the Jewish land. On the seventh day, the Jewish man does not work, but must rest, for it is his sabbatical, and all thirty-nine forms of labor are forbidden him, for they would disturb his rest. In the seventh year, the land itself is the worker and the Jewish man is the employer, the manager, he for whom labor is performed, and when the land rests, he is forbidden those forms of labor that would disturb its rest. Just as a Hebrew servant works six years and in the seventh year goes free, thus the land of creation works six years for the Jewish man as instructed by its Creator, blessed is He, and in the seventh year returns to His possession, for the land is only lent to the Jewish man for every six years: "And six years shall you plant your land and gather its produce, and the seventh—you shall relinquish it and leave it" (*Shemot* 23:10–11). "You shall relinquish it and leave it": this is the central element of the seventh [year]. The rest of the *shabbat* of Creation counteracts the sovereignty of the laws of time and space that the intellectual ego apprehends and admires and from which the bestial ego derives pleasure. The rest of the *shabbat* of creation liberates man from slavery to his civilization, prevents him from falling victim to mechanization and automation of his being; the rest of the *shabbat* of the land counteracts the sovereignty of man, the sovereignty of his rule of creation after its assumption of the form of nature, the tyranny of bestial aspiration and of intellectual aspiration, by revoking from them all authority for an entire year and by thus declaring that the function of the land is not to serve as a plaything in the hands of the exalted kingdom of man, for it too is a purposeful creation, just as man is a purposeful creation—one creation corresponding to the other—and only the common purpose of all creation, only the wishes of the Creator, blessed is He, and His Torah, the Torah of the Ten Utterances and of the Ten Commandments, brings them together in purposeful activity, man as manager and land as worker. "You shall relinquish it and leave it": renounce ownership of it, because for an entire year you cease to be its owner! That declared ownerless by the Creator, blessed is He, is ownerless! For six years it served you faithfully to the best of its ability: the year of its *shabbat* has arrived! Let it rest on its sabbatical! Its entire worth is not merely as your servant! Like you, it has independent worth that the Creator of it and you, blessed is He, instilled within it. For an entire year, throughout the days of its *shabbat*, you are to respect its independent worth. Only following its *shabbat* are you to begin to receive it again from the hands of the Creator, blessed is He, for the duration of six new years.

This is the land's "sabbatical year" (*Vayikra* 25:5), "the rest of the land" (*ibid.*, v. 6), the land's "sabbatical rest" (*ibid.*, v. 4), "a rest for Hashem" (*ibid.*, v. 1), a negative and a positive sabbatical—negative in voiding your sovereignty and demanding that you relinquish the land and leave it alone, positive in returning the land to the Creator, blessed is He, who rested from it on His seventh day— a *shabbat* for Hashem!

Rav Breuer continues that as the land rests, one gains a new perspective of God's interaction in the world and His plans for society.

Throughout the days of the land's *shabbat*, it is ready to fulfill only the order of its true Owner, and man must order it to do nothing. Its Owner, blessed is He, issued his order once, no more—issued [it] absolutely in His Torah: "the poor of your nation shall eat, and that which they leave over the beasts of the field shall eat" (*Shemot* 23:11); "the land's rest shall afford you what to eat: you and your servant and your maid and your hired worker and your resident who live with you, and for your animals and for the beasts that are in your land shall all its produce be to eat" (*Vayikra* 25:6–7)— an unparalleled transformative order!

Throughout the days of the land's rest, this order voids all private proprietary rights to the produce of the ground. Whatever grows this year does not grow for the benefit of any particular man. Let all come, among them the "owner" of yesterday, and receive their part from that which is ownerless. "It is an affirmative *mitzvah* to relinquish whatever the land grows in the seventh [year], as is stated, 'and the seventh—you shall relinquish it and leave it,' and whoever locks his vineyard or fences in his field in the seventh [year] contravenes an affirmative *mitzvah*, as is the case if one gathers all his produce into his home. Rather, he is to relinquish all, and all everywhere are equally entitled, as is stated, 'the poor of your nation shall eat.' One is permitted to bring a little into his home, as one brings from that which is ownerless: five jugs of oil, fifteen jugs of wine ..." (Rambam, *Hilchot Shemitta ve-Yovel* 4:24). This order counteracts sovereign private property! Private property is no inherent value, certainly no sublimely holy "vision," as thought by the tyrannical capitalist seated on his full wallet. Let every capitalist know that the true visions tolerate no abrogation, not even for a single year! When the land returns on its *shabbat* to the sole possession of the Creator, blessed is He, He immediately voids all private property, thus showing you that private property is in great need of justification, justifiable only by the purpose of creation, and that any ill use of private property destroys its entire foundation! If private property is sovereign property, then the Torah opposes private property,

for the Torah opposes any tyrannical sovereignty! The *shabbat* of the land thus is a
vigorous protest against sovereign private property!

This order destroys all divisions between the classes. "You and your servant and your
maid and your hired worker and your resident," all are equal before the Master of the
land, and all will come, you among them, to receive their portion from the table of
the supreme One and eat in the sanctity of the seventh [year]. Classes have no place
in any vision. The sabbatical year does not recognize them—it recognizes only man.
When you consider the history of the nations of the world, you can appreciate how
great—even revolutionary—Judaism is!

A Call to Unity

As mentioned above, *shevi'it*'s various interpersonal callings encourage unity, as the poor
become little different than the wealthy, and the wealthy are able to understand the plight
of the poor. This interpersonal achievement justifies *shevi'it* in its own right. However,
shevi'it serves as an interpersonal bridge to an openly religious experience as well.

All Jews experience what it means to be "landless", and this sense of equality is directed
toward a purpose – unity. The *Shem Mi-Shmuel* notes that this can be gleaned from the
fact that the *mitzvot* of *shevi'it* are addressed in the singular form. Their applicability to the
entire Jewish People indicates that the singular terminology is for the purpose of unifying
the nation.

He further sees this in the placement of the *mitzvah* of *Hakhel* during *Sukkot* following
shevi'it. The purpose of *Hakhel* is to unify the nation, just as was achieved at Har Sinai,
when we encamped by the mountain "as one man with one heart" (Rashi, *Shemot* 19:2).
The acceptance of the Torah and the spiritual benefits of *shevi'it* require the unity that the
interpersonal aspects inspire.

The unity enabled by *shevi'it* exists both in the physical and the spiritual plane. The
Lubavitcher Rebbe (*Hitvaaduyot* 5747, vol. III, p. 156) points that for the entire year of
shevi'it, people are not involved in their specific professions, something which ordinarily
separates individuals into various guilds, as all jobs require different strengths and different
interests. In addition, the division between those who have land to work and those who
do not are erased during *shevi'it*. Therefore, unity is achieved more easily, as everyone is
occupied with the common goal of spirituality.

The Rebbe points out, based on *Tanya* (chapter 32), that the more people "accentuate
their soul's importance and discount the significance of their bodily needs," the easier it is
to fulfill the *mitzvah* of loving one's fellow Jew (*Vayikra* 19:18). Deep inside, the Jews are
a united people; this unfortunately often goes unnoticed as physical distinctions between
people are accentuated. *Shevi'it* allows for removing the outer shell of the nation to reveal
this inner connection. The Rebbe adds that *shevi'it* is the ultimate preparation for the
experience of *Hakhel*, which achieves the unity of purpose and commitment of the whole
nation.

One might have viewed this message in a vacuum, seeing *shevi'it* only as an interpersonal year of kindness and not one of deepening the relationship with God. However, if the whole purpose were benefiting the needy, a year of planting and working the field might actually be more effective. Instead, the Torah merges the two ideals in perfect harmony – a year of relinquishing one's hold on the land while also providing for the poor.

Summary

The *bein adam la-chavero* messages of *shevi'it* are explicit in the Torah but go far beyond charitable opportunities. They provide an equalizing factor, uniting the nation as was experienced at Har Sinai. *Shevi'it* and the other *mitzvot ha-teluyot ba-aretz* eradicate extreme poverty while ensuring the nation collectively provides for others. In the process, we all recognize that we are "receivers" far more than "givers".

Chapter 15

Theme 4: *Bein Adam LeAtzmo-* A Year to Build Character

We have seen how *shevi'it's* various *mitzvot* present numerous tools for deepening one's relationship with one's neighbor and with God. What is even more fascinating is how *shevi'it's* impact on those relationships is supposed to be internalized and affect one's personality. Man is not only called upon to fulfill ritual commandments or to demonstrate interpersonal responsibility. He also has a responsibility to develop character in the process.

Mitzvot whose aim is to build character, are often referred to as *mitzvot bein adam le-atzmo*, and their part in the philosophy of *shemitta* is nothing short of astounding.

Emulating God

One source for the obligation of character development is the Biblical mandate of "וְהָלַכְתָּ בִּדְרָכָיו," *ve-halachta bi-derachav*, "And you should follow in His ways" (*Devarim* 28:9), which is essentially an obligation to develop an ethos of kindness. Following God's ways is neither about one's fellow nor even about God Himself, but rather about fostering a Godly persona.

The nature of *mitzvot bein adam le-atzmo* is expressed through several Talmudic statements. Many commentators note that there is an entire group of *mitzvot* whose primary purpose is to transform one's personality.

Rav Yaakov Ettlinger (*Aruch La-Ner, Makkot* 24a) refers to these *mitzvot* as "reflexive *mitzvot*… [which bear] the requirement of justice, weighing one's actions to ensure that one is wholesome." The prophet Micha taught the Jews of his generation that there are three fundamental requirements of religious life: "He has told you, O man, what is good, and what Hashem requires of you: Only to do justice, and to love goodness, and to walk modestly with your God" (*Micha* 6:8). The three pillars of life are acting kindly towards one's brethren, forging a humble relationship with God, and developing a virtuous personality of weighing carefully one's behavior, what Rav Ettlinger terms *bein adam le-atzmo*.

The Vilna Gaon and the Maharsha also invoke the concept of *bein adam le-atzmo* in other contexts in which the Talmud emphasizes three fundamental elements of religious observance. They observe that the focus of tractate *Avot* is this category of *mitzvot bein adam le-atzmo*, which calls for weighing one's actions objectively (doing justice) and serves as a primary focus of Torah-life.

In a broader sense, *mitzvot bein adam la-atzmo* focus on one's thought process — the command center of a person's body, the mind — allowing one to build a thoughtful and balanced personality. The *bein adam le-atzmo* element aims to ensure that we do not limit our focus to actions; instead, we must develop a rich inner core.

This extends our obligation above and beyond the performance of specific *mitzvot*. We are bound to develop the personality of one who is capable of walking in the ways of God consistently and constantly. We must not only learn what the Torah wants us to do, but who it wants us to be.

In the area of ethics, the *bein adam le-atzmo* element teaches us that even if we excel in bringing happiness and pleasure to others, we are still spiritually lacking if we fail to develop a personality to which these actions come naturally. In order to do so, we must look deeper into the Torah, weigh our actions, and identify those character traits (*middot*) that must be developed in order to nurture this divinely inclined ethos.

Self-improvement, viewed by many as a relatively modern fad, is, in fact, a perennial Jewish calling, reflecting a longstanding tradition of ethical discipline and moral improvement. The Sages explicitly mention the stress on character development. It permeates the works of many Jewish thinkers, particularly the Rambam, who clearly expresses the notion that perfection of character is not only a means to an end but a religious ideal in its own right.

Although the Rambam is known for his focus on the intellect in the religious realm, he repeatedly writes about the importance of developing a Godly character. The Rambam views developing *middot* as both a fulfillment of the *mitzvah* of walking in the ways of God and a component of the *mitzvah* of knowing God. In *Moreh Ha-Nevuchim*, he explains that while God is unchanging and what we term His *middot* are merely the ways in which we perceive His actions, the importance of knowing them lies in our being able to model our characters after them:

> For the chief aim of man should be to make himself, as far as possible, similar to God: that is to say, to make his acts similar to the acts of God, or as our Sages expressed it in explaining the verse, "You shall be holy" (*Vayikra* 19:2): "Just as He is called 'merciful,' so should you be merciful; just as He is called 'gracious,' so should you be gracious" (Sifrei, *Devarim* 11:22). (*Moreh Ha-Nevuchim* III, 54)

The Rambam's emphasis on knowledge is of utmost importance, but only so long as it moves its possessor toward a state of Godly conduct in this world.

The *bein adam le-atzmo* element of *mitzvot* is a goal in its own right while also a component of the other aspects of *mitzvot*. Therefore, when analyzing the *bein adam la-Makom* or *bein adam le-chavero* aspects of other *mitzvot*, we must also identify the elements of *mitzvot* that serve to transform a person's personality. One must not only act with mercy but become merciful.

Two Levels of Self-Improvement

In the Rambam's perspective on *emuna*, which involves actual knowledge of God and unwavering commitment to Him, character building is the only sign of true knowledge, as it expresses successful absorption of God's value system. The Rambam considers knowing God so important that he begins and ends his *halachic* compendium, *Mishneh Torah*, with the concept. However, it is specifically his conclusion to *Moreh Ha-Nevuchim*, the book directed to the confused intellectual, which reveals how much the knowledge of God is connected to the personality of man.

In that context, the Rambam discusses four primary areas of perfection that people attempt to achieve. The first three are the perfection of property, perfection of money, and perfection of moral behavior. Subsequently, the Rambam goes on to explain why these goals cannot be man's aim, as their sublimity is not inherent but rather ancillary to their unique identity.

Interestingly, the Rambam writes the third type of perfection, i.e., the perfection of moral behavior, cannot be man's true aim, because it only relates to actions performed in the presence of others. It is not inherent to man's being:

> For all moral principles concern the relation of man to his neighbor; the perfection of man's moral principles is, as it were, given to man for the benefit of mankind. Imagine a person being alone and having no connection whatsoever with any other person. All his good moral principles are at rest; they are not required, so they give man no perfection whatsoever. These principles are only necessary and useful when one comes into contact with others. (ibid.)

Self-improvement in knowing how to act with others, and acting with kindness is not a sign of one's character. Therefore, as important as it is, it is not true perfection.

In the following paragraph, the Rambam defines the fourth type of perfection as the only true form: perfection in one's knowledge of God. He cites the *pasuk* declaring that the only thing man can truly glorify himself in is "that he understands and knows Me" (*Yirmeyahu* 9:23). Knowledge of God is the only true perfection.

It is here that the Rambam adds a twist. The *pasuk* itself continues: "That I am God, who exercises mercy, justice, and righteousness on earth." The Rambam explains that if one's knowledge of God doesn't express itself in these refined Godly characteristics, then he does not truly know Him. If knowledge of God does not express itself in one's character, then one has not reached true perfection:

> The object of the above passage is, therefore, to declare that the perfection in which man may truly glory is attained by him when he has acquired — as far as this is possible for man — the knowledge of God, the knowledge of His Providence and of the manner in which it influences His creatures in their production and continued existence. Having acquired this knowledge, he will then be determined always to seek mercy, justice and righteousness, and thus to imitate the ways of God. We have explained this many times in this treatise. (Ibid.)

Viewing this statement in light of the third perfection, we can explain that knowing how to act towards others when it doesn't actually improve oneself is not self-improvement, and therefore it is not perfection. Only intellectual knowledge of God, which fosters a unique personality and a deep inner life in which the intellect transforms one's mindset, can be actual perfection. This fourth perfection, that of knowing God and expressing that knowledge in one's character, is wholly unique. One's character is a reflection of one's inherent holiness, not an expression of how well one has learned to deal with others, make friends, and influence them.

Shevi'it's Call for Self-Improvement and Character Building

While self-improvement is a constant goal, day-to-day commitments often push aside character development in the face of deadlines and responsibilities. Shabbat affords the opportunity for mindfulness and time to focus on and identify who one has become — and this is true both the sabbatical day and the sabbatical year. A year devoted to gaining a new perspective on his relationship with God, infused with the *emuna* and knowledge that God provides, as one lives with a newfound *bitachon* and trust in God being the One who provides his needs should impact one's outlook. A year where one has the opportunity to put down his shovel, pick up his book, and return to the study hall, must impact one's overall character as well.

If *shevi'it* only teaches one to give without becoming a giver, it has not done its job. A year of a radical departure from "the real world" is supposed to transform "the real world" that one comes back to, in the process altering one's personality and inner world. Although almost all (if not all) *mitzvot* contain a *bein adam le-atzmo* element, *shemitta's* entire structure rests upon it.

Shemitta calls for actions and a societal setup very different from that of the six other years. It is essentially a rest from the endless pursuit of wealth and control in order to take stock of what those six years have done to one's personality and to ensure the continuous improvement of one's character and outlook.

Working on one's character is of utmost importance, but it involves supreme difficulty. Rav Yisrael Salanter, the founder of the Mussar movement, declared: "It is easier to learn the entire Talmud than to change one character trait." It is easier to spend the year of *shevi'it* learning than to transform one's character – yet the challenge is also an essential aspect of *shevi'it*. Just as one does not hesitate to leave his field fallow, he must not refrain from taking stock of his personality, using *shevi'it* as a means to re-educate himself about his and society's potential.

Put in the Rambam's terms, *shevi'it* is more than just a year of learning how to give and to reconnect with God and *emuna*. *Shevi'it* calls upon man to "become" and to express knowledge of God through his actions. It represents both an obligation to improve one's character and an opportunity to do so.

A successful *shevi'it* impacts one's character, personality, and emotional connection to those in distress, simultaneously revolutionizing one's outlook on society as a whole.

The Practice of *Gevura*

The first attribute *shevi'it* inculcates is one we have already discussed. The *midrash* attributes to those who observe *shemitta* the distinction of *"giborei ko'ach,"* the angelic disposition of being able to overcome their desires and watch their fields lay ownerless for a year. This is true heroism, suspending "logical judgment" in order to adhere to God's call even amid uncertainty about one's food supply. But this attribute of *gevura* must be ingrained in one's personality as well.

During *shevi'it*, man must actively surrender ownership of his produce, relinquishing his hold on that which he usually assumes is entirely his. The Rambam explains the *mitzvah* in this way:

> We are commanded to disown everything which the land produces during the *shemitta* year, to release everything which grows on our property for the use of any living creature. (*Sefer Ha-Mitzvot*, positive command 134)

The *Sefer Ha-Chinuch* identifies the character traits of generosity and abnegation as essential elements of *shevi'it*:

> Once every seven years, a person must declare his field ownerless, not only in order to assist the poor, but also to learn how to relinquish his property, so that he may protect himself from greed and avarice. (*Sefer Ha-Chinuch, mitzvah* 84)

The *Sefer Ha-Chinuch* adds that doing so allows the nation to learn the art of generosity. The produce planter doesn't enjoy the right to a feeling of beneficence for providing for others, as the Torah gives equal access to all. Rather than focusing on the notion that the poor will receive sustenance from his fields and produce, the farmer is supposed to focus on the qualities necessary to do this in other situations as well. In fact, this is far more beneficial for the poor in the long run, as it develops a society in which generous character traits and a desire to give abound.

The Kli Yakar explains that this is why the post-*shevi'it* Hakhel is performed on Sukkot. *Shevi'it* enables one to discard the perspective of "what is mine is mine," identified by the *mishna* (*Avot* 5:10) as the primary character trait of Sodom. This outlook makes one very possessive, and *shevi'it* comes to eradicate it:

> That similarly is the reason for this assembly, for, in addition to taking up these four species on the first day of the holiday, God commands us to perform another such redolent act at the end of every seven years, for the *shemitta* year similarly is a cause of assembly and peace, for one neither plants nor cultivates during it, and the impoverished of one's nation have what to eat, as one is not permitted to take possession of the crop of the seventh year as if he were the owner. This, then, indubitably is the reason for this peace, for all matters of conflict stem from the attitude of "what is mine is mine," "This one says, 'It is all mine,'" etc. This is less the case in the seventh year, because though not all are equal in what they must do, all are equal in what they must not, and this truly is conducive to peace. Thus it is that on Sukkot, when everyone emerges from a permanent home to a temporary home and dwells under the *sukka* of His peace, the king is commanded on the first intermediate day of the festival to perform an act redolent of peace, and this is the principle of Hakhel. (Kli Yakar, *Devarim* 31:12)

Controlling Desire for Wealth and Acquisition

Beyond the specific messages regarding one's attitude and personality, *shevi'it* provides a broader lesson regarding the proper place of physical work in our existence. Many involve themselves in an endless pursuit of wealth which robs them of the time and headspace to focus on purpose. *Shevi'it* is a year in which the difference between the haves and have-nots is defined by one's personality and interests rather than one's ability to write a check, allowing one to inculcate other concerns.

The three negative character traits that remove man from the world are connected to wealth:

רַבִּי אֱלִיעֶזֶר הַקַּפָּר אוֹמֵר הַקִּנְאָה וְהַתַּאֲוָה וְהַכָּבוֹד מוֹצִיאִין אֶת הָאָדָם מִן הָעוֹלָם:

Rabbi Elazar Ha-kappar says: Jealousy, desire, and [the pursuit of] honor remove man from the world. (*Avot* 4:21)

Shevi'it allows man to put wealth into perspective. As R. Yitzchak Arama and others point out, *shevi'it* is supposed to provide the rest that enables returning to one's business afterward with a conception of wealth as a means and not an end. The desire for riches, the jealousy of those who have more, and the attempt to use wealth as a status symbol should be much less pronounced after *shevi'it*'s conclusion.

Although *sheiv'it* observance is primarily for the farmer, *shevi'it*'s calling is really for all of society to be able to gain this perspective. The character-building necessity of *shevi'it* at least once every seven years is so essential to individuals and society that efforts must be engaged to ensure it is realized.

Humility

Another trait attributed to those who keep *shevi'it* is humility. When Moshe Rabbeinu speaks to the Jewish People in the desert prior to their entering into the Land of Israel (*Devarim* 8:17), one idea that he repeats is that the nation should not interpret their physical success in the Land of Israel as the result of their own activity. They must recognize God's providence instead of attributing their achievements to the strength of their own hands. This humble approach lies at the heart of *shevi'it*.

The *Ktav Sofer* describes how *shevi'it* allows one to develop an outlook of humility, both financially and spiritually:

Due to *shemitta*, one humbles his heart, so that he does not say, "My strength and the power of my hand made me this wealth," for he sees distinctly that all is from Heaven and in His hand. One thus finds himself obligated to show humility before Him (may His name be blessed) and to observe His commandments, laws, and ordinances. This is [the meaning of] his comment, "Just as *shemitta* was proclaimed from Sinai, thus the entire Torah was proclaimed from Sinai," for *shemitta* is the foundation of faith and trust, and this rouses him to make himself meritorious, for all depends on God's will. One might add that when the Torah was given upon the small mountain Sinai, it was given there to teach that one ought not to be proud, for God dwells with the lowly. This is a great principle of the Torah — that one not be proud — and through *shemitta* one humbles his heart. (*Ktav Sofer*, *Vayikra* 25:1)

The *Ktav Sofer* adds that the humility factor is so significant that it explains the connection between *shevi'it* and Sinai that the Torah describes in *Parashat Behar*.

Experiencing and Enabling Empathy

We have already marveled at the fascinating form of *tzedaka shevi'it* embodies. Yet the purpose of this form of *tzedaka* is not only to give, but also to enable the one who at least bears the illusion of ownership to gain a keen understanding of the recipient's feelings.

In the absence *shevi'it*, great individuals had to find alternate means of giving with true generosity and empathizing with recipients. Stories abound regarding various rabbis who, when collecting on behalf of their communities during the frigid winters, would try to enable the wealthy benefactors to feel the harsh conditions. Rather than going inside the wealthy individual's home as he sat by the warmth of the fire, they would speak to the benefactor while he was standing at the doorway, lengthening the conversation so the homeowner could feel the plight of the poor.

Rav Eliyahu Chayim Meisel, Chief Rabbi of Lodz, did this, and when asked for an explanation, he responded:

> Satisfied individuals can never feel the pangs of the hungry people. I came to ask for your help in supplying wood for the poor people of our town. If we were seated comfortably in this warm house discussing this matter, you would never have realized the intense cold from which these people are suffering from. But now that you have had a taste of the cold, your entire attitude has changed and you are willing to give a sufficient amount to alleviate the suffering.

Rav Yitzchak Magriso explains *shevi'it's tzedaka* elements similarly; they allow the wealthy to feel the life of the poor:

> Furthermore, this commandment comes to teach the wealthy person how much grief the poor man has. His life hangs in the balance at all times, and he is constantly begging God for food. "In the evening he asks for the morning, and in the morning he wishes it were evening" (*Devarim* 28:67). He is constantly on the go, worrying about whether he will have food for himself and his family. A moment does not pass without worry.
>
> The wealthy person, on the other hand, is always happy and in good spirits. He walks through his fields and vineyards and sees the grain, and enjoys watching his crop grow. He does not even think about the poor man and is not concerned about his grief.
>
> God, therefore, commanded that in the seventh year one make a "release." One may not plow, plant, or harvest in this year, and one may not gather his crops. Rather, one must leave it as public property. The wealthy man is then also concerned: "Since I have not planted… how will I eat…" (*Vayikra* 25:20)
>
> This will allow the wealthy individual to realize that he only suffers with this uncertainty for one year: "What about the poor man who grieves at all times… and is always worried about how he will earn a living and from where he will get food?" By feeling the pain of the poor and supporting him in other years, God will make sure he will not become poor. (*Me-am Lo'ez, Behar*)

The Societal and Personal Effect

Beyond what has been described here, every aspect of *shevi'it* provides guidance towards a more virtuous character, inculcating throughout the six years of work the awareness of the impending *shevi'it*, leading people to be less cutthroat. They are encouraged not only to give but to be humble givers, willing to relinquish what they might otherwise feel rightfully entitled to. This allows them to express their knowledge of God and refine their character.

Summary

Shevi'it affords for a year to focus on one's character and personality. The various traits that *shevi'it* enables allow one to truly develop one's knowledge of God and attain true perfection. These *bein adam le-atzmo* elements of *shevi'it* are not only added benefits of this wonderful year, but integral to the entire *shevi'it* enterprise.

Chapter 16

Theme 5- *Bein Adam Le-Artzo*: Between Man, the Earth and His Land

In the last few chapters, we discussed *shevi'it*'s role in deepening one's relationships with God through its *bein adam la-Makom* messages, forging a healthier relationship with one's neighbors and society through its *bein adam la-chavero* elements, and aiding one in improving character and building a more kind and mindful personality through its *bein adam le-atzmo* elements. While all these facets are essential for understanding and appreciating *shevi'it*, they clearly do not tell the entire *shevi'it* story, and the reason is simple: *Shevi'it* is inherently connected to land. As we have seen, the Torah discusses *shevi'it* in several contexts, including agricultural, financial and spiritual matters. Nevertheless, the fact that almost all of *shevi'it* laws are limited to the Land of Israel indicates the central role land plays in the *mitzvot* of *shemitta*.

For this reason, we termed a fundamental theme behind *shevi'it* as *bein adam le-artzo*, directly related to our relationship with the land. In Section III we will discuss whether *shevi'it*'s restrictions of agricultural work fall upon the inhabitants of the land or on the land itself as well. Independent of that question, however, it is clear that *shevi'it* is uniquely connected to the Land of Israel; that is where it applies, and the Torah links *shevi'it* observance to the nation's rights to the Land of Israel.

What exactly is the nature of *shevi'it*'s land-based message? Does it merely present more agricultural *mitzvot* unique to the Land of Israel, or does it express a unique perspective regarding our attitude to nature in general and to the Land of Israel in particular?

This question should not be taken lightly, as there seems to be great diversity in perceptions of Judaism's general environmental and ecological concerns in general, and specifically as they relate to *shevi'it*. Of late, we have become increasingly aware of the rampant misuse and abuse of nature and the environment. Environmentalist groups have raised the banner of altering consumption, conserving natural resources, and changing our overall relationship with the environment. While there has been major pushback by those who deny the extreme dangers involved, even many who generally share ecological concerns have questioned whether environmentalist objectives should take precedence over other considerations.

A number of thinkers identify *shevi'it* as a set of *mitzvot* aimed at ingraining a different relationship with the environment. For some, this is virtually the sole purpose of all of *shevi'it*. In parallel to the general discourse on environmentalism, the emphasis that some have placed on *shevi'it*'s relationship to ecological concerns has led to pushback by those who see *shevi'it*'s connections to environmentalism as insignificant at best, and probably non-existent. Some, turned off by what they feel is an attempt to allow foreign influences to reinterpret the Torah's *mitzvot*, have gone so far as to deny that Judaism has any ecological concerns. Let's investigate a little into the Torah's environmental perspective and then attempt to identify *shevi'it's* role in the process.

Judaism and the Environment

It is clear that Judaism and environmentalism are two different "isms" and are not identical, though some concerns indeed overlap. The Torah is clearly against waste, requiring care for the environment and natural resources and sensitivity to all of God's creations. Yet, it's often hard to justify the aggressive environmental activism that often silences other needs and societal benefits because of perceived ecologically destructive results. Concern for the environment is a significant value, but not the only value, and it must be weighed alongside other values.

Similarly, concern for nature is undoubtedly part of *shevi'it*, but not all of *shevi'it*. We have already seen that the Torah's various descriptions of *shevi'it* portray a multidimensional year with a multifaceted identity. It is too broad to tie down to one theme. Of our seven themes, one certainly does seem to be a reconnection to nature in general, and our land in particular, but in its own terms. Nevertheless, *shevi'it* provides a good opportunity to reflect on the Torah's environmental concerns and see where it overlaps and diverges modern ecological and environmental movements.

Our study will attempt to obtain a general picture of *shevi'it's* relationship to our perspective on nature and investigate a broader outlook of the interplay between Judaism and ecological awareness.

A Jewish View of Ecology and the Environment

In our study of *Parashat Bechukotai*, we saw that man's actions affected the environment on a spiritual plane since the dawn of time. This is especially true in *Eretz Yisrael*, where observance of *shevi'it* determines whether the land will grow or lie desolate. But it is also clear that human action and inaction impacts the world physically. Neglect of our ecosystems and environment, coupled with abuse of the natural world, results in depleting resources, extinction of species, and human-caused natural disasters.

Some environmental activists place the blame regarding human's laissez-faire attitude to nature on certain religious perspectives that elevate the status of mankind. In their minds, if we portray humanity as the pinnacle of creation, the upshot is that humans will use their privileged status for the misuse and abuse of the environment. However, as we delve into the primary sources, we will discover that humanity's elevated status is also a source of responsibility for everything in existence, particularly the natural world.

We will begin by examining the *pesukim* that some view as the culprit for the abuse of nature. The closing *pesukim* of the first chapter of *Bereishit* describe how man was created in God's image and immediately afterward blessed:

וַיְבָרֶךְ אֹתָם אֱ-לֹהִים וַיֹּאמֶר לָהֶם אֱ-לֹהִים פְּרוּ וּרְבוּ וּמִלְאוּ אֶת הָאָרֶץ וְכִבְשֻׁהָ וּרְדוּ בִּדְגַת הַיָּם וּבְעוֹף הַשָּׁמַיִם וּבְכָל חַיָּה הָרֹמֶשֶׂת עַל הָאָרֶץ: וַיֹּאמֶר אֱ-לֹהִים הִנֵּה נָתַתִּי לָכֶם אֶת כָּל עֵשֶׂב זֹרֵעַ זֶרַע אֲשֶׁר עַל פְּנֵי כָל הָאָרֶץ

וְאֶת כָּל הָעֵץ אֲשֶׁר בּוֹ פְרִי עֵץ זֹרֵעַ זָרַע לָכֶם יִהְיֶה לְאָכְלָה: וּלְכָל חַיַּת הָאָרֶץ וּלְכָל עוֹף הַשָּׁמַיִם וּלְכֹל רוֹמֵשׂ עַל הָאָרֶץ אֲשֶׁר בּוֹ נֶפֶשׁ חַיָּה אֶת כָּל יֶרֶק עֵשֶׂב לְאָכְלָה וַיְהִי כֵן:

And G-d blessed them and G-d said to them: Be fruitful and multiply and populate the world and subdue it. And you will rule over the fish of the sea and fowl of the sky and all wild creatures roaming the Earth." And God said, "Behold, I have given to you all seed-bearing plants on the face of the Earth and every tree that has seed-bearing fruit; they shall be yours for food. And to all the animals on land, to all the birds of the sky, and to everything that creeps on earth, in which there is the breath of life, [I give] all the green plants for food." And it was so. (*Bereishit* 1:28-30)

The simple understanding of the *pesukim* is that humanity was granted dominion and mastery over the other creations. Indeed, if we stop here, one might view this as a license for misuse of the land and all other creatures. However, already in the next chapter, it is clear that the call of "*ve-kivshuha*" is much more a responsibility than a right.

Although Adam is given "all seed-bearing plants on the face of the Earth and every tree that has seed-bearing fruit," he is forbidden to consume meat. His mastery of nature requires, first and foremost, mastery of himself and his own desires. Furthermore, the Torah describes that Hashem places Adam in Gan Eden to serve and protect, not to use and abuse:

וַיִּקַּח ה' א-לֹהִים אֶת הָאָדָם וַיַּנִּחֵהוּ בְגַן עֵדֶן לְעָבְדָהּ וּלְשָׁמְרָהּ:

And the Lord, G-d took Adam and placed him in the Garden of Eden to serve and protect. (*Bereishit* 2:15)

Humanity's elevated status requires *shemira,* protecting the resources subservient to them. Humans are stewards of the world. Jewish thought teaches that the world belongs to God, who grants rights to individuals who recognize Divine ownership and use the world's resources for positive purposes. The *midrash* goes even further:

בְּשָׁעָה שֶׁבָּרָא הַקָּדוֹשׁ בָּרוּךְ הוּא אֶת אָדָם הָרִאשׁוֹן, נְטָלוֹ וְהֶחֱזִירוֹ עַל כָּל אִילָנֵי גַּן עֵדֶן וְאָמַר לוֹ, רְאֵה מַעֲשַׂי כַּמָּה נָאִים וּמְשֻׁבָּחִין הֵן, וְכָל מָה שֶׁבָּרָאתִי בִּשְׁבִילְךָ בָּרָאתִי, תֵּן דַּעְתְּךָ שֶׁלֹּא תְּקַלְקֵל וְתַחֲרִיב אֶת עוֹלָמִי, שֶׁאִם קִלְקַלְתָּ אֵין מִי שֶׁיְּתַקֵּן אַחֲרֶיךָ.

At the time that God created Adam, He led him past every tree in Gan Eden and said to him, "See how beautiful and praiseworthy are My creations. Everything that I created, I created for you. **Be careful not to damage or destroy My world**, for if you damage it, there will be no one to fix it up after you." (*Kohelet Rabba* 7:3)

The responsibility to safeguard Hashem's creations goes hand in hand with the license to use nature.

The *gemara* notes that two *pesukim* seem to contradict one another regarding whether humans are really given the right to use the world. The *gemara* explains that only purposeful usage with a proper perspective, expressed through the recitation of a *beracha*, provides the license for using it:

ר' לֵוִי רָמֵי כְּתִיב "לַה' הָאָרֶץ וּמְלוֹאָהּ" וּכְתִיב "הַשָּׁמַיִם שָׁמַיִם לַה' וְהָאָרֶץ נָתַן לִבְנֵי אָדָם" לָא קַשְׁיָא כָּאן קֹדֶם בְּרָכָה כָּאן לְאַחַר בְּרָכָה...

Rabbi Levi noted a contradiction: One verse states, "The Earth, and all that is contained therein, belongs to God" (*Tehilim* 24:1), and another verse states, "The heavens belong to God, but the Earth was given to man" (*Tehillim* 115:16). There is, in fact, no difficulty. The first verse refers to food before the recitation of a blessing; the second verse refers to food after the recitation of a blessing. (*Berachot* 35a)

Proper use of the land – recognizing through the medium of a *beracha* that Hashem granted one appropriate use of the world's resources – is the actual license for usage. Misappropriating the use by erasing God from the picture and failure to recite a *beracha*, is not only abuse of nature, but is viewed as illegal procuration of God's world. The *gemara* even refers to it as theft.

After Adam receives this limited license for using the world, he is told that he cannot eat from the *Eitz Ha-Da'at*, the Tree of Knowledge, and he quickly learns that abuse of his privileges gets him evicted from the Garden. These lessons of responsible use are similarly learned by his son and continue to be taught until the greatest early lesson of all – the *Mabul* (Flood). The *Mabul* eradicates the world's population who misuse life while simultaneously giving the world a new chance to get it right.

In this context, the previous license and responsibility to safeguard and be dominant over nature is possibly altered. In *Bereishit* ch. 9, when Hashem blesses Noach after he leaves the ark, there is no mention of "*ve-kivshuha.*" Although humanity is now permitted to eat animals, which were prohibited to Adam, "*ve-kivshuha*" is not repeated. Some commentaries understand that there is no real change. Radak (9:2) explains that the Torah repeats the notion of "*ve-kivshuha*", albeit with different terminology. The Malbim writes that although it still applies, it was unnecessary to repeat this directive after Noach elevated himself to a level far above animals and was permitted to eat meat. Others, however, understand the omission of "*ve-kivshuha*" as a limitation on that license[59].

Either way, at this point in time, it was clear to all that the rights to use the world are not unlimited; they come with responsibility, and humanity and the world will be reminded of that if they fail to heed the message.

Pinnacle of Creation?

Balancing humanity's role as creatures of the world and responsible partners with God leads to a philosophical debate among great Jewish thinkers regarding the degree by which mankind is truly the pinnacle of creation.

Parashat Bereishit describes that humankind was created after all other creatures and nature. Does this indicate that humanity is the pinnacle of creation? The *midrash* notes that this reality can be viewed in two lights, which are entirely dependent on how individuals use their enhanced skills:

---

59   See Rav Yair Kahn's analysis, https://www.etzion.org.il/en/tanakh/torah/sefer-bereishit/parashat-bereishit/ parashat-bereishit-man-and-nature.

אִם זָכָה אָדָם אוֹמְרִים לוֹ אַתָּה קָדַמְתָּ לְמַלְאֲכֵי הַשָּׁרֵת וְאִם לָאו אוֹמְרִים זְבוּב קְדָמְךָ יַתּוּשׁ קְדָמְךָ שִׁלְשׁוּל זֶה קְדָמְךָ.

If man is worthy, they say to him: You preceded the ministering angels. And if not, they say to him: A fly preceded you, a mosquito preceded you, this worm preceded you! (*Bereishit Rabba* 8:1)

Some of the great Chassidic masters describe the need to remember the great heights that people can attain alongside their ability to fall to even greater destruction if one's powers are abused. As Rabbi Simcha Bunam of Peshischa was known to say: "Keep two truths in your pocket and take them out according to the need of the moment. Let one be 'For my sake the world was created,' (*Sanhedrin* 37a) and the other, 'I am dust and ashes.' (*Bereishit* 18:17)"

Rabbenu Sa'adya Gaon and later the Maharal clearly express that man is the crown and ultimate end of creation. On the other hand, the Rambam (*Moreh Ha-Nevuchim* 3:13) takes issue with that conclusion, as he is unwilling to assume that there exists any singular goal to the creation of Hashem's vast world. He does concur that humans are the noblest and most important creatures on earth, but not in the entire universe.

Some later thinkers extend the approach that humanity is the focus of creation by arguing that humankind is also the focus of the celestial worlds and human actions influence those worlds. Rav Chayim of Volozhin describes how a Jew's study of Torah actually upholds the entire universe (see *Nefesh Ha-Chayim, sha'ar* 1, chaps. 4-6). He does, however, add a caveat. The more we recognize humanity's importance, glory, and authority, the more clearly we bear significant responsibility for the world as a whole. Humankind has the greatest power to influence the world, both for good and for bad. Its power to create is only matched by its power to act in an evil manner and destroy not only our universe, but the celestial worlds as well.

One of the strongest proponents of the immense power of every individual is the Saba (Alter) Mi-Slabodka, Rav Natan Tzvi Finkel, who emphasizes the majesty of man and his prized role in creation. At the same time, however, he tempers this with a realization of the immense responsibility it engenders:

All conduct of life, whether material life or moral life, whether the life of the community or that of the individual, is based on the measure of man's recognition of his own worth. A person of low self-esteem treats himself lightly and treats life itself lightly, to the point that he is liable at times to expose himself to dangers, without any regard, even for the most trivial of matters. Not so a person who enjoys high self-esteem; he values and cherishes live, and with all his strength he strives to elevate himself, and to elevate all of life along with him. (*Or Ha-Tzafon*, I, p. 270)

How can one balance this elevated status coupled with an intense responsibility?

Rav Yosef Dov Soloveitchik discusses this tension as a major focus of *homo religiosus*, the consciousness of the religious individual. Such a person recognizes his lofty status, but is not blind to his lowliness and weaknesses, often feeling insignificant. Rav Soloveitchik describes how *Halacha* provides a response to the tension:

> *Homo religiosus* is indeed highly subjective... It is in this light that we can understand the deep contradiction pervading the spiritual self-evaluation of *homo religiosus*. On the one hand, he senses his own lowliness and insignificance, his own frailty and weakness; he knows that even a "gnat preceded him, a snail preceded him." He sees himself as the one biological creature who has misused his own talents for destructive ends, who has failed in the task assigned to him. On the other hand, he is aware of his greatness and loftiness, how his spirit breaks through all barriers and ascends to the very heights, bores through all obstacles and descends to the very depths. Is he not the crown of creation to whom God granted dominion over all the work of His hands?... In the depths of his consciousness he is entangled in the thicket of two contradictory verses. One verse declares, "When I behold Thy heavens, the work of Thy fingers, the moon and the stars which Thou hast established; what is man, that Thou art mindful of him, and the son of man, that Thou thinkest of him" (*Tehillim* 8:4-5), while the other verse declares, "Yet Thou hast made him but a little lower than the angels, and hast crowned him with glory and honor. Thou hast made him to have dominion over the works of Thy hand; Thou hast put all things under his feet" (ibid. 8:6-7). And *homo religiosus* has yet to find the third harmonizing verse.
>
> However, halakhic man has found the third verse - the Halakha. He, too, suffers from this dualism, from this deep spiritual split, but he mends the split through the concept of Halacha and law...
>
> If "man hath no pre-eminence above a beast; for all is vanity," then what is the nature of the Day of Atonement? What is the meaning of pardon and forgiveness? What is the purpose of the sacrificial service of the day? The private, intimate encounter between the high priest and his Creator in the holy of holies? What is the whole nature of the holiness of the day, that holiness which bestows atonement upon us? Why should we be confronted at all with the concept of sin and iniquity on the one side and the obligation to repent on the other? Indeed, the Halakha set man at the very center of the world, and the Day of Atonement attests to this... Indeed, I am the one creature in this world who reflects the image of Divine Presence. Do I not study the Torah, the cherished plaything [see *Tehillim* 119:77] of the Holy One, blessed be He? The angels themselves long to learn Torah from me: Am I not at this very moment reaching out to my lover and beloved?...
>
> In the blinking of an eye the lowliest of creatures turns into the noblest of creatures, whom the Holy One, blessed be He, elected at the very inception and recognized as worthy of standing before Him. Standing before God! What self-esteem is present here! (*Halakhic Man*, pp. 66-70)

For Rav Soloveitchik it is not the power endowed to humanity that engenders responsibility as much as the opposite process: Recognizing one's duty gives rise to a sense of power. Halachic man recognizes that God's command imposes upon him serious responsibility and that he has a defined mission to execute – and thus a sense of power. He lives in this world not as a passing creature but an agent of God. One who recognizes this responsibility and power can truly be central to the world's creation.

In this vein, Rav Kook writes:

> There is no doubt in the mind of any educated and thinking person, that the rulership mentioned in the Torah ... does not refer to the rulership of a tyrannical despot who deals cruelly with his nation and his servants, with the sole purpose of achieving his personal desires and fancies. Heaven forfend that there should be such an ugly principle of servitude, stamped with an eternal stamp in the world of God Who is good to all, and Whose mercies extend to all His works, Who declared, "Kindness shall build a world."
>
> Since the Torah testifies that at one time all of humanity managed to attain this lofty moral state, as our Sages comment on the verses showing that Adam was not permitted to eat meat ... It was only when the children of Noach appeared, after the Flood, that it was permitted to them ... Hence, can we imagine the possibility that this greatly valuable moral good, which was once in actuality the way that mankind lived, will be lost for all time? ("The Vision of Vegetarianism and Peace,")

Partnering With God

One might wonder: If God created a wonderful world, which He Testified is *"tov me'od,"* exceedingly good (*Bereishit* 1: 31), why should humanity try to alter it at all? Isn't subduing the world a means of upsetting the natural world that God wished should endure?

This question has strong backing in the thought of enlightenment thinkers, such as Jean Jacques Rousseau in his "On the Inequality among Mankind," who take issue with the whole concept of civilization. Rousseau describes natural life as romantic and perfect, arguing that humanity can survive perfectly well without civilization and that technological and social progress has been detrimental to him.

It seems clear that Jewish thought rejects these notions out of hand. God specifically charged mankind with the responsibility of advancing this world, in essence, partnering with Him in helping the world achieve its grand purpose.

The *midrash* (*Pesikta, Bereishit* 43) interprets God's name associated with the creation of the world, ש – ד – י, as meaning "שאמר לעולמו די," "He who told the world enough." God retracted from completing the creation of the world in order to leave room for humanity to continue His work as His agents. When God declared the world to be *"tov me'od,"* He was describing a perfected state of imperfection. The world is the perfect arena for proper use by humanity to achieve the goals that Hashem set out for the world.

This reality is expressed in a beautiful *midrash* (*Tanchuma, Tazria* 5). Rabbi Akiva is asked by a wicked Roman, Turnus Rufus: "Whose actions are more beautiful, those of God or of man?" Rabbi Akiva replies that human actions are more beautiful than those of God. This surprising answer is lost on Turnus Rufus, who then questions that if God's actions are greater, why do Jews perform circumcision? Rabbi Akiva responds that it is clear that Turnus Rufus did not listen to his response. Man's actions are greater than God's, and this can be easily proven. Rabbi Akiva brings Turnus Rufus raw wheat and cake and notes that the cake is clearly superior. Rabbi Akiva concludes: "This (wheat) is the work of God, and this (cake) is the work of man."

Rabbi Akiva explains that we have no qualms mentioning that Hashem placed us in a world in which He created the raw materials that need to be perfected. Wheat's ability to naturally be worked into flour and bread is God's magnificent creation, but it will remain unsavory if humanity doesn't perfect it. Similarly, Hashem created males incomplete and charged humankind through a *brit*, a covenant, to partner with God and perfect ourselves through circumcision. Indeed, the *mitzvah* of *brit mila* was transmitted with God's name of ' – ד -ש. God said He would create the perfect raw materials for man to fully perfect.

Rav Joseph B. Soloveitchik goes so far as to explain *"ve-kivshuha"* as a divine calling to become a creator, just like Hashem:

> Man's likeness to God expresses itself in man's striving and ability to become a creator... Adam the First [described in *Bereishit* ch. 1] wants to be human... and to be human means to live with dignity... Man of old who could not fight disease and succumbed in multitudes to yellow fever or any other plague with degrading helplessness could not lay claim to dignity. Only the man who builds hospitals, discovers therapeutic techniques and saves lives is blessed with dignity. Man of the 17th and 18th centuries who needed several days to travel from Boston to New York was less dignified than modern man who attempts to conquer space... In doing all this, Adam the First is trying to carry out the mandate entrusted to him by his Maker who, at dawn of the sixth mysterious day of creation, addressed Himself to man and summoned him to "fill the earth and subdue it." (*The Lonely Man of Faith*, pp. 11-16)

Rav Soloveitchik does not view the development of civilization as a curse, but as a blessing – not as a sin, but as a mission and destiny. Indeed, man's dominion can become a source of pride and abuse, the proper usage of which is not a rebellion against God but the act of a reliable partner.[60]

As Rav Jonathan Sacks writes:

> The men on the plain at Shinar [in the story of the Tower of Babel] make a technological discovery. They learn how to make bricks by drying clay. As after so many other technological advances, they immediately conclude that they now have the power of gods. They are no longer subject to nature. They have become its masters. They will storm the heavens. Their man-made environment – the city with its ziggurat or artificial mountain – will replicate the structure of the cosmos, but here they will rule, not God. (*The Dignity of Difference: How to Avoid the Clash of Civilizations*, p. 52)

It is apparent that there is a necessary balancing act between serving as God's agents in advancing the world and understanding our place as fellow creatures of His world. But it is far easier said than done. Certain *mitzvot* help strike a balance.

---

60   Rav Soloveitchik continues that mankind must also embrace the persona of Adam II, the description of mankind in *Bereishit* ch. 2, who seeks transcendence much more than mastery.

Limits on Control

Man is called upon to inhabit the world – not only to "be fruitful and multiply," but to build up the world (see *Yeshayahu* 45:18). Populating the world means building a sustainable world that can continue to provide for a growing population, and we are therefore prohibited from wasting natural resources. A number of limitations ensure that humans partner with God rather than seeking to replace Him. Besides the prohibitions on wasting and destructive usage, certain creations are off-limits.

The various prohibitions of *kilayim* restrict one from making certain mixed species, as these hybrids are off-limits. The Torah presents these restrictions as *chukim*:

אֶת חֻקֹּתַי תִּשְׁמֹרוּ בְּהֶמְתְּךָ לֹא תַרְבִּיעַ כִּלְאַיִם שָׂדְךָ לֹא תִזְרַע כִּלְאָיִם וּבֶגֶד כִּלְאַיִם שַׁעַטְנֵז לֹא יַעֲלֶה עָלֶיךָ:

My statutes you shall keep; you shall not let your cattle mate with a different kind, you shall not sow your field with two kinds of seed, you shall not wear a garment of wool and linen. (*Vayikra* 19:19)

The *Yerushalmi* seems to view this as a broader injunction, prohibiting one from improperly altering the natural world:

"My statutes you shall keep ..." because they are laws that I legislated in My world. From here we learn that they were forbidden even to Adam, the first man. (*Yerushalmi, Kilayim* 1:7)[61]

The Ramban explains the reasoning for the prohibition of *kilayim*:

The reason for the *mitzvah* of *kilayim* is that God created specific species in the world in both the vegetable and animal kingdoms and instilled in them the ability to self-perpetuate and preserve their respective species forever, as long as God wants the continuation of the world. He commanded the propagation of each species and that they should never be altered, as it is stated, "And the Earth will bring forth self-perpetuating grasses according to their species ..." (*Bereishit* 1-12). One who mixes two species changes and denies the initial creation and shows that he believes that the Holy One Blessed be He did not make this world perfect. (Ramban, *Vayikra* 19:19)

While humanity contributes to the completion of creation by making the world serve its purpose, hybridization is prohibited as it attempts to create new entities not deemed necessary by God. Engaging in such activity implicitly denies God's omniscience, as if to say that He did not think of making such a hybrid. The license to use nature is to further it in line with God's purpose while recognizing that Hashem placed natural laws in the world itself (see Rav Hirsch, *Vayikra* 19:19)[62].

---

61   See the discussion in the Talmud (*Sanhedrin* 56a, 60b) regarding whether some *kilayim* prohibitions are incumbent on all of humanity, not only Jews.

62   Rabbi Jonathan Sacks expresses this idea as follows: It calls these rules chukkim or "statutes." The thirteenth-century scholar Nahminades understood this term to mean laws which respect the integrity of nature. To mix different species, he argued, was to presume to be able to improve on the order of creation, and thus an affront to the Creator. Each species has its own internal laws of development and reproduction, and these must not be tampered with: "One who combines two different species thereby changes and defies the work of creation, as if he believe that the Holy One, blessed be He, has not completely perfected the world and now wishes to improve it by adding new kinds of creatures." (The Dignity of Difference, p. 168)

The Torah places restrictions on certain forms of wasting, often referred to as *bal tashchit* (see *Devarim* 20:19). This serves as a general prohibition against all forms of destructive and wasteful activity. The Sefer HaChinuch explains the *mitzvah* as follows:

> The root of the *mitzvah* [of *bal tashchit*] is well known; it is to educate our souls to love goodness and meaning and to cling to it. In doing so we will attach ourselves to the good and distance ourselves from anything that is bad and any type of destruction. This is the way of *hasidim* (particularly pious people) and those with good deeds, those who love peace and seek the welfare of others, drawing them close to the Torah. They never waste anything, even a kernel of mustard, and are pained by any destruction that they see. If they are able to prevent it, they will put all their effort into saving something from being destroyed. . (*Sefer HaChinuch* 529)

Rav Hirsch explains that the essence of being a human means accepting the responsibility to respect the world and use its resources with dignity. He explains the prohibition of *bal tashchit* as an underlying principle in Judaism:

> "Do not destroy anything" is the first and most general call of God, which comes to you, Man, when you realize yourself as master of the earth ... If you should now raise your hand to play a childish game, to indulge in senseless rage, wishing to destroy that which you should only use, wishing to exterminate that which you should only exploit, if you should regard the beings beneath you as objects without rights, not perceiving God Who created them, and therefore desire that they feel the might of your presumptuous mood, instead of using them only as the means of wise human activity – then God's call proclaims to you, "Do not destroy anything! Be a *mensch*! Only if you use the things around you for wise human purposes, sanctified by the word of My teaching, only then are you a *mensch* and have the right over them which I have given you as a human.
>
> However, if you destroy, if you ruin, at that moment you are not a human but an animal and have no right to the things around you. I lent them to you for wise use only; never forget that I lent them to you. As soon as you use them unwisely, be it the greatest or the smallest, you commit treachery against My world, you commit murder and robbery against My property, you transgress against Me!" This is what God calls unto you, and with this call does God represent the greatest and the smallest [creations] against you and grants the smallest and also the greatest [creations] a right against your presumptuousness ...
>
> In truth, there is no one nearer to idolatry than one who can disregard the fact that things are the creatures and property of God, and who presumes also to have the right, having the might, to destroy them according to a presumptuous act of will. Yes, that one is already serving the most powerful idols – anger, pride, and above all ego, which in its passion regards itself as the master of things. (*Horeb*, ch. 56)

Rendezvous with Nature

Many *mitzvot* reflect the Torah's connection to the natural world. The entire calendar ensures that people are in touch with the times and the needs of seasons. Tefilla times change daily and seasonal tefillot reflected the natural needs of the times. Numerous *berachot* reflect recognition of natural phenomena, and we are tasked with seeing God's Hand in the natural and supernatural. The Rambam (*Hilchot Yesodei Ha-Torah* 2:2) recognizes that appreciating nature can be a religious experience. He explains that one can achieve love and awe of Hashem by "contemplating His great and wondrous actions and creations; [when] he sees His immeasurable and infinite wisdom, he will immediately love, praise, extol, and long to know the great God."

The *midrash* equates lack of appreciation of nature with wickedness:

> A wicked man even in his lifetime is considered dead, for he sees the sun shining, and he doesn't recite the blessing of "Who creates the lights"; [he sees the sun] setting, and he doesn't recite the blessing of "Who brings on the nights;" he eats and drinks, and doesn't recite the blessings over food. However, the righteous [are different, in that they] recite blessings on every single thing. (*Tanchuma, Ve-Zot Ha-Beracha*)

One aspect of wickedness is the inability to contemplate and recognize God's Hand in the basic aspects of nature.

Rav Yochai Rudik (*Be-Sod Ha-Shemitta*) notes that not everyone who recites the blessings connected to nature recognizes them as a call to analyze the fascinating aspects of daylight, nightfall, and God's overall Creation. These blessings are often recited inside synagogues from which the natural wonders may not even be visible. Initially, the various morning blessings were meant to be recited one by one as one performed the actions referenced in the *berachot*. When standing up straight, putting on his shoes, and the like, the appropriate *beracha* was recited. Now they are all said in one list in the morning, as our link to ourselves and our surroundings has been weakened.

One blessing that aims to encourage man to recognize God in nature is the blessing upon witnessing the blossoming of fruit trees in the month of Nissan. The *Shulchan Aruch* details the emotional connection to God upon observing this ritual:

> One who goes out in the month of Nissan and sees trees that are blossoming recites: "The source of all blessing are you, the Lord our God, King of the Universe, who has not made anything lacking in His world, and created in it good creations and good trees in order for mankind to benefit from them." (*Shulchan Aruch*, OC 226:1)

Unfortunately, for many people, this rendezvous with nature never occurs. Individuals need to seek out blossoming trees in order to be able to recite the blessing, while the Talmud and the language of the *Shulchan Aruch* refer to a natural, unplanned encounter with nature. The ideal setting for the *beracha* is one recognizing God's role in the blossoming of the natural world after a winter of stunted growth.

Given this approach to the natural world, it is not difficult to understand *Chazal's* description of how the greatest leader of all time showed *hakarat ha-tov*, gratitude, to elements of nature. Rashi (*Shemot* 7:14, 8:13) writes that Moshe Rabbeinu did not actively take part in the initiation of the first three plagues, as he felt indebted to the water and the ground, which saved his life. The idea that one can owe a debt of gratitude to natural, inanimate objects, such as the river and the land, indicates that they are far more than mere raw materials. They have personalities, just like humans.

The recognition of the purpose of every aspect of nature is expressed in *Perek Shira*, a description of the song that every aspect of nature "sings" to Hashem. Kabbalistic thought stresses the role of every creature, as nothing God created is purposeless.

Rav Aryeh Levin describes how this idea was impressed upon him by Rav Kook:

> I recall the early days from 1905 onward, when it was granted me by the grace of God, the Blessed One, to go up to the Holy Land, and I came to Jaffa. There I first went to visit our great master Rabbi Abraham Isaac Kook, who received me with good cheer, as it was his hallowed custom to receive everyone. We chatted together on themes of Torah study. After an early *Mincha*, he went out, as his hallowed custom was, to stroll a bit in the fields and gather his thoughts; and I went along. On the way I plucked some branch or flower. Our great master was taken aback, and he told me gently, "Believe me: In all my days I have taken care never to pluck a blade of grass or flower needlessly when it had the ability to grow or blossom. You know the teaching of our Sages that there is not a single blade of grass below here on earth which does not have a heavenly force above telling it, 'Grow!' Every sprout and leaf of grass says something, conveys some meaning. Every stone whispers some hidden message in the silence. Every creation utters its song." Those words, spoken from a pure and holy heart, engraved themselves deeply upon my heart. From that time on I began to feel a strong sense of compassion for everything. (Simcha Raz, *A Tzaddik in our Time*(

Every aspect of the natural world has its angel telling it to grow. We must assist the angels, not uproot their source. The more connected we become to the environment, the more we appreciate the divine purpose behind all facets of nature.

Interrupting Torah Study for Nature

Some might question the veracity of a positive view of nature and the spiritual potential a connection to it promises, based on the following *mishna*:

> רַבִּי שִׁמְעוֹן אוֹמֵר הַמְהַלֵּךְ בַּדֶּרֶךְ וְשׁוֹנֶה וּמַפְסִיק מִמִּשְׁנָתוֹ וְאוֹמֵר מָה נָאֶה אִילָן זֶה וּמָה נָאֶה נִיר זֶה מַעֲלֶה עָלָיו
> הַכָּתוּב כְּאִילוּ מִתְחַיֵּב בְּנַפְשׁוֹ:
>
> Rabbi Shimon said: If one is walking along the road and is studying [Torah], and then interrupts his studies and says, "How beautiful is this tree! How beautiful is this plowed field!" the verse considers it as if he has forfeited his life. (*Avot* 3:7)

This unusually harsh statement, declaring that one who interrupts Torah study to recognize the beauty of nature forfeits his life, indicates that nature is either religiously insignificant or at least inconsequential as compared to Torah study. Based on other statements of the Sages, including the blessings they codified to praise God's creations in the natural world, it is clear that the latter is the only valid interpretation. As inspiring as nature may be, Torah study is a more complete way of reaching God. One involved in it should therefore realize the repercussions for stopping to marvel at the natural world. This is the understanding of Rav Ovadia of Bartenura, who states that although the same liability holds true for any interruption from one's learning, the *mishna* specifically chooses the example of stopping to see a beautiful tree, for although one may make a blessing upon seeing it, it is nevertheless improper to halt one's learning for such a purpose.

Several commentators, however, tone down the harshness of the *mishna*. Some note that the *mishna* says it is "**as if** he has forfeited his life," indicating hyperbole. Rashi explains that it is not that one forfeits his life, but rather that amid the dangers of travel, especially in those days, Torah study serves as a constant protector. Even if nature is important, marveling at it is not direct Torah study, and therefore will not be sufficient to protect one from bandits.

One might go one step further: The *mishna* is not erasing or minimizing the religious importance of nature, but putting it in perspective. In fact, the *mishna* uses the term "*na'eh*" to describe the beauty of the tree, the same term that is used in the blessing made in the month of Nissan. Recognizing beauty can be a religious experience, a sign of righteousness, but only when it is in consonance with Torah study.

In an article entitled "The Beauty of a Tree," Rav Tzvi Yehuda Ha-Kohen Kook notes the unique phraseology of the *Mishna*. Unlike the law in *Shulchan Aruch* regarding one who is walking and notices a tree in bloom, the *mishna* refers to one who is *mafsik*, who interrupts his learning, to comment on the beauty of nature. Recognition of nature is truly holy when one views it as an extension of Torah study, rather than an interruption or distraction.

The *mishna*, in its carefully worded formulation, is informing us of the dangers of disconnecting the beauty of nature from our religious outlook. One should not reject the beauty of the world, but rather see it through the eyes of the Torah, the blueprint of creation.

Rav Tzvi Yehuda adds that although many texts of the Mishna attribute this teaching to Rabbi Shimon, he prefers the variant text that cites Rabbi Yaakov, as he is the one who teaches elsewhere in *Avot*:

> This world is like a portal before the World to Come. Prepare yourself in the portal so that you may enter the banquet hall. One hour of repentance and good deeds in this world is better than the entire life of the World to Come; and one hour of spiritual bliss in the World to Come is better than the entire life of this world. (*Avot* 4:16-17)

Rabbi Yaakov's primary message is consistent; one must never lose sight of the spiritual essence and must not be distracted by the appearance of nature as an end in itself. For this reason, Rabbi Yaakov warns that one's appreciation of the beauty of nature should never interrupt Torah study.

Since many scientists have been ardent atheists, it is clear that appreciating nature outside of the proper context can be detrimental and counterproductive. On the other hand, a Torah-based outlook allows one to realize how fantastic God's creations are.

Balancing Our Concern for Nature and its Religious Implications

We have made a case for appreciating nature being a fundamental religious ideal. Recognizing the beauty in Hashem's world also expresses concern for biodiversity, as everything created is divinely ordained for a purpose:

מָה רַבּוּ מַעֲשֶׂיךָ ה' כֻּלָּם בְּחָכְמָה עָשִׂיתָ מָלְאָה הָאָרֶץ קִנְיָנֶךָ:

How great are your handiwork Hashem, you created them all with wisdom, the world is full with your acquisition! (*Tehillim* 104:24)

But while environmental concern is part of our religion, it is not our religion. It is here where common environmentalist policies sometimes clash with Torah ones and lead many to discount the importance of ecology altogether.

For instance, there are clear limitations on the way humans can utilize animals (not causing *tza'ar ba'alei chayim*, pain to animals; the prohibition against improper forms of muzzling animals), but that doesn't mean that, under proper conditions, animals can't be used for human needs. It is specifically the Torah that determines the relative strength of our various values; otherwise, values can become their own religion, and hypocrisy and trampling of basic truths become rampant. It is precisely for this reason that we need the Torah to dictate ethical and value-based decisions. Reason can enable us to develop many values, but it often falls short in determining the relative strength of those values.

For instance, the prohibition of causing *tza'ar baalei chayim*, pain to animals, is clearly substantial in Halacha (see *Shulchan Aruch*, OC 305:20), but it pales in significance when compared to providing essential human needs and saving human lives. Instances of animal-lovers expressing disregard for human pain are examples of how an ethical doctrine can go haywire if not rooted in some deeper, divine system of thought.

Unfortunately, not too long ago, the Jewish People experienced the most heinous crimes against humanity at the hands of a society that considered itself highly cultured, ethical, and humanitarian. Many of the Nazi leaders who spent their days killing humans en masse were great lovers and protectors of animals. Deputy Führer Rudolf Hess, of cursed memory, was a mass murderer, but he was also a vegetarian and a member of an animal rights society. His care for animals developed when he saw a calf being led to the slaughter and could not bear the pleading look in the eyes of the animal, which sensed its impending doom. Similarly, SS head Heinrich Himmler, of cursed memory, penned a letter describing his love and care for animals, "creatures grazing at the end of the forest — innocent, helpless, unsuspecting creatures…"

Years before Hitler, of cursed memory, came to power, the story goes, the *Rosh Yeshiva* of Slabodka, Rav Moshe Mordechai Epstein, was on a trip to Germany, and he saw a woman sitting on a bench kissing her dog. In shock, he predicted: "They will be slaughtering people in this country one of these days, for it says in the *pasuk* (*Hoshea* 13:2), 'Butchers of people will kiss calves.'" If care for animals leads one to see animals as human, then one has failed to recognize the dividing line between man and animal – and that, in turn, may lead to the utmost cruelty toward one's fellow man.

George Steiner expresses the disillusionment of the rationalists themselves in the post-Holocaust era:

We know now that a man can read Goethe or Rilke in the evening, that he can play Bach and Schubert and go to his day's work at Auschwitz in the morning. To

> say that he has read them without understanding, or that his ear is gross, is cant. In what way does this knowledge bear on literature and society, on the hope, grown almost axiomatic from the time of Plato to that of Matthew Arnold, that culture is a humanizing force, that the energies of the spirit are transferable to those of conduct? (Language and Silence, preface)

A divine set of moral dictates ensures that one can maintain balance in interpersonal behavior. A higher authority directs each person as to how to balance different values. Therefore, when discussing the importance of nature, one must balance it with our other concerns.

However, it is clear that modern consumer-culture's abuse of the environment has no place in Jewish thought. In the words of Rabbi Sacks:

> Advanced consumer cultures are built on a rapid succession of artificially induced and temporarily satisfied desires. When the market becomes not a mechanism of exchange but the guiding paradigm of life, then meaning itself is undermined...
> What is therefore morally unacceptable about the new economy from a Jewish point of view is not the free market itself, but the breakdown it is creating in the sense of social solidarity, the increasing segregation of the wealthy from the poor, and the waning sense of the responsibilities of success – what J. K. Galbraith called "the culture of contentment." (*The Dignity of Difference* , pp. 76, 99)

We recognize the unity of creation, providing numerous gateways to developing a relationship with Hashem, but abuse of nature is not one of them.

With this background in mind, let's reinvestigate what *shevi'it* has to teach us about our connection to nature.

Shevi'it and Environmentalism

It is easy to see how *shevi'it* not only provides respite for the land and the workers, and a rest from the perspective that the goal is to create bigger, better, faster, and cheaper, increasing one's consumption along the way. Rather than being self-absorbed and focusing on how to increase gains, one grows by being outward-focused. For a year, the farmer stops working the land to further his wealth, and instead spends a year sharing his resources with everyone, especially those with less, and invests the greatest resource of all – time – with much more significant meaning.

There is good reason to believe that *shevi'it* bears a universal message for our attitude towards land in general. Several *halachot* of *shevi'it* seem to iterate agricultural concern – for example, refraining from working the land for a year, relinquishing possession of the produce growing in one's property, and treating *shevi'it* produce with specific sanctity, *kedushat shevi'it*.

We have already seen that the Rambam sees a benefit for the land itself:

> The laws... are meant to make the earth more fertile and stronger by letting it lie fallow. (*Moreh Ha-Nevuchim* III:39)

Since ancient times, it has been recognized that excessive planting of the same crops year after year is detrimental to the land. It was common practice for many to plant in certain fields only every other year, to ensure the land would not be depleted of its nutrients. According to the Rambam, *shevi'it*'s "resting" the ground for a year will enable it to become stronger, and it will then presumably produce greater yields in the future.

One might say that according to the Rambam, *shevi'it* is meant to strengthen the land, teaching us that abusing our natural resource of land will only come to hurt us in the long run.

In chapter 11, we saw that a number of commentators take issue with the Rambam's understanding. If *shevi'it* is an agriculturally beneficial set of *mitzvot*, why does it carry such dire consequences for non-fulfillment? Moreover, why would specifically the crops of the sixth year, the period in which the soil would be the most depleted, be blessed? Additionally, if this is exhibitive of a general calling for agricultural concern, why restrict it to the Land of Israel once every seven years?

It is possible that the Rambam, who presents this idea as his second reason for the laws of *shevi'it*, is merely raising an additional point: Alongside the social goals of *shevi'it* that he outlines in the same chapter, there is also a benefit for the land.

This is the approach of Rav Avigdor Miller. He explains that *shevi'it* is an entire year of awareness of God as the Creator of everything, a concept that is even more emphatically pronounced during *yovel*. Then he adds:

> But just as Shabbos is intended also "In order that your ox and your donkey should rest, and the son of your handmaiden should be refreshed" (*Shemos* 23:12), so also is the Shabbos of the Seventh Year and of the *yovel* also intended for the soil to recuperate its fertility and to refresh its resources. The practice of the fallow year ensured the land against the baneful results of over cultivation and allowed it to continue to "flow with milk and honey."
>
> This is in accordance with the principles that everything in the Torah Is intended also for the material happiness of the nation, and by fulfilling the laws of the Torah the nation is rewarded by material benefits. (*Kingdom of Priests*, p. 303)

A second understanding of the Rambam's view is that *shevi'it*'s agricultural goal is a lesson in its own right – to gain a proper perspective on nature and the use of the resources of the land.

In fact, the *mitzvah* of resting from work in the seventh year is twofold; not only does man rest, but "the land shall rest (*ve-shaveta ha-aretz*) a *shabbat* to Hashem." The *pesukim* themselves clearly indicate that the land itself has something to gain from this reality.

Although others commentators disagree with Rambam's view, it may have a source in the *midrash*, which states that the rest of the land is significant in its own right. The *midrash* states that the land "works hard" all the other years, as it expends serious effort to bring forth its yield as it suffers on account of man's sins. Therefore, God, who is merciful upon His creations, gives the land a year off once every seven years:

For the Holy One, Blessed be He, has compassion on His creations. As the Jewish People are most precious before Him, the land as well is precious before Him more than any other creation. It is worked and yields, giving birth throughout the whole year; it releases its produce before the Holy One, Blessed be He. When the creatures do God's will, the land blossoms... and when they sin, it is punished on their account. Adam sins, and the earth is punished on his account; Kayin sins, and the earth is punished on his account; the people of Sodom sin, and the earth is punished on their account... Therefore, the Holy One, Blessed be He mandates the law that [the land] rest during the seventh year. (*Midrash Aggada* (Buber), *Vayikra* 25)

This understanding only makes sense if we view the land not as an inanimate parcel of territory, but rather as something with a deeper essence.

The Rambam's reasoning of allowing the land to lie fallow to regain its strength might have even deeper significance. Throughout the everyday hustle and bustle that is so commonplace in our world, people often become preoccupied and fail to notice what is important. Rav Kook (in his *Haggada*) remarks that the distinction between a slave and a freeman is not determined by who wears shackles but rather by attitude. Freedom is the ability to be faithful to one's inner calling. When the land lies fallow, and the farmer has time to rest, he has the opportunity to reflect on his overall connection to the land. Some assert that one of the important lessons that one should take from this period is proper interaction with nature and one's environment.

As one stops his body and takes a rest, his mind begins to function. In the words of Rabbi Sacks:

[Shabbat] is a day that sets a limit to our intervention in nature and the pursuit of economic activity. We become conscious of being creations, not creators. The earth is not ours but God's. For six days it is handed over to us, but on the seventh day we symbolically abdicate that power. We may perform no "work," which is to say, an act that alters the state of something for human purposes. The Sabbath is a weekly reminder of the integrity of nature and the boundaries of human striving.

What the Sabbath does for human beings and animals, the sabbatical and jubilee years do for the land...

As Maimonides points out, land which is over exploited is eventually eroded and loses its fertility. The Israelites were therefore commanded to conserve the soil by giving it periodic fallow years and not pursue short-term gain at the cost of long-term desolation...

The power of the religious imagination is not that it has easy answers to difficult questions, but that it provides a framework of thought for such large and intractable issues. It is easier to understand the moral constraints on action when we believe that there is someone to whom we owe responsibility, that we are not owners of the planet, and that we are covenantally linked to those who will come after us... The simplest image, and surely the most sensible one, in thinking about our ecological responsibilities is to see the earth as belonging to the source of being, and us as its trustees, charged with conserving and if possible beautifying it for the sake of our grandchildren not yet born...

It is one thing to have an abstract conception of ecological responsibility, another to celebrate the Sabbath weekly – to renounce our mastery of nature one day in seven – and to make a blessing, as Jews do, over everything we eat or drink to remind ourselves of God's ownership of the world. Prayer, ritual and narrative are ways we shape what Tocqueville called "habits of the heart." They form character, create behavioural dispositions and educate us in patterns of self-restraint. (*The Dignity of Difference*, pp. 167-171)

Shevi'it is a time to focus on the effects that our actions, both physical and spiritual, have on the land.

Chazal note that God's instruction to Adam to "serve and protect" the land cannot be understood as a responsibility to work the land, as the curse requiring toiling in the land resulted only from Adam's later sin of eating from the *Eitz HaDa'at* (see Chapter 18). What, then, was his role in serving the land? *Chazal* explain that rain only began when Adam prayed for it (Rashi *Bereishit* 2:5). The ideal relationship between man and nature is that one's spiritual actions advance the land physically. *Shevi'it* provides a once-in-seven-year opportunity to return to that type of experience, in which we recognize that attention to Hashem's guidelines for living in the world actually engenders physical success. The Torah tells us that proper use of nature involves fulfilling its spiritual purpose and the essential *mitzvot* of the land, and these are necessary if we want the earth to continue to produce blessing. Through our demonstration of self-control and our focus on *emuna* and *bitachon* (see Chapter 13), we merit the supernatural blessing of the land promised by Hashem.

Furthermore, observing *shevi'it* requires understanding the needs of the land. For example, agronomists attest that most damage done to gardens, even by well-meaning gardeners or owners, results from a lack of understanding of nature's needs. Overwatering is not a sign of affection for nature; it suffocates the plants, which need oxygen just like a human. Even when not responsible for killing plants, overwatering prevents plants from developing a root system sufficiently strong to thrive and survive crises, such as storms.

When one limits his agricultural activities during *shevi'it* to only certain forms of permitted activities necessary for preserving growth, he spends the time prior to and during *shevi'it* attuning himself to what the ground and the plants actually need and what is harmful to them.

Letting the land rest is the first expression of recognizing that further working the land doesn't necessarily achieve greater growth. But beyond its physical benefits, it also allows for an opportunity to contemplate. One can transform his relationship to the land from one of control to one of intimate understanding and appreciation. He can realize that even well-meaning actions can be destructive to the land, and those aimed at abusing it for short-lived selfish goals certainly bring along deadly consequences. For one full year, there is no room for deforestation and destroying vital ecosystems. Hopefully, one emerges from the year recognizing that if a forest needs to be cleared, there is a way to do so without burning down its foliage and eroding its rich soil.

The Torah's description of the desolation that will befall *Eretz Yisrael* due to lack of fulfillment of *shevi'it* is reflected in many areas in which one tries to abuse nature and kills the future prospects of the ground in the process.

The concept of *shemittat karka'ot*, declaring one's produce as *hefker*, as well as the idea of treating produce in a special manner due to its *kedushat shevi'it* status, further emphasize the dangers of conspicuous consumption. The landowner may have worked the land and invested in its agricultural success, but he is just like everyone else when it comes to reaping the benefits of the growth. This reflects that possession is not a goal in its own right, but an opportunity. Consumption of the world's resources, even when justified, must be done with dignity. Furthermore, the produce that does grow during *shevi'it* must be eaten and not used for commercial purposes; it must be consumed in its natural manner, and it may not be wasted. This conveys a lesson regarding the sanctity of food in general.

In short, appreciating that we do not own the land is an essential part of *shevi'it*'s lesson for the world at large:

> וְהָאָרֶץ לֹא תִמָּכֵר לִצְמִתֻת כִּי לִי הָאָרֶץ כִּי גֵרִים וְתוֹשָׁבִים אַתֶּם עִמָּדִי:
>
> The land shall not be sold permanently, for the land in mine, for you are strangers and residents with Me. (*Vayikra* 25:23)

As Hashem told Adam, "Take heed so you not destroy my world," as "there is no one to fix it" after us.

The Torah refers to the ground as *adama*, and man, formed from the earth, is called *Adam*. However, the same letters spell *adameh*, reflecting that we are called upon to be similar to God Himself. Interestingly, the evil Nevuchadnetzar used this term to describe how he viewed himself as Godlike.

> אֶעֱלֶה עַל בָּמֳתֵי עָב אֶדַּמֶּה לְעֶלְיוֹן:
>
> I will ascend above the heights of the clouds; I will be like (*adameh*) the most High. (*Yeshayahu* 14:14)

One's interaction with nature can be uplifting or dangerous. One who sees beyond the physical beauty of nature and recognizes Hashem as the source of that beauty is able to make nature a part of his spiritual repertoire. One who misuses nature and views his accomplishments and the beauty of the natural world around him as expressions of his power, is liable to view themselves in place of G-d.

The Laws of Our Land

Shevi'it certainly includes an important universal *bein adam le-artzo* theme, but the Torah clarifies that *shevi'it* is inherently connected to a particular land – the Land of Israel.

The *pesukim* in *Parashat Mishpatim* don't explicitly mention *Eretz Yisrael*, but refer to the land that is to be released during *shevi'it* as "*artzecha*," "your land":

וְשֵׁשׁ שָׁנִים תִּזְרַע אֶת אַרְצֶךָ וְאָסַפְתָּ אֶת תְּבוּאָתָהּ: וְהַשְּׁבִיעִת תִּשְׁמְטֶנָּה וּנְטַשְׁתָּהּ וְאָכְלוּ אֶבְיֹנֵי עַמֶּךָ וְיִתְרָם
תֹּאכַל חַיַּת הַשָּׂדֶה כֵּן תַּעֲשֶׂה לְכַרְמְךָ לְזֵיתֶךָ:

And six years you shall sow your land (*artzecha*) and shall harvest its fruits. But [in] the seventh, you shall release it and let it lie fallow, and the poor of your nation will eat, and what they leave over the beasts of the field shall eat. So you shall do with your vineyard and with your olive grove. (*Shemot* 23:10-11)

Although the vague term "your land" could, on the face of it, refer to land owned by a Jew anywhere in the world, the commentators explain that it is a reference specifically to the Land of Israel. Some explain *b'artzecha* as an obvious reference to Israel, as this command precedes the sin of the Golden Calf, when there was no reason to imagine the possibility of a Jew in exile outside of the Land. Alternatively, we could suggest that although the application of *shevi'it* is limited to the Land of Israel, its lessons apply to our land wherever it may be. The messages of *shevi'it* should impact how we use the earth and its resources anywhere in the world.

However, the description of *shevi'it* in *Parashat Behar* clearly limits the laws of *shevi'it* to the Land of Israel, indicating that its message is primarily applicable there:

כִּי תָבֹאוּ אֶל הָאָרֶץ אֲשֶׁר אֲנִי נֹתֵן לָכֶם וְשָׁבְתָה הָאָרֶץ שַׁבָּת לַה'...וְהָיְתָה שַׁבַּת הָאָרֶץ לָכֶם לְאָכְלָה לְךָ וּלְעַבְדְּךָ
וְלַאֲמָתֶךָ וְלִשְׂכִירְךָ וּלְתוֹשָׁבְךָ הַגָּרִים עִמָּךְ:

When you come to the land which I shall give you, the land shall rest a Sabbath to God... But the Sabbath of the land (*shabbat ha-aretz*) shall be for you to eat, for you, and for your servant and for your maid, and for your hired servant and for the residents by your side that sojourn with you. (*Vayikra* 25:2, 6)

Shevi'it is the *shabbat* of the Land of Israel. In fact, it may be that according to the Rambam's explanation, the need for agricultural rejuvenation is a unique need of the Land of Israel. *Eretz Yisrael* should not just be a land of agricultural development but a beautiful country that retains its nutrients.

The Abarbanel (commentary on *Avot*) explains that *shevi'it*'s core message is that the Land of Israel is the chosen land, much as the Jewish people are the chosen nation, duty-bound to bear the banner of declaring God's kingship to the world. The Jews as a people fulfill this mission by resting on the seventh day of the week, and the land, which works on a yearly agricultural cycle, rests every seven years.

In fact, some commentators openly discourage focus on the utilitarian benefits of refraining from planting for a year, as the Land of Israel follows a different set of rules. The Chizkuni explains that this is the meaning of the phrase "the land shall rest a Sabbath to God":

This is to say, that your intention in not planting should not be to benefit and improve the land, but rather to fulfill the *mitzvah* of God. (Chizkuni, *Vayikra* 25:2)

The Kli Yakar similarly notes that the fact that we are instructed to sow our fields for six years, instead of letting them lay fallow every other year, indicates that the *mitzvot* of *shevi'it* are intended to ensure that the Jewish People view their agricultural settlement in

Eretz Yisrael against the backdrop of trust in God:

> God therefore wholly removes them from the natural order of things, for it is the way of the other nations during these six years to observe a cycle of two years planting and one year fallow, so as not to deplete its resources. Yet the Holy One, Blessed be He, says, "'Six years you may sow your field' — every year — and I promise you to augment its energy so that it is not depleted."
>
> Furthermore, there is a miracle within this miracle, for if anyone where to cultivate the land for six years in a row, even were its power not depleted, it would certainly not be strengthened. Yet God says that in the sixth year, on the contrary, He will bolster and increase its fecundity: "I shall command my blessing in the sixth year, and it shall produce the crop of the three years." If the miracle were that it produce the crop of three years, this would be miraculous enough, but on top of this, even if the crop that it produces in the sixth year is sufficient for the needs of only one year, God will send His blessing to their granaries, so that one eats a little and it is blessed in his innards — so much so that the crop will suffice for three years...
>
> God will increase the energy of the land so much that the same crop will suffice for three years, which certainly is the greatest and most manifest miracle of all: through all these proofs that I have demonstrated to you, know that the earth is mine. (Kli Yakar, *Vayikra* 25:2)

It is not simply that the Land of Israel has character, personality, and needs similar to those of man; it is directly affected by the Jewish People and their actions. Observance of *shevi'it* allows for the realization that *Eretz Yisrael's* nature is inherently connected to the Jewish people. The nature of the entire earth is important, but *shevi'it* relates specifically to the unique nature of *Hashem's* land. The supernatural quality of the Land of Israel is the ticket to appreciating *shevi'it*.

In the next theme, we will see how our relationship to the land as a whole, throughout our history and in modern times, can be seen through the eyes of *shevi'it* observance.

Chapter 17

Theme 6: Return to *Eretz Yisrael* and its *Mitzvot*

Eretz Yisrael's Agricultural Rebirth Upon the Jew's Return

Now that we have described how *shevi'it* binds us to nature in general and the Land of Israel in particular, we can begin to appreciate an additional theme, one which forms the basis of Rav Avraham Yitzchak HaKohen Kook's introduction to his *Shabbat HaAretz*.

Parashat Bechukotai's description of *shevi'it* observance as our license to secure living in our Land is coupled with a description of the devastating desolation that will befall the Land upon the exile of the Jewish nation from it due to lack of *shevi'it* observance. It is almost as though the Torah wants us to develop an understanding of the Jewish presence in the Land of Israel through the eyes of *shevi'it*. The Torah tells us that the land will rest one way or another – either through the observance of *shevi'it* by Jews in the land or through desolation that refuses to allow growth. Living in *Eretz Yisrael* entails weathering *shevi'it*'s challenges; returning to the Land without doing so is a recipe for disaster.

Although the primary sources for this outlook appear in early Rabbinic sources, Rav Kook presents an in-depth view based upon these sources and his overall philosophy on history and historical development. He discusses the goal of a Torah society and a Jewish State in the Land of Israel, the reason for exile, and the spiritual realities inherent in a nation that longs to return to its land. He describes the tension of longing to live in the land to fulfill its *mitzvot* while simultaneously realizing that the young settlement does not seem strong enough to weather that challenge. He speaks about the dream of living in the Land and observing its *mitzvot,* and the reality he hoped and envisioned would change very soon. Although Rav Kook wrote about the subject more than a century ago, he tackled issues that are still relevant and seemingly will remain that way for a long time.

But the discussion doesn't begin with Rav Kook or even the early Rabbinic sources, as the inherent connection between the Jewish People and the Land of Israel – and the fact that *shevi'it* is the glue that binds them to each other – appears already in the Torah itself.

The Gift of Israel — The Condition of *Shevi'it*

The most explicit description of the necessity of *shevi'it* observance for successful settlement in the land is found in *Parashat Bechukotai*, where the Torah details that lack of fulfillment of *shevi'it* will result in desolation of the land:

> וְאֶתְכֶם אֱזָרֶה בַגּוֹיִם וַהֲרִיקֹתִי אַחֲרֵיכֶם חָרֶב וְהָיְתָה אַרְצְכֶם שְׁמָמָה וְעָרֵיכֶם יִהְיוּ חָרְבָּה: אָז תִּרְצֶה הָאָרֶץ אֶת שַׁבְּתֹתֶיהָ כֹּל יְמֵי הָשַּׁמָּה וְאַתֶּם בְּאֶרֶץ אֹיְבֵיכֶם אָז תִּשְׁבַּת הָאָרֶץ וְהִרְצָת אֶת שַׁבְּתֹתֶיהָ: כָּל יְמֵי הָשַּׁמָּה תִּשְׁבֹּת אֵת אֲשֶׁר לֹא שָׁבְתָה בְּשַׁבְּתֹתֵיכֶם בְּשִׁבְתְּכֶם עָלֶיהָ:

I will scatter you among the nations and will unsheathe the sword to pursue you. Your land will be desolate and your cities in ruins. The land [*ha-aretz*] shall be appeased for its Sabbaths while it is desolate and you are in the land of your enemies; the land shall rest and have appeasement for its Sabbaths. All the days of its desolation it shall be at rest, according to the rest that it did not enjoy while you dwelt in it. (*Vayikra* 26:33-35)

The idea that *shevi'it* observance is a condition for living in the Land of Israel emerges from several other *pesukim* as well. The Torah emphasizes that *shevi'it* applies "in the land that I am giving you":

כִּי תָבֹאוּ אֶל הָאָרֶץ אֲשֶׁר אֲנִי נֹתֵן לָכֶם וְשָׁבְתָה הָאָרֶץ שַׁבָּת לַה':

When you come to the land that I am giving (**noten**) you, the land shall rest a Sabbath to God. (*Vayikra* 25:2)

The Alshich notes that it is through *Eretz Yisrael* that God exhibits His claim of ownership to the earth, showing the world that He is its Creator and therefore has the right to give the land to whomever He desires (see Rashi, *Bereishit* 1:1). Thus, during *shevi'it*, "a *shabbat laHashem*," the Land will continue to provide even when unworked.

Why does the Torah formulate the command such that the Land is described as resting? Man can rest, but how can land rest? The Alshich explains that although land cannot usually rest, *Eretz Yisrael* can:

It is possible that the Torah wishes to make the point that even land can be holy. Just as the Jew receives an additional spiritual force on the Shabbat, so does the land in Israel during the *shemitta* year. There is a precedent for this in the sanctity of Mount Sinai during the revelation experience, when the people are warned that they will die if they ascend or touch the mountain (*Shemot* 19:12).

The potential sanctity of *Eretz Yisrael* stems from the fact that God is giving it to us. The souls of the Jewish people are deeply attached to the Holy Land, as demonstrated by the terms for travelling to the land... Avraham is told "Go for yourself," as he is moving towards himself, to his true essence, as one is truly at home only in *Eretz Yisrael*.

Eretz Yisrael is a land like no other, as it is only there that the Jewish People may find their essence. As the Jews received an elevated soul, a *neshamat yeteira*, during *shevi'it*, the land does as well. This sanctified land can rest.

The *Ohr HaChaim* notes that this phrase is written in the present tense – "I am giving" – as opposed to the past tense, as it appears in other contexts – "the land which I have given" (see, for example, *Bereishit* 35:12). He derives from this formulation that the Land of Israel is a constant but conditional gift. He adds that this is the reason that the previous *pasuk* emphasizes that the *mitzvot* of *shevi'it* were taught at Har Sinai:

Why does the Torah finds it necessary to mention that... specifically this legislation was revealed at Mount Sinai?... Perhaps the fact that here God describes His gift to the Jewish People of *Eretz Yisrael* is a reason for Him to remind the people that the gift of the Land is conditional on the observation of the *mitzvot*, as they accepted when they stood at Mount Sinai and received the Ten Commandments. The present tense "that I am giving" ties the gift to Mount Sinai, where the Israelites undertook their oath to keep the Torah.

Eretz Yisrael is given anew every time the nation commits itself to observe *shevi'it* and the other *mizvot*.

The idea that *Eretz Yisrael* is given as a continuous gift to the Jewish People similarly emerges from the blessing that Yitzchak gives to Yaakov, which describes the future gifts that will be given to his descendants in *Eretz Yisrael*:

וְיִתֶּן לְךָ הָא-לֹהִים מִטַּל הַשָּׁמַיִם וּמִשְׁמַנֵּי הָאָרֶץ וְרֹב דָּגָן וְתִירֹשׁ:

And may God give you of the dew of the heavens and of the fatness of the earth and an abundance of grain and wine. (*Bereishit* 27:28)

Rashi cites from the *midrash* that the term וְיִתֶּן refers to repeated giving:

"וְיִתֶּן לְךָ" - יִתֵּן וְיַחֲזֹר וְיִתֵּן.

"And He will give to you" – He will give and give again. (Rashi *Bereishit* 27:28 citing *Bereishit Rabba* 66:3)

Eretz Yisrael and its blessings weren't given to the nation only once; instead, they are a constant gift from God. God chose *Eretz Yisrael*, a land that requires continual blessing, as the promised land, as it necessitates the nation to forge a constant relationship with God. It is a land that is dependent on rainfall, and its inhabitants are therefore always connected to the Source of bounty (see *Devarim* 11:12). This contrasts with the gift given to Esav, who, though not deserving of a blessing, is promised land rich in natural resources (*Bereishit* 27:39). Esav is given land that requires no relationship with God, as God would provide all of his needs once and for all upfront, essentially cutting off any need for a continuous affiliation (see *Chizkuni* 27:39).[63] The Jewish People remain connected to God and maintain an ongoing relationship with Him through the land, which requires a consistent flow of rainfall and divine beneficence to show its true, majestic colors.

The constant gift of *Eretz Yisrael* parallels the gift of Shabbat, as the Ohr HaChayim explains:

At the time God created the universe, He invested it with only enough power to endure six days, for reasons known only to Himself... So God created one day which would be able to invest the world with staying power for another six days. If God had not created the Shabbat, the nothingness and chaos preceding these six days would have returned and God would have had to start the process of creation ex nihilo all over again. Due to the infusion of the "soul" of Shabbat, the universe was fixed on a more permanent basis...The words "for on it He rested" indicate that by means of this special day, He was able to rest from all His work... i.e., creation ex nihilo, which

---

63   This is similar to the curse of the snake in Gan Eden (*Bereishit* 3:14). Since the snake is doomed to eat the dust of the earth, he will always have something to eat. His needs will always be met easily, and he will have no need for a relationship with God.

only He can do… (Ohr HaChayim, *Shemot* 20:11)

The idea that the world is created every Shabbat anew is a reappearing theme in works of the Chassidic masters. The *Shem MiShmuel* explains that it applies to the seventh year as well, as *shabbat ha'aretz* is also a period of renewal, *hitchadshut.*

> Just as the created world in general, so too is the inheritance of *Eretz Yisrael* for the Jewish people; it is given to them only for seven years at a time to work the land, and then it is given to them again after another seven years. Therefore, its fruits are holy… And this too is Shabbat: the weekly Shabbat for the world and *Shabbat ha-aretz* expressing the nature of *Eretz Yisrael* as a constant gift to the people. (*Shem MiShmuel, Vayikra* 25:1, p. 347)

The Torah refers to *shevi'it* as Shabbat because just as the world is created seven days at a time and is renewed every Shabbat for the next week, the gift of *Eretz Yisrael* is renewed every seventh year.

The *Sefat Emet* (*Toledot* 5634; *Behar* 5648; *Behar* 5635) similarly notes that the Torah's formulation, "the land that I am giving," indicates that *Eretz Yisrael* is a perennial gift, allowing constant renewal and a continual relationship between God and His people. This ongoing gift provides for a feeling of renewal in man's acceptance of the entire Torah and all its *mitzvot*, and this is why *shevi'it* is taught in the context of Sinai. (See *Shabbat UMo'ed B'Shvi'it*, ch. 9.)

With this in mind, it should come as less of a surprise that the Jewish presence in the Land of Israel depends on *shevi'it* observance. The constant gift of *Eretz Yisrael* requires the perpetual connection that *shevi'it* provides. Every *shevi'it* we observe, we are given another seven-year grant for the land, as we reaffirm our divine gift. Failure to observe *shevi'it* is almost tantamount to a refusal of the gift, and thus entails exile.

Impact on Our Perspective of the Land

This perspective, which views *Eretz Yisrael* as a constant divine gift to the Jewish people requiring renewal every seven years, calls into question a common, longstanding assumption.

How vital is *Eretz Yisrael* to the Jewish People? There is no doubt that Eretz Yisrael plays a pivotal role as the spiritual heartland of our nation. The *Sifrei* (Re'eh 80) declares that the *mitzvah* of *yishuv Eretz Yisrael*, settling the Land of Israel, is "equal to all [other] *mitzvot* in the Torah". Most authorities accept the Ramban's view (*Mitzvot SheShachah HaRav* 4) that this *mitzvah* of *yishuv Eretz Yisrael* is still applicable with all its glory in our times. *Chazal* do not spare words on the importance of living in the land (see Gemara at the end of *Ketubot*). But is *Eretz Yisrael* possibly just "extra-credit"? Is it really an essential part of our individual and national consciousness, or just a spiritual supplement to an otherwise full religious life?

The argument that *Eretz Yisrael* might just be an extra is usually advanced with a straightforward rationale. The Torah was given at Sinai, outside of the land of Israel.

Doesn't that indicate that the defining identity of our nation is through the Torah, no matter where one is in the world? Isn't *Eretz Yisrael* at most just the icing on top? Let's take a quick stroll through Jewish history to investigate this claim.

A Necessity or An Extra

After Avraham is commanded to leave his home and birthplace and to go to "the land which I will show you" (*Bereishit* 12:1), the destiny of the Jewish People is presumed to lie in *Eretz Yisrael*. His children will become a nation there, and it is there that they are destined to settle. From this point forward, every departure from the land — Avraham's in time of famine, Yaakov's to find a wife — is transitory. The people can only become God's nation in the Land that God gave them. Even as Yaakov prepares to bring his entire family to Egypt during the famine, he is full of trepidation. Despite his desire to see Yosef, Yaakov agrees to go only when God reassures him that this journey will be beneficial for the nascent nation: "Do not be afraid to go down to Egypt, for there I will make you into a great nation. I will go down with you to Egypt, and I will also bring you up" (46:3-4),

Yet, when Moshe Rabbeinu is given the task of bringing the people out of Egypt, he is presented with a new model. When he is invested with his mission at the burning bush, God tells Moshe that the ultimate sign of his leadership will be at Mount Sinai:

> וַיֹּאמֶר כִּי אֶהְיֶה עִמָּךְ וְזֶה לְּךָ הָאוֹת כִּי אָנֹכִי שְׁלַחְתִּיךָ בְּהוֹצִיאֲךָ אֶת הָעָם מִמִּצְרַיִם תַּעַבְדוּן אֶת הָא-לֹהִים עַל הָהָר הַזֶּה:
>
> And He said, "For I will be with you; and this is the sign for you that it was I Who sent you: When you take the people out of Egypt, you will worship God on this mountain." (*Shemot* 3:12)

Moshe becomes God's agent in redeeming the people, but he also emerges as "Rabbeinu," our master and teacher. The fact that the nation receives the Torah outside of *Eretz Yisrael* has convinced some that one may live a complete Torah lifestyle in the Diaspora. In fact, Moshe himself never enters the Land, although it is his most fervent wish. Indeed some mitzvot only apply in *Eretz Yisrael* but maybe the territory promised to our forefathers is really just the site God chose for building our nation. At least on an individual basis, perhaps the whole world is equally fitting for a deeply religious life.

Indeed, although our *Avot* were promised that their children would inherit *Eretz Yisrael*, they were also told that the nation would be exiled from the land. Although the ideal may be to live in *Eretz Yisrael*, where all the *mitzvot* of the Torah are applicable, some argue that *Eretz Yisrael* cannot be integral to a nation that will ultimately be exiled from its land. According to this approach, Torah is the only indispensable part of our nation; *Eretz Yisrael* is more like the "cherry on top." After all, our nation survived in exile for almost two thousand years, but wouldn't survive a day without our Torah.

While this approach presents a compelling argument, let us evaluate it from the perspective of *shevi'it*. Rav Yosef Carmel notes that there is good reason to interpret the Torah's introductory remarks in *Parashat Behar* about *shevi'it* as a divine demonstration of the fallacy of this approach. *Parashat Behar* teaches us that *shevi'it* was taught at Sinai.

If Sinai was the goal, the covenant of Sinai would not be expected to focus on *mitzvot* that apply only when the nation is living in *Eretz Yisrael*. He explains that although the Torah is given on Har Sinai, on foreign soil, emphasizing its relevance in the Diaspora, nevertheless, "one must remember that the purpose of the giving of the Torah is creating the complete Jewish life of our people in *Eretz Yisrael*. This complete Jewish life includes undoubtedly the central *mitzvot* of the *shemitta* year."

Notably, the *kedusha* of Har Sinai was transient; it vanished after the Har Sinai experience. The *luchot* (tablets) received at Sinai are placed in the *aron* (the Holy Ark), which stands at the center of the *Mishkan*. The Jewish People transport the *Mishkan* to *Eretz Yisrael*, where the *aron* is ultimately placed at the center of the *Mikdash* (the Temple). The Ramban (*Shemot* 25:1) explains that the *Mishkan's* role is to be a traveling Har Sinai. Through the *Mishkan*, the nation takes the supernatural Har Sinai experience with them in a more modest fashion, where God Rests among the nation constantly. The temporary *Mishkan* is but a stage with the end goal the building of a permanent *Mikdash* in *Yerushalayim*, which will serve as the epicenter of the developing nation's existence. The goal of the *Mishkan* is to ensure that Har Sinai "makes *Aliya*," as it is taken to *Eretz Yisrael*.

This alternative perspective sees Har Sinai as proof that, indeed, Judaism can exit in the diaspora where Torah study can even flourish. However, it will always be a transient existence. The goal will always be to bring the Jews and the Torah they study in the diaspora to a permanent home in *Eretz Yisrael*.

This outlook agrees that Torah is relevant and can even thrive in *chutz la'aretz*, at times more easily than in *Eretz Yisrael* – but a full Torah life cannot. The complete Torah only applies in *Eretz Yisrael*, as only there do all its *mitzvot* apply. The unique nature of our people is represented by the *mitzvot ha-teluyot ba'aretz*, as these were the ones Moshe hoped to be able to fulfill if granted permission to enter the land (*Sota* 11a). *Shevi'it* is the epitome of these *mitzvot*, and it is not surprising that it is used to refute the vision of Diaspora Judaism as complete.

Utter Destruction

According to this perspective, the Jewish nation's true home will only be in Eretz Yisrael. But if Eretz Yisrael is so essential to the Jewish identity, what does exile indicate about God's relationship with the Jewish people after they sin?

The *pesukim* in *Parashat Bechukotai* describe that Hashem will scatter the people into exile in a list of the harsh punishments that the nation will receive for their sins. However, a careful look at the *pesukim* indicates that the Torah focuses far more on the land's barrenness than the nation's exile. The Torah repeatedly mentions that the land will lie desolate on account of not observing *shevi'it* (*Vayikra* 26:31-2, 33-4, 43).[64]

---

64   The Torah begins by describing the desolation of the land (Vayikra 26:31-2), then mentions the exile (33), and then returns to mention the desolation of the land on account of lack of *shevi'it* observance (34-5, 43). Rabbanit Sharon Rimon (https://haretzion.linnovate.co.il/en/tanakh/torah/sefer-vayikra/parashat-behar/behar-exile-desolation-and-lying-fallow) noes that the Torah clearly focuses on the land and its desolation rather than the exile (repeating the word "land" sven times, and the root *sh-m-m* (desolation) seven times as well).

Offhand, the Torah's stress on the land's desolation requires explanation. Why does the curse of the nation's exile seem secondary to the land lying in waste?

The commentaries offer several explanations. The Ibn Ezra (ad loc.) notes the land's desolation causes shame to the exiled Jewish nation. The *pesukim* in *Sefer Melachim* (9:7-9) seem to add that the desolation testifies to the nation's sins that caused the destruction. Additionally, the *Torat Kohanim* (ch. 7) notes that the desolation impresses upon the nation that their exile will be long, as the desolate land lies beyond their reach. Desolation also has a very practical impact, as it makes returning to the land practically difficult. The nation cannot just return to a wasteland and pick up where they left off. This also causes psychological despair, as the nation wonders if it is even possible to return to the land.

A Blessing In Disguise?

The desolation certainly expresses grave destruction, however, the Midrash (*Torat Kohanim* ch. 6) cited by Rashi and others identify in it a hint of consolation as well. In the midst of the *tochacha's* horrifying message of destruction, the Torah provides a silver lining through the very reality of desolation. Indeed there will be exile, but it is temporary, as no other nation will succeed in cultivating the land in the Jews' absence. Rashi explains:

> וַהֲשִׁמֹּתִי אֲנִי אֶת הָאָרֶץ - זוֹ מִדָּה טוֹבָה לְיִשְׂרָאֵל שֶׁלֹּא יִמְצְאוּ הָאוֹיְבִים נַחַת רוּחַ בְּאַרְצָם, שֶׁתְּהֵא שׁוֹמֵמָה מִיוֹשְׁבֶיהָ:

> "And I will bring the land into desolation" — this is a good tiding for Israel, that their enemies will find no solace in the land and it will remain desolate. (Rashi *Vayikra* 26:32)

The Maharal (*Gur Aryeh*) explains that although the *pasuk's* context is divine retribution, we learn from the superfluous addition of the word "*Ani*," "I," that it is declared through the attribute of loving-kindness. The desolation is rooted in affection for the Jewish People. Specifically because the expulsion and desolation are due to divine retribution, they are also the secret of Israel's rehabilitation.

The Ramban elaborates that the punishment of exile and desolation is nothing short of a blessing in disguise, indicative of the Jewish people's inherent connection to the land even in the absence of Jewish settlement:

> That which God states here, "So devastated will I leave the land that your enemies..." constitutes a good tiding, proclaiming that during all our exiles, our land will not accept our enemies. This is a great proof and assurance for us, for in the entire inhabited world one cannot find such a good and large land which was always lived in, and yet is as ruined as it is [today]. For from the time we left it, it has not accepted any nation or people; they all try to settle it, but to no avail. (Ramban, *Vayikra* 26:32)

The Ramban's words are echoed in the commentary of his student, Rabbeinu Bechayei (ibid.):

> All the nations seek to do so but cannot build it up. This is a great sign for Israel: ever since the land was laid waste, it has refused to harbor any nation or tongue, nor will it do so in the future, until its scions return to it.

The Land will remain true to its people and will not grow crops for anyone else. God will indeed exile the people from the Land, but that does not indicate that He doesn't want them to return to the Land when they are ready. This good tiding is nothing less than God's commitment to the Jewish People and their return to the land.

Even when there comes the point where the Jewish nation must be exiled from the land, that in no way indicates a disconnect from the land. As the desolate wasteland testifies to the punishment, it also testifies that the land is waiting faithfully for its nation to return. While history illustrates that

Desolation and Rebirth

To appreciate the Ramban's comment, made in the thirteenth century, it is important to be somewhat familiar with his biography. The Ramban lived the majority of his life in Spain, but after recording his successful defense of the Jewish religion in print, his life was in danger. Although there were closer and safer places to run to, he chose to follow his dream and travel to *Eretz Yisrael*. After initially arriving in Acre, he refused the entreaties of the locals to stay there in the relative safety of the city, as he desired to travel to Jerusalem. After arriving there and bearing witness to the devastation, he wrote to his son these unforgettable words describing the sad reality of destruction:

וּמָה אַגִּיד לָכֶם בְּעִנְיַן הָאָרֶץ? - כִּי רַבָּה הָעֲזוּבָה וְגָדוֹל הַשַּׁמָּמוֹן! וְכָלְלוּ שֶׁל דָּבָר: כֹּל הַמְקֻדָּשׁ מֵחֲבֵרוֹ חָרֵב יוֹתֵר מֵחֲבֵרוֹ: יְרוּשָׁלַיִם חָרְבָה מִן הַכֹּל, וְאֶרֶץ יְהוּדָה יוֹתֵר מִן הַגָּלִיל. וְעִם חָרְבָּנָהּ הִיא טוֹבָה מְאֹד, ...

What can I tell you regarding the land? Many are [the Land's] forsaken places, and great is the desecration. The rule of thumb is: The more sacred the place, the greater the devastation it has suffered. Jerusalem is the most desolate place of all, and Judea is more [desolate] than the Galilee, yet with its destruction it is [an] exceedingly good [land]...

The Ramban observed the situation with his own two eyes. The Land of Israel, despite numerous empires vying for it, lay in ruins and agricultural desolation. He recognized the destruction yet reiterated his belief that it was the ultimate proof that the Jewish People would return.

In the Ramban's "Prayer at the Ruins of Jerusalem" (1267), after extolling the once beautiful city of Yerushalayim, he describes its current state; it not only lacks Jews, but is uncultivated. Utter desolation does not befit the land, which deserves more, but it will only produce for the Jewish nation. He powerfully describes that any small yield it provides for other nations may be likened to a nursing mother who has lost her child; she may still provide some milk for a time, but it is only a trifle to be given to the animals. The same may be said of the land flowing with milk and honey; it may provide for the other nations for a bit, but its true sustenance is reserved for its children alone:

And the fruits of the land, a pride and adornment (*Yeshayahu* 4:2)
Its fruit and produce are plentiful;
It is still a land which flows
With milk and honey for its dwellers!

> I have likened you, my mother,
> To a woman in birth whose child died in her lap.
> The milk in her breasts causes her pain,
> And so she gives suck to the pups of dogs.
> And with all this, "Your lovers despise you" (*Yirmeyahu* 4:30),
> And your enemies find you desolate…
> "And the forsaken places are many
> In the midst of the fat and large land" (*Nechemya* 9:35)
> For they are not befitting you,
> Nor are you fit for them…

The Ramban, while bemoaning the destruction, recognizes the divine displeasure with the situation at hand, as the land anxiously awaits the return of the people who will succeed in bringing back the beauty that is so natural to it.

The Ramban spent the last three years of his life in Jerusalem, taking the first steps to reinstate the Jewish presence in the land that would allow it to flourish. He awaited the day when it would bloom again, signaling the end of the period of destruction and the commencement of the period of return, which will only happen with the return of the Jewish nation.

The Torah's words indeed were proven true throughout history. The best word to describe the Land of Israel in all the years that various nations fought over it is desolation.

The Abarbanel, who served as a high official in the Spanish government prior to the Expulsion of 1492, examines the *pasuk* in the *tochacha*, "I will scatter you among the nations and will unsheathe the sword to pursue you" (*Vayikra* 26:33). He explains that any haven in exile is only temporary; sooner or later, the sword will be unsheathed against the Jewish People. Those who dwell in foreign lands with a feeling of security will realize it is an illusion. At some point, the people will feel the need to return, and in the process, *Eretz Yisrael* will return to itself.

Modern Arabs claim a lengthy period of successful settlement in the Land of Israel under the banner of a Palestinian people, but the truth is very different. While the Ramban could only testify to prior history and the reality he witnessed, what was true at the time of the Ramban remained true as long as the Jewish People had not returned to the land as a nation. Mark Twain – in a famous passage in *Innocents Abroad* (1867), his best-selling work in his lifetime – describes the desolation of Israel and the Torah's prophetic reality, about twenty years before Jews begin to return to Israel in order to settle and develop agriculturally:

> Palestine sits in sackcloth and ashes. Over it broods the spell of a curse that has withered its fields and fettered its energies. … Where the hosts of Israel entered the Promised Land with songs of rejoicing, one finds only a squalid camp of fantastic Bedouins of the desert; Jericho the accursed, lies a moldering ruin, today …. Renowned Jerusalem itself, the stateliest name in history, has lost

all its ancient grandeur, and is become a pauper village... the wonderful temple which was the pride and the glory of Israel, is gone.... Palestine is desolate and unlovely. And why should it be otherwise? Can the curse of the Deity beautify a land? [It is] a desolate country whose soil is rich enough, but is given over wholly to weeds — a silent mournful expanse... A desolation is here that not even imagination can grace with the pomp of life and action... We never saw a human being on the whole route... There was hardly a tree or a shrub anywhere. Even the olive and the cactus, those fast friends of the worthless soil, had almost deserted the country.

Mark Twain merely puts into words the reality of the Land of Israel without its Jewish inhabitants. His description of Yerushalayim having lost its ancient grandeur is almost a carbon copy of the *pasuk* in *Eicha* (2:15):

All who pass by clap their hands at you, They hiss and shake their heads over the daughter of Yerushalayim: Is this the city that is said to be 'the epitome of beauty, the joy of the entire earth'?

It is almost as if the land still lies in its initial state of destruction. Twain recognizes the divine curse responsible for this devastation, and in the process, unwittingly gives voice to the view of the Ramban: the land is waiting for a change. The land is waiting for its children to return.

During the almost two-thousand-year exile, no other nation successfully cultivated the land. It became a series of unfertile deserts surrounded by "oases" of malaria-infected marshes. The land remained sparsely populated. According to the nomadic individuals who tried to cultivate the land, the land was cursed; growth was impossible. In fact, in 1880, the American Consul in Jerusalem reported: "The population and wealth of Palestine has not increased during the last forty years" (Ben Halpern, *The Idea of a Jewish State*, p. 108).

This desolation was the reality encountered by the *Chovevei Tziyon*, those who returned to *Eretz Yisrael* in the late 1800s. Areas that had been fertile in biblical times were now infested wastelands. *Eretz Yisrael* had indeed remained true to the Jewish people, waiting for the only nation that could be its redeemer. Scattered throughout the four corners of the earth (see *Avoda Zara* 10b), the small numbers of Jews intent on returning had new goals. Besides heralding the beginning of the period of the ingathering of the exiles, they would come to agriculturally advance the land, building agricultural settlements in a land that had been desolate since the Jewish People's expulsion almost two thousand years earlier.

As Jews returned to their land and Jewish settlements began to arise, so did the reality that the only places where there was agricultural growth were in Jewish villages. The Report of the Palestine Royal Commission quotes an account of the Maritime Plain in 1913:

The road leading from Gaza to the north was only a summer track suitable for transport by camels and carts... no orange groves, orchards or vineyards were to be seen until one reached [the Jewish village of] Yavne... (*The Idea of a Jewish State*, p. 233)

It is not surprising that many individuals who were not sympathetic to the Zionist cause nevertheless accepted the fact that the land began to blossom amidst Jewish settlement, and they, therefore, deemed the arrival of Jews a necessity. In fact, of all people, Sharif Hussein, the Guardian of the Islamic Holy Places in Arabia, stated:

> The resources of the country are still virgin soil and will be developed by the Jewish immigrants. One of the most amazing things until recent times was that the Palestinian used to leave his country, wandering over the high seas in every direction. His native soil could not retain a hold on him, though his ancestors had lived on it for 1000 years. At the same time we have seen the Jews from foreign countries streaming to Palestine from Russia, Germany, Austria, Spain, America. The cause of causes could not escape those who had a gift of deeper insight. They knew that the country was for its original sons (*abna'ihi-l-asliyin*), for all their differences, a sacred and beloved homeland. The return of these exiles (*jaliya*) to their homeland will prove materially and spiritually [to be] an experimental school for their brethren who are with them in the fields, factories, trades and in all things connected with toil and labor. (Samuel Katz, *Battleground — Fact and Fantasy in Palestine*, p. 126)

As Hussein foresaw, the regeneration of Palestine and the growth of its population would come only after Jews returned in massive numbers. This was not the result of the Jewish People taking over Arab lands, as there was little or nothing that grew, and the land couldn't support Jewish inhabitants. Instead, as the Jewish settlement grew and the divinely promised reawakening of prosperity came to life, Arabs from surrounding lands begin to come to the land to take advantage of the newfound growth.[65]

Even though there was always a small Jewish presence in the Land of Israel, it had not engaged in farming for the most part. Investment of efforts in agriculture began only when the students of the Vilna Gaon and others arrived in the Land for the express purpose of bringing about an agricultural revolution that would herald the ultimate redemption. In fact, the Talmud explicitly links the physical rebirth of the land to promising indications of the upcoming redemption:

---

65 Numerous sources reflect the dearth of population in *Eretz Yisrael* when it lay desolate. Far from a Palestinian nation residing in the land, before Jewish settlement in the late nineteenth-century, virtually only nomadic tribes could be found in the land. As the Jewish nation began to return to the land, *Eretz Yisrael* came to life, as if awakened from a slumber, bringing prosperity and, in turn, rapid immigration from neighboring Arab areas. Because *Eretz Yisrael* only grows for the Jewish People, the Arab immigrants found themselves trying to live in Jewish areas of the land. As the British Peel Commission Report recorded: "The increase in Arab population is most marked in urban areas affected by Jewish development. Jews have been building in Haifa, and Arab population has increased there by 86 percent between 1922 and 1931" (*Spokesman-Review*, Nov. 7, 1937).

These numbers continued to increase as the British government buckled down on Jewish immigration while showing indifference to Arab immigration: "Illegal immigration into the country...continues and according to an authoritative estimate, Arabs illegally entering Palestine are outnumbering the Jews by 20 to one. The Arab newspaper 'Aldifar' today reported that an appeal may be made to the neighboring Arab countries to organize dispatch of Arabs illegally into Palestine as counter to the Jewish immigration. According to police authorities it is far more difficult to keep a check of Arab smuggling of immigrants than it is of the Jewish" (*Indian Express*, Oct. 22, 1945).

The Arab immigrants retained their last names, attesting to their identity with their land of origin (such as Al-Turki [Turkey], Al-Baghdadi [Iraq], and Husseini/Hussein [Saudi Arabia; Hussein was the fourth Imam]. See The Origins of Arab Settlers in the Land of Israel (mida.org.il) for a historical record of the various surnames found in Israel's Arab population, all aimed at indicating the various countries of origin of the families and clans. See http://www.eretzyisroel.org/~peters/depopulated.html for a further sources.

וְאָמַר רַבִּי אַבָּא: אֵין לָךְ קֵץ מְגֻלֶּה מִזֶּה, שֶׁנֶּאֱמַר יְשָׂרָאֵל וְאַתֶּם הָרֵי יִשְׂרָאֵל עַנְפְּכֶם תִּתֵּנוּ וּפֶרְיְכֶם תִּשְׂאוּ לְעַמִּי יִשְׂרָאֵל וְגוֹ'.

Rabbi Abba said: There is no *ketz meguleh,* clearer indication of the End [of days], than this, as it is stated (*Yechezkel* 36:8): "But you, O mountains of Israel, you shall shoot forth your branches and bear your fruit for my people Israel [when they are soon to come]." (TB *Sanhedrin* 98a)

Rashi explains that the land's bringing forth fruit in abundance acts as a sign of the impending redemption.

Israel is currently viewed as an agricultural powerhouse, the world's leader in agricultural innovation and success. Yet, one need look no further than Wikipedia ("Agriculture in Israel") to realize that Israel's agricultural leadership is anything but a given:

Agriculture in Israel is a highly developed industry. Israel is a major exporter of fresh produce and a world leader in agricultural technologies, despite the fact that the geography of the country is not naturally conducive to agriculture. More than half of the land area is desert, and the climate and lack of water resources do not favor farming. Only 20% of the land area is naturally arable.

Could this success be attributed to natural causes or an expression of brainpower and commitment? Or are those reasons coupled with the Land's embrace of its nation upon its return to its borders?

The Promised Land's Promise

The sorry agricultural state of most of the Middle East was the argument adopted by many detractors of the Zionist push for Jewish settlement in the land. Mark Twain's findings, coupled with the sad reality in Arab lands, led to "concerned voices" to argue that Jewish settlement in what was then the British Mandate of Palestine would result in certain death for the Jewish pioneers. The malaria-infested wastelands couldn't support a large increase in population.

Twain's testimony, so true at the time, would quickly become outdated in Jewish areas of the land. A year after Twain's trip, planning for Israel's first agricultural school, "Mikveh Yisrael",[66] began. Jewish agricultural settlements and colonies arose and, against all odds, began to drain the swamps and restore the land to its natural beauty. As they return to the land, the land returns to them, and Israel's agricultural miracle comes in full swing.

Many of these pioneers viewed themselves as implementing the teachings of the Vilna Gaon and great Chassidic leaders who advocated agricultural redemption of the land as a means of initiating the first steps of the *geula,* redemption.[67] Rabbi Abba's statement about

---

66   It opened in 1871. A tailor in Yerushalayim, R' Gershon, who made the uniforms for the agricultural students, suggested the name "Mikveh Yisrael", hope of Israel, based on the *pasuk* in the *haftorah* of *Parashat Bechukotai,* Yirimyahu (17:3): "O Lord, *Mikveh Yisrael,* the hope of Israel, all who forsake you will be put to shame". Charles Netter, the school's founder, accepted the suggestion. A further indication that *Parashat Bechukotai* described the tragic exile and desolation, but also the secret to the Jewish return.

67   See https://jewishaction.com/books/two_hundred_years_in_eretz_yisrael_the_seminal_aliyah_of_the_

Israel's agricultural rebirth heralding the redemption process was now being witnessed, and these pioneers were playing an active role in bringing it about.

In the words of Rav Kook (*Chazon ha-Geula*, 5701): "The beginning of the redemption is unquestionably unfolding gradually before us. From the time when the mountains of Israel began to shoot forth branches and to yield fruit for Am Yisrael, who had started to come back, this beginning commenced...."

Lowdermilk's Findings

In 1938 a Christain soil conservationist, Walter Clay Lowdermilk, was sent by the United States Department of Agriculture to survey the use of land in Europe, North Africa, and the Middle East. His mission was to bring back information that could assist the American Southwest. In the process, he found the beauty of Israel while witnessing the Jewish nation's agricultural revolution in the land. He used his scientific expertise to further the agricultural rebirth in the land, playing a pivotal role in developing Israel's Mekorot national water carrier system. Upon his return to the United States, he wrote *Palestine: Land of Promise*, and served as a primary advocate for Jewish settlement in the land. Although he would return to live in Israel, his works influenced Harry Truman and others, and his influence positively impacted the United States' acceptance of the Jewish State.

Interestingly, he wrote that his findings while surveying greater Palestine essentially indicated that while Mark Twain's words still rang true in most of the Middle East, they no longer applied to the Jewish settlements. He accused "poor stewardship of the land" by non-Jewish populations as responsible for the once fertile land becoming a wasteland. Centuries of abuse depleted the soil.

The areas inhabited by Jewish settlers, however, were rather impressive. He notes that specifically those "who fled to Palestine from the hatreds and persecutions of Europe" were able to astonishingly build three hundred colonies by "defying great hardships and applying the principles of co-operation and soil conservation." They have, he continued, "demonstrated the finest reclamation of old lands that I have seen in three continents." And "they have done this by the application of science, industry, and devotion to the problems of reclaiming lands, draining swamps, improving agriculture and livestock and creating new industries." All this was accomplished against "great odds and with sacrificial devotion to the ideal of redeeming the Promised Land."[68]

He was convinced that some of the Jewish success in Israel could be exported to the United States and elsewhere while proclaiming that Israel's agricultural success ensured it could become a viable home for the Jewish nation. He wrote: "The Holy Land can be reclaimed from the desolation of long neglect and wastage and provide farms, industry, and security for possibly five million Jewish refugees from the persecutions and hatreds of Europe ..."

Armed with his Bible, the Christian Lowdermilk recognized that both the land's desolation

---

talmidei_hagra/

68   See http://www.jbooks.com/interviews/index/IP_Radosh.htm, where quotes are taken from.

and the Jewish pioneers' remarkable regeneration of the soil should not be a surprise to anyone. He attests: "When Jewish colonists first began their work in 1882... the soil was eroded to bedrock over fully one-half of the hills – streams across the coastal plain would choke with erosional debris from the hills to form pestilential marshes infested with dreaded malaria... Those who can read the record that has been written in the land know that this state of decadence is not normal... Rural Palestine is becoming less and less like Trans-Jordan, Syria and Iraq and more like Denmark, Holland and parts of the United States."

Lowdermilk was so amazed by his findings that he and his wife eventually made Israel their home to contribute his expertise and further advance the land. He remarked: "If we were interested in the regeneration of Man, let all the righteous forces on earth support these settlements in Palestine as a wholesome example for the backward Near East, and indeed for all who seek to work out a permanent adjustment of people to their lands."

Yet Lowdermilk recognized that his world-class knowledge could not explain everything. Science was of limited value in interpreting the extent of agricultural success in the land. The Divine promise was the only fully "rational" explanation for the agricultural miracle that Jewish agricultural settlements brought to the land that had remained faithful to its people for so long. If only Lowdermilk could see the country now.

The Pioneer's Challenge of *Shevi'it* Observance

One can only imagine the passion of the Jews returning to the Land from all four corners of the world, as they witnessed their hard work assist the Land bear fruit, when it had not done so for generations. Simultaneously, those with a historical perspective and a religious outlook understood that maintaining the right to continue settling the land meant doing so in line with God's Will. The return meant an opportunity for fulfilling the *mitzvot hateluyot ba'aretz*. At the same time that these opportunities were embraced, however, they were often accompanied by recognition of their observance's challenges. No set of *mitzvot* was as challenging as those of *shemitta*; moreover, none would have the same repercussions for non-observance.

This brought the question to the forefront: Was *shevi'it* to be viewed as an obstacle to this reawakening or as its guarantee? The connection between observance of *shevi'it* and the return to the Land of Israel also explains a bit of the contention surrounding what is known to many as the *heter mechira* controversy.

An important factor in the discussion is that an overwhelming majority of *halachic* authorities rule that *shevi'it* in our day and age is only Rabbinically mandated, as the Biblical requirement only pertains when the nation is settled in the land in an ideal manner, according to its tribes (as discussed at greater length in section III). Since *shevi'it* is so challenging and its nonobservance has brought about exile, why did the Sages make it Rabbinically binding at all? The question is its own answer. If such a challenge has been revived by Rabbinic injunction, its message is evidently still relevant. Therefore, as the nation returns to its Land's embrace, proper *shevi'it* observance becomes an essential question as to how to view the modern return and its future implications.

For some, the newfound opportunity for *shevi'it* observance would demonstrate the recognition that the Jewish return to the land was a miraculous expression of the divine promise. Attempting to rebuild the land without complying with *shevi'it* would be tantamount to blasphemy, raising the threat of returning to exile, as non-observance of *shemitta* brought about originally.

Others viewed the observance of *shevi'it* as an obstacle to Jewish return; if there was going to be an agricultural revolution in Israel, the nation needed to plant as much as possible. Before each group of pioneers' first *shevi'it* year, there could only be a maximum of six years of planting, leaving little to live off of during the *shevi'it*. Some of the nonobservant farmers viewed the laws of *shevi'it* as proof that the new settlement in *Eretz Yisrael* could not observe the traditional laws if it wanted to survive. Even religious settlers who personally acknowledged the importance of *shevi'it* observance felt that for practical reasons caused by the extenuating circumstances of the time, traditional *shevi'it* observance was not yet possible. Could the observance of Rabbinically mandated laws be worthy of the divine promise that sufficient produce would grow in the sixth year for the nation to continue to survive during the *shevi'it* year as well? The settlers reasoned that the situation was one of *pikuach nefesh*, mortal danger, and in order to save lives (and deal with a host of other challenges), *shevi'it* could not be observed. Many people, including some of the financial sponsors of the new settlements, viewed *shevi'it* as an obstacle that might destroy any chance for successful resettlement of the Land of Israel. In their minds, a means had to be found to permit working the land.

As the numbers of pioneers grew, the challenge of *shevi'it* became all the more formidable, as there were more mouths to feed and greater fear that the *shevi'it*-year harvest would not provide sufficient yields. Through a series of *halachic* deliberations beyond the current purview, one suggestion became known as the *heter mechira* –permitting the selling of the land's Jewish soil to non-Jews to allow working the land during *shevi'it*.

In the context of our philosophical analysis of the issues, more important than discussing the controversy surrounding the *heter mechira*, is appreciating the historical destiny that brought about this challenge. The rebirth of Israeli agriculture is the sign of the Jews' return, and any issues it might raise, *shevi'it* observance chief among them, are a welcome reflection of the land's faithfulness to its people, as well as a call for man's faith in God.

With this in mind, we can appreciate the work of Rav Avraham Yitzchak Ha-Kohen Kook (1865-1935), who witnessed in his lifetime the early stages of the ingathering of exiles into *Eretz Yisrael*. Rav Kook's broad vision for the future of the Land and the nation was expressed in the context of *shevi'it*. In his introduction to his *Shabbat HaAretz*, he discusses the concept of *shevi'it*, its goals, its challenges, and its implications. To understand Rav Kook's words, we must take a moment to review some of the philosophical underpinnings of his approach to *Eretz Yisrael*, which was highly influenced by Rav Yehuda HaLevi's *Kuzari*.[69]

Rav Yehuda HaLevi's Perspective on the Land of Israel

The theme of the uniqueness of *Eretz Yisrael* and its special character appears throughout the *Kuzari*. The king's interlocutor, the *Chaver*, describes the necessity of *Eretz Yisrael* for the Jewish People, both as individuals and as a collective (an idea he also alludes to in 1:95). He presents a parallel to the natural world, in which only specific things grow in certain locations. *Eretz Yisrael* is a unique land, especially suited to nurture the Jewish People and to allow it to achieve its spiritual aspirations:

> You will have no difficulty in perceiving that one country may have superior qualities to others. There are places in which particular vegetables, minerals, or animals are found, or where the inhabitants are distinguished by their form and character, since perfection or deficiency of the soul are produced by the mingling of the elements. (*Kuzari* 2:10)

In response to the king's wondering what unique aspects are the lot of those who live in the Land, the *Chaver* responds:

> In the second instance, it would belong to the country on account of the religious acts connected with it, which I would compare to the cultivation of the vineyard. No other place may share the distinction of the divine influence, just as no other hill country may be able to produce a variety of fine wine. (*Kuzari* 2:11-12)

The land can bring the nation to realize its potential, as it is only in *Eretz Yisrael* (or on account of it) that prophecy is attainable for mankind. It is in this context that the *Chaver* explains that the uniqueness of the Land is expressed through *shevi'it*:

> Do you not see that even the land was given its Sabbaths, as it is said: "Sabbath of the land" (*Vayikra* 25:6), and "When you come to the land which I am giving you, the land shall rest a Sabbath to God." (ibid. v. 2). It is forbidden to sell it forever, as it is said: "For Mine is the land" (v. 23). Observe that the "feasts of God" and the "Sabbaths of the land" belong to the "land of God." (*Kuzari* 2:17)

Rav Kook's Outlook on the Land

Rav Avraham Yitzchak HaKohen Kook was born in Griva, Latvia in 1865. He was a child prodigy and later a prized student in the Volozhin Yeshiva, where he was a close disciple of the Rosh HaYeshiva, Rav Naftali Tzvi Yehuda Berlin (the Netziv). At the age of 23, Rav Kook took his first rabbinical position. In his thirties, he began spreading his thought through three articles that anticipated the fully-developed philosophy he developed in the Land of Israel.

An ardent lover of the Land of Israel, Rav Kook moved to *Eretz Yisrael* in 1904 and assumed the position of the Chief Rabbi of Yaffo (Jaffa). He served not only the Orthodox population in the area but the new secular Zionist agricultural settlements nearby, as well.

---

69   The Kuzari is Rabbi Yehuda HaLevi's book on Jewish thought. It describes a discussion between the Khazar king (who converted to Judaism in the eighth century) and the *chaver*, a learned Jew, who answers the spiritually searching king's questions.

His influence continued to spread, even when he was stuck in Europe during World War I. While in London, Rav Kook played an active role in diplomacy that led to the Balfour Declaration. Upon returning, he was appointed the Chief Rabbi of Jerusalem, and soon after, the first Chief Rabbi of Israel (although this was prior to the founding of the State).

Rav Kook was a prolific writer and thinker whose mastery of all areas of Torah, unique personality, and familiarity with some modern thought and philosophy combined to form a towering individual. Many credit him with prophetic views of what would occur in Israel as the Jewish nation returned and rebuilt the Land. Although he passed away in 1935, before the founding of the State of Israel, he wrote extensively of a State that would play an integral part in enabling the Jewish nation to achieve its primary role in the world.

Rav Kook's outlook on *Eretz Yisrael* is heavily based on the *Kuzari*. In his well-known opening statement regarding the Land, he takes issue with two perspectives about *Eretz Yisrael* that view in it primarily practical significance. In his rebuttal, he echoes the *Kuzari's* sentiments and takes them further:

> *Eretz Yisrael* is not a superficial matter, a superficial asset of the nation, merely a means to achieve the objective of overall unity and material, or even spiritual, survival. *Eretz Yisrael* is an essential element bound with a living connection to the people, linked by its inner essence to the people's existence. (*Orot, Eretz Yisrael* 1)

Rav Kook is adamant that the Land is not merely "a means to achieve the objective of overall unity and material… survival" of the nation, what is sometimes referred to contemporarily as a "safe haven." Additionally, it is not necessary merely for the "overall unity and… even spiritual survival" of the nation. Rav Kook posits that this perspective "cannot survive, for its foundation is shaky…" Such a conception fails to recognize how the destiny of the Jewish People is intertwined with that of the land.

What is the source that forms the basis of the views of Rav Yehuda HaLevi and Rav Kook regarding this level of connection between the people and the Land? Quite simply, *shevi'it*. The Torah conditions the Jewish presence in the Land of Israel upon its observance, the terminology "which I am giving to you" connects it to the right to receive the gift of *Eretz Yisrael*, and it is through the re-emergence of *shevi'it* that the Jewish People's return to the land is manifest.

Therefore, it is understandable that Rav Kook chooses to explain the nature of the Jewish connection to *Eretz Yisrael* and the significance of the rebirth specifically in the introduction for his work on *shevi'it*.

Nevertheless, this choice may be seen as counterintuitive. One primary focus of his work *Shabbat HaAretz* is creating a *halachic* basis for the rationale of the *heter mechira*, the controversial means of selling *Eretz Yisrael* to non-Jews in order to permit cultivation during *shevi'it*. The *heter* appears to be an attempt to employ leniencies rather than to rise to the challenge of *shevi'it* observance. Yet, it is specifically in the introduction to that work that Rav Kook expresses his historical outlook on the people, their land, their exile, and their restoration — amid the challenges and opportunities of *shevi'it* observance.

On the one hand, Rav Kook fully acknowledged that the agricultural rebirth of the land was a fulfillment of the initial stages of redemption, so long as it was accompanied by the *mitzvot* that uniquely expressed the land's sanctity. Yet, at the same time, Rav Kook felt that the time had not yet come when full *shevi'it* observance was practical. This was the impetus for the publication of *Shabbat HaAretz* on the eve of the 1909-1910 *shevi'it* year.

The gist of Rav Kook's entire preface is that the *heter mechira* is, as summarized by Rav Aharon Lichtenstein, a *halachic* tragedy. The resettlement of the land, due to historical necessity, must commence without full observance of the agricultural *mitzvot*. It is this preface that deserves special attention in order to appreciate *shevi'it*'s role in Jewish history, according to Rav Kook.

Rav Kook's Historical Perspective

To understand Rav Kook's approach, we must first consider his overall perspective on history. Rav Kook viewed history as constantly advancing, albeit with setbacks. According to his outlook on the "evolutionary" advancement of the world, the world is moving towards greater perfection. In a section of his *Orot HaKodesh* entitled "The Ascending Development," Rav Kook describes the general advancement of the world towards the absolute perfection of God, the *Ein Sof* (a Kabbalistic phrase meaning the infinite one), which he saw as the goal of creation. In this context, he defines the evolutionary process of natural, historical progress as a philosophical theory, not a scientific one:

> The theory of evolution (*hitpatchut*) is increasingly conquering the world at this time, and, more so than all other philosophical theories, conforms to the kabbalistic secrets of the world. Evolution, which proceeds on a path of ascendancy, provides an optimistic foundation for the world. How is it possible to despair at a time when we see that everything evolves and ascends? When we penetrate the inner meaning of ascending evolution, we find in it the divine element shining with absolute brilliance. It is precisely the *Ein Sof in actu* which manages to bring to realization that which is *Ein Sof in potentia*. (*Orot HaKodesh* 2:537)

For Rav Kook, Darwin's biological theory of evolution, which was just beginning to gain traction at the time, was nothing new; it was merely a means of Western thought embracing at least one aspect of the Kabbalistic worldview regarding the unfolding of reality.

Rav Kook's philosophy sought to synthesize all aspects of truth, even what he viewed as scientific half-truths. His thought makes use of dialectical analysis. A dialectic postulates opposing concepts – a "thesis", and its negation, the "antithesis." A dialectic that reaches a conclusion achieves "synthesis", a proper balance between the concerns of the thesis and antithesis. Two general forms of dialectics exist. A dialectic that never reaches a harmonious resolution is known as a Kierkegaardian dialectic (after nineteenth-century Danish theologian Soren Kierkegaard), whereas a dialectic that ends in "synthesis" is termed a Hegelian dialectic (after nineteenth-century German philosopher Georg W. F. Hegel).[70]

Great thinkers such as Rav Yosef Dov HaLevi Soloveitchik viewed Judaism as a system of thesis and antithesis, a Kierkegaardian dialectic:

> Judaic dialectic, unlike the Hegelian, is irreconcilable and hence interminable... To Hegel, man and his history were just abstract ideas; in the world of abstractions, synthesis is conceivable. To Judaism, man has always been and still is a living reality... In the world of realities, the harmony of opposites is an impossibility. ("Majesty and Humility," p. 25)

For the Rav, Jewish philosophy requires *chakira*, investigation of various possibilities, and the adopting of sometimes irreconcilable dialectics, not always reaching harmony. Although, at times, the Rav does achieve harmony between opposing concepts, he views the dialectical challenge as innate in our existence.

On the other hand, Rav Kook espoused a harmonious approach to life, viewing history as constantly moving toward synthesis. Many credit Rav Kook's Kabbalistic approach and the influence of the Ramchal (Rav Moshe Chaim Luzzato, author of *Derech Hashem* and *Mesillat Yesharim*, among numerous other works) as impacting his worldview.[71] Others argue that Hegel's philosophy also influenced Rav Kook, as he too saw history as having an ultimate purpose that would unfold through the resolution of the dialectical tension of opposing historical forces.[72]

Rav Kook presents his dialectical approach to history in numerous contexts, emphasizing the dialectical tensions whose resolutions propel history forward towards its ultimate purpose.[73] History, in his view, is not simply an amalgam of different societies; rather, one leads into another. One synthesis becomes the basis for the next thesis, followed by antithesis and ultimately a new synthesis. For Rav Kook, divine perfection is reflected through this process of constant growth, which is ultimately optimistic but is not linear. There will be stages of imperfections and contradictions (*"shevira,"* shattering), as they

---

70 Hegel himself attributed the terminology to philosopher Immanuel Kant.

71 Rav Kook's student, the *Nazir*, identifies the Ramchal as the primary influence on Rav Kook's philosophy of history; see *Orot HaKodesh*, vol. 1, pp. 31-38.

72 For a detailed analysis of Hegelian influence on Rav Kook, see Shlomo Fischer, "Self-Expression and Democracy in Radical Religious Zionist Ideology" (Ph.D. diss., Hebrew University, 2007), pp. 75-126.
    It is clear that Hegel's approach to history had influence on a number of Jewish thinkers, among them Nachman Krochmal, who lived in the early years of the Emancipation. Krochmal notes that in the Hegelian world view, nations take turns climbing onto the world stage and preaching their outlook to the world, but at some point disappear from the world stage, even as their central ideas are passed on. Krochmal writes that while this is indeed true of other nations, it is not true of the Jewish People, who have never disappeared from the world stage, stubbornly disproving Hegel's universal rule that all nations will decline and demise. Krochmal notes that it is because Judaism is God-centered, and God is eternal and omnipotent, that the nation can never complete teaching its message. It is everlasting like God Himself (see https://www.shalomrosenberg.com/wp-content/uploads/2020/03/KUZARI-ENGLISH.pdf).
    Rav Kook seems to have accepted a similar understanding, although never explicitly reconciling his worldview with that of Hegel. For Rav Kook, the Jewish nation is inherently connected to God and the Torah and cannot be explained independently of those eternal truths. Hegel's outlook on history is useful for terminology that can help us uncover patterns in Jewish history, but Jewish history is the history of the eternal nation, which does not operate by the temporal rules guiding world history.

73 See *Eder HaYakar*, pp. 13-14; *Orot HaKodesh*, vol. 1, p. 15; *Shemonah Kevatzim* 5:61; *Iggerot HaRa'ayah*, vol. 1, Letter 110.

are necessary ingredients for ultimate *tikkun* (rectification). The ongoing process of reconstructing the broken pieces results in a more potent, perfected form that can better reveal the divine light ("*achdut hahafachim*," the unity of opposites).

Following this worldview, Rav Kook viewed the desire to return to *Eretz Yisrael* not as merely another stage in Jewish history, but as leading to history's culmination. For Rav Kook, redemption is a historical process filled with dialectical contradictions (national/universal, physical/ spiritual, etc.) that will ultimately reach a stage of higher synthesis.[74]

Indeed, for this reason, Rav Kook saw significant spiritual importance in all modern political movements and cultural sensibilities. He viewed modern historical phenomena, such as atheism and Zionism, as serving a role in this process, particularly because they appear antagonistic to traditional religious life. They present an opportunity for elevating Judaism as they pave the way for a more exalted form of faith. Atheism, he argued, should not be seen as a rejection of God, but rather a rejection of the outwardly religious individuals who lack a true relationship with God. Hearing the cry of the atheist can actually ensure that we better understand Judaism and strengthen our relationship with God. Similarly, the cultural Zionism that seeks to serve as a secular replacement for Jewish religious identity includes a love of Jewish peoplehood and lays the groundwork for Judaism's eventual renewal as a spiritual nation in its land.

This outlook plays a major role in Rav Kook's introduction to *Shabbat HaAretz*. Rav Kook viewed the destruction and desolation of the Land as playing a pivotal role in the unfolding of the historical process leading to redemption.

Rav Kook's Introduction to *Shabbat HaAretz*

Shabbat HaAretz begins with a description of the deep significance of *shevi'it* and *yovel*, specifically within the context of the role they play from a Jewish national perspective:

> The very same effect that is produced for every individual by the Shabbat is produced by the *shemitta* for the nation as a whole.

In addition to *shevi'it's* general purpose and the implications of the Shabbat of an entire nation in its land, Rav Kook emphasizes *shevi'it's* unique role in history, particularly during his lifetime.

To understand Rav Kook's perspective, we must first recognize the radical nature of his thinking. A nation that had all but lost its connection to its land could not imagine a mass return if not by the miraculous coming of the Messiah. Rav Kook explained that the return of the Jewish pioneers to the land proved a tremendous miracle, as the Land of Israel had started growing again for the Jewish People. This blessing indicated that the time of the revealed redemption was at hand.

---

74   See Betzalel Naor's collection of essays, *When God Becomes History*, where he points out that Rav Kook took traditional Jewish views of history one step beyond, such that God not only reveals Himself through history, but actually becomes part of it.

Shevi'it, symbolizing both exile and redemption, was re-emerging historically as a reality for the Jewish People, indicating the significance of the period but also calling for temporary measures to ensure the new settlements would be capable of dealing with these new realities.

For this reason, a major portion of Rav Kook's preface is devoted to his penetrating description of the nation's connection to the Land and *shevi'it*'s role in maintaining that connection. He also explains why exile is the only available option for a nation that has lost sense of the connection:

> The special character of the land and the special character of the nation fit well together. In the same way that the nation is distinguished by divine elevation in the deepest parts of her being, so in the same way it is the land, the land of God, which prepares and refines the people who inhabit it as an everlasting inheritance and which is theirs through a covenant and an oath based on trust in the eternal glory of Israel. This is firmly founded on the divine nature which is fixed in the very nature of this wonderful, desirable land, a land that is betrothed to this people that God has chosen for His special treasure. The soul of both the nation and the land function together at the very basis of their existence, fulfilling their roles in realizing during the sabbatical year the full potential of their longing and yearning which emanate from the depths of their holiness.
>
> On the one hand, the people work with their spiritual strength on the earth, and so the seed of God becomes manifest through His spiritual influence. On the other hand, the land acts on the people in refining its inner qualities to suit the desire for a godly life that is perfect in its form and structure. A sabbatical year is an absolute necessity for the nation and for the land.

Rav Kook goes on to describe exactly how the sabbatical year fulfills this role of liberating and educating the people, inculcating the holiness that is so natural and necessary for the Holy Land. He discusses why when the nation falls and loses sight of their treasured status and the behavior required for maintaining that status; they lose perspective. They no longer understand *shevi'it*'s message and cease to observe it. As the nation regresses spiritually, the land is contaminated and can no longer maintain its physical beauty, as it is a land that responds physically to the spiritual status of its beloved people.

Due to the national character of *shevi'it*, losing touch with its message is equivalent to losing touch with the essence of national life in Israel. If the People model their national existence in Israel after other nations, they lose touch with the singular, unique spiritual core of the nation. This involves becoming disconnected from the Torah, both as individuals and as a collective.

Rav Kook advances one of his innovative ideas in this context. He argues that if the nation completely distances itself from the spiritual aspects of its national character by attempting to cultivate the land at all costs, even nonobservance of *shevi'it*, their remaining in the Land is not beneficial. When the connection to the Land is detrimental for the spiritual solitude of the nation, they must be distanced from their Land for their own good. Misuse of the land will only bring about destruction. The people contaminate the Land through their actions, and something must be done.

At this point, there are essentially two options: God can choose to eradicate the people, as they are, in fact, deserving of punishment for their sins. Alternatively, God can put in place a system that will rehabilitate and heal the misguided nation and pave the way for their ultimate return to their Land.

A strict measure of justice would indeed entail the former option. A nation that failed to heed numerous warnings, worshiped other gods, mistreated its unfortunates, and deviated so significantly from its mission, should be deemed hopeless. Exile would provide a future chance for the nation; wouldn't eradication be far more appropriate? Rather than leave the land desolate, logic would dictate that the Land should remain intact, and it, with the *Mikdash*, be given over to another people who will more faithfully fulfill the word of God.

While this might be the logical response of un-tempered justice (and some faiths have embraced this philosophy), this is certainly not God's plan. God made his selections of a nation, a land, and a place in the land to serve as His *Mikdash*. God doesn't make bad choices; people do. God invests within the eternal nation the ability to repent and one day return to their land with a new perspective, one that can allow them to successfully build a model society. For this reason, God does not eradicate the Jewish People, but instead sends them into exile.

This is the blessing in disguise. The land might be desolate, but it remains an indication of God's plan for the Jewish nation to return when they are fit to, and to then rebuild the land. The second blessing in disguise is that the land would be punished for the people's sins, rather than eradicating the nation. This proves that there is a chance for altering destiny.

The idea that some of the worst moments of destruction in our nation's history are blessings in disguise is a tradition with firm roots. The *pasuk* in *Tehillim* states:

> מִזְמוֹר לְאָסָף אֱ-לֹהִים בָּאוּ גוֹיִם בְּנַחֲלָתֶךָ טִמְּאוּ אֶת הֵיכַל קָדְשֶׁךָ שָׂמוּ אֶת יְרוּשָׁלַם לְעִיִּים:
>
> A song of Asaf: O God! Nations have come into Your heritage, they have defiled Your Holy Temple, they have made Jerusalem into heaps. (*Tehillim* 79:1)

The Sages question why this chapter, which describes the Temple's destruction, is termed a "song." Logic would dictate that the destruction of the Temple should not be a cause for song, but rather a cause for lamenting (see Rashi, *Kiddushin* 31b). The *midrash* explains that the joy in the devastation is that "God exhausted His fury on the wood and stones of the Temple," allowing the Jewish People themselves to survive.

Along these lines, the Vilna Gaon explains that the mourning of the Ninth of Av is lightened at midday because that is when the Temple actually started burning. Although logic would dictate that specifically at the moment of destruction one should be more overcome with pain, it is at the moment that the Temple burns that permission is granted for the mourners to rise from the floor and sit on chairs. Although the destruction is no cause for celebration, the fact that God takes out his anger on the physical building of the Temple is a cause for some modicum of consolation. The moment of destruction reflects God's immense love for the Jewish People and His desire to give them another chance.

This historical outlook is the only approach that can explain a phenomenon described in another of Mark Twain's well-known remarks regarding the Jewish People:

> If the statistics are right, the Jews constitute but one quarter of one percent of the human race. It suggests a nebulous puff of star dust lost in the blaze of the Milky Way. Properly, the Jew ought hardly to be heard of, but he is heard of, has always been heard of. He is as prominent on the planet as any other people, and his importance is extravagantly out of proportion to the smallness of his bulk... He has made a marvelous fight in this world in all ages; and has done it with his hands tied behind him. He could be vain of himself and be excused for it. The Egyptians, the Babylonians and the Persians rose, filled the planet with sound and splendor, then faded to dream-stuff and passed away; the Greeks and Romans followed and made a vast noise, and they were gone; other people have sprung up and held their torch high for a time but it burned out, and they sit in twilight now, and have vanished.
>
> The Jew saw them all, survived them all, and is now what he always was, exhibiting no decadence, no infirmities, of age, no weakening of his parts, no slowing of his energies, no dulling of his alert but aggressive mind. All things are mortal but the Jews; all other forces pass, but he remains. What is the secret of his immortality? (*Concerning the Jews*, Harper's Magazine, March 1898)

The Purpose of Exile

With this outlook in mind, it is possible to understand one of Rav Kook's radical explanations of the purpose of the exile. If the scattering of the nation is a sign of divine love for the people, then the exile must serve a purpose other than punishment. But what could that purpose be?

Rav Kook begins by explaining why the rights and even benefits of remaining in the land were not applicable during the exile:

> When Israel's awareness of its own spirit became foggy... forgetting their inner strength and pride, looking superficially at the underdeveloped and wild environment made them forget their inner greatness. The yearning for a refined godly life slipped from their hearts... The light of justice was dimmed. In its place came the coarse imagination of a lawless society... (*Shabbat HaAretz* p. 117)[75]

As Rav Kook enunciates the horror of such a situation, he also notes that, due to the connection between man and the land, this reality affects the land as well.

> As the people became spiritually weaker, the special quality of the land could no longer find fulfillment... the people absorbed bad influences, which coarsened its pure nature... when national life became defiled, the power of ethics increased [i.e. although there were outbursts of moral intensity, in the absence of supporting political institutions, they were unsustainable], but with the surrounding political turmoil, the result was simply inner anguish and confusion. These two elements, the

---

75   All citations of *Shabbat HaAretz* are from Rabbi Julian Sinclair's bilingual edition, *Rav Kook's Introduction to Shabbat HaAretz* (Hazon, 2014).

> people and the land, which, when healthy, had given each other so much grace and power for good — made each other sicker and more corrupt. Finally they had to take the cruel-kind medicine, the dreadful surgical operation of separating the people from the land.

Allowing another nation to conquer and subjugate Israel isn't an option when *shevi'it* observance is forgotten and with it the sense of understanding of the nation's purpose. Subjugation within the boundaries of the land will not suffice when the whole national life, from the economy to the festivals, has become rotten to the core.

The sad result is the curses described in *Parashat Bechukotai*. A nation that has lost understanding of its purpose needs to undergo surgery – to be excised from its land.

> Finally they had to take the cruel-kind medicine, the dreadful surgical operation of separating the people from the land …

As the *Musaf* prayer states, "Due to our sins we have been exiled from our land." For Rav Kook, this is not mere punishment, but a necessary process after sin. Rav Kook builds on this to explain how exile serves as the antidote to this deeply-rooted dilemma of national proportions.

Specifically because national life in Israel seeks to create a commonwealth and society that merges the physical and the spiritual, the stakes are so high and the challenge so great. It is when this fails that the frightening prophecies in *Parashat Bechukotai* result. But this is not the end. The process concludes with hope, as the Torah describes. Rav Kook explains that the purpose of exile is not to supplant life in Israel, nor to make exile a lasting option. Rather, the nation can only survive and exist as a nation in the Land that God has destined for it.

Rav Kook describes how a misguided society and corrupted government in the Land of Israel cannot be fixed from within. He sharply delineates the bitter conflict between moral values and "the oppression, coercion, and grubbiness stemming from [the desire for] acquisition and property, which must be manifest in the world of action." When the negative influence of national life becomes too morally injurious, writes Rav Kook, there is no avoiding "the terrible detachment, the expulsion of the nation from the land." In exile, the Jews may change focus and begin a process of spiritualization.[76]

Exile allows the Jewish people to develop a spiritual focus. When the nation is outside of its land, it cannot apply itself to building up the physical part of the nation; it has no land,

---

76   The Talmud says something similar: "Since the day the Temple was destroyed, God only has in His world the four cubits of Halacha" (*Berachot* 8a). While the Temple stood, the opportunity and challenge of merging the physical with the spiritual was keenly felt. The Temple, after all, was a physical structure, the place where God took the dust from the place of the altar in order to form man. It is there that the *kohanim* partook of many of the offerings, attributing spiritual significance to the act of eating. The Temple allowed the merging of heaven and earth, giving spiritual significance and greater enjoyment to all of man's physical pursuits. However, physical presence and control of the site without the necessary spiritual connection is meaningless. The Talmud (*Sanhedrin* 96b) informs us that when Titus became haughty, feeling as if he had destroyed the holy Temple, a voice came out from the heavens and informed him: "You are making a mistake; you are simply grinding flour that was already milled." In other words, once the edifice lost its spiritual core, the Temple was as good as demolished.

no national economy, and no connection to the challenges of merging a secular society with a divine mission. In exile, it would be possible to refocus on at least the spiritual aspects of existence in order to prepare for a return to *Eretz Yisrael*, as individuals prepare to reform the nation.

> In exile, Israel abandoned its preoccupation with secular matters that concerned the people as a whole, and turned its eyes and hearts toward heaven. It stopped trying to amass power, chariots, and horses like every other people on earth, and the nation as a collective ceased all materialistic pursuits. It no longer desired the debaucheries of the surrounding peoples. The spirit of God began to beat within the people once again and to awaken them to the true heights of the human soul. So too, they became aware once more of the Jewish people's spiritual potential… Their eyes and hearts, which were habitually cast heavenward, began to recuperate from the backslidings and sins of their national life.

The Temple's destruction and the exile that followed were a resounding blow for the aspirations of the nation as a whole, but at the same time, the exile of the people from the land provided an opportunity to focus on the purely spiritual aspects of religious life. Religious life is much more limited in the Diaspora but much easier. To be a Jew in the exile, one must study and pray, do kindness, and the like. Still, one need not try to build a redeeming economy, a national army, a political hierarchy, and all other aspects of human society. The challenges of attempting to build a commonwealth are well worth it. Still, they are challenges nonetheless, as is described extensively in the accounts of the biblical kings and their struggles to create a Jewish commonwealth.

> Indeed, observance of the general, national Torah is especially difficult, far more difficult than observing the Torah of the individual. For Torah and *mitzvot* come to purify mankind, and the process of purifying the entire people, as a society which requires national-governmental matters, is much more complicated than the purification of each individual as a specific person… (*Ma'amarei Re'iya* 1:174)

Rav Kook saw the reality of his day, in which the people were beginning to return to the land with the goal of settling it, and not only as individuals. Broad agricultural development was on the agenda, and political aspirations as well. In his writings elsewhere, Rav Kook describes the state and commonwealth of the Jewish People as being capable of expressing *yesod kisei Hashem ba-olam*, "the foundation of God's Throne in the world, whose entire desire is that God shall be one and His Name shall be one."

Although Rav Kook recognizes the challenge of developing moral character in the exile, he also states that our "obligation is not merely to be holy as individuals, but additionally and especially to be 'a kingdom of priests and a holy nation.'"

Mark Twain's observations about the survival of the Jews and the obliteration of the ancient empires which once threatened and wreaked havoc upon them dovetails with Rav Kook's perspective. The Jewish nation can only find its complete self and fulfill its mission in the Land of Israel; when undeserving of the gift, the people can derive no benefit from inhabiting the Land of Israel. For this reason, every empire that has had its moment in history to usurp the throne and glory of the Jewish People has served its national purpose after destroying the Land and dispersing the people. Thus, they shortly faded and disappeared from the historical arena, while the Jewish nation, bruised and beaten, uses its time in exile to reconnect to its roots and focus on spirituality, until it longs to return to the Land and build a society and a commonwealth based on the Torah's glorious principles.

The Newfound Relationship to the Land While in Exile

The reality of exile not only serves as a training ground for focusing on the spiritual aspects of the law; it also helps the Jews reshape their relationship with the Land. Throughout the millennia of exile, there have been many golden ages of Jewry in many countries, when wealth, genius, and political acumen catapulted the Jews to positions of authority and protected status – yet none of these periods endured. The results were often depressing, as the sense of insecurity belied the initial feelings of safety. For both practical and spiritual reasons, life in exile produces a longing for the ultimate return, as Rav Kook writes:

> From the time they were separated from the land, they turned toward it — not with the greedy gaze of one who sits in his house and desires to reacquire the land that he had sold because it supplied him with bread and other physical needs, but rather with a look of holy love for its inner character, befitting the Godly desire that had begun to return to the people....

The Jewish People will undergo a healing process in exile, until there comes a time when individuals will return to recreate the nation in the Land of Israel. Distance will make the heart grow fonder of the aspects of *Eretz Yisrael* that were forgotten when abuse of power and misuse of the spiritual foundations of the land were prevalent. In the process, the people will embrace *shemitta* and its message.

Exile also gives the Jewish People the opportunity to realize what sort of society they must strive to build:

> We were forced to leave the international political stage, although there was an inner desire that we do so, until the glorious time when it would be possible to conduct a government without evil or barbarism; this is the era for which we long... Our souls have been sickened by the terrible crimes of governments during evil times. But now, the time has come; very soon the world will sweeten and we will be able to prepare ourselves, for it will already be possible for us to conduct our government on the foundations of goodness, wisdom, uprightness and clear, divine illumination... It is not worthy for the Nation of Israel to involve itself in government so long as governing has to be full of bloodshed, while governing requires the skill of evildoing. (*Orot HaMilchama*, p. 14)

Rav Kook's optimism sees the growing numbers of Jews interested in returning to Land as a possible indication that the lessons of exile have been inculcated and that there is an opportunity to reform a purified government and society in *Eretz Yisrael*. He asks, how one can know when the process of purification has been completed and the time to renew our national existence in our land has arrived?

> To whom has been revealed the divine secret, to know when the nation and the land have been totally purified from their contamination? ... No one among us knows. Therefore, our eyes look to find the hidden secrets where they can be found - in the vision of the revealed time of redemption, of which our Sages said: "There is no clearer indication of the End (*ketz meguleh*) than this, as it is stated (*Yechezkel* 36:8): 'But you, O mountains of Israel, shoot forth your branches and bear your fruit for my people Israel [for their return is near].'" (*Shabbat HaAretz*)

Rav Kook explains the Sages' statement connecting the redemption to the physical rebirth of the Land of Israel, as it arises from desolation and destruction to become an agricultural wonderland, not as a secondary sign, but rather as a direct response to the essence of the need and purpose of exile. It inherently indicates the renewed encounter between the nation and their land; it is the *ketz meguleh*, the clearest sign. The fact that the nation successfully resettles the land and brings forth fruits in ways that no conquering nation achieved, is the divine proof that the promised time has arrived.

Past Settlement During the Exile

Rav Kook mentions that even during the exile, there has always been at least a small Jewish presence in the Land of Israel. In fact, the Rambam indicates that the absence of Jews from *Eretz Yisrael* would be tantamount to the destruction of our nation (*Sefer HaMitzvot*, positive commandment 254). Given this, what changes with the establishment of the new settlement?

Rav Kook explains that those who came to live in *Eretz Yisrael* throughout the past generations did so in the face of great danger, as they were drawn to the spiritual character of the land, recognizing its superiority. However, those *olim* did not attempt to build up the land physically. They didn't plant in the land and therefore weren't representative of a *ketz meguleh*, an indication of the time for redemption:

> After a long time, scattered individuals gradually began returning to the land, drawn there by God's hand and by the holiness of the land rather than by any concern with material wellbeing or with reestablishing national government... So long as the anger has not been assuaged, and so long as the sickness in the depths of the people's soul has not been fully cured, there was every reason for them to turn only to heaven for support. Because of the extent of the land's destruction, people were not interested in trying to live a life closely tied to the earth; if dreams of restoring political sovereignty had occurred to them then, their confusions and ancient corruptions would like have been to return and reawaken. So their spiritual vision was blocked, and most people forgot about the land, and the scattered individuals who were concerned with it related to it as a spiritual ideal rather than as a physical reality. (*Shabbat HaAretz*, p. 129)

In fact, Rav Yosef Karo, although a resident of the Land of Israel, did not record any of the *halachot* of agricultural *shemitta* in the *Shulchan Aruch*, the Code of Jewish Law. Evidently, the majority of *shevi'it's halachot* were not yet practically applicable for a nation who had returned to reside in the Land, but not settle its farms. In his responsa, Rav Yosef Karo analyzes the most applicable relevant *halacha*, regarded the status of produce in Israel grown by non-Jews and whether it is accorded the special sanctity of *shemitta* produce. The Jews in his time lived in the land, but they did not live off the land.

This was the painful reality for almost two thousand years, but Rav Kook found himself in a different situation. The Jews of his day had awakened and had begun to follow a dream calling not only for the physical return of seekers of spirituality but a mass movement. They succeeded in reviving the land's agricultural beauty, transforming the sackcloths and ashes described by Mark Twain into sacks filled with produce. The sign discussed in the Talmud, the *ketz meguleh*, symbolizes the people's recognition of the need to merge the physical with the spiritual – that God has deemed the time for the return has arrived:

> But with the fulfillment of the whole measure of God's rebuke (which refines not just individuals, who began to return from the early days of the exile, but also the spirit of the nation as a whole, which was uplifted along with the degraded spirit of the land), the mourning for Zion began to seek outlets in action.

Rav Kook continues with a passionate description of the people's recognition that a return to the Land would allow for the nation's healing both spiritually and physically. The nation's heart had begun to beat again; though it was imperceptible to most at first, it was becoming more and more apparent. He describes the corporeal desires of the people to settle the Land and physically work it as expressions of the "exalted spirits of this long-suffering person that had generally forgotten the ways of physical existence…" He points out that in order to merit prophecy, it is not enough to be intellectually wise and spiritually solid; one must also be strong and materially self-sufficient. If these are necessary components for an individual to merit divine revelation, the same applies on the national plane as well. The nation must be physically strong to merit the revelation it is waiting for.

Rav Kook's description of the nation's awakening from its slumber, the initial effects being felt in the secular Zionist world's desire to return to the Land and build it up physically, may best be understood with an analogy. When one wakes up from a long rest, some parts of the body might be slower than others in arising. One might find that a leg or arm is still asleep and isn't yet ready to move. The heart is pumping, however, and it is just a matter of time before the whole body feels rejuvenated and ready to arise like a lion.

Rav Kook views the events in his lifetime as a sign that the Jewish heart — not only that of individuals, but of the collective — has started to pump again on its own. The nation has awoken from a coma, but it initially shows movement only in some of the physical areas. Looking for a display of restored brainpower and wisdom, the loved ones are troubled, yet the doctor is excited. If there is any movement, that means that the heart is pumping and the brain is sending signals. It might take some time to see the expression of intellectual rejuvenation, but it is on its way. The brainpower, the intelligence, the Torah greatness of the nation will once again show itself if we remain patient enough to let the body of the nation physically arise. In fact, the importance of physical restoration is more profound in the Land of Israel, as even prophecy itself is limited to the extraordinary land, which allows for the bridging of the physical and the spiritual.

The Beginning of the Redemption

Rav Kook continues with a vivid description of the initial pioneers who had begun settling the land:

> With souls that were paralyzed with shock, and with legs that stumbled from the evil and wearying oppression of enemies and with the humiliation of constant wanderings, as people without hope or comfort on foreign soil, there came to the Land of Israel a few survivors who had been scattered in the diaspora. Their eyes bleary from the darkness of exile after exile, they could no longer bear the full force of the great light that is implanted in the land. The backbone has not yet been straightened, the spirit has not yet revived, the divine soul has not yet become manifest in its full soaring flight. But a few single rays of light are scattered in all directions, the revealed end is becoming closer all the time, and all in whom the spirit of the Lord pounds hurry to be among the first builder who will build up the nation in the land of eternal delight.

Rav Kook, who exudes optimism, is not blind to the fact that this return is far more modest than what had been originally envisioned or expected. Yet at the same time, Rav Kook sees this not as an end, but as the beginning of a process, which will be revealed step-by-step through the return and the observance of *mitzvot* like those of *shevi'it*:

> Just as the resurrection of our people upon the holy land is still young, so is what it has erected small and poor as compared with our great hope, which becomes strong with the help of the right hand of the Lord that is raised on high "to plant the heavens and to securely establish the earth, and to say to Zion: 'You are my people,'" so is the spirit that is within us poor and weak from the high elevation of the land of desire. And the splendor of God that becomes manifest through the holiness of the *yovel* and of the *shemitta* on the holy land, which gives strength and might to the people, is only visible to us from afar.

Here again, Rav Kook informs us of the role that the *mitzvot* of *shemitta* and *yovel* play in this return, such that "the splendor of God" will become manifest.

Although the return to the Land will present the opportunity to fulfill all *mitzvot hateluyot ba'aretz*, Rav Kook presents this analysis as an introduction to *shevi'it* and describes specifically *shevi'it*'s message as the antidote for the misplaced perspective that necessitates exile. As we noted, this approach is especially potent considering Rav Kook is often associated with his rabbinic backing of the *heter mechira*, allowing for the legal sale of some of the land to non-Jews to enable farming under certain conditions.

Jewish pioneers facing the challenges of observing *mitzvoth ha-teluyot ba-aretz* is nothing new. Great Jewish thinkers throughout the generations noted that one can not imagine a return to the Land agriculturally without fulfillment of the land's *mitzvot*, despite the difficulty inherently part of this observance. For example, the *Shelah HaKadosh* (sixteenth century) expresses the difficulty of coming to the land and failing to uphold its agricultural *mitzvot*:

> One year after I arrived in the Holy City of Jerusalem, it is the sabbatical year. Many of the inhabitants of the Holy Land wish to exempt themselves because of the great

difficulty; the year preceding *shemitta* there was a famine in the land and there was insufficient food, day by day…I have contemplated the matter to myself and have thought, "I have a greater obligation to observe than they do, and even to sell the shirt off my back. God will say to me: Why have you come from a place where you were exempt from this and come to a place of obligation? And now in this place you will abandon this *mitzvah*? Why have you come to profane my land?"…The *mitzvah* of dwelling in the Land of Israel should not come through the sins of ignoring the *mitzvot* of the Land, in which case what is lost will be more than what is gained.

Contemporaries of Rav Kook advanced similar arguments. Rav Yaakov Dovid Ridbaz settled in *Eretz Yisrael* at the end of his life, leading the battle for strict adherence of *shevi'it*. He argued that the Torah leaders who were behind the resettling of the Land of Israel did so for the express purpose of fulfilling the agricultural *mitzvot* and observing *shevi'it* without reliance on the *heter mechira*. He describes his fears that the violation of *shevi'it* will lead to *galus*, concluding as follows:

I sink down on our sacred soil: My land, my land, do not turn into your children's prosecutor before our heavenly Father. Behold the suffering of the learned men and of the holy people, writhing in pain and hurt, dissolved in tears at the desecration of your sacred Shabbat. O, entreat the Creator that He bestow mercy on us and redeem us soon, that His children may return from foreign soil and preserve your Shabbat in sanctity and purity, for His Will is our will. (*Kuntres Halacha LeMa'aseh Shevi'it*)

Similarly, Rav Kook's own mentor, the Netziv (Rav Naftali Tzvi Yehuda Berlin), writes that specifically due to *Eretz Yisrael*'s spiritual nature, one should not judge the need for reliance on a *heter* based on a purely natural financial analysis:

If our people in *Eretz Yisrael* could only be convinced that ignoring the *shemitta* might, God forbid, entail punishment, the threat of drought and locust and plague. For we have to realize the following premise: As the preservation of the Jewish People is immediately dependent on God, completely independent of normal and lawful conditions, so *Eretz Yisrael* is set apart from other lands, for its development and prosperity does not depend on the material prerequisites so essential for other lands, but depends, as the object of Divine providence, on the conscientious fulfillment of God's Law.

The conclusion of Rav Kook's introduction to *Shabbat HaAretz* addresses these points. He continues his line of reasoning that the return to *Eretz Yisrael* is a historical process, which in his day was only in its infancy. In that context, he attempts to explain that although *shevi'it*'s message is a necessity, its complete observance is not yet a possible reality. Only when *shevi'it* can be fully fulfilled will this potential be realized and the utopian society that *shevi'it* engenders achieved.

Rav Kook was himself concerned that inobservance of *shevi'it* could jeopardize the entire settlement enterprise, but he also felt that the return to the Land and the fulfillment of all its *mitzvot* would come at separate stages in the redemption process. The Talmud Yerushalmi (*Berachot* 1:2) describes redemption as unfolding in stages, similar to the morning dawn.

The sun's light begins slowly enlightening the darkness, little by little (*kima kima*); only then does the light take hold and take over the sky. Similarly, the redemption begins slowly, and there might still be darkness alongside the light until further stages of redemption:

> We must recognize that we are obligated to strive with all of our strength to bring matters so that, in the end, the sabbatical year will be increasingly observed in all of its holiness in the Holy Land.... But how to arrive at this sacred goal? Which means should we use to attain it? This matter must be considered carefully.
>
> In my opinion, we need to arrive at our desired goal precisely by graduated efforts. Rabbi Chiya Rabbah described the overall redemption of Israel as beginning slowly, little by little (*kima kima*). So too, the spiritual redemption of establishing the Land's holiness will progress in stages, step by step. (p. 330)

Rav Kook's Position on the *Heter Mechira*

Although Rav Kook is known as a staunch defender of the *heter mechira*, he did not begin that way. Indeed, his perspective on the Jewish return to the land being part of a redemptive process and a return to the fulfillment of the *mitzvot hateluyot baaretz* precluded a perspective that would champion the *heter*. In his letters (p. 258), Rav Kook notes that before arriving in *Eretz Yisrael*, he and his father-in-law, Rabbi Eliyahu David Rabinowitz-Teomim (known as the Aderet, rabbi of Ponevezh and later Chief Rabbi of Jerusalem), both opposed the *heter*. That changed, however, when the Aderet arrived in Israel and saw that "it is impossible to even consider not making some sort of arrangement for the sabbatical year." When Rav Kook saw firsthand the precarious nature of the fledgling settlements, he too conceded that the *heter* was an unfortunate necessity. In addition to the fact that the settlers earned their living through the sale of agricultural produce, he understood that the Arabs recognized the success of the Jewish farmers. If Jews, lacking means to protect their land, did not work it during *shevi'it*, the Arabs "will take control of Jewish land during the sabbatical year by grazing their herds on them" (*Letters*, p. 285).

A further fear was that failure to resettle the land due to *shevi'it* would have disastrous consequences regarding the overall perspective of Judaism's compatibility with the contemporary world:

> Even worse is the potential condemnation of Judaism and widespread rejection of Torah observance that could result from a strict ruling, heaven forbid. For the anti-religious actually hope that the rabbis will forbid [all agricultural activity]. Then they will have gained a great victory. They will prove to all that by listening to the rabbis, the land will be laid waste, the fields and vineyards will become desolate, and all commercial ties for the sale of wines, oranges and other produce will be broken — ties that the survival of the Jewish settlement truly depends on. (p. 258)

These reasons led Rav Kook to reluctantly agree to use of the *heter* as a temporary measure for farmers who felt they had no other option, although he described "my heart aches continually because of this priceless *mitzvah*" (*Letters*, p. 296). He also defended those who refused to rely on the *heter* and ensured that they not be penalized by the Jewish organizations purchasing farmland for Jewish farmers. However, Rav Kook distinguished between farmers and consumers. While a farmer could be stringent and choose not to rely on the *heter mechira*, Rav Kook took issue with consumers who decided not to purchase Jewish produce so as to be strict regarding *shevi'it* observance.

Although Rav Kook defended the *heter*, he also very much limited its application. In essence, Rav Kook's generally strict rulings about *shevi'it* practice left little room for a fledgling society to successfully support itself without adopting the *heter mechira*. The Chazon Ish, Rav Avraham Yeshayahu Karelitz, who is known for his strict approach prohibiting use of the *heter mechira*, was actually generally far more permissive in *shevi'it* practice than Rav Kook was. Indeed, some understand that the Chazon Ish's lenient rulings regarding *shevi'it* observance actually enabled a model for sustaining the nation while observing *shevi'it*. Rav Kook's more strict rulings required a different model, and he, therefore, he adopted the *heter mechira*, although he felt it must be reevaluated every *shevi'it* to see if it is indeed necessary.

Rav Kook anxiously awaited full *shevi'it* observance and had no intention of circumventing its compliance. He felt the rabbinic nature of *shevi'it* observance in our day, coupled with other *halachic* factors, allowed for the temporary sale of Jewish farmland to non-Jews for the express purpose of allowing the settlements to prosper and moving towards the goal of full *shevi'it* observance when possible.

In another letter, Rav Kook explains that he didn't advance all his arguments to allow use of the *heter*:

> All this was in order that the *heter* should not become too accepted, but will always be considered a temporary measure (*hora'at sha'ah*), something that was permitted grudgingly due to the needs of the time. But when these issues are analyzed in the way of true Torah scholarship... the prohibition would become too weakened — and I certainly did not desire that. (*Letters*, pp. 348-349)

Indeed, some authorities maintain that Israel's economy is currently strong enough to endure *shevi'it* observance without reliance on the *heter mechira*.

Between Optimism and Reality

Rav Kook saw a temporary need for reliance on the *heter mechira* before *shevi'it* could be fully observed and *yovel* would return to educate the nation about a redeemed society. But how long is this process supposed to take?

Rav Yehuda Amital's remarks regarding what parts of Rav Kook's vision still remain unfulfilled serve as a powerful reminder that we are still not at the finish line. Rav Amital describes how Rav Kook's Torah played an essential role in his survival while in a labor camp during the Holocaust, but that very catastrophe, coupled with the imperfect nature of the State born in its aftermath, convinces him of the limits of Rav Kook's optimism:

> My spiritual outlook is based on and nourished by the writings of Rav Kook. His works sustained me during my difficult days in a Nazi labor camp, and in their merit I managed to withstand the difficult trials I have encountered. But specifically because

of what I learned from his teachings, I believe that we, the followers of his approach, must view the current situation in accordance with reality, and not quote passages written eighty years ago without considering their applicability to our period...

Our love of our country must not blind us from criticizing its shortcomings. We remain very, very far from the ideal Jewish State, and we must therefore do whatever we can to bring about its realization. A more just society and stronger public values are necessary prerequisites for its actualization. If we want to hasten the ultimate redemption, we must work harder to ensure moral values on both the individual and communal levels. Closing the social gaps, concern for the vulnerable elements of society, fighting poverty, and respectful treatment of the non-Jews in Israel - all these measures will bring us closer to the day for which we long. We hope and believe that our State will develop into the ideal Jewish State, "the foundation of the Divine Throne in the world, whose entire desire is that God shall be One and His Name shall be One." (Elyashiv Reichner, *By Faith Alone* (Maggid, 2011), pp. 108-110.

As noted, Rav Kook identifies an educational purpose of exile, as it purifies the nation, enabling it to focus its efforts on spiritual matters in the absence of the physical needs of a state. Rav Kook's optimistic view indicates that upon the nation's return, they would reconnect with the value system expressed in *shevi'it* and create a spiritually-driven society capable of effectively dealing with the physical needs of the nation. While certain aspects of Rav Kook's historical perspective seem right on the mark, Rav Amital notes that some of his optimism has remained as yet unjustified. The return to the Land often witnesses repeated expressions of the depraved behavior that made the Jewish People deserving of exile in the first place. Even if this is a process, Rav Kook seems to envision a much shorter one.

Whether Rav Kook's vision played out fully or not, we can certainly recognize some fascinating historical perspectives in his writings, some of which even seem prophetic given that they were written prior to the founding of the State.

Rav Kook's introduction to *Shabbat HaAretz* describes the role that the agricultural *mitzvot* in the Land of Israel, primarily those of *shevi'it* and *yovel*, assume in preparing the society for its historic role. This is the ticket to understanding the aspects of *shevi'it* that, if understood properly, may guide the nation towards achieving these optimistic goals. It is possible that Rav Kook's vision is less flawed than our application of his teachings. It is our perseverance in realizing *shevi'it's* messages that has fallen short. Thus, studying it and remaining faithful to its calling will illuminate the path towards all we can hope for.

Limiting adoption of the *heter mechira* to the specific situations in which it is still absolutely necessary, such as in the case of produce designated for export, and allowing *shevi'it's* messages to extend beyond the farmers but to all of society, hold the promise for realizing the remainder of Rav Kook's optimistic vision.[77]

---

77   See the final chapter of Rav Eliezer Melamed's *Peninei Halacha Shevi'it*, where he offers a fascinating description of a process through which in the near future there will be no need for the *heter mechira* at all.

Theme 7- A Succesful Spiritual Economy- The Torah's System for Social Justice

One clear theme of *shevi'it* and *yovel* relates to the type of economy the Torah wishes the Jewish nation to have. When the nation resides in their own land without foreign rule, they are able to create a society with a model economy and serve as "a light onto the nations" in this respect.

Some of the most formidable questions that *shevi'it* and *yovel* raise relate directly to the economy. Every seven years, all agricultural economic advancement comes to a halt. Rather than focusing on planting and furthering growth, the nation spends a year focused on growth in other realms. Produce temporarily ceases to be a commodity and simply remains food meant for consumption. The laws of ownership are suspended, as all members of society share the produce. At the conclusion of the year, *shemittat kesafim* sets in, and collection of all outstanding loans is held in abeyance. *Yovel* takes these ideas one step further, impacting the economy in additional ways. Slaves are set free, and all land in non-walled cities throughout *Eretz Yisrael* returns to its ancestral owners. This essentially means that land can never be sold, but can only be rented out for the number of harvests until the following *yovel*.

Examining these *halachot* in the context of the Torah's broader economic vision provides great insight for the Torah's recipe for a "redeemed economy". Financial *mitzvot* which apply throughout the world, including providing interest-free loans and charity to the poor, are coupled in the land with its unique agricultural *mitzvot*, the *mitzvot ha-teluyot ba'aretz*, that similarly provide for those in need. Together, these *mitzvot* provide a portrayal of a "redeemed economy."

The Two Extremes

Two contemporary economic models (with many offshoots) are generally advanced as the ideal forms of economy: Market Economies and Command Economies. Although these modern economic models may not be entirely applicable to ancient systems, they help outline the moral dimensions that are outgrowths of monetary policy:

> Market economies and command economies occupy two polar extremes in the organization of economic activity. The primary differences lie in the division of labor (also known as factors of production) and price-determining mechanisms. The activity in a market economy is unplanned, as it is not organized by any central authority. Private ownership generates economic activity through voluntary contracts, and supply and demand of goods and services determine their price. Market economies are generally referred to as Capitalist. Businesses and consumers are expected to protect their own interests, and there is no central authority including fairness and equal opportunity or support for the less fortunate. These economies advocate "laissez faire" (French for "let [people] do [as they please]") as the best

policy. Financial success determines allocation of resources.

Alternatively, in a command economy, governments own the factors of production (including land and other resources) and these centralized governments direct all the factors of production. Hence, it is known as a planned economy. The government controls supply and sets demand as well as prices. It also provides basic necessities to all its citizens.

Generally, the differences between these economies don't limit themselves to the types of economies, but expand to the overall nature of society and governance. Command economies are generally the model for authoritarian societies and governments, while nations that promote economic liberty often are defined by greater personal freedoms.[78]

While these two models represent fundamentally different approaches to economic issues, most economies embrace one approach while adopting elements of the other. The two primary debates between advocates of these forms of economy relate to the factual question of which economic system is most efficient and the value-driven disagreement regarding which model is most moral.

Advocates of a planned economy claim that free markets generate waste, as they are not planned with the true interests of the population in mind. Market economists counter that free markets allow for a natural means of arriving at the ideal allocation of resources, as the market allows for an "invisible hand" to guide it. They add that free markets ensure motivation, as the greatest human motivator is personal interest. The more one is rewarded with success; the more one will be pushed to success, as a natural selection of affordability and efficiency determines success and even survival. Market economists also note the rampant corruption that often plagues planned economies. In contrast, free markets recognize the need to suit themselves to the actual needs of the market and let freedom reign.

In terms of the debate regarding which economy is more moral, planned economy advocates hold the greatest value to be equality. A command economy can assure that values such as equality are met by being planned from above, with governments incentivizing their values. They point to the unbalanced wealth in free markets, where the poor cannot claim to be free to choose as they please, as they are limited due to the dearth of resources.

The primary moral value for free-market advocates is liberty, which is severely curtailed when a government declares what role every individual must take. They note the inefficiency and often corrupted public sectors full of inflated bureaucracy and the need to support non-productive societal needs in order to maintain equality. This, in turn, they claim will hurt the needy most, as the successful individuals must contribute larger amounts of taxes. This will restrict their ability to develop the industries and companies that could provide needed jobs for others and thereby help elevate society.

Command economies present themselves as value-based, with centralized state-controlled

---

78 A shortened summary from https://www.investopedia.com/ask/answers/100314/whats-difference-between-market-economy-and-command-economy.asp.

and regulated welfare systems. Free-market proponents counter that they share many similar values, but support for the underprivileged must come from private individuals deciding to do so out of their own free will. When supporting the needy is relegated to each individual, one can do it effectively, not as a sense of requirement but rather through a real desire to help the less financially fortunate.

The dissenters say that private charities cannot compete with government welfare programs, incentivized investment in poorer areas, and social programs. More importantly, they argue that private charity is humiliating for the recipient and breeds arrogance in the giver. Public welfare, in their opinion, isn't dehumanizing, as it applies equally to all of society.[79]

The Torah's Value System

While no modern economic system bases itself solely one model, one might question what the Torah advocates and what type of balance between a market and command economy it advocates.

It seems clear that the Torah seeks a society with a balance of three aspects: *mishpat*, *tzedaka*, and *chessed*. The Torah tells us that Hashem chose Avraham Avinu specifically so that he educate his descendants to adopt these traits (*Bereishit* 18:19).

What is a society of *mishpat*? *Sefer Tehillim* expresses the importance of benefiting from one's own toil:

> יְגִיעַ כַּפֶּיךָ כִּי תֹאכֵל אַשְׁרֶיךָ וְטוֹב לָךְ:
>
> When the toil of your palms you eat, you are praised and it is good for you. (*Tehillim* 128:2)

The Talmud (*Berachot* 8a) cites this *pasuk* and concludes: "Greater is one who benefits from his own toil than one who fears God." In a number of contexts, the Sages cite the *pasuk* in *Mishlei* (15:27), שׂוֹנֵא מַתָּנֹת יִחְיֶה, "one who hates gifts shall live," as proof that one should aim never to accept gifts (see *Kiddushin* 59a). The Torah not only allows individuals to benefit from their successful production but seems to view that as an ideal. "*Mishpat*" calls for individuals being able to reap the results of their efforts.[80]

On the other hand, Torah society is an extremely charitable society (as will be discussed

---

79   See Rav Chaim Navon's article on the Torah's approach to economics which provides an erudite summary of some of the issues, https://torah.etzion.org.il/en/torahs-approach-economics.

80   As Rabbi Jonathan Sacks (*Covenant and Conversation, Behar- Bechukotai* 5772) notes:
Unlike aristocratic cultures, such as that of ancient Greece, Judaism was never dismissive of work or the productive economy. It did not favour the creation of a leisured class. "Torah study without an occupation will in the end fail and lead to sin" (*Avot* 2: 2). Next, unless there are compelling reasons otherwise, one has a right to the fruits of one's labours. Judaism distrusts large government as an infringement of liberty. That is the core of the prophet Samuel's warning about monarchy: A king, he says, "will take the best of your fields and vineyards and olive groves and give them to his attendants … He will take a tenth of your flocks, and you yourselves will become his slaves" (*Shmuel* I 8). Judaism is the religion of a people born in slavery and longing for redemption; and the great assault of slavery against human dignity is that it deprives me of the ownership of the wealth I create. At the heart of the Hebrew Bible is the God who seeks the free worship of free human beings, and one of the most powerful defences of freedom is private property as the basis of economic independence. The ideal society envisaged by the prophets is one in which each person is able to sit "underneath his own vine and fig tree" (*Micha* 4:4).

at length in the following chapter). A society of *chessed* and *tzedaka* is one of care and concern for others, especially those in need. The Torah requires that both individuals and the community as a whole provide financial assistance to the poor. However, the Torah's perspective on charity is different than the common perspective in contemporary society. There is no governmental welfare system; rather, we have *mitzvot* placed on the individual and adopted by society. One who experiences financial success must learn to share.

The Charitable *Mitzvot HaTeluyot BaAretz*

Although the Torah's recipe for a charitable economy applies globally, its complete system is unique to *Eretz Yisrael*. The entire concept of *tzedaka* is radically different in Israel than it is elsewhere. Several *mitzvot hateluyot ba'aretz*, agricultural *mitzvot* that apply specifically in the Land of Israel, have a significant charitable focus that educates us towards a fundamentally different type of *tzedaka*. Giving/receiving is replaced with sharing/partaking. In all but one of the philanthropic *mitzvot hateluyot ba'aretz*, the needy are not "given" anything. Instead, they partake of certain parts of the field and produce that are rightfully theirs, not the farmers'.

The Torah describes several charitable *mitzvot hateluyot ba'aretz* that define portions of a farmer's field or certain forms of produce as belonging to the poor (*Vayikra* 19:9-10; 23:22; *Devarim* 24:19-22):

Pe'ah: The corner of the field. 1/60 of each field is not harvested by the owner, as it belongs to the poor.

פֵּאָה

Shichecha: Forgotten produce. Sheaves of wheat or other crops forgotten in the field belong to the poor.

שְׁכְחָה

Leket, Peret: Gleanings. Grains (*leket*) or grapes (*peret*) that fall to the ground while harvesting belongs to the poor.[81]

לֶקֶט, פֶּרֶט

Olelot: Incompletely formed grape clusters belong to the poor, not the owner.

עוֹלְלוֹת

Pe'ah and *shichacha* apply in all types of fields (see *Devarim* 24:20). Wheat fields have a requirement of *leket*, while vineyards have two unique requirements of *peret* and *olelot*.

In wheat fields:	In vineyards:	From all trees:
פֵּאָה, לֶקֶט, שְׁכְחָה	פֵּאָה, פֶּרֶט, עוֹלְלוֹת שְׁכְחָה	פֵּאָה, שְׁכְחָה

Each of these five concepts includes a pair of *mitzvot* – a positive command to leave items

---

81   This only applies if less than three stalks fall in one place during the harvest. If three stalks fall at once, then the owner it permitted to collect them. Our Sages (*Shabbat* 113b) state that Rut was aware of this law and was careful to only pick up one or two fallen stalks.

for the poor and a prohibition to take them (*Sefer HaMitzvot aseh* 120-4, *lo ta'aseh* 210-214). Together these *mitzvot* transform one's field into a center for agricultural charity, allowing one to provide for the poor in a dignified manner.

These *mitzvot* apply to produce growing in *Eretz Yisrael* throughout the six years leading up to *shevi'it*. During those six years, a farmer owns only the parts of his field that are not affected by these *mitzvot hateluyot ba'aretz*. Yet, even what remains does not belong to him entirely. The produce of *Eretz Yisrael* has the status of *tevel* and cannot be eaten until certain portions of it are separated for different purposes.

The farmer must first separate *teruma gedola* (Biblically any small amount, rabbinically between 1/60th and 1/40th of the produce), which is set aside for a *Kohen's* use and is forbidden for consumption by any non-*Kohen*.[82] A number of tithes are also separated. The first, known as *ma'aser rishon*, is separated in all years and is given to a Levi, although it does not enjoy any special sanctified status. The identity of the second tithe is dependent on the appropriate year in the *shevi'it* cycle. During the first, second, fourth, and fifth years of the *shevi'it* cycle, a tenth of the produce is separated as *ma'aser sheini*. This produce is sanctified and set aside to be eaten in Yerushalayim, ideally by the owner, ensuring that an individual will go to the spiritual center of the nation and celebrate one's crop while basking in holiness.[83] In the third and sixth years of the cycle, a portion of the produce is given to the poor in what is known as *ma'aser ani*. This produce is not sanctified and is unique in that it is the sole example of an owner actually giving an agricultural gift to the poor. For this reason, some authorities (see Tosafot, *Ta'anit* 9a, s.v. *aser*) cite this as a source for the concept of *ma'aser kesafim*, giving a tenth of one's income to charity.[84]

Thus, even the produce that "belongs" to the farmer must first be dedicated to supporting the spiritual echelon of the nation (*teruma* and *ma'aser rishon*), connecting one's physical success with one's own spiritual progress (*ma'aser sheini*), and directly supporting the needy (*ma'aser ani*).[85]

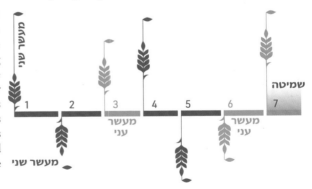

The laws of *shevi'it* go far beyond that, of course. During *shevi'it*, the owner releases his

---

82   *Terumat ma'aser*, the *teruma* taken from the first tithe by the Levi, is similarly sanctified for use by a *Kohen*.

83   One who is unable to bring the fruits to Yerushalayim before they will spoil is permitted to perform an act known as *chilul*, redemption, by transferring the sanctity of *ma'aser sheini* produce onto coins, which will be used to purchase produce in Yerushalayim that will be consumed in sanctity.

84   There is a difference of opinion as to whether the obligation of *ma'aser kesafim* is Biblical, Rabbinic, or a *minhag.*

85   The *shivat haminim*, the seven species of produce with which *Eretz Yisrael* is blessed, have an additional gift of *bikkurim*, the first-fruits, which are brought to the *Beit HaMikdash* and given to the *Kohen*.

rights to all produce grown in his field, allowing the poor to eat it in a manner no different than the owner himself. This is the explicit goal of the equal access to *shevi'it* produce described in *Parashat Mishpatim*:

> וְהַשְּׁבִיעִת תִּשְׁמְטֶנָּה וּנְטַשְׁתָּהּ וְאָכְלוּ אֶבְיֹנֵי עַמֶּךָ וְיִתְרָם תֹּאכַל חַיַּת הַשָּׂדֶה כֵּן תַּעֲשֶׂה לְכַרְמְךָ לְזֵיתֶךָ:
>
> But [in] the seventh you shall release it and let it lie fallow, and the poor of your nation shall eat, and what they leave over the beasts of the field shall eat. Thus shall you do with your vineyard [and] your olive grove. (*Shemot* 23:1)

The produce that grows in the farmer's field during *shevi'it* is declared *hefker*, ownerless; it has special sanctity (*kedushat shevi'it*) and is dedicated "*l'ochla*" – for consumption alone.

The overwhelming trend of *mitzvot hateluyot ba'aretz* seems to be a transformation of one's yield from a marketable possession to a means of connecting with other members of society and injecting values into goods. Understanding how this model was accomplished in a fully agrarian society can help us appreciate the Torah's approach to economics and social justice, and hopefully, help us learn how to ensure these values are achieved in a more cosmopolitan economic environment as well.

Dignity Based on Sanctity

One theme that repeats itself in the context of *mitzvot hateluyot va'aretz* is that the Torah seeks as little "giving" as possible. Most of the charitable gifts are taken by the poor; only regarding the produce that the owner keeps for himself is a portion given to others. The Torah seems to be concerned with the dignity (*kavod*) of the individual in need. Since the ideal is to eat of one's own efforts without receiving gifts, the Torah recognizes the difficulty involved in accepting from others and ensures that everyone will have their basic needs met in a dignified fashion.

The intent of the *mitzvot hateluyot ba'aretz* seems to be to transform one's outlook on wealth and accomplishments. They prevent the need for a welfare state, as they seek personal involvement in building up the land and achieving success through divine blessing. The poor will always have somewhere to go for their basic food needs, but they will be able to do so in a dignified manner. They partake of the produce that is designated for them; they do not take the produce that belongs to others.

The Torah recognizes that pauper has not only physical and economic needs, but emotional needs as well. The indignity of being dependent on others, the loss of pride when asking others for one's basic needs, is the psychological dimension that the *mitzvot hateluyot ba'aretz* seek to ameliorate. The Torah clearly recognizes that there will always be poor people among us (*Devarim* 15:11), but it still argues that their dignity must be preserved in every way possible.

We can attain a greater appreciation of this model by studying the story of *Megillat Rut*. Rut is a widow who recently converted and arrived in *Eretz Yisrael* with her mother-in-law, herself a widow still mourning the passing of her husband and sons. They live in abject poverty after previously enjoying great wealth. Rut supports herself and her mother-in-law by gathering the charitable agricultural gifts, thereby attaining food in dignity.

By divine arrangement, she finds herself in the field of Boaz, a relative of her deceased husband, and she ultimately marries him, eventually becoming the great-grandmother of Dovid HaMelech.

This rags-to-riches story is more than the story of Rut alone. It is the story of the *mitzvot hateluyot ba'aretz* and their role in forging a society in which all members are not only accounted for but also accepted in dignity. The most unfortunate member of society, the poor woman lacking a family, is not only able to partake of the bounty of the field of the wealthy through these gifts, but even to be noticed and appreciated.

The protection of one's own dignity and the dignity of others is a fundamental principle of Judaism known as *kevod ha-beriyot*. The *gemara* teaches (*Berachot* 19a) that the principle of *kevod ha-briyot* is so great that it at times outweighs other *halachic* considerations. While certain individuals, such as one's parents or teachers, are accorded extra honor, every individual deserves a tremendous level of respect as a *tzelem Elokim*, a being created in the image of God.

The *mishna* in *Pirkei Avot* emphasizes that one's concern for the honor of others is what defines one's own honorableness:

אֵיזֶהוּ מְכֻבָּד? הַמְכַבֵּד אֶת הַבְּרִיּוֹת, שֶׁנֶּאֱמַר "כִּי מְכַבְּדַי אֲכַבֵּד וּבֹזַי יֵקָלּוּ" (שְׁמוּאֵל א' ב'):

Who is honored? He who honors others, as it is said: "For those who honor Me I will honor, and those who scorn Me shall be degraded" (*I Shemuel* 2:30). (*Avot* 4:1)

The Tiferet Yisrael explains:

> When one honors his fellow man because he is created in God's image, one is in essence honoring God. Therefore, God will bestow honor upon this individual, as his own Godliness will shine, causing others to honor him.[86]

Protecting the honor of all individuals created in the image of God requires treating others, and oneself, in an honorable manner, but herein lies a danger. Sometimes, *kevod haberiyot* becomes a goal in its own right, as individuals seek personal honor. The *mishna* issues a clear warning against the pursuit of honor:

רַבִּי אֱלִיעֶזֶר הַקַּפָּר אוֹמֵר הַקִּנְאָה וְהַתַּאֲוָה וְהַכָּבוֹד מוֹצִיאִין אֶת הָאָדָם מִן הָעוֹלָם:

Envy, desire, and honor remove a man from the world. (*Avot* 4:19)

Many people are driven by an endless appetite for honor, and they are never satiated. Rav Chaim Shmuelevitz (*Sichot Mussar*, ch. 82) offers an interesting suggestion regarding how one's feelings of entitlement can be channeled to better suit oneself and others. The more one feels the desire to be honored, the more he may recognize that others may feel the same way. Showing others *kavod* allows one to be an honorable individual, rather than being lost in the constant hunt for honor. However, one truly fulfills the obligation only

---

86   Rabbeinu Yona explains that honoring others does not provide them with anything, as they are either worthy of the honor or not. However, honoring another person allows the one showing the honor to express honorable behavior, thereby imitating God, Who created the whole world for His glory and yet provides honor to all of mankind. Rashi explains that the *mishna* is essentially teaching one how to be honored by Heaven, as one's sensitivity to human dignity causes God to provide the same concern for one's own dignity.

after finding a trait in another worth honoring; the *kavod* must be real.[87]

Rabbi Jonathan Sacks explains how finding dignity in others is a religious imperative:

> The question is: To what extent will we see our present interconnectedness as a threat or a challenge? As the work of man, or as a call from God to a greater humanity, as well as to a greater self-restraint? As for me, I believe that we are being summoned by God to see in the human other a trace of the divine Other. The test — so lamentably failed by the great powers of the twentieth century — is to see the divine presence in the face of a stranger; to heed the cry of those who are disempowered in this age of unprecedented powers; who are hungry and poor and ignorant and uneducated, whose human potential is being denied the chance to be expressed. That is the faith of Abraham and Sarah, from whom the great faiths, Judaism, Christianity and Islam, trace their spiritual or actual ancestry. That is the faith of one who, though he called himself but dust and ashes, asked of God himself, 'Shall the judge of all the earth not do justice?' We are not gods, but we are summoned by God — to do His work of love and justice and compassion and peace. (*The Dignity of Difference: How to Avoid the Clash of Civilizations*, p. 208)

This is not only a duty; it is the very basis of the concept of human rights. Rav Ahron Soloveichik argues:

> This key concept of *k'vod habriyos*, the dignity of all human beings, constitutes the basis of human rights. The maxim of "Man was endowed by his Creator with certain inalienable rights" was not an innovation of the founders of the American republic. These men were impressed with the doctrine of human rights which flows naturally from the concept of "the dignity of man" and the "image of God in which He created Man," as they knew from their Biblical background. (*Logic of the Heart, Logic of the Mind*, p. 62)

The difference between the secular doctrine of human rights and that of Judaism is that Judaism concerns itself not only with the rights of man, but with man's duties to espouse the doctrine of *tzedek u-mishpat*:

> In modern society, assaulting a person is a crime but failure to save a human life is not. Civil law finds it inconceivable that a person should have the right to demand help and generosity from another. The Torah's concept of *tzedek*, however, gives the person the right to demand aid. (Ibid., p. 64)

---

87   The Rambam (*Hilchot De'ot* 3:1) cautions against living an undignified existence:
A person might say, "Since envy, desire, honor, and the like support a wrong path and drive a person from the world, I shall separate from them to a very great degree and move away from them to the opposite extreme." For example, one might not eat meat; nor drink wine; nor live in a pleasant home; nor wear fine clothing, just sackcloth, coarse wool and the like, as the pagan priests do. This, too, is a bad path and it is forbidden to walk upon it. Whoever follows this path is called a sinner...
Although one should not be driven by honor, one should recognize that an honorable attitude and feeling of self-worth are essential in order to act honorably. Although this is a difficult balancing act, Rav Shmuelevitz explains that this attitude is an essential aspect of the religious personality and the mission of fulfilling God's word. Understanding one's worth allows one to stand up to those doubting the significance of spiritual pursuits and to embrace one's *tzelem Elokim*.

Rav Aharon Lichtenstein notes that Yosef Dov HaLevi Soloveitchik often emphasized that while the Western tradition customarily speaks of "the dignity of man," we speak of "the sanctity of man":

> The dimension of sanctity is the basis and foundation of our conception, and the "dignity" is integrally connected to it. By that token, our concern for *kevod ha-beriyot* is not just an obligation towards others or ourselves, but also an obligation towards the Almighty. When man is viewed as a divine creature, then our perception of reality changes. [88]

The connection between the charitable *mitzvot hateluyot ba'aretz* and man's inherent *kedusha* is reflected in the placement of these *mitzvot* in *Parashat Kedoshim*, which begins with the call to sanctify ourselves, "because I, Hashem your God, am holy" (*Vayikra* 19:2). The Seforno comments:

> The Torah explains that once we have accepted Him as God, it is proper that we walk in His ways, to do righteousness and justice, and among these are the gleanings, forgotten sheaves, and corner of the field mentioned in the chapter. This is explained by His saying: "I am Lord your God" — that is to say: Since I am your God and all My ways are kindness and truth, it is fitting that you observe these categories of righteousness, which are desirable before Me... (Seforno, *Vayikra* 19:9-10)[89]

Rav Hirsch develops this concept further:

> The foundation for a holy life, *"Kedoshim tihyu,"* starts with the fundamental laws of the family and the individual, namely with respecting parents and Shabbat. This foundation is completed with the fundamental law of society, namely the *mitzvah* of *tzedaka*, the right to receive it and the duty to give it. It is significant that the social foundation is woven into one unit with laws pertaining to the service of God, laws of sacrifices. For, in Jewish life that is sustained by God, there is no antithesis of religious and social; they are not even separate, coexisting parts of one higher whole. Rather, they are interrelated in organic unity, like root and stock, blossom and fruit. Judaism says: "Love God and love mankind" (*Avot* 6:1), for the love of God includes the love of his creatures. The foundation of the peace offering, which is the joy of happiness, is also the foundation of our responsibility for the happiness of others. (Rav Hirsch, commentary on *Vayikra* 19:10)

The call to holiness, *"Kedoshim tehiyu,"* requires not only dignified giving, but doing so in a way that transforms the giver. Just as there is a proper way to offer a sacrifice, there is a proper way to harvest one's crops.[90] One must focus not on the bounty; rather, one should develop real concern for others. One's field should become a field for the community's needs. One should give in a way that ensures he avoids haughtiness and high-handedness, as property should be a means of bringing peace and connection to God and one's fellow

---

88   See https://www.etzion.org.il/en/halakha/studies-halakha/philosophy-halakha/human-dignity-halakha.

89   See also *Ha'amek Davar, Vayikra* 19:9.

90   It may be that for this reason that the *mitzvah* of *shichecha* is omitted from the command in *Parashat Kedoshim*, as it is fulfilled entirely passively, focusing on the result rather than the intent of the giver. In the context of *kedusha*, how one gives is more important than what one gives.

man. Just as the peace-offering is consumed by the priest, the altar, and the one who offers the sacrifice, one's yield should be enjoyed by all. Doing so allows one to transform one's wealth into a holy part of religious life.

Thus, in the context of *Parashat Kedoshim*, we are instructed regarding the *bein adam l'atzmo* element of the charitable agricultural *mitzvot*.

Social and Ritual Obligations

Interestingly, the agricultural gifts to the poor are mentioned to other times in the Torah, in *Parashat Emor* and *Parashat Ki Teitze*. A careful look at each mention recognizes that each *Parasha* focuses on a different aspect of the *mitzvah*.

Four chapters after introducing the *mitzvot ha-teluyot ba'aretz* in *Parashat Kedoshim*, the Torah repeats them in *Parashat Emor*, in the midst of the discussion of the festivals (*Vayikra* 23:22). Why are these *mitzvot* mentioned in between the command to bring the *omer* offering on Pesach and the two loaves on Shavuot?

On the simple level, this indicates that one cannot be joyous on the festivals without expressing care and concern for the underprivileged. Furthermore, *Torat Kohanim* states that this juxtaposition equates providing for the poor with the offering of sacrifices. One who gives these gifts to the poor is considered as if he has offered sacrifices, and one who neglects his obligations to the poor is akin to one who neglects his sacrificial duties.

The Ibn Ezra (ad loc.) explains that these *mitzvot* are mentioned in the context of the festivals of Pesach and Shavuot because they are observed during the harvest season, and the Torah reminds one harvesting his crop to provide for the poor. The Ramban (ad loc.) adds that one might think that if he uses his crop for *mitzvot* such as the *omer* offering of Pesach or the two loaves of Shavuot, there is no need to be concerned with the poor. The Torah repeats these commandments here to convey the critical idea that the attention one pays to his ritualistic duties must never diminish his sensitivity to the plight of the underprivileged. Social justice cannot be pushed aside for ritual obligations, partly because God views one's giving to the poor as an obligation to Him as well.

Rav Hirsch takes this idea further, explaining the similarity in message of these specific offerings and the gifts to the poor:

> Fulfillment of the *mitzvot* of *peia* and *leket* is the practical corollary to the *omer* and the two loaves, for through them every individual is guaranteed the means of an independent existence. However, this is guaranteed only by the power of Torah and *mitzvot*. Were it not for God's Torah, only the landowners would enjoy an existence worthy of human dignity; only they would benefit from the bounty of the fields. The landless, however, the poor and the strangers, would be dependent on the sympathy and judiciousness of the landowners. Yet, in our "progressive" times, to appeal to the landowners for support borders on a crime, and the few coins of charity given by them humiliate the recipients.
>
> But such is not to be done in Israel. For this nation carries the first cuttings of its fields to the sanctuary of the Torah, and there waves the *omer* before God. And on the day

that commemorated the receiving of the Torah, the nation brings two loaves to the sanctuary of the Torah, and there vows to fulfill its duty as the people of the Torah. The prosperity that is granted to the community is to bestow upon every individual a dignified existence. In this nation, the produce of the land and the labor of man are not solely for the benefit of the landowners. The landless and the strangers are rightful partners in the harvest, and their upkeep is the obligation of the wealthy and the privilege of the poor...

For the wealthy man who cares for the needy of his people merely fulfills thereby his duty to God. This duty is thrust upon him with every grain of produce that God caused to grow in his field. This concept of *tzedaka* is the greatest of the Torah's social triumphs. (Rav Hirsch, commentary on *Vayikra* 23:22)

Thus, in the context of *Parashat Emor*, we learn of the ritual element of social justice. The *mitzvot hateluyot ba'aretz* are not only meant to provide for the poor; they are gifts to God as well.

The Interpersonal Element

The most straightforward aspect of the *mitzvot hateluyot ba'aretz*, of course, is the interpersonal element; they provide for the needs of others. This explains the placement of these *mitzvot* in *Parashat Ki Teitzei* (*Devarim* 24:19-20), alongside many other commands of the same genre.[91]

Rav Hirsch points out that it seems rather evident that the purpose of this *mitzvah* is not to solve the issues of poverty, as it is left to chance whether the poor will take anything from one's field. Indeed, the poor themselves are obligated to leave these gifts from any fields they may own for other unfortunates. Rather, he explains, these *mitzvot* serve a different purpose altogether:

At harvest time, a person surveys what nature has done for him and what he is about to take home as the fruit of his own labor. At this time he utters the proud and momentous words: "My own." Precisely at this time, every member of the nation must bear in mind and signify in deed that anyone who can say "This is mine" is obligated to care for others as well. His field and his vineyard do not yield their produce for him alone (this is the message of *peia* and *olelot*). In the labor of his hands he is not to work for himself alone (this is the message of *leket* and *peret*). For in the state governed by the Law of God, the care of the poor and the stranger is not left to feelings of sympathy; it is not dependent on property owners' fears of the threat posed to them by the despair of the poor. Rather, it is a right that God has given to the poor and a duty that He has assigned to property-owners. And over all of them, God proclaims, "I am Lord your God", thereby assuring all of them of His personal care, encompassing all with equal love and justice and the obligating all equally to be just

---

91   The addition of *shichecha* in this context – which, as mentioned can be fulfilled even without any awareness at all – underscores the importance of achieving the result of providing for the needs of the poor. This is the essence of what distinguishes interpersonal *mitzvot* from their ritual counterparts; regarding interpersonal *mitzvot*, the result can be significant, even without the proper intent.

> and loving toward others. Thus, He unites them all to form a holy community that is sustained by justice and charity. (Rav Hirsch, commentary on *Devarim* 24:19)

Rav Hirsch emphasizes that the various *mitzvot* of the field "counter the pride of ownership" while providing the means for the poor to support themselves. They remind man that he shouldn't view the whole harvest as being his alone; he should not exploit the field down to the last stalk, but leave to the poor at least whatever falls. The harvest gifts do not actually provide for the poor as much as remind us of our duty to provide for the poor.[92]

The *Sefer HaChinuch* explains how the *mitzvah* of *pe'ah* develops one's character:

> God wished His chosen people to be graced with every good moral quality, that they should be generous in spirit and blessed in soul. I have already written that actions mold the character, improving it and making it receptive for divine blessing. There is no doubt that by leaving a portion of his produce and declaring it free to everyone so that the needy may enjoy it, man's spirit will become more unselfish and he will enjoy divine grace. But he who gathers in everything into the house, leaving nothing for the needy who saw the field full of standing corn and hoped to satiate their hunger, will no doubt do harm to his character, breeding selfishness, ill-will and miserliness. (*Sefer HaChinuch, mitzvah* 216)

The same reason suffices to explain the other agricultural laws as well.[93] The agricultural *mitzvot* serve an essential purpose in transforming the harvester from a greedy individual counting all his crops to one who realizes that his wealth can also be used as a means of providing for the poor.

The *mitzvot ha-teluyot ba-aretz* are repeated three times in the Torah as they are far more than charity (*Parashat Ki Teitze's bein adam la-chavero* focus). They present an ideal opportunity to enhance one's relationship with God (*Parashat Emor's bein adam la-Makom* focus) and help one develop a holy personality (*Parashat Kedoshim's bein adam le-atzmo* focus).

---

92 This explains how even *shichecha*, although fulfilled unintentionally, can build one's character:
    To the foregoing is now added the *mitzvah* of *shichecha*. The *mitzvah* serves to purge your thoughts of possessiveness and greed. It teaches you that your mind, too, which works at increasing wealth, must not be focuses solely on your own welfare. Rather, whatever has once escaped your attention at harvest time must be left for the poor. The *mitzvah* of *shichecha* serves to uplift harvest thoughts, just as the *mitzvah* of *leket* serves to uplift harvest labor...

93 Regarding *Shichcha*, the *Chinuch* adds:
    What lies at the root of the precept? The poor and the needy, in their want and their penury, set their eyes on the crop of grain when they see the owners of the fielding bringing in sheaves from the field according to God's blessing. "If only I might be granted to gather in sheaves to my house! If only I had one, I would rejoice in it!" It was therefore part of God's beneficent will to fulfill their desire and yearning when it happens by chance that the owner forgets a sheaf.
    Shichecha helps foster the proper mindset by encouraging the farmer to realize that the things he has forgotten are probably not important at all, allowing him to put himself in the shoes of the needy. The Malbim quotes the *Chinuch's* reasoning, explaining that through this *mitzvah*, God allows man to be the conduit for taking care of the needs of the indigent — not only feeding them, but allowing them to feel important as well.

The Torah Economy

The model that emerges from the *mitzvot hateluyot ba'aretz* is one of a caring society in which income is not a status symbol or the basis of a caste system. Any economic progress has portions that are shared by all. The goal is ensuring *kavod* for others while preventing the pursuit of *kavod*.

As we noted in Section I, political economist and economic philosopher Henry George (1839-1897) noted that the Torah system is a radical deviation from the economic models known in the past, which call for the privileged members of society with means to forgo their possessions and wealth in order to provide a more equitable distribution of resources and create a redeemed, socially-concerned, and value-based economy.

Indeed, certain economic elements are only possible in a God-driven society, in which divine blessing ensures there will be enough growth in the sixth year to provide through the eighth year. As Howard Jonas points out[94], only the true God could make the promises necessary for this society to exist. Most of these agricultural *mitzvot* are limited to *Eretz Yisrael*, because the high stakes of a redeemed utopian economy require clear recognition of Hashem's role in the process and the nation living in God's Land.

The Torah welfare system is operated through individuals, not forced upon by government; its economic system certainly does not entail government control of resources. The needy are provided for by each and every member of society with means, and portions of all prosperity are shared with those who lack their own personal success. In that sense, it appears to be a "capitalist" system. In many respects, however, it differs from classical market economies.

The most well-known advocate of the market economy was thinker Adam Smith, who called for competition based on the premise that human beings act in an egotistical manner:

> It is not from the benevolence of the butcher, the brewer, or the baker that we expect our dinner, but from their regard to their own interest. We address ourselves, not to their humanity but to their self-love... Nobody but a beggar chooses to depend chiefly upon the benevolence of his fellow-citizens. (Adam Smith, *An Inquiry into the Nature and Causes of the Wealth of Nations*, Book 1, Chapter 2)

Competition allows for a market driven by self-interest, not concern for the less fortunate. This is the "natural selection" of economics. Those who succeed will hopefully give charity, but that is not a part of the economic model.

Although the Torah clearly calls for financial progress and requires that individuals plant for six out of seven years, never does the Torah allow one to become egotistical or driven completely by self-interest. Furthermore, even competition is limited to some degree, as it is improper to encroach on another's business and to open up a competing business in the same locale (see C.M. 157).[95] The Torah is willing to forgo economic efficiency in

---

94   See chapter 13.

95   Although the *Chavat Yair* (42) argues that this is not an outright prohibition and that refraining from competing is

situations where it will drive others out of business.

The *Chatam Sofer* notes that even in the economic realm, personal conduct must be distinguished by compassion and lovingkindness. Even when competition is allowed legally, it is incumbent upon the Sages to ensure that when:

> "strife will increase and livelihood will decrease [through competition] and ruin lies in the waiting, it is fitting that ordinances be enacted so that people not conduct themselves like the fish of the sea that swallow one another" (*Responsa Chatam Sofer, Choshen Mishpat* 5:44; see also 5:61).

As Rav Chaim Navon writes:

> Unrestrained and unbridled competition is unfit not only because of what will happen to the loser – that he will lose his livelihood, but also because of what will happen to the winner – that he will lose his human sensitivity and moral consciousness.
> The Torah does not content itself with concern for an efficient economic system, or with concern with a morally correct division of economic resources. The Torah fashions an economic system that considers moral factors on the individual level as well. An economic system of a particular bent encourages people to develop particular traits and characteristics. The Chatam Sofer emphasizes that according to the Torah the economic system must encourage people to develop the traits of mercy and compassion, rather than rapacious competition ... An absolutely free market economy nurtures the development of negative character traits on the part of the individual.[96]

On the other hand, the Torah does not adopt a socialist outlook to solving the problem of poverty, as has been noted by both non-rabbinic thinkers and great Torah scholars.

In 1930, Ze'ev Jabotinsky wrote that although the Torah derides a social order in which the rich live in comfort at the expense of the suffering poor and shares the socialist movement's protest of that reality, the Biblical Economic Plan decidedly rejects socialism's concrete plan to solve the problem of social inequality and is in fact based on an idea diametrically opposite to it. While socialism averts the possibility of accumulating wealth by expropriating the means of mass production from private ownership, preventing the possibility of social inequality, exploitation, and economic competition, "the Bible seeks to preserve economic liberty, but to reform it by certain limitations and antidotes." Jabotinsky lists Shabbat rest for all one's workers, the agricultural gifts to the poor, and charity as some of the "reforms of economic liberalism; they leave the principle of private enterprise intact."

Jabotinsky notes that the Torah's concept of *yovel* clearly illustrates a different antidote for eliminating inequality. He views Yovel as "an attempt to institutionalize periodic social upheavals":

> The main difference between the biblical revolution and socialist revolutions is

---

an act of piety, the *Chatam Sofer* disagrees.

96   See https://torah.etzion.org.il/en/torahs-approach-economics.

that the latter are supposed to occur once and for all, while the jubilee revolution should occur at regular intervals. According to plans based on the socialist ideal, a just distribution of land (and measures of social justice in general) will be set one day and admit no further changes. According to the Biblical plan, economic life will preserve after the jubilee full liberty for further changes. People will continue to make projects, to scheme, to struggle and compete; some will become rich, some will become poor; life will keep the character of an arena in which it is possible to lose or win, show initiative and fail or succeed.

This economic liberty would have only two limitations. The first limitation (or rather, an entire system of limitations) functions continuously: work is prohibited one day a week; one must leave the corner of his field and the gleanings of his vineyard for the poor; the tithe will be paid, being "holy unto the Lord". Translated into modern terminology, this means limiting and regulating the working hours, and generally all legislation for employee protection, all social security and progressive taxing. The other limitation, or rather antidote, to economic liberalism is the jubilee. It is as if a huge axe sweeps once in a while like a storm over the forest of humanity, and cuts down those treetops which have grown above the average; debts are cancelled, the impoverished regains his property, the slave goes free. Balance is restored, and the economic game starts over again, until the next upheaval...

[*Yovel* is] the very antithesis of socialism. The concept of repeated economic upheavals is an attempt to correct the ills of economic liberalism, not to forestall them. Quite on the contrary, this concept is clearly based on the conviction that free economic competition is one of the most powerful motivations in life. Let people struggle, lose and win. It is only necessary to cushion the arena with soft grass, so that whoever falls will not be too painfully injured... once in a while the referee's whistle is heard in the arena: winners and losers return to their starting positions, and line up shoulder to shoulder. Precisely because the game must go on...

[The *yovel* system] it retains the one thing which socialism has sworn to eradicate, and without which life may not be worth living - the eternal possibility of upheaval, the volcanic element in social life; a field of action, not a pasture. ("The Jubilee: The Biblical Plan for Expanded Ownership")

Although some elements of Jabotinsky's thought may be debatable, he does seem to effectively articulate that the Torah calls for a capitalist system in which there is private enterprise in six out of seven years, but with significant safeguards to ensure it never reaches a point of immoral competition and individuals sinking into debt for eternity with no opportunity for a fresh start.[97]

The Torah seems to accept a capitalist economic model, but with checks and balances through the *mitzvot hateluyot ba'aretz*, most explicitly *shevi'it* and *yovel*. As Rabbi Jonathan

---

97   Similarly, Heinrich Heine pointed out, "Moses did not want to abolish ownership of property; he wished, on the contrary, that everyone should possess something, so that no man might, because of poverty, be a slave with a slavish mind. Liberty was forever the ultimate thought of this great emancipator, and it still breathes and flames in all his laws which concern pauperism" (Israel Tabak, *Judaic Lore in Heine* [Johns Hopkins University Press, 1979], p. 32).

Sacks notes, the Torah's "aim is to correct the tendency toward radical and ever-increasing inequality that result from the unfettered play of free-market economics." *Shevi'it, yovel,* and all the social legislation in the Torah addresses the phenomenon of "There's nothing surer: The rich get rich and the poor get poorer":

> However, the market economy is better at producing wealth than at distributing it equitably. The concentration of wealth in a few hands gives disproportion power to some at the cost of others... This is not a critique of market economics, which he believes is still the best system there is. But it needs careful regulation and steering. That is what the legislation contained in Behar represents. It tells us that an economic system must exist within a moral framework. It need not aim at economic equality but it must respect human dignity. No one should become permanently imprisoned in the chains of debt. No one should be deprived of a stake in the commonwealth, which in biblical times meant a share in the land. No one should be a slave to his or her employer. Everyone has the right – one day in seven, one year in seven – to respite from the endless pressures of work. None of this means dismantling the market economy, but it may involve periodic redistribution.
>
> At the heart of these laws is a profoundly humane vision of society. "No man is an island." We are responsible for one another and implicated in one another's fate. Those who are blessed by God with more than they need should share some of that surfeit with those who have less than they need. This, in Judaism, is not a matter of charity but of justice – that is what the word tzedakah means. We need some of this spirit in advanced economies today if we are not to see human misery and social unrest. (*Covenant and Conversation-Behar-Bechukotai (5772) – The Limits of the Free Market*)

This perspective of the Torah system as a free market with a moral compass through *mitzvot* that serve as checks and balances is similarly expressed by Rav Azriel Ariel. He notes that another unique aspect of the Torah system is that the poor do not have the right to demand gifts. The Torah emphasizes the givers and their responsibilities. Instead of empowering the government to assist the needy, the Torah system places responsibility on the individual. Although it is unheard of to have a Jewish city without a charity fund for the poor (see *Hilchot Matanot Aniyim* 9:1-3), at its root, the Torah is concerned not only with ensuring the needs of the poor are met, but that individuals are involved in altruistic giving. A government might be able to force an individual to give money, but it can't ensure it is given from the heart. In contrast, when a community groups together to form a charity fund, individuals choose to perform acts of loving-kindness with their fellow Jews.

Rav Ariel characterizes the Torah's "unique therapeutic social policy as actually rooted in deemphasizing the poor's social rights." Socialists highlight the plight of the socially disadvantaged individual and view society itself as responsible for the welfare of those individuals. Capitalism, in contrast, emphasizes personal responsibility, initiative, and effort. The individual does not see himself responsible for the fate of others:

> The Torah, as is wont to do, unites these antipodes into one comprehensive system. Rambam counts eight levels in the *mitzvah* of charity (*Hilchot Matanot Aniyim* 10:7-

14). At the top of the list is a loan. Loans, as we know, are to be repaid. One cannot take a loan to buy alcohol and drink to intoxication; no one would loan money to a person who acts in this way. Loans are given to purchase a means of creating revenue, through which the poor person will be able to emerge from the circle of poverty. The weakness of socialism is that it habituates the poor person to leave his fate in the hands of society at large. In this way, the *mitzvah* of giving a loan leaves the yolk of responsibility on the shoulders of the individual in need. It is his responsibility to return the loan on time—down to the last penny.

Additionally, forging a partnership with a person in need or finding them employment are other ideal forms of charity, as they assist the individual in pulling himself out of poverty, instead of living at the expense of others.

The higher the level of personal responsibility a person has, the higher his emotional health and the greater his happiness… In the Torah's system, though, even the gifts of the poor are not a given. The Torah does not provide social insurance to anyone. There is no nationwide taxation system that would facilitate gathering extensive resources, making it possible to cover all of the poor's needs. Instead, the charity taxation system is local and small-scale…. Which can tailor itself to the unique needs of each poor individual.[98]

The agricultural gifts to the poor similarly place a large measure of responsibility on the poor individual, who must gather the produce from the fields; even during *shevi'it*, when produce is ownerless, whoever comes first can harvest it. In this manner, "The poor person is forced to leave the apathy that marks a harsh socioeconomic situation; he must be proactive and take personal initiative. This facilitates the impoverished individual to break out of the poverty mentality and paves the path towards self-rehabilitation."

The Torah's laws create a society that does not advocate either of the extremes of socialism or capitalism, but instead creates a free market celebrating human initiative while ensuring that everyone's needs are actively served rather than passively achieved. Indeed, the numerous failed socialist revolutions coupled with the failed societies of unequal wealth call for a return to the Torah's ideals. Rav Ariel concludes:

The time is not yet ripe to set down a new social constitution in the State of Israel. Much work lays ahead of us—both halachic investigation and assessment of the situation in the field—to create a new, just system of charity that will cultivate a healthy, loving, and supportive society, one that gives with loving kindness and will serve as a beacon of light unto the nations and a shining example of a just society to the entire world.

Although organizing the contemporary economy based on these principles is beyond our current capabilities, the more we understand them and the Torah's goal of ensuring that economic and agricultural progress do not become moral quagmires, the more we can inculcate these values in society.

---

98   See a translation of his article at https://en.toraland.org.il/beit-midrash/halachic-guides/hilchot-haaretz/hilchot-matanot-aniyim/matanot-aniyim-preface-matanot-aniyim-as-a-model-for-social-policy-in-justice-shall-you-be-established/.

The Connection to the Land of Israel

Now that we understand the significance of the agricultural gifts to the poor, we are faced with an obvious question. Why are these *mitzvot* dependent on the Land of Israel? If they are so essential for ensuring that one who is involved in planting a field develops and fosters a holy character, why should they not apply throughout the world? Why is the Torah's full economic vision limited to *Eretz Yisrael*?[99]

In order to answer this question, we must take a broader look at the challenges and benefits of agricultural work.

Farmer vs. Shepherd

In our day and age, and the idea of dedicating one's life to agriculture is a foreign concept for most people. Yet before the Industrial Revolution, a person's professional choices were far more limited. In the time of the Torah, the essential choice was between shepherding and agriculture.

In the Torah's description of the first conflict between brothers – that of Kayin and Hevel – very little is explicit regarding what brought about the dispute. The only thing that the Torah clearly tells us about the brothers is their different professions: Kayin was a farmer, while Hevel was a shepherd (*Bereishit* 4:2). Kayin was the first to offer a sacrifice to God, which he brought from his produce, but God accepted only Hevel's sacrifice, which he brought from his sheep. Some commentators explain that Kayin's offering was not accepted, despite his initiative, because he did not bring the best of his produce, while Hevel offered the choicest of his sheep. Others, however, suggest that Kayin's very choice of profession was indicative of his personality and constituted a challenge that, if not confronted successfully, could lead to his downfall.

Rav Hirsch notes that the root of the name קַיִן is קָנָה, "acquisition," observing that working the land is indeed a means of attaining and acquiring wealth:

> Agriculture demands all a person's physical strength ... He needs to devote his whole life to his bodily existence. The concept of "Kayin," i.e. "*kana*" (acquisition) – self-recognition – and the pride associated with acquisition, implicit in the terms *kayin* and *kana*, are most evident in the farmer. The ground that the farmer has fertilized by the sweat of his brow has become part of his personality. He has made his ground bear fruit, and it becomes something of ultimate value for him – it becomes part of his personality, he holds onto it and settles it.
>
> To be sure, agriculture stimulates and develops civilization. Most inventions and skills may be credited to agriculture. The settlement of the land implicit in agriculture

---

99 There are some agricultural *mitzvot* that are not *teluyot ba'aretz*. The *mitzvah* of *orla*, which prohibits consumption of fruit from a tree during its first three years of growth, applies in *chutz la'aretz* as well, as long as it is certain that the fruits are from the first three years. Similarly, some of the laws of *kilayim* (*kila'ei hakerem*, planting wheat and vines in proximity, and *kila harkava*, grafting of different species) also apply outside of *Eretz Yisrael*. The laws of *hafrashat challa* apply in *chutz la'aretz*, and according to many authorities, the *halachot* of *chadash* (partaking in the new grain before the 16th of Nissan) apply outside of *Eretz Yisrael* as well. However, these laws do not relate to social justice and care for the needy, in the manner of *shevi'it*, *yovel*, *pe'ah*, and the like.

leads to the formation of society and state and the administration of justice.

Nevertheless, Rav Hirsch notes, though agriculture does have these positive elements, it also poses a tremendous spiritual challenge to the farmer, as seen in the agricultural societies of old:

> On the other hand, the farmer is a slave to his field, and the field draws him towards it. Once he has placed the yoke of pursuit of acquisition upon his neck, his spirit also becomes subservient ... This leads to slavery ... Moreover, he will easily be brought to admiration of the forces of nature, upon whose influences the success of his field depends. Faith in God and in the superiority of man was first lost among the agricultural nations. It was there that idol worship first developed.

Hevel's choice of profession, continues Rav Hirsch, is entirely different:

> In contrast, the life of the shepherd is most elevated. He is concerned principally with living things. His care of them arouses within him humane feelings and sympathy for suffering. His acquisitions are portable. The flock needs the shepherd's care, but their existence is not in his hands. Thus, the shepherd is protected from the danger of overestimating his own value and that of his property. His profession does not occupy all his strength and efforts. His spirit is invested in his labor to a lesser degree, and remains open to godly and humane values. For this reason our forefathers were shepherds, and Moshe and David also shepherded flocks.
>
> Working the land is fundamentally tied to the concept of private ownership. There is much significance to the fact that Hevel became a shepherd, while Kayin, obsessed with *kinyan* (acquisition), became a tiller of the soil. (Rav Hirsch, commentary on *Bereishit* 4:2)

It is clear from God's words to Kayin that though one who works the land is faced with a challenge, his pursuit need not be an evil one. Although sin does indeed "crouch at the door" – at the plowed field of the tiller of the soil –"you can rule over it" (*Bereishit* 4:7). Man's free choice and moral independence afford him the ability to be an upright worker of the soil with a deep religious consciousness.[100] As Rav Hirsch notes:

> Man's natural labor was agriculture. Man needed to "work the land" in order to provide himself with food for sustenance .... This is also Israel's destiny according to the Torah. (Rav Hirsch, commentary on *Bereishit* 4:2)

Obviously, the land must be planted and built up to provide food for humans and for the flocks they tend. However, one who chooses to focus on building the land as his profession is liable to become overly attached to it and even intoxicated by its physical qualities, thereby losing his spiritual perspective.

One of the greatest examples of this danger is that of Noach. Noach is introduced to us as the righteous individual building the ark, the head of the lone family to survive the Flood. Yet immediately after his departure from the ark, he turns to agriculture and

---

100 For further discussion of this point, see Rav Elchanan Samet, "Why Did God Not Accept Kayin's Offering?" http://www.vbm-torah.org/parsha.60/01bereis.htm.

plants a vineyard (9:20). To introduce his choice of a pursuit that ultimately leads to his inebriation and humiliation by one of his sons, the Torah uses the term "*vayachel*," connoting an act of *chullin*, that which is unsacred (see Rashi).[101]

The *midrash* (*Bereishit Rabba* 31:3) comments that although Noach is first described as a "righteous man" (6:9), when he turns to agriculture, he becomes a mere "man of the land" (9:20). Rav Aharon Lichtenstein points out that the Torah does not refer to him simply a "*worker* of the land," but as a "*man* of the land." Noach was consumed by his profession to the point that it became a part of his very identity. He became a man of the land, with all the implications of that title. It was admirable for Noach, upon exiting the ark, to immediately begin cultivating the earth. However, despite his good intentions, the earth consumed him and changed his perspective.[102]

Given the dangers of agriculture, it is not surprising that most Jewish leaders turned to shepherding, an occupation through which they could harness their feelings of care and concern for others. This dynamic is noted in the *midrash* (*Shemot Rabba* 2:2), which notes that Moshe's care for each and every individual sheep in his flock showed God that he would care for every Jew as well.

The only exception to this rule is Yitzchak, who not only amassed a vast quantity of livestock (*Bereishit* 26:14), but also planted crops, obtaining a one-hundred-fold return on the seeds he planted (26:12).

Yitzchak's two sons, Yaakov and Esav, were both supposed to take part in shaping the future of the fledgling Jewish nation (see Malbim on *Parashat Vayishlach*), but they chose different paths: "Esav was a skillful hunter, a man of the field, but Yaakov was a simple man, who dwelled in tents" (25:27). Interestingly, "Yitzchak loved Esav, for he hunted [and provided food] in his mouth" (25:28). Yitzchak loved Esav due to his choice of profession, hunting, as opposed to Ya'akov's pursuit of shepherding, the usual Jewish profession of the day.

Yitzchak had planted a field, rather than restrict himself to shepherding, because he knew that the Jewish future would require planting as well as shepherding. The Jewish People would need to build the Land of Israel, and Yaakov's abilities as a shepherd would be only a part of that endeavor. Yitzchak never discounted Yaakov's greatness, but he understood that Esav too had something positive to contribute. He was supposed to be the physical provider that enabled Yaakov to educate the world toward spirituality. Yet, the Torah tells us, Esav did not fulfill this responsibility, because he failed to gain a correct perspective on his pursuits. He made no effort to cultivate the land, preferring to see it merely as a place to indulge himself and hunt wild animals. The concept of working hard to achieve results – a key positive aspect of agriculture – was totally lost on Esav.

The *Midrash Ha-Gadol* (cited in *Torah Sheleima* 199) underscores the difference between

---

101 Although Rashi, citing the *midrash*, specifically faults Noach's decision to plant a vineyard, the *Chatam Sofer* explains that Noach began with the righteous motive of planting grapes to use as libations for sacrifices to God. Yet in practice, he partook of the wine himself before offering a libation. He thus became intoxicated, and the enterprise became unsacred.

102 See www.etzion.org.il/vbm/archive/7-sichot/01noach.rtf.

the brothers' personalities in its account of the purchase of the birthright:

When Esav entered, he found Yaakov standing and cooking, his eyes tearing from the smoke.

Esav said, "Why do you go to all this trouble? Open your eyes and see how all people on earth eat whatever they find – fish, insects, crawling creatures, swine, and such – but you trouble yourself to prepare a dish of lentils!"

Yaakov said to him, "But if we act in that way, what will we do to prepare for the day about which it is said, 'Seek justice, seek humility; perhaps you will then be protected on the day of the Lord's wrath' (*Tzefanya* 2:3), the day when the reward of the righteous is dispensed?"

He said to him, "Is there a World to Come, or perhaps a resurrection of the dead …?"

Yaakov said to him, "If there is no World to Come and no resurrection of the dead, why do you need the birthright? Sell your birthright to me today!"

Yaakov was prepared to invest time in accomplishing his goals. Esav wanted only quick results.

Yitzchak knew that despite Esav's failure, the Jewish nation would at some point need to revert to farming – to planting seeds, as Yitzchak himself had done. Yaakov understood, however, that this time had not yet arrived, and he, therefore, became a shepherd. Yet, one of Yaakov's sons understood that a day would come when shepherding would no longer suffice as the sole occupation of the Jewish People.

In Yosef's first dream, he envisioned that his brothers' sheaves were bowing down to his sheaves. Although his brothers were taken aback by the implication that they would be subjugated to Yosef, they may also have taken issue with the very subject of this dream, which implied that Yosef had left the family tradition. As Rav Hirsch explains:

It is remarkable that he should have dreamt of binding sheaves. That was something with which they ordinarily had no connection: they were shepherds. Becoming an agricultural people was still only their destiny in the distant future. If agriculture was so much in his mind that he even dreamt of it, the brothers were justified in thinking that this only could be due to the teaching and information given to him by his father, Yisrael, regarding the expected national destiny of the family. All the more, then, could the brothers believe themselves justified in saying: Will you indeed in the future be king over us, or perhaps even now already rule over us? (Rav Hirsch, commentary on *Bereishit* 37:9)

Rav Yosef Dov Soloveitchik explains that the brothers were, in fact, not wrong. Yosef dreamed of a different reality that would soon face the Jewish People:

Biblical Joseph was not persuaded that "Jacob dwelt in the land of his father's wanderings" (37:1) would endure for long. The words "Your seed shall be strangers in an alien land" (15:3) kept tolling in his ears. He saw himself and his brothers in an alien environment, far from the land of Canaan, in new circumstances and under new conditions of life. In his dream he saw "behold we are binding sheaves"; we are no longer in Canaan, we are in the land of Egypt and we can no longer be shepherds. We are integrated into a new economy with new styles of living, characteristics, and laws .... Basically he dreamt of a new framework within which the unity of the family could be preserved, even in the far-flung places where the Creator of the Universe would scatter them. His constant preoccupation was the continuation of Abraham's tradition amidst a new economic structure and civilization. (*Five Addresses*)

While his brothers were not yet ready to accept this reality, Yosef dreamed of a future in which agriculture would become a necessity for the Jewish People.

Indeed, Yosef's identification of the positive aspects of agriculture later enabled him to correctly interpret Pharaoh's dream. Pharaoh, like Yosef, had two dreams, one relating to livestock and one about sheaves of grain (*Bereishit* 41). Although Pharaoh was surrounded by the greatest dream-interpreters of the day, they failed to interpret the dream in a way that sat well with him. Why did Pharaoh's advisers fail to interpret his dreams correctly? It is possible that the idea of gathering in sheaves seemed to them an act so devoid of spiritual significance that it could not possibly convey a message from God. Yosef, meanwhile, understood that although agriculture is a challenging profession, where "sin crouches at the door" (4:7), man can "rule over it" and apply it in a spiritually positive manner. Yosef, therefore, had no difficulty seeing how an agricultural, earthly dream contained within it a divine message.

Importantly, the Egyptians had already chosen agriculture as their prime pursuit, and the Torah pointedly notes that the Egyptians abominated shepherds (46:34). Rav Hirsch details the contrast between our forefathers' choice of shepherding and the Egyptians' disdain for that profession:

Consider the antipathy of the ancient Egyptians toward shepherds and pastoral peoples. All the negative outgrowths of the agricultural mentality discussed above were found in Egypt. Egyptian culture was based on agriculture; its characteristic features were polytheism on the one hand and human enslavement on the other. Work was the purpose of man. The individual per se had no value, no dignity, no freedom. The Egyptian was born a slave to his occupation. Faith in God, faith in the freedom of man and man's likeness to God remained alive only in the hearts of one tribe of shepherds – our forefathers. The Egyptian leaders were very shrewd in instilling in their people an implacable hatred for pastoral peoples.

The Egyptians, explains Rav Hirsch, specifically chose agriculture because it was a mode of acquisition, and one that allowed the wealthy and successful to take advantage of the weak and poor. Work that centered around tending to the needs of the animal kingdom was antithetical to their way of life.

Yosef, who did not believe that agriculture was all bad, looked forward favorably to a Jewish agricultural future. However, in view of the prevailing culture, he warned his family to stay far away from agriculture while in Egypt and to announce loudly that they were shepherds. This, he felt, not only would help them maintain their separation from the Egyptians, but would also enable them to maintain the positive qualities of the shepherd without being confounded by the spiritual challenges of working the land. (Rav Hirsch, commentary on *Bereishit* 46:33)

The Point of Transition

Rav Soloveitchik discusses why shepherding remained the preferred profession until the people arrived in the Land after the Exodus:

> I believe that there is a serious reason for the preference given to the pastoral over the farming community. The land was promised to Avraham, Yitzchak and Yaakov in the form of a covenant concluded between the Almighty and the patriarchs. However, there was a stipulation in the agreement: its implementation was contingent on the sojourn of Avraham's children in a strange land as bondsmen and servants. Prior to the fulfillment of this stipulation, the gift was held in abeyance; the finalization and the full consummation of the covenant took place after the Israelites met the challenge of "Your seed shall be strangers" (*Bereishit* 15:13). Thus their rights to the Promised Land were limited. The most they had was a *kinyan peirot*, the right to use the land and enjoy its produce. Later, after the exodus, they acquired *kinyan ha-guf*, full ownership. Therefore, before the exodus they had no right to develop an agricultural economy, to dig, to build, to destroy, to change the structure of the land. All they possessed was the right to enjoy the fruit, and that is exactly what the pastoral community did. It did not exploit the land as would an agricultural society. It took whatever the land offered. (*Festival of Freedom*, pp. 127–128)

Before the sojourn in Egypt, the time for agriculturally building the Land had not yet arrived. After the exodus, as the people made their way from Egypt to the Land of Israel, Moshe began to prepare them for the new challenge they would face as they changed from shepherds into farmers and as the nation transformed from a simple, pastoral society into a more complex, agricultural civilization.

Aside from completing the acquisition of the Land, the shift to agriculture would allow the people to put down roots, so that they would not easily give up their place even in the face of adversity:

> As an agriculturalist, man will be connected to his environment. He will not willingly leave it in famine, as Yitzchak who planted and did not leave Israel in the face of famine. The farmer will defend his property because it is his lot, but the Torah teaches the Jew how to be involved in the land while maintaining the kind and gentle demeanor of the legendary shepherd. (Ibid.)

Life after the conquest of the Land would not be as it had been in the time of the Patriarchs. Rav Soloveitchik notes (*The Emergence of Ethical Man*, pp. 150-156) that although Avraham had previously planted the seed of the Jewish People in the Land of Israel, his presence there had not been of a permanent nature. With the words "*lech lecha*" (*Bereishit* 12:1), God had removed Avraham from his stable home in civilized and urbanized Mesopotamia to live as a nomad in a foreign land. Avraham's travels throughout the land – fulfilling the divine directive, "Rise, walk about in the Land, along its length and along its breadth, for I will give it [all] to you" (13:17) –enabled him to establish his presence throughout the Land, but prevented him from fully settling in any one place. He thus was able to throw off the societal mores of his day and forge a new bond with God. Just as the time had not yet come for an agricultural society in the Land, the time was not yet ripe for a sedentary Jewish presence there.

The great transition from nomadic tribe to a nation settled in its land and from a society of shepherds to one built on agriculture took place upon the entry of the Jewish People into *Eretz Yisrael* after their wanderings in the desert. Indeed, this transition is the theme of Moshe's final messages to the Jewish People before they enter *Eretz Yisrael*. In order to make sure that the growth of the Holy Land would not become a physical trap for its Jewish inhabitants, Moshe had to explain what life in the Land had in store for the Jewish People. His guidelines regarding the proper attitude once in the Land constitute a core component of his final speeches to the nation.

Settling *Eretz Yisrael* Agriculturally

At the end of Moshe's life, he shares a historical perspective on the Jews as a people and on what they must do to successfully enter the Land of Israel and dwell there in physical and spiritual sublimity. He spares nothing in his descriptions of the vastness and physical beauty of the Land, but he also does not shy away from the challenges that will attend the settlement of the Land.

In *Parashat Ekev* (*Devarim* 8), Moshe reminds the Jewish People that adherence to the *mitzvot* will enable them to possess the land that God promised them. He continues by contrasting the Land of Israel with the places where the people lived previously:

וְזָכַרְתָּ אֶת כָּל הַדֶּרֶךְ אֲשֶׁר הוֹלִיכְךָ ה' א-להיךָ זֶה אַרְבָּעִים שָׁנָה בַּמִּדְבָּר....: וַיְעַנְּךָ וַיַּרְעִבֶךָ וַיַּאֲכִלְךָ אֶת הַמָּן אֲשֶׁר לֹא יָדַעְתָּ וְלֹא יָדְעוּן אֲבֹתֶיךָ לְמַעַן הוֹדִיעֲךָ כִּי לֹא עַל הַלֶּחֶם לְבַדּוֹ יִחְיֶה הָאָדָם כִּי עַל כָּל מוֹצָא פִי ה' יִחְיֶה הָאָדָם:

You shall remember all the way that the Lord, your God, led you these forty years in the desert... He afflicted you and made you hungry, and fed you manna, which you had never known and your fathers had never known, in order to make you know that it is not by bread alone that man lives. (*Devarim* 8:2–3).

These *pesukim* serve as both an introduction and a contrast to life in the Land, whose praises Moshe proceeds to enumerate:

כִּי ה' א-להיךָ מְבִיאֲךָ אֶל אֶרֶץ טוֹבָה אֶרֶץ נַחֲלֵי מָיִם עֲיָנֹת וּתְהֹמֹת יֹצְאִים בַּבִּקְעָה וּבָהָר: אֶרֶץ חִטָּה וּשְׂעֹרָה וְגֶפֶן וּתְאֵנָה וְרִמּוֹן אֶרֶץ זֵית שֶׁמֶן וּדְבָשׁ: אֶרֶץ אֲשֶׁר לֹא בְמִסְכֵּנֻת תֹּאכַל בָּהּ לֶחֶם לֹא תֶחְסַר כֹּל בָּהּ אֶרֶץ אֲשֶׁר אֲבָנֶיהָ בַרְזֶל וּמֵהֲרָרֶיהָ תַּחְצֹב נְחֹשֶׁת: וְאָכַלְתָּ וְשָׂבָעְתָּ וּבֵרַכְתָּ אֶת ה' א-להיךָ עַל הָאָרֶץ הַטֹּבָה אֲשֶׁר נָתַן לָךְ:

For the Lord, your God, is bringing you to a good land, a land with streams of water, [with] fountains and depths that flow from the valleys and the hills. A land of wheat and barley and vines and fig trees and pomegranates, a land of oil-bearing olives and honey. A land in which you will eat bread without scarceness, in which you will lack nothing, a land whose stones are iron and from whose mountains you will mine brass. You will eat, you will be satisfied, and you will bless the Lord, your God, for the good land that He has given you. (*Devarim* 8:7–10)

These praises of the Land reiterate its superior physical properties, especially relative to the desert in which the Jews had sojourned. Yet, involvement in the physical beauty of the land does not come without spiritual challenges. The next *pesukim*, therefore, warn the Jews of the dangers of involvement in physical bounty and excessive pride in physical wealth and possessions:

> הִשָּׁמֶר לְךָ פֶּן תִּשְׁכַּח אֶת ה' א-לֹהֶיךָ... פֶּן תֹּאכַל וְשָׂבָעְתָּ וּבָתִּים טֹבִים תִּבְנֶה וְיָשָׁבְתָּ: וּבְקָרְךָ וְצֹאנְךָ יִרְבְּיֻן וְכֶסֶף וְזָהָב יִרְבֶּה לָךְ וְכֹל אֲשֶׁר לְךָ יִרְבֶּה: (יד) וְרָם לְבָבֶךָ וְשָׁכַחְתָּ אֶת ה' א-לֹהֶיךָ...

> Beware lest you forget the Lord, your God ... Lest when you eat and be satisfied, and you build good houses and dwell in them; And your herds and flocks multiply, and your silver and gold multiply, and all that you have multiply, So that your heart becomes haughty and you forget the Lord, your God ... (*Devarim* 8:11-14)

The message of these *pesukim* is clear: The Land's physical largess, if misused, can lead to disaster. One who views their agricultural success as the result of human effort – rather than that of man's divinely blessed partnership with God in building the Land – he is liable to become distanced from God and forget Him.

The Torah then once again contrasts the Land of Israel with the desert:

> הַמּוֹלִיכְךָ בַּמִּדְבָּר הַגָּדֹל וְהַנּוֹרָא נָחָשׁ שָׂרָף וְעַקְרָב וְצִמָּאוֹן אֲשֶׁר אֵין מָיִם הַמּוֹצִיא לְךָ מַיִם מִצּוּר הַחַלָּמִישׁ: הַמַּאֲכִלְךָ מָן בַּמִּדְבָּר אֲשֶׁר לֹא יָדְעוּן אֲבֹתֶיךָ לְמַעַן עַנֹּתְךָ וּלְמַעַן נַסֹּתֶךָ לְהֵיטִבְךָ בְּאַחֲרִיתֶךָ:

> Who led you in the great and terrible desert, [with] snakes, poisonous serpents, and scorpions, and thirst for lack of water; Who brought forth water for you from the rock of flint. Who in the desert fed you the manna, which your fathers had never known, in order to afflict you that I may put you to the test, to provide good for you in the end. (*Devarim* 8:15–16)

The desert served an educational goal; the people's sustainment by manna from Heaven conveyed the eternal message that it is really God Who supplies food. Yet, as the repeated contrast of the Land and the desert reminds the people, it will be challenging to recall this truth once they have arrived in the Land. If the people forget Who is really helping them, the state of affairs culminates with the famous declaration denying God's role in human prosperity:

> וְאָמַרְתָּ בִּלְבָבֶךָ כֹּחִי וְעֹצֶם יָדִי עָשָׂה לִי אֶת הַחַיִל הַזֶּה:

> And you will say in your heart: My power and the strength of my hand made me this wealth. (*Devarim* 8:17)

The desert experience itself was fraught with challenges, which were largely addressed in a miraculous manner. The Jews were fed manna, drank from the well of Miriam, and were protected by seven clouds of glory. Yet, when these verses contrast the period in the desert with that following entrance into the Land, the consumption of the manna is described as a test. Rashi views the test with reference to the specific laws associated with the manna, such as not leaving any over and not attempting to gather it on Shabbat. Other commentators, however, see here a test of outlook. Seforno states the test is to see "whether you will do His will when he grants you sustenance without suffering." Ramban goes one step further, explaining that the test involved being totally dependent on the manna while in a desert lacking any source of other food. The manna taught reliance on God, as the people were in a position in which they could not provide for themselves.

Settlement in the Land would similarly present a test. Would the Jew recall amid the plenty that God's rain is the new manna from Heaven? Would man recall that even when all is fertile, it is the divine blessing that fuels this growth?

Rav Hirsch notes how these questions stem from the *pesukim*:

> After you have attained independence and wealth, you are likely to forget that you were a slave in Egypt and helpless in the wilderness, and that you attained independence and wealth only with God's help. The fullness of plenty you enjoy by means of the ordinary course of nature is equivalent to the revealed miracle of the sustainment of the wilderness; it is the work of God's hand and the gift of His providence.
> The manna, "bread from Heaven" (*Shemot* 16:4), contrasts strongly with the bread that man eats in the Land of Israel, with whose blessing we recognize that it too is from God, "Who brings forth bread from the land" (*"ha-motzi lechem min ha-aretz"*). In this way, the test of the manna was to be supplanted by the ultimate test of living in the lap of luxury in the Land of Israel, yet not taking its yield for granted. (Rav Hirsch, commentary on *Devarim* 8:14–17)

Moshe was well aware that the challenge awaiting the people in the Land was liable to cause them to deny God's hand in their prosperity. It might even elicit in them the same types of inhumane behaviors that characterized the people of Egypt. Egypt was also land of physical prosperity – but, as discussed previously, a sort of prosperity that drove its inhabitants towards utter cruelty to others.

The nomadic existence of the desert had helped the people to distance themselves from the unholy philosophies of Egyptian society, in favor of developing a covenant with God and becoming God's mouthpiece to the world. In view of the great change that would come upon the return to the Land of Israel, Moshe emphasized to the people that their transitory desert existence, which echoed the life of the Patriarchs in the Land, would be short-lived. Upon entering the Land, the people would be obligated to build not only a home for God, but a homeland.[103] While their behavior and actions would serve to consecrate the Land spiritually, they would also have to create a model physical society in which they could live a life of acquisition while maintaining a sterling character.

Moshe was well aware that the difference between the sojourn in the desert and the settlement of the Land was not all the people needed to understand in order to develop a civil, agricultural society. At the time of the Exodus, the people had emerged from Egypt while displaying, at least outwardly, only a small part of their unique national character. The Jewish People could easily be physically removed from Egypt, but obliterating their

---

103 Furthermore, as long as the Jews were nomads, roving and wandering from place to place and pitching their tent everywhere, building houses nowhere, God's sanctuary was simply a tent – the *Ohel Mo'ed*. When the Jews gave up their nomadic civilization and became a settled, agricultural people, the divine tent was converted into a house – the *Beit Hashem*.

Egyptian mentality would take much longer.

In particular, the Jewish people would find building an entire social structure especially difficult. The returning Jews, who were tasked with creating an economy, settling the Land, and building it up, were familiar with only one model for building a national economy: the Egyptian model.

A nation amassing wealth might very well be tempted to mimic the Egyptian economy, to work the fields in the way it knew only too well from Egypt. It was this Egypt, this agricultural economy, from which Yosef had warned his brothers to keep their distance. Yosef had dreamed of an agricultural future for the Jewish people, but he was well aware that it must be built upon the principles of fairness and justice that had characterized the lives of the Patriarchs, and not the corruption of the Egyptian economy.

Although the Egyptians did not succeed in transforming Yosef's brothers into acquisition-minded farmers, the brothers' descendants, whom the Egyptians later subjugated and who even took some of Egypt's wealth upon leaving, had a soft spot for the Egyptian way of life. During the sojourn in the desert – for instance, in the episode of the Spies – the people frequently desired to return to Egypt:

וְלָמָה ה' מֵבִיא אֹתָנוּ אֶל הָאָרֶץ הַזֹּאת לִנְפֹּל בַּחֶרֶב... הֲלוֹא טוֹב לָנוּ שׁוּב מִצְרָיְמָה: וַיֹּאמְרוּ אִישׁ אֶל אָחִיו נִתְּנָה רֹאשׁ וְנָשׁוּבָה מִצְרָיְמָה:

"Why is the Lord taking us to that land to fall by the sword? … Would it not would be better for us to return to Egypt?" They said one to another, "Let us head back to Egypt." (*Bamidbar* 14:3–4)

This attraction to Egypt was due not to a lack of appreciation of Moshe's beautiful descriptions of the Land of Israel. Instead, it stemmed from the failure to recognize the Land's incomparable spiritual superiority, which would make the difficulties of its settlement worthwhile (see *Reflections of the Rav*, Chapter 11).

God did not bring the Jewish people out of Egypt to mimic degenerate Egyptian society (see *Vayikra* 18:3), nor did he want to recreate the Egyptian economy or outlook in the Land of Israel. Therefore, three chapters after Moshe uses a contrast of the Land of Israel and the desert to warn the Jews not to forget God when they live prosperously in the Land, he details just how different it is from Egypt, so that the people would understand that God had tailored the Land of Israel to facilitate the formation of a relationship with God and a spiritually elevated society and economy:

וּשְׁמַרְתֶּם אֶת כָּל הַמִּצְוָה אֲשֶׁר אָנֹכִי מְצַוְּךָ הַיּוֹם לְמַעַן תֶּחֶזְקוּ וּבָאתֶם וִירִשְׁתֶּם אֶת הָאָרֶץ אֲשֶׁר אַתֶּם עֹבְרִים שָׁמָּה לְרִשְׁתָּהּ: וּלְמַעַן תַּאֲרִיכוּ יָמִים עַל הָאֲדָמָה אֲשֶׁר נִשְׁבַּע ה' לַאֲבֹתֵיכֶם לָתֵת לָהֶם וּלְזַרְעָם אֶרֶץ זָבַת חָלָב וּדְבָשׁ: כִּי הָאָרֶץ אֲשֶׁר אַתָּה בָא שָׁמָּה לְרִשְׁתָּהּ לֹא כְאֶרֶץ מִצְרַיִם הִוא אֲשֶׁר יְצָאתֶם מִשָּׁם אֲשֶׁר תִּזְרַע אֶת זַרְעֲךָ וְהִשְׁקִיתָ בְרַגְלְךָ כְּגַן הַיָּרָק: וְהָאָרֶץ אֲשֶׁר אַתֶּם עֹבְרִים שָׁמָּה לְרִשְׁתָּהּ אֶרֶץ הָרִים וּבְקָעֹת לִמְטַר הַשָּׁמַיִם תִּשְׁתֶּה מָּיִם: אֶרֶץ אֲשֶׁר ה' א-להֶיךָ דֹּרֵשׁ אֹתָהּ תָּמִיד עֵינֵי ה' א-להֶיךָ בָּהּ מֵרֵשִׁית הַשָּׁנָה וְעַד אַחֲרִית שָׁנָה:

You shall observe all of the mitzvot that I command you today, in order that you be strong, and come and possess the land to which you are passing over to take possession of it. And in order that you prolong your days upon the land that God promised your

Patriarchs to give to them and their seed, a land flowing with milk and honey. For the land to which you are coming to take possession of it is not like the land of Egypt, from which you came out, where you sowed your seeds and watered with your foot, like a vegetable garden. The land to which you are passing over to inherit it is a land of mountains and valleys; it drinks water from the rain of heaven. It is a land for which the Lord, your God, cares: the eyes of the Lord, your God, are always upon it, from the beginning of the year to the end of the year. (*Devarim* 11:8–12)

The Land, Moshe points out, is irrigated in a very different manner from Egypt – one that makes clear the need for God constantly to tend to it. In the Land of Israel, creating an immoral, slave-driven caste society would not bring about agricultural success, as in Egypt, but total destruction.[104] Moshe warns the people not to attempt to recreate the Egyptian wealth regime in the Land of Israel. The Land is indeed beautiful and fertile, but its geography, uniquely suited for spiritual growth, requires a certain kind of work.

Agriculture as a *Mitzva* in the Land of Israel

At what point would shepherding cease to be the main Jewish occupation? When would

---

104 This is not the first instance in the Torah in which the Egyptian mentality and economy are contrasted with those appropriate for the Land of Israel. The aura and attractiveness of the Egyptian economy are subtly described in earlier contexts as well. Then, as in Moshe's day, resisting the lure of the Egyptian economy was not easy, but it was essential for developing the correct outlook for building an economy in the Land of Israel.

Just as his descendants had to go to Egypt and then strive to free themselves of it upon leaving, Avraham was compelled to go to Egypt after fulfilling God's commandment to travel to the Land of Israel. Rav Soloveitchik explains (*Abraham's Journey*, pp. ?) that the famine that led Avraham to Egypt served as a test to see how he would react to Egyptian culture. The test was repeated when Yaakov had to go to the alien culture of Charan, and again when Yosef went to Egypt. The Jew had to show that he could live in exile and still retain his spiritual identity. Avraham not only passed this test, but emerged with an even greater disdain for what Egypt stood for and a greater appreciation of God. But even this first time the covenantal community stepped foot in that country, the temptation to mimic Egypt and live by its rules plagued Avraham's family. Although Avraham's nephew Lot is described as an integral part of his family (*Bereishit* 12:5), when he returns with Avraham to the Land of Israel from Egypt, he makes the fateful decision to part from Avraham and settle instead in Sodom, which is compared to Egypt: "Lot lifted up his eyes and saw that the entire plain of the Jordan, all the way to Tzo'ar, was extremely fertile … like the Garden of the Lord, like the land of Egypt… (13:10) Perhaps the experience of seeing people take what they wanted from others – as Pharaoh had done in snatching Sarah – had enticed Lot, who then chose the closest equivalent to Egyptian culture in the vicinity.

By choosing to live elsewhere from Avraham, Lot parted ways with his uncle's moral compass (see Rashi, *Bereishit* 13:11). When Lot lifted up his eyes, he saw the pasturelands of Sodom (*Bereishit* 13:10), unlike Avraham, who lifted up his eyes to see Mount Moriah (22:4). Whereas Avraham set the stage for the Jewish People to return from Egypt without being enamored of its Egyptian culture, Lot served to illustrate the danger of trying to recreate the Egyptian economy in the Land of Israel.

The juxtaposition of the evil of Sodom with its prosperity and its comparison to Egypt seem intended to warn the Jewish people of mimicking the Egyptian economy. Fertile Sodom was the epitome of a merciless society that refused to share its wealth and openly battled hospitality (*Bereishit* 19:5; Rashi, *Bereishit* 18:21, 19:26; *Sanhedrin* 109a). The ultimate destruction of Sodom for the utter lack of fairness and justice that characterized it is indicative of the moral decay of a prosperous society that is unwilling to share with others. Much as the Garden of Eden was not maximized by Adam, the prosperity of Egypt was not good for the spiritual needs of Avraham's descendants. The Land of Israel, Moshe taught the Jews, is fundamentally different from Sodom of old, whose physical makeup was one cause of its destruction. Sodom's fertility kept its people prosperous even as they became more and more evil, to the point of destruction. There was no hope of rehabilitation, no hope for Avraham's prayers to save the city, where even ten righteous individuals were nowhere to be found. The fertile valley, which was not conducive to a moral, righteous economy, became a wasteland.

working the land and gathering sheaves become a legitimate profession?

The *mitzvah* of *orla*, the prohibition against making use of the fruits of a tree's first three years of growth, is introduced as follows:

וְכִי תָבֹאוּ אֶל הָאָרֶץ וּנְטַעְתֶּם כָּל עֵץ מַאֲכָל וַעֲרַלְתֶּם עָרְלָתוֹ אֶת פִּרְיוֹ שָׁלֹשׁ שָׁנִים יִהְיֶה לָכֶם עֲרֵלִים לֹא יֵאָכֵל:

When you will come to the land and you will plant (*u-netatem*) all types of trees for food, you shall consider their fruit forbidden (*orla*). Three years shall it be forbidden to you: it shall not be eaten. (*Vayikra* 19:23)

Given that some elements of *orla* apply outside the Land of Israel, why does the Torah introduce this *mitzvah* with the phrase, "When you come to the land"? The answer to this question may be found in the midrashic understanding of the word "*u-netatem*" as not merely a condition – "and you will plant" – but a commandment in its own right – "**then** you will plant." The *midrash* explains that the Torah commands planting, as cultivating fruit trees in the Land of Israel is a *mitzvah*:

Rabbi Yitzchak son of Rabbi Shimon said: "You shall follow after the Lord, your God" (*Devarim* 13:5) – Is it then possible for mortals to follow the Holy One, blessed be He, concerning Whom it is written, "Your way is in the sea, and Your path in many waters" (*Tehillim* 77:20)? And you say, "You shall follow God"?!

"And you shall cleave to Him" (*Devarim* 13:5) – Is it then possible for a mortal to ascend to the heavens and cleave to the divine presence, concerning which it is written, "For the Lord your God is a consuming fire" (4:24)?!

[How then are we to understand this idea of adhering to God?] From the very start of the world's creation, the Holy One occupied Himself with planting, as it is written, "The Lord God planted a garden in Eden" (*Bereishit* 2:8). So, too, when you enter the Land, you must first occupy yourselves with planting. Thus, it is written, "When you come to the land, then you shall plant all types of trees for food ..." (*Vayikra Rabba* 25:3)

When the time comes to enter the Land of Israel, planting a fruit tree becomes a holy act of walking in God's ways.[105]

As Rav Aharon Lichtenstein points out:

---

105 The physical development of the Land of Israel is an essential part of the *mitzvah* of settling the Land. It is for this reason that the *gemara* (*Sanhedrin* 98a) describes the physical growth of produce in the Land of Israel as a sign of the impending redemption: "Rabbi Abba said: There is no clearer indication of the End than this, as it is stated (*Yechezkel* 36:8): 'But you, O mountains of Israel, you shall shoot forth your branches and bear your fruit for My people Israel [when they are soon to come].'" Growth in the Land of Israel is a harbinger of a spiritual return to the land and a testimony to the unique connection between the Land and its people. (See chapter 17, where we discuss this idea at length.)

Rav Yissachar Teichtal (*Eim HaBanim Semeicha*, p. 84) states that development is such an essential part of the *mitzvah* of settling the Land and so necessary for the ultimate redemption that "the simple Jew who builds the Land without any spiritual intent (*kavvana*), merely for his own benefit, accomplishes a greater rectification (*tikkun*) in the supernal worlds than the most righteous man with his tearful, mournful midnight prayers (*tikkun chatzot*) recited for the Divine Presence and the end of the exile." Although his position is subject to debate, it is abundantly clear that the physical growth of the Land of Israel is spiritually significant, as is eating the physical bounty of the Land.

> The "planting" with which God occupied Himself was not the mere planting of trees; it was the very creation of the world, the infrastructure for all that would follow. Thus, upon entering *Eretz Yisrael*, we are also commanded to plant trees and to cultivate the land – not only in relation to the *mitzvot* of *orla* and *reva'i*,[106] but to establish the infrastructure for national existence. If God builds an entire world on the foundation of planting trees, then we too are required to plant in *Eretz Yisrael* so that there will be a healthy economy and a basis for communal life.

Yosef indeed foresaw that there would be a need to work the land – but only the Land of Israel. By the same token, the Torah's negative approach to agriculture is temporary, limited to the period before Jewish settlement of the Land.

Rav Hirsch, following his discussion of Kayin's unfavorable choice of profession, explains how all the agricultural *mitzvot* comprise a foundation for a positive spiritual experience in the realm of farming:

> The Torah anticipates the chronic dangers inherent in agriculture and prescribes the remedy, legislating against deification of property. Shabbat and *shemitta* forever testify that the earth belongs to God, and man is His servant. The agricultural laws, such as the prohibitions of *kilayim* and *orla*, on one hand, and the positive injunctions of *leket*, *shichecha*, and *pe'ah*, on the other, remind man of God's presence, cautioning him to maintain brotherly and neighborly love. Thus the Torah solves the moral problem of agriculture; in this way a society of God-fearing farmers is created, all sharing brotherly love and equality. But outside of the Torah framework, a danger is presented to faith in God and to the freedom and equality of all men. (Rav Hirsch, commentary on *Bereishit* 4:2)

Based on this approach, it is not difficult to understand why of all the forefathers, it was specifically Yitzchak who was involved in agriculture. Yitzchak was the one most intimately connected to the Land of Israel, even planting the Land in the midst of a famine (*Bereishit* 26); of the forefathers, only Yitzchak never left the Land. Yitzchak understood that a Jew must view the Land of Israel not only as a place to graze livestock, but as the place where the Jewish People engage in agriculture. Yosef similarly dreamed of a new future in which the agricultural profession would be embraced by the Jewish People, and planting and harvesting would be a core part of Jewish life. But this could become a reality only once the Jewish People came to the Land of Israel and settled it. Only then would the agricultural *mitzvot* become binding. At that point, these *mitzvot* would be needed to allow the Jewish People to weather the challenge of tilling the soil – being involved in acquisition, yet not consumed by it.

We can similarly understand why the agricultural *mitzvot* are limited to the Land of Israel. Outside of *Eretz Yisrael*, one should focus on shepherding rather than farming. There, the challenges of a life of acquisition cannot necessarily be solved by agricultural *mitzvot* to reframe one's outlook. Only in the Land of Israel is the farmer God's partner in transforming His barren land into a spiritual wonderland of physical beauty. Only in the

---

106 The *mitzvah* of *reva'i* requires the owner of a fruit tree to bring the produce of its fourth year to Jerusalem, where the fruit is to be eaten in a state of ritual purity.

Land of Israel do a land's holiness and the *mitzvah* of building it up transform every act of acquisition into a spiritual act.

Even in the Land of Israel, difficulties and challenges accompany a life of tilling the soil. Farming is no longer the facile pursuit that it was in the Garden of Eden. If the Jewish farmer were to work hard yet lack agricultural *mitzvot* to help him build a holy character, he would be liable to forget God. The *mitzvot hateluyot ba'aretz* not only recognize the holiness inherent in all that grows in the Land of Israel, but foster the creation of a God-fearing agricultural society in which physical acquisitions bring one closer to spiritual success.

This point is reflected in the great desire of Moshe Rabbeinu to enter *Eretz Yisrael*. Moshe's description of the Land's beauty in his final speech is particularly poignant, as it comes on the backdrop of God's refusal to allow him to enter it. The *gemara* asks why, despite repeated refusals by God, Moshe continued with his desperate supplications to enter the Land of Israel:

> Rabbi Simla'i expounded: Why did Moshe desire to entire the Land of Israel? Did he perhaps need to eat of its fruit or to satisfy himself with its goodness? Rather, this is what Moshe said: There are many *mitzvot* that the Jewish People received that can be fulfilled only in the Land of Israel. Let me enter the land so that they are all fulfilled by me. (*Sota* 14a)

The *gemara* is unwilling to accept that Moshe desired to step foot in the Land solely due to its physical fruits and beauty that he himself so effectively described. Rather, the *gemara* explains, Moshe desired to fulfill the unique *mitzvot* of the Land.

Although it is understandable that the spiritual giant Moshe would not have been enticed by the physical beauty of the Land of Israel alone, it is notable that the physical pleasures of the Land that the *gemara* downplays are the very heart of what we say regarding the Land in both the *Birkat HaMazon* and the *Beracha Achat MeEin Shalosh*.[107] In these blessings, we describe our gratitude for the Land of Israel, given to us so that "we can eat of its fruit and satisfy ourselves with its goodness" – the precise wording of the *gemara* regarding the pleasures that Moshe did not seek!

Perhaps we can suggest that Moshe did, in fact, desire to partake of the fruit and goodness of the Land of Israel – but only after performing the agricultural *mitzvot*, as he so passionately desired. The Land's bounty alone, if acquired without the mindset fostered by these *mitzvot*, is not reason enough to come to the Land of Israel. Indeed, the Spies (*Bamidbar* 13) brought back with them some of the Land's beautiful fruits, yet ultimately discounted its significance. Moshe desired to take part in the agricultural *mitzvot* of the land, which would enable him to eat of its fruit with the correct spiritual perspective. Only in this way would the Land's fruit be good reason to come there.

---

107 *Birkat HaMazon* is recited after one eats bread; the *Beracha Achat MeEin Shalosh* is recited after the consumption of other grain products, fruits of the seven species, wine, and grape juice.

The Jewish Ethic of a Redeemed Economy in the Land of Israel

It is clear that these various *mitzvot* present a recipe for what we have referred to as a "redeemed economy", i.e., an economy that seeks to elevate society. How is it that the Land of Israel can give rise to a "redeemed" economy so different from the Egyptian economy the nation just left? To answer this question, we must first identify the underlying principles of a redeemed economy.

The Underlying Principles of a Redeemed Economy

Rav Soloveitchik (*Hapardes*, vol. 11, pp. 32ff.) identifies two different economic models that the people experienced in the desert: that of the manna and that of the quail. The manna, as described by the Torah, epitomizes an economic idyll in which everyone receives what he needs and easily recognizes God's hand in the process:

זֶה הַדָּבָר אֲשֶׁר צִוָּה ה' לִקְטוּ מִמֶּנּוּ אִישׁ לְפִי אָכְלוֹ עֹמֶר לַגֻּלְגֹּלֶת מִסְפַּר נַפְשֹׁתֵיכֶם אִישׁ לַאֲשֶׁר בְּאָהֳלוֹ תִּקָּחוּ: וַיַּעֲשׂוּ כֵן בְּנֵי יִשְׂרָאֵל וַיִּלְקְטוּ הַמַּרְבֶּה וְהַמַּמְעִיט: וַיָּמֹדּוּ בָעֹמֶר וְלֹא הֶעְדִּיף הַמַּרְבֶּה וְהַמַּמְעִיט לֹא הֶחְסִיר אִישׁ לְפִי אָכְלוֹ לָקָטוּ:

Gather of it, every man according to his consumption – an *omer* per person, for the number of souls for whom you are responsible: let every man take for those in his tent. The children of Israel did so and gathered, some more and some less. When they measured with an *omer*, he who had gathered most had no more and he who had gathered least had no less: each had gathered according to his consumption. (*Shemot* 16:16–18)

Here there obviously was no need for cutthroat capitalism, as greater efforts failed to gather more manna. In order to perpetuate this mindset in the Land of Israel, the Jewish People are commanded to remember the period when they ate divine manna and their clothes miraculously never wore out (*Devarim* 8:2–4). Indeed, many Jews recite the passage from *Shemot* every morning, because it so succinctly encapsulates the Jewish economic ethic.[108] Rav Soloveitchik describes the period in the desert:

> The Israelites in the wilderness were free from daily cares and worries. They ate their bread, not by the seat of their brow, but in the knowledge that God was with them. There was no need to till, plant, watch, and reap. The curse imposed upon Adam was suspended. (*Festival of Freedom*, p. 165)

But when the people protested about the manna (*Bamidbar* 11), God brought them quail, the *selav*. Overcome by desire, they gathered as much as they could – and were struck by a plague. Hoarding, with the false security it offers, is clearly rejected by the Torah:

---

108 In view of its underlying significance, we can well understand the *gemara*'s statement (*Berachot* 48b) that Moshe composed the first blessing of *Birkat HaMazon* when the manna first fell. This ideal is reflected by the sacrifice of one *omer* of barley flour in the *Beit HaMikdash* on the second day of *Pesach* – the same amount as the manna allotted to every individual in the desert. The people's needs were met and their desires were fulfilled, but they were not devoured by them.

וַיָּקָם הָעָם כָּל הַיּוֹם הַהוּא וְכָל הַלַּיְלָה וְכֹל יוֹם הַמָּחֳרָת וַיַּאַסְפוּ אֶת הַשְּׂלָו הַמַּמְעִיט אָסַף עֲשָׂרָה חֳמָרִים
וַיִּשְׁטְחוּ לָהֶם שָׁטוֹחַ סְבִיבוֹת הַמַּחֲנֶה:

The people arose all that day and all that night and all the next day, and they gathered the quail. He who [gathered] least gathered ten stacks. (*Bamidbar* 11:32)

Rav Soloveitchik comments:

These verses beautifully describe the greed that manifested itself in a craze for hoarding and accumulating the quails .... This portrayal is typical not only of the Israelite tribes in the Sinai desert, but also of modern man, who overemphasizes his ability to safeguard himself, resulting in a form of self-idealization. (*Festival of Freedom*, p. 11)

The greedy gathering of the quail, says the Rav, is the gathering of an economy that plays by the rules of the sea: The big swallow the little; all is permitted in the name of acquisition. This destructive economic ethic is antithetical to the Jewish ethic.

The Rav notes that the ideal Jewish economy must be based on the principle that man is permitted to search for economic security, but must not be maddened by it:

Man is commended for his preoccupation with his economic needs and his endeavors to develop the means for their satisfaction. Yet he must never ascribe unlimited worth to economic goods and absolutize their significance for the enhancement of human happiness and welfare ...

Human economic behavior fluctuates between two poles: economic activism (which the Bible sanctions) and trust in God. The latter is an important motif which should guide the *homo economicus* in his actions. There are two central themes in the prophets. First, God feeds and sustains all living creatures. Second, feeding is an act of grace on the part of God... We all eat out of God's hand. Eating means receiving alms-bread from the Almighty: "You open Your hand and satisfy every living thing with favor" (*Tehillim* 145:16) ...

God, in His infinite mercy, allows man to work for his sustenance and to devise means of increasing the yield of his labors. He also permits him to strive for material comfort and riches. Yet man must never entertain the illusion that the bread he eats is his. This would result in the profanation of the bread and in man's self-absolutization and self-deification. Man must know that he is not a creator in either the metaphysical or the economic sense. He cannot create matter, life, or economic goods. His world of material wealth was given to him gratuitously by the Creator of the universe. (*Festival of Freedom*, pp. 9–10)

In the absence of this knowledge, man, driven by the search for wealth, knows no boundaries:

Economic man is determined to succeed at any price. If necessary, he is ready to destroy his competitor. The Darwinian struggle for survival is related mainly to economic survival. In economic life, the fittest and strongest survive; the weak perish. Marxism introduced the concept of the class struggle as shaping historical events. In a word, economy and sanctity, or economy and spirituality, are two mutually exclusive concepts … Judaism disagrees with this entire philosophy …. Another economy can be organized, however, in which a spirit of cooperation and mutual understanding prevails. (*Festival of Freedom*, p. 168–169)

The first principle of a redeemed economy is that the human urge for acquisition must be controlled by the intellect; it is given boundaries. The people's failure in the episode of the quail was a failure to implement this principle, and their limitless greed drew the wrath of the Almighty and destroyed them.

Importantly, Shabbat is presented for the first time in the passage in *Sefer Shemot* about the manna. Together, the manna and Shabbat represent an economy that sees God's hand in its sustenance and can allow for a holy day, dedicated to spiritual pursuits, to sanctify all the physical efforts of the week.

וַיֹּאמֶר מֹשֶׁה אִכְלֻהוּ הַיּוֹם כִּי שַׁבָּת הַיּוֹם לַה' הַיּוֹם לֹא תִמְצָאֻהוּ בַּשָּׂדֶה:

Moshe said, "Eat it today, for today is God's Sabbath. Today you will not find it in the field." (*Shemot* 16:25)

Shabbat does not make economic sense; a day off logically means working a day less than one's competitors. However, it brings holiness to a person's economic activity, so that the six days of creative activity are sanctified with their culmination, expressing the higher purpose of man's endeavors. Through this sanctity, divine blessing comes to the activities of those who refrain from labor on Shabbat.

The second principle of a redeemed economy is thus that acquisition serves a higher purpose and goal – one of holiness.

Finally, the third characteristic of a redeemed economy is generosity:

If man looks upon himself as the sole possessor, as the only proprietor of economic goods, then his economy is an ugly affair, then there is exploitation and unfair competition. However, if man is ready to surrender at any time the call comes through, to return whatever I possess to the rightful owner, to give up whenever the demand for return is made, then holiness is possible. (*Festival of Feedom*, p. 171)

The Economy of the Land of Israel

These pillars of a redeemed economy are fundamental to the Jewish People's model economy in the Land of Israel. The entire economic enterprise of the land is built to ensure that even while reaping the fruits of his work in the field, man retains a humbling connection with God and uses his wealth to further justice and righteousness. But how?

The first avenue is the knowledge that the physical building of the land is a fulfillment of the *mitzvah* of settling the Land of Israel, and therefore actually a spiritual pursuit. This idea is vividly expressed by the *Chatam Sofer*, who was not a political Zionist but whose writings evince great love of the Land. In his defense of the European Jewish educational curriculum, which did not include secular studies, the *Chatam Sofer* explains that although the gemara (*Berachot* 35a) concludes in accordance with the view of Rabbi Yishmael that alongside Torah study, one must work for his living (and that occupational training must therefore be provided) – against the view of Rabbi Shimon bar Yochai that one should occupy himself only with spiritual pursuits and trust that God will support him – that holds true only in *Eretz Yisrael*. It is there that "the work of the field is a *mitzvah* in its own right of settling the Land of Israel and bringing forth its holy fruit …" He then adds: "The same holds true for any other occupation that has a role in settling the Land of Israel, as any such thing is included in the *mitzvah*" (Chatam Sofer, *Sukka* 36a, s.v. *domeh*). Work in the diaspora has no spiritual element; work in the Land of Israel is a *mitzvah*.

The most important difference between Egypt and *Eretz Yisrael* lies in the personal relationship with God facilitated by the produce that the Land of Israel brings forth. As noted above, Moshe Rabbeinu points out the difference between the irrigation of Egypt and that of *Eretz Yisrael* (*Devarim* 11:8-12). Whereas Egypt can always rely on the Nile River as a source of water (barring severe drought), *Eretz Yisrael* has no comparable source of river water and must rely on "the rain of heaven."

The primordial snake was cursed to "eat dust all the days of your life" (*Bereishit* 3:14). Although food would be readily available, the snake would never need to ask God for food or maintain a relationship with Him. The Egyptians similarly were "blessed" with a Godless economy, given the ever-present Nile. Man worked hard to irrigate the fields, building an economy without thinking of the heavens.[109]

In *Eretz Yisrael*, in contrast, the Jewish People enjoyed the blessing given to Yaakov: "God shall give you of the dew of heaven" (*Bereishit* 27:28). This is an active gift from God, Who continues to give it as long as the people are worthy.

Man's responsibility for bringing rain from heaven was an essential element of Creation. The Torah describes:

וְכֹל שִׂיחַ הַשָּׂדֶה טֶרֶם יִהְיֶה בָאָרֶץ וְכָל עֵשֶׂב הַשָּׂדֶה טֶרֶם יִצְמָח כִּי לֹא הִמְטִיר ה' א-להים עַל הָאָרֶץ וְאָדָם אַיִן לַעֲבֹד אֶת הָאֲדָמָה:

No shrub of the field was yet on the earth and no herb of the field had yet sprouted, for the Lord God had not brought rain upon the earth and there was no man to work the ground. (*Bereishit* 2:5)

Rashi explains:

"For the Lord God had not brought rain." And what is the reason he had not brought rain? Because "there was no man to work the ground" – there was no one to recognize the goodness of rainfall. When Adam came and realized that rain is essential for the world, he prayed for rain, it came down, and the trees and vegetation of the world sprouted. (Rashi, *Bereishit* 2:5, s.v. *ki*)

The first rain in history resulted from man's prayers, teaching man that physical growth on Earth is a product of heavenly grace, to be deserved through spiritual pursuits.

---

109 Interestingly, like Egypt, Sodom was situated adjacent to a river and developed a Godless economy and depraved social norms. The city of Sodom is compared not only to Egypt (as noted above, n. 67), but also to "the Garden of God" (*Bereishit* 13:10), i.e. the Garden of Eden, where man picked fruit without need for work. Only after man ate from the Tree of Knowledge was he cursed to work the ground with difficulty (ibid. 3:17–19). (A number of commentators opine that when Adam was initially commanded to tend to and protect the garden [ibid. 2:15], the intent was only that he occupy himself with spiritual pursuits, through which the garden would grow. There was to be no need for physical work; the garden's plants would grow as a response to spiritual efforts.)

Life in the Land of Israel is a return to the Garden of Eden. Just as God's presence was apparent in the Garden of Eden, it is apparent in the Land – "a land for which the Lord, your God, cares: the eyes of the Lord, your God, are always upon it, from the beginning of the year to the end of the year" (*Devarim* 11:12). As part of the people's natural existence in the Land of Israel, its climate reacts to their spiritual condition (see Ramban, *Vayikra* 18). In the words of Rashbam (*Devarim* 11:10): "This land is better than all other lands for those who observe His commandments, and worse than all other lands for those who do not observe them."

The Mishna (*Ta'anit* chapter 1) prescribes fast days when rain is lacking in the Land of Israel, because physical drought is simply an expression of God's hiding His face from His people. The local weather serves as a kind of religious feedback mechanism. Through drought or famine, God indicates that the people must change their ways to avoid a more drastic punishment. Natural existence, fed by heavenly rain, is actually a prerequisite for healthy spiritual existence in the physical Land. In the Land of Israel, the dependence upon heavenly rain facilitates the development of an economy that is aware of God, devotes itself to Him, and maintains its interpersonal focus.

The dependence on rain in *Eretz Yisrael* brings us to another component of its suitability for the development of a redeemed economy. Although the fact that Egypt has a constant water supply might be viewed as an asset over *Eretz Yisrael's* dependence on rain, in truth, the irrigation of Egypt is far more labor-intensive. There, the people must transport the water from the Nile to their fields; indeed, the Egyptians worked hard to amass manpower to support an economy that did not see the divine hand in its activities, enslaving people to work the land as hard as possible and to distribute water from the Nile through canals and irrigation systems. In *Eretz Yisrael*, in contrast, the people can sit back and watch the divine rainfall give life to the vegetation. Although the water supply is not constant, when it is deserved, it allows man to reap its benefits with a minimum of work:

> In the Land of Egypt, if one does not work with spade and shovel, giving up his sleep for water, then he has nothing, but in the Land of Israel it is different: they sleep in their beds, and God makes the rain fall. (*Yalkut Shimoni, Eikev* 857)

The divine manna in the desert not only enabled the Jews to clearly recognize God as the provider of bread, but also allowed them to occupy their time with spiritual pursuits rather than physical needs. It is no surprise that Rabbi Shimon bar Yochai – whom we quoted previously as advising the Jew to spend all his time studying Torah, while relying on God for his physical needs (*Berachot* 35a) – had a very positive view of the Jews' time in the desert: "Rabbi Shimon bar Yochai says: Interpretation of the Torah was given only to those who eat manna. How so? One sits and expounds [Torah] and does not know from where his food and drink will come, or from where his clothing will come" (*Mechilta, Vayissa* 2).[110] This is Rabbi Shimon bar Yochai's motto for all. He advocates that man focus

---

110 The *midrash* concludes: "This is [the meaning of the statement that] interpretation of the Torah was given only those who eat manna, and second to them are those who eat *teruma*." It seems from this *midrash* that this is how the *Kohanim* lived. They did not own land, but were designated as the teachers and spiritual voice of the people, and they were therefore sustained by the *teruma* provided to them by others (see Rambam, *Hilchot Shemitta VeYovel*, ch. 13).

all his energies on Torah and rely on God to provide for him in the same manner that He provided manna.

Notwithstanding the view of Rabbi Shimon, however, the *gemara* (*Berachot* 35b) seems to rule in accordance with the opposing view of Rabbi Yishmael, at least for most people (see *Bei'ur Halacha* 156, s.v. *sofa*). In order to provide for himself in the Land of Israel, man must engage in at least a minimum of agriculture.

Rabbi Yishmael surely was cognizant of the spiritual dangers of working the land, but he realized that the time for manna from heaven ceased when the Jews entered the Land. An economy based on "bread from heaven" (*Shemot* 16:4) is neither the reality nor the ideal for the masses settled in the Land of Israel. The experience of the desert allowed the Jewish people to forge their identity as a people, with all their needs provided. In the Land of Israel, however, the people would live a natural existence. Man would work the field. Instead of receiving bread from heaven, he would recite a blessing over bread from the earth.

Unlike the manna, which the Torah describes as bread God rains down (*mamtir*) from heaven (*Shemot* 16:4), in the Land of Israel, the bread of the earth is nourished by rain (*matar*) from heaven (*Devarim* 11:11). Man does work the field, but he is to recognize that nothing grows without heavenly intervention. In the Land of Israel, it is clear that even earthly bread comes from God. The *matar* of the manna raining from the Heavens was replaced with the *matar* of rain itself, expressing God's providence on the crops of the land.

The Torah refers to the manna in the aforementioned *pasuk* as *lechem min ha-shamayim*, bread from the Heavens (*Shemot* 16:4), and the Rema Mi-Pano (*Ma'amar Shabbatot* 4) explains that the blessing the Jews recited upon eating manna was *hamotzi lechem min ha-shamayim*. Although we are active partners in planting the seed and the various processes necessary before one can thresh, winnow, knead and bake his bread, he still recognizes God as the provider. The *beracha* recognizes God in the process as *hamotzi lechem min ha-aretz*.

The Alshich (commentary to *Vayikra* 19:9) notes that successful agricultural growth, more than success in other occupations, is clearly indicative of God's role. Not only are crops susceptible to natural disasters such as hurricanes and tornados, but even abnormal winds, insufficient rainfall, and heatwaves can completely destroy the crop yield. Indeed, this is why God "takes a percentage" of that yield, giving it to the poor instead of taking it for Himself. He is our partner in agricultural success.

Agriculture and Faith

In light of this connection between spiritual and physical existence in the Land, we can understand why the *gemara* characterizes the section of the Mishna dealing with agricultural laws, *Seder Zera'im*, as epitomized by faith:

> Reish Lakish said: What is the meaning of that which is written, "The faith [*emunat*] of your times shall be a strength of salvation, wisdom, and knowledge; fear of the

Lord is His treasure" (*Yeshayahu* 33:6)? "Faith" – this is the section of *Zera'im*...[111]
(TB *Shabbat* 31a)

The farmer knows that all of his efforts in the field are mere attempts at sustenance, in the hope that weather conditions will not destroy the crop. Only the One who gives life can determine whether physical crops will grow. Nevertheless, the farmer "puts his faith in the One who gives life to the world, and he plants" (Tosafot ad loc., s.v. *emunat*).

The superiority of faith in God's hidden agricultural miracles over a manna-based existence is further evident from an important comment of the Ramban. Noting that God performed many manifest miracles when bringing the Jews out of Egypt and through the desert, he explains that such miracles served as proof of the Creator's existence and the truth of the Torah. Nevertheless, God does not want to prove His existence anew in every generation. Manifest miracles are not the ideal, as they demonstrate God's existence only at the moment they happen. The overarching goal is that man forge a relationship with God and constantly recognize Him. He, therefore, issued numerous *mitzvot* requiring us to remember the Exodus and transmit its memory to his children:

All these [commandments] are intended to bear witness to the wonders throughout the generations, so that they will not be forgotten, and so that the heretic will not have any justification for rejecting the belief in God ... As a result of the great manifest miracles, one grants the truth of the hidden miracles, which constitute the foundation of the entire Torah, for no one can have a part in the Torah of Moshe Rabbeinu without believing that all things and events that befall us are entirely miraculous, not in any way natural or inevitable, whether public affairs or individual affairs. (Ramban, commentary on *Shemot* 13:16)

During the entire period the people sojourned in the desert and were fed manna, bread from heaven; the goal was that they one day arrive in the Land of Israel, where they would eat natural bread, yet appreciate God's role in performing the "hidden miracle" of sending rain from heaven. Since *Eretz Yisrael* blooms in response to the actions of the people, it is the perfect setting for an economy permeated with the recognition of God's hidden hand in every facet of human existence.

Sanctifying the Physical World

Life in the Land of Israel is a life of holiness, which entails not escape from the physical world, but the sanctification of it – living in and beautifying the physical world while remaining committed and connected to the ideals of the Jewish People. It is a life of working in the field while one's assets and attitude remain oriented toward heaven.

The agricultural *mitzvot* of the Land of Israel allow us to maintain this perspective. A farmer who offers *bikkurim*, first fruits (*Devarim* 26) in the *Mikdash*, is required to recite a declaration tracing the historical background of his crops. He recalls God's promise to the Patriarchs that their descendants would inherit the Land of Israel, remembers the exodus from Egypt, and recognizes God as the One who has given the Jews their land and their crops. Providing *terumot* and *ma'asrot* from one's produce to feed the *Kohen*, the

---

111 The *gemara* proceeds to associate each of the remaining orders of the Mishna with a different element of the verse.

Levi, and the poor allows one always to provide for others with his financial gains. The farmer reserves part of his field for the poor, as if they are its true owners, and provides the charitable gifts of *leket* and *pe'ah*.

Yet the ultimate act of charity and ultimate recognition of the limits on one's ownership comes with the year of *shevi'it*, when the farmer must waive ownership of his fields, declaring all that grows to be ownerless and allowing everyone to partake of his produce.

An Israeli farmer who had spent years cultivating expensive, exotic fruit trees once described to me the amount of inner strength necessary to watch teenagers come during the sabbatical year and take fruits from his trees without even realizing what had gone into planting them. Those who observe the *mitzvot* of *shevi'it* are, with good reason, described by our Sages as *giborei ko'ach*. This strength of character brings with it an appreciation of God's involvement with the land and of who is the true owner of the field.

Just as Shabbat is an essential part of the Jewish economic ethic, so is the sabbatical year. During this year, man almost reaches the point of being sustained by manna: "Then I will command My blessing upon you in the sixth year, and [the land] shall bring forth produce for the three years" (*Vayikra* 25:21). Rav Yaakov Moshe Charlop goes one step further, describing the growth of crops during the sabbatical year as equivalent to the growth of vegetation in the Garden of Eden. Both, he notes, come forth without the need to work the land. This is a time when an agriculturist can dedicate himself to the study of Torah and spiritual rejuvenation.[112]

In the next chapter, we will see that many *mitzvot ha-teluyot ba-aretz* only apply Biblically when a majority of the nation resides in Israel. This is a further expression of the link between the land and the people. It also indicates that Jewish society strives for a united nation, expressed through the mutual responsibility that Jews have for one another in the land. Because of the intimate connection between Jewish peoplehood and Jewish agriculture, a number of agricultural *mitzvot* are applicable only when the majority of the Jewish people reside in the Land of Israel. As long as the link between nationhood and

---

112 See also our discussion of the *mitzvah* of *Hakhel*, which is fulfilled on the Sukkot following *shevi'it*. Importantly, due to the difficulty of maintaining a healthy perspective, spiritual renewal cannot be limited to every seventh year. Therefore, explains the *Sefer HaChinuch* (*mitzvah* 360), the yearly tithe of kosher domestic animals is brought to Jerusalem, where it is eaten by the owner after the blood and fat have been offered on the altar:

This precept is causally rooted in that God, blessed is He, chose the people of Israel and desired, for the sake of making them righteous, that they be those who occupy themselves with His Torah and know His name. So in His wisdom He brought them close with this *mitzvah*, that they might learn and accept moral teaching. For God knows that most people are drawn after the inferior, lowly physical element, "being also flesh" (*Bereishit* 6:3), and do not devote their spirit to toiling in the Torah and being constantly occupied with it. Therefore, with His understanding, He arranged matters so as to give them a location where all would know the words of His Torah under all circumstances ...

Every man would take up the tithe of all his flocks to... Jerusalem, where the Sanhedrin was ... and would likewise take up the tithe of our crops in four years of the seven-year cycle (*ma'aser sheini*) ... and eat his fruit there: either the owner of the stock would go there himself to study Torah, or he would send one of his sons there, so that he would study there and be sustained by that produce. As a result, in every single Israelite's house there would be a wise man versed in the Torah, who with his wisdom would teach his entire family.

Benefitting from the physical bounty of the Land of Israel is associated with the Torah and spirituality, which spread from Jerusalem into every home in the Land. The more successful one's business endeavors, the more one will have to bring to Jerusalem to reconnect with the spiritual core of the nation.

agriculture is a healthy one, the field owner provides for those who lack, and the pursuit of wealth will never descend to the survival of the fittest.

Outside the Land

In the Land of Israel, everything from the terrain to the agricultural *mitzvot* is designed to foster a redeemed economy. Although many agricultural *mitzvot* do not apply outside the Land, the same economic principles must be applied globally. The economic model of the Land of Israel serves as the ethical ideal even for those whose bread is not brought forth by rain from heaven. Even where agricultural *mitzvot* do not apply, their message should be expressed in business endeavors in every way possible.

In order to maintain a redeemed economy, we must ensure that we remain conscious of God and develop a society that cares for the weak and needy. We must ensure that our Shabbat is a time of spiritual renewal and focus on the fact that it is God who delivers His bounty to those engaged in physical work. Reciting blessings that recognize God as the source of our food, subordinating our wealth to a higher purpose, and finding opportunities for spiritual renewal help us to maintain the Jewish economic ethic, wherever we reside.

The sabbatical year symbolizes this concept. Although the agricultural aspects of the year apply only in the Land of Israel, the release of loans (*shemittat kesafim*) applies throughout the world. At the conclusion of the year, all unpaid loans are released, and while it is proper that one who owes money repay it, he cannot be required to do so. Because the Jewish ethic of a redeemed economy applies everywhere, the entire world needs a sabbatical year. The release of loans not only is a *mitzvah*, but teaches us the proper attitude towards lending, charity, and interaction with employees and clients.

Shevi'it and the system of *mitzvot hateluyot ba'aretz* force us to ask some difficult questions. To what degree is our spiritual progress connected to our physical wealth? To what degree are we giving charity, and at what point do we recognize that divine blessing is a necessary ingredient in our wealth – that and our silent partner, God, wants some of his share set aside for the needy in society?

Section 3

A Deeper Look into *Hilchot Shevi'it*

A Deeper Look into *Hilchot Shevi'it*

Section I of this work focused on *shevi'it* as presented in different *parashiyot* in the Torah. In Section II, we identified the multifaceted nature of *shevi'it* and elaborated on seven primary themes that help elucidate *shevi'it's* messages. In this section, our focus will be on analyzing some basic *halachot* of *shevi'it*.

This is in no way meant to be a comprehensive *halachic* work, but rather a bridge between the *pesukim* and some of the practical *halachic* issues. The goal is to appreciate the *halachic* questions associated with *shevi'it* rather than present all the answers. Our objective is to provide an overview of the issues, uncover some underlying rationale and themes, and hopefully engender a greater appreciation of *shevi'it* and its *mitzvot*. The aim is to present a general analysis, but we focus only on those areas that best capture the nature of the topics.

We hope that this section will serve as an invitation to further research the *halachic* topics with an appreciation of their underlying worldview and outlook.

In Section I, we noted that agricultural *shevi'it* refers to four separate periods:

1	**2**	**3**	**4**
The Land Before Planting	**The Land During the Growing Season**	**The Vegetation and Crops While Growing (on trees or in the ground)**	**The Produce After it is Harvested**

Understanding this led us to divide agricultural *shevi'it* into two categories:

שַׁבָּת הָאָרֶץ

Shabbat HaAretz refers to the first two stages, focused on one's interaction with the land.

שְׁמִטָּה

Shemitta focuses on one's interaction with the crops and the produce of the land in the last two stages.

With this in mind, we will divide our *halachic* discussions into four categories as well: two focused on the interaction with the land and two on the interaction with the land's produce. This organization will illuminate the unique nature of *Eretz Yisrael* and how its interaction with the Jewish nation impacts its *halachot*. We will then analyze the *halachot* associated with the land during *shevi'it*, followed by those related to its crops as they grow and are subsequently harvested. The topics include:

הִלְכוֹת הָאָרֶץ / *Hilchot Ha'Aretz*
The *halachot* of the land as they relate to *shevi'it* (the status of modern-day *shevi'it* observance and the borders of the land)

הִלְכוֹת שַׁבַּת הָאָרֶץ / *Hilchot Shabbat Ha'Aretz*
The *halachot* of the land's rest during *shevi'it* (including permitted and prohibited agricultural activity and an introductory discussion of gardening during *Shevi'it*)

הִלְכוֹת שְׁמִיטָה / *Hilchot Shemitta*
Halachot regarding relinquishing rights to one's produce and crops during *shevi'it*

הִלְכוֹת פֵּירוֹת שְׁבִיעִית / *Halachot* of *Shevi'it* Produce
Halachot regarding the sanctified status of *shevi'it* produce

Chapter 19

Kedusha and *Kedushat Eretz Yisrael*

We are privileged to be discussing *shevi'it* at a time when *shevi'it* observance is not merely a dream but a reality. That has not been the case for nearly two thousand years, since the time of the second *Beit HaMikdash*. *Tehillim* (122) describes the return to Jerusalem with the words, *hayinu k'chlomim*, "we were like dreamers". For centuries, even the concept of stepping foot on the holy soil of the land was but an unattainable dream.

In our day, the dream has become a reality. We still continue to dream for a full redemption, but we have witnessed the return of a large portion of the Jewish People to our land, heralded by an agricultural revolution that places Israel at the pinnacle of agrarian advancement and innovation. Nevertheless, observance of *shevi'it* today may be only Rabbinic in nature, a point that has significant *halachic* implications for contemporary *shevi'it* observance. In order to understand the status of *shevi'it* observance today, we must first explore the concept of *kedushat Eretz Yisrael*, the sanctity of the Land that in turn leads to the requirements of the *mitzvot hateluyot ba'aretz*. To do so, we must first understand what *kedusha* is all about.

Defining *Kedusha*

The term *kedusha* is often used colloquially without careful attention to its meaning. Rav Mayer Twersky notes that etymologically, *kedusha* denotes separateness, which is why Hashem is described as *Kadosh* (*Vayikra* 19:2), but it also indicates consecration and designation. These two elements are clearly related, as consecration is based on a state of separateness.[113]

Understanding *kedusha* as consecrated separateness is essential for appreciating many areas of Jewish law and thought. First of all, it indicates why the idea of *kedusha* applies to the physical world. If *kedusha* were rooted in separation alone, one could imagine *kadosh* objects being completely other-worldly, and one would achieve a life of "*kedusha*" only by separating himself from worldly matters, attempting to reach the heavens through a celibate life of clinging to the "spiritual." However, a life of consecrated separateness enables one to sanctify physical objects with *kedusha*, as focus and consecration assume separateness. Separating from the mundane as an end unto itself allows one to consecrate himself to Hashem.

Jewish holiness is a holiness of life. We do not view martyrdom as the goal. The imperative of "'You shall live by them' – and not die by them" (*Sanhedrin* 74a) also has a positive implication: to live through the *mitzvot*. Physical acts and physical places can be endowed with *kedusha*, if consecrated to be dedicated towards a separate and sanctified existence.

---

113 See http://www.torahweb.org/torah/2003/parsha/rtwe_kedoshim.html

There are primarily three forms of *kedusha*:

> *Kedushat Makom*: Sanctified space
>
> *Kedushat Zeman*: Sanctified time
>
> *Kedushat Ha'Adam*: Sanctity of Man

In all three areas, there seem to be contradictory indications as to whether it is Hashem who sanctifies or whether He charges mankind with the responsibility of sanctifying.

Rav Aharon Lichtenstein describes the two possible approaches:

> It seems to me that there are two basic approaches one can take to the concept of sanctity...
>
> One can say that a sanctified object has certain intrinsic characteristics, and that is why specific laws apply to it. Conversely, one may say that specific laws apply to an object and that therefore these laws differentiate it from other objects. For example, the fact that a *kohen* and a *nazir* are not allowed to become impure through contact with a dead person effectively removes them from this aspect of life. This separation, this delineation, creates sanctity...
>
> One perspective is that holiness flows from above. The Almighty creates sanctity, He manifests sanctity, and He transmits of His sanctity to some of the matter He created, and to which the Halacha has accorded sanctity. The other approach is that sanctity is created primarily by man, that man has been authorized by the Almighty, by the Torah, by the *Halacha*, to create sanctity...
>
> Does God bestow sanctity, or is man deputized to confer it? This is a fundamental question. Its primary application is halachic, but it is also a critical question regarding ones' conception of how man serves God...
>
> When we speak of holiness originating with the Almighty, we mean that the very presence of sanctity, its existence in a particular object that has a certain inherent nature, all stems from God...
>
> Some people find the very notion that sanctity could be created by man to be inconceivable. After all, they claim, how can man create sanctity? Man is a material being. Who authorized him? Where does he derive such capabilities? What mystical power could enable man to create sanctity? ...
>
> By contrast, the Rav maintained the opposite perspective... The Rav said that holiness is created by man. God created a neutral world with raw materials that can be endowed with holiness. The Rav said that it is true that there are things that possess intrinsic holiness, but, essentially, sanctity is created by man. Man receives neutral raw materials and fashions them with the sanctity of his personality, and that is the core from which sanctity develops.
>
> Sometime later I saw that Rav Meir Simcha of Dvinsk advances a similar approach in his *Meshech Chochmah* (on Exodus 19:13). "Divine acts do not instill sanctity; only sanctification by man effects holiness." (*Seeking His Presence*, pp. 136-52)

Rav Soloveitchik's perspective appears throughout his writings, at times expressed in a rather radical formulation:

Holiness is created by man, by flesh and blood. Through the power of our mouths, through verbal sanctification alone, we can create holy offerings of the Temple treasury and holy offerings for the altar. The Land of Israel became holy through conquest, Jerusalem and the Temple courts – through bringing two loaves of thanksgiving. It is man who sanctifies space and makes a sanctuary for his Creator. (*Halakhic Man* p. 47)

Rav Soloveitchik views this as the craving of Halakhic Man, his dream of creating:

Halakhic man craves to bring down the Divine Presence and holiness into the midst of space and time, into the midst of the finite, earthly existence... (ibid. p. 41)
The dream of creation finds its resolution in the actualization of the principle of holiness. Creation means the realization of the ideal of holiness... If a man wishes to attain the rank of holiness, he must become a creator of worlds. If a man never creates, never brings into being anything new, anything original, then he cannot be holy unto his God... Therein is embodied the entire task of creation and the obligation to participate in the renewal of the cosmos. The most fundamental principle of all is that man must create himself. It is this idea that Judaism introduced into the world. (ibid. pp. 108-9)

Despite the formulations of Rav Soloveitchik and the *Meshech Chochma*, Rav Lichtenstein notes that both sources of *kedusha* seem to exist – the naturally intrinsic and the consecrated by humans. The *gemara* itself (*Pesachim* 117b) distinguishes between the *kedusha* of Shabbat, which is "*kevia v'kayama*," established and permanent from when Hashem sanctified it at the dawn of time, and the sanctity of the festivals, regarding which God transferred to humanity the power and jurisdiction to sanctify (see *Pesachim* 117a). Nevertheless, Rav Lichtenstein points out, even those days that are innately holy, such as Shabbat, include a human role as well; man was commanded to "remember the Sabbath day *leKadsho*, to keep it holy" (*Shemot* 20:8), which contributes and adds an element of sanctity.[114]

Rav Lichtenstein explains that *kedusha* stems from Hashem, but humankind is empowered to endow *kedusha* when connected to Hashem:

There is ultimate sanctity, which stems from the Almighty. Man, by connecting to God, absorbs some of this holiness, and becomes sanctified such that he is then capable of transmitting holiness into the world.
All three types of *kedusha* – *kedushat makom*, *kedushat zeman*, and *kedushat ha'adam* – include a dual nature, partially innate and partially endowed by man. The ultimate expression of the merger of the three forms of *kedusha* is found in *shemitta*. It is then that the consecrated land (*makom*) is uniquely sanctified at the specific time of the seventh year (*zeman*), sanctifying the *shevi'it*-observant individual with it (*adam*).

---

114 Rav Soloveitchik himself notes this dichotomy in his *Shiurim L'Zecher Abba Mari* (*Kiddush K'Mekadesh HaShabbat*). See also *The Lord is Righteous in All His Ways* (ed. Jacob Schachter), p. 201: "There is something called *yom kadosh*, holy time. Indeed, the whole concept of *kedushat ha-yom* ...indicates that there is substance to the day that can be filled with sanctity. Days and hours are endowed or saturated with holiness. The day is a substance of which I can predicate a variety of adjectival designations."

For this reason, *shemitta* is referred to as *shabbat ha'aretz*, and much like the weekly Shabbat, it is *Shabbat laHashem*. *Shemitta* is necessary for the nation and essential for the land. Similarly, *Shemitta* imparts in each individual a *neshama yetera*, an expanded soul (see section II theme 2). In the words of Rav Kook:

> The *segula* of the land and the *segula* of the nation complement each other. Just as the nation is unique in its aptitude to reach spiritual heights from the depths of its everyday life, so too, the land, God's land, prepares the nation who dwells in it as an everlasting inheritance, which comes with a covenant and an oath, with faith in the eternity of Israel, founded upon Godly nature, which is immovably infused in this glorious land, married to the nation which God chose as His *segula*. The soul of the nation and the land together act to bring about the foundation of their existence; they demand their purpose: to actualize their potential and holy longings in this sabbatical year. (*Shabbat HaAretz*, Introduction)

Implications for *Kedushat Eretz Yisrael*

Based on this understanding, we may question the nature of the sanctity of *Eretz Yisrael*. At what point did *Eretz Yisrael* attain its status as a *kadosh* land? Is it inherently *kadosh*, sanctified by God from time immemorial, or does it require an act of consecration by mankind? If it indeed requires an act of sanctification, at what point did that happen? If human acts of consecration are necessary, what happens when those actions are overturned? Do exile and destruction affect that status?

Sanctity From the Dawn of Time?

Chazal imply that *Eretz Yisrael* enjoyed special significance from the dawn of Creation. In fact, even *Yerushalayim* and the location of the *Mikdash* were already set aside as sanctified places:

> Hashem created the world as a human child is created. Just as the navel is placed at the center of the human body... so too Hashem created the world from the *even shetiya* and from the Holy of Holies, and from it the world was founded. This is why it was called *even shetiya*, for from it Hashem began to create His world. And Hashem created the *Beit HaMikdash* above in the Heavens, and the *Beit HaMikdash* below on the land, each in line with the other. (*Masechet Semachot, Chibut HaKever* 1:1)

In many context, *Chazal* emphasize that *Eretz Yisrael* was unique from its inception. Rashi cites several of these sources in his comments on the Creation account, including his first comment on the Torah. There he cites Rabbi Yitzchak's question of why the Torah describes the cryptic story of Creation rather than begin with the first *mitzvah* commanded to the Jewish People. He responds:

> Because of [the thought expressed in the text (*Tehillim* 111:6)]: "He declared to His people the strength of His works [i.e. He gave an account of the work of Creation] in order that He might give them the heritage of the nations." For should the peoples of the world say to Israel, "You are robbers, because you took by force the lands of

the seven nations of Canaan," Israel may reply to them, "All the earth belongs to the Holy One, blessed be He; He created it and gave it to whom He pleased. When He willed He gave it to them, and when He willed He took it from them and gave it to us." (Rashi, *Bereishit* 1:1; see *Yalkut Shimoni* 187).

Elsewhere (*Bereishit* 2:7), Rashi cites a *midrash* (*Bereishit Rabba* 14:8) that *Adam HaRishon* was created from the dust of the *Makom HaMizbeach* (the place where the *mizbeach* (altar) would stand in the *Mikdash* in Yerushalayim).

From the Period of the *Avot*?

The early significance of *Eretz Yisrael* is also apparent in the lives of the *Avot*. Avraham Avinu is charged with the mission of *Lech Lecha* – leaving the land of his forbearers, where he was born and grew up, in order to move to the land that Hashem would show him, *Eretz Yisrael*. Through the experiences of the *Avot*, *Eretz Yisrael* is transformed into *Eretz Avoteinu*, the land of our forefathers, in addition to Hashem's land. Did the *Avot* play a role in the human element of imparting *kedusha* to the land?[115]

There seems to be some indications that the first acts of consecration occurred during the lifetime of the *Avot*:

וַה' אָמַר אֶל אַבְרָם אַחֲרֵי הִפָּרֶד לוֹט מֵעִמּוֹ שָׂא נָא עֵינֶיךָ וּרְאֵה מִן הַמָּקוֹם אֲשֶׁר אַתָּה שָׁם צָפֹנָה וָנֶגְבָּה וָקֵדְמָה וָיָמָּה: כִּי אֶת כָּל הָאָרֶץ אֲשֶׁר אַתָּה רֹאֶה לְךָ אֶתְּנֶנָּה וּלְזַרְעֲךָ עַד עוֹלָם: וְשַׂמְתִּי אֶת זַרְעֲךָ כַּעֲפַר הָאָרֶץ אֲשֶׁר אִם יוּכַל אִישׁ לִמְנוֹת אֶת עֲפַר הָאָרֶץ גַּם זַרְעֲךָ יִמָּנֶה: קוּם הִתְהַלֵּךְ בָּאָרֶץ לְאָרְכָּהּ וּלְרָחְבָּהּ כִּי לְךָ אֶתְּנֶנָּה:

And God said to Avram after Lot had parted from him: "Now raise your eyes and see, from the place where you are, northward and southward and eastward and westward. For all the land which you see I will give to you and to your seed forever. And I will make your seed like the dust of the land, so that if a man will be able to count the dust of the land, so will your seed be counted. Go walk the land, to its length and to its breadth, for I will give it to you." (*Bereishit* 13:14-17)

Avraham is told to survey the land in all directions, as he will acquire the Land and bequeath it to his children.[116] Then he is told to walk the length and breadth of the land, as it will be given to him.

Hashem subsequently forged two covenants with Avraham Avinu, the *Brit Bein HaBetarim*

---

115 A parallel question relates to the sanctification of Yerushalayim, and the *Makom HaMikdash* in particular. During the time of the *Avot*, Yerushalayim already began to play a major historical role, although it is described merely as "*HaMakom*," the place, without any description of where this sanctified place is. It is there that *akeidat Yitzchak* takes place, and Avraham recognizes it as the place where Hashem's presence would one day be manifest: "And Avraham called that place 'God will see (*Hashem yireh*),' concerning which it is said to this day, 'God will make Himself seen upon the mountain (*behar Hashem yera'eh*)'" (*Bereishit* 22:14). Later, that same mountain is where Yaakov dreams of a ladder connecting the Heavens to the earth. Thus, Yerushalayim seems to be already sanctified, but every indication of its holiness is shrouded in secrecy and described as a future destiny. Even when Hashem commands that the *Mikdash* be built in that place so the *Shechina* can rest there, He does not reveal its location; it remains "*hamakom asher yivchar Hashem*," the place that Hashem will choose (see, for example, *Devarim* 12:5). Is Yerushalayim chosen from the dawn of time, historically significant due to the experiences of the *Avot*, or destined to be chosen at a later point in history (apparently at the time of David HaMelech)?

116 See the comment of the Keli Yakar on these *pesukim*, cited in chapter 8.

(Covenant Between the Parts; *Bereishit* ch. 15) and *Brit Milah* (circumcision; *Bereishit* ch. 17). Both of these covenants promise the Land of Israel to the Jewish People.

Based on these sources, *Chazal* indicate that our nation's possession of the land actually began with the *Avot*. For example, Rabbi Elazar states (*Avoda Zara* 53b) that *Eretz Yisrael* "was [already] an inheritance for them from their forefathers." Furthermore, we learn from Hashem's instruction to Avraham to walk the length and breadth of the Land that one legal means of taking ownership of land is accomplished by walking through it (*Bava Batra* 100a) – which clearly assumes that Hashem provided Avraham with the means to acquire the land. Additionally, the Yerushalmi cites Rabbi Yose's statement:

> When [the Jews] entered [the Land], they inherited it retroactively, for Rav Huna said in the name of Rabbi Shmuel ben Nachman: [The Torah] does not say, "To your progeny I will give [the Land]," but rather, "To your progeny I have given" (*Bereishit* 15:18)—already given. (*Yerushalmi, Challa* 2:1).[117]

Later Acts of Sanctification

While these sources clearly suggest that the Jewish people's claim to the land goes back to Avraham Avinu, other sources seem to indicate that Eretz Yisrael was only consecrated by the Jewish nation at later points in history. The *gemara* (*Yevamot* 82b) cites from the historical anthology called *Seder Olam*, regarding the *pasuk* concerning the Jewish People's return to Eretz Yisrael following their exile: "And Hashem your God will bring you into the land that your fathers inherited, and you shall inherit it" (*Devarim* 30:5). Rabbi Yose, the author of *Seder Olam*, understands this *pasuk* as indicating that there are two separate *yerushot*, inheritances, of the Land of Israel. The first one, *yerusha rishona*, the inheritance of "your fathers," is temporary, but the second one, *yerusha sheniya*, will last, and there will be no need for a third inheritance.

This idea of two inheritances is phrased in the *gemara* as two separate *kedushot* of the Land of Israel – the *kedusha rishona*, the initial *kedusha* of the land, which did not last past Destruction, and the *kedusha sheniya*, a second sanctification, which, according to some opinions, did last. The simple understanding of the historical points of these two *yerushot* and *kedushot* can be gleaned from a *gemara*:

> הַרְבֵּה כְּרַכִּים כָּבְשׁוּ עוֹלֵי מִצְרַיִם וְלֹא כְּבָשׁוּם עוֹלֵי בָּבֶל מִפְּנֵי שֶׁקְּדוּשָׁה רִאשׁוֹנָה קִדְּשָׁה לְשָׁעָתָהּ וְלֹא קִדְּשָׁה
> לְעָתִיד לָבֹא וְהִנִּיחוּם כְּדֵי שֶׁיִּסְמְכוּ עֲלֵיהֶן עֲנִיִּים בַּשְּׁבִיעִית
>
> Many cities were conquered by those who came up from Egypt, but they were not conquered by those who came up from Babylonia, because the initial sanctification sanctified it for that time, but did not sanctify it for all future times. And they [those who came up from Babylonia] left [some areas unsanctified] in order that the poor should rely on them during the Sabbatical year. (*Chagiga* 3b)

Most commentaries identify the *yerusha/kedusha rishona* as the conquest and sanctification

---

117 See *Parashat Derachim* by R. Yehuda Rosanes (author of the *Mishneh LaMelech*), sermon #9; see also Rabbi Dr. Judah Goldberg, *Lifnei Sinai* series, "Before Sinai: Jewish Values and Jewish laws," who discusses these sources. https://haretzion.linnovate.co.il/en/authors/rav-dr-judah-goldberg?from=48

of *Olei Mitzrayim,* the nation led by Yehoshua when they entered the Land. This included a seven-year period of conquering the Land followed by seven years of dividing the Land among the tribes (*kibbush v'chiluk*).[118] More than merely a technical necessity, this process played a critical role in ensuring Jewish ownership over the land and imparting it with *kedusha.* The *yerusha/kedusha sheniya,* the second sanctification, was accomplished by the *Olei Bavel,* the Jews who returned from the Babylonian exile after the destruction of the first *Mikdash,* led by Ezra the Scribe.[119]

Dual Sanctity of the Land

Thus, *Eretz Yisrael* appears to have a degree of innate *kedusha* and *kedusha* imparted by human activity, paralleling the two types of *kedusha* discussed above. In the terminology of Rav Kook (based on the writings of Rabbi Yehuda HaLevi in the *Kuzari* and the Maharal), there are two concepts at play: *segula,* an innate treasured uniqueness, and *bechira,* a practical chosenness.[120] Rav Kook illustrates this distinction in terms of the Jewish People, who always constitute a *segula,* but are only actually chosen (*bechira*) at a later point. Similarly, *Eretz Yisrael* is inherently *kadosh,* but it requires human activity to endow it with its complete *kedusha.*[121]

Rav Shimon ben Tzemach Duran (*Tashbetz*) distinguishes between two forms of *kedusha* found in the Land of Israel:

> There are two separate concepts: *Kedushat Shechina,* the sanctity of the Divine Presence, and *Kedushat Mitzvot,* the sanctity regarding *mitzvot.* The sanctity of the Divine Presence is specific only for the western bank of the Jordan, but the sanctity of the *mitzvot* [is present] both in [the western bank] and [the eastern bank]. (*Tashbetz* 3:200)

The *Tashbetz* notes that there are two aspects to *kedushat Eretz Yisrael.* First, *Eretz Yisrael* is the home of the Divine Presence, which is to be found throughout the broadest borders of

---

118 It is notable that the number seven appears repeatedly in this context. Indeed, the nation's arrival in the land opens with the conquest of Yericho, which involves encircling the city over a period of seven days, and seven times on the seventh day (*Yehoshua* 6:2-6).

119 Interestingly, Rabbeinu Chananel (cited by *Tosafot, Yevamot* 82b) understands that "the first possession" was that of Avraham, Yitzchak, and Yaakov ("your fathers"), and the second was that of Yehoshua. According to the primary opinion, *Eretz Yisrael* was evidently not yet sanctified at the time of the *Avot,* who seemingly anticipated a future sanctification when the nation would return from exile to sanctify the land. Rabbeinu Chananel, in contrast, appears to identify their acts as actual forms of sanctification.

120 Rav Soloveitchik (*Kol Dodi Dofek*) used different terminology to distinguish between two aspects of the covenant: "*brit goral*" (covenant of fate) and "*brit yi'ud*" (covenant of destiny). The former refers to a historical reality forced upon the individual, whereas the latter describes the person's conscious decision to accept this reality and lend it meaning.

121 Rav Yitzchak Levi, in his vast writings about Yerushalayim (See https://www.etzion.org.il/en/search?authors=5830&from=0&size=12), notes a similar distinction to explain much of Yerushalayim's history. It is clear that Yerushalayim possesses a unique nature, an inner *segula* from the Dawn of Time, but the *bechira* of Yerushalayim only materializes after a human act of consecration. The *Shem MiShmuel* (*Parashat Re'eh,* s.v. *v'hinei*) notes that this reflects that even inherent *kedusha* requires seeking out by the Jewish nation for it to come to fruition: "Since no one stirred himself in the matter except for [David], it was therefore impossible that they would find the place… According to our approach, it was because they didn't seek that they did not find."

Eretz Yisrael. Second, there is a unique *kedushat Eretz Yisrael* necessary for the fulfillment of the *mitzvot hateluyot ba'aretz*. These borders are far more limited, as they require a separate act of consecration performed under specific conditions.

Rav Ishtori HaParchi (*Kaftor VaFerach*) also speaks of two forms of *kedusha* of the land, but he identifies the innate *kedusha* as stemming from the consecration of the *Avot*, not the Divine Presence:

> The sanctity of the Land and its uniqueness are from the time of its granting to the holy *Avot*, not just from the time of conquest alone. (*Kaftor VaFerach*, p. 247). [122]

With that in mind, he explains the terms "*kedusha rishona*" and "*kedusha sheniya*" not as new acts of consecration but rather as rededications of what was already holy (p. 257). This leads him to a radical conclusion that from the time of the *Avot*, the land always retains its sanctity; the changes over time do not reflect the underlying sanctity of the land, but rather impact the *mitzvot hateluyot ba'aretz* and the *shemitta* year.

While both the *Tashbetz* and the *Kaftor VaFerach* note dual aspects of the *kedusha* of the Land of Israel, they differ on the implications of those distinctions and their practical ramifications.

All of Eretz Yisrael is inherently *kadosh* and unique, but its inherent destiny has to be actualized by the Jewish nation. Their presence in the land and intent to designate it as a sanctified land for living and fulfilling the land's unique *mitzvot* is essential for this status to take effect. No matter what history has in store, *Eretz Yisrael* is always *Nachalat Hashem*, but Hashem made its *kedusha* dependent on it being His nation's land as well. Only through the living and sanctification of the Jewish people does the land gain its unique status. Eretz Yisrael's *segula* is everlasting, but its *bechira*, and the reflection of that in its special *mitzvot*, requires human action and, at times, continued possession of the land.

The Rambam's Rulings

A great deal of the literature surrounding this topic deals with the Rambam's explanation of the distinction between the first and second sanctifications of the land:

> All of the lands that the *Olei Mitzrayim* took possession of were sanctified in the *kedusha rishona*. When they were exiled, that sanctity was nullified. [The rationale is that] the initial consecration came about because of *kibbush*, the conquest. Hence, its consecration was effective for the time [it was under their rule], but not for all time. When, by contrast, *Olei Bavel* came and took possession of a portion of the land (*chazaka*), they consecrated it with *kedusha sheniya*. [This consecration] is perpetuated forever, for that time and for all time. (*Hilchot Terumot* 1:5)

The Rambam accepts Rabbi Yose's position that there were two sanctifications of the

---

122 The *Kaftor VaFerach* dedicates a long chapter (10) to enumerating the unique properties, both metaphysical and *halachic*, of the Land of Israel. He discusses the *mitzvot* that apply in the Land and makes reference to some of the Rambam's rulings regarding the areas where there is *kedusha rishona* but lack *kedusha sheniya*, explaining that there are very few differences between the borders of the commonwealths and that they are only distinctions associated with the produce of the land, not the land itself.

land: The first was that of the *Olei Mitzrayim*, which was only temporary, and the second was that of the *Olei Bavel*, which was eternal. The presumption is that just as *kedusha* can be created, it can be destroyed. If whatever was responsible for the sanctification ceases, the *kedusha* goes with it.

Accordingly, the expansive borders of the Land of Israel for purposes of the *mitzvot ha-teluyot ba-aretz* ceased to obligate the nation in those *mitzvot* after the first exile. The obligation returned only to the more narrow borders of the *Olei Bavel* when a portion of the nation returned to the Land after the seventy-year exile.

This understanding lends itself to several questions, as Rav Aharaon Lichtenstein notes:

> What was the status of the Land during the Babylonian Exile? Was it simply identical with Iceland's or Manchuria's? Or, to put the same question differently: What of areas settled by Joshua and during the First Commonwealth but not during the Second? Are they now simply part of *chutz la-aretz*, their past dead and forgotten? (*Leaves of Faith: The World of Jewish Living*, pp. 65-66)

Furthermore, while the Rambam distinguishes between the two different acts of sanctification – the first through *kibbush*, conquering the land, and the second through *chazaka*, taking hold of the land – he does not fully explain his distinction. Why is the first sanctification of *kibuush* obliterated when the Land is conquered by others, whereas the second sanctification of *chazaka* remains despite the nation's exile?

It is further notable that the Rambam's ruling regarding the essential erasure of the *kedusha rishona* of *Eretz Yisrael* differs from his view regarding the sanctification of Yerushalayim. The Rambam rules that Yerushalayim's additional sanctity remains intact even after the city and the *Mikdash* were destroyed. Unlike the first sanctification of the land itself, which is erased after destruction, Yerushalayim's *kedusha* is everlasting (to the point that we could, in theory, offer *korbanot* in our day even without the *Mikdash*, provided that we were to do so on the *mizbeach*):

> Why do I say that the original sanctification sanctified the Temple and Yerushalayim for all time, while in regard to the consecration of the rest of *Eretz Yisrael*, as regards the sabbatical year, tithes, and other laws of this nature, [the first sanctification] did not sanctify it for all time? It is because the sanctity of the Temple and Jerusalem stems from the *Shechina*, and the *Shechina* can never be nullified. (*Hilchot Beit HaBechira* 6:15-17)

Evidently, the Rambam understands that once the identity of *Yerushalayim* as *HaMakom* is revealed[123] and the Jewish People consecrate it, its *kedusha* is everlasting. In contrast, the rest of the land's *kedusha* requires a constant connection to the Jewish People.

An additional factor is that other rulings of the Rambam seem to imply that even areas of *Eretz Yisrael* only sanctified by the *kedusha rishona* of *Olei Mitzrayim*, nevertheless, enjoy a unique sanctity even in our day. For example, the Rambam rules that *semicha* (the passing on of the rabbinic title) and *egla arufa* (the beheading of a calf in the atonement process for

---

123 See note 3 above.

an unwitnessed murder) still apply in the expansive borders of the *Olei Mitzrayim*.

To explain the Rambam's rulings, the Brisker tradition, beginning with Rav Chaim Soloveitchik and continuing down his line of children, distinguishes between "**shem Eretz Yisrael**," areas contained in land **known** as Eretz Yisrael, and areas of Eretz Yisrael that possess *kedusha* for the purposes of the *mitzvot ha-teluyot ba-aretz*. Whereas certain *halachot* pertain to any area defined in name as *Eretz Yisrael*, and therefore apply to the land under all circumstances. In contrast, the *halachot* that are connected to the *kedusha* of the Land require a constant Jewish presence to retain their *kedusha* status.[124]

Rav Ahron Soloveichik (*Parach Mateh Aharon, Sefer Ahava*, p. 178) explains that the land is known as Eretz Yisrael, the "Land of Israel," because it is the property of the people of Israel. The geographic "Land of Israel" is the land granted to the Jewish nation, which is immutable, but the sanctity of that land for certain *mitzvot* may require added conditions.

Rav Yosef Dov Soloveitchik offers a fascinating explanation for *kedusha sheniya* remaining even though the *kedusha rishona* ceased upon the Jewish exile. He notes that the *Olei Bavel* initiated the second *kedusha* of Eretz Yisrael by immediately starting with rebuilding the *Mikdash* and extending *Yerushalayim*'s everlasting *kedusha* to the rest of Eretz Yisrael. The *Olei Mitzrayim*, however, conquered the expanses of *Eretz Yisrael* but left *Yerushalayim* for the end. It was only fully conquered and sanctified more than four hundred years later under King David:

> The First Temple was built after the Land of Israel was already sanctified…. The Temple was only built giving a special sanctity to Jerusalem after the peripheral parts of the land were sanctified. However, the situation was different during the time of Ezra… Ezra did not go about reclaiming areas of the Land of Israel; he first set about to build the Temple and to restore the walls of Jerusalem… When the holy Temple, the chosen dwelling place for the *Shechina*, was built, it bestowed sanctity on the whole Land of Israel. This time the sanctity … was established first in the center itself and from there it spread outward… to the rest of the Land of Israel, until all of it was completely sanctified. .. The rebuilt walls [of Jerusalem and the Temple] held it in their power to radiate sanctity upon their surroundings and to bestow the holiness of the *Shechina* upon the entire Land of Israel. (*On Repentance*, p. 315)

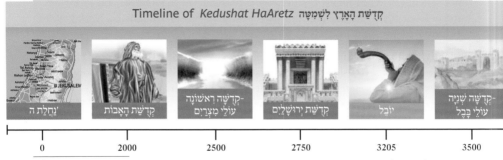

Timeline of *Kedushat HaAretz* קְדֻשַּׁת הָאָרֶץ לִשְׁמִטָּה

נַחֲלַת ה׳ ⸱ קְדֻשַּׁת הָאָבוֹת ⸱ קְדֻשָּׁה רִאשׁוֹנָה-עוֹלֵי מִצְרַיִם ⸱ קְדֻשַּׁת יְרוּשָׁלַיִם ⸱ יוֹבֵל ⸱ קְדֻשָּׁה שְׁנִיָּה-עוֹלֵי בָּבֶל

0	2000	2500	2750	3205	3500

---

124 See *Chiddushei HaGra"m HaLevi*, end of *Hilchot Shemitta VeYovel*; see also Rav Aharon Lichtenstein's opinion, as presented by Rav Elyakim Krumbein, https://www.etzion.org.il/en/tanakh/torah/sefer-bereishit/kedushat-aviv-harav-aharon-lichtenstein-zt%E2%80%9Dl-sanctity-time-and-place.

The Borders of the Land – Practical Implications

The Rambam's ruling has important practical implications for the observance of the *mitzvot ha-teluyot ba-aretz*, and *shemitta* in particular. Where is it prohibited to work the land during *shevi'it*? Does the produce of the region have *kedushat shevi'it* status? Which crops must be relinquished as *hefker*? Does the injunction of *sefichin* apply? Does the produce require *bi'ur*?

It is notable that the borders of the land during the First Commonwealth were much larger than during the Second, A smaller geographic area of *Eretz Yisrael* was sanctified in the second *kedusha*, with ramifications for the *halachot* that depend on the status of the land.

It is also important to note that some of the Land's borders described repeatedly in the Torah are more expansive than they were during either the First or Second Commonwealth.[125] As Professor Yoel Elitzur summarizes:

> These passages speak of expansive borders, which include all the inhabitable land east of the Mediterranean Sea. Defined another way: all of Greater Syria between Egypt and Mesopotamia, the middle portion of which is known as the Fertile Crescent. This vast region was defined in a national sense, in a manner typical of the zeitgeist of Isaiah's time: "In that day, Israel shall be a third partner with Egypt and Assyria as a blessing on earth" (Isaiah 19:24).[126]

However, *Parashat Masei* (*Bamidbar* 34) delineates entirely different borders for the Land of Israel. The *pesukim* describe the borders in great detail, but they are far more limited than the expansive borders generally mentioned in the Torah.[127] The actual conquest of the Land of Israel adhered to these more limited borders.[128]

Additionally, we must consider the implications of the fact that the modern State of Israel

---

125 The future borders of *Eretz Yisrael* are mentioned four times in the Torah and are described as extraordinarily vast; see *Bereishit* 15:18, *Shemot* 23:31, and *Devarim* 1:6-8 and 11:23-24. In these four descriptions, the *pesukim* provide six geographical points delineating the borders of the land, including borders for each of the four directions: In the north, the Euphrates River; in the west, the Mediterranean Sea (referred to as the Sea of Philistia or the Western Sea in these passages); in the south, the Sea of Suf (in *Bereishit* 15, the river of Egypt); and in the East, the wilderness (in *Devarim* 11, the wilderness and the Lebanon).

126 https://www.etzion.org.il/en/tanakh/studies-tanakh/core-studies-tanakh/mishpatim-destined-borders-land-israel.

127 There are several opinions regarding the identification of the northern and southern borders. Rabbi Menachem Leibtag summarizes (https://tanach.org/bamidbar/matot/matots1.htm):
The "minimalist" approach identifies the northern border in the area of today's Southern Lebanon, i.e. along the Litani river until the Metulla area. The southern border, according to this view, runs along the Be'er Sheva - Gaza line in the northern Negev. On the other hand, the "maximalist" opinion identifies the northern border somewhere up in Turkey and Northern Syria, while the southern border is said to be situated somewhere deep in the Sinai desert.

128 The two different borders are generally referred to by clichés based on *pesukim* in *Tanach*: **The Expansive Borders:** "From the Nile to the Euphrates" – encompassing almost the entire Middle East; **The Limited Borders:** "From Dan to Be'er Sheva" (see *Shmuel I* 3:20) – indicative of a much smaller country. The *pesukim* describing Avraham's two covenants with Hashem may refer to the two sets of borders mentioned in the Torah. The more limited borders of *Parashat Masei* may be rooted in the second covenant of Avraham Avinu and Hashem, *Brit Mila*, while the more expansive borders seem to refer back to *Brit Bein HaBetarim*. See Rabbi Leibtag's explanation, ibid. Interestingly, *Sefer Yehoshua* also mentions both borders. It begins by presenting the expansive borders (*Yehoshua* 1:3), using language that closely resembles the passage from *Devarim* 11. However, in chapter 13, it presents the borders of *Parashat Masei* as a point of contrast for the achievements of the conquest.

controls large areas of Eretz Yisrael that were under foreign rule during the Second Commonwealth. Are they sanctified simply by dint of current Jewish control?

Conversely, what is the status of parts of the Biblical Land of Israel that are not currently within the boundaries of the State of Israel? The northern borders of Eretz Yisrael described in the Torah would seem to include a great deal of modern-day Lebanon, and possibly Syria as well. Since there is no real trade between Israel and these countries, there is not much need to clarify the *halachic* status of produce grown in those areas. On the other hand, the southern border of the land of Israel is subject to much dispute. What are the southern borders described in *Parashat Masei*, and which areas are included in the regions sanctified by the *Olei Mitzrayim* and *Olei Bavel*?

This is an important practical question. Suppose there are Jewish-owned lands that are part of the State of Israel but are not endowed with *kedusha* for the purposes of *hilchot shevi'it*. In that case, those areas might provide us with a critical method of supporting Jewish agriculture even when options are limited due to *shevi'it* restrictions. In fact, *Chazal* explain (*Chagiga* 3b, cited above) that the *Olei Bavel* deliberately did not sanctify all of the areas they occupied so that the poor would be able to procure local produce during *shevi'it* from the unsanctified areas.

In our day and age, the question posed in *Parashat Behar* – "What will we eat in the seventh year?" – is less relevant due to advance refrigeration and the ability to import inexpensive produce from abroad. In contemporary Israeli society, only two percent of the workforce is involved in agriculture. Even if all of those farmers were to dedicate the year of *shevi'it* to spiritual pursuits, as anticipated by the Torah, the rest of society would still be able to operate more or less normally. The overwhelming majority of the population can easily avoid the challenges of *shevi'it* entirely, and most are not interested in simply coping with a limited selection of produce during *shevi'it*.

The decision to import produce from abroad (or to buy from local non-Jewish farmers) should not be taken lightly. This goes beyond the importance of "buying local." Immediately after describing the *halachot* of *shabbat ha'aretz*, the Torah introduces a discussion of the laws of buying and selling:

וְכִי תִמְכְּרוּ מִמְכָּר לַעֲמִיתֶךָ אוֹ קָנֹה מִיַּד עֲמִיתֶךָ אַל תּוֹנוּ אִישׁ אֶת אָחִיו:

When you sell property to **your colleague**, or buy any from **your colleague**, you shall not wrong one another. (*Vayikra* 25:14)

The *Sifra* (ad loc.) explains that the seemingly unnecessary mention and repetition of "*amitecha*," your colleague, indicates that one should prefer doing business with one's co-religionists. The simple understanding is that this is an outgrowth of the fact that a kinship of brotherhood binds all Jews; we are all part of a larger whole, and we recognize that another Jew's success is ours as well.

Notably, choosing to import produce during *shevi'it* has long-term implications, as experience has proven that any inroads non-Israeli produce makes during *shevi'it* continue at least to some degree afterward. *Shevi'it*-observance thus becomes a long-term obstacle to the success and even solvency of many farmers. Modern business models also present unique challenges for farmers, as produce is generally marketed both locally and in international markets. Israeli produce is sold throughout the world, winning numerous awards. If during the seventh year, Jewish farmers cannot sell their produce, they would likely lose their contracts. Is there a way for Israeli agriculture to invest in its growth without risking *shemitta* and without *shemitta* jeopardizing its business prospects?

It would be ideal to find a means to ensure maximum consumption of Jewish produce alongside full *shevi'it* observance. One possibility is buying produce grown in the State of Israel but outside the borders that are endowed with *kedusha*. If there are areas of the modern State where *hilchot shevi'it* do not apply, or do so only in a limited capacity, that will allow for *shevi'it* observance alongside supporting *"amitecha."*

Three Areas of *Shevi'it* Observance

The *mishna* delineates three separate areas of the land regarding its *kedusha* for *Shevi'it*:

> There are three regions in regard to the sabbatical laws. All land that was controlled by the *Olei Bavel* – that is, from the Land of Israel until Kiziv – [its produce] may not be eaten and it may not be cultivated. And all land that was controlled by those the *Olei Mitzrayim* – that is, from Kiziv until the river and until Amanah – [its produce] may be eaten, but it may not be cultivated. From the river and from Amanah and further, [its produce] may be eaten and it may be cultivated. (*Shevi'it* 6:1)

While one area is considered beyond the borders of Eretz Yisrael entirely and, therefore, not subject to any of the *shevi'it* limitations, the Mishna is clear that all *halachot* of *shevi'it* apply to the area of *kedusha sheniya* (*Olei Bavel*). Within the borders of *kedusha rishona* (*Olei Mitzrayim*), one may not work the land, but one can eat the produce. There is a difference of opinion among the commentaries regarding whether this means that the laws of *bi'ur* do not apply there (Rash) or if the limitations of *sefichin* do not apply (Rambam, *Hilchot Shemitta VeYovel* 4:26). Additionally, there is a debate about whether the produce of those areas has *kedushat shevi'it* (see Rav Kook's *Shabbat HaAretz* 4:26:2).[129]

The primary area of the State of Israel that may be included in *kedusha rishona* (*Olei Mitzrayim*) but not *kedusha sheniya* (*Olei Bavel*) is known as *Arava Dromit*, the southern Arava. Its status is subject to a dispute partially due to disagreement regarding the identification of the southern border described in *Parashat Masei*. According to Rav Tukachinski (*Sefer Eretz Yisrael*, pp. 34-7), those borders include Eilat, while others draw the border at Wadi El Arish, much further north. Still, others maintain that we must observe the *mitzvot ha-teluyot ba-aretz* in all areas under Israeli control.[130]

Many perform what is referred to as a *"heter mechira lechumra"* in the areas in question. Due to the lack of clarity regarding whether these areas are within the borders of *Eretz Yisrael*

---

129 Virtually all other *mitzvot hateluyot ba'aretz*, including *terumot* and *ma'asrot*, do apply in the borders of *kedusha rishona*. The *mitzvah* of *yishuv Eretz Yisrael/Eretz Yisrael* applies in the entire area described in the Torah, which, as noted, is significantly larger than the borders of either *Olei Mitzrayim* or *Olei Bavel*.

130 Additionally, there is discussion about whether five areas of modern day Israel are included in the borders of *Olei Bavel*: the western Negev, the Beit Shean Valley, the Jordan Valley, the Chermon, and the Shefeila around Akko.

for the purposes of *shemitta* observance, these areas are cultivated during *shevi'it* with an additional precaution that the land is sold to non-Jews for the year, as in an ordinary *heter mechira*. Some who are generally unwilling to rely on the *heter mechira* are willing to do so in these regions. Others treat the land as though it has no *shevi'it* sanctity at all. This is the primary means of supplying Jewish produce during the *shemitta* year for some kashrut agencies.[131] Other authorities, however, question the *halachic* permissibility of relying on produce from these areas[132].

Shemitta BeZman HaZeh-
The Obligation of *Shemitta* in our Times

Another critical question stemming from the *kedusha* status of *Eretz Yisrael* regards the level of obligation of contemporary *shevi'it* observance. The observance of *shevi'it* and *yovel* became Biblically obligatory after the Jews entered the Land of Israel. Indeed, the very last passage of *Tanach* mentions that the lack of *shemitta* observance was the cause of the seventy years of exile from the land. When a small portion of the Jewish People returned to the Land and re-sanctified a more limited area (the *Olei Bavel*), did *shemitta* and *yovel* observance gain the same Biblical level of obligation?

This issue is discussed in the *gemara* in *Arachin*, although the *gemara's* intent is subject to dispute. The *gemara* learns that the Torah's requirement that *yovel* be observed when "freedom can be proclaimed in the land, to **all** its inhabitants" (*Vayikra* 25:10) indicates that the *mitzvah* applies only when all the inhabitants live in their apportioned territories in the Land, and not when some of the nation has been exiled:

> Upon the exile of the tribes of Reuven and Gad and half the tribe of Menashe, *yovel* was annulled, as it is written: "And you should proclaim freedom unto the land for all its inhabitants" – during the time that all its inhabitants are on it, and not at a time that some have been exiled. Perhaps if they were all on it, however mixed together, the tribe of Binyamin with Yehuda, and the tribe of Yehuda with Binyamin, yovel should be observed? We learn from what is written, "For all its inhabitants" – at a time that its inhabitants are settled properly, but not when they are mixed. (*Arachin* 32b)

The *gemara* seems to state that *yovel* is applicable only when all twelve tribes are present in the Land of Israel, living according to their tribes in their ancestral *nachalot* (portions). Therefore, from the time that the Ten Tribes were exiled (over a period beginning during the reign of Achaz, king of Yehuda), *yovel* was no longer observed. Nevertheless, the *gemara* states, they continued to count the *yovel* years so as to know the appropriate year for *shevi'it* observance. The *Rishonim* offer a number of understandings regarding whether *yovel* and *shemitta* were observed Biblically during the latter years of *Bayit Rishon* and

---

131 See the summary of opinions by Rabbi Eli Ozarowski: https://www.torahmusings.com/2015/01/food-consumption-shemita-year-israel-diaspora-ii/

132 See Rav Yaakov Ariel, https://en.toraland.org.il/beit-midrash/halachic-guides/hilchot-haaretz/hilchot-shemitah/shemitah-introduction1-shemitah-a-national-mitzvah/.

during *Bayit Sheini*, as well as the implications for our times.[133]

A related question has to do with the extent of the relationship between the three "*shemitta-related*" *mitzvot*: agricultural *shevi'it*, *shemittat kesafim*, and *yovel*. Does each one carry its own set of rules, or are they dependent on each other, such that if one or another no longer applies Biblically in our time, the others do not as well?

The Torah's description of *shevi'it* in *Parashat Behar* describes *shevi'it* observance alongside the observance of *yovel*. In fact, the Torah seems to explicitly connect them:

וְסָפַרְתָּ לְךָ שֶׁבַע שַׁבְּתֹת שָׁנִים שֶׁבַע שָׁנִים שֶׁבַע פְּעָמִים וְהָיוּ לְךָ יְמֵי שֶׁבַע שַׁבְּתֹת הַשָּׁנִים תֵּשַׁע וְאַרְבָּעִים שָׁנָה:

And you shall count for yourself seven sabbaths of years, seven years seven times over, and the seven sabbaths of years shall number for you forty-nine years. (*Vayikra* 25:8)

Yovel is observed on the fiftieth year, after seven *shevi'it* cycles, and *yovel's* existence, therefore, appears to depend on the existence of *shevi'it*. But does the relationship go both ways? Can *shevi'it* exist even if *yovel* no longer applies?[134]

According to many authorities, given the Torah's linkage of the two *mitzvot*, and since *yovel* is no longer Biblically obligated, neither *yovel* nor *shemitta* are obligatory in our day and age on a Biblical level, but *shemitta* observance is nevertheless Rabbinically mandated.[135]

The Rabbinic status of *shemitta* in our day is indicated, for example, by the *gemara* in *Mo'ed Katan* (2b), which questions why the *mishna* permits watering certain fields that do not receive sufficient rainwater during the *shevi'it* year, providing two possible answers: 1) The *mishna* expresses the view of Rabbi Yehuda HaNasi that *shevi'it* is only

---

133 Some understand the *gemara* to indicate that even in the latter years of *Bayit Rishon*, *shevi'it* was only Rabbinically obligated, while the Ramban (*Gittin* 36) understands that *shevi'it* observance remained a *mitzvah deOraita*. Most opinions agree that *yovel* was no longer observed during *Bayit Sheini*, although Rabbeinu Tam (*Tosafot*, *Arachin* 32b and *Gittin* 36a) differs.

134 The relationship between the two is further discussed in the *gemara* (*Nedarim* 61a) regarding a dispute as to how the *yovel* cycles are counted. Is the *yovel* year in year 50 the beginning of the next seven *shevi'it* cycles (i.e., year 1 of the following count), or is it a "gap year," with the next *shevi'it* beginning only after *yovel* concludes?

135 The *Yerushalmi* (*Shevi'it* 10:2) cites a second reasoning for the Rabbinic obligation of *shemitta* (accepted by the *Sefer HaTeruma* 45:4): *Shemitta* observance is only Rabbinically obligated because the Land presently lacks the sanctity of *kedushat hamitzvot* (as when the second *kedusha* of the Land was nullified). The *Ba'al HaMaor* (cited in *Sefer HaTeruma*, and possibly the Ra'avad) understands that because we lack a *Beit Din* to count the years of the *shemitta* cycle, *shemitta* is not even Rabbinically ordained nowadays; it is observed only as a *minhag* or *middat chassidut*.

The widely accepted explanation – that *shemitta* is Rabbinically mandated in our time due to its connection with *yovel*, which applies only when the majority of the nation lives in the land – leads to an important practical question. According to recent statistics, Israel is currently the country that is home to the greatest number of Jews, although not a majority of the world Jewish population. (The world Jewish population is approximated at 15.7 million, and about 6.135 million Jews live in Israel. The United States is second with about 5.7 million Jews.) The Jewish population of Israel grows yearly around 1.7 percent (through birth and *aliya*), while the Jewish population in most other countries is unfortunately declining. If these trends continue, Israel will become home to the majority of Jews in the world at some point in the not-so-distant future. Will this change the status of *yovel* and *shemitta*? Although some authorities conclude that other *mitzvot hateluyot ba'aretz* will become biblically ordained under those circumstances, most *poskim* rule that even then, *shemitta* and *yovel* will remain only Rabbinically obligated, as the Biblical obligation requires that the Jewish People reside in the Land according to tribal territory.

Rabbinically obligated in our day; 2) Even when *shevi'it* is Biblically mandated, watering fields is prohibited only Rabbinically. The upshot of both answers is that whenever *shevi'it* observance is Rabbinically mandated, either in general or specifics, there are certain dispensations when great financial loss is at stake.

Importantly, Rabbi Yehuda HaNasi further links the obligation of *shemittat karka'ot* and that of *shemittat kesafim*, such that when *yovel* is no longer Biblically obligatory, the other *mitzvot* are similarly not Biblically mandated:

> Abaye said: [The *mishna* is referring] to the sabbatical year in the present time [when its prohibitions are only by Rabbinic decree], and it is in accordance with the opinion of Rabbi Yehuda HaNasi. As it is taught [in a *baraita*] that Rabbi Yehuda HaNasi says: [When the verse states:] "And this is the manner of the release, every creditor will release [that which he has lent to his neighbor]" (*Devarim* 15:2), the verse speaks of two releases: One is the release of land, and the other is the release of money. [This verse equates these two releases, indicating that] when you [are mandated by Torah law to] release land, you must release money, and when you are not mandated to release land, you need not release money. (*Moed Katan* 2b)

This question is significant, as designating contemporary *shemitta* observance as either Biblically or Rabbinically mandated has *halachic* implications. In addition to the resolution of questions in cases of doubt (*safek*), certain allowances are built into Rabbinic requirements that may enable leniencies in situations where a loss is at stake, as reflected in the *mishna* in Mo'ed Katan. If *shemitta* is obligatory only on a Rabbinic level in our day, this might lead to a more measured practice of *shemitta*. In fact, one significant implication might be the ability to enact the *heter mechira*.[136]

The Tur (Y.D. 331) rules that *shemitta* is only Rabbinically mandated nowadays, and most authorities accept this view (see, for example, *Chazon Ish* 3:8).[137] Rav Kook (Letter 555) generally agrees with this approach, but he notes that since one question regarding *shevi'it*'s Rabbinic status is whether the *kedusha* of Eretz Yisrael remains in our day, we should be stringent for the opinion that *shevi'it* is Biblically ordained whenever possible.

Why is there a Rabbinic Obligation?

Why did *Chazal* obligate us in *shemitta* and not *yovel*, if both are linked?

---

136 Another implication of the distinction between Biblical and Rabbinic obligation relates to the applicability of the promised blessing for *shemitta* observance. If the *mitzvah* is no longer obligatory by Torah law, can we rely on the Torah's promise that Hashem will provide for those who observe *shemitta* properly? The Sema (C.M. 67:2) appears to state that since *shevi'it* observance is only Rabbinic, the *bracha* no longer applies, but the *Chazon Ish* (18:4) disagrees, noting that the Heavenly tribunal accepts the rulings of our earthly Sages. However, the *Chazon Ish* writes that the *bracha* is dependent on two realities: preparation and *hishtadlut*. One cannot merely rely on Divine blessing, as one must prepare in advance all that is permitted in order to allow for maximal *shevi'it* observance with blessings.

137 The Beit HaLevi (3:1) writes that *shemitta* is obligated *midivrei kabbala* in our day, citing *pesukim* from *Sefer Nechemia* that describe that in the days of Ezra, the nation swore to uphold a pact that included *shevi'it* observance. The Rambam's opinion on the matter subject to dispute, as he seems to contradict himself, and the rulings of Rav Yosef Karo in the *Beit Yosef* (Y.D. 331) and *Kesef Mishna* also appear inconsistent.

The requirements of *"kol yoshveha aleha"*, that the Jewish People reside in the land according to *shevet*, is unique to *yovel* and *shemitta*. Specifically, due to *shemitta* and *yovel's* connection between *Eretz Yisrael* and the Jewish people, the *mitzvot* do not apply on a Biblical level when the Jewish nation does not live in the land.

Yovel is a vision with an agricultural component that sets the tone for Jewish society and the economy throughout the forty-nine years from one *yovel* to another. That glorious vision can only apply when the people reside in their Land in the optimal state. The ethical sensitivities that inspire these laws always apply. Still, when some of the tribes are no longer in Eretz Yisrael, the nation can no longer function as an organic whole. The vision of "liberty throughout the land, unto all the inhabitants thereof" is no longer attainable.

Nevertheless, *shemitta* is so central to our core that *Chazal* could not imagine a time without it. Therefore, *Chazal* instituted a rabbinic obligation of *shemitta*. It serves as a means of connecting us to Hashem, our land, and our fellow Jews, and shapes our character and outlook. *Chazal* wanted us to uphold as much of *shevi'it's* goal as possible, expressing our nation's initiative to further our relationship with Hashem even when the ideal setting is impossible. The Torah deputized the Sages to enact Rabbinic obligations that would preserve Torah values, and they clearly felt that *shemitta* observance was a critical component of those values.

According to the ruling that *shemitta* is observed only rabbinically due to the lack of sufficient Jewish inhabitants in the Land, the implications of the *pesukim* in *Bechukotai* linking lack of *shemitta* observance and the exile are even more astounding. The destruction of *Eretz Yisrael* and the exile of its inhabitants has implications for the applicability of the *mitzvah* of *shemitta* itself. The Jews failed to keep *shemitta* properly, and were therefore expelled; as a result, the land loses a *mitzvah* integral to its character and deeply implanted in its nature.

As we noted above, since the *mitzvah* of *shemitta* is Rabbinically ordained nowadays, *Chazal* devised a system with certain allowances in extenuating circumstances. However, due to the importance of the *shemitta* framework even when Rabbinically ordained, we will find certain Rabbinic restrictions that apply across the board, aimed at ensuring that *shemitta* is appropriately observed even when its status is Rabbinic and not Biblical.

Concluding Thoughts

The ideal society that *shemitta* and *yovel* envision requires merging the three forms of *kedusha* – *makom*, *zman*, and *adam* – with the nation in its land. The Torah made the full-fledged *kedusha* of *Eretz Yisrael* regarding these *mitzvot* inextricably connected to the Jewish nation's presence in *Eretz Yisrael*. Our fulfillment of *shevi'it* brings much *beracha*, but our violation of it forfeits our right to live in the Land and to observe it to its fullest extent.

We have come a long way in realizing the dream of an ingathering of the exiles and returning to our land, but we still have a ways to go. The Rabbinic obligation of *shemitta* in our times allows us to taste a little bit of the dream and do what we can to make it a reality.

Chapter 20

Shabbat Ha-aretz- The *Halachot* of the Land's Rest

As we have seen, the *pesukim* in *Parashat Behar* describe *shevi'it* as a year of agricultural rest, *shabbat ha'aretz*. We are familiar with the weekly Shabbat as a day of refraining from all *melacha*. Does the same hold true regarding *shevi'it*? Does it require cessation from all agricultural *melacha* for an entire year? It is notable that the *pesukim* explicitly prohibit only a limited number of agricultural activities.

As we will see, *shabbat ha'aretz* of the seventh-year, entails refraining from a host of agricultural activities, many of which are not explicitly mentioned in the Torah. At the very least, they are Rabbinically prohibited due to their compromising the year as a year of agricultural rest.

Determining if a prohibition is Biblical or Rabbinic is important for at least two significant reasons. First of all, Rabbinic prohibitions involve certain leniencies, especially in cases of impending financial forfeiture. The Sages lifted certain *shevi'it* prohibitions when they would lead to certain losses. They prohibited only the advancement of new growth but did not prohibit maintaining that which is already growing. *Shevi'it* is not supposed to be a year when everything growing on the land dies, but rather a year focused on advancing spiritual growth while maintaining the land's beauty. Thus, identifying specific acts as Rabbinic prohibitions will indicate which activities can be performed to avert losses.

Second, understanding the nature of Rabbinic injunctions and requirements will help us not only understand *shevi'it*, but provide a glimpse into the nature of Rabbinic injunctions in general. Additionally, it might help us understand why the Sages imposed *shemitta* prohibitions altogether when they often involve significant difficulty.

Clarification of what is permitted and what is prohibited during *shevi'it* is vital due to the *halachic* ramifications for farmers, garden owners, and possibly all residents of and visitors to *Eretz Yisrael*. But the questions also reach the heart of one of our primary themes in this work – the relationship between *shevi'it* and *Eretz Yisrael*.

Eretz Yisrael is a beautiful land, endowed both physically and spiritually with Divine blessing. Just as we are commanded to sanctify the land through our actions and realize its *kedusha* by consecrating it to be fit for *mitzvot ha-teluyot ba-aretz*, the *mitzvah* of *yishuv Eretz Yisrael* teaches us that we should be doing the same thing in the physical realm as well. Besides living in Israel, we should beautify it and make it an aesthetically pleasing place to live (see Section II themes 5-6). This raises questions regarding *Shevi'it* observance. After all, if the land is supposed to be beautiful, how can we afford to refrain from working the land for a year? Understanding what is really permitted and prohibited during *shevi'it* will make it clear that abstaining from advancing the land is in no way, shape, or form a call to abandon our beautiful land or allow it to turn into a wasteland.

The *Halachot* of the Four Stages

We have seen that the *halachot* that impact agriculture during the seventh year can be divided into two primary categories:

1. *Halachot* on the Land, which we referred to as the *halachot* of *shabbat ha'aretz*

2. *Halachot* on the produce of the Land (both while it is growing and after it is harvested), which we referred to as the *halachot* of *shemittat karka'ot*

We further noted that each category can be divided into two:

Halachot of *Shabbat HaAretz:*

- Before anything grows on the land

- Improving the trees or crops while they are already growing

Halachot of *Shemittat Karka'ot:*

- Dealing with crops while still growing on the land

- Dealing with the produce after the harvest

We will identify these four stages by the following graphics:

1	**2**	**3**	**4**
The Land Before Planting	**The Land During the Growing Season**	**The Vegetation and Crops While Growing (on trees or in the ground)**	**The Produce After it is Harvested**

The agricultural *halachot* primarily concern themselves with *shabbat ha'aretz*, with the first two stages involving preparing the land for growth and improving the crops after they or the trees are already growing.

The *Melachot* Explicitly Mentioned in the Torah

Parashat Behar

Parashat Behar contains the most explicit description in the Torah of the *halachot* of *shabbat ha'aretz*. After introducing *Parashat Behar* as laws transmitted at Har Sinai, the Torah mentions a general goal of the cessation of agricultural activity during the seventh year, alongside an explicit mention of four prohibitions:

דַּבֵּר אֶל בְּנֵי יִשְׂרָאֵל וְאָמַרְתָּ אֲלֵהֶם כִּי תָבֹאוּ אֶל הָאָרֶץ אֲשֶׁר אֲנִי נֹתֵן לָכֶם וְשָׁבְתָה הָאָרֶץ שַׁבָּת לַה': שֵׁשׁ שָׁנִים תִּזְרַע שָׂדֶךָ וְשֵׁשׁ שָׁנִים תִּזְמֹר כַּרְמֶךָ וְאָסַפְתָּ אֶת תְּבוּאָתָהּ: וּבַשָּׁנָה הַשְּׁבִיעִת שַׁבַּת שַׁבָּתוֹן יִהְיֶה לָאָרֶץ שַׁבָּת לַה' שָׂדְךָ לֹא תִזְרָע וְכַרְמְךָ לֹא תִזְמֹר: אֵת סְפִיחַ קְצִירְךָ לֹא תִקְצוֹר וְאֶת עִנְּבֵי נְזִירֶךָ לֹא תִבְצֹר שְׁנַת שַׁבָּתוֹן יִהְיֶה לָאָרֶץ: וְהָיְתָה שַׁבַּת הָאָרֶץ לָכֶם לְאָכְלָה לְךָ וּלְעַבְדְּךָ וְלַאֲמָתֶךָ וְלִשְׂכִירְךָ וּלְתוֹשָׁבְךָ הַגָּרִים עִמָּךְ:

When you come to the land which I shall give you, the land shall rest (*ve-shaveta ha-aretz*) a sabbath to God. Six years you may sow your field and six years you may prune your vineyard and gather in the produce. But in the seventh year the land shall have a sabbath of complete rest, a sabbath to God; you shall not **sow** your field nor **prune** your vineyard. You shall not **reap** the after-growth of your harvest nor **gather** the grapes of your untrimmed vines; it shall be a year of complete rest (*shenat shabbaton*) for the land. But the sabbath of the land (*shabbat ha-aretz*) shall be for you to eat, for you, and for your servant and for your maid, and for your hired servant and for the residents by your side that sojourn with you. (*Vayikra* 25:2-6)

The *pesukim* mention six years of planting fields (*sadeh*) and vineyards (*kerem*) and gathering the crops of each, followed by the seventh year where one ceases from both planting and normal harvesting in both the *sadeh* and the *kerem*. These seem to serve as representative examples of fields of annual crops (planted yearly) and trees on which perennial crops grow. While a field is replanted every year, the trees of perennials are pruned and prepared for a new crop, without being directly planted.

The Four Explicit Prohibitions

Four acts are explicitly mentioned as entailing prohibitions – two in the field and two in the vineyard. In both the field and the vineyard, one is prohibited from promoting growth and harvesting like any other year, but fostering growth in a field is done through planting (*zeria*), while in a vineyard, which already has vines, this is done through pruning (*zemira*). There is also a different term used for harvesting wheat in fields (*ketzira*) and grapes in vineyards (*betzira*).

	שָׂדֶה In the Field	כֶּרֶם In the Vineyard
Promoting Growth	לֹא תִּזְרַע Do not plant seeds	לֹא תִזְמֹר Do not prune
Harvesting (Regularly)	לֹא תִקְצוֹר Do not harvest	לֹא תִבְצֹר Do not harvest grapes

These four prohibited activities are *mitzvot lo ta'aseh*. When Jewish courts had the authority to adjudicate such matters, violation of a prohibition in the Torah that involves action generally incurred a punishment of *malkot* (lashes) when violated after a warning (*hatra'ah*).

It is notable that although the Torah prohibits planting fields, regarding trees it restricts only pruning vineyards. This leads to the question of whether נְטִיעָה (*netia*), planting trees, is also included in the Torah's prohibitions (and whether the Biblical prohibition of pruning is limited to vineyards and not applicable to all trees).

The General *Mitzvat Aseh*

In addition to these four prohibitions, the Torah repeatedly mentions the command, "*veshavta ha'aretz*," which would seem to be a general requirement for the land to rest. This *mitzvah* is a *mitzvat aseh*, a positive commandment. At the very minimum, this phrase indicates that one must refrain from working the land through these four activities, as doing so will prevent the land from resting. What remains unclear is whether this *mitzvat aseh* requires resting from additional agricultural activities as well.

	מצוות עשה Mitzvot Asseh	מצוות לא תעשה Mitzvot Lo Ta'aseh
Fields of Grain (Land)	וְשָׁבְתָה הָאָרֶץ (maybe also בֶּחָרִישׁ וּבַקָּצִיר תִּשְׁבֹּת) And numerous other ways of repeating it	שָׂדְךָ לֹא תִזְרַע -Prohibition of panting fields. אֶת סְפִיחַ קְצִירְךָ לֹא תִקְצֹר- Prohibition of harvesting fields.
Vineyard (Trees)	וְשָׁבְתָה הָאָרֶץ	וְכַרְמְךָ לֹא תִזְמֹר וְאֶת עִנְּבֵי נְזִירֶךָ לֹא תִבְצֹר -Prohibition of pruning and harvesting vineyards.

Parashat Ki Tisa

We noted in Section I that there is a Tannaitic debate regarding whether a *pasuk* in *Parashat Ki Tisa* refers to the weekly Shabbat or to *shevi'it*:

> שֵׁשֶׁת יָמִים תַּעֲבֹד וּבַיּוֹם הַשְּׁבִיעִי תִּשְׁבֹּת בֶּחָרִישׁ וּבַקָּצִיר תִּשְׁבֹּת:
>
> Six days you shall work, but on the seventh day you shall rest; in plowing and in harvesting, you shall rest. (*Shemot* 34:21)

Since thirty-nine *melachot* are prohibited on Shabbat, including plowing and harvesting, there is no need to single out these two acts if the *pasuk* is referring to Shabbat. For this reason, Rabbi Akiva teaches that the *pasuk* is instructing us about a different Shabbat – the *shabbat* of the Land:

> דְּתַנְיָא בֶּחָרִישׁ וּבַקָּצִיר תִּשְׁבֹּת רַבִּי עֲקִיבָא אוֹמֵר אֵינוֹ צָרִיךְ לוֹמַר חָרִישׁ וְקָצִיר שֶׁל שְׁבִיעִית שֶׁהֲרֵי כְּבָר נֶאֱמַר
> שָׂדְךָ לֹא תִזְרַע וְגוֹ' אֶלָּא חָרִישׁ שֶׁל עֶרֶב שְׁבִיעִית הַנִּכְנָס לִשְׁבִיעִית וְקָצִיר שֶׁל שְׁבִיעִית הַיּוֹצֵא לְמוֹצָאֵי שְׁבִיעִית

> "In plowing and in harvesting, you shall rest" – Rabbi Akiva says: There is no need to be told to desist from plowing or reaping in the seventh year, for it is already stated: "You shall not sow your field..." [It can be taken] only [to prohibit] plowing in the pre-sabbatical year [which may cause agricultural benefits] extending into the seventh year and [likewise] to the harvesting of the seventh year's crops which mature in the post-sabbatical year. (*Rosh Hashana* 9a)

This is the basis for the concept of *tosefet shevi'it*, which we discussed at length in Section I.

According to Rabbi Akiva, one agricultural act that is prohibited in advance of the *shemitta* year, at least by way of a positive commandment, is חֲרִישָׁה (*charisha*), plowing one's field.

The *mishnayot* in *Masechet Shevi'it* begin with the laws of *tosefet shevi'it*, indicating that during Temple times, in the latter part of the sixth year, any plowing that directly benefits growth during the seventh year is prohibited. If plowing is prohibited during the sixth year due to the positive commandment of *tosefet shevi'it*, it would seem logical that plowing would undoubtedly be forbidden during *shevi'it* as well. However, some sources seem to indicate that at least certain forms of plowing are only Rabbinically prohibited.

Parashat Mishpatim

The first time we are introduced to *shevi'it* in the Torah is in *Parashat Mishpatim*, where the Torah tells us that unlike the six years, when one works in the field and harvests:

> וְהַשְּׁבִיעִת תִּשְׁמְטֶנָּה וּנְטַשְׁתָּהּ וְאָכְלוּ אֶבְיֹנֵי עַמֶּךָ וְיִתְרָם תֹּאכַל חַיַּת הַשָּׂדֶה כֵּן תַּעֲשֶׂה לְכַרְמְךָ לְזֵיתֶךָ:

> But the seventh year you shall let it rest and lie fallow, that the poor of your people may eat; and what they leave, the animal of the field shall eat. In this manner you shall deal with your vineyard and with your oliveyard. (*Shemot* 23:11)

We noted that the meaning of the words "*tishmitena untashta*" is elusive and is understood to be anything from a reference to releasing one's hold on the produce of their field to releasing loans as part of *shemittat kesafim*.

The *gemara* cites an opinion that this refers to refraining from additional agricultural activities, a view that Rashi cites in his commentary on the Torah (as his second explanation):

> דָּבָר אַחֵר תִּשְׁמְטֶנָּה מֵעֲבוֹדָה גְמוּרָה, כְּגוֹן חֲרִישָׁה וּזְרִיעָה. וּנְטַשְׁתָּהּ מִלְּזַבֵּל וּמִלְּקַשְׁקֵשׁ:

> Alternatively, "rest" from full labor, such as plowing and sowing. "And lie fallow" – [refrain from] fertilizing and removing stones. (Rashi *Shemot* 23:11)

The Ramban and others question Rashi's explanation, noting that this understanding doesn't seem to be accepted in the *gemara*. Rashi may be indicating that refraining from *melacha* during *shevi'it* is not only on account of the land's need for rest (the *mitzvat aseh* of *shevita*), but also for the people. The *mitzvat aseh* of *shemitta* requires relinquishing one's agricultural pursuits of conquering the land. For a year we will focus on improving ourselves rather than advancing our fields.

Two Questions that are Basically One

Two questions immediately jump out from reading the text, one based on what the Torah omits and one based on what the Torah explicitly mentions.

First, there are clearly many agricultural activities beyond the four explicitly mentioned in the Torah that make up the farmer's regimen, but they seem to be omitted. A basic understanding of what a field or tree needs for proper growth indicates that agriculture involves far more than the two forms of promoting growth mentioned in the *pesukim*.

All living organisms have basic needs of water, gases, and the like to thrive and even survive. Much like a person requires nutrients, sources of energy, and water, plants have similar needs; they receive light from the sun, water from the ground, and carbon dioxide from the air. Their roots (xylem) absorb water and nutrients from the soil.

Notably, while plants are often the food we eat and they produce the oxygen we breathe, although they have similar energy needs to humans, they produce their own energy through photosynthesis, from the sunlight, water, and air. While some of the glucose created from photosynthesis is stored as starch for periods without sunlight, the plant cannot survive without sunlight and water. Every plant has its own unique needs, needing more or less sun or water, but no plant can grow without the resources it needs to thrive.[138]

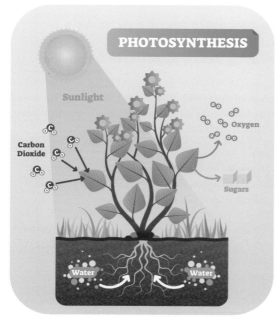

Thus, planting is only a small part of cultivating the land. The area for planting must be carefully prepared, the field fertilized, and the plant breeded, weeds removed, and protected from animals. Planting without providing the necessary irrigation and tending to the plants is futile, yet the Torah doesn't explicitly mention any of these additional activities. Does that mean that the Torah permits them, and if so, under what circumstances?

Second, the specific acts that the Torah mentions seem to be repetitive. Of the four actions that the Torah explicates, it really just lists two prohibited actions – two prohibitions in the field and their corresponding prohibitions in the vineyard. Why does the Torah need to specify

---

138 This is one element of the comparison between humans and plants in the *pasuk*, "כִּי הָאָדָם עֵץ הַשָּׂדֶה" (*Devarim* 20:19).

the prohibitions in this manner? Wouldn't it have been sufficient to prohibit promoting growth and regular harvesting? We would intuitively understand that this includes both fields and trees.

Essentially, both questions boil down to one general query: Did the Torah mention these four actions as guiding principles, examples of prohibited activities that include prohibitions of similar activities that perform the same goals? Or are these four activities four unique prohibitions, such that anything omitted from the list is permitted during *shevi'it*?

Four Specific Prohibitions or Four Principles?

Our question is essentially: Did the Torah prohibit four actions or did the Torah formulate four principles, i.e., any actions promoting growth or a form of harvesting for either annuals or perennials would be prohibited? To answer this question, let us take a look at the Shabbat Model for prohibited activities on the weekly Shabbat.

The Shabbat Model

Chazal refer to the four activities explicitly prohibited on *shevi'it* as *melachot*, a term used by the Torah to describe the prohibited acts on Shabbat:

וְיוֹם הַשְּׁבִיעִי שַׁבָּת לַה' אֱלֹהֶיךָ לֹא תַעֲשֶׂה כָל מְלָאכָה אַתָּה וּבִנְךָ וּבִתֶּךָ עַבְדְּךָ וַאֲמָתְךָ וּבְהֶמְתֶּךָ וְגֵרְךָ אֲשֶׁר
בִּשְׁעָרֶיךָ:

The seventh day should be a Shabbat for Hashem your God, do not perform any *melacha*... (*Shemot* 20:10)

The Torah describes Hashem's Creation of the world as *melacha*, from which He rested when completing the world on Shabbat. Obviously, then, it cannot refer to physical labor, which is not relevant to God. As Rav Hirsch explains:

> The word *"melacha"* appears two hundred times in Scripture and never once refers to physical labor. The *melacha* that is forbidden on Shabbat is conceived as the execution of an intelligent purpose by the practical skill of man: i.e., any production, creation, or transforming an object for human purposes; but not physical exertion.
> Even if you tired yourself out the whole day, as long as you produced nothing within the meaning of the term *melacha*, as long as your activity has not been a constructive exercise of your intelligence, you have produced no *melacha*. On the other hand, if you have engendered, without the slightest exertion, even the smallest change in an object for human purposes, then you have profaned the Shabbat, and undermined your calling as a Jew ... (*Horeb* 21:24)

Thus, while *melacha* is generally translated as "work," it in fact refers to creative, transformative activities in the physical realm. Actions on Shabbat that may be simple to perform can still be classified as *"melachot"* if they entail creative, physical activity. The same way Hashem rested on the first Shabbat of Creation, we rest from our creative activities on Shabbat.

The Torah identifies the activities that qualify as "*melacha*" in using the same term to refer to the activities performed in the construction of the *Mishkan*, the Tabernacle in the wilderness. After the commandment to build the *Mishkan*, the Torah states that one must nevertheless observe Shabbat:

וַיֹּאמֶר ה' אֶל מֹשֶׁה לֵּאמֹר: וְאַתָּה דַּבֵּר אֶל בְּנֵי יִשְׂרָאֵל לֵאמֹר אַךְ אֶת שַׁבְּתֹתַי תִּשְׁמֹרוּ כִּי אוֹת הִוא בֵּינִי וּבֵינֵיכֶם
לְדֹרֹתֵיכֶם לָדַעַת כִּי אֲנִי ה' מְקַדִּשְׁכֶם:

Hashem said to Moshe saying: And you speak to the children of Israel saying: But my Shabbatot you must safeguard, as it is a sign between Me and you to know that I am Hashem who sanctifies you. (*Shemot* 31:12-13)

In their commentaries, Rashi and the Rashbam explain that the Torah thereby indicates that any *melacha* necessary for building the *Mishkan* is prohibited on Shabbat.

The activities that were actually performed in the *Mishkan* are referred to as *avot melacha*, but because the Torah does not present a list of those *melachot*, but rather only the general principle that we should not perform any *melacha* on Shabbat, all activities that perform creative functions are prohibited on Shabbat as well. We refer to these actions as *toladot*.

Every *melacha* has two components:

1. *Ma'aseh hamelacha* – the act that was performed in the *Mishkan* (the *av melacha*)
2. *Melechet machshevet* – the creative purpose of the act that was performed in the *Mishkan*

Any act that achieves the same goal and purpose as the *av melacha* through an alternate action is referred to as a *tolada*. Both *avot* and *toladot* are prohibited *mideoraita* (Biblically) on Shabbat.

For example, in the *Mishkan*, the *melacha* performed was planting wheat kernels, and that therefore constitutes an *av melacha*. Every other form of advancing growth, such as watering plants (and even putting seeds in water outside of the ground), is a *tolada* and is also Biblically prohibited.

Avot and *Toladot* on *Shevi'it*

Based on the comparison between *shevi'it* and Shabbat, we can now reformulate our original question: When the Torah prohibited these four *melachot* during *shevi'it*, were they mentioned as *avot melacha*, thereby including in the negative commandment all similar acts that achieve the same goals as *toladot*? Or are only these specific actions prohibited, meaning that the Torah did not extend the *avot* and *toladot* model to *shevi'it*? In the *gemara*'s formulation (*Mo'ed Katan* 3a): Did the Torah prohibit both *avot* and *toladot* on *shevi'it*, or only *avot*?

The *gemara* there first cites Abaye's view that the explicitly prohibited acts are general categories of prohibited farming that include other acts of promoting growth or normal harvesting. However, Rava offers a different approach:

רָבָא אָמַר אָבוֹת אָסַר רַחֲמָנָא תּוֹלָדוֹת לָא אָסַר רַחֲמָנָא
Rava states: ... The Torah prohibited *avot*, but it did not prohibit *toladot*.

As proof of his assertion, Rava notes that if the Torah viewed the four explicit prohibitions as *avot* that include *toladot*, there would have been no need to mention the same types of activities in field and in the vineyard. We would have learned that harvesting a vineyard is prohibited from the fact that harvesting a field is prohibited! The fact that the Torah mentions the parallel activities in a vineyard indicates that only the specific actions mentioned are prohibited.

> מִכְּדֵי זְמִירָה בְּכָלַל זְרִיעָה וּבְצִירָה בְּכָלַל קְצִירָה לְמַאי הִלְכְתָא כַּתְבִינְהוּ רַחֲמָנָא לְמֵימְרָא דְּאַהָנֵי תּוֹלָדוֹת
> מִיחַיֵּיב אַאַחְרָנְיָיתָא לָא מִיחַיֵּיב
>
> Since pruning is a kind of sowing, and grape-gathering a kind of reaping, what law did the Merciful One desire to include by writing these [derivative acts]? To indicate that only for these derivative acts [specified in the text] is one held liable; and for any other [derivative process] one is not held liable.

The issue at hand in this discussion is not whether additional activities are permitted during *shevi'it* or not; all opinions agree they are not. Rather, the question is whether activities that achieve the same goals as the *avot melacha* are prohibited as *mitzvot lo ta'aseh min haTorah* (Biblical prohibitions) or as Rabbinic prohibitions (or possibly something in between, as we will see). The activities that would fall in this disputed category include watering plants or seedlings, trimming or pruning dry branches of a tree to help it grow better, fertilizing the soil, cutting weeds, and fumigating crops to kill insects.

Distinguishing Between Shabbat and *Shevi'it*

According to Rava – who maintains that additional *melachot* that serve the same purpose as the *avot melacha* are not prohibited as *toladot* – why doesn't the *avot/toladot* model apply to *shevi'it*? After all, *shevi'it* is referred to as *shabbat ha'aretz*, why wouldn't any agricultural activities that impede the land's rest be included?

The simple explanation is that the Torah presents the two "*shabbatot*" differently. The weekly Shabbat is a day when we, much like Hashem did after six days of Creation, cease from all *melacha*. The Torah issues a general command, "לֹא תַעֲשֶׂה כָל מְלָאכָה," and does not delineate specific actions that are prohibited. All *melachot*, creative, transformative physical activities, are prohibited. Those performed in the *Mishkan* are the archetypical *avot melachot* and other acts that achieve the same purpose in a different manner are Biblically prohibited as *Toladot*.

Regarding *shevi'it*, in contrast, the Torah mentions four (possibly five) agricultural activities that are prohibited, without ever referencing a general prohibition of *melacha*. This seems to indicate that the Torah seeks to prohibit only the specific actions listed.

Rav Hirsch offers a significant rationale to distinguish between the overarching Shabbat prohibitions and the more limited *Shevi'it* ones:

> The prohibition of labor on Shabbat does not apply only to *avot*, but also to *toladot*. However, the prohibition of working the land during *shemitta* applies only to the labors specified in the Torah: sowing, pruning, harvesting. This difference between *shevi'it* and Shabbat is based on the difference between their meanings. Shabbat

expresses the surrender to God, who is the Creator of the world and its King, and man is subservient to God, who rules the whole universe with His powers. Man rests from creative action through his acknowledgement of Creation. Of course, all creative physical activity is considered forbidden labor on Shabbat. Any difference between *avot* and *toladot* is merely a formality.

In contrast, *shemitta* expresses the surrender to God, in that the Land of Israel is in His possession, and for that purpose, one subjugates his land to the rule of God. The Jewish man recognizes that his land belongs to God, and he is merely a sojourner with God. In that moment, he does not work his field and does not gather his produce in order to ensure its existence. And when he refrains from sowing and pruning- and when he refrains from harvesting the fruit that grew on its own to bring to his home- still his land does not provide his food in that year, and it is found that the seal of lack of ownership on produce exists across the entire land. And that entire year it is publicly announced that Israel is not the master of the land. (Rav Hirsch, Commentary on *Vayikra* 25:4)

Indeed, the difference between Shabbat and *shevi'it* is so blatant that it calls into question the use of the terminology of *avot* and *toladot* regarding *shevi'it* altogether.

The terms *avot* and *toladot* are used by *Chazal* in a number of disparate contexts: Shabbat, *shevi'it*, *avoda zara*, and monetary damages. Rav Moshe Taragin (VBM, Shevi'it Series 1) summarizes Rav Aharon Lichtenstein's explanation for when the terms are appropriate. He notes that the common denominator of all the cases where the *Avot/ toladot* models appear involves instances where specific forbidden acts are prohibited for a broader purpose. They involve an affront to the *kedusha* (sanctity) that underlies the system behind the prohibitions:

A violation of Shabbat is not just a forbidden act; it also entails an attack upon the over-arching *kedusha* of Shabbat and *Am Yisrael*. This aspect of Shabbat – the *kedusha* which permeates the seventh day – has a definite *halachic* impact too. Violation of Shabbat defines someone as a *nochri* (gentile), since his actions carry broader implications – the reduction of the *kedusha* of Shabbat and of his own personal *kedusha* as a Jew. Thus, the act is forbidden not merely because Hashem defined it as "*assur*," but also because its violation damages a broader system or framework. Consequently, not only is the "*ma'aseh*" (action) forbidden, but also the "*totza'a*" (result). In this case, then, *toladot*, which are slightly different actions achieving the same net result, should also be forbidden. For instance, if the Torah forbade baking as an *av* on Shabbat partially because it profanes the holiness of Shabbat, then its *tolada*, cooking, should be forbidden as well. Had only the act of baking *per se* been forbidden, we would have no right to extend it to cooking, which is similar but not identical to baking. However, since the prohibition is based partly upon the consequences of the act and the resulting damage to the holiness of the day, we might allow expansions. After all, cooking is similar to baking and seems to damage the *kedushat Shabbat* in the very same manner...

This could also be claimed about *shemitta*, which is referred to as "*shabbat laHashem*" and is considered to be a form of Shabbat (*kedushat hazman*). The overall holiness of

Shabbat Ha-aretz- The Halachot of the Land's Rest

> the seventh year is denigrated by working during *shemitta*. Thus, only when the result comprises an integral part of the *issur* can a *tolada* be forbidden...
>
> In summation, we might justify the existence of *toladot* in areas of *halacha* in which the general consequences, and not just the inherent act, comprise part of the prohibition.

Essentially, *shevi'it* like Shabbat, is a *mitzvah* whose sum is much greater than its parts. There is a clear goal – ensuring that the land rests – and the prohibitions stem from this. This explains why *Chazal* use the terminology of *avot* and *toladot* for *shevi'it* despite its apparent inapplicability due to the Torah's formulation of the prohibitions in an explicit rather than overarching manner.

Although we accept Rava's position that the Torah's formulation of the *shevi'it* prohibitions indicates that only the explicitly mentioned acts are prohibited as *melachot*, that doesn't mean all other acts are permitted. Any agricultural activity not prohibited *min haTorah* will at the very least be rabbinically restricted. Although fulfilling these enactments may demand additional *gevura*, the rabbinic restrictions actually ensure that the spirit of the law is maintained alongside the letter of the law of *shevi'it*. The Torah indicates that the seventh year is meant to be a year of refraining from normal agricultural processes to ensure that one can devote the period for the spiritual and character growth that it allows for its adherents.

Alternatively, even if other agricultural activities are not prohibitions, they still might be prohibited Biblically through the *mitzvat aseh*, positive commandments, requiring *shevita*, rest, and/or *shemitta*, relinquishing.

The Positive Commandments of *Shevi'it*

We have noted that there are two positive commandments associated with *shevi'it*, "*veshavta ha'aretz*"/ *Shabbaton* and "*tismitena untashta*." These *mitzvot aseh* parallel the positive command of "*tishbot*"/ *Shabbaton* regarding our weekly Shabbat observance. One who performs a *melacha* on Shabbat violates both a negative prohibition and this *mitzvat aseh*.

Regarding both Shabbat and shevi'it, there is a dispute about whether the mitzvat aseh merely reiterates the need to rest from prohibited melacha on Shabbat and shevi'it putting an overall positive spin on the goal of the cessation of *melacha*, or adds additional prohibitions as well. According to the first view, the *mitzvat aseh* does not require additional forms of rest, but simply indicates the Torah's goal for the day or year, which drives *Chazal*'s establishment of additional rabbinic prohibitions to ensure that the spirit of the law is maintained. According to the latter view, however, the *mitzvot aseh* instruct us that we are supposed to rest from any activities that would compromise our weekly Shabbat rest or the land's rest during *shevi'it*. Proponents of this view argue that according to Rava, additional growth-enhancing activities are prohibited on *shevi'it* not due to rabbinic enactments, but rather due to the *mitzvot aseh* of *shevi'it*. In this view, those prohibitions are not *mitzvot lo ta'aseh*, and are therefore not punishable by *malkot*, but they do entail Biblical – and not Rabbinic – prohibitions.

This idea is accepted by the *Aruch HaShulchan* (*HeAtid* 19:3) and is expressed powerfully by Rav Moshe Feinstein (*Iggerot Moshe YD* 5:47), who agrees to the general principle that the *mitzvat aseh* is more expansive and that when the *gemara* limited the scope of the Biblical prohibitions, it was referring only to the *mitzvot lo ta'aseh*.

A deeper understanding of the interplay between rabbinic restrictions and Biblical *mitzvot* should help us concretize a clear understanding of the relationship between the various prohibitions of *shevi'it*.

Understanding Rabbinic Restrictions

The Torah explicitly deputizes the Sages to enact rabbinic laws and restrictions in order to ensure that a number of goals are maintained. Although these enactments may appear cumbersome and restrictive, they serve an essential function.

The Torah instructs our Sages to make enactments to protect the Torah:

רַב אַשִׁי אָמַר: וּשְׁמַרְתֶּם אֶת מִשְׁמַרְתִּי - עֲשׂוּ מִשְׁמֶרֶת לְמִשְׁמַרְתִּי.

Rav Ashi said: "And safeguard My commandments" (*Vayikira* 18:30) – make a protection for My commandments. (*Mo'ed Katan* 5a)

Chazal must safeguard the Torah by developing enactments that will protect it. As the Men of the Great Assembly instruct in the first *mishna* in *Pirkei Avot*: "וְעֲשׂוּ סְיָג לַתּוֹרָה," "Make a fence around the Torah." Just as a fence around a vegetable patch protects what is inside and indicates the value ascribed to what is inside (see Rabbeinu Yonah's commentary ad loc.), *Chazal* both protected and showed their love and appreciation of *mitzvot* through their restrictive fences.

At times, Rabbinic enactments serve an equally important role – ensuring that the spirit of the law is maintained, not only the letter of the law. Often, the Torah prohibits specific actions with the goal that we inculcate the overall lessons of the prohibitions and refrain from additional activities in order to enable us to reach that goal. When the Torah's letter of the law expresses an underlying spirit, the Sages ensure that we don't lose sight of the spirit.

In turn, the community is commanded to abide by the rulings of Chazal:

כִּי יִפָּלֵא מִמְּךָ דָבָר לַמִּשְׁפָּט בֵּין דָּם לְדָם בֵּין דִּין לְדִין וּבֵין נֶגַע לָנֶגַע דִּבְרֵי רִיבֹת בִּשְׁעָרֶיךָ וְקַמְתָּ וְעָלִיתָ אֶל הַמָּקוֹם אֲשֶׁר יִבְחַר ה' אֱלֹהֶיךָ בּוֹ: וּבָאתָ אֶל הַכֹּהֲנִים הַלְוִיִּם וְאֶל הַשֹּׁפֵט אֲשֶׁר יִהְיֶה בַּיָּמִים הָהֵם וְדָרַשְׁתָּ וְהִגִּידוּ לְךָ אֵת דְּבַר הַמִּשְׁפָּט: וְעָשִׂיתָ עַל פִּי הַדָּבָר אֲשֶׁר יַגִּידוּ לְךָ מִן הַמָּקוֹם הַהוּא אֲשֶׁר יִבְחַר ה' וְשָׁמַרְתָּ לַעֲשׂוֹת כְּכֹל אֲשֶׁר יוֹרוּךָ: עַל פִּי הַתּוֹרָה אֲשֶׁר יוֹרוּךָ וְעַל הַמִּשְׁפָּט אֲשֶׁר יֹאמְרוּ לְךָ תַּעֲשֶׂה לֹא תָסוּר מִן הַדָּבָר אֲשֶׁר יַגִּידוּ לְךָ יָמִין וּשְׂמֹאל: וְהָאִישׁ אֲשֶׁר יַעֲשֶׂה בְזָדוֹן לְבִלְתִּי שְׁמֹעַ אֶל הַכֹּהֵן הָעֹמֵד לְשָׁרֶת שָׁם אֶת ה' אֱלֹהֶיךָ אוֹ אֶל הַשֹּׁפֵט וּמֵת הָאִישׁ הַהוּא וּבִעַרְתָּ הָרָע מִיִּשְׂרָאֵל: וְכָל הָעָם יִשְׁמְעוּ וְיִרָאוּ וְלֹא יְזִידוּן עוֹד:

If theres hould arise a matter too hard for you in judgment, between blood and blood, between plea and plea, and between lesion and lesion, matters of controversy within your gates; then you shall arise and go up to the place which Hashem your God shall choose. And you shall come to the priests, the Levites, and to the judge that shall be in those days; and you shall inquire; and they shall declare unto you the sentence of judgment. **And you shall do according to the sentence, which they shall declare unto you from that place which Hashem shall choose; and you shall observe to do according to all that they shall teach you. According to the law which they shall teach you, and according to the judgment which they shall tell you, you shall do; you shall not turn aside from the sentence which they shall declare unto you, to the right, nor to the left.** And the man who acts illicitly, in not obeying the priest that stands to minister there before Hashem your God or unto the judge, that man shall die; and you shall eliminate the evil from Israel. And all the people shall hear, and fear, and cease to act illicitly. (*Devarim* 17:8-13)

Thus, abiding by the enactments of *Chazal* is actually the fulfillment of a Biblical commandment[139]. For this reason, we recite a *bracha* indicating a divine command when performing Rabbinically-enacted *mitzvot*, such as lighting the Chanukah *menora* and reading the *Megilla* on Purim:

מַאי מְבָרֵךְ? מְבָרֵךְ אֲשֶׁר קִדְּשָׁנוּ בְּמִצְוֹתָיו וְצִוָּנוּ לְהַדְלִיק נֵר שֶׁל חֲנֻכָּה. וְהֵיכָן צִוָּנוּ? רַב אַוְיָא אָמַר: מִלֹּא תָסוּר .

What blessing does one make? One blesses "who sanctified us with His commandments and commanded us to light a Chanukah candle." And where were we commanded? Rav Avya said: From "do not turn away" (*Devarim* 17:11). (*Shabbat* 23a)

Although the Torah empowers the Sages to make enactments, it requires that we clearly differentiate between Rabbinic and Biblical obligations. Regarding scope, Biblical prohibitions generally apply even in pressing situations, barring danger to life. On the other hand, Rabbinic prohibitions often have built-in leniencies in circumstances of loss and the like. If the Torah did not prohibit a particular activity but left it to the Sages to ensure that we refrain from it, that indicates that the prohibition should not apply under all circumstances.

The *Mitzvah* of *Shabbaton* for Shabbat and *Shevi'it*

In the context of Shabbat and *shevi'it*, Rabbinic enactments further advance the goal of "*shabbaton.*" This term is used to describe the year in *Parashat Behar* (*Vayikra* 25:4), and it is similarly used in the context of Shabbat and the Festivals in *Parashat Emor*. The Torah repeatedly describes Shabbat as a day of "*shabbaton*" and commands a *mitzvat aseh* of "*Tishbot*", rest. One who performs *melacha* on Shabbat violates not only the prohibition of "*Lo ta'aseh kol melacha*", do not perform *melacha*, but also a positive mitzvah of resting on Shabbat (Rambam Hilchot Shabbat 1:1).

A number of authorities explain that this *mitzvat aseh* of *Shabbaton* is more expansive than the prohibition, as it includes acts that don't fit the *melacha* classifications. The Ramban (*Vayikra* 23:24) explains that *Shabbaton* injects a spirit into the Shabbat experience. He notes that many acts not prohibited as *melacha* will nevertheless prevent one from focusing on Shabbat. He illustrates this by pointing out that a store-

---

139 This is clearly the understanding of the Rambam (Hilchot Mamrim ch. 1) who equates *Beit Din HaGadol's* interpretive role (as explicitly derived in the pesukim) with its legislative role. The Ramban takes issue with the Rambam's understanding (see *Shorashim l'Sefer HaMitzvot* 1).

owner well-versed in *Halacha* could operate his business on Shabbat more or less going about his regular weekday practice while being careful not to perform *melacha*. He would be engrossed in thinking about what to buy and sell, but would ensure a non-Jewish assistant performed any *melacha* acts. The Ramban explains that while this individual would not be in violation of *lo ta'aseh kol melacha*, he would be robbing himself of the Shabbat spirit, and the day of rest it seeks. The Ramban explains that the *mitzvah* of *"shabbaton,"* is a *mitzvat aseh* which requires that beyond refraining from *melacha*, one must cease one's normal activities – disconnecting from habitual labor for a day of mindfulness and purpose: We are commanded by the Torah to rest … by abstaining even from activities that do not constitute *melacha*, rather than exerting oneself the whole day… measuring grain, weighing fruits and gifts, filling barrels with wine, moving utensils and stones from house to house and place to place. … None of this involves *melacha*. The Torah therefore demands *shabbaton*, a day of cessation and rest, and not a day of exertion.

The Ramban adds that if this were not true, one could make a mockery of Shabbat, through careful selection of his actions:

And if it were a walled city with its doors locked at night, they would load wine, grapes and figs onto the donkeys and bring all types of cargo on Yom Tov, and the market would be fully open for all transactions. Stores would be open, storekeepers would sell, money-changers would sit at their tables with their gold coins in front of them, and laborers would arise early for work and hire themselves out for these and similar jobs like during the week. This is [otherwise] permissible on Yom Tov, and even on Shabbat itself, for none of this involves *melakha*. The Torah therefore said *shabbaton* – it should be a day of cessation [from activity] and rest, and not a day of exertion.

Based on this understanding, the Ramban explains that this *mitzvat aseh* of *Shabbaton* actually prohibits many of the usually thought to be rabbinic prohibitions known as *Issurei Shevut*, (*"Shevut"* prohibitions). When the Torah prohibited *melacha* it also set the guidelines for what activity is inappropriate for Shabbat. The *mitzvat aseh* of *Shabbaton* teaches that the Torah requires everyone to maintain that spirit by refraining from actions that negate this spirit, even when not classified as actual *melacha*.

The notion that *Shevut* are not just rabbinic prohibitions but actually violate the *mitzvat aseh* of *Shabbaton*, appears in other sources as well. The Ritva (*Rosh HaShana 32b*) cites this as a "pearl from the Ramban", and the Aruch Ha-Shulchan summarizes:

The Ritva wrote in the name of the Ramban that there is a tradition in our hands that the *shevutim* of Shabbat are not like other rabbinical prohibitions, but rather they are like Torah prohibitions… The primary essence of the matter is that the Torah declared liability for stoning for performing biblically defined *Melacha*, and the Torah did not declare liability for stoning for performing *Shevut* prohibitions. However, a *Shevut* prohibition is indeed a full prohibition, to be equated with the biblical prohibitions.

When do *Shevut* acts constitute Biblical violations and when are they only rabbinic? If the basis for prohibition is really Biblical, why doesn't the Torah specify these acts among the prohibited *melachot*?

A popular understanding of the Ramban (expressed explicitly by Rav Yaakov Ariel, *BiOhala Shel Torah* 5:23) is that one who performs one *Shevut* act only violates a rabbinic prohibition, as they are still overall maintaining the *Shabbat* experience. However, one who repeatedly performs such acts, and treats Shabbat ostensibly as a weekday, only refraining from actual *melacha*, they have totally undermined Shabbat's spirit and violate the Biblical prohibition of *Shabbaton*.

Addtionally, the Torah's model for a general *mitzvat aseh* and specific *mitzvot lo ta'aseh* actually enables ideal fulfillment of Shabbat with some leeway in extenuating circumstances. A *melacha* explicitly prohibited by the Torah is almost never permitted, barring extreme circumstances. On the other hand, the general *mitzvat aseh* describes an overarching goal of rest, and it includes additional actions when they detract from this goal. These acts, generally viewed as Rabbinic bans, fall in the parameters of the Biblical prohibition only when they detract from the spirit of the period, and the latitude is therefore much greater. *Melachot* are prohibited acts; the Rabbinic restrictions are acts banned for a purpose, and therefore are at times permitted when that goal is not compromised.

Shabbaton During *Shevi'it*

As mentioned, a similar *mitzvat aseh* of *shabbaton* is mentioned in the Torah regarding *shevi'it* as well. Indeed, the Ramban notes that the formulation of *shabbaton* found in *Parashat Behar* expands the prohibitions of *shevi'it* just as it does on Shabbat:

> The Torah prohibits labor on Shabbat through a negative commandment punishable by excision and death and prohibits exertion and toil on Shabbat through this positive *mitzvah* [of *shabbaton*] ... Similarly [regarding *shevi'it*, the Torah states], "There shall be a *shabbat shabbaton* for the land" (*Vayikra* 25:4), a sabbath of rest, that one should not plow or work the field at all ... (ibid.)

The same way the Ramban understands the positive command of shabbaton on Shabbat should apply to shevi'it. Just as *shabbaton* provides the mandate for the Sages to delineate *issurei Shevut*, the types of actions that detract from the spirit of Shabbat, a similar model would apply to the Rabbinic restrictions of *shevi'it* as well. Similar to Shabbat, beyond the explicit prohibitions delineated in the Torah regarding *Shevi'it*, the Torah also indicates that Shevi'it must be a *Shabbaton* and requires *ve'shavta ha'aretz Shabbat LaHashem*, that the land rest. In other words, the acts prohibited by the Sages are essentially mandated by the Torah's positive requirement that the seventh year be a period of *shabbaton*.

Like *Shabbat*, where the *melachot* are almost never permitted but the *Shevut* prohibitions may not apply in some extenuating circumstances, *shevi'it* would be no different. The general *mitzvat aseh* describes an overarching goal of the land resting, and it includes additional actions when they detract from this goal. These acts are rabbinically banned on a one-time basis but included in the Biblical prohibition when they detract from *shevi'it's* overal spirit of the land resting. Banned for a purpose, at times they will be permitted when that goal is not compromised.

Rav Avraham Yitzchak HaKohein Kook explicitly links the *mitzvah* of *shabbaton* in reference to *shevi'it* to the Ramban's understanding of the term regarding Shabbat.

> The fact that there is no negative commandment prohibiting any field activities other than those explicitly mentioned in the Torah… only refers to instances in which someone would perform other agricultural activities on a non-constant basis. However, if one were to work the field on a constant basis as one does every other year, only refraining from those *melachot* which are explicitly prohibited in the Torah, one would nevertheless violate the positive *mitzvah* of *shevita*, which is a *mitzvah* [explicit] in the Torah. (*Shabbat HaAretz Kuntres Acharon 7*)

Rav Kook explains that there is clearly a positive commandment prohibiting normal field activity and treating *shevi'it* as any other agricultural year, even if one refrains from the explicit prohibitions of planting or harvesting. This *mitzvah* of *Shabbaton* ensures that one maintains the spirit and grasps the unique message of *shevi'it*. It also sets the guidelines for what additional acts should be prohibited for undermining *shevi'it's* spirit. These additional "rabbinic" prohibitions will be prohibited rabbinically on a one-time basis and Biblically prohibited when done consistently, subverting the overall purpose of *shevi'it*. This also provides leeway for permitting some of these activities in extenuating circumstances, as we will see.

Veshavta Ha'aretz- Rest for the Land or for the Individual

It is notable that the Torah's formulation of the positive *mitzvah* of agricultural rest during *shevi'it* – "*veshavta ha'aretz*" – is ambiguous:

דַּבֵּר אֶל בְּנֵי יִשְׂרָאֵל וְאָמַרְתָּ אֲלֵהֶם כִּי תָבֹאוּ אֶל הָאָרֶץ אֲשֶׁר אֲנִי נֹתֵן לָכֶם וְשָׁבְתָה הָאָרֶץ שַׁבָּת לַה': … וּבַשָּׁנָה הַשְּׁבִיעִת שַׁבַּת שַׁבָּתוֹן יִהְיֶה לָאָרֶץ שַׁבָּת לַה' …

When you come to the land which I shall give you, the land shall rest (*ve-shaveta ha-aretz*) a sabbath to God… in the seventh year the land shall have a sabbath of complete rest, (*Shabbat Shabbaton*) a sabbath to God… it shall be a year of complete rest for the land. (*Vayikra 25:2, 4*)

Is there a *mitzvah* that man let the land rest, or there is a *mitzvah* requiring that the land itself rest?[140] The entire idea of a *mitzvah* of rest incumbent upon the land is somewhat

---

140 A similar question pertains to other aspects of *shevi'it* as well. Is the Torah describing the situation that must be created, or is it instructing man what he must personally do? This question pertains to the obligation of *hefker*, releasing ownership of the produce of one's field during *shevi'it*. Does the *mitzvah* fall upon each person to actively declare his *shevi'it*-produce ownerless, or does it require that we actively recognize that God has repudiated all private ownership of produce during this year? A similar question is asked regarding the financial *shemitta*. Does the Torah cancel the rights of collection for all loans, no matter whether the lender is interested or not, or is it the

difficult to understand. How can an inanimate object fulfill a *mitzvah*? Although the Torah describes *Eretz Yisrael* as a living organism, only humans can fulfill *mitzvot*. Thus, to rephrase the question: Is it man's obligation to refrain from working the land, or is it incumbent upon him to ensure that the land doesn't produce?

This question is not merely academic, as it has both legal and philosophical ramifications. If the land must rest – which seems to be the implication of the *pasuk* – then even if man is not personally involved in encouraging growth, there might be reason to prevent allowing plants to grow!

Ibn Ezra refers to this question:

> It is a *mitzvah* upon the Jew not to allow a stranger to plant during the seventh year, the same way in which one must not let the stranger under one's control perform labor on Shabbat. (*Ibn Ezra, Vayikra* 25:2)

According to Ibn Ezra, the land itself must rest. Man's obligation is to ensure that no one under his control works the land.

This question of whom the *mitzvah* addresses, the man or the land (or both), is the subject of a dispute related to a discussion in the *gemara* (*Avoda Zara* 15a) involving the Torah's instruction to allow one's animal to rest on Shabbat (*Shemot* 23:12). The Talmud cryptically compares the *mitzvah* of animal rest on Shabbat with the *mitzvah* of agricultural rest during Shemitta. *Tosafot Rid* (*Avoda Zara* 15b) explains that the laws of *shevi'it* require that a Jew's field rest[141]; it is not sufficient that man refrain personally from working the land. *Tosafot* (ad loc.) and others, however, explain the passage differently, without employing the radical idea that Jewish land must rest.

Both understandings emerge from an apparent contradiction in the Rambam's formulation of this *mitzvah*. In his introduction to *Hilchot Shemitta*, he writes:

> The land should rest during the seventh year from its *melacha*.

In the actual laws, however, he states:

> There is a positive commandment to rest from working the land and working the trees during the seventh year, as it says: "*Veshavta ha'aretz …*" (*Hilchot Shemitta* 1:1)

The simplest explanation of the Rambam's view is that both ideas are correct. The *mitzvah* is in fact that the land must rest, but that *mitzvah* is accomplished by man, ensuring that no work is done in the field. In essence, *shevi'it* calls for a partnership between man and the land.

Rav Kook illustrates the significance of this question:

> Some say that even if a non-Jew works in a Jew's field, the Jew is considered to be violating the commandment of the land's sabbath… since the Torah associated the sabbath with the land, as is stated, "The land shall rest a sabbath to God." Whether it

---

obligation of a lender to cancel the loan?

141 Much has been written on this subject, including various interpretations of the Tosafot Rid's exact opinion. See *Minchat Asher Shevi'is*.

is a Jew or a non-Jew who labors to cultivate the land, therefore, does not matter...
Others, meanwhile, take the position that one may allow his land to be cultivated by
a non-Jew. (*Shabbat Ha-Aretz* 1;1)

This point has significant implications. First of all, if the *mitzvah* is not only incumbent
upon one's own personal soil but even that of others (and maybe even non-Jews), then
the entire basis for permitting the agricultural development of land when sold to non-Jews
would be voided, as one must make sure that even non-Jews do not work the soil of the
land of Eretz Yisrael during *shevi'it*.

The *Minchat Chinuch* (112) points out several other practical ramifications for this
question: Is it permissible to plant before *shevi'it* if the seeds will take root during *shevi'it*?
May one hire non-Jewish workers to cultivate a field during *shevi'it*? Is one permitted to
use a pre-programmed watering system?

An interesting ramification of this debate was discussed in modern times when the idea
arose of planting through a *gerama* device. This mechanism essentially separates an
individual's action from its result by employing a separate microprocessor. If one uses
such a device, he does not directly perform the agricultural activity, but is responsible for
the result, as due to him, the land did not rest. Although the *Aruch HaShulchan* (*HeAtid*
19:6) permits *melacha* performed through *gerama* during *shevi'it*, Rav Tzvi Pesach Frank
prohibits it, as it violates the land's *shabbat*[142].

A Message to the Entire Nation

The extent of the *mitzvat aseh* of *shevi'it* is also relevant to the question of who it addresses
– the entire nation or only the individual farmer. Rav Yerucham Fishel Perla argues that
according to the Behag, the *mitzvah* is for every individual in all of *Eretz Yisrael* to make
sure that that the land rests:

> The Behag and those who follow him omitted the positive command of the land
> resting during *shevi'it*... It seems that their understanding is that the *aseh* is derived
> from the *pasuk*'s instruction that the land rest... and, therefore, it applies to every
> individual, not only on his own field, but on the entire land, as it doesn't say " you
> must rest your [singular] land." Therefore, one is obligated not only regarding himself,
> but regarding others as well. As the *gemara* states: "Man is commanded that the land
> rest during *shevi'it*" (*Avoda Zara* 15b), i.e., even having someone else work his land
> is a violation of this law. Thus, this *mitzvah* applies to all of the Jewish People, for it
> applies to all the fields of Israel, and it applies to everyone for their own work as well
> as the work of others.
>
> Thus, the Behag and those who follow him reason that this law is one of the laws that

---

142 "Even if you say that *gerama* is not included in the negative commandment [of "you shall not sow"] because
the Torah forbids [only] the act of planting, and here he is merely the indirect cause [of planting], one can still
claim that it violates the positive commandment of *"veshavta ha'aretz,"* even though it is only the indirect cause
[of planting]... For one is required to ensure that his field rests, so that even if he is only the indirect cause of his
land being worked... he has not fulfilled the positive commandment of *"ve-shavta ha-aretz."*" (*Har Tzvi, Zera'im*
2:32–34). See also Har Tzvi OC 208.

> are commanded to the public, and it is therefore not counted among the positive commandments that apply to each individual on his own, but rather among the select laws that apply to the entire public. (*Commentary on Rav Saadia Gaon's Sefer HaMitzvot*, positive command 64)

This understanding helps us appreciate the Torah's message. *Shevi'it* is not only for the farmer, every Jew is connected to the land, and everyone shares the responsibility to ensure it rests. In a similar vein, Rav Yisrael Zev Mintzberg discusses how those who do not own fields can fulfill the positive command of *shevi'it*:

> The prohibitions of *shemitta* are conveyed in the second person ("do not sow and do not harvest"), but the *aseh* of the land resting is written in the third person, as it is commanded of all of Israel, for whom it is incumbent to strengthen those who wish to rest in the seventh year from their work in the fields and to fulfill the law and to assist the workers who earn from their labor in the fields of others to find other work or to support them financially during this year, so that they may engage in Torah study and divine service. (*Peirot Shevi'it* 10)

This understanding indicates that the *mitzvat aseh* addresses the non-farmer just as much as the farmer. The Torah insists that everyone does his share in ensuring the land's rest, including finding alternative means of sustenance for the farmers.

For some, that means offering financial support to those who observe *shevi'it*. This can be done in a number of ways. One, is the initiative known as *Keren HaShevi'is*, a fund for non-farmers to donate money to support *shevi'it* observant farmers. There are other initiatives where individuals buy areas of farmland from the farmers to both help support them while at the same time fulfilling the *mitzvah* of letting their land rest. Others feel that the best way to support *shevi'it* is through joining an *Otzar Beit Din* such as that of *Otzar HaAretz*.[143] No matter what, the *mitzvat aseh* of *v'shavta ha'aretz* requires that everyone of us take an active part in giving the land its rest, and hopefully using that time to connect to all of *shevi'it's* themes.

Tishmettena- Relinquish

We noted above that according to one view cited in Rashi, the *mitzvah* of "*tishmettena untashta*," the command to "abandon" the land, includes an obligation to refrain from specific *melachot*:

> "Rest" from full labor, such as plowing and sowing. "And lie fallow" – [refrain from] fertilizing and removing stones. (Rashi, *Shemot* 23:11)

The Ramban questions this comment, noting that the *gemara* concludes that the *melachot* mentioned by Rashi are prohibited Rabbinically, not Biblically.

The Maharal responds that Rashi understood the *gemara's* conclusion differently:

---

143 See chapter 26.

> The *gemara* (*Avoda Zara* 3a) refers to these *melachot* as being Rabbinically prohibited because the Torah granted the ability to the Sages to define which labors are prohibited and which are permitted, and therefore they are all Rabbinic. But this is all included in the Torah's instruction, "and lie fallow" – from all other *melachot*; it is simply that the details of which actions are prohibited and which are permitted were given to the Sages, and in that sense they are *miderabbanan*.
>
> This is similar to the prohibited *melachot* on *Chol HaMo'ed*, which the Torah forbids but were given to the Sages to determine, and they are considered *miderabbanan* (*Chagiga* 18a).
>
> Although the *gemara* indicates that the *pasuk* [of "*tishmittena untashta*"] is merely an *asmachta* (textual support), and we have argued that it is a proper derivation, it is considered an *asmachta* because there is no explicit mention of a specific *melacha*. Rashi does not mean that the *pasuk* explicitly refers to these *melachot*, but rather that the Sages taught that it refers to fertilizing and removing stones. (*Gur Aryeh, Shemot* 23:11)

Essentially, the Maharal explains that indeed Rashi agrees that additional agricultural prohibitions beyond those explicitly enumerated in the pesukim are rabbinically prohibited; however, while they are rabbinic in practice they are not rabbinic in origin. The Torah expressly required that one release their hold on their fields through an act of *tishmetenna*. The Torah deputized the Sages to provide the illustrations of which agricultural actions are prohibited and under what conditions. However, refraining from them fulfills one of the fundamental goals of the year, *shemitta*, releasing and relinquishing.

We have seen opinions that understand both *mitzvat asei* mentioned in the Torah regarding *shevi'it* observance as extending the *issur melacha* beyond the explicit prohibitions. Both *mitzvot aseh* of *Shabbaton* and *Tishmetenna* focus on the goal, rather than the specifics. "*Shevita*" and "*shemitta*" underscore the dual goals of *shevi'it* as a year of rest and relinquishing. When one physically rests from working the land, relinquishes his hold on it and its produce, one truly allows a year dedicated to Hashem.

The Practical Implications- The Perfect Balance

The Torah's model of four explicit prohibitions and overarching *mitzvot aseh* that call for limiting additional agricultural activities provides the perfect balance for maintaining the beauty of Eretz Yisrael while giving the land rest. The four prohibitions explicit in the Torah are essentially completely off limits for the seventh year. Refraining from planting and pruning prevents advancing the land but doesn't negatively impact the beauty of what already exists. For a year, alongside all the other goals of *shevi'it* which rest from the planting allows, farmers are free to develop the land in non-agricultural means. Building roads, terraces, and any other infrastructure is permitted and even advisable during the year.

On the other hand, the additional agricultural activities of the field are often absolutely necessary for ensuring the continued growth of that which has already been planted. The positive *mitzvot* of *shemitta*, releasing one's hold on the land, and *shevita*, letting the land rest, indicates that additional agricultural activities are inappropriate only when unnecessary. For this reason, either the *mitzvat aseh* restricts additional activities or guides the *rabbanan* to do so, but these prohibitions are dependent on circumstance.

The Gemara (Avoda Zara 50b) provides criterion for when these additional prohibitions are permitted. It asks:

> What is the underlying difference between *zihum* (treating a tree to protect it from worms) which is permitted and *gizum* (cutting dry branches) which is prohibited?

The Gemara answers:

> *Zihum* is done for U'kumei ilana, the preservation of the tree and is therefore permitted, whereas *gizum* is done for Avruyei ilana, to strengthen the tree, and is therefore prohibited.

The Gemara indicates that promoting new growth is prohibited, while maintaining the crops is permitted. Since only improving the growth is not permitted, a farmer or the owner of a garden would be allowed to remove weeds, water plants, mow the grass, etc. in situations where the field or garden would otherwise be ruined[144]. This is because Shemitta's calling is to refrain from planting new items, but the upkeep of what already exists is permitted.

Additionally, the Gemara Moed Katan (3a) indicates that the rabbinic restrictions of *shevi'it* were never prohibited in instances of *hefseid*, significant financial loss. There is a discussion if this is an alternative way of stating *leumkei*, maintaining is permitted, or this is an additional dispensation. According to Rashi (ad loc.), preventing loss is a reason to permit otherwise prohibited actions, while the Ritva (ad loc.) seems that only acts designated for stimulating growth were prohibited, while other acts were never included in the rabbinic prohibitions in the first place.

The Rationale- *Yishuv Eretz Yisrael*
The Rambam (*Hilchot Shemitta v'Yovel* 1:10) provides an explanation for why rabbinically restricted *melachot* are permitted when necessary to maintain growth.

> Why were all these activities allowed? For if he will not irrigate [the field], the land will become parched and all the trees in it will die. Since the prohibition against these activities and the like is Rabbinic in origin, they did not impose their decrees in these instances. For according to Scriptural Law, a prohibition applies only to the two primary categories and their two derivatives, as explained.

The Rambam notes that the intention of the laws of Shemitta was never that one not tend to the land at all, leaving all the crops to die. Not only would this ruin a person's fields

---

144 For the exact *halachic* parameters of when this is permitted please see Rav Rimon's *Shemitta* or other *halachic* works on the topic.

and possibly their permanent livelihood, but it would also destroy the beauty of the land of Israel. The Shemitta year is a year of refraining from promoting new growth, allowing one to focus on maintaining what they have, and seeking to grow their spiritual garden. The goal of the rabbinic additions is to ensure that the spirit of the law, *Shabbaton*, be maintained. *Yishuv Eretz Yisrael* will be advanced through infrastructure and developing the spiritual backbone of the country and its inhabitants.

Shevi'it observance will never destroy the beauty of *Eretz Yisrael* or leave the land desolate. Quite the contrary, *Eretz Yisrael* only became a wasteland when *shevi'it* wasn't properly observed, leading to the nation's exile and the land's barrenness. The two secrets to ensuring *Eretz Yisrael's* beauty during *shevi'it* involve learning the *halachot* and preparing in advance.

One who learns the *halachot* of *shevi'it* in-depth recognizes that they can perform just about all necessary agricultural needs throughout the year with proper preparation. In fact, this preparation involves really getting to know one's fields and gardens. Much of what people do in their gardens is actually detrimental. The time one takes to learn the needs of one's garden in order to limit one's gardening to the bare minimum actually ensures greater long-term growth and stability to the beauty of one's garden.

אָבוֹת וְתוֹלָדוֹת הָאֲסוּרוֹת בִּשְׁנַת הַשְּׁמִטָּה

אַב מְלָאכָה-דְּאוֹרָיְיתָא

שָׁלָב שֵׁנִי:	שָׁלָב רִאשׁוֹן:
שְׁפּוּר מַה שֶׁכְּבָר גָּדַל	הֲכָנַת הָאֲדָמָה לִזְרִיעָה

וְשָׁבְתָה הָאָרֶץ שַׁבָּת לַה'

תּוֹלָדוֹת-דְּרַבָּנָן

Acts of Promoting Growth | Promoting Tree Growth | Improving the Land | Cutting other branches

Improving לְאַבְרוּיֵי   Maintaining לְאוֹקְמֵי

Chapter 21

The *Mitzvah* of *Shemitta*

Having discussed Shabbat HaAretz, the agricultural halachot that impacts the land and the crops before the produce growing is available for consumption, we will now move on to the second area of agricultural *hilchot shevi'it, shemittat karka'ot*. This affects both the stage when produce is available on the trees as well as after it has been picked. These *halachot* affect the consumer almost as much as the farmer and are relevant for all those in *Eretz Yisrael* (and beyond).

❶	❷	❸	❹
The Land Before Planting	**The Land During the Growing Season**	**The Vegetation and Crops While Growing (on trees or in the ground)**	**The Produce After it is Harvested**

Shabbat HaAretz

Shemittat Karka'ot

For six out of seven years the farmer is involved in *yishuv Eretz Yisrael*, cultivating the land and beautifying it. Imagine a farmer who has toiled to plant and harvest.

It has been a challenging year of storms, natural disasters, sickness, but "he" has persevered. The harvesting season has arrived, and he is all too excited to pick the fruits. In comes someone he doesn't know, he is on a backpacking trip cross country, he tells his friend "I told you there was no need to waste any of our money on buying fruit, look as these scrumptious fruits, someone must have worked really hard for them, but they are all ours. "on the house", that is, "his house" of course".

To a certain degree, there are constant reminders in *halacha* that growing fruit in *Eretz Yisrael* is a culmination of a promise to our forefathers that was materialized a generation after leaving Egypt. Unlike the Egyptian government-owned land where the wealthy landowners enslave anyone who wants to survive and not succumb to hunger, in our land, certain portions of the field constantly belong to the poor.

Yet at no point is this recognition as apparent as it is during *Shevi'it*. All growing produce is declared ownerless. For as long as the crop is growing, the farmer must refrain from restricting access to others. The food should not be guarded (*shamur*), as it should be free for the taking. In addition, he must actively abrogate ownership of the produce and allows all to take.

As the produce is ready to be picked, one can imagine that the landowner who has toiled would want to harvest it, feed himself and his family, and sell the rest of the crop as a return on investment and hopefully a little profit. Indeed, this is how the Torah describes the appropriate practice for the first six years. But in the seventh year, the Torah teaches that one must put that practice to rest, releasing his hold on his produce and his field. He opens up the gates that generally restrict outsiders from traversing his property, replacing them with a giant sign: "These fruits are *hefker*, ownerless. Come one, come all, and partake!"

The majority of individuals who will benefit from the generosity of *halacha* allowing fruit to be free for the taking will be the poor. Individuals who currently own no land, though they may have in the past but came on hard times. It could be young families just starting out, scraping all their money together to get an education and improve their lot. It could be individuals whose business ventures went sour… it could be anyone. In short, most of those who stand to gain are those who can't reap produce from their own fields, either because they lack fields or trees. It is a year of sharing the wealth. The produce of *shevi'it* is unique, and it is therefore treated with a special set of *halachot*.

Tishmetenna Untashtah

In our discussion of the presentation of *shevi'it* in *Parashat Mishpatim* (Section I *Parasha* I), we noted that the Torah introduces us to the uniqueness of the seventh year by introducing the obligation of "*tishmatenah untashtah*":

וְשֵׁשׁ שָׁנִים תִּזְרַע אֶת אַרְצֶךָ וְאָסַפְתָּ אֶת תְּבוּאָתָהּ: וְהַשְּׁבִיעִת תִּשְׁמְטֶנָּה וּנְטַשְׁתָּהּ וְאָכְלוּ אֶבְיֹנֵי עַמֶּךָ וְיִתְרָם תֹּאכַל חַיַּת הַשָּׂדֶה כֵּן תַּעֲשֶׂה לְכַרְמְךָ לְזֵיתֶךָ:

And six years you shall sow your land (*artzecha*) and shall harvest its fruits. But in the seventh (*shevi'it*), you shall release it (*tishmetenna*) and let it lie fallow (*untashta*), and the poor of your nation will eat, and what they leave over the beasts of the field shall eat. So you shall do with your vineyard and with your olive grove. (*Shemot* 23:10-11)

As opposed to the previous six years, during which one plants and harvests, this is not the case during the seventh year. The Torah focuses on the social benefits of such acts – that "the poor of your nation will eat," and even the wildlife will be able to eat the leftovers. We noted that the placement of this aspect of *shevi'it* in *Parashat Mishpatim* has great significance, as besides the entire *parasha* being enclosed in the larger description of the Har Sinai experience, it generally focuses on the social laws. *Shevi'it* is one of the quintessential expressions of a society built on bridging the spiritual and interpersonal.[145]

Although we translated this phrase as "you shall release it and let it lie fallow," we noted that its meaning is the subject of dispute. This phrase is unlike the lengthy description of

145 In the following *pasuk*, the Torah describes how one's animals also benefit from the observance of the weekly Shabbat. As noted by the Alshich (see Section I *Parasha* 1), a human's rest also enables the goal of *veyinafesh*, reaching one's soul, and this is true both on Shabbat and during *shevi'it*.

the agricultural laws of *shevi'it* in *Parashat Behar*, which refers to the idea of *shabbat ha'aretz* but makes no mention of the term *shemitta*. Although the Ibn Ezra and Seforno explain the phrase as an earlier iteration of the financial *shemitta* described at length in *Parashat Re'eh*, most authorities maintain that the *pasuk* in *Mishpatim* is referring to a concept that parallels *shemittat kesafim* – *shemittat karka'ot*, a release of the land during *shevi'it*.

What form of agricultural release is called for? Some understand *tishmetenna* and/or *untashtah* as obligations regarding releasing the land from various forms of work. Rashi explains:

> **Tishmetenna** — [release] from real work, such as plowing and sowing. **Untashtah** — and abandon it from fertilizing and hoeing.

We noted in last chapter that *tishmatenna* might be an overall positive requirement to refrain from agricultural activities that are not explicitly prohibited in the Torah.

The more common understanding of *tishmatenna* is a requirement of releasing one's hold on the produce that grows on his property. According to this view, *shemitta* as an act of release associated with the **produce** of the field, rather than the field itself.

The *Mechilta* offers an understanding of the term *tishmetenna untashtah* that views the phrase as a reference to **how** one is to relinquish his hold over the agricultural produce in the field:

> דָּבָר אַחֵר: וְהַשְּׁבִיעִית תִּשְׁמְטֶנָּה וּנְטַשְׁתָּהּ, מִפְּנֵי מָה אָמְרָה תּוֹרָה, לֹא שֶׁיֹּאכְלוּ אוֹתָהּ עֲנִיִּים?! הֲרֵי אֲנִי מַכְנִיסָהּ, וּמְחַלְּקָהּ לַעֲנִיִּים! תַּלְמוּד לוֹמַר: 'וְהַשְּׁבִיעִית תִּשְׁמְטֶנָּה וּנְטַשְׁתָּהּ' - מַגִּיד שֶׁפּוֹרֵץ בָּהּ פְּרָצוֹת. אֶלָּא שֶׁגָּדְרוּ חֲכָמִים מִפְּנֵי תִּקּוּן הָעוֹלָם.

> Another explanation: "And on the seventh year you shall release and abandon": Why did the Torah state this? [Is the purpose not] that the poor should eat it?! So I will bring in the [produce] and distribute it to the poor! Therefore, the verse teaches: "And on the seventh year you shall release and abandon it" – this teaches that [one really should] break down the fences [and leave the field open], but the Sages limited it due to *tikkun olam*, the benefit of society. (*Mechilta DeRebbi Yishmael, Mishpatim* 20:18)

The *Mechilta* notes that it is insufficient to merely release one's hold on their crops or to gather them on behalf of the poor. Rather, "*untashta*," "and you shall abandon," indicates that one must abandon ownership even of the grass and let the poor (and everyone else) enter his field and partake of the fruits as if they own them.

The concluding phrase of this passage is unclear. Who should break down the field's fences, and what benefit to society did *Chazal* envision when they limited the practice?

The simplest understanding is that this obligation falls upon the owner of the field. Ideally, to fulfill the *shemitta* obligation, one should break down all the fences around his property. The Sages, however, did not require this, as they felt it would be best for society if it were not done. Alternatively, the *Kesef Mishna* (*Hilchot Shemitta* 4:4) explains that this is not a reference to the owner's obligation, but rather permission granted to the poor, who were initially entitled to break down any fences or barriers preventing them from reaching the produce. Although the Sages ruled that no one may break down the farmer's fences, the farmer himself is not permitted to erect fences that will inhibit the access of others, even if he intends to collect all the produce and allocate it to the poor. It is not his to give.[146]

This understanding of *tishmatenna* is accepted by the Rambam, who sees the farmer's release of his hold on his produce – almost abandoning his field – as the primary agricultural responsibility of the "*shemitta* year":

> We are commanded to disown everything that the land produces during the *shemitta* year, to release everything that grows on our property for the use of any living creature. The source of this commandment is God's statement, "But in the seventh, *tishmetenna u-ntashta*." (*Sefer HaMitzvot*, positive commandment 134)

In his *Mishneh Torah*, the Rambam expands upon the requirements of declaring one's produce *hefker* (ownerless) as an act of *shemitta* (using the term from the verse):

> It is a positive commandment to divest oneself from everything that the land produces in the *shemitta* year ... Anyone who locks his vineyard or fences off his field in the *shemitta* year has nullified a positive commandment. This also holds true if he gathers all his produce into his home. Instead, he should leave everything ownerless. Thus, everyone has equal rights in every place, as the verse states: "And the poor of your nation will eat." One may bring a small amount into one's home, just as one brings from ownerless property, e.g., five jugs of oil, fifteen jugs of wine.

Any act of locking one's vineyard or actively preventing others from taking possession of one's fruits is a violation of this *mitzvah*. This *mitzvah* applies not only to the farmer, but to anyone who has a vegetable garden or fruit trees.[147]

For the Rambam, the year is a *shemitta* year. That is how the Torah introduces it, and through that prism we should view its other *halachot* as well. The *Sefer HaChinuch* (*mitzvah* 84) points out that this requirement earns the year its appellation – *shemitta*.

The Goals

The Torah itself explicitly presents the rationale for this act of *shemitta*: "And the poor of your nation will eat." The Zohar (*Vayikra* 108) explains that the poor are often limited in their means of mobility; logic dictates that during the *shemitta* year, despite the depletion of resources, they must largely remain where they are. Therefore, during the *shemitta* year, they are to be allowed to enjoy the crops. Although all may partake of these ownerless fruits, the primary benefit is to the poor, who have nothing of their own (see Ralbag, *Vayikra* 25).[148]

---

146 The *Merkevet HaMishna* (commentary to *Mechilta* 20:18) explains that the *Mechilta* did not mean that one could ever literally break down the field-owner's fence. Rather, it intended to illustrate in a graphic way that it is almost as if the field owner retains no ownership over his field at all.

147 Rav Shlomo Zalman Auerabach (*Ma'adanei Eretz* 5:6) notes that if only a small amount grows in one's field, just sufficient for one's own needs, then it is not *hefker*.

148 Abarbanel (*Shemot* 23:10) notes that this social benefit of *shemitta* is somewhat present during the weekly Shabbat as well, as the underprivileged receive a day of rest, as do one's animals.

In addition to these social *bein adam lechavero* benefits, there are goals in the theological *bein adam laMakom* and character-building *bein adam le'atzmo* realms as well.

Religiously, relinquishing one's hold on the land allows the owner to "remember that the land which brings forth its fruits yearly does not bring forth fruits through its own powers, but because there is a master over the land and over the land's owners" (*Sefer HaChinuch, mitzvah* 84). Through this recognition, man also fortifies his *bitachon* in God, as he realizes that in the absence of "his" fields, his survival and success are dependent upon the Almighty.

Rabbeinu Bechayei (*Vayikra* 25) adds that since the purpose of the *shemitta* year is to recognize God's mastery over the land, one releases the hold on the land "in order to allow man to contemplate in his heart that God is the true owner and Master." The *Kli Yakar* (ad loc.) states that the primary reason for relinquishing ownership is in order to recognize God's possession, but once one is already doing so, it is proper that it then be abandoned so that the poor can benefit from it (see also *Shem MiShmuel*, ad loc.).

The Ibn Ezra explains that this is why *shemittat kesafim* is described as a "*shemitta laHashem*" (*Devarim* 15:2), just as the entire year is referred to as a *Shabbat laHashem* (*Vayikra* 25:2, 4):

> A *shemitta* to Hashem – In honor of Hashem, who provided him with the wealth. And the reason for attaching the phrase *laHashem* is because it is a *shabbat* to Hashem.

Although the entire seventh year is a *shabbat* to Hashem, the culminating moment of the seventh year is when *shemittat kesafim* takes effect. At that moment, the overall *shemitta* message is compounded: Our wealth is *laHashem*, provided by God, Who informs us how to use it.[149]

Rabbeinu Bechayei observes a distinction between how the Torah phrases the obligations of *shemitta* ("your land") as opposed to those of *yovel* ("the land"), as follows:

> The Torah uses direct language when speaking about either the Shabbat day or the Shabbat year, whereas when speaking of the jubilee year, it uses the third person, speaking in more general terms... Seeing that immediately after Shabbat one may resume work and immediately after the *shemitta* year the farmer may recommence his usual activities of plowing and sowing etc., the Torah used direct language as the farmer considers the land as his own. After the seventh year preceding the jubilee year, which is also a *shemitta* year, i.e. a year when he did not work his field, the farmer must not wait another year before he can again treat the land as if it were his own. The Torah hints at this by using indirect language in speaking of the land in question. Even the manner in which the Torah describes the abandoning of the land during *shemitta*, "you shall release it (*tishmetenna*) and let it lie fallow (*untashtah*)" indicates that the land has ceased to belong to the farmer during that year. The relationship between us and the land during the *shemitta* year is that whereas we abandon **it, it**

---

149 See *Sifra* 2, *Gittin* 36, where the *gemara* cites Rabbi Yehuda HaNasi's connection between *shemittat kesafim* and *shemittat karka'ot*.

does not abandon us. The reason is that once again we will resume our activities upon it demonstrating that it is ours. The same is not the case with the jubilee year, as many fields will return to owners who had previously been forced to sell them for one reason or another. It is therefore appropriate to speak of such land in the third person, i.e., not addressing a specific owner. (Rabbeinu Bechayei, *Vayikra* 23:10)

When *yovel* comes, many individuals will "lose" possession of the fields they have "purchased", as they will return to their owners. Therefore, it is far easier to recognize that they are not the true owners of their fields. However, the same is not true concerning *shemitta*. During the seventh year, man knows that he will return to his fields the following year, and he will even be charged with the task of working the land and harvesting its bounty. The land remains one's own, but man must fulfill *tishmetenna*, abandoning his claim to it and relinquishing his rights to its fruit.

Rav Hirsch explains that doing so will allow one to recognize who really is in control of the land:

By observing the *mitzvah* of *shemitta*, an entire nation proclaims before the world that its land belongs to God, and that He is the land's one, sole true Master. In the seventh year, the nation refrains from exercising its rights of ownership and humbly returns its land to the Lord of all the earth. By doing so, the people acknowledge that they are strangers and sojourners on their own land, dwelling on it only by the grace of the Owner. Then the arrogance that causes men, secure on their own land, to become callous and harsh in dwelling with those without property, melts away, yielding to love and kindness toward the stranger and the poor. Even the wild animals, as God's creatures, are considered endowed with rights on God's earth, upon which all are to dwell together. (Rav Hirsch, commentary on *Shemot* 23:10-11)

Halachic Ramifications

There are a number of important ramifications of the fact that the produce that grows during *shevi'it* is declared *hefker*.

The Rambam explains that two *halachot* of *shemitta* mentioned in *Parashat Behar* are a direct outgrowth of the status of the produce of one's fields as *hefker*:

We are forbidden from harvesting in the normal way crops that the ground produces on its own during the seventh year... The intention of the verse is that one may not harvest in the same way one harvests grain during other years. One may only gather it as if it was ownerless. (*Sefer HaMitzvot*, negative commandment 222)

Since the produce is ownerless, no one can use it by harvesting it professionally. Instead, one should only take a small amount at a time.

שֶׁלֹּא כְּדֶרֶךְ הַקּוֹצְרִים

The Rambam adds that even that which one takes from the produce should be attained with a *shinuy*, a change from the normal method:

We are forbidden from gathering in the normal manner fruit which trees produce during *shemitta*. We must make a change in order to demonstrate that it is considered ownerless. (*Sefer HaMitzvot*, negative commandment 223)

The *mishna* (*Shevi'it* 5:7) writes that one may sell up to 5 oil pitchers and 15 wine pitchers at a time, "as that is normal to bring from *hefker*." The *mishna* adds that if one took more from *hefker*, the produce is nevertheless permitted. The *mishna* seems to maintain that the primary obligation is to declare the produce *hefker*; once this is done, it should be treated as such, and one should not take more than one normally would from *hefker*. However, since the produce is ownerless, there is no prohibition on taking too much (see Ri Kurkus, *Hilchos Shemitta VeYovel* 4:24). However, the Rambam (Hilchot Shemitta VeYovel 4:24) rules that one who takes more produce than the allotted amount violates a prohibition (see *Chazon Ish* 12:5).

Furthermore, from the time the produce growing has *kedushat shevi'it*, the farmer cannot do anything that will harm the produce, as it doesn't belong to the owner (see *Ma'adanei Eretz* 5:6).

Ideally, besides a verbal declaration of *hefker* regarding one's produce, one should place a sign indicating that one's produce is *hefker* and free for all to take.

Rav Kook requires one to obtain permission from the owner before entering his property to partake of the produce. The *Chazon Ish* permits owners worried about other property being stolen to leave a note stating that the owners will give produce to anyone who wants it.

In *Hilchot Mattenot Aniyim* (6:5), the Rambam notes that ownerless produce, such as the seventh year's produce, is not liable to the obligations of separating the gifts of teruma the like (see also *Hilchot Terumot* 2:9-12).

Whose Declaration? The Individual or the King?

There is a fascinating dispute among the authorities regarding what creates the *afkata*, the removal of the ownership over the produce, which has important ramifications for these *halachot*. Is it the farmer (*afkata degavra*) or the King (*afkata deMalka*), i.e., God, who declares the produce *hefker*?

Rav Yosef Karo (*Teshuvot Avkat Rochel* 24) understands that the mitzvah is that every Jew must declare his or her produce ownerless during the seventh year. This is known as *afkata degavra*, personal expropriation. This obligation obviously does not apply to non-Jews. Therefore, produce from non-Jewish land, even if processed by a Jew, will not be deemed ownerless by the gentile owners and will therefore carry an obligation of *teruma* (as all non-*hefker* property does).

However, the Mabit (1:11) argues that *shemitta* produce is ownerless by "royal" expropriation, *afkata deMalka*. The King, God, annuls private ownership of produce during the seventh year through an automatic, divine act of *hefker*. Thus, by definition, all *shemitta* produce – even that of a non-Jew – is *hefker* and free from any *teruma* obligation. For this reason, he explains, the Rambam rules that one violates the *mitzvah* by fencing in his land. Essentially, any attempt to exhibit ownership over produce that God has already declared not to be in one's possession is a violation of the *mitzvah* of *shemitta*.

The *Minchat Chinuch* (84, s.v. *ve'ani mistapek*) points out that this dispute has several ramifications. For instance, is there a verbal obligation incumbent upon each landowner to declare his produce ownerless, as the Rambam implies? Although this is certainly the ideal (see *Dinei Shevi'it, Degel Yerushalayim*, 14:3), according to some authorities, it is unnecessary; the only demand placed upon owners is to leave the gates to their property open to allow access to those who wish to enter, as the produce is by definition ownerless.

Rav Moshe Feinstein (*Iggerot Moshe*, Y.D. 3:90) offers an interesting middle position: There is a requirement to renounce ownership of his produce, but even if one fails to do so, the Torah declares his produce ownerless in any case. Rav Yosef Rimon explains:

> The logic underlying the first approach is that when a person willingly declares his produce ownerless, he internalizes the message that the land and the produce growing on it do not belong to him.
> On the other hand, the very act of repudiating title to produce can infuse a person with the sense that he is the owner, because only an owner can declare his produce ownerless. Thus, according to the second approach, it is precisely the Torah's insistence that all produce is automatically regarded as ownerless during the *shemitta* year that will bring a person to internalize the message that "the land is Mine; for you are strangers and sojourners with Me" (*Vayikra* 25:23).

One might add that according to Rav Moshe Feinstein's middle position, both are true. God has at His disposal the means of repudiating ownership of produce for all those who fail to do so on their own. The *shemitta* year provides man with an obligation and an opportunity — *tishmetenna* — for inculcating all the messages delineated above.

The Ground Itself

According to the simple understanding, although the farmer's produce is *hefker*, the land itself remains the owner's property. However, at least one opinion in a passage in the Talmud (*Nedarim* 42b) may maintain that the poor gain certain rights in the land itself. Rav Yekutiel Asher Zalman Anzil (glosses to the *Avnei Milu'im* 72:2, 9) explains that this is because the Torah declares that the agricultural *shevi'it* limitations are due to "*Ki li ha'aretz*," "for the land is Mine" (*Vayikra* 25:23). All share the produce because the land is God's, and there is no reason to limit the access of the poor to the land.

The Rambam (*Hilchot Shemitta VeYovel* 7:18) rules that there is a distinction between the seventh and eighth years. Although *shemitta* produce retains its *kedushat shevi'it* status throughout most of the eighth year and is *hefker* until the second rain during the eighth year, the poor can no longer enter the fields the *shemitta* produce. Rav Shaul Yisraeli (*Chavat Binyamin*, vol. 3, p. 642) and Rav Chaim Kanievsky (*Derech Emuna* 7:18) explain that although *shemitta* produce is *hefker* (*tishmetenna*) even into the eighth year, the obligation of *netashta*, calling for abandoning one's property and allowing others to come in to partake of the produce, only applies during the seventh year.

Accordingly, Rav Yisraeli explains, during the seventh year, one still owns his fields and can perform non-agricultural activities there (including building on the property), but the rights of the poor to the produce enable them to come into the property even if doing so will damage the property. However, in the eighth year, their rights to the produce only apply if taking it won't damage the property. Rav Kanievsky adds that, under those circumstances, the owner would have to remove the produce from his field to enable others to partake.

A Simple "Thank You"

To what degree does the owner get any credit for working the fields and cultivating the produce that grows during the *shemitta* year? Does he at least retain enough rights in the produce that those who partake of it should thank him for it?

The *mishna* (*Eduyot* 5:1) cites a dispute between Beit Shammai and Beit Hillel as to whether one eats *shevi'it* produce "*betova*" or "*shelo betova.*" Beit Shammai maintains that one eats in both manners; there is a question regarding whether Beit Hillel argues by stating that one cannot eat *betova* (Bartenura) or that one must eat *betova* (Ra'avad). The simple explanation is that these terms refer to whether there is an obligation, or even an allowance, to thank the owner. Beit Shammai maintains that there is no obligation or prohibition to do so, whereas Beit Hillel either requires or prohibits doing so, depending on the proper text.

The *Tosafot Yom Tov* (ad loc.) explains the Ra'avad's understanding of Beit Hillel, that one must eat *betova*. Since the produce is *hefker*, there is no legal obligation for the poor to ask permission from the landowner. Nevertheless, the Sages required him to do so in order that people do not become accustomed to taking from others without asking permission and expressing gratitude. Rav Kook explains that according to the Ra'avad, one must ask permission and the landowner must grant it, but if he refuses to do so, one is not permitted to partake of the produce.

There seems to be an important lesson in this discussion. As we have seen, the *shemitta* obligation of releasing one's produce and abandoning one's hold on the field for that purpose is a difficult obligation that reminds the farmer who the real owner of the land and the produce is. On the other hand, this farmer has partnered with Hashem in the mitzvah of yishuv Eretz Yisrael, cultivating the land and helping the desert bloom for the past six years. So long as he recognizes Hashem's partnership in his success, he is to be commended, and the produce is his during all other years. When the owner ceases to act as a landowner in the seventh year, poor and rich alike take from his property without any limitation, which has social benefits and a positive effect on the farmer's outlook.

The Torah, however, is also concerned for the outlook of those who benefit from the farmer's generosity. The goal of the Torah is not to have capable individuals receive handouts in a welfare state (see chapter 18), and it, therefore virtually always requires action from the needy to actively get what is available for them. This allows for the disadvantaged to partake with honor and dignity, but it runs the risk of the poor becoming accustomed to benefitting from the labor of others without proper gratitude. It also presents a danger that they might not see the need to exert effort to achieve, as others work on their behalf. Rather than creating equality, this system could potentially breed laziness, and in turn discord between those who work and those who live off their efforts.

In short, there is a danger in the poor man's "thank you," as the landowner might focus on the righteousness of his *shemitta* act, but there is a danger in refraining from doing so, as it runs many risks for those who take. For this reason, the Ra'avad maintains that although asking permission and saying thank you isn't required, the Sages wanted one to do so to ensure that society as a whole gains maximal benefit.

Chapter 22

Kedushat Shevi'it- The Sanctity of Shemitta Produce

The most common application of *hilchot shevi'it* for the non-farmer (and even the non-Israeli) relates to *kedushat shevi'it*, the sanctified status of seventh-year produce. Many consumers find these *halachot* to be stress-inducing, as their normal routine of purchasing produce, cooking, and even disposing of excess is interrupted. However, one who recognizes what lies behind these halachot will hopefully be less overwhelmed and possibly even inspired.

Shevi'it produce has a special status at two different stages:

1. While the crop is growing in nature

2. After the produce is no longer growing (on the tree or in the ground)

As we have seen, while the produce is growing, several *halachot* restrict the landowner's natural feeling of ownership and control. Although he has probably invested great effort and expense in fulfilling the *mitzvah* of *yishuv Eretz Yisrael*, settling the land and cultivating its growth, he must nevertheless release his hold on "his" produce during this year and declare the crops *hefker*.

Even after the produce is taken from the ground, however, special halachot apply to it. The produce is special and must be treated with *kedushat shevi'it*, a unique degree of sanctity.

The Sanctified Produce of Shemitta

In *Parashat Behar*, after delineating the limitations of working the land, the Torah goes on to mention the unique laws regarding produce:

וְהָיְתָה שַׁבַּת הָאָרֶץ לָכֶם לְאָכְלָה לְךָ וּלְעַבְדְּךָ וְלַאֲמָתֶךָ וְלִשְׂכִירְךָ וּלְתוֹשָׁבְךָ הַגָּרִים עִמָּךְ: וְלִבְהֶמְתְּךָ וְלַחַיָּה אֲשֶׁר
בְּאַרְצֶךָ תִּהְיֶה כָל תְּבוּאָתָה לֶאֱכֹל:

But the produce of *shabbat ha'aretz* shall be for you to eat (*l'ochla*), for you, and for your servant and for your maid, and for your hired servant and for the residents by your side that sojourn with you. And for your cattle, and for the beasts that are in your land, shall all the produce of it be for food. (*Vayikra* 25:6-7)

The Torah here uses an interesting terminology to refer to all that grows during the seventh year without human input – "shabbat ha'aretz," i.e., the (product of the) rest of the land. While everything that grows in the Land of Israel has a special *kedusha* status, the limits on human interaction in the growth process make the seventh-year produce even more unique. Produce associated with the seventh year is not only the product of *shabbat ha'aretz*, but *shabbat laHashem*; it is a unique expression of Hashem's direct blessing on the land, and it must be treated as such.

The Talmud Yerushalmi derives the sanctified status of seventh-year produce from a verse in the next passage in the Torah, which discusses *yovel*:

> כִּי יוֹבֵל הִוא קֹדֶשׁ תִּהְיֶה לָכֶם מִן הַשָּׂדֶה תֹּאכְלוּ אֶת תְּבוּאָתָהּ:

For it is the *yovel*; it shall be holy to you. You may only eat the growth direct from the field. (*Vayikra* 25:12)

> יוֹבֵל הִיא - מָה הִיא קוֹדֶשׁ אַף תְּבוּאָתָהּ קוֹדֶשׁ :

"For it is the *yovel*; it shall be holy to you" – Just as it is holy, so too its produce is holy. (Yerushalmi *Shevi'it* 4:7, cited by Rashi, *Vayikra* 25:12)

From this source, it seems that the special status of the produce is derived from the Land: Just as the Land is sanctified, so is the crop growing on it.

Similarly, the *gemara* (*Sukka* 40b) explains that not only is the produce sanctified, but when purchased, the sanctity transfers to the money:

> *Shevi'it* transfers its holiness to the money used to purchase it, as the verse states, "For it is the *yovel*; it shall be holy to you." Just as with holy objects the money assumes the sanctity and becomes forbidden, so too with *shevi'it*, the money assumes the same sanctity and becomes forbidden.

For this reason, produce with *kedushat shevi'it* that is available in stores must be acquired in a special manner.

Tosafot point out that the unique *kedusha* of this produce is reflected in its many unique *halachot*:

> There are countless laws and prohibitions that govern the produce of the seventh year, which must be treated with *kedushat shevi'it*! (Tosafot, *Sukka* 39a, s.v. *she-ein*)

Notably, the Torah declares that seventh-year produce is designated *l'ochla*, for consumption – by human or animal, by the owners or anyone else. Given that the produce that grows on its own during *shevi'it* is supposed to be declared *hefker*, why does the Torah state that we are entitled to consume it? Rashi (based on *Torat Kohanim, Behar* 1) explains: Although I have prohibited the produce to you, I did not prohibit you to eat it or to derive benefit from it, only that you should not treat it as if you were its owner. Instead, everyone is deemed equal — you, [your slaves,] and your hired worker and resident.

The basis of a number of the limitations regarding *shevi'it* is the fact that one must recognize his lack of ownership over the produce, as any effort to the contrary might remove any license to benefit from it.

The primary *halachot* regarding *kedushat shevi'it* produce are learned from the Torah's emphasis on what rights we have to that produce – "*l'ochla*," to eat. It is obvious that edible produce is to be eaten; the fact that the Torah stresses this end must indicate something more. *Chazal* thus derived a number of *halachot* from this terminology, and there is a possibility that there is even a *mitzvah* to eat *shevi'it* produce:

לְאָכְלָה וְלֹא לְהֶפְסֵד	לְאָכְלָה וְלֹא לִסְחוֹרָה
	 "For eating and not for business" (*Bechorot* 12b).
"For eating and not for wasting" (*Pesachim* 52b). *Shevi'it* produce cannot be wasted.	*Shevi'it* produce is not commercial merchandise. In an ordinary year, farmers use whatever they do not eat themselves as a commercial commodity. During *shevi'it*, that is not permitted, as the crops are supposed to be shared equally by all.

Additionally, other halachot learned from the terminology include:

- לְאָכְלָה וְלֹא לִכְבִיסָה- "For eating and not for laundering" (*Sukka* 40)- *Shevi'it* produce is designated for eating and not for removing stains.

- לְאָכְלָה וְלֹא לִמְלוּגְמָא- "For eating and not for medicine" (*Sukka* 40)- *Shevi'it* produce is not to be used for medicinal purposes.

לֹא לְיֵצוּא No Exporting

Shevi'it produce is pure food, not a commodity to use as one pleases. Other *halachot* are learned from the *pasuk* as well. For instance, from the word בְּאַרְצֶךָ, *b'artzecha*, "in your land," we learn that one may not export *shevi'it* produce outside of Eretz Yisrael (*Shevi'it* 6:5). The Torah refers to the food being left for both humans and animals, indicating that one may consume *shevi'it* produce for as long as it is available to animals in the field (*Pesachim* 52b). This is the *mitzvah* of *biur*, which will be discussed in its own chapter.[150]

---

150 We have noted previously (see chapter 19) that the term *kedusha* generally refers to consecrated separateness. Is the *kedusha* status a mere offshoot of the limitations inherent in its use, or do the prohibitions reflect a consecrated and sanctified status?

Rav Chaim Ilson (*Peri Chaim*) notes that the term *l'ochla* serves as a source for both the unique requirements of the produce and its limitations. *Shevi'it* produce is designated for consumption through eating, drinking, or anointing with it in the normal way it is used. Because it is so designated, one is also restricted in using it for any other purposes. In the language of the *mishna*, the produce has "*kedushat nitan*" (*Shevi'it* 8:2), holiness based on its designation.

Its *kedusha* is also reflected in the inability to remove its sanctity. As we noted, the *kedusha* status of *shevi'it* produce is transferred when it is purchased with cash. In this sense, *shevi'it* produce should be compared to *hekdesh*, the property of the Temple. If sacred property is sold, the money becomes holy. *Shevi'it* produce differs in this sense from agricultural gifts such as *teruma*, which do not transmit their holiness to cash used for their purchase. This power is known as *tefisat damim* (*Avoda Zara* 54b); the sacred character of *shevi'it* "grips" the object given in exchange for it.

There are only three objects that have this power of *tefisat damim* – *hekdesh*, *avoda zara* (pagan artifacts), and *shevi'it*. Interestingly, however, *tefisat damim* operates differently with regard to *shevi'it* produce than it does with other similar products. Rav Yosef Zvi Rimon offers one explanation:

The added sanctity of *shemitta* produce stems from the fact that, unlike *teruma*, *shemitta* produce is holy from its inception. The sanctity of *teruma* (and *hekdesh*) is attached to produce (or other objects) through human action

A *Mitzvah* to Consume?

The formulation *l'ochla* also seems to be a requirement. The Ramban writes that it actually should be counted as one of the *mitzvah* obligations:

> The Torah states concerning *shevi'it*, "But the sabbath of the land shall be for you to eat," regarding which the rabbis taught: "'For food,' but not for trade ..." And this *mitzvah* was repeated through the expression, "And the poor of your nation will eat." (Ramban, addenda to the Rambam's *Sefer HaMitzvot*, positive commandment 3)

The *Megillat Esther* commentary (ad loc.) understands the Ramban to be stating that there is an actual *mitzvah* to eat *shevi'it* produce. He challenges this view, supporting the Rambam's decision not to count it as a *mitzvah*, and explains that the *pasuk* merely permits one to consume the produce so long as one does not waste it or use it for commerce. Others (Chazon Ish 14:10) assert that the Ramban does not mean that the consumption is a *mitzvah* per se, but rather that using *shevi'it* for one of the proscribed purposes has the status of a prohibition derived from a positive commandment[151].

In a similar vein, some understand the Tosefta to prohibit use of *shevi'it* produce in a state of ritual impurity:

> One must not apply oil of the seventh year with impure hands. (Tosefta, *Shevi'it* 6:9)

Although some understand that the Tosefta is only restricting usage of *shevi'it* with hands that are known to be impure, Rav Kook (*Shabbat HaAretz* 5: 7) understands that according to the Tosefta there is a requirement to wash one's hands before using the produce. He notes that this is unnecessary in our day, as we no longer observe the laws of ritual purity, but it is still a meritorious practice. This practice is advocated by the *Chayei Adam* as well. Others suggest that being stringent to wash one's hands before eating *shevi'it* will lead one to consume less of it; thus, for practical reasons, this ostensibly meritorious practice is ill-advised (see Rav Rimon, *Hilchot Shemitta*, p. 234).[152] Either way, these special laws underscore the unique status of *shevi'it* produce.

The general *halachot* learned from *l'ochla* can be summarized:
The Rambam summarizes the principles of proper usage of *Kedushat Shevi'it* produce:

> A great principle was stated with regard to the produce of the Sabbatical year: Whatever is distinguished as being for human consumption, e.g., wheat, figs, grapes, and the like, should not be used as a compress or a bandage, even

לְאָכְלָה

---

when a person sets aside *teruma*, with the caveat that man can also redeem the produce and transfer the sanctity to the money. The sanctity of *shemitta* produce, on the other hand, is natural and innate, and therefore the owner cannot remove the sanctity even if he tries to redeem the produce ... Yet, despite the stringency stemming from this innate sanctity, given that the consumption of *shemitta* produce is available to every Jew, the Torah did not require that it be safeguarded from ritual impurity. (*Hilchot Shemitta*)
See Rav Hirsch, *Vayikra* 25, for another explanation

151 For a summary of some of the sources on the topic see Summary http://www.eretzhemdah.org/Data/UploadedFiles/SitePages/8119-sFileRedir.pdf.

152 In fact, when it comes to other produce, the Talmud (*Chullin* 106a) states: "A person who washes his hands for fruit exhibits a haughty spirit."

for a person, as implied by the *pasuk*: "It shall be a Shabbat of the Land for you, so that you may eat of it," i.e., whatever is distinguished as being for you [your consumption] should be used as food. (*Hilchot Shemitta V'Yovel* 5:11)

In practice, *shevi'it* produce must be eaten in a usual manner, and it may not be used for non-food uses. Even the leftovers of *shevi'it* produce are treated differently. *Shevi'it* produce is not discarded normally, but is instead either placed in a protective bag (or two) in the garbage or placed in a special bin designated for *shevi'it* leftovers. Although some refer to it this bin as a "*pach shemitta*," that term is somewhat disparaging, as it literally means "*shemitta* garbage bin," and *shevi'it* produce is holy – not garbage. Rav Yosef Zvi Rimon suggests that a more appropriate name might be *kli l'she'eriot kedushat shevi'it*, a vessel for leftover *kedushat shevi'it*. A user-friendly approach might refer to the vessel as a *Kli-Lekdush*, a shortened form of *Kli LeKedushat Shevi'it* that puts the stress on the *kedusha* found in *shevi'it* produce.

Despite the financial value of food, there is a great amount of waste in our modern industrial society. Wasteful food practices begin in the fields and continue through all forms of food production, all the way through the modern kitchen. During *shevi'it*, we are supposed to become more attuned to how we treat our food. Learning the lessons of *kedushat shevi'it* will hopefully ensure our food doesn't go unnecessarily to waste during all years, not only the seventh.

כְּלִי לְקְדֻשַׁת שְׁבִיעִית

What and When?

Does the status of *kedushat shevi'it* pertain to all types of produce? The *gemara* (*Sukka* 40a) explains that the sanctity attaches to produce "that gives benefit at the same time as it is consumed." The *gemara* and later commentaries discuss this designation at length.

Importantly, even among the produce that clearly obtains the status of *kedushat shevi'it*, that status begins at different points of the year depending on the type of produce. Although the laws associated with the land commence on Rosh Hashana of the seventh year and conclude with Rosh Hashana of the eighth, the *kedushat shevi'it* status of any particular product applies only during a specific time during the year.

Rabba said: The Rabbis have said that [the year of] a tree is determined by the [time of the] emergence [of fruit]; that of grain and olives by one third of their ripening; that of vegetables by their picking. (*Rosh Hashana* 13b)

Any vegetables **picked** during the seventh year have *kedushat shevi'it*, but fruits have *kedushat shevi'it* only if they **blossom** during *shevi'it*. As a result, fruit may be assigned *kedushat shevi'it* status only later in the year, but it also may continue to possess that status until significantly into the eight year.

There is a question whether produce of non-Jewish owned land has kedusha

Produce of the land of Israel

יְרָקוֹת
Vegetables

פֵּירוֹת
Fruit

תִּירוֹשׁ וְיִצְהָר

דָּגָן וְקִטְנִיּוֹת
Grains and Legumes

לְקִיטָה
Picking

חֲנָטָה
Formation of the fruit

Vegetables picked (harvested) during Shemitta have kedusha (they will be available almost immediately after Rosh Hashana through the first few months of the eighth year)

Fruit are kadosh if the formation of the fruit (chanata, approximately identical to hava'at shelish, reachinga third of its growth) is during the shemitta year. (They are available in the last few months of the Shemitta year through most of the eighth year, and at times the beginning of the ninth). [Some treat citrus fruits (especially lemons) like an Etrog]

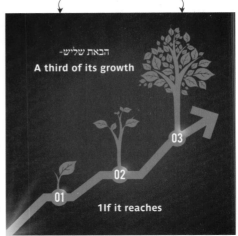

הבאת שליש-
A third of its growth

03

02

01

1If it reaches

Whatever reaches a third of its growth during the shemitta year is kadosh. (Grains, legumes, grapes and olives with kedusha are available from the end of the seventh year through the end of the eighth).

אֶתְרוֹג

There is a discussion if Etrogim should be treated as fruits or vegetables. Therefore we treat all etrogim that are picked or blossom during the shemitta year as Kadosh (the etrogim available during the eighth year are kadosh)

The Lessons of *Kedushat Shevi'it*

As noted, the greatest expression of the produce's unique status is reflected in the Torah's designation of it "*lachem l'ochla*," "for you for consumption," as opposed to commodity, waste, or even irregular consumption. The *Ohr HaChaim HaKadosh* derives an important idea from the term "for you":

> The principal reason for this verse is to inform us that contrary to other sacred matters, which are restricted to the altar or to the priests, in this instance everyone is entitled to consume what has grown during the seventh year. (*Ohr HaChaim, Vayikra* 25:6)

Sanctified fruit is generally limited to the *Kohanim* or eaten specifically in Yerushalayim or the *Mikdash*, but this fruit is for everyone and can be eaten throughout the land. "*Lachem*" refers to society as a whole. Everyone is on the same playing field, no matter how wealthy one is.

The Chizkuni explains that this is the reason one doesn't tithe the produce of *shevi'it*:

> You are not obligated to tithe any part of it, nor to set it aside for the poor, **as it is not yours to distribute**. Neither is what it produces to be converted into libations to be offered in the Temple.

Whatever grows in the holy soil of the Land of Israel requires tithes to be taken from it; until they are separated, the produce is considered *tevel*. *Shevi'it* is ownerless and therefore is not *tevel*. It is meant to be consumed only, reflecting its inherently sanctified status. One cannot even "decide" to use it for a holy purpose, as it is not a personal possession at all.

Even animals have to be taken into account when determining if the produce can be eaten:

> This indicates that the *shevita* mentioned in the verse is for you to eat of the fruit alongside the servants and animals, that all should be able to eat of the produce during this year without working the land. (Ramban, 25:5)

"For consumption but not for..."

All fruit in the Land of Israel wears a *kippa*. Whatever grows in the holy soil requires tithes to be taken from it; until they are separated, the produce is considered *tevel*. *Teruma* is only fit for *kohanim* and must be eaten in purity; the first tithe is given to Levites... These are just some of the laws which express the *kedusha* of all that grows in the Land of Israel. *Shevi'it* is ownerless and therefore is not *tevel*. It is meant to be consumed only, reflecting its inherently sanctified status.

Kedushat Shei'it produce also helps us appreciate the uniqueness and significance of *Eretz Yisrael*. Produce of the seventh year is "holy fruit from a holy land." If we recognize the fruit's *kedusha*, we are reminded that the land is also holy. We should make sure to appreciate the land every time *kedushat shevi'it* foods are consumed.

Rav Hirsch notes how all these laws express a limitation on man's ownership, transforming *shevi'it* from a commodity associated with business, trade, or non-food use to a food that one can enjoy not only through its physical taste, but through the spiritual serenity of eating sanctified produce in the Holy Land.

Rav Eliyahu Blumenzweig similarly emphasizes that the prohibition of wasting *shevi'it* produce is an expression of the central, underlying principle of *shemitta* – that God is the owner of the land, not man. When a person rents or borrows an object, he has no right to destroy it, despite his right to make use of it. Indeed, there is no greater sign of ownership than being allowed to destroy the object. During the *shemitta* year, the produce is not the property of its human "owner," and he, therefore, has no right to destroy it.

The Broader Lessons

There is good reason to believe that the laws of *shevi'it* are supposed to impart broader lessons as well. These lessons will help gain a healthier perspective of both property and proper food usage for other years as well. *Shevi'it* invites us to question the nature of our ownership over any property we might "possess". If the inability to exclusively use the produce in our property is a lesson for life, that everything really belongs to G-d, so what do we really own in other years?

The Torah has great concern for property rights and ownership. The prohibitions on all forms of stealing are just one indication of the Torah's protection of property rights. The Torah guides us to show great concern for the property of others, as the Mishna teaches that others money should be as precious to you as your own (Avot 2:12).

Nevertheless, the Torah's perception of "possession" differs from our customary perspective.

The *gemara* (*Bava Kamma* 68b) notes that if the legal owner of an object (*shelo*) does not have that object (*b'reshuto*) – such as when it has been stolen – neither he nor the present possessor are considered the full-fledged owner. The lesson appears to be that ownership of an item without the ability to use it is meaningless; it is, for all intents and purposes, not actually yours. Ownership is meaningful only when one's objects can be used purposefully.

While this might seem strange, there seems to be a clear lesson. While we might attach a great deal of importance to Net-worth, money that is just gathered with no possession to ever use, is in all intents and purposes not really yours. Possession is indicative of the ability to use something. One's possession can be compromised when someone forcefully steals something from you, or even when one consciously decided not to use one's wealth.

A miserly individual who has a large bank account but won't spend a cent does not fully possess wealth, even if it is legally his. Conversely, an individual whose bank account is nearly empty is truly wealthy if he uses what he has for positive purposes. This is one explanation of the famous teaching: "Who is wealthy? One who is happy with his lot" (*Avot* 4:1).

This does not mean the Torah advocates reckless spending, quite the contrary, it is against the waste of one's resources, but simultaneously against the perspective that acquisition is synonymous with having. Wealth is not a race to see who can rank higher on Forbes wealthiest list, but a question of what role one's wealth plays in one's life.

One year out of seven the Torah reminds us the purpose of the food is for consumption, and not merely to be viewed as a commodity. During this year, one's lack of possession in their field open for all to partake is actually a great lesson in real wealth. One who has what they need and is able to help others through their successful efforts, will be adding much more to their spiritual bank account than could be housed in their physical bank if they were selling the produce they don't really need for food.

Gan Eden, Manna, and *Shevi'it*

In addition to the context of *shevi'it* produce, the term *le-ochla* appears only in three other contexts in the Torah. It is initially mentioned when God informs Adam that the fruit of the trees are his to consume (*Bereishit* 1:29-30), a permission repeated to Noach (before and after the Flood (ibid. 6:21, 9:3); it later appears regarding consumption of the manna in the desert (*Shemot* 16:15).[153] "L'ochla" thus indicates eating when there is no need to work the land.

When Adam lived in Gan Eden, his efforts in working the land did not determine the land's output. Adam was placed in *Gan Eden,* and granted permission to eat of all the produce of the garden barring the *Eitz HaDa'at,* the Tree of Knowledge. Adam was placed in the garden and received a command:

וַיִּקַּח ה' אֱלֹהִים אֶת הָאָדָם וַיַּנִּחֵהוּ בְגַן עֵדֶן לְעָבְדָהּ וּלְשָׁמְרָהּ:

And the Lord God took Adam and placed him in the garden *le'ovda u'leshomra,* to serve and protect. (*Bereishit* 2:15)

This command *leOvda u'leShomra,* often translated "to work and protect the land", cannot be a requirement to physically work the land, as this command appears before Adam's sin and subsequent curse: "from the sweat of your brow you shall eat bread" (*Bereishit* 3:19). *LeOvda* could best be translated as "to serve". Adam's service involved maintaining a proper perspective regarding who really the provides the produce and all blessing. This understanding of *leOvda* is supported by the Torah's description of the agricultural growth at the beginning of creation waiting for "man to work the soil" (ibid. 2:5).

וְכֹל שִׂיחַ הַשָּׂדֶה טֶרֶם יִהְיֶה בָאָרֶץ וְכָל עֵשֶׂב הַשָּׂדֶה טֶרֶם יִצְמָח כִּי לֹא הִמְטִיר ה' אֱלֹהִים עַל הָאָרֶץ וְאָדָם אַיִן לַעֲבֹד אֶת הָאֲדָמָה:

And no shrub of the field was yet on earth and no grasses of the field had yet sprouted, because the Lord God had not sent rain upon the earth and there was no man *la'avod,* to work, the soil, (*Bereishit* 2:5)

Rashi (*ad loc.*) there explains that this *avoda* was not physical work, but rather *tefilla;*

Why had God not yet brought rain? Because "there was no man to till the ground";

153 The Torah uses similar terminology regarding a description of kosher animals (*Vayikra* 11:39), but only in the four contexts described in the text is there a description of something meant to be eaten.

there was no-one to recognize the goodness of rain. When man appeared and understood that rain is essential for the world, he prayed for it, and rain came down, and then the trees and plants grew.

The growth of the land all comes directly from Hashem (Bereishit 2:8-9, 15-16). In Gan Eden one could feel the direct relationship between one's spiritual recognition of Hashem's role and the successful growth in the land. All the (super)natural growth of the land was *lachem leOchla* , to be eaten for mankind. Yet, it is only fitting for one who fully recognizes the true owner of the land and who is indeed responsible for its success. When Adam eats from the tree against Hashem's wishes, he acts as if it really belongs to him, and as a result, the land is cursed and he is banished from the garden.

As long as Adam retains the proper outlook, he eats from God's hand, without physical toil. However, when Adam ate from the Tree of Knowledge against Hashem's wishes, he acted as though it belonged to him; as a result, the land was cursed, and he was banished from the garden.

Noach, who leads the world in its second chance of existence, is reminded of the call of *l'ochla*. Before and after the flood Hashem tries to remind him that nature's produce is placed in humankind's hands to use properly, while recognizing God as the true Provider. Noach's first act of planting is a vineyard (*Bereishit* 9:19), but the Torah records that instead of eating the grapes he drinks the wine derived from them. He becomes inebriated, losing control of his intellectual cognition, and the repercussions are disastrous (ibid. 21-27). Noach's failure to live by the creed of *l'ochla* and to impart it to future generations ultimately requires *l'ochla* to be reserved for the Jewish people.

The next time we find the term *l'ochla* is in reference to the Jewish nation's eating of the manna in the desert. For forty years it was entirely clear who was supplying the food. The challenge would be, what happens when the manna stops. As the Jewish nation enters into *Eretz Yisrael* they will begin to work the land. At this point, *le'ovda ule' shomra* will require actually working the land alongside spiritual activity. Will the nation recognize that *Eretz Yisrael* will become a *Gan Eden* if we abide by the *halachot* of the land and recognize that we eat from Hashem's blessing (*l'ochla*)?

Matar- The Different "Rains"

The Torah seemingly adds another term to help us recognize the proper perspective we require when living in the land and eating from its blessings. There are two primary Hebrew words in the Torah associated with rain, *geshem* and *matar*. Interestingly, the root *matar* appears only fourteen times in the Torah and in limited contexts.

It is used to describe the irrigation in *Gan Eden* at the beginning of the world (*Bereishit* 2:5, cited above), the raining down of the manna in the desert, and the rain that will fall in *Eretz Yisrael* when the Jewish nation acts properly. These three contexts are the same contexts where the term *l'ochla* appears. But here the Torah goes one step further. The Torah also describes three instances of destruction which rained down from the heavens with the term *matar*: the destruction of the world during the flood (*Bereishit* 7:4), the destruction of Sodom (ibid. 19:24), and the destruction of Egypt with the plague of hail (*Shemot* 9:18). All three of these instances, integrally connected to *Gan Eden* and life in *Eretz Yisrael*[154] express the power of *matar*. *Matar* are heavenly lessons[155] for the good or bad. Misuse of the world results in *matar* of destruction, while proper use of the world and divine blessings merits manna, *shevi'it* produce, and a return to Gan Eden.

Through the term *matar*, however, the Torah distinguishes between the blessing of the manna and the blessings of *Eretz Yisrael* in general and *shevi'it* produce in particular. The manna was edible "bread of the heavens" that rained down in the desert for the benefit of the nation (**"mamtir min hashamayim"**; *Shemot* 16:4). It was not hard to see Hashem as responsible for the substance of the nation. Life in *Eretz Yisrael* also has *matar*. Hashem placed us in a land that requires rain (see chapter 19), but the rain doesn't provide bread, but the power for human planting and cultivating to bring forth fruit. As the Torah details, the land will be sustained **"l'matar hashamayim"** (*Devarim* 11:11) by the heavenly rain. As we build up the land every six out of seven years, it is easy to lose sight of who is responsible for growth. We work the land (*leOvda*) and guard our produce (*leShomra*) in the most literal sense of the terms. Yet, the Torah wants us to remember the initial *matar* that brought forth growth on the land. That rain (*ki lo* **himtir**) only came when man was ready *la'avod*, to serve, which Rashi explains is a reference to spiritual service, *tefilla* (*Bereishit* 2:5, Rashi ad loc., cited above). Recognizing God is the ticket to physical blessing in the land and in our lives.

The generation of the desert woke up every morning for forty years to the clear recognition of Hashem as the physical provider, while the nation focused on Torah study and spiritual pursuits. However, after entering into the land of Israel we directly experience this message of *l'ochla* only every *shevi'it*.

Six years out of seven, we cultivate the land and build it, as we are no longer in *Gan Eden*. Although we know that our spiritual state plays a significant role in the blessing we see in the growth, because we are involved in cultivating the land, there is the danger that we will see ourselves as responsible for the output. There is one year where we live in Eretz Yisrael as if we are in *Gan Eden* and partaking of the divine blessing of the manna – the year of *shevi'it*.

The Torah assures us that there is no need for concern regarding what we will eat during the seventh year, as Hashem will bless the produce of the sixth year so that it will provide for all our needs. This parallels the double portion of the manna provided on the sixth day in the desert, which provided enough to sustain the people through their rest on Shabbat.

Rabbi Shimon bar Yochai states (*Mechilta D'Rabbi Yishmael* 2): "The Torah was given to expound upon to those who eat the manna..." The Jews in the desert could wield proper effort in the learning of Torah, as they were supported by the divine blessing of the manna

---

154 The flood is a description of the failure of the world to see God's Hand in life (the second usage of *l'ochla* mentioned above), and the Torah explicitly equates Sodom and Egypt. Sodom was "like the Garden of God, like Egypt" (*Bereishit* 13:10). Life in Eretz Yisrael is meant to be the direct contrast to life in Sodom and Egypt (see chapter 19).

155 As expressed explicitly in the Torah's final use of the term in *Parashat Ha'azinu, ka-matar likchi*, my lesson like rain.

and didn't have to exert themselves to make a living. Similarly, the seventh year allows for a return to Har Sinai; instead of working the land, the divine blessing is there *l'ochla*. For an entire year, man can return to the Garden of Eden, spending a year involved in spiritual pursuits without any physical effort and partaking of the physical bounty that comes as a direct blessing from God. Rabbi Shimon bar Yochai even felt that this divine blessing will be so apparent if the Jews "fulfill the will of God," they won't even have to gather the produce, as others will do it on their behalf (*Berachot* 35b), similar to the manna in the desert.

However, if the land doesn't rest, the Torah tells us in *Parashat Bechukotai* that the punishment is expulsion from the land, which will lie in utter desolation (*Vayikra* 26:34). In other words, if we are unable to live in Gan Eden by Hashem's rules, recognizing His ownership of the land, there will be no blessing and there will be no crops. Much like Adam, we will be expelled from Gan Eden. The blessing will not only be lost during the seventh year, but as long as the Jews remain in exile, unable to return until they recognize the divine contract between the Land and God. Eretz Yisrael flourishes when we recognize it as the Gan Eden it is supposed to be.

The privilege of eating *kedushat shevi'it* produce – something that numerous generations of Jews in exile could not do – is an opportunity that should not be taken for granted. The laws of *kedushat shevi'it* should help us recognize not only Who provides for our needs during this year, but at all times.

Appreciating *Kedushat Shevi'it*

Like the Land of Israel itself, *shevi'it* produce possesses *kedusha* and requires special treatment. Because of the many laws entailed, however, many people avoid it altogether. Instead of consuming it, as the Torah instructs, they treat it as though it were prohibited entirely.[156]

Rav Kook summarizes the beauty of *kedushat shevi'it* produce as expressed through its *mitzvot* and its accompanying limitations:

There is no desecration of sanctity, expressed by the strict claims of private property, regarding anything that grows during this seventh year; the endless desire of wealth, which is stimulated by trade, will be forgotten, as *shemitta* food is "'For food,' but not for medicine, 'for food,' but not for trade." A beneficent eye and deep appreciation will rest on all with the blessing of God in the fruit of the land, "'For food,' but not for loss." Mankind will return to their healthy nature in a manner where they will not need healing for sicknesses, which mostly come on account of harming one's balance in life while distancing oneself from the pure spiritual nature of man: "'For food,' but not for an emollient; 'for food,' but not for perfume; 'for food,' but not for an emetic." A holy and elevated spirit will be poured out on all of life, "It will be a year of complete

---

156 Many *hechsherim* include a line that "there is no concern for *tevel, orla,* or *shevi'it.*" *Tevel* (un-tithed produce) and *orla* (fruit grown during a tree's first three years) are two prohibitions that should certainly be avoided. *Shevi'it,* on the other hand, when consumed properly, is a *mitzvah*.

rest for the land, a sabbath to God." (*Shabbat HaAretz*, Introduction)

Man may achieve *ayin tova*, a positive point of view, realizing that not everything in life is about ownership and amassing wealth.

Rav Tzadok HaKohen adds that *shevi'it* produce has a positive spiritual impact on the individual who eats it:

> The fruits sanctified with the seventh-year [holiness] should inject within the people Godly holiness, as the fruits are holy... and the fruits will also inject holiness within those who eat them... Shemitta is similar to Shabbat... and eating the fruits of the seventh year will inject the holiness of Shabbat into the hearts of those who eat the fruit... (*Pri Tzaddik, Vayikra* 25)

The *Shem MiShmuel* (*Vayikra* 25) describes one who consumes the fruit as one who eats directly from the heavenly table (*mishulchan gavo'ah*). Rabbi Chaim Vital (*Eitz HaDa'at Tov, Vayikra* 25) writes that the significance of eating sabbatical fruit is not only due to its holiness, but additionally in that it aids one to occupy oneself in the study of Torah, which is part of the goal of the *shemitta* year. Similarly, Rav Kook continues:

> What the Shabbat achieves regarding the individual, the *shemitta* achieves with regard to the nation as a whole. A year of solemn rest is essential for both the nation and the land, a year of peace and quiet without oppressor and tyrant... It is a year of equality and rest, in which the soul reaches out towards divine justice, towards God who sustains the living creatures with loving kindness. There is no private property and no punctilious privilege but the peace of God reigns over all in which there is the breath of life. Sanctity is not profaned by the exercise of private acquisitiveness over all this year's produce, and the covetousness of wealth stirred up by commerce is forgotten. For food – but not for commerce.

Chapter 23

The Kashrut of *Shevi'it* Produce–
Shamor and *Ne'evad*

As we have seen, the unique status of the land and the produce that grows from it – both while growing as well as after it is harvested – is a direct outgrowth of the overall goals of *sheviit*. The themes of *shevi'it* observance, including eliminating one's feelings of possesion and equalizing ownership over produce, serve an essential role in the Torah's recipe for a religiously focused, socially directed, and character-building year emphasizing the unique role of our nation in our land.

The *halachot* of *shevi'it* inform us what we must do and what we should not do with the land and its produce during the seventh year. Any produce that grows on its own or under proper *halachic* conditions must be treated with *kedushat shevi'it*.

We have seen in previous chapters that *kedusha* is best translated as "consecrated separateness." Consecrated status demands distinct treatment. The *kedusha* of produce grown in Eretz Yisrael often leads to prohibitions. Thus, produce is designated as *tevel* (un-tithed and therefore forbidden produce) until all *terumot* and *ma'asrot* are taken. Is the same true of produce improperly grown during *shevi'it*? Is acting improperly with the produce reason to prohibit them?

This is an important question when it comes to purchasing produce (and possibly even flowers) during *sheviit*. Indeed, some people are wary of buying produce with *kedushat shevi'it*, for fear that it was not grown or procured in a permissible fashion. Is this a legitimate concern?

Protecting *Shevi'it*

As we have noted, *Chazal* recognized the unique challenges posed by *shevi'it* observance, especially in an agricultural society, labeling the farmers who keep it properly "*gibborei koach*" (see Section II, Theme 3). Indeed, the difficulties entailed are what ultimately enable the successful inculcation of *shevi'it*'s multifaceted messages.

On the other hand, the repercussions of failure to observe *shevi'it* are extreme, as the Torah clearly indicates the *shevi'it* observance is essential to our right to live in Hashem's Land. The Torah promises that nonobservance of *shevi'it* leads to *galut* (*Vayikra* 26), and *Tanach* attests that this is what indeed took place (*Divrei HaYammim II* 36:21). For this reason, when a small part of the nation returned to Eretz Yisrael to build the Second Commonwealth, the covenant Ezra and Nehemiah made with the people specifically mentions observing *shevi'it*:

> וְעַמֵּי הָאָרֶץ הַמְבִיאִים אֶת הַמַּקָּחוֹת וְכָל שֶׁבֶר בְּיוֹם הַשַּׁבָּת לִמְכּוֹר לֹא נִקַּח מֵהֶם בַּשַּׁבָּת וּבְיוֹם קֹדֶשׁ וְנִטּשׁ אֶת הַשָּׁנָה הַשְּׁבִיעִית וּמַשָּׁא כָל יָד:

And as for the peoples of the land who bring merchandise and all grains on the Sabbath day to sell, we shall not purchase from them on the Sabbath or on holy days,

and we shall abandon [the land] during the seventh year [and] the loan given by every hand. (Nechemia 10:32)

Rav Kalman Kahana cites sources from Chazal and from the books of Hasmoneans and Josephus' Antiquities of the Jews, attesting to the extensive observance of shevi'it during the Second Temple period. The Jews had endured the painful ramifications of exile due to shevi'it violations, and they took steps to ensure that it would be properly observed the second time around.[157]

Based on their responsibility of "וַעֲשׂוּ סְיָג לַתּוֹרָה, "building a protective fence around the Torah" (Avot 1:1), and keeping in mind the difficulty of shevi'it observance, Chazal introduced measures to ensure that shevi'it is kept properly. Furthermore, because shevi'it is a public mitzvah, ensuring that the shevi'it atmosphere is maintained was a prime concern to Chazal. For this reason, even when certain non-agricultural activities are performed in the fields, they must be done in such a manner that is clear to all that no shevi'it restrictions are violated in the process. Thus, even some permitted acts that appear like working the land were outlawed (see Shevi'it 3:4; Moed Katan 4b). Chazal also issued restrictions to prevent the aiding of shevi'it offenders (Shevi'it 5:6-9).

Another example of a Rabbinic enactment intended to protect shevi'it is that of sefichin (discussed in chapter 25), annual produce that is harvested on shevi'it and was prohibited in order to prevent misrepresentation of produce planted during shevi'it.

However, the question remains regarding the status of produce that was grown in violation of the Torah's prescription for a year of "shabbat ha'aretz" and "shemittat karka'ot."

	Meaning of the Concept	Product of its violation
Shabbat HaAretz	The prohibition to work the land before and while produce is growing	נֶעֱבָד: Produce derived from fields improperly worked during shevi'it
Shemittat Karka'ot	Releasing one's hold on the produce on his property through an act of declaring it hefker, so that all can partake of the produce equally	שָׁמוּר: Produce that was guarded during shevi'it and not declared ownerless

Is shamur or ne'evad produce essentially non-kosher? Does the fact that produce was procured through a violation result in a prohibition of the produce itself?

This question is significant, as the people who stand to gain by violating shevi'it will likely distribute their produce in the markets. In addition, some detractors of the heter mechira assume that produce grown through reliance on the heter mechira is at the very least considered shamur v'ne'evad and may also be prohibited as sefichin.

---

157 "Shemitta BeMahalach HaZemanim," Shenat HaSheva (Jerusalem, 1985), pp. 118-124.

Status of *Shamur V'Ne'evad* Produce

The status of *shamor v'ne'evad* produce is subject to debate among the *Rishonim*, who discuss the meaning and relationship between two statements in the *Torat Kohanim*.

The first statement seems to indicate that one is not permitted to harvest any produce that was not properly declared *hefker*:

> "And the grapes you have set aside for yourself you cannot harvest" – From guarded produce (*shamur*) of the land you may not harvest, but you may harvest of *hefker* produce. (*Torat Kohanim* 1:3)

Immediately afterwards, we read:

> "Do not harvest" – Do not harvest in the manner of the [professional] harvesters ... but you must do so [abnormally, deviating from the usual manner].

The *Rishonim* differ as to whether the requirement to harvest in an abnormal manner applies to *shamur* produce, while *hefker* produce can be harvested normally, or if guarded produce is totally prohibited and the provision of abnormal harvesting relates to *hefker* produce.

Another statement of the *Torah Kohanim* similarly seems to prohibit *shamur* produce. The *Torat Kohanim* discusses the Torah's intent in describing the permitted and sanctified produce of *shevi'it* as "*shabbat ha'aretz*":

> "וְהָיְתָה שַׁבַּת הָאָרֶץ לָכֶם' - מִן הַשְּׁבוּת בָּאָרֶץ אַתָּה אוֹכֵל, וְאֵין אַתָּה אוֹכֵל מִן הַשָּׁמוּר. מִכָּאן אָמְרוּ: שָׂדֶה שֶׁנִּטַּיְּבָה, בֵּית שַׁמַּאי אוֹמְרִים - אֵין אוֹכְלִים פֵּרוֹתֶיהָ בַּשְּׁבִיעִית, וּבֵית הִלֵּל אוֹמְרִים - אוֹכְלִים".
>
> "And the *shabbat ha'aretz* should be for you" – From the rested [i.e. unworked] produce in the land you may eat, but you may not eat from the guarded produce (*shamur*). From here they stated: A field that has been worked on *shevi'it* – Beit Shammai maintains: One cannot eat the produce, and Beit Hillel maintains: One can eat. (*Torat Kohanim* 1:5).

This passage seems to explicitly state that guarded *shevi'it* produce (*shamur*) is prohibited; one should only eat from "*shabbat ha'aretz*" produce, which grew in a field that rested from work during the seventh year and was not guarded.[158] Beit Shammai adds that one similarly may not eat the produce of fields that were worked during *shevi'it* (*ne'evad*). Beit Hillel, on the other hand, appears to reject the prohibition of *ne'evad*. The *Rishonim* dispute whether Beit Hillel permits *shamur* produce as well.

Thus, some maintain that guarded produce does not become prohibited, but something unique must be done during their harvesting to fulfill the responsibility of declaring it *hefker*. In contrast, a prohibition of *shamur* and/or *ne'evad* produce would indicate that any attempt to retain ownership over one's produce has the result that no one can derive benefit from it. *Shevi'it* produce belongs to everyone equally; any attempt to deny that

---

158 The *Torat Kohanim* uses the term *shabbat ha'aretz* to refer not only to non-worked land, but also non-guarded land, apparently because by both working his field and guarding his produce, the farmer acts as though whatever grows belongs to him.

reality has serious repercussions. The *halacha* regarding ne'evad might be less strict than that of *shamur* because working the land does not necessarily constitute an exhibition of ownership of the produce, whereas guarding produce denies that it is a divine gift.[159]

Shamor Produce- Purchasing and Eating

The Gemara (Sukka 39b) states that even according to the opinion that guarded produce (Shamor) isn't prohibited, one shouldn't purchase it from an ignorant individual. Rashi there and Rambam (8:2) seems that the prohibition stems from the fact that one is prohibited to purchase or do any form of business with shevi'it produce, and any money used for that purchase has *Shevi'it* sanctity and will probably not be treated with sanctity by the ignorant seller. For this reason, it is almost impossible to find a practical case where *shamor* produce is available without being sold, as one who guards their produce intends to sell it, and the purchase of it runs a series of other issues.

Regarding the outright permissibility of guarded fruits, there are several contradictions as to what the Chazon Ish's ruling on the matter, and it is explained (see Mishpetei Eretz 5767 ed. P. 291) that since practically even if the produce isn't prohibited there is no way to purchase them, they are essentially always prohibited. Bottom line, however, if one finds *shamor* produce in front of them (possibly as a guest in someone's home) they aren't prohibited (*Minchat Shlomo* 44).

Ne'evad Produce- Purchasing and Eating

It is clear from several *mishnayot* (see *Terumot* 2, 3; *Shevi'it* 4,2) that Chazal prohibited benefit from those who performed certain agricultural work in the fields. The Ramban cites this as a proof that *ne'evad*, produce gained from prohibited agricultural work, is prohibited. The *Ra'avad* (gloss to Hil. *Shemitta* 4,15) adds that the *Sephichim* prohibition further illustrates that products of Shevi'it violations are prohibited.

The Rambam personally debated this issue, initially citing the view of the Ritz Geut that ne'evad is prohibited, but later (*Hilchot Shemitta* 4, 15) adopting the view that ne'evad produce is permitted. Rav Shlomo Zalman Auerabach (*Minchat Shlomo* 44) rules that the minhag is to permit *ne'evad*, and so is cited in the name of the Chazon Ish. Nevertheless, here as well, most cases of *ne'evad* produce will run into problems regarding their purchase. The main instance where this is significant is whether one who is stringent regarding *heter mechira* and feels that the sale is invalid can eat from produce of others who rely on it.

Deeper Implications of *Shamor* and *Ne'evad*

The question of the permissibility of *shevi'it* produce where the laws of *shevi'it* weren't observed seems to underscore a Gbunch of broader issues. Besides the *halachic* issues

---

159 Interestingly, a number of authorities maintain that there is there is a Rabbinic injunction that those who work their fields during *shevi'it* are prohibited from working them the following year. Nevertheless, Beit Hillel permits eating produce cultivated in such fields. The Radvaz (*Hilchot Shemitta V'Yovel* 4:1) explains that while the individual is punished for worked his land, since the produce of the field is not his own, but rather belongs to the entire Jewish People, the produce is not restricted and is permitted for everyone to eat.

mentioned above regarding the *kedusha* status of *shevi'it* produce, there is another issue.

We mentioned that once every seven years our produce consumption is supposed to mirror the eating of the manna, and to a certain degree the intended eating of *Adam Ha-rishon*, the first human, in the Garden of Eden. *Ne'evad* and *Shamor*, the terms we use for produce on worked land or guarded while growing, are the exact terms commanded to *Adam Ha-rishon*: *Le'ovda u'leshomra*.

וַיִּקַּח ה' אֱלֹהִים אֶת הָאָדָם וַיַּנִּחֵהוּ בְגַן עֵדֶן לְעָבְדָהּ וּלְשָׁמְרָהּ:

And the Lord God took man and placed him in Gan Eden *le'ovda u'leshomra* (to serve and protect). (*Bereishit* 2:15).

We have seen several times how the term *l'ochla* returns us to the bliss of *Gan Eden*, where we eat of the bounty of the land with deep recognition of Hashem as our Provider. *Le'Ovda u'leshomra* in the context of Gan Eden involves dedicating one's time to spiritual service, strengthening one's relationship with God, the one who really determines what grows.

After being kicked out of *gan eden* we as a nation experienced direct sustenance from Hashem in the *midbar*, throughout our forty-year sojourn in the desert. There, the commandment of *l'ochla* reappeared, as once again we would eat with clear recognition of Hashem as the Provider.

In *Eretz Yisrael* we would physically work the land, fulfilling the *mitzvah* of *yishuv Eretz Yisrael*, settling the land and watching the deserts bloom. But once every seven years we take a step back. We don't physically work the land (*ovda*) and we don't even protetct our crops (*shomra*) as they are free for all to take. *Le'ovda u'leshomra* regain their initial meaning from the time of *gan Eden*. There is no need for farming, as the year can be dedicated to the spiritual service *shevi'it* allows involving a focus on Torah study and a return to "Har Sinai". The divine blessing provides significantly more crops in the sixth year and we consume it alongside the blessed produce throughout the seventh year (*l'ochla*). Produce of the seventh year is sanctified with *kedushat shevi'it* and its *halachot* help us recognize that we are consuming manna-like produce in a year of *Gan Eden*.

The only individuals who are able to ruin this bliss are those who deny the divine blessing and think they accomplish more by working the land (*leOvda*) literally. Those driven by greed deny the shared ownership of all the produce of the land and try to guard it (*leShomra*) by restricting others from taking it. Generally, these same individuals will have commercial objectives for doing so (violating *l'ochla v'lo l'schora*, for consumption and not for selling).

The opinions we presented about the *halachic* validity of eating such produce seem to revolve around the question: Does undermining the blessing of *shevi'it* produce by working the land and guarding it in violation of *shevi'it* relegate this produce as unviable and prohibited? Anyone who does so will not be partaking of manna-like produce, nor will they be blessed with a year of *Gan Eden*. Unfortunately, those who don't follow the rules of *Gan Eden* are banished from the garden much like Adam and instead of the blessing they are cursed with "by the sweat of your brow you will eat bread…" (*Bereishit* 3:15).

These are the exact punishments and curses described in *Parashat Bechukotai* of what will befall the nation if they fail to observe *shevi'it*, banishment and desolation (*Vayikra* ch. 26). However, will the produce be prohibited?

Although produce of *ne'evad* and *shamor* should not be appetizing to us, the opinions who permit such produce might reason as follows: All one's efforts to futher the growth of *shevi'it* produce are doomed to failure; Hashem's blessing surrounds *shevi'it* crops whether one chooses to recognize that or not. One's punishments for *shevi'it* violations will be felt after the seventh year, but no matter what you try to do, divine blessing will encapsulate the produce of the seventh year.

Chapter 24

Sefichin: Produce that Grows on Its Own

We noted previously that the Torah and *Chazal* were very concerned that individuals would violate *shevi'it*. The severity with which the Torah views *shevi'it* violations requires that we take precautions to ensure that individuals can express the *gevura* necessary to be *gibborei koach* of *shevi'it*. Thus, produce designated as "*shamur*" (guarded produce) or "*ne'evad*" (produce of worked fields) may be prohibited *mid'orayta* (Biblically). We also saw that *Chazal* were concerned regarding permitting activities that could easily be used by the disingenuous as a cover for *shevi'it* violations.

One area of *shevi'it* that poses difficulty in observance relates to annuals – that is, grains, legumes (*kitniyot*), and vegetables that generally have to be replanted again every year in order to grow. While fruit will continue to grow on trees during *shevi'it* regardless of the farmer's actions, vegetables and annuals will only be available part of the year. At the beginning of the year, there may still be crops that were planted during the sixth year, but they certainly won't last for the entire year of *shevi'it* or into the eighth year, when crops can be planted again.

Because annual crops grow from seeds, there is always the possibility that seeds planted in previous years will grow even when not planted during *shevi'it*. This produce that grows on its own is known as סְפִיחִין, *sefichin*, after-growths.

Does *shevi'it* prevent us from making use of such vegetation, which was not planted on *shevi'it* itself?

The Torah Law
·····························

We noted elsewhere that the *pesukim* in *Parashat Behar* seem to present contradictory expressions regarding the permissibility of produce that grows on its own during *shevi'it*.

סְפִיחַ קְצִירְךָ לֹא תִקְצֹר (*Vayikra* 25:5)	וְהָיְתָה שַׁבַּת הָאָרֶץ לָכֶם לְאָכְלָה (*Vayikra* 25:6)
"Do not harvest the produce in the fields." This seems to indicate that one is restricted from harvesting and consuming that which grows during *shevi'it*.	"The produce of the Shabbat of the land will be for you to eat." This seems to indicate that the Torah specifically designated the produce of the seventh year to be consumed.

We noted that the *Torat Kohanim* (*Behar* 4:5) offers a few explanations. The primary understanding is that although *shevi'it* produce is designated for consumption, as long as it is treated with the requisite *kedusha*, it cannot be harvested in the usual manner: "לֹא תִקְצֹר כְּדֶרֶךְ הַקּוֹצְרִים." The owner of the field may not express his ownership through the harvesting process. Rabbi Akiva, however, explains that anything that grows on its own during the *shemitta* year is prohibited to harvest. This is why the Jews are likely to question what they are going to eat during *shevi'it*:

וְכִי תֹאמְרוּ מַה נֹּאכַל בַּשָּׁנָה הַשְּׁבִיעִת הֵן לֹא נִזְרָע וְלֹא נֶאֱסֹף אֶת תְּבוּאָתֵנוּ:

And if you will say: "What will we eat in the seventh year? Behold, we may not sow, nor gather our produce" (*Vayikra* 25:20)

According to Rabbi Akiva, the people are expressing two fears: they will not be able to plant new produce, and additionally they will not be able to gather and harvest that which grows on its own:

אִם אֵין אָנוּ זוֹרְעִים, מָה אָנוּ אוֹסְפִים? אָמַר רַבִּי עֲקִיבָא: מִכָּאן סָמְכוּ חֲכָמִים עַל הַסְּפִיחִים, שֶׁיִּהְיוּ אֲסוּרִים בַּשְּׁבִיעִית.

If we do not sow, what are we gathering? Rabbi Akiva says: This is the source of the prohibition of *sefichin* during *shevi'it*, as articulated by the Sages. (*Torat Kohanim* 4:5)

As the Tosafot Rid (*Pesachim* 51b) explains, Rabbi Akiva understands that the designation of the produce of *shevi'it* as being "*l'ochla*," set aside for consumption, only relates to fruit of the trees. However, produce that grows directly from the ground is prohibited Biblically, even if it was not planted on *shevi'it*. There is, therefore, no contradiction between the *pesukim* quoted above.

The Sages cited in the *Torah Kohanim* disagree with Rabbi Akiva's understanding of the *pesukim*. In the view of the Sages, the Torah designates all *shevi'it* produce, both fruits and vegetables, as *l'ochla*, prohibiting only normal harvesting, and therefore clearly the Torah does not prohibit gathering that which grows on its own. In their view, the concern expressed by the Jews regarding what they will eat during *shevi'it* given that "לא נאסף," "we will not gather," refers to the requirement of *biur shevi'it*. Even though they are able to gather produce that grows on its own, they are not permitted to store it for long periods. *Sefichin* are prohibited Rabbinically, such that the *pasuk* cannot possibly refer to the prohibition.

Examination of this Rabbinic prohibition will help us understand its scope and provide greater insight into the balance between safeguarding *shevi'it* observance and ensuring that the people need not be concerned that they will lack food during *shevi'it*.

The Rabbinic Prohibition

The *Torat Kohanim* does not provide an explicit reason why *sefichin* are prohibited Rabbincally. Especially according to the Sages, who understand that all produce growing during *shevi'it* is designated *l'ochla*, shouldn't we want to guarantee that it all can, in fact, be eaten? Furthermore, the Torah's allowance of consumption of produce that grows on its own would help ensure that the people have ample food. What would warrant such a prohibition? Why would *Chazal* limit the consumption of produce of the sixth year, which the Torah specifically indicates is blessed?

The *mishna* in *Shevi'it* (9:1) quotes Rabbi Yehuda's opinion that mustard *sefichin* are permitted, and the reasoning he provides is "שֶׁלֹּא נֶחְשְׁדוּ עֲלֵיהֶם עוֹבְרֵי עֲבֵרָה"– there is no fear of bad actors regarding them. A number of *Rishonim* explain that this indicates that *Chazal* generally prohibited *sefichin* due to the fear of dishonest efforts to continue growing produce during *shevi'it*, pretending that it was an after-growth of the previous year's planting. So rules the Rambam:

> All consumption of *sefichin* is prohibited on a Rabbinical level. And why was this decree made? Because of sinners, so that they do not go surreptitiously and sow grain and legumes and other produce in their fields and eat from them when they grow and claim they are *sefichin*. Therefore, a decree was made banning all *sefichin* from *shevi'it*. From this we learn that we do not eat from the produce of *shevi'it* with the exception of the fruits of the trees and crops that are not commonly planted, for example: rue, goosefoot, and others. However, vegetables that are commonly planted in gardens and grains and legumes are Rabbinically prohibited. And one who gathers them is punished with lashes. (Rambam, *Hilchot Shemitta* 4:2)

Despite the desire to enable consumption of all *shevi'it* produce, after experiencing exile due to rampant *shevi'it* violations during the first *Mikdash*, the Sages felt that permitting *sefichin* under general circumstances would create a dangerous means for illegitimate actors to violate *shevi'it*. The Sages therefore, prohibited most *sefichin* consumption.

This perspective still requires some explanation. After all, if the Torah designates food for consumption during a year when there is less to eat, why would *Chazal* prohibit it, even given the fear of *shevi'it* violation[160]? We noted elsewhere (Chapter 19) that *Chazal* went so far as to refrain from sanctifying certain areas of the Land to ensure that the needy would have food to eat on *shevi'it*. Why do they seemingly do the opposite here?[161]

It seems that the distinction is based on the fact that this prohibition reflects *Chazal's* concern that individuals will make a mockery of *shevi'it* observance, abusing the trust that the Torah places in the people by using illicit methods to eat away at *shevi'it*'s core under a façade of righteousness. These *"ovrei aveira"* act as though they have been divinely blessed, when they are in fact attempting to rebel against God and His connection to His nation and His Land.

The prohibition of *sefichin* seems to be a commentary on how disingenuous individuals can negatively impact society through the medium of underhanded deceit. Allowing that practice to continue would undermine society as a whole; the moment that these types of practices became known to the public, no one would be able to trust his neighbor. Despite the *mitzvah* to consume *shevi'it* produce, and despite the need for as much permitted produce as possible, the Sages evidently felt it necessary to limit our consumption so that we would remain a society of honest adherents.

---

160 See the Aruch Hashulchan 22:3-10 questions extensively why *Chazal* prohibited *sefichin*.

161 The truth is that in practice, there were generally not many prohibited *sefichin* available for consumption. Some annuals are permitted because the probability or possibility of *shevi'it* violation is low. In our day, the problem is expanded, because if one does not rely on the *heter mechira*, any vegetables grown through that method might be prohibited as *sefichin*.

Halachic Implications

Understanding that the accepted position of the Sages is that *sefichin* are prohibited to prevent illicit violations of *shevi'it* leads to important *halachic* limitations of the prohibition. Essentially, *sefichin* are prohibited due to the fear of *ne'evad*, that the fields might be worked through planting, which generates a restriction on the produce. Thus, the only *sefichin* that should be prohibited are those regarding which there is a well-founded fear that they come from clandestinely cultivated crops.

Thus, although the *sefichin* prohibition applies to wheat, legumes, and vegetables, there is a dispute regarding growths that do not have *kedushat shevi'it*, such as some forms of flowers. Several authorities rule that the logic of the prohibition should apply to any situation in which one stands to gain by planting the produce during *shevi'it*, and the prohibition thus includes flowers (*Mishnat Yosef* 1:9:1). However, Rav Shlomo Zalman Auerbach (*Minchat Shlomo* 1:51:11) rules that only produce with *kedushat shevi'it* is included in the prohibition.[162] There is no prohibition of *sefichin* regarding fruits that grow on trees, as even if the trees were planted "illegally" on *shevi'it*, the fruit is *orla* during the first three years, and fruit rarely grows immediately in any event.

Another important implication of the reasoning behind the prohibition relates to the stage of growth at which a crop is considered *sefichin* prohibited on *shevi'it*. The Rambam (*Hilchot Shemitta V'Yovel* 4:9-13) rules that the prohibition applies to legumes that reach a third of their growth during *shevi'it* ("hava'at shlish")[163] and all vegetables with *kedushat shevi'it* that are harvested during *shevi'it* ("lekita"). The Ra'sh (9:1) agrees regarding legumes, but argues regarding vegetables. He notes that it is clear from some *mishnayot* that there is a possibility of permitted *shevi'it* vegetables. Thus, the determinant must not be whether the vegetables have *kedushat shevi'it*, but whether it appears that they were actually planted in the seventh year. Any growth that breaks ground during the sixth year is considered *sefichei shishit*, after-growths of the sixth year, and is permitted for consumption, even if they are harvested (properly) on *shevi'it* itself.[164] If the vegetables sprouted before *shevi'it*, they do not carry Chazal's concern for dishonest farmers.

The Ra'sh's understanding helps respond to a question we posed above: If the vegetables of the sixth year are blessed produce, meant to ensure the nation has food to eat during *shevi'it*, why did Chazal prohibit it? The answer seems to be that Chazal did not, in fact, prohibit the produce of the sixth year; any vegetable that sprouts during the sixth year is not included in the *sefichin* prohibition and should be eaten with *kedushat shevi'it* when picked in the seventh year, with the understanding that it is divine bounty.[165]

---

162 Since flowers are not consumed, there is reason to believe that even if the *sefichin* prohibition does apply to such flowers and the like, one would not be prohibited from benefiting from their beauty; see *Shemitta KeHilchata*, ch. 12, note 12.

163 This is explicit in the *Yerushalmi, Ma'asrot* 5:2.

164 The Ramban (*Vayikra* 25: 5) and Rosh (9:1) concur with this view.

165 The Rambam (*Hilchot Shemitta V'Yovel* 4: 18) rules, based on the Tosefta, that prohibited *sefichin* should be uprooted and not permitted to grow, either due to fear that people will think they were planted during *shevi'it* (see Mahari Curcus ad loc.) or because people will think the owner of the field intends to eat them (see *Chazon Ish* 9:4).

The *Pe'at HaShulchan* (22:3) and the *Chazon Ish* (9:17) rule like the Ra'sh. The *Chazon Ish* even explains that the mere sprouting before *shevi'it* is sufficient to permit an entire vegetable field. For this reason, the practice is to plant vegetable fields in enough time before *shevi'it* to ensure that the vegetables will sprout before Rosh Hashana of *shevi'it*. Stories (some might say legends) are told of the lengths to which the elderly *Chazon Ish* would go to investigate vegetable fields to identify if anything had sprouted before *shevi'it* so as to permit the entire field.[166]

For this reason, there will be vegetables with *kedushat shevi'it* for some time at the beginning of *shevi'it*. Calendars are published every *shevi'it* listing until when one will be able to find each type of vegetable in the marketplace, as until that time, it can be assumed to have sprouted during the sixth year. These vegetables possess *kedushat shevi'it* when harvested during the seventh year.

The reasoning behind the prohibition is also the basis for permitting the consumption of perennial vegetable plants during *shevi'it*. A number of vegetable plants are planted only once and will then continue to grow vegetables every year. Although the vegetables of a particular year might only sprout during *shevi'it*, since the initial sprouting of the vegetables from the plant occurred before *shevi'it*, the prohibition of *sefichin* does not apply to these vegetables (see *Katif Shevi'it* 16:7).[167]

Similarly, the *sefichin* prohibition does not apply to produce that grows in a *sadeh bar*, a wild field, or a *sadeh hefker*, as in those cases, the logic of the prohibition does not apply. Produce that grows in fields that are not meant for planting or in which planting annuals is detrimental are also not included in the prohibition (Rambam, *Hilchot Shemitta V'Yovel* 4:4).[168]

If the crop has already been harvested, some rule that it should be left to rot on its own, as *shevi'it* produce is still inherently holy and may not be actively destroyed (see *Chazon Ish* 4:6 and *Aruch HaShulchan* 22:9).

166 Although Rav Shlomo Zalman Auerbach (*Minchat Shlomo* 49-50) felt that one should be stricter and require that vegetables reach a third of their growth prior to *shevi'it* in order to be excluded from the prohibition, *l'Halacha* he accepted the opinion of the *Chazon Ish*. Importantly, Rav Auerbach maintained that there may be other reasons that we can be lenient regarding *sefichin* in today's day and age. First of all, planting can no longer be done in secrecy, as it entails tractors and other heavy machinery, and the possibility of clandestine illegal planting is thus far more unlikely. Second, anyone who wishes to plant during *shevi'it* nowadays can simply rely on the *heter mechira*; there is no need for him to surreptitiously plant during *shevi'it*. Based on this, Rav Zev Weitman (*Likrat Shemitta Mamlachtit* 8:2-3), Rabbinic supervisor of Tenuva Dairies and one of the major Religious Zionist figures pushing for greater observance of *shevi'it* without reliance on the *heter mechira*, suggests that we rely more heavily on planting during the sixth year in order to ensure readily available Jewish crops of vegetables and the like during the seventh year. This advances the important endeavor of providing Jewish-grown produce without any *halachic* questions throughout the year of *shevi'it*. This may sometimes entail planting annual crops in the sixth year at a non-optimal time, something that is risky agriculturally, but one who accepts such risks for noble reasons can recognize the divine *beracha* that his actions will hopefully elicit. "Devout farmers who recognize that the measure of their bounty isn't dependent on themselves, but on divine assistance, will recognize with faith that fulfilling the *mitzvot* of *shemitta* will not lead to damage or loss, but rather the opposite: it will lead to blessing, as the Torah promises."

167 It is important to note that advancements in refrigeration allow for a number of vegetables from the sixth year to be marketable for some time during the following year. In the absence of a reliable *hechsher*, it is therefore difficult to determine whether one is dealing with produce of the sixth year or the seventh. It is often very difficult to clarify the status of produce exported from the State of Israel.

Importantly, since a non-Jew is permitted to plant during *shevi'it*, produce from fields owned by non-Jews are not prohibited as *sefichin* (Rambam, ibid. 4:29). This is the basis for the dispute regarding *heter mechira* produce. According to those who view the *heter mechira* fields as non-Jewish owned, their vegetables can be eaten throughout the year, as the prohibition of *sefichin* does not apply. However, according to those who question the validity of the sale, the annuals and vegetables will be prohibited as *sefichin*.

Sefichin During Year Eight

The reasoning behind the prohibition of *sefichin* is also relevant to its application in the eighth year. As *shevi'it* ends, immediately after Rosh Hashana of the eighth year, Israeli agriculture comes back to life and farmers begin planting again. At what point can we assume that the vegetables and annuals are from the eighth year and there is no reason to prohibit them due to concerns of *sefichin*? The *mishna* asks this question:

> When may one buy vegetables at the outgoing of the sabbatical year [without fear that they are sabbatical produce]? When enough time has passed for similar [vegetables] to grow. Where produce ripens quickly, even that which is late in ripening is also permissible. Rabbi [Yehuda HaNasi] used to allow the buying of vegetables immediately after the sabbatical year was over. (*Shevi'it* 6:4)

The first opinion in the *mishna* states that one should not purchase vegetables after *shevi'it* within the timeframe in which it would take such produce to grow anew in the eight year.

The Rambam (ibid. 4:29) and others explain, based on the Tosefta (4:7), that this prohibition applies even when one knows that the produce was harvested during the eighth year. As long as bad actors still stand to gain from surreptitiously planting during *shevi'it* and marketing their products before *shevi'it*-observers can do so, the prohibition still has relevance. Therefore, there exists a concept of *sefichin b'motza'ei shevi'it*, a continued prohibition of *shevi'it* during part of the eighth year.

The Rambam rules (ibid. 4:6), based on the Yerushalmi (*Demai* 2:1), that *sefichin* are prohibited only until Chanuka of the eighth year. The *Chazon Ish* explains that any vegetables harvested after Chanuka of the eighth year (even those that could possibly have been planted during *shevi'it*) are permitted, as by that time bad actors have little to gain from their illegitimate plans. However, vegetables harvested during *shevi'it* itself always remain prohibited.

There are calendars that provide information as to when different vegetables could have grown entirely during the eighth year and from what point their consumption is permitted. Vegetables that grow quickly, such as cucumbers and zucchini, will appear on the shelves relatively quickly, but most other vegetables will be permitted only permitted from Chanuka time. Certain vegetables that have a long shelf-life and could still be from *shevi'it* (e.g. onions) will only appear as permitted eighth-year produce later on in the year.[169]

---

168 Vegetables that grow in one's home or in a non-perforated flower pot are permitted, since this is not the primary method of vegetable growth, and it is not even clear that cultivating them is prohibited during *shevi'it* itself; see *Sefer HaShemitta*, ch. 6, n. 2.

169 Legumes are permitted from the time they reach a third of their growth during the eighth year; see *Chazon Ish* 9:16.

Only Applies to Vegetables and Annuals

That grow in the borders of Olei Bavel   In Jewish owned land:

Only if grows outside (not inside a home)

According to the Chazon Ish, as long as any sprouting began in the sixth year it is permitted:

Only applies where the reason for the Gezeira applies, Excluding:

Chapter 25

מַה נֹּאכַל בַּשָּׁנָה הַשְּׁבִיעִית-What Can We Eat During *Shevi'it*?

The most practical question that concerns *shevi'it* observers in Eretz Yisrael is a take-off on the Biblical question:

> וְכִי תֹאמְרוּ מַה נֹּאכַל בַּשָּׁנָה הַשְּׁבִיעִת הֵן לֹא נִזְרָע וְלֹא נֶאֱסֹף אֶת תְּבוּאָתֵנוּ:
>
> And if you say: What shall we eat during the seventh year, for we will not plant or gather our grains? (*Vayikra* 25:20)

Since normal planting and harvesting are restricted throughout the year and there are limitations on eating *sefichin* and the like, the question seems legitimate. What does Hashem want us to eat during shevi'it?

Not so long ago – due to lack of refrigeration, funds, and secure shipping routes – this question was particularly pertinent, as the Jews who had returned to Eretz Yisrael were living off the land, and the arrival of *shemitta* brought fear of literal starvation.

In our day and age, the vegetable stores in Israel are certainly not empty during *shevi'it*. There is plenty of produce available, but what type is most appropriate? What are the special *halachot* regarding how they must be eaten?

A Little History

As we have noted, the reality faced by the initial pioneers of Jewish agricultural settlement in the late 1800s in *Eretz Yisrael* was very different than that of today. They encountered a land of infertile swamps that aptly fulfilled the Biblical curse of *shemama* (desolation) during the exile. The Land of Israel only grows for its Jewish inhabitants, and when the Jewish nation returned to its land, it began to flourish. As the *navi* states:

> So says the Lord God, to the mountains and to the hills, to the streams and to the valleys, to the desolate wastes and to the abandoned cities, which have become a prey and a derision to the rest of the nations around...
> As for you, you mountains of Israel – you shall shoot forth your branches and yield your fruit to My nation, Israel, for they will soon come. For behold, I am for you, and I shall turn to you, and you will be tilled and sown. And I will multiply men upon you – all of the house of Israel, in whole; and the cities will be inhabited, and the desolate places rebuilt. (*Yechezkel* 36:4, 8-10)

The Talmudic description of the echoes of redemption rung loudly in the ears of the pioneers:

> Rabbi Abba said: There is no more revealed sign of the redemption than this, as it is written (*Yechezkel* 36), "As for you, you mountains of Israel – you shall shoot forth your branches and yield your fruit to My nation, Israel, for they will soon come." (*Ketubot* 68a)

Yet here the *shevi'it* challenge began. Would the fledgling agricultural settlements succeed in weathering *shevi'it*? Would *shevi'it* observance result in starvation or even worse? The Biblical question of "what will we eat?" was on everyone's mind.

Some viewed the challenge of *shevi'it* as a call to *gevura*. It provided the opportunity to exhibit how our success in the Holy Land requires fulfillment of the agricultural *mitzvot hateluyot ba'aretz*. But the challenges were very real. Adding to the difficulty was that Baron Rothschild, the benefactor of many agricultural communities, was unwilling to continue supporting those who couldn't find a way to continue developing the land during *shevi'it*. It was clear that some sort of *halachic* response was necessary.

הֶתֵּר מְכִירָה

The majority of Rabbinic authorities ruled that *shevi'it* observance when most of the nation is not living in Israel in their ancestral plots is only Rabbinically mandated, allowing for certain leniencies. Beginning in the *shemitta* year of 5649 (1888-1889), some great Rabbinic leaders, lead by Rav Yitzchak Elchanan Spector and Rav Shmuel Mohliver, permitted reliance upon the *heter mechira*, which grants a permit (*heter*) of temporarily selling (*mechira*) the Jewish farmland to a non-Jew prior to *shevi'it*. This would allow some cultivation of the land and remove prohibitions such as *sefichin* from the vegetables that grew during *shevi'it*.

This approach was a source of great debate. Some of its detractors saw it as a violation of a Biblical injunction of "*Lo Techanem*" (*Devarim* 7:2), which is broadly understood as including a prohibition of giving non-Jews ownership of land in Eretz Yisrael (see *Avoda Zara* 20b). Others focused on what they viewed as an ineffective means of sale and other *halachic* issues.

Nevertheless, even the *heter mechira*'s detractors recognized its noble intentions – providing a means of support, and at times even survival, while assisting the continued growth of Jewish agriculture in Israel. Rav Avraham Yeshaya Karelitz – known by the name of his magnum opus, the *Chazon Ish* – was a fierce opponent of the *heter mechira*, but he issued numerous lenient rulings regarding *shevi'it* observance that enabled survival even without it. Interestingly, Rav Avraham Yitzchak HaKohen Kook, who ultimately became one of the main Rabbinic backers of the *heter mechira*, generally ruled far more strictly then the Chazon Ish on matters of *shevi'it* observance, which lead to a greater need for reliance on the *heter mechira* (see Rav Rimon, *Shemitta*, p. 418).

Those who did not accept the *heter mechira* advocated what they referred to as a strict observance of *shevi'it*, founding the *Keren HaShevi'is*, a fund to help support farmers who let their fields lie fallow during *shevi'it*.

The stakes of this dispute were always very high. Those who denied the *heter mechira*'s validity felt that it would result in the nation's exile and the desolation of the land, as lack of *shevi'it* observance had done in the past. On the other hand, the alternative options often involved forgoing purchasing Jewish produce available through the *heter* and purchasing from the non-Jewish inhabitants of the land. At times, these residents were openly hostile to

Jews and Jewish agricultural advancement, yet some observant Jews preferred supporting them at the expense of their brethren who relied on the *heter mechira*. This decision impacted other years as well, as Jewish land that remained uncultivated during *shevi'it* was often usurped by hostile inhabitants who embraced the increased opportunities and resources in an effort to take over more land in order to provide for the needs of *shevi'it* observers.

For the proponents of the *heter mechira*, the temporary sale to non-Jews through the *heter* was a fulfillment of helping one's fellow Jew in distress. The true violation of *Lo Techanem* was by individuals who were giving enemies of the nation a permanent foothold in the land through increased farmland. Some questioned whether those who advocated a "strict approach to *shevi'it*," which indeed did not rely on the *heter mechira*, were being strict at all, as their approach was overall much more permissive.

With battle lines drawn and each camp accusing others of spiritually destructive decision-making, the differences of opinion seemed insurmountable. At times, it seemed as though each camp viewed the other as the true enemy of the continued existence of the Jewish nation in their land.

The Current Debate

The question now is far different than it once was. The agricultural revolution Israel has witnessed over the past one hundred fifty years is unheard of in the annals of history. Israel is the only country in the world with more forests than it had one hundred years ago, and it is the number-one agricultural exporter in the world.

The Tony Blair Institute for Global Change's 2019 report on Israeli agriculture notes that Israel is an agricultural leader despite numerous challenges. It has a shortage of natural water resources, it is far from potential export markets, two-thirds of the land is arid or semi-arid, its original agricultural pioneers arrived with no farming experience, and the land was barren and swampy. Nevertheless, it has the highest tomato yield in the world (six times the global average), the highest cow-milk productivity (more than double the European average), and the lowest post-harvest grain loss (40% less than the global average). Israel has made the desert bloom and has become a "light unto the nations" for developed and developing countries.

The report seeks answers on the secret to Israel's success. It notes several factors, including effective decision-making, well-organized farmers, a market-oriented approach, and a multidisciplinary innovation system focused on problem-solving. The report expresses hope that these elements can be replicated in some way in African countries. However, it notes that some elements of Israel's success are unique to Israel, including strong ideological ties to agriculture and a pioneering spirit.

While all that is true, the report misses the most fundamental factor: Divine blessing stemming from a prophetic promise. When the Jewish nation returns to the Land, the Land returns to them and comes back to life.

This promise, however, carries with it the same conditions it did in the past. If we want to merit divine blessing, we must abide by the Torah's guidelines for being worthy of the blessing.

For many, Israel's current agricultural standing indicates that there is no longer a need for the *heter mechira*, as it was always intended as a temporary measure; it was never intended to be institutionalized. The question of "what can we eat" can now be answered simply: non-Jewish produce, either imported from other countries or purchased from our local neighbors. No one is going to go hungry nowadays – except, perhaps, the farmers, who will continue to be supported by a small government allowance, and primarily the *Keren HaShevi'is*.

Advocates of the continued use of the *heter mechira* argue that although circumstances have changed, it is necessary in order to sustain the Israeli agricultural enterprise. In our day, when only a small percentage of the Jewish residents of Israel are farmers or work in agriculture, *shemitta* may pose a different question: מַה נֹּאכַל בִּשְׁאָר הַשָּׁנִים, what will we eat in other years? In today's globalized economy where farmers don't only sell to local markets, the inability to work the field during *shemitta* translates into the inability to supply global contracts for a year. In a world where contracts are rarely for one year at a time, *shevi'it* observance is seen by some as a barrier to exporting produce abroad. Can Israel's farmers possibly invest and advance if there is a hiatus in its exportable produce every seven years? Should all Israeli produce be provided by outsiders, such that there will be no sanctified Jewish produce at all?

Advocates of continued reliance on the *heter mechira* argue that although it is noble for farmers to let their fields lie fallow, we are obligated to support our Jewish brethren who work in agriculture and feel they won't survive the other years as well if they don't rely on the *heter*.

Over time, the *heter mechira* has been fortified both *halachically* and legally to ensure that it responds to the objections of its detractors, although the objection of using a means to circumvent *shemitta* remains. The advocates argue that opting to purchase produce from local enemies instead would certainly be criminal.

Another Way?

שִׁשִּׁית

In modern times, alternative options have been developed to respond to the challenges of *shevi'it*. The most basic option is reliance on produce from the sixth year. Although there is discussion as to whether the Biblical blessing promising a particularly bountiful sixth year continues when *shevi'it* observance is only Rabbinic (see *Sema*, C.M. 67), there certainly seems to be great blessing every year preceding *shemitta*. It was difficult to harness all the blessing in the past, as lack of suitable refrigeration did not allow for *shishit* produce to be available throughout the year. Nowadays, some sixth-year produce (such as onions, gourds, and the like) lasts throughout most of the seventh year.

Other options include reliance on hydroponic produce and produce grown in areas of the

State of Israel that are not considered sanctified for the purposes of *shevi'it* (see ch. 19). These options seek to provide a means for Jewish farmers to continue to supply produce, both nationally and at times even internationally, during the seventh year. In addition, they seek to limit the need to import produce from overseas or to purchase from hostile neighbors.

There is, however, another option that is agreed upon in principle by both the Chazon Ish and Rav Kook.[170] This option, if executed properly, allows not only for supporting local Jewish farmers, but also partaking of sanctified *shevi'it* produce. Additionally, it is not a modern innovation at all, as its basis is explicit in the Tosefta, which states:

אוֹצַר בֵּית דִּין

> Originally, agents of the *Beit Din* would sit at the city gates, and if someone came with *shemitta* produce in his hand, they would take it from him and provide him with enough food for three meals, and they would put the rest into a storehouse in the city. When the time for harvesting figs arrived, the court's agents would hire workers to pick them and make them into cakes of pressed figs, put them in barrels, and put them in the city storehouse. When the time for harvesting grapes arrived, the court's agents would hire workers... And on Fridays, they would distribute the food from the storehouses to each and every person according to the needs of his family. (*Tosefta, Shevi'it* 8:1-2)

The Ramban (*Vayikra* 25:7) understands that the *Tosefta* describes a means of distributing produce throughout *shevi'it* through the aegis of *Beit Din*. Since *shevi'it* produce (other than *sefichin*) is not only permitted but possibly a *mitzvah* to eat, the primary issue is how individuals throughout the land can get the produce. The issue is not one of ownership, as the produce has been declared *hefker* by its owners; it simply remains impractical for all the residents of Israel to go field by field in order to gather the various different crops they need for a vegetable salad or soup. The *Tosefta* describes a means of harvesting the produce in a way that would otherwise be prohibited and distributing it throughout the land.

The modern equivalent of this practice is known as *Otzar Beit Din*, through which a court serves as a public treasury enabling distribution of *shevi'it* produce. The Chazon Ish (*Shevi'it* 11:7) accepts this practice and explains (*ibid.* 12:6) that the prohibition of harvesting normally applies when one exerts his ownership over produce by harvesting it as if it is one's own. However, the agents harvesting on behalf of *Beit Din* do the opposite; they harvest for the benefit of all the Jewish families who will receive the produce for free through the *Beit Din*. The goal is to provide *shevi'it* produce to everyone – especially the poor – without profiting from the fruit.

Even this approach has its detractors, both due to alternative understandings of the

Tosefta[171] and questions regarding its implementation.[172] *Otzar Beit Din* produce cannot be sold, and therefore, any money used to distribute *Otzar Beit Din* must not be for the fruit itself. Although *Otzar Beit Din* does not allow for profiting from the produce, the reality is that the cost of distributing the produce in line with the laws of *shemitta* is far more expensive than in a normal year. Therefore, *Otzar Beit Din* produce is rarely cheaper than other produce.

Nevertheless, several Otzar Beit Din systems in Israel serve virtually all sectors of the religious public, although they often operate differently. Some arrangements ensure the produce is not "sold" in stores or by weight or not sold at all.

Otzar Beit Din produce has full *kedushat shevi'it* and therefore must be treated as such, including proper use and proper disposal of leftovers (see ch. 24).

Value-Based Decision Making

Two of the primary determinants for deciding which form of produce is ideal for *shevi'it* are the *halachic* concerns and the practicalities. Obviously, if one feels that a certain approach is not *halachically* valid it ceases to be a viable option. On the other hand, even if something is *halachically* ideal, if it is practically difficult, it will probably be marginally available, if at all. For instance, *matza menutak*, use of detached platforms, is expensive and available primarily for leafy vegetables only.

The farmer must consider if he should fulfill *shevi'it* in the most straight-forward manner, dedicating the year to Torah study or other pursuits, or if he should adopt one or more of the other options, continuing to supply at least some produce, with *shevi'it* observance a daily part of the year.

Some consider any farmer who doesn't fulfill *shevi'it* literally as abrogating his responsibility, but most have little understanding of what doing so entails. Some point out that most, if not all, of the non-farmers who make such claims draft a *prozbul*, ensuring they can collect outstanding loans after *shemittat kesafim*; they don't fulfill financial *shemitta* as it is written in the Torah. One shouldn't attempt to judge others and their decisions, but should focus on the decisions that apply directly to them.

Non-agricultural residents of Israel have far less complicated decisions. The question is not whether they will work but what they will consume. After learning about *shevi'it*, its themes, and the value system that accompanies its *halachot*, it is clear that any *halachic* considerations should seemingly take *shevi'it's* broader picture into consideration. It is here that the non-farmer consumer is given the opportunity to choose between "observing *shevi'it*" or circumventing it.

---

171   See Rash Sirlio, *Shevi'it* 8:6, who interprets the *Tosefta* differently. The Radbaz (*Hilchot Shemitta V'Yovel* 7:3) notes that the Rambam does not cite the *Tosefta* as *halacha*.

172   *Otzar Beit Din* produce does not have any issues of *shamor* or *ne'evad*, as the ground is not worked in violation of *shemitta* and the *Beit Din* ensures the produce is distributed to all. The *sefichin* prohibition, however, still applies to *Otzar Beit Din*. This means that at the point when the *sefichin* prohibition sets in for each crop where it applies, *Otzar Beit Din* will no longer be able to supply those crops.

In 5761 (2001), Rav Aharon Lichtenstein delivered a powerful speech in which he painted a vivid description of the beauty of the Torah's concept of *shevi'it*. He decried the situation nowadays, when the issue of reliance or lack of reliance on the *heter mechira* has turned a year designated as one of brotherhood into a year of dissention and divisiveness. He notes that he personally does not advocate reliance on the *heter mechira* – not because he questions its *halachic* validity, but because it seeks to bypass *shemitta* rather than observe it:

What remains today of this spectacular vision? Virtually nothing. The transition from an agrarian to industrial economy eliminated – for the vast majority of society – the direct relevance of the forbidden farming activities. Yet, in this area the situation is relatively good: We neither circumvent nor distort the prohibitions; the majority of us simply do not encounter them. Regarding, however, the prohibitions pertaining to eating and the sacred status of the produce, the situation is ten times worse.

What options avail themselves to those reverently concerned about the sanctity of *shemitta* produce and the detailed laws relevant thereto? They can rely on a legal fiction, according to which – woe unto the ears that hear such a thing! – the fields of the entire land, from Lebanon to Egypt and from the sea to the Jordan River, are sold or leased to a gentile ... Even should we assume the halakhic propriety of the lenient position, the phenomenon itself must make us tremble.

Alternatively, those who feel skeptical about the "*heter*" can purchase produce grown overseas or in Arab fields (if he is prepared to rely on the ruling of the Beit Yosef, who allows doing so). But how vast a gap exists between running to special greengrocers in order to pay exorbitant prices for non-Jewish produce – grumbling over the schlep and expense while priding oneself for his piety – and the biblical vision that "You may eat whatever the land during its Shabbat will produce"! Can we find any commonality between that sense of arrogance and the sense of human submission and divine greatness that stand at the center of the institution of *shemitta*? Of those who are diligent in their observance of the prohibition of "*sefichim*" (vegetables that grew during *shemitta*), what percentage go through the *shemitta* year with genuine joy, as opposed to those who long, almost desperately, for relief from its burden?. ..

Virtually no other area exists where we sense so acutely the fierce tension between the pain of the Almighty on the one hand and that of *Kenesset Yisrael* on the other...
Over the last generation we have earned the privilege of reinstating Jewish settlement in Eretz Yisrael, and we dealt with the *mitzvot* related to the land with considerable success. Yet the *mitzvah* of *shemitta* remains a particularly hard nut to crack. We cannot put a hold on the country's agriculture for an entire year without losing all world markets the following year, resulting in the collapse of Jewish agriculture in the Holy Land. We could, perhaps, distinguish between the farmer, who cannot let his field lay fallow, and the consumer, who can conduct himself stringently and not rely on the "*heter*." Clearly, however, without consumers purchasing their produce, the farmers and agricultural industry at large will collapse. Moreover, even if a single individual or limited sector of the population can act stringently without inflicting irreparable damage to agriculture, such an option clearly does not live up to the standard articulated by Kant, by which one must act in a manner in which he wishes others to act. The interests of *Kenesset Yisrael* demand the leniency of the sale in order

to prevent a total breakdown of the Zionist agricultural enterprise in Israel.

Concurrent with our concern for the welfare of *Kenesset Yisrael*, we sense ever so strongly the pain of the Giver of the Torah. Specifically the *mitzvah* of *shemitta* – a *mitzvah* of such critical importance, whose underlying idealistic depth is so clear and so easy to identify with – we circumvent, hiding behind a trick of sorts rather than properly fulfilling it...

Some people classify themselves in terms of *yirat Shamayim* based on their reliance on, or opposition to, the "*heter mekhira*." Those who choose not to rely on the "*heter*" paint themselves in the eyes of others – and at times even their own eyes! – as God-fearing and meticulous in *mitzvah* observance. Those who do rely on the "*heter*," from their perspective, are religiously weak. Thus, the "*heter mekhira*," which should have been the subject of a legitimate halakhic debate, takes on a factional dimension. Those supporting the "*heter*" view the issue as a sacred battle, as if no real basis for stringency exists; from the other side, we face a world of dissension and divisiveness.

Rav Lichtenstein noted that he did not see a solution on the horizon, but advised that "we acknowledge the reality and weep over it." In his conclusion, he noted that both those who circumvent *shemitta* through the *heter* and those who purchase non-Jewish non-*shemitta* produce might have taken care of the formal responsibilities, but neither are "*meshamet*" (observing *shemitta*); instead, they are both "*mishtamet*" (shirking responsibility).

In the years that have passed since Rav Lichtenstein's speech, the horizon has shifted. More and more cities have realized that with proper preparation, they can observe *shemitta* properly while maintaining beautiful gardens. Similarly, many farmers have realized that for many crops, *Otzar Beit Din* can provide for most needs for the local Israeli population. A number of leading Religious Zionist rabbis have advocated limiting reliance on the *heter mechira* to situations in which *Otzar Beit Din* is not an option (such as most exports and crops with *sefichin* issues), encouraging use of *Otzar Beit Din* whenever possible. They have noted that doing so allows for fulfilling the *mitzvot* of *shemitta* as well as the values of *shemitta*, without trying to circumvent it. This allows for eating sanctified Jewish-grown produce while observing the *mitzvot* that are the ticket to our continued living and flourishing in the land.

In this manner, we announce that *shevi'it* isn't a problem or a period we must survive, but a challenging *mitzvah* we are overjoyed to have the opportunity to fulfill. This allows for eating the sanctified *shevi'it* produce (possibly a *mitzvah*) and supporting farmers who want to observe *shevi'it* through the *Otzar Beit Din*. Furthermore, in this manner, *shevi'it* observance does not lead to neglect of other *mitzvot*, such as supporting one's fellow Jew (a *mitzvah* found in *Parashat Behar* in the context of *shevi'it*; *Vayikra* 25:36). It is possible that many of the values that Rav Lichtenstein bemoaned being lost can be achieved through the contemporary proliferation of *Otzar Beit Din*.

One of the leading proponents of this approach is Rav Yaakov Ariel, former Chief Rabbi of Ramat Gan and a leading Religious Zionist *posek*. He notes Rashi's citation of the *midrash*'s response to the question, "What does shemmita have to do with Har Sinai?" – that *shevi'it* serves as the model for the fact that both the *kelalim* and *peratim* of all *mitzvot* were taught at Sinai. In context, *kelalim* and *peratim* refer to the general broad principles of *mitzvot* and the details of each *mitzvah*. Rav Ariel notes that there is an additional meaning to these terms; *kelal* refers to the Jewish nation as a whole, and *perat* refers to the individual. *Shemitta* requires decision-making that is concerned not only with the *perat*, every individual on his own, but for the *kelal*, the greater good of society and everyone in it. This is especially true given that many of *shevi'it*'s goals are for the *kelal*. One should adopt an approach that best suits the greater society and helps the farmer's observe *shevi'it*:

> One of the most basic principles in the laws of *shemitta* is that the land and its agricultural produce are taken from the individual and given over to the whole—the population at large... The main idea behind this *mitzvah* is to remove people from their egocentric worldview and develop their sensitivity towards others, public responsibility, and patriotism. Interestingly, we find another distinction in the laws governing the collective group versus the individual. As the individual is concerned, it is forbidden to pressure borrowers from repaying their debt. However, a rabbinical court—that is, the representatives of the public—may collect the debt...
>
> Mutual responsibility is an even more significant component of this *mitzvah*. We have already seen that the Torah removes the farmer's private possession of the crops of his fields and transfers it to the general public: "Let the needy among your people partake of it" (*Shemot* 23:11). The Torah's vision for the *shemitta* year is that the "haves" will share their wealth with the "have nots" ... It is apparent that the spirit of the law during the *shemitta* year insists that responsibility is mutual: Just as the farmer is responsible to take care of the poor, so too consumers should take the farmers' situation into consideration. We should all shoulder the responsibility to observe this *mitzvah*. Thus, it seems that the *hidur mitzvah* for consumers during the *shemitta* year is to help farmers shoulder their financial burden. Otherwise, consumers would not fully observe the *mitzvah* of *shemitta*: they do not own fields or orchards, so they cannot remit their ownership of the land and its produce. How can consumers nevertheless fulfill this great and important *mitzvah*? It seems that the only way is through helping farmers to observe the *mitzvah*. (Introduction to *Katif Shevi'it*[173])

Rav Ariel notes that *hiddur mitzvah* often focuses on each individual, determining what the appropriate way to fulfill a *mitzvah* is. This would lead to a consumer-oriented focus for *shemitta*, determining what would be the least *halachically* questionable decision and the most economical. However, Rav Ariel writes, this is completely antithetical to *shemitta*'s community-oriented approach, in which *hiddur mitzvah* involves determining what is ideal for the community as a whole. There is one option that allows for observing *shevi'it*, ensures that produce doesn't rot but can be eaten in sanctity throughout the land, and concerns itself with the community as a whole, sharing the burden with the farmer:

> It is possible that the cost of Israeli produce is higher than other produce. Here, however, lies the litmus test of one who wants to perform *mitzvot* in their most *mehudar* form. If one is willing to pay more for meat with a higher standard of *kashrut*,

173 See https://en.toraland.org.il/beit-midrash/*halachic*-guides/hilchot-haaretz/hilchot-shemitah/shemitah-introduction1-shemitah-a-national-mitzvah/

אוֹצָר בֵּית דִין

גִדּוּלֵי עֲרָבָה

Otzar Beit Din: This refers to produce that is marketed by *beit din* (the courts) in order to ensure that produce will reach all communities. All the produce marketed in this manner has *kedushat shevi'it*. The produce itself is not sold; the only charge of the produce is for the work involved in bringing it to market. Although some question this method's practical validity, others view it as the ideal means of supporting Jewish farmers while enabling people to eat fruit with *kedushat shevi'it*.

Jewish agriculture from areas of the State of Israel that are not within the borders of Eretz Yisrael (at least not for *shevi'it* purposes). Many of these areas are subject to dispute, and this option thus often includes an additional *heter mechira*.

יְבוּל חוּ"ל (חוּץ לָאָרֶץ)

Produce imported from outside Israel: Obviously, this involves no *shevi'it* prohibitions. However, it supports foreigners instead of "the poor of your nation."

יְבוּל נָכְרִי

Produce of gentiles living in Israel: This certainly involves no violations of *shevi'it* prohibitions, as non-Jews have no obligation to observe *shevi'it*. However, there is a dispute as to whether this produce has *kedushat shevi'it*, and relying on it often entails buying from Israel's enemies and giving them more of a foothold in Israel.

הֶתֵּר מְכִירָה

The *heter mechira* is a controversial solution to the challenges posed by *shevi'it*. It involves an arrangement through which Jewish-owned Israeli farmland is sold to a gentile. This legal sale (according to those who adopt it) permits gentiles to work the land and continue agricultural production during *shevi'it*. However, its *halachic* basis is subject to dispute, and at the very least it seems to bypass *shemitta* rather than fulfill it.

הֶתֵּר מְכִירָה · גְּדּוּלִים בְּלִי קְדֻשַׁת שְׁבִיעִית · שְׁשִׁית

גְּדּוּלִים בְּלִי קְדֻשַׁת שְׁבִיעִית

Hydroponics

Produce without *kedushat shevi'it*: This option includes plants that are not grown directly in the ground, such as "*matza menutak*," plants grown on detached bedding inside a house (i.e., in a greenhouse in an above ground planter), hydroponics, etc.

שְׁשִׁית

Sixth-year produce: In the case of vegetables, this indicates that the produce was harvested during the sixth year; in the case of fruit, it means the produce blossomed during the sixth year, even if it was harvested only in the seventh.

would he also be willing to pay more for agricultural produce that is more *kosher*? ...
The topic of *shemitta* is complex. It necessitates a high level of fear of Heaven while
considering the big picture, as well as all of the details. This combination, in which we
constantly strive to observe *shemitta* in its entirety and in the most *mehudar* fashion,
while taking into consideration the constraints that do not yet make it possible—
brings us forward on a path of safe and steady progress as both the Land and its
sabbatical year will be best safeguarded and observed.

The key question for anyone involved in the laws of the *shemitta* is as follows: Is Israeli
agriculture in the Land of Israel a value or only a necessity? The *mitzvah* of *shemitta*
answers this question. It sanctifies the land, its crops, and its growers, elevating them
from a necessity to a value....

Our goal is not to rule regarding the disputes as to what the ideal produce during *shevi'it* is.
However, after numerous chapters elucidating *shevi'it*'s themes and goals, it seems essential
to ensure that our decision-making includes *shevi'it*'s value system and a communal
outlook, especially when it allows for not only fulfilling *shevi'it*'s *mitzvot*, but also fulfilling
the mandate of *l'ochla* and eating *shevi'it* produce in sanctity.

Chapter 26

בְּעוּר פֵּרוֹת שְׁבִיעִית -
The Obligation of *Biur*

The requirement of *biur peirot shevi'it* entails eliminating produce that grew during *shevi'it* after a certain point in the year. Each crop has its own *biur* time. (A list is put out by the Israeli Chief Rabbinate and other rabbinic groups every *shemitta*.) When a particular crop's time of *biur* arrives, if one has only three meal's worth of produce in one's possession for each member of his family, no *biur* is necessary, but any additional produce requires *biur*.

The exact parameters of *biur* and the nature and implications of the obligation are subject to dispute and will be discussed in this chapter. Of interest is that this *halacha* may be one of the greatest reflections of the Torah's insistence that one recognize the true owner of *shevi'it* produce – and, for that matter, everything else.

The Source

In the context of eating *shevi'it* produce, the *pesukim* in *Parashat Behar* state:

בְּעוּר פֵּרוֹת

וְהָיְתָה שַׁבַּת הָאָרֶץ לָכֶם לְאָכְלָה לְךָ וּלְעַבְדְּךָ וְלַאֲמָתֶךָ וְלִשְׂכִירְךָ וּלְתוֹשָׁבְךָ הַגָּרִים עִמָּךְ: וְלִבְהֶמְתְּךָ וְלַחַיָּה אֲשֶׁר בְּאַרְצֶךָ תִּהְיֶה כָל תְּבוּאָתָהּ לֶאֱכֹל:

And the produce of the Shabbat of the land shall be for food for you: for you, and for your servant and for your maid-servant, and for your hired worker and for the settler by your side that resides with you; and for your cattle, and for the animals that are in your land, shall all the produce thereof be for food. (*Vayikra* 25:6-7)

כָּל זְמַן שֶׁחַיָּה אוֹכֶלֶת

Later in the same chapter, the Torah makes a similar statement regarding the produce of *yovel*:

כִּי יוֹבֵל הִוא קֹדֶשׁ תִּהְיֶה לָכֶם, מִן הַשָּׂדֶה תֹּאכְלוּ אֶת תְּבוּאָתָהּ.

For it is a jubilee; it shall be holy unto you; you shall eat the produce thereof **out of the field**. (*Vayikra* 25;12)

In *Parashat Mishpatim* as well, the Torah makes reference to *shevi'it* produce being eaten by wild animals:

וְהַשְּׁבִיעִת תִּשְׁמְטֶנָּה וּנְטַשְׁתָּהּ וְאָכְלוּ אֶבְיֹנֵי עַמֶּךָ וְיִתְרָם תֹּאכַל חַיַּת הַשָּׂדֶה כֵּן תַּעֲשֶׂה לְכַרְמְךָ לְזֵיתֶךָ:

But [in] the seventh year you will let it rest and lie fallow, that the poor of your people may eat; and what they leave, the **animal** of the field shall eat. In this manner you will deal with your vineyard and with your oliveyard. (*Shemot* 23:11)

The *Torat Kohanim* (1:9) derives from these *pesukim* that one's right to eat *shevi'it* produce is limited to the period when the produce is still growing in the field and is thereby accessible to *chayot*, undomesticated animals. One must remove produce from his home when it is no longer available to non-domesticated animals. At that point, not only can an individual not eat the food, but even one's domesticated pets or farm animals cannot eat it. As soon as non-domesticated animals cannot attain the crop in the wild, it requires *biur*.

Indeed, one of Rashi's explanations of the word "*untashta*" is that one forgoes use of his produce entirely after the time for *biur*, recognizing a further limitation on one's ownership during *shevi'it*.

It seems that one of the messages that emerges is that during *shevi'it*, one has a right to produce – even that which grows in his own field – only when it is permitted for consumption to all. Man has no rights in the produce above and beyond the rights of wild animals.

Defining the *Biur* Requirement

Chazal's use of the term "*biur*" in this context is important, as the term carries varied connotations: At times it refers to getting rid of something (e.g. *biur ma'asrot*), while at other times it calls for destruction (e.g. *bi'ur chametz*). In parallel, there is a debate among the *Rishonim* as to the implication of *biur peirot shevi'it*. Is it a form of relinquishing ownership, such that the produce is declared *hefker* (Ramban, *Vayikra* 25:7), or does it entail eradication through burning (Rambam, *Hilchot Shemitta V'Yovel* 4:28)? Some (Ra'avad on *Torat Kohanim* 1:9) view it as both: Declaring produce *hefker* is required when the produce is no longer growing in one's local area, and eradication is necessary when it is no longer found in the larger region.

We accept the opinion that one takes any produce that requires *biur* out of one's possession into the public domain and declares it *hefker* by relinquishing ownership of it in the presence of three individuals.[174] After performing *biur* by declaring the produce *hefker*, one can reacquire the produce.[175] If *biur* was not performed at the proper time, the produce is prohibited for consumption and should be burned or buried.[176]

Although we do not adopt it as the *halacha*, the Rambam's view is instructive. The *mishna* (*Shevi'it* 9:8) states that one may distribute three meals worth of the leftover *shevi'it* produce to everyone before *biur*. Many understand this to mean that one can retain three meals worth of the produce for every member of his family. The Rambam, however, understands that when the time for *bi'ur* arrives, before eradicating the leftover *shemitta* produce, one should try to give three meals worth of it to others. Only what is left over and not distributed for consumption must be eradicated through burning.

---

174 The three individuals can be people one knows personally and who one doesn't fear will want to acquire the produce for themselves.

175 When this is impossible, there may be alternative forms of *biur* as well; see *Mishpitei Eretz*, ch. 31). Although *biur* can be momentary, the hope is that its lessons still have an impact.

176 There is a dispute as to whether this prohibition applies even if *biur* wasn't performed accidently (*shogeg*) or because one was unable to do so (*ones*).

The idea that *shevi'it* produce is supposed to be physically destroyed, as the Rambam maintains, is difficult to understand. After all, the sanctity of *shevi'it* produce requires that the produce be eaten – *l'ochla* (*Vayikra* 25:6) – and nothing done to destroy it or compromise its ability to be consumed. Why, then, would the Torah now command us to eradicate the produce? In fact, this question also applies to the opinion that *biur* entails declaring the produce *hefker*, as the Torah clearly states that *shevi'it* produce is meant to be consumed.

This is especially difficult according to the authorities who view the *biur* obligation as Rabbinic in nature (see Ramban, *Vayikra* 25:7). Why would the Sages determine that after a specific date, sanctified *shevi'it* produce that carries with it the *mitzvah* of *l'ochla* should be eliminated?

Rav Asher Weiss (*Minchat Asher, Shevi'it, Biur*) explains that the Rambam's view reflects that *biur* is trying to ensure that, in fact, all *shevi'it* produce is eaten. If there is a time limit for eating and the food will possibly go to waste afterward, people will do their utmost to eat the fruit by that point. The Rambam's view is essentially rooted in the same premise of that of the other *Rishonim*:

> In truth, the primary *mitzvah* of *biur* is removing produce from one's home and ensuring it is eaten by individuals and domesticated animals... Even the Rambam maintains that the *mitzvah* is that produce should be equally available to all for consumption. Therefore, when the time for *biur* arrives, one must remove any produce he has in his home and distribute it to others. Although the Rambam states that any produce that is not consumed must be destroyed, that is not really the *mitzvah* of *biur*, but rather an outgrowth of it (*Minchat Asher Shevi'it, Biur*).

In other words, *biur* is a means of ensuring that the produce is actually eaten. Knowing that all produce that is not eaten by people or animals will have to be destroyed, one will do his utmost to make sure it is eaten. This is in essence the ultimate expression of the goal of *l'ochla*. The Torah ensures that *shevi'it* produce will be consumed in the appropriate time.

Rav Hirsch (*Vayikra* 25) notes that the requirement of *biur* entails even further reliance on God's assistance and blessing. Given that people generally eat from the previous year's crop, there is an expected shortage of food during the eighth year, following *shevi'it*. But the Torah requires *biur* on all stored produce, leaving no produce at all for the eighth year!

Rav Hirsch explains that this is why the Torah refers to the nation questioning what they will eat in the seventh year, rather than the eighth. Were it not for the promise of divine blessing, people would refrain from eating their stored produce even in the seventh year, out of fear that they would be left with nothing in the eighth.

The *Ketav VeHaKabalah* (*Vayikra* 25:21) notes that due to the requirements of *biur*, any planting that takes place in the eighth year is dependent on seeds from the sixth year. For this reason, the Torah emphasizes that the blessing of the sixth year lasts for three years.

Through the requirement of *biur*, it is almost as if Hashem ensures that we need His blessings during the eighth year.

Lessons of *Biur*

This unique requirement of *biur* carries with it a host of important lessons that we should carry with us beyond the *shevi'it* year.

Some understand that *biur* calls for "seasonal eating" – that is, eating produce at the time that nature makes it available. When foods are in season, they can be freely harvested and stored, but when they are no longer in season, all harvests must be shared with the public. Eating food according to its natural seasons, much like wild animals do, helps one connect to the land and realize that one can probably endure a season without his favorite fruits.

In addition to assisting us in appreciating produce when it is not available, the *halacha* of *biur* might be a reminder that one can look at their food like an elevated human or like a wild animal, which consumes whatever is available. Although humans may feel that they can outdo wildlife, preserving food for longer periods, during at least one year on the calendar, the *halacha* of *biur* reminds us that this attitude is inappropriate and even beastly. Humans, created in the Divine Image, are to use their ingenuity to ensure everyone has food – not to hoard it for themselves and their pets.

Several commentaries note that there is a clear lesson here as to who actually owns *shevi'it* produce:

> Let us visualize the *Shevi'it* laws, realized in practice. They constitute an act of homage unparalleled in its sublimity. Through its fields, gardens and meadows, through every fruit and every blade of grass, a whole nation proclaims for a full year: "Our national soil belongs to God, and we are merely 'strangers and sojourners', with Him." Without haughtiness and without pride of ownership they join, in complete equality, with the poorest of men and become equal even to the beasts of the field; God alone is exalted on that day. (Rav Hirsch, commentary on *Vayikra* 25)

Rav Avigdor Miller notes the attention the Torah accords to the needs of animals and what it represents.

> This unusual commandment demonstrates the special attention to herbivorous wild animals. On the seventh year the fields remain uncultivated, and the deer feed at will on the spontaneous after-growth of produce. And in order to emphasize the importance of this lesson, the command is given that when there is nothing left for the wild beasts, we must make *bi'ur* to abandon even that produce or after-growth that we had kept for our cattle. This demonstration of the Sabbatical Year as a symbol of the Creator's kindliness parallels similar demonstrations of Hashem's kindliness in the commandments of the weekly Shabbos: "That your ox and your donkey may have rest" (*Shemot* 23:12). (*A Kingdom of Kohanim, Parashat Behar* 25:7)

Rav Miller notes that this is a small part of the overall message of the *shevi'it* year aimed at eliminating the ego. One realizes that all the control he has over other people, and even animals, is an illusion; the only One with control is Hashem:

> The sabbatical year does not recognize classes—it recognizes only man. Yet what

is most startling is its declaration of equal rights for man and beast! "And for your animals and for the beasts that are in your land shall all its produce be to eat!" Animals and beasts have the same right to the produce of the seventh [year] given to man, and this right of animals and beasts is of such significance that it directly influences the right of man: "One eats produce of the seventh [year] only as long as the given species is to be found in the field"...

Only in partnership with animal and beast may man eat the produce of the *shabbat*, for the *shabbat* is a demonstration against the sovereignty of the bestial and the intellectual ego. Even sovereign private property and the terrible division between classes stem from the sovereign bestial ego and the sovereign intellectual ego. This great *shabbat* thus comes to declare rest so as to put an end to the obnoxiousness of the bestial and the intellectual ego, and this rest places the land; man, with his bestial and his intellectual aspiration, and animal in precisely the same rank, for all are equal before their Creator, blessed is He. All are His creatures, all are His servants, none exceeding the others, and now only—only—the liberated visionary ego stands— *alone*—before Him who "alone" is exalted.

The *mitzvah* of *biur* reminds us of our place and breaks the illusions of our lofty status. At the same time, it reminds us of the Torah's concern for all of Hashem's creatures, as we live in His world.

Some emphasize that *biur* provides an additional lesson about food security; once the time of *biur* has passed and the produce is no longer available in the wild, one can no longer eat food he has stored. Instead, this food must be made available to the public until it is fully consumed. *Biur* seems to obliterate any possibility of food hoarding, as one gains nothing by taking more for himself; the time will come when it will become forbidden.

Others note that one's sense of food security focuses not only on his own needs, but on those of his neighbors and community. Instead of storing food for personal use, one shares it with others, increasing his social awareness and concern.

The *mitzvah* of *"l'ochla"* tells us not only that *shevi'it* produce should be consumed, but the way in which it should be consumed. We have noted in the past that the same term is used in the context of the manna (*Shemot* 16:15) and Gan Eden (*Bereishit* 2). The *pesukim* make clear that manna cannot be stored for later consumption (see 16:20). Every day, one would receive a new portion of manna. Only on Friday, before Shabbat, would they receive a double portion, and only then would it last until the next day. One's lot was set. There was no hoarding and no saving – only eating what Hashem gave him and his family for that day.

While this is something very difficult to live with on a daily basis, for one year we recognize that we essentially eat from the manna. Everything is given to us through divine blessing. As much as we want to hoard and save for ourselves, we are instructed to share with others and eat it with a sense of blessing and appreciation. Eating in this manner provides a year in Gan Eden, eating from the manna, as we see God's blessing in all we have. Inculcating the values of *biur* should extend its lessons throughout the other six years as well.[177]

177 Interestingly, we accept the opinion *leHalacha* that after the time of *Biur* arrives, one can retain three meals worth of produce for each family member and the rest should be declared *hefker*, ideally in the presence of three individuals. However, *halacha* states that one can re-acquire their own produce after *Biur* is performed.

While one might wonder what this accomplishes, evidently its role is to ensure that the lesson is learned. Indeed if anyone fails to perform *Biur,* the produce becomes prohibited. While *Biur* can be momentary, the hope is that the lesson lasts for a lifetime, or at least until the next *Shemitta.*

Some basic *halachot* of *biur* include:

The *Biur* Requirement: When *sha'at habi'ur* arrives, i.e., the time that a particular crop is no longer available in the fields, one must perform *Biur* or the produce in one's possession will become prohibited for consumption

When is it done: Each crop has its own *Biur* time. A list is put out by the Israeli Chief Rabbinate (and other rabbinic groups as well) every *Shemitta.*

Which Produce: When a particular crop's time of *Biur* arrives, if one only has three meal's worth of produce in one's possession for each member of their family, then no *Biur* is necessary. Any additional produce requires *Biur.*

How is *Biur* done: We saw a difference of opinion how to perform *Biur.* We accept the opinion that one takes any produce that requires *Biur* out of one's possession into the public domain and declares them *hefker* by relinquishing ownership of them in the presence of three individuals. After performing *Biur* by declaring them *hefker*, one can reacquire the produce.

If *Biur* was not performed at the proper time: If *Biur* wasn't performed at the proper time, the produce is prohibited for consumption and should be burned or buried. There is a dispute whether this prohibition applies even if *Biur* wasn't performed accidently (*shogeg*) or when unable to do so (*ones*).

Note: The *halachot* of *Biur* are full of subtle intricacies and this overview should not be relied upon for practical *halacha.*

Section 4

Shevi'it's Lasting Messages
Hakhel and *Shemittat Kesafim*

Chapter 27

Shemittat Kesafim:
Monetary Shemitta

Introduction

Although most of the *halachot* of *shevi'it* are limited to the Land of Israel, one aspect of the *shemitta* year applies everywhere in the world – *shemittat kesafim*, "monetary release."

The Torah instructs that all outstanding loans are "released" at the concluding moment of the *shemitta* year and cannot be forcibly collected. The implications of this are wide-ranging, affecting debtors and creditors and impacting the whole credit system and, thereby, the entire economy.

Despite its ramifications and application throughout the world, *shemittat kesafim* is largely unknown, even in many observant circles. The simple reason for this is that during the Second Temple Period, the great Sage Hillel the Elder instituted the *prozbul*, an enactment enabling loan collection even after the onset of *shemittat kesafim*.

The topic of *shemittat kesafim* presents us with several questions: What is the goal of *shemittat kesafim*? What are its objectives for debtors and creditors and society as a whole? How is the financial *shemittat kesafim* relatd to the agricultural sabbatical year? Why isn't the Torah concerned that forgiving loans will ruin the credit system and prevent individuals from loaning money? How could Hillel institute *prozbul* if, by doing so, he was seemingly uprooting the Torah's institution of *shemittat kesafim*?

Analyzing the source and the *mitzvah* will provide a better understanding not only of *shemittat kesafim*, but will also deepen our appreciation of *tzedaka*, agricultural *shevii't*, and the Torah's overall prescription for a charitable society.

The *Mitzvah* of *Tzedaka*
·····································

The Torah seems to explicitly relate the general *mitzvah* of *tzedaka* with *shemittat Kesafim*. The source for this monetary *shemitta* is found in the Torah's lengthiest discussion of the *mitzvah* of *tzedaka*. Additionally, the two discussions of the *tzedaka* obligation in the Torah both appear alongside *shemitta*.

צְדָקָה

The Torah's first mention of *tzedaka* appears in *Parashiyot Behar*:

וְכִי-יָמוּךְ אָחִיךָ, וּמָטָה יָדוֹ עִמָּךְ--וְהֶחֱזַקְתָּ בּוֹ, גֵּר וְתוֹשָׁב וָחַי עִמָּךְ. אַל-תִּקַּח מֵאִתּוֹ נֶשֶׁךְ
וְתַרְבִּית וְיָרֵאתָ מֵאֱלֹהֶיךָ וְחֵי אָחִיךָ עִמָּךְ: אֶת-כַּסְפְּךָ לֹא-תִתֵּן לוֹ בְּנֶשֶׁךְ וּבְמַרְבִּית לֹא-תִתֵּן
אָכְלֶךָ:

When your brother becomes poor, and his ability to support himself fails where he is with you, you shall support him, [even if he is] a stranger or a sojourner, and he shall live with you. Do not exact from him advance or accrued interest, but fear your God. Let him live by your side as your kinsman. Do not lend him your money at advance interest, or give him your food at accrued interest. (*Vayikra* 25:35-37)

The second, including the *mitzvah of Shemittat Kesafim*, appears in *Parashat Re'eh.*

מִקֵּץ שֶׁבַע שָׁנִים תַּעֲשֶׂה שְׁמִטָּה: וְזֶה דְּבַר הַשְּׁמִטָּה שָׁמוֹט כָּל בַּעַל מַשֵּׁה יָדוֹ אֲשֶׁר יַשֶּׁה בְּרֵעֵהוּ לֹא יִגֹּשׂ אֶת רֵעֵהוּ וְאֶת אָחִיו כִּי קָרָא שְׁמִטָּה לַה': אֶת הַנָּכְרִי תִּגֹּשׂ וַאֲשֶׁר יִהְיֶה לְךָ אֶת אָחִיךָ תַּשְׁמֵט יָדֶךָ: אֶפֶס כִּי לֹא יִהְיֶה בְּךָ אֶבְיוֹן כִּי בָרֵךְ יְבָרֶכְךָ ה' בָּאָרֶץ אֲשֶׁר ה' אֱלֹהֶיךָ נֹתֵן לְךָ נַחֲלָה לְרִשְׁתָּהּ: רַק אִם שָׁמוֹעַ תִּשְׁמַע בְּקוֹל ה' אֱלֹהֶיךָ לִשְׁמֹר לַעֲשׂוֹת אֶת כָּל הַמִּצְוָה הַזֹּאת אֲשֶׁר אָנֹכִי מְצַוְּךָ הַיּוֹם: כִּי ה' אֱלֹהֶיךָ בֵּרַכְךָ כַּאֲשֶׁר דִּבֶּר לָךְ וְהַעֲבַטְתָּ גּוֹיִם רַבִּים וְאַתָּה לֹא תַעֲבֹט וּמָשַׁלְתָּ בְּגוֹיִם רַבִּים וּבְךָ לֹא יִמְשֹׁלוּ:

כִּי יִהְיֶה בְךָ אֶבְיוֹן מֵאַחַד אַחֶיךָ בְּאַחַד שְׁעָרֶיךָ בְּאַרְצְךָ אֲשֶׁר ה' אֱלֹהֶיךָ נֹתֵן לָךְ לֹא תְאַמֵּץ אֶת לְבָבְךָ וְלֹא תִקְפֹּץ אֶת יָדְךָ מֵאָחִיךָ הָאֶבְיוֹן: כִּי פָתֹחַ תִּפְתַּח אֶת יָדְךָ לוֹ וְהַעֲבֵט תַּעֲבִיטֶנּוּ דֵּי מַחְסֹרוֹ אֲשֶׁר יֶחְסַר לוֹ: הִשָּׁמֶר לְךָ פֶּן יִהְיֶה דָבָר עִם לְבָבְךָ בְלִיַּעַל לֵאמֹר קָרְבָה שְׁנַת הַשֶּׁבַע שְׁנַת הַשְּׁמִטָּה וְרָעָה עֵינְךָ בְּאָחִיךָ הָאֶבְיוֹן וְלֹא תִתֵּן לוֹ וְקָרָא עָלֶיךָ אֶל ה' וְהָיָה בְךָ חֵטְא: נָתוֹן תִּתֵּן לוֹ וְלֹא יֵרַע לְבָבְךָ בְּתִתְּךָ לוֹ כִּי בִּגְלַל הַדָּבָר הַזֶּה יְבָרֶכְךָ ה' אֱלֹהֶיךָ בְּכָל מַעֲשֶׂךָ וּבְכֹל מִשְׁלַח יָדֶךָ: כִּי לֹא יֶחְדַּל אֶבְיוֹן מִקֶּרֶב הָאָרֶץ עַל כֵּן אָנֹכִי מְצַוְּךָ לֵאמֹר פָּתֹחַ תִּפְתַּח אֶת יָדְךָ לְאָחִיךָ לַעֲנִיֶּךָ וּלְאֶבְיֹנְךָ בְּאַרְצֶךָ:

At the end of seven years you shall perform a release (*shemitta*). And this is the substance of the release: that every creditor release his hand from that which he has lent to his friend. He shall not exact from his friend or from his brother, because he will have declared the time of the release for the Lord. You may exact from the foreigner; but you must release whatever is due you from your kinsmen. But there shall be no needy among you, since Hashem your God will bless you in the land that Hashem your God is giving you as a hereditary portion. If only you heed Hashem your God and take care to keep all this instruction that I enjoin upon you this day. For Hashem your God will bless you as He has promised you: you will extend loans to many nations, but require none yourself; you will dominate many nations, but they will not dominate you.

When there is a destitute person among you, any of your brothers, in one of your settlements in your land that the Lord, your God, is giving to you, you shall not harden your heart and you shall not shut your hand against your destitute brother. Rather, you shall generously open your hand to him, and extend to him any credit necessary for providing that which he lacks. Beware lest there be a lawless thought in your heart saying, "The seventh year, the year of remission, is approaching," and you treat your destitute brother with miserliness and refuse to give to him. You shall surely give to him, and let your heart not feel bad when you give to him, because for this the Lord, your God, will bless you in all of your deeds and in all of your endeavors. For there will never cease to be needy ones in your land, which is why I command you: open your hand to the poor and needy kinsman in your land. (*Devarim* 15:7–11)

The Rambam cites both of the above passages as sources for the *mitzvah of tzedaka:*[178]

---

178 Unlike the Rambam, who views both passages as referring to the *mitzvah* of tzedaka, the Ramban (*Shichechat HaAsin* 16) does not view the passage in *Parashat Re'eh* as referring to tzedaka.

> It is a positive commandment to give *tzedaka* to the poor among the Jewish people …
> as it is said, "generously open your hand to him," and it is said, "you shall support him,
> [even if he is] a stranger or a sojourner, and he shall live with you," and it is said, "and
> your brother shall live with you" (*Vayikra* 25:36). (*Hilchot Matenot Aniyim* 7:1)

The Rambam might have identified the need for two *pesukim* as each one expresses another aspect of *tzedaka*. *Parashat Behar* focuses on the *bein adam la-chavero* responsibility to ensure those in need receive the necessary support. *Parashat Re'eh* focuses on the concern one should have for others, illustrating the *bein adam la-Makom* element of the *mitzvah*.

Additionally, our connection to *tzedaka* should not only be out of a sense of obligation, but due to general concern for the plight of others. The Rambam, therefore, illustrates that beyond the two explicit Biblical requirements, giving *tzedaka* exhibits our connection to our forefather Avraham and his legacy:

> We must be more meticulous about the mitzvah of *tzedaka* than about any of the other
> positive commandments. *Tzedaka* is the trademark of the righteous descendants of
> our forefather Avraham, as it is written, "For I [God] have known him to the end that
> he will command his children and household after him to keep the way of the Lord,
> to do righteousness [*tzedaka*] and justice [*mishpat*]" (*Bereishit* 18:19). The throne
> of Israel can be established and the true faith can stand only through the merit of
> *tzedaka* … (*Hilchot Matenot Aniyim* 10:1–2)

The Rambam sees *tzedaka* as an expression not only of the values with which Avraham would educate his children, but the essential spiritual DNA of the Jewish People, who inherited from Avraham the inner nature of compassion and the practice of kindness. *Tzedaka* is thus more than a responsibility. It is an opportunity to express our innate nature as descendants of Avraham Avinu. This expresses the *bein adam le-atzmo* element of the *mitzvah*.

Furthermore, the *mitzvah* entails more than a call to giving, require us to contribute gladly. Rav Hirsch notes that the Torah's description of *tzedaka* in *Parashat Re'eh* is more concerned with the compassionate heart than the giving hand. The natural state of the Jewish heart is generosity. For this reason, the *gemara* casts doubt on the Jewish ancestry of a person who is cruel and uncompassionate (*Yevamot* 79a).

Two Sources, Two Focuses

A deeper look at the two sources of the *mitzvah* of *Tzedaka* reveals some essential similarities alongside some striking differences:

Similarities between *Behar* and *Re'eh*	Differences between *Behar* and *Re'eh*
Both appear alongside mention of *shevi'it*. In both places, the Torah specifies *achicha*, "your brother." The *mitzvah* of *tzedaka* entails one brother providing for another. Both emphasize the giving of loans.	The extent of the obligation: *Behar* requires essential support, while *Re'eh* requires maintaining the poor man's dignity in every way, דֵּי מַחְסֹרוֹ אֲשֶׁר יֶחְסַר לוֹ, everything he is missing. *Behar* focuses on giving; *Re'eh* focuses on how to give (with an open hand, joyously)

One striking similarity is that, as mentioned, both *parashiyot* discuss *tzedaka* in the context of *shevi'it*.[179] Evidently, the *mitzvot* of providing *tzedaka* can only be properly understood upon the backdrop of *shevi'it* and the culture of generosity that it seeks to nurture.

Furthermore, both *parashiyot* include loans to the poor as part of their discussion of *tzedaka*. The discussion in *Parashat Behar* is juxtaposed to the command not to loan on interest, and the lengthy description in *Parashat Re'eh* introduces the *mitzvah* of *tzedaka* only in the middle of a host of other *mitzvot* for the benefit of those in need. It begins with the tithe that is given to the poor in two years of the seven-year cycle (*ma'aser ani*) and then describes the release of loans at the conclusion of the seventh year. The Torah then mentions lending and giving *tzedaka* to the poor, only to return to *shemittat kesafim*, prohibiting individuals from withholding loans as the sabbatical year approaches.

As we noted above, whereas *Parashat Re'eh* defines the proper attitude for giving *tzedaka*, *Parashat Behar* is where the Torah describes how best to assist those in need. Nevertheless, *Behar* also contributes a critical dimension of the requisite attitude for giving *tzedaka*, as the Torah introduces each related *mitzvah* using the same term: "your brother."

> כִּי-יָמוּךְ אָחִיךָ, וּמָכַר מֵאֲחֻזָּתוֹ--וּבָא גֹאֲלוֹ, הַקָּרֹב אֵלָיו, וְגָאַל, אֵת מִמְכַּר אָחִיו.
>
> If your brother becomes poor and has sold some of his property ... (*Vayikra* 25:25)
>
> וְכִי-יָמוּךְ אָחִיךָ, וּמָטָה יָדוֹ עִמָּךְ--וְהֶחֱזַקְתָּ בּוֹ, גֵּר וְתוֹשָׁב וָחַי עִמָּךְ.
>
> And if your brother grows poor and his hand fails with you ... (25:35).

The Torah requires a Jews to redeem the estate and home of his brother who has been unable to pay off his debts, as well as to provide him with an interest-free loan. The key term is "you shall strengthen him." As Rashi explains, the primary obligation is to ensure that one's brother does not sink into debt. This is done by providing him with assistance before he is broken. Even if it gets to a point where those efforts were unsuccessful, the

---

179 *Parashat Behar*, the primary *parasha* of the agricultural laws of *shevi'it*, is the first source of the *mitzvah* of *tzedaka* in the Torah. *Parashat Re'eh* discusses *tzedaka* in the context of the discussion of *shemittat kesafim*, the release of loans at the final moment of the sabbatical year.

Torah places additional restrictions on how we mus treate our financially needy brothers.

וְכִי-יָמוּךְ אָחִיךָ עִמָּךְ, וְנִמְכַּר-לָךְ--לֹא-תַעֲבֹד בּוֹ, עֲבֹדַת עָבֶד.

And if your brother who dwells with you grows poor and is sold ... (25:39)

וְכִי תַשִּׂיג, יַד גֵּר וְתוֹשָׁב עִמָּךְ, וּמָךְ אָחִיךָ, עִמּוֹ; וְנִמְכַּר, לְגֵר תּוֹשָׁב עִמָּךְ, אוֹ לְעֵקֶר, מִשְׁפַּחַת גֵּר.

And if a sojourner or stranger grows wealthy with you and your brother who dwells with him grows poor and sells himself to the stranger ... (25:47)

Pasuk 39 refers to a case in which one's brother is forced to sell himself into slavery and requires care and concern on the part of the master. *Pasuk* 47 introduces the requirement to redeem a Jew who has been sold as a slave to a non-Jew, describes how he must be treated if he is not redeemed, and notes his right to go free come *yovel*. The *pesukim* make clear that even when an individual is forced to sell himself into servitude, he should never be treated as a mere object. A Jew always retains his identity as a brother and must not be overworked or abused.[180]

The Rambam emphasizes this point:

> All of the Jewish People are brothers, as it is written, "You are children of Hashem your God" (*Devarim* 14:1). If a brother is not compassionate toward his brother, then who will show compassion to him? (*Hilchot Matenot Aniyim* 10:2)

Despite the focus on brotherhood in *Parashat Behar*, however, the message of that passage is broader in scope, applying even to non-Jews who have accepted their Noachide responsibilities (גר ותושב) and not limited to the Land of Israel. The passage in *Parashat Re'eh*, in contrast, focuses on giving to Jews in the Land of Israel. Furthermore, unlike the passage in *Behar*, the section in *Re'eh* requires supplying anything the person needs. The description in *Re'eh* revolves entirely around the theme of brotherhood. Because the one in need is our brother, it follows that we must do much more than obliterate his hunger; instead, we must provide all that he lacks, even if his poverty is a product of his personal habits. As codified by the Rambam:

> Even if this particular indigent man used to ride on a horse and have a servant run before him heralding his arrival, and he then became poor, one must purchase for him a horse and a servant. (*Hilchot Matenot Aniyim* 7:3)[181]

Since the obligation of *tzedaka* revolves around brotherhood, there is an order of priorities as to whose needs should be provided first. One's first obligation is to oneself (Rema, YD 251:3). Afterward, as the *pesukim* indicate, come one's family members, according to their degree of closeness, and then the needy of one's city. Since the *pesukim* also refer to the poor "in your land," the poor of the Land of Israel receive precedence over the poor of

---

180 The Torah requires that one treat an indentured worker so well that the worker not only shares his master's standard of living, but is even granted precedence, to the point that the *gemara* (*Kiddushin* 20a) declares, "Whoever acquires a Jewish slave acquires a master for himself." What, then, is the point of the Torah's institution of slavery for a fellow Jew? The placement of these *pesukim* in *Parashat Behar* indicates that this is a means of *tzedaka* as well.

181 Rav Shlomo Wolbe (Alei Shur, vol. 2, p. 198) notes that the undefined call for "providing that which he lacks" indicates that there are no objective standards in tzedaka. Rather, a person must train himself to identify another's needs by listening to him and seeing what he truly lacks, even if we consider them luxuries. This subjective requirement is an expression of true concern for our brothers in need.

other lands.[182]

Rav Hirsch further discusses how the Torah's emphasis on brotherhood highlights closeness and solidarity as hallmarks of *tzedaka*:

> Even if there is only one brother in your city or your country who is in need of help, then there is a needy man among you, in the sphere of your responsibility, and you may not turn away from him ... Again and again in this chapter the needy man is referred to as *achicha*, "your brother." Every needy person who stands before you, even if you do not know him, is your brother, a child of your Father in heaven, and when he turns to you, he does so with a letter of recommendation, as it were, from God, who is the Father of you both. (Rav Hirsch, commentary on *Devarim* 15:7)

The fact that the laws of *shemittat kesafim* are included in the *Parashat Re'eh* – and not in *Parashat Behar*, along with the other laws of *shevi'it* – is notable. The placement in *Re'eh* appears to be based on the inherent connection between *shemittat kesafim* and the "brotherhood" element of *tzedaka*. At the same time, the placement of the discussion of *tzedaka* in *Parashat Behar* reveals that there is a connection between *tzedaka* and *shevi'it* as well.

The Nature of *Tzedaka*

Although the Torah encourages us to assist the needy based on a sense of brotherhood, the *gemara* (*Bava Batra* 8b and *Ketubot* 49b) indicates that a court may force a person to give *tzedaka*. (See also Rambam, *Hilchot Matenot Aniyim* 7:10, 9:12.)

The commentators question how this is appropriate, as there is a general halachic principle that a court may not coerce a person to perform any positive *mitzvah* whose reward is stated explicitly in the Torah (*Chullin* 110b). The Torah would seem to put *tzedaka* in this category, as the reward for *tzedaka* is explicit in the *pasuk*:

נָתוֹן תִּתֵּן לוֹ וְלֹא יֵרַע לְבָבְךָ בְּתִתְּךָ לוֹ כִּי בִּגְלַל הַדָּבָר הַזֶּה יְבָרֶכְךָ ה' אֱלֹהֶיךָ בְּכָל מַעֲשֶׂךָ וּבְכֹל מִשְׁלַח יָדֶךָ:

Make every effort to give to him, and do not feel bad when you give to him, because for this the Lord, your God, will bless you in all of your deeds and in all of your

---

182   Chazal learn from the pasuk's verbosity ("When there is a destitute person among you, any of your brothers, in one of your settlements in your land that the Lord, your God, is giving to you..." Devarim 15:7) that priority is to be given to those who are closest to the giver (see Shulchan Aruch, YD 251). "The Torah does not wish love of humanity or patriotism to be built up at the expense of our omission of our obligations to those nearer to us" (Nechama Leibowitz, Studies in Shemot, p. 409).

Furthermore, Chazal learn from the words "with you" (Vayikra 25:35) that one must view himself as though he were poor himself (Midrash Tanchuma, Mishpatim 15). One way to understand this comment is that a person can better appreciate the need to help others if he imagines a reality in which he is in poverty and requires assistance. Alternatively, we might interpret this midrash as indicating that before helping others, one must ensure that his own needs are met. One should not give away more than a fifth of his assets to the poor, lest he himself become needy (see Ketubot 50a). Indeed, the gemara (Bava Metzi'a 33a) concludes one's own financial needs take precedence over those of others. As Rav Yitzchak Berkowitz explains (in an audio shiur), although a person has a financial responsibility to his relatives and others, his closest relative is himself. He has a responsibility not to impoverish himself, as he has a responsibility toward himself and his own needs. An individual who recognizes that he must ensure that his own needs are met before he helps others acts rationally and correctly, like a passenger on a plane who fastens his own oxygen mask before helping others. Otherwise, it is likely that no one will receive help and one will only increase the number of people in need.

endeavors. (*Devarim* 15:10)

Some commentators explain that *tzedaka* qualifies as an exception to this rule. In explaining why, they underscore the uniqueness of this *mitzvah*.[183]

Rav Hirsch writes that there are two simultaneous *tzedaka* obligations – one incumbent upon every individual and one as a member of the community. The reward promised to the giver of *tzedaka* only applies to fulfilling one's personal obligation, not to fulfilling one's obligations as part of a community, and the latter can therefore be compelled. (See also Rav Chaim Soloveitchik, *Reshimot Shiurim, Nedarim* 1:208.)

The *Ketzot HaChoshen* cites a number of sources that demonstrate that the obligation to provide *tzedaka* creates a lien on one's property. There is an actual debt that requires *tzedaka* be provided from every estate. Even though the court cannot compel the performance of the *mitzvah*, it can force an individual to pay his debts. In a similar vein, the *Ohr HaChaim* (*Devarim* 15:4; see also commentary on *Shemot* 22:24) writes that God accords wealth to individuals as custodians, responsible for sharing that wealth with other children of God. Those with means are to be God's emissaries for a more equitable distribution of wealth. One who is unwilling to perform their duty willingly, can be forced to do so.

Notably, the Torah mentions the reward for giving *tzedaka* in the context of the *mitzvah* in *Parashat Re'eh*, which focuses on the manner in which *tzedaka* is given: "You shall not harden your **heart** and you shall not shut your hand against your destitute brother…You shall surely give to him, and let your **heart** not feel bad when you give to him" (*Devarim* 15:7, 10). What role does the heart play in extending *tzedaka* to another person?

The Ramban understands the Torah's instruction not to harden one's heart against giving *tzedaka* as a negative commandment:

> We should not feel pained by giving *tzedaka*, nor should we give without generosity, nor think of it as a financial burden. (Addenda to *Sefer HaMitzvot*, no. 17; see also *Semak*)

The Ramban emphasizes that the Torah explicitly requires giving with a caring heart. Hardening one's heart, even if one is giving a generous amount, would be a violation of a *mitzvah*. A generous attitude is as essential as a generous gift.

Indeed, Rav Hirsch (*Devarim* 15:7) observes that the Torah's warning against hardening one's heart, rather than commanding to open one's heart, indicates that heartfelt concern for the needy is the natural reaction to a request for *tzedaka*. The Jew's hand and heart are naturally open, but they are subject to the sway of the evil inclination, which might convince him not to give. The Torah instructs one to find his inner kindness and give with a genuine desire to help.

This idea is beautifully expressed in the *Sefer HaChinuch*, in which the title of the *mitzvah* to give *tzedaka* reflects the inner experience of the giver:

> "To Perform *Tzedaka* Toward Those Who Need It **with Joy and Gladness**." (*Sefer*

183　*Tosafot* (*Bava Batra* 8b; *Ketubot* 49b) take a different approach, distinguishing between verbal coercion, which can be implemented, and phyisical coercion, which is not acceptable.

HaChinuch, mitzvah 479)[184]

This analysis solves the aforementioned querry. The Torah indeed promises a reward for those who give *tzedaka*, which should prevent the courts from forcibly requiring individuals to contribute their share of the tzedaka. However, the promise of blessing to the charitable appears in *Parashat Re'eh*, focusing on how to give. One who gives due to compulsion or even with a "hardened heart" does not fulfill the *mitzvah* described in *Parashat Re'eh* and is not worthy of any blessing. On the contrary, he violates a prohibition.

The idea that the hallmark of *tzedaka* is not simply giving money, but relishing the opportunity to unleash one's heartfelt desire to assist others sheds light on several *halachot* regarding *tzedaka*. The *Shulchan Aruch* codifies:

> One must give *tzedaka* with a pleasant countenance, with joy and with gladness, empathizing with the plight of the poor person and offering words of comfort. If one gives with a sad or demeaning face, then he loses the benefit of giving. (*Shulchan Aruch*, YD 249:3)[185]

The *gemara* teaches (*Sukka* 49b), "*Tzedaka* is measured only according to the kindness through which is is performed." Rashi explains that "kindness" refers to the effort extended in giving *tzedaka* in a manner that provides the greatest benefit to the pauper.[186]

This perspective on *tzedaka* explains the Rambam's well-known eight levels of *tzedaka*, a hierarchy based on the values of protecting the dignity of the recipient, enabling him to become self-sufficient, and generosity expressed by the giver:

> There are eight levels of *tzedaka*, each greater than the next. The highest level, above which there is no other, is to strengthen the name of another Jew by giving him a present or loan, or forming a partnership with him, or finding him a job in order to fortify him until he no longer must rely on *tzedaka* …
>
> The second level is where one gives *tzedaka* to the poor, but does not know to whom he gives, nor does the recipient know his benefactor, for this is performing a *mitzvah* for the sake of Heaven. This was the manner of giving in the *Beit HaMikdash*, where the righteous gave secretly and the virtuous poor drew sustenance anonymously.
>
> The third level is where one knows to whom he gives, but the recipient does not know his benefactor …
>
> The fourth level is where one does not know to whom he gives, but the poor person does know his benefactor … and is not ashamed.
>
> The fifth level is where one gives before being asked [when contact is unavoidable]. The sixth level is where one gives after being asked. The seventh level is where one

---

184   See also Rabbeinu Yonah, *Sha'arei Teshuva* 3:35–36.

185   See also *Avot DeRabbi Natan* 13, which states that giving nothing but a smile is greater than giving a large donation with a frown.

186   See also Rambam's comment on the *mishna*, "All is according to the majority of the deed" (*Avot* 3:15), where he emphasizes that "Good character traits do not come to a person by virtue of the greatness of a deed, but rather by the frequency with which he performs it." Every act of *tzedaka* has an impact on one's heart and character. Thus, what is significant is not so much the size of a donation as the repeated act of opening up one's heart and extending one's hand to others in need. See also Maharsha, *Bava Batra* 9a, s.v. *gadol*.

gives to the poor less than is required, but gladly and with a smile. The eighth level is where one gives to the poor person begrudgingly. (*Hilkhot Matenot Aniyim* 10:7–14)[187]

Since the *mitzvah* of *tzedaka* as an opportunity to express concern for the poor, even those who are poor themselves must give, even though this does not solve any societal problems and indeed makes the poor needier:

Every man is obligated to give charity. Even a poor man who himself lives off charity is obligated to give from what he is given. (*Shulchan Aruch*, YD 248:1)

Every member of society must take part in the *mitzvah* of opening his heart and exhibiting his care and concern for others.

Mitzvat Halva'ah: The *Mitzva* of Extending Loans

Understanding the Torah's stress on giving *tzedaka* with a heartfelt desire to help others may explain why the ultimate level of *tzedaka* might not be a charitable gift at all, but rather lending money.

Tzedaka is often translated as "charity" and is usually understood as a reference to gifts to the needy. However, although *tzedaka* includes such contributions, every time the Torah discusses *tzedaka*, it specificly discusses interest-free loans and not charitable gifts. In *Parashat Behar*, the *mitzvah* of *tzedaka* is presented in the context of the prohibition of charging interest on loans. In *Parashat Re'eh*, the *mitzvah* of *tzedaka* is conveyed in the context of the *mitzvah* of releasing loans at the end of the *shemitta* year. In fact, the Torah does not seem to explicitly refer to what we classically call *tzedaka*, monetary gifts to the poor, as such. Assistance to the needy is always mentioned through the mechanism of interest-free loans.[188] The *Nevi'im* and *Ketuvim* are replete with calls to give gifts of *tzedaka*, reinforcing it as a Jewish value, but it is not explicit in the Torah!

The Benefits of Lending Money vs. Giving *Tzedaka*

Chazal emphasize that lending money is of greater value than *tzedaka*:

Rabbi Abba also said in the name of Rabbi Shimon ben Lakish: He who lends [money] is greater than one who performs *tzedaka*, and he who forms a partnership [thus providing employment] is greater than them all. (*Shabbat* 63a)

The Rambam codifies this *mitzvah* and its relationship to *tzedaka*, noting that the highest form of *tzedaka* is described in *Parashat Behar*[189]:

---

187 The Rambam's final two levels indicate a preference for one who gives less than is needed in a generous manner over one who provides the required amount without the proper attitude. He nevertheless seems to view a begrudging gift as *tzedaka*, unlike the *Shulchan Aruch* (cited above) and Maharil Diskin, who states that one who gives begrudgingly is worse than one who gives nothing at all.

188 The Torah does discuss giving the second tithe in the third and sixth year of the seven-year agricultural cycle as a gift to the poor – *ma'aser ani* – but that is taken only from agricultural produce one harvests.

189 See the Rambam above (*Hilchot Matenot Aniyim* 10:7) who mentions providing loans as an example of the highest form of charity.

We are commanded to lend money to a poor person, so as to help him and to ease his burden. This *mitzvah* is even greater and of more magnitude than that of giving charity, for one who has already reached the point where he has to openly ask people for money is less bothered and pained by [needing to ask for assistance] than one who has not yet reached this level. He therefore needs assistance to prevent his situation from becoming known and reaching such a point. (*Sefer HaMitzvot*, positive *mitzvah* 197)

Although the economic vision of *Parashat Behar* includes means of assisting those who have lost their financial footing, the Torah prefers that one assist his fellow before he degenerates to that point (*Vayikra* 25:35). The most effective way of doing so is to find a job for a person who needs help or to extend a loan. Free loans provide an opportunity for the recipient to chart his own course of rehabilitation. The hope is that he will be able to return the money he borrowed, thereby ensuring that there will be no need for outright charity.

Rav Hirsch similarly explains that it is desirable to lend to a poor person, or preferably help him to start a business, so that he can earn a living without embarrassment:

This is the highest form of benevolence, for by supporting the needy person in this way, one treats him as an absolute equal and enables him to earn his own living, and one does not hurt the feelings of the recipient in any way. (Rav Hirsch, commentary on *Devarim* 15:8)

It is notable that the Rambam describes giving charity as being on a lower level than providing support through a loan. This is not self-evident, as one who gives charity transfers his own money or material items to another, whereas providing a loan does not necessarily entail any sacrifice on the part of the giver.

Rabbi Yehuda HeChasid expresses our surprise at finding that the highest levels of *tzedaka* do not seem to be *tzedaka* at all:

There is a form of *tzedaka* that does not seem like *tzedaka* at all, but is nevertheless considered by God to be the highest form thereof. For example, when a poor person has merchandise to sell or [has written] a book that no one wishes to buy, and you buy it from him. So too, if a poor person wishes to be a scribe but no one wishes to hire him and you hire him – there is no greater *tzedaka* than this. (*Sefer Chasidim* 1035)

While both Rambam and Rav Hirsch focus on how a loan retains the borrower's dignity, there may be an additional reason for the preferred status of loans. Giving *tzedaka* in a way that does not feel like charity prevents the giver from fooling himself into thinking that he has "saved" a poor individual. Thus, a loan does more to build one's character than a charitable gift. This sort of character growth, says the *Sefer HaChinuch* (66), is the reason for the *mitzvah* of lending to the poor:

The reason for this commandment is that God wanted His creatures to be habituated and accustomed to the attribute of compassion and kindness, because it is a praiseworthy character trait, and by virtue of inculcating good character traits, they will be worthy of receiving good [from God], for good and blessing can be bestowed only on good and not on its opposite. Through God's bestowal of goodness on those who are good, His desire to bring goodness to the world is fulfilled. Were it not for this purpose, God, blessed is He, would give the poor all they need without our involvement: it is out of His kindness that He permits us to be His emissaries, in order to make us meritorious. (*Sefer HaChinuch, mitzvah 66*)

This point is reflected in the *pasuk* in *Parashat Mishpatim*, which emphasizes the proper perspective that one should have when giving to others. The *pasuk* appears to be unusually verbose, referring to the poor as *Ami,* "My people," and describing the poor man as "the poor person who is with you." The midrash explains Hashem refers stresses that the needy are "His" people:

Israel asked the Holy One, blessed be He, "Who are Your people?"
He answered them, "The poor," as it is stated (*Yeshayahu* 49:13), "For the Lord will console His people and have mercy on His poor" ...
This is why it states, "If you provide a loan to My people." (*Shemot Rabba* 31:5)

The *midrash* (31:13) continues to observe that by not only acknowledging the poor as connected to Him, Hashem distinguishes Himself from wealthy individuals who seek to distance and disassociate themselves from any poor relatives. The *mitzvah* of providing loans thus educates the financially-secure individual regarding the proper perspective when giving. A giver is to appreciate that the needy are God's people. He cares for them, and He has given excess money to their brothers so that the latter can assist them.

Additionally, there is a practical benefit to lending instead of giving charity: Lending enables funds to be donated again and again. When one gives a charitable gift, he has fulfilled his *mitzvah* but won't be able to give that money again. On the other hand, when the funds one has set aside for charitable loans are returned, he can make a loan to another needy person.

Furthermore, a society of lenders assists everyone when they need it most. Some individuals have excess funds in the winter but need more in the summer. Others are the opposite. If everyone lends others when possible and can borrow when in need, everyone stands to benefit. Thus, through lending, many more members of society can be givers and share their wealth with others.

The Rights of Borrowers and Lenders

לֹוֶה

In addition to championing the right of the needy to request and almost demand assistance, the Torah shows concern for the needy by restricting the creditor from harassing the debtor if he is unable to pay:

מַלְוֶה

אִם כֶּסֶף תַּלְוֶה אֶת עַמִּי אֶת הֶעָנִי עִמָּךְ לֹא תִהְיֶה לוֹ כְּנֹשֶׁה לֹא תְשִׂימוּן עָלָיו נֶשֶׁךְ:

When you lend money to My people, to the poor man among you, do not press him for repayment. [Also] do not take interest from him. (*Shemot* 22:24)

This prohibition of pressing the borrower seems to be a further example of the Torah's extreme compassion for those in need. The lender is not supposed to act as a creditor commonly acts toward one who has borrowed from him. Rashi cites *Chazal*'s practical explanation of how to fulfill this *mitzvah*:

> You shall not demand it of him forcibly (*Tanchuma* 9, *Shemot Rabba* 31:6). If you know that he lacks [money to repay you], do not appear to him as if you have lent to him, but as if you have not lent to him – that is, do not embarrass him (*Bava Metzia* 75b). (Rashi, *Shemot* 22:24)

In such a situation, a creditor is required to go so far as to avoid encountering the borrower. Rav Hirsch notes that while in every other society, the borrower hides from the creditor, in Jewish society, the opposite is true; the creditor who knows the borrower can't pay should avoid him to prevent embarrassment.

Moreover, the Torah notes, if one does hound a person who owes him money, God will hear the debtor's cries and punish the lender. This is quite an extreme punishment, considering that the money was lent without interest and that any leverage employed is for the sole purpose of recovering the lender's own money.

Nevertheless, lenders have rights as well. Although the Torah commands us to provide loans, a lender may take steps to ensure that he can collect his borrowed money. Thus, for example, a lender may take collateral for his loan. Rabbi Yishmael (in the *Mechilta*) comments on the juxtaposition of the laws of collateral and the *mitzvah* of lending:

> The Torah wishes to teach you that you should do your *mitzvah* [of lending], and you are entitled to receive back what is yours.

Nevertheless, although the Torah allows one to take collateral for a loan to incentify its repayment, the Torah places a number of rules on the collateral to ensure that the security taken is productive for both the lender and borrower. Collateral must only be a security for the loan, not a way of creating hardship for the borrower by way of pressuring him:

> אִם חָבֹל תַּחְבֹּל שַׂלְמַת רֵעֶךָ עַד בֹּא הַשֶּׁמֶשׁ תְּשִׁיבֶנּוּ לוֹ: כִּי הִוא כְסוּתֹה לְבַדָּהּ הִוא שִׂמְלָתוֹ לְעֹרוֹ בַּמֶּה יִשְׁכָּב
> וְהָיָה כִּי יִצְעַק אֵלַי וְשָׁמַעְתִּי כִּי חַנּוּן אָנִי:

> If you take your neighbor's garment as security, by the time the sun sets you shall return it to him. For it is his only covering, it is his garment for his skin – with what should he lie? And it shall be that if he cries out to Me, I will hear, for I am gracious. (*Shemot* 22:25–26)

The Torah ensures that the pledge should be made through a positive arrangement; it should not be counterproductive and prevent the borrower from earning a livelihood:

> לֹא יַחֲבֹל רֵחַיִם וָרָכֶב כִּי נֶפֶשׁ הוּא חֹבֵל:

> Do not take an upper or lower millstone as security for a loan, since that is like taking a life as security. (*Devarim* 24:6)

The Torah further requires that one take the security in a manner that does not violate the borrower's dignity or privacy:

> כִּי תַשֶּׁה בְרֵעֲךָ מַשַּׁאת מְאוּמָה לֹא תָבֹא אֶל בֵּיתוֹ לַעֲבֹט עֲבֹטוֹ: בַּחוּץ תַּעֲמֹד וְהָאִישׁ אֲשֶׁר אַתָּה נֹשֶׁה בוֹ יוֹצִיא

אֵלֶיךָ אֶת הָעֲבוֹט הַחוּצָה:

When you make any kind of loan to your neighbor, do not go into his house to take something as security. You must stand outside, and the man who has the debt to you shall bring the security outside to you. (*Devarim* 24:10-11)

Thus, any garment needed by the borrower for the night must be returned by then, and any item that is essential to the debtor's livelihood must be returned when the debtor requires it. This arrangement clearly significantly reduces the creditor's leverage for collecting a loan to a very needy individual.[190]

A Binding Conditional *Mitzva*

The Torah introduces the rules pertaining to loans in *Parashat Mishpatim*, which primarily discusses monetary laws. These *pesukim* appear following the prohibition of mistreating widows and orphans. The Torah makes clear that it does not view loans as just another form of *chessed*, but rather commands a unique *mitzvah* to extend loans to the needy:

אִם כֶּסֶף תַּלְוֶה אֶת עַמִּי אֶת הֶעָנִי עִמָּךְ לֹא תִהְיֶה לוֹ כְּנֹשֶׁה לֹא תְשִׂימוּן עָלָיו נֶשֶׁךְ:

If you provide a loan to My people, to the poor person who is with you, do not act toward him as a creditor; do not lay interest upon him. (*Shemot* 22:24)

The first word in the *pasuk*, אם, "if," usually indicates a choice. In other words, in the event one chooses to provide a loan, these are the guidelines (see Malbim on the *pasuk*). Thus, the *pasuk* does not seem to require that one to lend money to others, but merely states that he may not collect interest if one does so.

However, this reading is difficult to accept as the *pesukim* in *Parashat Re'eh* that we previously encountered indicate that one must open his hand and provide a loan when approached by the needy. Due to the difficulty of reading the *pasuk* in *Mishpatim* conditionally, Rabbi Yishmael explains that although the word "if" generally indicates an optional or conditional act, this *pasuk* is one of the three instances where there word "if" is used to express an obligation:

Every time the Torah uses the word "if," it indicates that which is optional, with three exceptions, and this is one of them ... You might say so, but perhaps it is only optional? When the Torah states, "Extend to him any credit" (*Devarim* 15:8), it indicates that which is obligatory, not optional. (*Mekhilta*, quoted by Rashi)

Thus, there is as a unique *mitzvah* obligation to provide loans to the poor. But if so, why, then, is the *pasuk* phrased conditionally, "**if** you provide a loan..."?

Some commentators explain that although there is an obligation to lend money, it is subject to outside factors. For example, Ibn Ezra explains that "if" merely indicates that

---

190 Why would a lender take collateral at all, given the restrictions? There are a few reasons. First, the laws of *shemittat kesafim*, which ordinarily release outstanding loans at the close of the sabbatical year, do not apply when collateral has been taken. Second, if collateral is taken, the lender's heirs can collect the loan even after his death. Furthermore, Ibn Ezra cites Rav Sa'adya Gaon as noting that taking collateral prevents the borrower from borrowing from someone else against the same item. Finally, we should note that a creditor may choose to take collateral out of compassion, believing that if a borrower takes advantage of those who help him, he may find himself unable to receive help from others in the future.

the ability to lend depends on the availability of funds. In effect, he reads the *pasuk*, "If the Lord has given you wealth so that you can lend to the poor..." The *Ohr HaChaim* conjectures that the Torah's choice of words relates to the reason some individuals have money to lend, while others do not:

> In general, God in His great kindness provides generously for the needs of all His creatures. He allocates a fixed amount for these needs. When a person has not qualified to receive his needs at the hands of God directly, because he is guilty of sinful conduct, God does not recall the amount that would have been allocated to such a person, but redirects it to another. As a result, the person who does not receive his livelihood from God directly either suffers deprivation or is forced to receive his livelihood through another channel. Receiving one's livelihood through a fellow human being instead of from the hands of God is demeaning for the recipient...
>
> The Torah suggests that if we find ourselves in possession of more than we need, we ought to lend it to someone whom the Torah describes as "My people." The meaning of this *pasuk* is that if you become aware that you have more money than you need for your personal requirements, it is clear that the excess originally belonged to another person, i.e., "the poor person who is with you." This is a clear hint that you should open your hand to lend to the poor person part of what used to be his or was intended for him. (*Ohr HaChaim, Shemot* 22:24)

The *Sefer Chasidim* writes that the needs of society and the character of the would-be borrower must be taken into account as well:

> This is to cover the following contingencies: if you are dealing with a rogue who never pays his debts or one who has plenty of money but pretends to be poor; or one who has no money but has food, but would rather do business and keep his children short of food ... In such cases it is better to give him food and not lend to him, even if you put him to shame by providing him food as charity every week. Since he is dishonest, he deserves to be shamed... (*Sefer Chasidim*)

The Maharal explains that the word "if" is used here because lending should stem from the kindness of the lender, not from a sense of obligation:

> For if a person would fulfill these dictates because he is obligated to fulfill the decrees of the King, this would not be the desire of God, for God wants man to fulfill the commandment out of his own desire to do so... Indeed, if a person would do ... [this] out of a sense of being commanded to do so by the King, unwillingly, this would not be something of which God could be proud...
>
> If someone were to loan money because he is commanded to do so, it would not be a *mitzvah*, as the *mitzvah* of providing loans must be performed out of the desire of a good heart, as it is written (*Devarim* 15:10), "and let your heart not feel bad." (*Gur Aryeh, Shemot* 22:24)

The use of "if" to connote a desire to assist fits well with our explanation of *tzedaka* discussed above. *Tzedaka* requires that men of means care about those who are struggling and be willing to provide generously for them, and that they do so with graciousness and joy.[191]

Two Types of Loans

The Abarbanel presents an alternative explanation that reunderstands loans and their relationship to *tzedaka*. Abarbanel interprets "if" literally – as referring to an optional act. Furthermore, he argues that the laws limiting pressure from the lender, coupled with God's promise to listen to any borrower who calls out to him, demonstrate that a loan is essentially a gift that may be returned.

He derives this from a *gemara* that learns from the language of *Parashat Re'eh* that if a person in need of charity is reluctant to accept a gift, one should instead give him a loan:

> "Lend" refers to a man who has no means and yet is unwilling to receive his sustenance [through charity]. The pasuk teaches that [money] must first be given as a loan [and then presented to him as a gift]. (*Bava Metzia* 31b; *Ketubot* 676b)

Here, a loan is provided only because the recipient refuses to accept a gift. This implies that a gift would be preferable.

The Abarbanel explains that the basic *mitzvah* of *tzedaka* is really to provide money as a charitable gift. Since loans are relevant only if an individual is unwilling to accept a gift or if the benefactor is unwilling to provide one, the *pasuk* introduces the laws of loans with the word "if." He differs with the common understanding, elucidated by the Rambam, that providing a loan is the highest form of *tzedaka*.

The Abarbanel argues that the laws of *shemittat kesafim* are intended to cause the loan to become a gift, which is considered ideal. With the conclusion of the sabbatical-year cycle, if the loan has not been returned and collateral has not been received, the debt will in practice be transformed into *tzedaka*. This holds true, however, only if the borrower is very poor. If the borrower is not needy, but simply in need of capital, then he should be lent money, but there is much more leeway to ensure that the loan will be returned. In such a case, the creditor is not obliged to return the collateral every day. His collateral retention prevents the loan from being released during the sabbatical year.

Based on the Abarbanel and some other sources, we can conclude that there are two different types of loans. One is a form of *tzedaka* that allows us to provide money to those in need if giving a gift is not feasible, as described in *Parashat Re'eh*. The second type of loan is a *mitzvah* distinct from *tzedaka*, serving to assist those who are not poor, but, nevertheless, require additional funds. This *mitzvah* is presented in *Parashat Mishpatim* and introduced as conditional. There is no reason that such a loan should not ultimately be collected. The Torah, therefore, provides means for ensuring repayment – while limiting these means so that they are not used against the poor, who should receive gifts rather than in actuality loans. In effect, the Torah's laws on debt collection reflect who needs the money more: the lender or the borrower.

This distinction is relevant to the *halachic* discussion regarding whether one can include

---

191 Rabbi Yitzchak Arama (*Akeidat Yitzchak, Shemot*, ch. 46) notes that by providing loans in this manner, one emulates God: "Our own experience in Egypt, if nothing else, should provide us with sufficient motivation. Just as God listened to our outcry then, He will listen to the outcry of the stranger, the orphan, and the widow, should they feel compelled to appeal to Him on account of our callousness. This concept extends to require that we help people in need with loans etc. without becoming oppressive creditors…"

loans in their counting of *ma'aser kesafim*, tithing one's income for charity[192]. If loans are a form of *tzedaka*, they should count toward *ma'aser* (see *Eliya Rabba* OH 156:18). In addition, the amount of money one ought to lend should be limited, since the *halacha* states that people of average means generally should not give more than twenty percent of their income as *tzedaka* (*Shulchan Aruch*, YD 149:1). Nevertheless, if a person has money that he will not need for the next two years and someone requests a loan that stands to be repaid by then, one should lend to him. This lending is not a form of *tzedaka*, but the distinct *mitzvah* of providing free loans.

Another distinction between types of loans is relevant to the question of interest on business loans. A look into the prohibition of taking interest seems to further express the differences between two forms of loans, though possibly diferent than presented by the Abarbanel.

The Prohibition of Collecting Interest

The *pasuk* in *Parashat Mishpatim* makes clear that loans must be free of any interest: "לֹא תְשִׂימוּן עָלָיו נֶשֶׁךְ", "do not lay interest upon him" (*Shemot* 22:24). This prohibition is repeated elsewhere as well (*Vayikra* 25:36–37; *Devarim* 23:20). The Torah not only prohibits usury (lending at extremely high interest rates), but any sort of predetermined interest payment. The Sages later prohibited many other practices that share even a remote possibility of lending with interest. The prohibition against charging interest on loans to a fellow Jew is so severe that the Torah and the Sages took pains to distance Jews from it.

This severity is reflected in the fact that the prohibition applies not only to the lender, but even to the borrower. He is forbidden to accept a loan with interest terms. Additionally, the prohibition includes anyone else who is a party to such a loan, including witnesses to the transaction and any judge who might uphold it.

Notably, the Torah does not permit charging interest on a loan even to a person who is capable of paying it. Thus, although the *pesukim* focus on a needy individual ("the poor person who is with you"), the prohibition applies even to loans to the wealthy.

Although it is a great act of kindness to lend without interest, we might legitimately wonder why a person is not permitted to "rent" out his money. After all, a person may rent out his tools, bicycle, or other property for a fee. Essentially, the fact that the lender's property is in the form of money, as opposed to an object, prevents him from investing it! Moreover, why does the Torah forbid taking interest on loans to those who do not need charity?

One explanation is based on economic logic: Goods lose value with wear and tear, whereas money never loses its value. For this reason, it has been argued, a person has the right to rent out objects that may be ruined, but money, which is not subject to wear, may not be rented. This logic is not entirely satisfactory, however. After all, a coin – especially in Biblical and Talmudic times – could be defaced, and thus lose value. Furthermore, due to the fluctuating buying power of money, a person may, in fact, lose value by lending his

---

192 There is a dispute whether *ma'aser Kesafim* is a Biblical obligation, rabbinic obligation, or a righteous custom (*minhag*), but everyone agrees it is an appropriate minimum amount of charity for those who have the capabilities of giving.

money.

Since economic logic fails to explain the Torah's prohibition, it seems that the logic of this *mitzvah* is one of education and character-building.

The commentators discuss whether one who lends on interest is comparable to a robber who takes money that is not his or to a person who consumes non-kosher food or violates another prohibition. Essentially, the question is whether the Torah views lending on interest as illegitimately profiting at the expense of another person or as an ordinary action that would be morally acceptable if not prohibited by Divine decree.

The Torah itself provides some insight into this question in its presentation:

לֹא תַשִּׁיךְ לְאָחִיךָ נֶשֶׁךְ כֶּסֶף נֶשֶׁךְ אֹכֶל נֶשֶׁךְ כָּל דָּבָר אֲשֶׁר יִשָּׁךְ: לַנָּכְרִי תַשִּׁיךְ וּלְאָחִיךָ לֹא תַשִּׁיךְ לְמַעַן יְבָרֶכְךָ ה'
אֱלֹהֶיךָ בְּכֹל מִשְׁלַח יָדֶךָ עַל הָאָרֶץ אֲשֶׁר אַתָּה בָא שָׁמָּה לְרִשְׁתָּהּ:

You shall not lend upon interest to your **brother** – interest of money, interest of food, interest of anything that can be lent upon interest. Unto a foreigner you may lend upon interest, but unto your **brother** you shall not lend upon interest, so that Hashem, your God, will bless you in all your endeavors in the land to which you are going to possess it. (*Devarim* 23:20–21)

אַל תִּקַּח מֵאִתּוֹ נֶשֶׁךְ וְתַרְבִּית וְיָרֵאתָ מֵאֱלֹהֶיךָ וְחֵי אָחִיךָ עִמָּךְ: אֶת כַּסְפְּךָ לֹא תִתֵּן לוֹ בְּנֶשֶׁךְ וּבְמַרְבִּית לֹא תִתֵּן
אָכְלֶךָ: אֲנִי ה' אֱלֹהֵיכֶם אֲשֶׁר הוֹצֵאתִי אֶתְכֶם מֵאֶרֶץ מִצְרָיִם לָתֵת לָכֶם אֶת אֶרֶץ כְּנַעַן לִהְיוֹת לָכֶם לֵאלֹהִים:

Do not take from him interest or increase, but fear your God, and let your **brother** live with you. Your money you shall not give to him for interest, and for increase you shall not give your food. (*Vayikra* 25:36–37)

The Torah empasizes that the only individual to whom one is obliged to lend without interest is one's brother. The meaning is clear: Brothers who fall on hard times must be helped with extreme kindness. Indeed, it is difficult to understand the concept of lending without interest as anything but an act of brotherhood. A Jew does not charge interest to a fellow Jew in his time of need.

One of the terms that the Torah uses to refer to interest is *neshech*, which the commentators explain is from the same root as *nosheich*, "to bite." A person who borrows on interest starts with a small loan, but the amount due may quickly balloon into a huge debt from which he is unable to extricate himself. It may be logical to allow to rent out his money, but the Torah prohibits as one should never increase his brother's debt by doing so.

There is a personal message here: The Torah wants us to value our brotherhood more than monetary gain. The fact that we are permitted to lend on interest to non-Jews is not due to discrimination against them, but rather is built upon the premise that lending without interest is an extreme kindness. Mandating such extraordinary kindness makes sense only if it is limited to family members. Additionally, even lending with fair interest rates is an act of kindness, as many individuals are untrusting and unwilling to do so. The Torah's permitting lending to non-Jews with interest actually provides them with opportunities to bankroll projects they might need, just without the exclusive kindness of interest-free loans limited to brothers.

Another educational element of the prohibition, which appears in numerous sources, is that money should be viewed not as a goal in its own right, but rather as a means to an end. A person may be tempted to amass great wealth simply for the purpose of having money, but the Torah disapproves of doing so. One is entitled to use his money to buy something and then rent out that property, but he must not view one's money as a self-contained means of attaining more wealth through lending on interest. Rav Hirsch comments:

> The Torah does not regard collecting interest as an intrinsically wrongful act. Interest is not antithetical to the concept of justice, but is antithetical to the basic principle on which Jewish society is to be built…
> The prohibition of interest should be counted among those *mitzvot* – such as Shabbat, the sabbatical year, and the jubilee year – that serve as testimony and reminders of God's dominion over the world and over Israel.

The *mitzvah* is rooted in the perspective that all money belongs to God. If a person is granted excess money to lend to others, he should view the extension of such loans not only as an act of goodwill, but as a duty to his nation – "My people" – the member of God's community.

Rav Hirsch notes an additional societal benefit of the prohibition of taking interest:

> The prohibition against interest nullifies the corrupting influence of money, which is the prime cause of social inequality, and breaks the immense power of capital. If this prohibition is strictly kept, all capital is in itself useless and unproductive, and is of use only if wedded to labor. Labor is thus made the primary and essential factor of social prosperity. Capital is forced to recognize the equal value of labor. The wealthy man must either engage in labor himself, for only thus will his money bear fruit for him (otherwise it remains dead capital), or associate himself with the working capacity of one who lacks wealth, share with him profit and loss, and for his own benefit further the lot of labor.
> A depressed labor market triggers an even more serious depreciation of capital, and capital can never profit from the ruin of labor. The prohibition against interest nullifies the basis for the existence of that shocking contrast where the wretchedness of the working class is found side-by-side with the most luxurious opulence. (Rav Hirsch, commentary on *Shemot* 22:24)

Essentially, Rav Hirsch explains that the prohibition of interest makes for a fairer society, as capital can be used only for creative investment or to pay for labor, and cannot be used just to make more money. This reality narrows the gap between rich and poor. One can only wonder to what extent Rav Hirsch's intention was to respond to the arguments of Marx's *Communist Manifesto*, which was written in his lifetime.

This understanding of the *mitzvot* of lending to those in need is far removed from the contemporary viewpoint that one's unspent capital is a potential means of making additional income – and which, by extension, views interest-free lending as foolish. The Torah clearly identifies a loan of any kind as an extreme kindness. It is not foolish, but sacrificial, as one person forfeits his gain for the benefit of another. Graciousness is the essence of the obligation to lend and a character trait that God wishes for lenders to cultivate through giving.

Distinguishing Between Two Types of Loans

Our explanation for the prohibition of lending on interest may also leave room for distinguishing between different forms of loans. The Torah is clear that the primary reason to prohibit lending with interest is that one shouldn't increase their wealth on account of a Jewish brother in financial need.

Nevertheless, the Torah distances us from all forms of interest, prohibiting lending on interest to both a poor individual or a wealthy businessman looking for investors. Still, one might possibly distinguish between situations when one's loans assist the poor, and instances where one's money will be used for those with a slight cash-flow problem or looking for additional funds for financial investment.

We introduced above the Abarbanel's distinction between two forms of loans. Similarly, there may be a practical difference between different loans regarding how willing we should be to use legal maneuvers to circumvent the interest prohibition. A *heter iska* is a *halachic* means of providing a loan for a joint business venture, which ostensibly enables something akin to charging interest. Entering a *heter iska* for a loan to the poor is certainly against the spirit of the law, but when lending to a businessman, it is hard to imagine that the spirit of the law is intended to allow the borrower to benefit financially instead of the lender. A *heter iska* would be necessary in such a case, as no outright lending on interest is permitted, but wouldn't necessarily be inappropriate.

Thus, for example, Rav Chaim David HaLevi (*Aseh Lekha Rav* 1:60) writes that it is inappropriate to use a *heter iska* when lending money to an individual who is poor or has fallen on hard times and needs financial assistance. On the other hand, a person may seek large sums because he wishes to start a business or invest. If collection of interest were never permitted, such an individual would never find anyone willing to lend him money; others would sooner use their money for themselves than give it to him as a free loan. This is the logical basis for the concept of the *heter iska*.[193]

One could argue that the Torah issued an outright prohibition on interest in order to protect the needs of those who should not be paying interest. Based on this line of reasoning, if there are legal means of providing interest-bearing loans to those who seek loans for profit, these do no violence to the spirit of the law.

The Abarbanel differs, however. Although he is one of the main sources we referred to previously to illustrate that there are two different types of loans, he sees no difference when it comes to the prohibition against interest. Abarbanel unequivocally states that under all circumstances, the spirit of the law is opposed to lending to another Jew with interest. The Torah's command is based on brotherhood, and it, therefore, applies no matter his financial state.

Responsibility of the Borrower

Until now, we have focused on the extraordinary rights granted to a debtor. Although a

---

193 Rav HaLevi argues that if a person seeks a loan to purchase a home or to marry off a child, use of a *heter iska* is not appropriate.

creditor is entitled to take collateral, that permission is severely limited when it comes to loans to the poor. Furthermore, all loans – no matter the wealth of the recipient – must be interest-free. Nevertheless, although the Torah focuses on the responsibilities of the lender, the borrower must not take advantage of the lender's philanthropy. A person who borrowed money but finds that he is liable to default must find a way to repay his debt; failure to do so would damage both him personally and society.

Providing interest-free loans is an extremely difficult *mitzvah*, as one is essentially requested to forego the use of his money and give it to another person who may not be able to return it, while collecting no charge in return. Although lending money that may not be repaid is an act of kindness, this is true only when the money is given to a needy person. Only in such a case does the Torah allow a person to receive a loan but not return it until he has the money to do so. In such a case, the recipient is genuinely aided by the funds and will not be driven further into debt by interest. However, in instances in which the lender does not view the money as charity but as a temporary loan, the lack of interest may cause damage by dampening the borrower's eagerness to return the loan, leading him to incorrectly view it as a gift. In the absence of interest, the recipient lacks a powerful incentive to return what he has borrowed as quickly as possible.

The Talmud (*Ketubot* 86a) declares that *"pri'at ba'al chov mitzvah,"* paying back loans is a *mitzvah*. On the most basic level, one who receives a free loan must repay the sum in full and punctually. Repayment is not only necessary as part of the agreement to repay and a basic civil duty; failure to do so on a mass level might threaten the institution of interest-free loans and lending altogether. If borrowers fail to pay their debts, people will become wary of lending, fearing that their loans will never be returned, and the institution of lending will suffer accordingly. [194]

There are also implications for the borrower: What will happen to a person's character if he is not concerned with returning money he has borrowed or returning it in a timely manner?

A loan creates a responsibility on the borrower's part and causes him to feel indebted to the lender. As the *pasuk* puts it, "The borrower is servant to the lender" (*Mishlei* 22:7). Thus, a proud, poverty-stricken individual who is unwilling to accept charity will be committed to returning the money he borrows. If all goes well and he successfully uses the loan to get

---

194 Just as a borrower might take advantage of the lack of interest, he might take advantage of other *mitzvot* meant to prevent abuse by lenders. If in fact he feels that he can avoid payment without incurring severe ramifications, his behavior will not only hurt the lender, but also impact detrimentally on society by discouraging people from lending money. Furthermore, this behavior might result in severe damage to his character. Some organizations that teach responsible financial behavior have developed a method for preventing such a development. When a person gives a loan to a recipient who does not seek charity, the means of repayment are made clear at the onset. They may require postdated checks and a strict schedule of reimbursement. One should think twice before providing a loan to someone who is not in need of charity without following such a protocol. Although it may feel as though doing so cheapens the act of kindness, establishing such guidelines helps the borrower internalize his responsibility to return the borrowed funds. Additionally, having a reimbursement schedule allows people to lend more, because they feel secure in the knowledge that they are almost guaranteed to receive their money when they expect it. See also Rav Aharon Lichtenstein's general discussion of the obligations of a person who receives charity: http://www.vbm-torah.org/archive/halak67/04halak.htm.

back on his feet, all parties will ultimately feel that the loan was a positive experience. The borrower received assistance without feeling degraded. The lender, for his part, receives the money he loaned and is satisfied that he has assisted another individual and can now use the funds for further acts of kindness.

The Torah strives to improve the lender's character (by ensuring he doesn't boast about his giving or belittle the recipient), guiding him to feel privileged to be God's agent in providing for those in need. The Torah also wishes to cultivate the recipient's character, facilitating a loan when he is unwilling to accept gifts and giving him confidence in his ability to repay while maintaining his desire to do so. The Torah is not concerned only with the mechanical act of lending, but with its impact on the character development of all involved.

	From The Recipient's Standpoint	For the Benefit of Society
Reasons to Pay Back the Loan	The borrower has promised to repay the loan and should do his best to do so.	Individuals will cease to provide free loans if they know that borrowers won't pay them back.

What should the recourse be for one who cannot pay off a debt? The Torah describes the course of action for one who dedicated an endowment (*erech*) to the *Mikdash* and is unable to pay it:

וְאִם מָךְ הוּא מֵעֶרְכֶּךָ וְהֶעֱמִידוֹ לִפְנֵי הַכֹּהֵן וְהֶעֱרִיךְ אֹתוֹ הַכֹּהֵן עַל פִּי אֲשֶׁר תַּשִּׂיג יַד הַנֹּדֵר יַעֲרִיכֶנּוּ הַכֹּהֵן:

If he is too poor to pay the endowment, he shall present himself before the priest, so that the priest can determine the endowment valuation. The priest shall then make this determination on the basis of how much the person making the vow can afford. (*Vayikra* 27:8)

The *mishna* provides more specifics:

Although the Sages said that assessment-debtors may have their property seized, they must be left enough food for three meals, and clothing for twelve months, a bed and bedclothes and *tefillin*. . . If he is a workman we leave him his work tools, from each kind. (*Arachin* 6:3)

The Talmud (*Bava Metzia* 114a) declares that the rules of arranging a means for a debtor to retain some of his assets surely apply to one who has borrowed money and is unable to repay. Just as arrangements are made to alleviate the situation of one who owes the Temple, arrangements would be made for one who is poor and requires financial assistance.

In fact, as we have seen, the Torah explicitly ensures that a worker receiving a loan retains his means of making a living, going so far as to declare that taking someone's livelihood is akin to taking his life:

Do not take an upper or lower millstone as security for a loan, since that is like taking a life as security. (*Devarim* 24:6)

Rabbi Dr. Asher Meir notes that although there is a practical reason for this law – as one who can't earn a living won't be able to pay back his debt – the Torah emphasizes its moral aspect. Similarly, the Torah rejects a punitive approach to debt repayment, instead obligating a constructive and rehabilitative approach. He cites the Rambam, who emphasizes that an insolvent debtor cannot be imprisoned or put to work:

> According to Torah law, when the creditor demands his debt from the debtor, if the debtor has assets, we leave the debtor essential assets and give the rest to the creditor, as we explained. And if we cannot find any assets of the debtor, or only those assets that we leave him, we let him go his way. We do not arrest him, nor ask him to bring proof that he has no other assets. (*Hilchot Malveh* 2:1)

One might be inclined to view bankruptcy laws as an outgrowth of the Torah's laws regarding debt repayment, but the truth is that historically, bankruptcy laws were initially orchestrated to protect the creditors, while only later taking into account the needs of debtors.[195] Furthermore, although the Torah exempts some of an insolvent debtor's basic assets and arranges a repayment schedule, it does not seem to allow for a discharge of the debt, as we find in many bankruptcy settlements. Instead, the debtor is given a bit of relief from counterproductive or vindictive collection action; he must continue to pay back his debts to the best of his ability.

Release of Loans: שְׁמִטַּת כְּסָפִים

שְׁמִטַּת כְּסָפִים

We have discussed a number of reasons that lending money takes precedence over *tzedaka*, specifically because it allows the receiver to retain as much dignity as possible. On the other hand, sometimes *tzedaka* is the best provision for those who are unable to pay loans back. As we noted, the borrower is indebted to the lender, to the degree that the *pasuk* in *Mishlei* refers to a debtor as a slave to the creditor. At times, a straight-out gift, which wouldn't cause such worry, might be better appreciated, even if it entails a little less dignity in receiving.

This delicate balance is managed through the *mitzvah* of *shemittat kesafim*, which essentially turns every loan into a gift at the end of the sabbatical cycle.

שְׁמִטַּת כְּסָפִים

שְׁמִטַּת קַרְקָעוֹת

Shemittat Kesafim and *Shemittat Karka'ot*

Let us look again at the *pesukim* in *Parashat Re'eh* that describe this *mitzvah*:

מִקֵּץ שֶׁבַע שָׁנִים תַּעֲשֶׂה שְׁמִטָּה: וְזֶה דְּבַר הַשְּׁמִטָּה שָׁמוֹט כָּל בַּעַל מַשֵּׁה יָדוֹ אֲשֶׁר יַשֶּׁה בְּרֵעֵהוּ לֹא יִגֹּשׂ אֶת רֵעֵהוּ וְאֶת אָחִיו כִּי קָרָא שְׁמִטָּה לַה': אֶת הַנָּכְרִי תִּגֹּשׂ וַאֲשֶׁר יִהְיֶה לְךָ אֶת אָחִיךָ תַּשְׁמֵט יָדֶךָ: אֶפֶס כִּי לֹא יִהְיֶה בְּךָ אֶבְיוֹן כִּי בָרֵךְ

---

195 See https://www.aish.com/ci/be/92962939.html.

יְבָרֶכְךָ ה' בָּאָרֶץ אֲשֶׁר ה' אֱלֹהֶיךָ נֹתֵן לְךָ נַחֲלָה לְרִשְׁתָּהּ: רַק אִם שָׁמוֹעַ תִּשְׁמַע בְּקוֹל ה' אֱלֹהֶיךָ לִשְׁמֹר לַעֲשׂוֹת
אֶת כָּל הַמִּצְוָה הַזֹּאת אֲשֶׁר אָנֹכִי מְצַוְּךָ הַיּוֹם: כִּי ה' אֱלֹהֶיךָ בֵּרַכְךָ כַּאֲשֶׁר דִּבֶּר לָךְ וְהַעֲבַטְתָּ גּוֹיִם רַבִּים וְאַתָּה לֹא
תַעֲבֹט וּמָשַׁלְתָּ בְּגוֹיִם רַבִּים וּבְךָ לֹא יִמְשֹׁלוּ:
כִּי יִהְיֶה בְךָ אֶבְיוֹן מֵאַחַד אַחֶיךָ בְּאַחַד שְׁעָרֶיךָ בְּאַרְצְךָ אֲשֶׁר ה' אֱלֹהֶיךָ נֹתֵן לָךְ לֹא תְאַמֵּץ אֶת לְבָבְךָ וְלֹא תִקְפֹּץ
אֶת יָדְךָ מֵאָחִיךָ הָאֶבְיוֹן: כִּי פָתֹחַ תִּפְתַּח אֶת יָדְךָ לוֹ וְהַעֲבֵט תַּעֲבִיטֶנּוּ דֵּי מַחְסֹרוֹ אֲשֶׁר יֶחְסַר לוֹ: הִשָּׁמֶר לְךָ פֶּן
יִהְיֶה דָבָר עִם לְבָבְךָ בְלִיַּעַל לֵאמֹר קָרְבָה שְׁנַת הַשֶּׁבַע שְׁנַת הַשְּׁמִטָּה וְרָעָה עֵינְךָ בְּאָחִיךָ הָאֶבְיוֹן וְלֹא תִתֵּן לוֹ
וְקָרָא עָלֶיךָ אֶל ה' וְהָיָה בְךָ חֵטְא: נָתוֹן תִּתֵּן לוֹ וְלֹא יֵרַע לְבָבְךָ בְּתִתְּךָ לוֹ כִּי בִּגְלַל הַדָּבָר הַזֶּה יְבָרֶכְךָ ה' אֱלֹהֶיךָ
בְּכָל מַעֲשֶׂךָ וּבְכֹל מִשְׁלַח יָדֶךָ: כִּי לֹא יֶחְדַּל אֶבְיוֹן מִקֶּרֶב הָאָרֶץ עַל כֵּן אָנֹכִי מְצַוְּךָ לֵאמֹר פָּתֹחַ תִּפְתַּח אֶת יָדְךָ
לְאָחִיךָ לַעֲנִיֶּךָ וּלְאֶבְיֹנְךָ בְּאַרְצֶךָ:

At the end of seven years you shall perform a release (*shemitta*). And this is the substance of the release: that every creditor release his hand from that which he has lent to his friend. He shall not exact from his friend or from his brother, because he will have declared the time of the release for the Lord. You may exact from the foreigner; but you must release whatever is due you from your kinsmen. But there shall be no needy among you, since Hashem your God will bless you in the land that Hashem your God is giving you as a hereditary portion. If only you heed Hashem your God and take care to keep all this instruction that I enjoin upon you this day. For Hashem your God will bless you as He has promised you: you will extend loans to many nations, but require none yourself; you will dominate many nations, but they will not dominate you.

When there is a destitute person among you, any of your brothers, in one of your settlements in your land that the Lord, your God, is giving to you, you shall not harden your heart and you shall not shut your hand against your destitute brother. Rather, you shall generously open your hand to him, and extend to him any credit necessary for providing that which he lacks. Beware lest there be a lawless thought in your heart saying, "The seventh year, the year of remission, is approaching," and you treat your destitute brother with miserliness and refuse to give to him. You shall surely give to him, and let your heart not feel bad when you give to him, because for this the Lord, your God, will bless you in all of your deeds and in all of your endeavors. For there will never cease to be needy ones in your land, which is why I command you: open your hand to the poor and needy kinsman in your land. (*Devarim* 15:7–11)

Although the seven years described in *pasuk* 9 clearly refer to the sabbatical cycle, it is not clear from the *pesukim* that this financial *shemitta* has anything to do with the agricultural sabbatical year, what is commonly referred to as *shemitta*.

For example, the *halachot* associated with the agricultural *shemittat karka'ot* are in effect for the entire seventh year. The obligation of *shemittat kesafim*, in contrast, is a momentary reality that takes effect at the conclusion of the seventh year, in its final moments as the agricultural *shemittat karka'ot* comes to an end.

Importantly, as we have previously noted, although the Torah uses the term *shemitta* in the context of the agricultural laws ("*tishmetenna untashta*," *Shemot* 23:11), the Torah's description of those laws in *Parashat Behar* repeatedly refers to *shabbat ha'aretz*, whereas the *mitzvah* of cancelling loans is described as *shemitta*.

As we discussed, most commentators view the command of "*tishmetenna untashta*" as referring entirely to the agricultural laws of *shevi'it*; *tishmetenna* focuses on the ground, while *untashta* focuses on the produce.[196] The Rambam (*Sefer HaMitzvot, asei* 134) and others maintain that "*tishmetenna*" refers specifically to the requirement to relinquish one's hold over the agricultural produce in the field and to declare it *hefker*. For this reason, the Rambam refers to the entire sabbatical year as *shemitta*, and this is the term that has been widely accepted as the description for all of the year's laws.

Given that these *mitzvot* coincide and are both referred to as *shemitta*, there appears to be some deep connection between them. In fact, the *gemara* derives an important *halacha* from that connection:

> As it is taught in a *baraita* that Rabbi [Yehuda HaNasi] says: "And this is the manner of the release (*hashemitta*); [every creditor] will release (*shemot*)" – the *pasuk* speaks of two releases: One is the release of land, and the other is the release of money. [This *pasuk* equates these two releases, indicating that] when you are mandated [by Torah law] to release land, you must release money, and when you are not mandated to release land, you need not release money. (*Mo'ed Katan* 2b)

Rabbi Yehuda HaNasi derives that the Torah's use of the double term "*shemitta-shemot*" that *shemittat kesafim* applies fully only when *shemittat karka'ot* applies fully. He sees a direct connection between the two mitzvot and views "*shemitta*" as the Torah's description for both.

Essentially, all aspects of the seventh year are rooted in *shemitta*, relinquishing, setting aside what one feels is his – the fruit he worked hard to plant and cultivate and the hard-earned money he has lent to the needy. At the end of the year of *shevi'it*, lenders are required to release their right to repayment of loans, just as a farmer is required to release his rights to the fruit growing in his field.

The Ibn Ezra notes that just as the agricultural laws pertaining to *shevi'it* are encapsulated in the term "*shabbat laHashem*" (*Vayikra* 25:2, 4), the release of debts at the end of *shevi'it* is referred to as "a *shemitta* to Hashem" (*Devarim* 15:2):

> A *shemitta* to Hashem – In honor of Hashem, who provided him with the wealth. And the reason for attaching the phrase *laHashem* is because it is a *shabbat* to Hashem. (Ibn Ezra, *Devarim* 15:2)

Although the entire seventh year is a *shabbat* to Hashem, at the culminating moment of the seventh year, when *shemmitat kesafim* takes effect through the release of loans, the message is compounded. Our wealth is *laHashem*, provided by God, who informs us how

---

196 As we noted, Ibn Ezra and Seforno interpret the word "*tishmettena*" as referring specifically to financial *shemitta*, as that is the context in which the root *sh.m.t.* appears, while "*untashta*" requires that the land remain fallow. According to this understanding, *Parashat Mishpatim* introduces us to two social concepts of the seventh year simultaneously, financial and agricultural. Thus, debt relief is an essential part of the *shemitta* year, both naming and initially defining it. Moreover, the agricultural and the financial components are connected, as both indicate a serious deviation from normal conduct, combining to give *shevi'it* its unique flavor.

Interestingly, the root *sh.m.t.* appears in *Parashat Re'eh* six times; in contrast, the root *sh.b.t.* appears in *Parashat Behar* seven times. Perhaps the "missing" seventh reference to *sh.m.t* is in *Parashat Mishpatim*, such that there are seven mentions of release for the entire seventh year, combining the agricultural and monetary elements.

to use it.

There is, of course, an additional difference between the *halachot* of *shemittat karka'ot* and *shemittat kesafim*: The agricultural laws of *shevi'it* apply only in the Land of Israel, whereas the release of loans applies everywhere in the world.[197] Notably, however, the *mitzvah* of *tzedaka* that appears in the same context as the *mitzvah* of *shemittat kesafim* makes explicit mention of "your land" (*Devarim* 15:7, 11). Rabbeinu Bechayei clarifies the relationship between the Land of Israel, the *mitzvah* of *tzedaka*, and the *halachot* of the sabbatical year:

> An alternative understanding of the words "in your land" is: "**even** when you are in your land," that is, even when you already have demonstrated that you believe that the earth is the Lord's by releasing your debtor from his debts and allowing all to pick the harvest of your field every seventh year, the Torah still commands you to perform deeds of charity as outlined in the present paragraph.
>
> If you must perform charity even in an environment where you have demonstrated the virtue that charity symbolizes, then when you are in the Diaspora and cannot demonstrate this virtue in any other way, you are most certainly obliged to practice charity even more meticulously ...
>
> The Torah concludes by saying "in your land," i.e. "even in your land," where you have already given up so much of what you would normally consider yours, you are not to withhold your generous contributions to the poor. It follows that your duty to be generous to the poor while you are in the Diaspora is even greater, as you have fewer means of manifesting this positive virtue. (Rabbeinu Bechayei, *Devarim* 15:10)

In the Land of Israel, there are numerous agricultural gifts to the poor that develop and express one's generosity. Outside of the land, it is only through more limited avenues – most importantly *tzedaka* and release of loans – that one can support the underprivileged and thereby come closer to God by developing one's character.

The Three *Mitzvot*

A careful look at the *pesukim* indicates that there are actually three *mitzvot* associated with *Shemittat Kesafim*. The Rambam explains the basic *mitzvat aseh* of *shamot*, releasing the loan, and the prohibition of *lo yigos*, restricting one from actively collecting the loan after *shemitta* takes effect:

> There is a positive *mitzvah* to release debts during the seventh year, as it is stated: "Every creditor that lends anything to his neighbor shall release it" (*Devarim* 15:2). One who demands a debt over which the sabbatical year passed violates a negative commandment, as it is stated: "He shall not exact it of his neighbor, or of his brother." (*Hilchot Shemitta* 9:1)

In addition, there is another prohibition barring one from refusing to lend as the sabbatical year approaches. These three *mitzvot* are:

---

197 Although the *Sifrei* (*Devarim* 111–112) and the *gemara* (*Kiddushin* 38b) entertain the possibility that the financial *halachot* of the sabbatical year have the same geographic limitations as its agricultural *halachot*, they ultimately conclude that the release of loans applies throughout the world.

שְׁמוֹט	לֹא יִגֹּשׁ	הַלְוָאָה
מצוות עשה	מצוות לא תעשה	מצוות לא תעשה
Mitzvot Asseh	Mitzvot Lo Ta'aseh	Mitzvot Lo Ta'aseh
Release - שְׁמוֹט	**Do not exact – לֹא יִגֹּשׁ**	**Beware – הִשָּׁמֶר לְךָ**
The lender releases the borrower from feeling that he must pay the loan back.	One is prohibited from demanding payment of a loan after *shemittat kesafim*.	Do not refrain from giving loans as the *shemitta* year approaches.

In the context of the third mitzvah requiring one to continue providing interest-free loans even as *shemitta* is approaching, the Torah describes how one should not only assist but should do so graciously with a joyous heart.

The *Sefer HaChinuch* provides two reasons for the positive *mitzvah* to release loans. First, it is aimed at teaching us beneficence, just as the agricultural *shemitta* does:

> …To teach us the great traits of generosity and feeling content with one's lot, and to set trust in God in our hearts. Then we will be prepared to receive the blessing and mercy from the Master. (*Sefer HaChinuch, mitzvah* 477)

These *mitzvot* are also a means of encouraging lenders to distance themselves from anything that smacks of theft or desiring what belongs to others:

> And from this we see an iron-clad safeguard to distance oneself from theft and coveting the property of others. We make the following *a fortiori* argument: Even if I lent my money, the Torah commands me to leave it come the *shemitta* year; all the more so that I should distance myself to the extreme!

Rabbeinu Bechayei suggests an additional reason, pointing out that the *mitzvah* teaches the lender that he is not in control:

> But in *shemitta*, only the lender was warned not to exact the borrower to pay off his debt and not to lord himself over the borrower to force him to pay. (Rabbeinu Bechayei, *Devarim* 15:2)

Through *shemittat kesafim*, the creditor learns to be truly gracious and beneficent, eradicate any desire for that which belongs to others, and realize that the financial resources one has are really gifts from God treated by His rules.

Rav Yonatan Eibeshitz explains that the *mitzvah* of *shemittat kesafim* essentially assures that the economy of the Jewish People will not depend on loans and investments:

> And this *mitzvah* caused Israel not to be settled in business more than is necessary, or to over-engage in financial dealings like those in such trades, or to be engrossed day

and night like the gentiles. For one who immerses himself in business does not always gain wisdom, because such dealings require loans from others or to be a creditor for extended periods of time. And this is incompatible with keeping the *mitzvot*, because when the *shemitta* year arrives, the creditor must relinquish his hold on the debtor, who is then absolved of all debt. And if so, it becomes incumbent on us to achieve a level of self-sufficiency as needed and to work for what we need without channeling all our abilities and powers for vanity and tricks to amass wealth in violation of the Torah. Rather, one should be of the pure in walking in the ways of God, who grants sustenance to all and whose Torah is to be studied day and night. Just as our forefathers did not seek to become wealthy, Hashem's blessing will enrich, as He gives and takes by His will, and the tricks of man are for naught. (*Tumim* 67:1)

Rav Chayim David HaLevi explains that *shemittat kesafim,* alongside other agricultural *mitzvot* for the poor, seeks to eradicate poverty as much as possible:

In general, the law of *shemitta* is inherently linked to numerous other *mitzvot* that were designated to give to the Jewish nation and to its state financial stability, by ensuring the stability of the poorer members of society.… If for whatever reason a poor man lost hold of his land, he is able to sustain himself by collecting the agricultural gifts of the poor, including gleaning, forgotten sheaves, the corner of the field and the poor man's tithe, and also through the *mitzvah* of *tzedaka*… If he needs a loan, he can get a free loan… And in the seventh year the poor man is freed from any financial worries, as any vegetation growing can be taken by him for the benefit of his family. And if he did not succeed in cancelling out all his debts, the end of the *shemitta* year comes and does so for him… And if even this doesn't work and he must sell his land — and in the worst case, he sells himself as a slave — the *yovel* year comes and frees all slaves and returns all land to its ancestral holders. At that point, everyone can begin their financial life anew. (*Mekor Chayim*, ch. 5, *shemittat kesafim*)

The Rambam explains that the various *mitzvot* surrounding *shemitta* and *yovel* serve a number of social and religious purposes:

As to the precepts enumerated in the laws concerning the year of release and the *yovel*, some of them imply sympathy with our fellow men and promote the well-being of mankind; for in reference to these precepts it is stated in the Law, "That the poor of thy people may eat" (*Shemot* 23:11); and besides, the land will also increase its produce and improve when it remains fallow for some time. Other precepts of this class prescribe kindness to servants and to the poor, by renouncing any claims to debts [in the year of release] and relieving the slaves of their bondage [in the seventh year]. There are some precepts in this class that serve to secure for the people a permanent source of maintenance and support by providing that the land should remain the permanent property of its owners, and that it could not be sold: "And the land shall not be sold for ever" (*Vayikra* 25:23). In this way, the property of a person remains intact for him and his heirs, and he can only enjoy the produce thereof. (*Moreh Nevuchim*)

Thus, in addition to providing a socially beneficial financial "restart" for the borrower, the obligation to release loans provides several lessons for the lender. As the Rambam notes, these goals combine for a multifaceted social construct built around the seventh year of *shemitta* and the fiftieth year of *yovel*.

The Severity of Withholding Loans

However, it is notable that the *mitzvah* of providing free loans to borrowers is built upon trust between the parties; lenders need to be confident that borrowers intend to repay their debts. *Shemittat kesafim* seems to call this into question. If the *mitzvah* frees borrowers of any obligation to return outstanding loans, why indeed should a lender extend a loan to begin with? The lender is already forfeiting interest on his loan. Now the Torah requires him to forfeit even the principal! How can the Torah instruct one not to withhold a loan based on the knowledge that the upcoming *shemitta* will inevitably cancel it?

In fact, Rav Shlomo Zalman Auerbach (*Minchat Shlomo* 1:47) rules that the prohibition against withholding loans has limits. It does not apply when one has a legitimate reason to fear that the borrower will not repay the loan. Instead, it pertains only to one who entertains the unfounded thought that a trustworthy Jew will take advantage of the approach of the sabbatical year and not repay the loan, not because one has a justified concern regarding the would-be borrower. Thus, this *mitzvah* addresses a person who would stop himself from performing an act of kindness due to ungrounded fears.[198]

Although the prohibition against withholding loans appears specifically in the context of *shemittat kesafim*, many commentators assume that it applies to one who withholds a loan at any time, as the *mitzvah* of giving *tzedaka* appears in these *pesukim* as well.[199] Even the commentators who maintain that the prohibition of withholding loans applies uniquely

---

198 Rav Moshe Sternbuch (*Ta'am VaDa'at*) similarly writes that the prohibition against withholding loans before *shemitta* applies only when the borrower expresses his sincere intention and desire to repay the money before *shemitta*. If the borrower does not indicate his willingness to repay the money before *shemitta*, in which case the loan essentially constitutes ordinary charity, the lender is not required to grant the loan if he cannot afford to sustain such a loss. There is no requirement to knowingly lend money that will not be returned, beyond the standard obligation of *tzedaka*.

199 For example, Rabbeinu Yonah (*Sha'arei Teshuva* 3:67) seems to understand the *mitzvah* as a general prohibition. The Torah simply introduces the prohibition in the context of a circumstance in which it is likely to be violated. In truth, it bears no inherent connection to *shemitta*, but rather applies any time a person refuses to grant a loan to a person in need. The Rambam, in contrast, clearly understands the *mitzvah* as specific to refraining from lending before *shemitta*, as indicated by the fact that he places it in *Hilchot Shemitta VeYovel* (9:30) and not in *Hilchot Malveh VeLoveh*, where he discusses the obligation to give loans. It is also notable that whereas Rabbeinu Yonah writes of refusing to lend to a poor person, the Rambam refers to a prohibition before *shemitta* to refuse to "lend to his fellow," as the prohibition before *shemitta* applies regardless of the borrower's financial status.

One practical ramification of this debate relates to whether or not the prohibition applies in contemporary society. It is generally assumed that nowadays, *shemittat kesafim* applies only on the level rabbinic enactment. Rav Yechiel Michel Tuketchinsky held that if the Torah obligation of *shemittat kesafim* does not apply, then certainly the accompanying prohibition against refusing loan requests before *shemitta* also does not apply. He clearly accepted the Rambam's outlook that this prohibition directly relates to the *halacha* of *shemittat kesafim*. By contrast, Rav Shlomo Zalman Auerbach argued that the prohibition forbids refusing a loan because of "false, imaginary concerns." It therefore makes no difference whether the anticipated remission of the debt will occur due to Torah law or rabbinic enactment. The moment a person refuses a debt out of fear of losing the money, he has violated this prohibition. This approach corresponds to the position of Rabbenu Yonah, that this prohibition relates to the general obligation to lend money to the poor.

prior to *shemittat kesafim* note that it is more likely that people will refuse to give other forms of *tzedaka* during that time. For example, the Abarbanel (ad loc.) interprets the *pesukim* as referring to the giving of *ma'aser ani*, the tithe to the poor, in the sixth year. The Torah warns that the capable individual who refuses to lend may also justify his failure to give *ma'aser ani* to the poor based on the fact that in the following year, everything will become ownerless and the poor will have equal access to all produce.[200]

The medieval commentator Rav Yosef Bechor Shor (ad loc.) explains that the *pesukim* directly link the agricultural and financial *shemitta*, by stating that one should not demand repayment of loans at the time of *shemittat kesafim* because "he has declared a *shemitta* to Hashem" (*Devarim* 15:2). He explains that specifically because the debtor has declared *shemitta* – that is, he refrains from working his land during the sabbatical year – he has no means to repay his debt at this time. One may demand repayment only from a non-Jew, who is not presently observing *shemitta*.[201]

Rav Elchanan Samet explains that this interpretation helps us understand the glaring time differential between the agricultural *shabbat ha'aretz*, which applies the entire seventh year, and the relinquishment of debts, which only come into force at the end of that year. He suggests that the reason for the difference is that in an agricultural society, a farmer takes loans at the beginning of a year and generally repays them at the end of the year when he harvests his crops. However, the Jewish farmer, who refrains from working the land during the seventh year and reaps no commercial harvest, obviously has no means by which he can repay his loans. Therefore, the Torah requires that one who observes *shemitta* not be penalized for being unable to repay:

> The problem with repaying debts is a problem that actually relates to the eighth year, since the borrowing farmer has no harvest from which to be able to repay the loan. At the beginning of the seventh year, no such problem exists, since the harvest of the sixth year is still available to the farmer, and he can use that for repaying a debt. During the course of the seventh year itself, it seems, the poor and the wealthy are nourished alike from the produce that grew in everyone's fields, as these are declared *hefker*, ownerless, as the *pasuk* teaches, "That the poor of your nation may eat."
>
> Thus we can understand the date for *shemittat kesafim*: It occurs at the transition from the seventh year to the eighth. We can also understand the dependence of *shemittat kesafim* on the *shemitta* of the land, even though the latter is an obligation on the individual that is not, in itself, dependent on the land. When the *shemitta* of the land is not observed, there is no need for this protection for a borrowing farmer, as during the seventh year he will be sowing and reaping as usual, and he will therefore be able

---

200 See also *Chasam Sofer* and *Ketav VeHaKabbala*, who writes that the prohibition is directed at a person who has lent on collateral, so that halachically the loan will not be cancelled at the conclusion of *shemitta*, yet who still refuses to lend, on the pretext that the poor will have equal access to his produce during the approaching sabbatical year and do not deserve a loan on top of that. Such refusal is liable to rob the would-be borrower of his dignity, as there are poor people who are uncomfortable taking from the produce of others, even when it's legal to do so. They prefer to work harder in order to repay their loans, rather than relying on the *shemitta* year to legally collect produce from fields. Therefore, the Torah requires one continue to lend even as the *shemitta* year approaches.

201 See also the Netziv, *Ha'amek Davar, Devarim* 15:2. Unlike the Bechor Shor, most commentators read the *pasuk* as "it has become a *shemitta* to Hashem" or as a reference to the court, which is given the responsibilities for establishing the calendar (see the commentaries of the Rashbam and Chizkuni, ad loc.).

to repay his debts.

This explanation provides a fascinating rationale not only for the *mitzvah* of *shemittat kesafim*, but also for Rabbi Yehuda HaNasi's understanding as to why the Torah here refers to the agricultural *shemitta* year as "*shemitta*," rather than "*shabbat ha'aretz.*" It is specifically the element of relinquishing one's produce during *shevi'it* that engenders the requirement to ease the farmer's debts.

One might question this understanding based on the fact that *shemittat kesafim* seems to apply throughout the world, even though agricultural *shemitta* is limited to Israel, apparently indicating that the two *shemittot* can exist independently. Perhaps we can explain that the *shemitta* ideal can only be achieved by a combination of *shabbat ha'aretz* and *shemittat kesafim*. However, Jews throughout the world, while lacking the ability to connect to the complete ideal because they live in lands that lack the holiness and divine providence essential for *Shabbat ha'aretz*, still long for a piece of the *shemitta* experience. The agricultural *shemitta* is an impossibility for them, yet the Torah still wants the *shemitta* experience to be felt by people outside of Eretz Yisrael to whatever degree possible.[202]

A Lawless Thought

The Torah terms one who refuses to extend a loan to a trustworthy individual as one who entertains "*beliya'al*" thoughts (*Devarim* 15:9).[203] This is a harsh term, whose only other use in the Torah is in reference to idol worship: "יָצְאוּ אֲנָשִׁים בְּנֵי בְלִיַּעַל מִקִּרְבֶּךָ וַיַּדִּיחוּ אֶת יֹשְׁבֵי עִירָם," "People of *beliya'al* went forth from among you and misled the residents of their city" (*Devarim* 13:13-14). On the basis of this parallel, the *gemara* (*Ketubot* 68a) establishes that "whoever hides his eye from charity is considered as though he worshipped idols." The use of the same term in reference to these two transgressions indicates a kind of equation between them. Notably, the *gemara* applies the prohibition of having a "lawless thought" to withholding *tzedaka* in general, not only to withholding loans. Indeed, most of the rationales for the use of the word "lawless" for a person who hesitates to lend seem applicable to reluctance to give *tzedaka*.

In what manner is refusal to financially assist the poor akin to soliciting idol worship? The *Panim Yafot* explains that anyone who truly believes in Divine Providence should recognize that no one becomes poor by fulfilling the *mitzvah* of *tzedaka*. One who questions that reality is deficient in his faith:

> The reason for this is that one who believes in God's Providence over the people of Israel – and in the land of Israel in particular – also accepts that one will not become

---

202 As we note below, however, the practice of many communities who failed to observe *shemittat kesafim* outside of the Land of Israel, as attested to by the Rosh, might indicate that after the *mitzvah* was no longer Biblically required, it was felt that the *shemitta* ideal could not be achieved in the absence of an agricultural *shemitta*.

203 Although the *gemara* assumes that the words "beware" and "lest" indicate a prohibition – as in the *pasuk*, השמר לך פן יהיה עם לבבך דבר בליעל – Rav Shlomo Zalman Auerbach (in his glosses to *Mishneh Kesef*) states that although it is improper to contemplate withholding a loan because the sabbatical year is coming, only following up on such a thought with actually withholding a loan is forbidden.

destitute through *tzedaka*, because God watches over us and blesses us. However, one who lacks sufficient faith says each person receives according to his random luck and will lack in the *shemitta* year. And this is idol worship at its core, as the *gemara* says one who lives in the Diaspora is like one who worships idols, for both individuals live according to random chance like the gentiles ... (*Panim Yafot, Re'eh* 15:9)

In a slightly different vein, Rav Shimshon Raphael Hirsch (*Devarim* 15:9) explains that when one is approached with a request for financial assistance, he should view it as a Divine request, as Hashem commanded one to respond in the affirmative when capable. Any refusal to accede to such a request is akin to an act of idol worship – worshipping wealth rather than Hashem.

Rabbi David Silverberg offers another explanation for the comparison drawn by the *gemara*:

By comparing a prospective lender's refusal in this case to idolatry, the *gemara* perhaps seeks to impress upon us the importance of personal sacrifice as an integral component of Jewish observance. It is not enough to believe in God as the Creator and Ruler of the world, to denounce pagan beliefs and accept the basic tenet of God's existence. This fundamental acceptance also requires the willingness to make sacrifices to fulfill the Divine Will, as expressed in the obligation of *shemittat kesafim* (the remission of debts on the seventh year). A person who refuses to make sacrifices for the sake of *avodat Hashem*, the *gemara* teaches, is equivalent to an idolater, because although he acknowledges the existence of the one, true God, he fails to acknowledge the practical implications of that belief. He as yet overlooks his obligation as a servant of God to set his personal interests and concerns aside for the sake of fulfilling the will of his Creator. (*S.A.L.T.*)

Rav Yehuda Leib Ginsburg (*Yalkut Yehuda*) notes that the word *beliya'al* is mentioned specifically in relation to an *Ir HaNidachat*, a city in which lawless individuals solicit others to idol worship, turning them away from God. Similarly, one who refuses to lend others in need when he has the ability to do so often causes the needy to question God's righteousness and to turn away from Him. The poor might even question God's Hand in the world, given that money is entrusted in the hands of the uncompassionate.

Perhaps we can take this observation further. If we understand the prohibition of withholding *tzedaka* as an aspect of the Torah's perspective on wealth allocation, refraining from financially assisting others is more than simply a lack of compassion; it is a form of rebellion against God's institution of providing for everyone's needs in allocating money to stewads who will provide it for others in their time of need. On the other hand, one who gives *tzedaka*, especially with a joyous heart as the Torah prescribes, not only fulfills a *mitzvah* but has a positive impact on society. He forges a partnership with God, the ultimate Provider, by acknowledging that his financial success is a reflection of his trustworthiness as a partner with Hashem for making the world a better place. He follows in the path of Avraham Avinu, who was chosen for his commitment to *tzedek umishpat*, righteousness and justice.

The Torah concludes the passage regarding free loans and *shemittat kesafim* by noting that poverty is a necessary component of the world in which we live: "For there will not cease to be poor in the land" (*Devarim* 15:9). One reason this is true is that God does not want to directly right all the socio-economic inequalities of the world Himself, and He, therefore, charged humanity to do so. His *mitzvot* are the recipe for how to do this, and fulfillment of those *mitzvot* recognizes the Divine plan. It also elicits a recognition of compassion, righteousness, and justice and promotes that message for all to see, including the needy themselves. On the other hand, failure to partner with Hashem in this noble mission elicits a harmful view of Divine justice and is comparable to idolatrous practices.

As we noted, the Torah emphasizes the element of brotherhood in the context of *tzedaka*, charging one to treat others in need as he would treat his own brother. The Maharal explains that this message underlies the prohibition against withholding loans, as well as the use of the word *beliya'al* in connection with idolatry. One who fails to recognize the bond of brotherhood by refusing to help other Jews who are in need expresses alienation from one's brothers and fails to acknowledge the kinship and shared responsibility of all Jews. His refusal is thus essentially an act of rebellion against the Jews as a people.

Others note that the character flaws that lead one to refuse to lend to others are rooted in idolatrous outlooks and a refusal to see G-d's role in life. For example, the *Yismach Moshe* attributes the refusal to lend to arrogance. Thus, the use of the word "*beliya'al*" can be understood through the prism of the dictum that equates arrogance with idolatry. One who is excessively proud of his wealth and financial attainment and therefore unwilling to assist the needy is comparable to an idolater. Others (see Nachshoni, *Parashat Re'eh*, citing Rav Shmelke of Nikosburg) attribute the would-be lender's insensitivity to a sense of predetermination, the belief that the needy are unworthy of support, which is akin to idolatry.[204]

The fact that the Torah goes out of its way to emphasize that one should refrain from rationalizing one's unwillingness to provide *tzedaka* makes it clear that although there are times when one might legitimately refrain from extending a loan (such as when the requester is not really in need), one must be careful never to rationalize his refusal when support is genuinely necessary.

The *Shemitta* Vision

Rav Shaul Yisraeli (*Shemitta through the Generations*) illustrates how the various economic aspects of *shevi'it* aim not only to give pride to the poor "recipient" but also to alleviate his financial instability and give him the ability to start again:

---

204 This assumption is reminiscent of the logic of Turnus Rufus that is refuted by Rabbi Akiva in *Bava Batra* (10a).

> First, the social aspect of the mitzvah stands out. That the lands rests entails putting to rest private proprietary rights to all fruits of this year… If, during the six years of labor, class-based disparities have come about and taken root, for this year they are null and void. The master has no more right than the servant, the native no more than the sojourner; even the social disparities that normally develop with economic classes dissipate, as it were, for this year; moreover, they are muted going forward.

Rav Yisraeli adds that *shevi'it's* economic interpersonal message affects the approach to money of both the wealthy and the poor. The *mitzvah* to lend money ensures that deep economic and class differences won't remain in place for long.

> Firstly, the Torah prohibits keeping money inert like some unmovable rock if someone is in need of it at any time: you bear an ongoing obligation to lend it to him, and this loan must be made gratis. The Torah, after all, prohibits interest with the full force of law and with quite a number of admonitions to the borrower, the creditor, and the witnesses. Yet the Torah does not make do with that: in addition to *Shemitta* of the land and renouncing ownership of produce comes the mitzvah of relinquishing debts, by which all debts not collected by the end of the *Shemitta* year expire and cease to be subject to collection.

He goes on to explain how extreme this mitzvah is, especially in light of all the *mitzvot* mandating honesty in business.

> The money which has accumulated in a person's possession is thus his own money, and he has achieved it conscientiously and with much effort — and now you require him to lend it to his fellow gratis! He does this wholeheartedly; he does not demand any part of the profit that this money may bring his fellow. There is just one thought that gnaws at his heart, just one thing that he would assure himself: that he will in fact be returned his money — his own money, without any sort of profit. He merely seeks that his fellow not profit from his toils and travails and give back nothing. Our natural course of thought would tend to side with him entirely. Yet the Torah does not think thusly: it would be "contemptible" for such a thought to cross one's mind. It demands geniality and kindheartedness of you when the loan is given, despite your knowledge that it is to be lost.

With this in mind, it is understandable how *Shemitta* presents the recipe for a financial revolution:

> One who walks in the way of the Torah, who observes this mitzvah once admonished severely regarding it — no less than regarding any other mitzvah — will effect a complete social revolution that quietly and peacefully, in one fell swoop, voids the economic and social disparities that have occupied human society since time immemorial. With the conclusion of the *shemitta* year, the whole nation's course of work and creativity begins anew, in a state where all people have virtually the same means at their disposal.

Rav Yisraeli concludes that the *mitzvah* of *yovel* once every fifty years seals this interpersonal economic message:

And if this is still not enough, since the tool that is the *mitzvah* of relinquishing debt can be implemented for cash in hand but not for money invested in real estate, where conspicuous disparities remain between the one who has succeeded in concentrating land under his ownership and the other who has been compelled to sell his, the *mitzvah* of *yovel* comes, and every person returns to his inheritance and family. All transactions that might have concentrated land under the ownership of a few while another social stratum grows impoverished are null and void; every person again stands upon the inheritance of his fathers, ready to turn a new page.

Shemittat Kesafim and Modern-Day Bankruptcy Law

An oft-discussed topic in contemporary discourse is the concept of debt relief. For example, in the wake of the Covid-19 pandemic, many governments provided loans to businesses, with an option for cancellation in line with government guidelines. These are loans that from their inception had the opportunity to become gifts. Is this comparable to *shemittat kesafim*, which "releases" loans that were meant to be repaid?

As we noted above, the Halacha takes into account the prospect of a debtor's insolvency and provides solutions regarding repayment. Although one is required to repay a loan, if a debtor cannot do so, he cannot be imprisoned or otherwise punished; he is simply required to repay what he can. We further noted that it is difficult to compare Halacha's accommodations in cases of insolvency to the modern-day concept of bankruptcy. However, it is possible to argue that bankruptcy does parallel the idea of *shemittat kesafim*. Rabbi Dr. Asher Meir notes:

The rationale for such a release [during *shemittat kesafim*] is clear: It is sometimes in everyone's interest to give debtors a fresh start, a new lease on life that will give them the ability and the incentive to become productive citizens. If the debts were incurred in good faith but hardship intervened, then the creditor will gain little by demanding full repayment from an indigent debtor and a fresh start is called for.

Some commentators question the existence of a parallel between the Sabbatical year discharge and modern bankruptcy. They point out that the Sabbatical year discharge applies equally to rich and poor, and that only loans are exempt, not other kinds of debts. They also point out that it is considered praiseworthy to pay back cancelled Sabbatical debts when possible.

I don't think these objections are decisive. Debts are only cancelled in the Sabbatical year when they came due before the year begins but were left uncollected. In most cases, this would apply specifically to insolvent debtors; debtors of means would have paid up beforehand or have their assets seized. We should add that throughout the Torah the assumption is that loans, which in ancient times were interest-free, were given to poor people. Indeed, the release passage itself refers to this, pointing out that if we fulfill this commandment ultimately we will not lose from it because the result will be that "there will not be any more poor among you."

Rabbi Dr. Meir notes that although the institution of *prozbul* limits the application of *shemittat kesafim*, that might indicate that the wholesale release of all loans – even those that could be repaid – would be inappropriate in certain situations. Allowing the religious courts the discretion as to when it is appropriate might be the balance of the letter and the spirit of the law. He concludes:

> Judaism considers paying debts a positive obligation – a *mitzvah*. Any time a person incurs a debt, he must do so with good faith and with reason to believe that he will be able to repay. He must then make every effort to obtain the means to fulfill his obligation.
>
> But if unexpected setbacks make it impossible to pay, the Torah suggests an ideal of giving the debtor a fresh start. In many jurisdictions, legislatures have identified with this ideal and introduced the ability for debtors to obtain such a fresh start, subject to various legal conditions and review. It is ethical to avail yourself of these laws if indeed your obligations were assumed with good faith, if you are properly eligible for the release, and if you need the discharge in order to obtain a true and fair fresh start in your affairs.

The Mechanism of *Shemittat Kesafim*

Although this analysis of *shemittat kesafim* as the rationale for the institution of bankruptcy certainly seems strong, a deeper study of the mechanism of *shemittat kesafim* points us to a significant question regarding its basis. Is the release of debts automatic, or is it the lender who declares that the borrower is not required to pay it back? Moreover, as we discussed above, the Torah prohibits withholding loans as the *shemitta* year approaches. Why isn't the Torah concerned by the possibility that excessive taking advantage of *shemitta's* discharge of debt will put the entire institution of debt relief in jeopardy?

Furthermore, it is notable that the Torah commands specifically that the lender "*shamot*," release his loans, not that he cancel them. Indeed, if the loan were canceled entirely, there would be no need for the *mitzvat lo ta'aseh* of "*Lo yigos*," which prohibits collecting debts after *shemittat kesafim*. What aspect of the loan is released, and does the lender have any discretion regarding the release?

Analysis of the *halachic* mechanism of *shemittat kesafim* will provide us with some clarity regarding its goals.

Rabbi Eliezer of Metz, author of the *Sefer Yerei'im*, proposes that the release of loans during *shemittat kesafim* is not automatic.[205] Rather, the *mitzvat aseh* is for the lender to actually release the loan:

> Repayment of a loan that passed through the *shemitta* year cannot be withheld by the borrower unless the lender says so. For as long as the lender has not relinquished ownership of the debt, the borrower is liable to pay. Rather, the borrower brings the lender to court to force him to relinquish the debt as is commanded by the Creator, and the court requires the lender to say "I relinquish," as is commanded by the

---

205 There is a similar question regarding *shemittat karka'ot*. Is the *hefker* of *shemitta* produce automatic, or is it the prerogative of the owner of the field to decide if he will fulfill his divinely ordained *mitzvah* of abandoning ownership of his produce?

> Sages… If he does not wish to say "I relinquish," the court forces him to do so, as the *beraitta* in *Ketubot* teaches: "[The court] lashes him until the point he perishes." (*Sefer Yerei'im* 164)

The *Yerei'im* rules that since there is a *mitzvah* incumbent on the lender to release the loan, the courts can force him to do so, but until he has actually declared that he released the loans, he has the right to collect them. In other words, until the lender actually releases the loan – either willingly or due to pressure from *beit din* – the borrower does not have the right to refrain from paying back the loan. According to the *Yerei'im*, loans are not automatically canceled; the Torah guides the lender how to act, requiring him to play an active role in the release.

Other *Rishonim* reject this conclusion, explaining that although there is a *mitzvah* incumbent upon the lender to declare that he relinquishes all his outstanding loans, the Torah releases them whether the lender agrees to or not. According to this accepted understanding, the Torah proclaims all loans to be released, but nevertheless commands the lender to declare so orally and accept the Torah's release.[206]

According to both of these views, the lender plays an active role in the process of transforming the status of the loan. What is the role of the borrower in this process?

Release or Cancelation?

מִשְׁמֵט אֲנִי

Throughout our discussion of *shemittat Kesafim* we have been careful to refer to *shemittat Kesafim* as loan release, not loan cancelation. Many understand *shemittat Kesafim* as a real cancelation of the loan. However, there is good reason to believe otherwise.

Significantly, the *mishna* clarifies that although *shemitta* obligates lenders to release their loans, borrowers are allowed to pay back the loans after the *shemitta* year:

הַמַּחֲזִיר חוֹב בַּשְּׁבִיעִית, יֹאמַר לוֹ מְשַׁמֵּט אֲנִי. אָמַר לוֹ אַף עַל פִּי כֵן, יְקַבֵּל מִמֶּנּוּ, שֶׁנֶּאֱמַר (דברים טו) וְזֶה דְּבַר הַשְּׁמִטָּה. כַּיּוֹצֵא בוֹ, רוֹצֵחַ שֶׁגָּלָה לְעִיר מִקְלָטוֹ וְרָצוּ אַנְשֵׁי הָעִיר לְכַבְּדוֹ, יֹאמַר לָהֶם, רוֹצֵחַ אָנִי. אָמְרוּ לוֹ, אַף עַל פִּי כֵן, יְקַבֵּל מֵהֶם, שֶׁנֶּאֱמַר (שם יט) וְזֶה דְּבַר הָרוֹצֵחַ:

[If a borrower wishes to] return a loan after the sabbatical year, [the lender] should say to him, "I release the obligation." If the borrower replies, "Nevertheless, [I wish to repay it,]" then the lender should accept the repayment, as it states, "this is the substance [literally, word] of the release" (*Devarim* 15:2). (*Shevi'it* 10:8)

The *mishna* derives from the Torah's terminology that the release of loans is essentially a matter of words. The lender is not required to refuse repayment, but rather merely to state

---

206 See Mordechai, *Gittin* 380, citing Rabbeinu Avigdor HaKohen, who draws a parallel between this law and the sanctification of a firstborn animal; although the animal is sanctified from birth, its owner is required to orally declare it sanctified. The *Ohr Zarua* (*Piskei Avoda Zara* 108) argues that because the release is automatic, a lender's refusal to relinquish his loans is ignored; however, he is only required to verbally declare, "I relinquish," if the borrower brings payment for the debt. See Rav Matan Glidai (*Shiurei Shemitta*)for a discussion of the difference between these views.

that he releases the obligation.

The next *mishna* goes one step further, clarifying that not only may a borrower repay his loans, but such behavior is praiseworthy:

הַמַּחֲזִיר חוֹב בַּשְּׁבִיעִית, רוּחַ חֲכָמִים נוֹחָה מִמֶּנּוּ.

If one who repays a debt after the sabbatical year, the Sages are pleased with him.

נוֹחָה הֵימֶנּוּ

These *mishnayot* indicate that at the very least, it is good practice to pay back one's loans after *shemitta*. But if the sabbatical year cancels loans, why should one be encouraged to return it? Rabbeinu Bechayei suggests a practical reason:

> If the borrower does not repay his debts even though he is legally in sound financial condition, he risks that the lender will shame him by spreading the word that his borrower took advantage of the lender's good nature and simply consumed his money. (Rabbeinu Bechayei, *Devarim* 15:2)

Since the lender borrowed the money with intent to repay it, it is in his best interest to do so if he can. Only if the borrower cannot afford repayment does he stand to benefit from the technical cancellation of the obligation.

Although Rabbeinu Bechayei understands the *mishna* on a practical level, the *gemara*'s discussion of the nature of the release calls into question the basic assumption that the sabbatical year indeed cancels loans.

The *gemara* cites the *mishna*'s statement that when a borrower attempts to return a loan after *shemitta*, the lender must state that he releases the loan, and the proper response is for the borrower to then declare that nevertheless, he wants to repay the loan. The *gemara*'s cites Rabba as stating that if a lender says that he releases an obligation and the borrower decides to take advantage and not repay the loan, the lender can take certain action until he agrees to pay:

> Rabba said: [The creditor] is permitted to "*tali*" [the debtor], until [the debtor] says this [that he nevertheless wishes to repay him]. Abbaye raised an objection from a *baraita*, which states: When [the debtor] gives [the creditor payment for a debt that has been cancelled], he should not say to him, "I give this to you in payment of my debt"; rather, he should say to him, "This is my money and I give it to you as a gift." [This indicates that the debt is repaid only due to the initiative of the debtor.] [Rabba] said to him: [The creditor] is permitted to "*tali*" [the debtor] as well, until he says [that he gives it as a gift. Thus, the initiative may come from the creditor.] (*Gittin* 37b)

The definition of "*tali*" is debated by the commentators. Rashi explains it literally: The lender may hang the borrower up high on a tree until he acquiesces to pay the loan. The Rosh is very troubled by Rashi's explanation, as it seems to be in total contradiction to the *mitzvah* of the lender releasing the loan and not exacting it from the borrower. The Rosh thus offers another explanation: The lender can exert psychological pressure upon the borrower by staring at the borrower after he comes to return the loan but refuses to pay after the lender says he released the loan.

Why is the lender permitted to put any amount of pressure, either psychological or physical, on a borrower who seeks to take advantage of the cancellation of his debt? The reason might be because *shemittat Kesafim* doesn't entail canceling debt at all. Instead, it calls for an act of *shemitta*, relinquishing one's rights to collect the loan, and a prohibition of *lo yigos*, restricting one from attempting to force collection of the loan.

For this reason, in a situation like that discussed in the *gemara*, where the lender has the means to pay, he should do so. The debt-release consists of a verbal obligation by the creditor not to exact a loan from anyone who is incapable of paying it. This release is a remarkable kindness, allowing the borrower an opportunity for a new financial beginning. However, although the borrower bears no legal obligation to repay the money, if he is in a position to reimburse his benefactor, he has a moral obligation to do so. Therefore, a solvent individual not only is permitted to repay a loan after the close of the sabbatical year, but may even be pressured to.[207]

The understanding that *shemitta* does not truly cancel a loan obligation is expressed in the *Sefer Yerei'im*, who writes that *shemitta* entails only ceasing to demand repayment; the borrower should repay the loan on his own volition:

> It appears to me that "*shemitta*" does not mean "forgiving" [a loan]. Rather, the Holy One commands that one "release" – i.e. leave it alone, not demand it – until the borrower returns it of his own accord… For whenever the Torah uses the word *Shemitta*, it means "to leave alone," not "to relinquish altogether," as it is written, "and during the seventh [year], you shall release [the land] and abandon it" – meaning, "you shall leave it alone."
>
> Thus a loan always has the condition that the debtor not keep [the creditor] waiting forever for repayment from his storehouse. If he does so, then he is termed an "evil debtor," as in the *pasuk*, "The evil debtor does not pay back" (*Tehillim* 37:21). (*Sefer Yerei'im* [older edition] 278)

In this view, the loan has not been canceled at all. Rather, instead of the lender having the power to force collection through the courts, repayment is now up to the borrower. He can postpone repayment as long as he needs to, but he should repay the loan the moment he has available assets. Later editions of the *Yerei'im* do not cite this extreme formulation, possibly indicating that his later view was that the entire loan is indeed canceled.[208] Nevertheless, several of *Acharonim* accept the overall premise that the loan is not completely voided after *shemittat kesafim* and that the borrower should repay it if he can.

This idea that the sabbatical year does not in fact cancel loans is expressed by Rav Kook:

> The purpose of the sabbatical year is not prevention of repayment of the loan and swaying of property rights, for the foundation of the Torah and its laws is the

---

207 See *Terumat HaDeshen* 304; Bach, *Choshen Mishpat* 67:36.

208 Rav Matan Glidai notes that the continuation of the *gemara* in *Gittin* may indeed indicate that the loan is cancelled entirely.

upholding of the property rights of every individual with respect to what is truly his. Rather, while ownership rights are upheld, there must be a spirit of generosity to prevent society from incurring damage due to wealth. Thus, the main purpose of the release of loans is that the loan not be demanded ... (*Ein Ayah* on *Pei'ah*)

Rav Hirsch similarly argues that *shemittat kesafim* obligates the lender to release the obligation to pay, while never obliterating the borrower's obligation when he is capable of repaying:

One who releases a debt in the seventh year allows the debt to be "released from his hand," but this release is strictly a one-sided action. The creditor, the *ba'al*, who holds the legal claim to the debt and thereby has become the debtor's master, renounces forever his right to exert this claim. The debtor, however, remains forever morally in his debt ... Moreover, it is not the Torah's intention to exempt people who can pay from the moral obligation of paying their debts, and from such people the creditor is entitled to expect that they will not exploit the privilege granted to them by the sabbatical year.

The Torah requires that the creditor declare a remittance, but this does not exempt the debtor from his duty. In this respect, the law of the seventh year differs from that of interest, as there the debtor is forbidden to pay interest just as the creditor is forbidden to accept it...

At the end of each sabbatical-year cycle, the repayment of every previously contracted debt remains only as a moral obligation: payment of the debt is left to the discretion of him who incurred it. Because of the trust that the Torah thus places in him, the debtor, instead of feeling weighed down by the burden of his debt, feels morally uplifted. Repaying the debt of his own free will now be a matter of personal honor for him. (Rav Hirsch, commentary on *Devarim* 15:2).

Shemittat Kesafim - Explained

If *Shemittat Kesafim* indeed doesn't call for loan cancellation, instead requiring one to relinquish the rights to forcibly collect outstanding loans, then a broader understanding of *Shemittat Kesafim* is in order. A loan is essentially a form of charity, according to the Rambam, the highest form. As the Abarbanel noted, at times, a loan is only provided in lieu of an outright gift because the recipient is unwilling to accept one. In such an instance, when the debtor can't afford to repay the loan, even the lender will rejoice as *Shemittat Kesafim* relieves the receiver of any sense of responsibility to return the loan.

Suppose the lender initially gave a loan, intending that it be returned. In that case, *shemittat Kesafim* provides him with a new *mitzvah* – to courageously state: "*Meshamet Ani* (I release the obligation)," recognizing that the borrower is incapable of returning the loan.

This understanding helps explain how a system of interest-free loans aimed at helping the needy can be maintained if *shemittat kesafim* essentially uproots the lender's rights to receive his money. *Shemittat kesafim* does not constitute cancellation of loans, but rather a denial of the lender's rights to demand payment of the loan and take the legal action necessary to ensure it is repaid.

The Torah requires that after the *shemitta* year ends, the lender perform an act of release, enabling the borrower to decide if he is capable of repaying the loan or not. The borrower is given a chance for a fresh start; he will be able to step out of his home without fear that he will be spotted by one of his creditors. He will be entitled to walk around in dignity and use any money he makes to invest in a brighter financial future, rather than to pay off one debt at a time. However, the moment he is on safe financial footing and is in a position to repay the loan, using *shemittat kesafim* as an excuse to avoid repayment is both morally inappropriate and devastating to the Torah's system of social concern and justice.

When *shemittat kesafim* is abused, it is not only a personal insult to the lender who went above and beyond to grant an interest-free loan to the borrower in his time of need, but it is an affront to the institution of free loans, which demands trust and security. Although lenders are commanded to allow *shemittat kesafim* to give borrowers a new start, they are allowed to be concerned when *shemittat kesafim* is abused by disingenuous borrowers to play insolvency in order to refrain from paying their benefactors. As we will see, this understanding of *shemittat kesafim* helps explain Hillel's enactment of *prozbul*.

Shemittat Kesafim in Our Day

We noted elsewhere that in the view of Rabbi Yehuda HaNasi (*Arachin 32*), *yovel* is observed only when at least a majority of the nation lives in the Land in their appropriate tribal portions. Whenever *yovel* is not operative, there is similarly no Biblical obligation of *shevi'it*. Similarly, Rabbi Yehuda HaNasi derives (*Moed Katan* 2b) that *shemittat kesafim* applies fully only when *shemittat karka'ot* applies fully.

Nevertheless, the practice and important lessons of *shemittat karka'ot* and *shemittat kesafim* are so crucial that the Sages understood that even when there is no Biblical obligation, it was their duty to require the observance of these *mitzvot* rabbinically. Therefore, *shemittat karka'ot* applies rabbinically in the Land of Israel in our day, and *shemittat kesafim* applies throughout the world.

The Yerushalmi adopts this perspective:

Rabbi Yose returned and said: "And this is the matter of *shemitta*: release …", when the [agricultural] *shemitta* applies Biblically [in the Land of Israel], then *shemittat kesafim* applies both in the land of Israel and in the Diaspora on a Biblical level; but when the [agricultural] *shemitta* applies only Rabbinically [in the Land of Israel], then *shemittat kesafim* applies both in the Land of Israel and the Diaspora Rabbinically. (*Yerushalmi* 10:2)

Regarding the practical obligation of *shemittat kesafim* in our day and age, however, we find two additional views.

The *Itur* (*Prozbul* 1), one of the *Rishonim*, notes that according to the opinion that *shemittat karka'ot* applies Biblically even in our day, *shemittat kesafim* is a Biblical requirement as well. Additionally, he notes that even if *shemittat karkaot* is dependent on the obligation of *yovel*, and, therefore, rabbinic, that is not necessarily true for *shemittat Kesafim*. *Shemitat Kesafim* is observed globally, and since not limited to the Land of Israel it should apply Biblically even in our times. Although the *Itur's* position is not accepted, it highlights the universal application and message of *shemittat kesafim*.

Although nearly all authorities maintain that *shemittat kesafim* is Rabbinically obligated nowadays, there were periods during the time of the *Rishonim* when *shemittat kesafim* was not practiced outside of the Land of Israel. Some *Rishonim* (including the Rosh, Maharik, and *Terumat HaDeshen*) attempted to defend this practice. Nevertheless, they note that it is improper, as *shemittat kesafim* is a universal concept.[209] However, the Ra'avad (in his commentary to the Rif, Gittin) expresses a more lenient opinion, reasoning that *shemittat kesafim* is indeed dependent on *yovel* and therefore does not apply Biblically. Additionally, it was never required even on a Rabbinic level. In his view, it is a *middat chassidut,* a pious practice, to observe *shemittat kesafim* in our day and to release one's loans, but it is not an obligation.

Although the *Shulchan Aruch* (*Choshen Mishpat* 67) accepts the prevalent position that *shemittat kesafim* applies as a Rabbinic obligation nowadays both in the Land of Israel and throughout the world, the Rema notes the dissenting opinion of the Ra'avad and suggests this as the basis for the *halacha* having fallen into disregard.

Interestingly, Rav Yonatan Eibeshitz notes that although the *mitzvah* of *shemittat kesafim* applies everywhere in the world, it is specifically outside of the Land of Israel that it takes on greater significance, as that is the only element of the *shemitta* structure that applies in *chutz la'aretz*:

> And if this is the case, why isn't there an attachment of loving and cleaving to this *mitzvah*? And if a scholar of philosophy or an ethicist said one should do this to acquire good traits, I know people would hasten to accept his word and remark what a great and wise scholar he is, speaking the Word of God. And our scholars of the Oral Law established these laws even for the present day. Is it not appropriate for any God-fearing individual to follow and keep these laws, even if they're merely a reminder of the laws we kept when we were present on our land? ... If so, it is crucial for each man to be stringent and follow these laws today through *prozbul* and other mechanisms, so as not to forget these laws. (*Tumim* 67:1)

Shemittat Kesafim is the primary opportunity for Jews throughout the world to connect to *shemitta* and its messages. For many non-farmers even in Israel, it is the only opportunity they have to release and relinquish what they own during *shemitta*. The more we appreciate it, the more we connect to shemitta and Eretz Yisrael as a whole and play our part in implementing the redeemed economy the Torah envisions.

The *Halachot* of *Shemittat Kesafim*

Two important questions regarding the *halachot* of *shemittat kesafim* are "when" and "what." When does *shemittat kesafim* take effect, and what forms of owed money are included in the release?

---

209 The Rosh describes the efforts he extended to reinstitute its observance.

When?

The Torah notes that *shemittat kesafim* takes effect *"miketz sheva shanim"* (*Devarim* 15:1). The *Sifrei* (*Re'eh* 111) concludes that the *shemitta* release of loans takes effect at the conclusion of the seventh year, in the final moment of the agricultural *shemitta* (see also *Arachin* 28b). One version of the Tosefta (*Shevi'it* 8:11) seems to rule otherwise, as it states that a *prozbul* (the document intended to limit the effects of *shemitta* on outstanding loans) should be written on Erev Rosh Hashana of the seventh year. This would seem to indicate that the limitations on collecting loans already come into existence at the beginning of the *shemitta* year.

The Rosh's Understanding

The Rosh (*Gittin* 4:18) offers a fascinating explanation intended to resolve the apparent contradiction. He explains that although the positive *mitzvah* of *shamot*, the release of the loan, takes effect only at the conclusion of the year (as explained by the *Sifrei*), the prohibition of actively seeking payment of the loan, *lo yigos*, takes effect at the beginning of the seventh year. The prohibition of *lo yigos* coincides with the commencement of the agricultural *shemitta* year, which is why a *prozbul* is written at that point.

Most *Rishonim* had a different text of the Tosefta than the Rosh and therefore disagree with his conclusion. They explain that both the *mitzvat asei* and *mitzvat lo ta'aseh* take effect simultaneously at the conclusion of the agricultural *shemitta* year. The *Shulchan Aruch* (*Choshen Mishpat* 67:30-31) accepts this majority opinion, and therefore rules that the *prozbul* should be written at the conclusion of the seventh year. Nevertheless, there are those who write an additional *prozbul* at the beginning of the year to take into account the Rosh's position (see *Shulchan Aruch HaRav, Hilchot Halva'ah* 37).

Although not accepted, the Rosh's opinion underscores a further connection between the agricultural and financial *shemittot*. When the *shemittat karka'ot* of *shabbat ha'aretz* takes effect, all loans are held in abeyance; the lenders have not yet released them, but at the same time, they cannot actively collect them. By the conclusion of the agricultural *shemitta* year, the lender should have absorbed the lessons of the year and should want to convert his loans into charitable gifts by fully releasing them.

Additionally, because *shemittat kesafim* applies throughout the world, the Rosh's understanding identifies that as the Jews of the Holy Land usher in the agricultural *shemitta*, reverberations of this powerful year are felt universally, as loans throughout the world are held in abeyance.

What? Which Debts are Included?

Any debt that began as a loan and has come due is clearly obligated in *shemittat kesafim*. However, the exact parameters of which debts are included are subject to dispute. *Shemittat kesafim* releases outstanding loans that were due before the conclusion of the *shemitta* year, but there is a discussion regarding outstanding loans whose due date is after the *shemitta* year. The *halachot* apply to loans of objects as well. Thus, for example, even one who loaned some condiments to a neighbor must release the obligation unless they enacted a *prozbul*.

Many opinions maintain that even bank accounts are included, as one essentially loans their money to a bank to utilize as it sits in their account. Therefore, the common practice is for everyone to write a *prozbul* to ensure that all forms of outstanding debts are included.

(Mis)Understanding *Prozbul*

As we noted in the introduction to this chapter, many observant Jews aren't at all familiar with the existence of *shemittat kesafim*. Although this is the aspect of *shemitta* that clearly applies throughout the world, it is rare to find an individual who feels uncomfortable lending someone money for fear that the loan will be erased. The simple reason for this is that during the Second Temple period, the great sage Hillel instituted what is known as *prozbul*, a legal means of enabling loan collection even after *shemittat kessafim*.

Hillel's enactment was a response to the reality in his time; lenders were no longer lending due to *shemittat kesafim*. The *mishnayot* in *Masechet Shevi'it* indicate that there were always legal means of ensuring that certain loans could be forcefully collected, as *shemittat Kesafim* didn't apply to all forms of loans. For instance, *moser shtarotav l'beit din*, one who hands over the deed of his loan to *beit din*. Since *beit din* is not included in the obligation of *shemittat Kesafim*, they can continue to collect the loans.

Nevertheless, Hillel's enactment allowed for a far simpler means to ensure loan collection after the *shemitta* year. Through the *prozbul* document, a lender gains the advantages of transferring his loans to *beit din* in a more user-friendly manner.[210]

Hillel's rationale is clearly stated in the *Mishna* (*Shevi'it* 10:3):

> A *prozbul* prevents the remission of debts in the *shemitta* year. This is one of the regulations made by Hillel the Elder. For he saw that people were unwilling to lend money to one another, disregarding the warning laid down in the Torah, "Beware lest there be an unworthy thought in your heart saying, etc." He therefore decided to institute the *prozbul*.

Prozbul was enacted to ensure that lenders don't violate the Torah prohibition of withholding loans for fear that *shemitta* will prevent their forced collection. A number of commentaries [211]ask why Hillel enacted *prozbul*, which seems to hold the *mitzvah* of *shemittat kesafim* in abeyance, in order to prevent the violation of another *mitzvah* (withholding loans). In reality, however, Hillel did not upend *shemittat kesafim*, since it essentially wasn't taking place; people were not loaning money altogether. This undermined the entire Torah loan system, which is aimed at ensuring easy credit for the needy so they can get their financial situations back on track. Hillel's *takana* improved the situation across the board.

---

210 The exact parameters of how this is done, and whether a *prozbul* must be signed in the presence of a respected *beit din* are subject to dispute. Another Biblical means of ensuring loan collection even after *Shemittat Kesafim* sets in is by extending a loan on the condition that it will always be collectible. This condition however, must be explicated at the initial time of the loan. *Prozbul* allows one to ensure the loan is collectible years after it was originally granted without preconditions.

211 See *Bach, Choshen Mishpat* 67:20 and *Tosafot Anshei Shem* on the *mishna*, in the name of the Maharshal.

The Dual Benefit of *Prozbul*

Many assume that *prozbul* was enacted on behalf of lenders, the more well-to-do members of society. In fact, however, *Chazal* explain that the word פרוזבול is an abbreviation for the word פרוזבוליבוטי, which means "enactment (פרוז) for the rich (בולי) and the poor (בוטי)." Rashi in his commentary on the *mishna* (and other *Rishonim* as well) explain that this enactment ensures that the rich will receive their money back and that the poor will find people who will agree to lend them money. Although *shemittat kesafim* prohibits lenders from forcibly collecting outstanding loans, an option that would enable them to receive repayment would generate a society in which there would always be ample lenders for the poor. This would indicate that the primary benefactors of *prozbul* are actually poor people in need of constant availability of interest-free loans.

Interestingly, the Vilna Gaon (*Shenot Eliyahu* on the *mishna*) explains that the enactment is known as *prozbul* (enactment for the rich), and not *prozbuliboti* (enactment for the rich and for the poor), because the primary basis for it was it ensured the rich would not violate the prohibition of withholding loans (as explicit in the *mishna*); the benefit to the poor was only secondary. Even according to the Vilna Gaon's understanding, however, it is abundantly clear that even if the rich gain spiritually by not violating a commandment, the poor gain the most, as *prozbul* ensures people can continue to lend money for the benefit of the needy.

This is understandable, as the Torah presents the system of free loans as a two-way street. The borrowers share responsibility with the lenders to guarantee that the Torah's interest-free credit system can continue. *Prozbul* benefits potential borrowers by ensuring available loans, but it also makes sure there will be little incentive for borrowers to take advantage of *shemittat kesafim* if they indeed have the means to pay back loans. The existence of borrowers who flaunt the system would be reason for lenders to no longer consider extending interest-free loans.

The *Prozbul* Choice

Prozbul provides a choice; the lender can decide whether he can afford to forego the collection of the loan. After a year in which the landowners compromised their exhibition of ownership of both their land, which wasn't worked, and their produce, which was essentially shared with all of society, they are faced with the question of what to do with their outstanding loans. Should they guarantee legal means of collection, or should they give the borrower a free pass to forgo forced collection hanging on his head, although still with an expectation to pay if possible?

The common time for enacting a *prozbul* is Erev Rosh Hashana at the end of the *shemitta* year. Thus, during the final moments of the *shemitta* year, as one has hopefully soaked up the *shevi'it* messages, one makes a decision whether to perform his part of *shemittat kesafim* or not.

Prozbul and Legal Fictions

Although we may recognize the brilliance and importance of Hillel's rationale for instituting *prozbul*, we also must acknowledge that his means of doing so was through a *ha'arama,* a legal circumvention of what would otherwise be *halacha.* The term *ha'arama* stems from the word *arum,* the adjective the Torah uses to describe the sly primordial snake, clearly giving the concept a negative connotation. There are a number of legal fictions employed in certain situations, but only some of them are explicitly given this title of *ha'arama.*

The reason why every legal fiction is not classified as a *ha'arama* is that the term, although often misused, specifically refers to *halachically* sanctioned circumventions. In his commentary on one of the *mishnayot* that sanctions certain circumventions while forbidding others, the Rambam writes:

> A permitted strategem is called a ha'arama (circumvention), whereas one that is forbidden is called mirma (deception). (Rambam, commentary on the Mishna, Temura 5:1).[212]

Although some *ha'aramot* entail acting in an out of the ordinary manner to permit certain otherwise prohibited activities, most *ha'aramot* entail a legally valid means of circumvention in *halacha,* whose efficacy is unmistakable. The question is not whether *ha'arama* works, but rather whether it is appropriate to rely on.

Indeed, although the concept of *ha'arama* carries a negative connotation, there are instances when *Chazal* actively instruct us to use a *ha'arama,* explaining that the Torah not only authorizes but at times even advises such behavior.[213]

Some use the innovation of *prozbul* as proof that there are always legal fictions that can be used to circumvent difficult-to-perform *halachot,* if not to "reform" *Halacha* altogether. The *prozbul,* they argue, may adhere to the letter of the law, but not its spirit, and yet the Sages instituted it in order to solve a particular problem. This view has generated the derogatory phrase, "Where there is a Rabbinic will, there is a halachic way." Proponents of this view claim that with a bit of ingenuity, there are always ways to "beat the system." If we can avoid the "problem" of *shemittat kesafim* through *prozbul* (and, some might add, obliterate the obligation of *shemittat karka'ot* through the *heter mechira*), we can essentially "modify" the Torah's *mitzvot* almost with impunity.

In truth, however, *prozbul* is actually a prime example of an attempt to ensure that the spirit of the law is maintained, even when circumstances make the fulfillment of *mitzvot* difficult.

If *shemittat kesafim* only takes effect when borrowers who genuinely have no means of repayment are offered an opportunity to start fresh with a clean financial slate, and if lenders are always individuals with additional assets who will not be overly affected by the

---

212 See also *Ma'aser Sheni* 4:4; *Shevi'it* 10:3; *Beitza* 11b. A number of commentators (see, for example, Rashba, *Beitza* 11b, s.v. Rav Ada) state that one cannot compare various *ha'aramot,* as there are many factors to be weighed before determining which are to be approved and which not. Some commentaries offer qualifiying factors to determine when a *ha'arama* is appropriate.

213 See Rav Yisrael Rozen, "Ha'aramot Hilchatiyot K'takanot Tzibbur," *Techumin* 21. For example, the *mishna* (*Ma'aser Sheini* 4:4-5) provides instructions for how one can perform certain *ha'aramot* regarding sanctified firstborn animals and *ma'aser sheini.*

lack of repayment, the *shemittat kesafim* system serves a fundamental role in eradicating the existence of the perpetually poor and indebted. However, when this system is abused or when it's applied to greater numbers of individuals, there is liable to be widespread reluctance to lend to the needy, particularly as *shemittat kesafim* approaches.

We noted above that according to Rav Shlomo Zalman Auerbach, the harsh terminology the Torah attaches to one who fails to lend as *shemitta* approaches does not apply to a non-trustworthy borrower. But it is not always easy to distinguish between those who are trustworthy and those who are not. Suppose potential lenders can not determine who can be relied upon to return loans. In that case, it is not surprising that there might come a time when the free-loan institution is in existential danger, despite the Torah's warnings.

The *prozbul* thus actually strengthens the spirit of the law. *Shemittat kesafim* was never intended to absolve landowners of their financial obligations to repay loans when they could afford to do so. As we explained, *shemittat kesafim* is not a cancellation of debts, but rather an abeyance of forced collection; it puts the prerogative in the borrower's hands as to whether he can afford to repay his debt. *Prozbul* equalizes the playing field by enabling the lender to decide if he can financially allow the borrower to determine if this loan needs to be paid back.

The Torah advocates using appropriate legal maneuvers to reach certain goals, depending on the situation. What might seem at some times to be a deviation from the spirit of the law is often an appropriate means of ensuring that the law is maintained.

The *halachic* system involves much more than a series of "dos" and "don'ts". Indeed, the word ה.ל.כ.ה. includes the spirit of the law as although generally translated as "law," *halacha* really means "walking." The Torah provides a path in life to walk on and actions to achieve the goals of the path. All legal systems incorporate a letter of the law and the spirit of the law, but we recognize that unlike a man-made legal sytem, the Torah's system is divinely planned, with all of the intricacies. Suppose a legal fiction exists to enable circumvention of what otherwise would be *Halacha*. In that case, it is not a means of trying to outsmart a system, as the omniscient Creator of the law cannot be outwitted. It is an opportunity to employ a legal means when the spirit of the law deems it appropriate.

Shemitta's Message Still Emerges

Hillel's enactment did not uproot the Torah's message of the requirement of concluding the *shemitta* year with an added new start for the borrower who legitimately, despite every effort, is unable to pay back his loans.

It is hard to view *prozbul* as seeking to benefit the wicked, as the lender who advances an interest-free loan to begin with is the one who should, in fact, be entitled to use it. Hillel's *prozbul* serves the role of ensuring the Torah's system of available loans is maintained, ensuring that no one capable of lending will violate the Torah's prohibition of refraining from lending due to *shemitta*'s release of the loans. It provides optional means of protection for any lender who feels the need to ensure repayment, and will not lend otherwise. It is essentially an alternative means of ensuring that the poor will not suffer from lack of credit options.

In a similar vein, one would be hardpressed to view the use of *prozbul* in the modern banking system as against the spirit of the law. As we have explained, the Torah's advancement of free loans is for the benefit of those in need; the intent was not to require one to forgo his capital and business opportunities in order to provide that opportunity for others. The banking system enabling investment and mortgages requires means of collection.

While Hillel's objective of *prozbul* was to ensure continued loans and benefit the poor, it can be used even when inappropriate. Similarly, once a *heter iska* provides a legal means of advancing even interest-bearing loans, the method can be employed even for loans to the poor. Although a *heter iska* and *prozbul* can possibly be misused, the system allowed for their usage when appropriate. A loan shark who lends the poor with interest and uses *prozbul* as a legal recourse of collection even when the ideal of *shemittat kesafim* would be appropriate, is misusing the tools meant to benefit society as a whole. But that is not a reason to disallow the existence of a *ha'arama* when it appropriately provides a legal means of ensuring the spirit of the law.

Rav Moshe Lichtenstein similarly explains when *ha'arama* constitutes a protection of the spirit of the law:

> *Ha'arama* is a halakhic mechanism intended to circumvent the formal aspect of a prohibition. In other words, it is a stratagem that provides the possibility of evading the obligating imperative, by creating conditions in which the details of the *mitzvah* do not apply. However, all that this can do is provide an exemption from the letter of the law, but it is incapable of providing an answer to the fact that the spirit of the law is not fulfilled and is not achieved, and that the person who utilizes the circumvention fails in that way. Formally, he does not violate any prohibition, but spiritually, his course is flawed. *Ha'arama* is, therefore, regarded as a negative phenomenon, and despite its efficacy, there is no justification to use it.
>
> All this is true in a case where there is no great gap between the *mitzvah* and its objective. To the extent that the reason for the *mitzvah* and the details of its laws no longer go hand in hand, the situation changes. If the reason for the *mitzvah* is no longer meaningful to us and our entire obligation to the *mitzvah* stems from the absolute imperative of Master of the universe, then creating a mechanism that evades the formal prohibition is no longer problematic, for the reason is no longer a factor. In all such cases, *ha'arama* becomes legitimate, and perhaps even desirable.

The idea that we can understand the inner rationale of every mitzvah and determine when it is appropriate to be circumvented is very dangerous, and is clearly inappropriate. Nevertheless, there are certain *mitzvot* regarding which the Torah seems to make its reasoning clear, and great sages the likes of Hillel can determine when *ha'arama* is appropriate:

> Let us take as an example the *mitzvah* of releasing debts in the seventh year. The Torah inserts it next to the *mitzvah* of giving charity and relates in its context to the social dimension of helping one's neighbor. Releasing debts was intended to provide a poor person who had been forced to take a loan with the opportunity to open a new page once every seven years, without the burden of past debts preventing him from ever

rehabilitating himself. The classic borrower in the Torah is a poor person who needs a longer economic breathing space ("If you lend money to my people, to the poor man among you..."), and if he fails to rid himself of the burden of debt that is oppressing him, the *mitzvah* of charity requires that the debt be released. It is clear as day that the Torah never meant that every seven years this *mitzvah* should give a windfall profit to large economic concerns like banks or insurance companies. However, even though the Torah never intended to make the banks richer on the backs of the simple saver, the *mitzvah* is defined as a release of debt, and as such it formally applies to all loans. A situation is created of a great gap between the purpose of the *mitzvah* and its practical application. Paraphrasing the prophet, this is a case of "that which I commanded, but never entered My mind."

Desirable *ha'arama* entered the world to resolve such a problem. *Ha'arama* resolves the technical halakhic problem without effecting a parallel change in the reason for the *mitzvah*. Therefore, if the original reason is still valid and a person extends a private loan to his poor neighbor or to a pauper who came to his door, the writing of a *prozbul* will provide him with the legal authority to collect his loan, but all of his actions and goals will stand in contradiction to the will of the Creator with respect to this *mitzvah*. It is important to emphasize that even today, such conduct is expected from one who lends money to a neighbor or relative. However, with respect to a financial institution, the relations with which are of a business nature, the goal of helping the poor is never fulfilled, and the only thing that prevents a person from collecting his debt is the legal reality in itself. With the writing of the prozbul, that problem altogether disappears, and there is no moral complaint or religious criticism of his actions. Whoever writes a prozbul in such a situation is to be praised.

Hillel's considerations when he enacted the prozbul were based on this principle, though his enactment related to "domestic loans" and not to savings accounts or business loans. Hillel saw that people were hesitating to extend loans, and thus they were in violation of a biblical prohibition, that the poor were left without a source of financing their basic needs, and that the objective of the *mitzvah* was not being fulfilled whatsoever. In such a situation, Hillel decided that the Torah's objective would better be reached through the writing of a *prozbul*, through the waiving of the lofty social vision of the Torah. However, the question remained regarding the substance of the law and the definition of the details of the *mitzvah* as an absolute imperative that prevent such a waiver. In order to deal with this problem, the *prozbul* was enacted as a desirable circumvention in the new circumstances. (*Ha'arama in Halakha*)

As we noted above, according to the Bechor Shor's understanding, *shemittat kesafim* was intended to protect the *shemitta*-observant farmer who was unable to pay back his loans after the *shemitta* year. In times when most debtors are not *shemitta* observant farmers, the protections of *shemittat Kesafim* are less relevant to many. *Shemittat Kesafim*, nevertheless, protects all borrowers, but using a *prozbul* becomes more understandable. However, the overall rationale for using a *prozbul* seems to be based on the nature of *shemitta*'s release of a loan. Far from eradicating a debt, *shemittat kesafim* requires that the lender release the borrower from forced repayment. Nevertheless, the debt of gratitude and morality still exists, as long as the borrower can afford to pay it. If the debt isn't canceled, ensuring through a *prozbul* that the lender will recognize the need to pay back the loan when he can is truly understandable.

In Summary

The Torah teaches us that the primary form of *tzedaka* is helping the needy in a way that maintains their dignity and honor. Thus, *tzedaka* is ideally fulfilled through the extension of interest-free loans, such that the recipient does not feel that he has been given a free gift. We further noted that the mechanism of *shemittat kesafim* essentially tranforms a loan into a gift if the borrower is unable to repay, providing him with a fresh start so that he is not saddled by endless debt. This calls for self-sacrifice on the part of the lender, as he no longer has legal recourse to recoup the loan. The responsibility to repay is now fully in the borrower's court; he knows that he should make an effort to return the money if the opportunity ever presents itself.

Nevertheless, the institution of free loans requires that lenders be given the security to lend money knowing that borrowers will do whatever they can to repay the loan. If borrowers were to take advantage of the letter of the law, avoiding repayment of loans that are rightfully owed, it is not surprising that lenders may stop lending altogether. Although the Torah warns creditors against refraining from lending due to *shemitta*, that applies to borrowers in good faith. Abuse of the system thus has ramifications for both lenders and borrowers, who will not be able to attain loans in the future.

Hillel recognized the affront to the needs of both the *buli* and the *boti*. He expanded the already existing mechanisms to ensure that loans are collectible even after *shemitta* for the benefit of both, thereby protecting the spirit of the law.

There is no obligation for a lender to write a *prozbul* or to include all of his loans in a *prozbul*. The lender can decide if he should do so based on two primary criteria: 1) Is this a loan that I can afford to transfer into a charitable gift? 2) Is the borrower capable of paying it back, or will he likely be at some time? When the lender asks these questions, he connects to the spirit of the law that Hillel maintained. There is also a custom that at least a small amount of money is not included in the *prozbul*, and *shemittat Kesafim* will take effect. This ensures that one can actually fulfill these *mitzvoth* of *shamot* and *lo yigos* at least with some of their loans.

The beauty of *shemittat kesafim* is that it applies throughout the world. It gives a taste of *shemitta's* message to Jews everywhere, and in the twilight moments of Eretz Yisrael's *shemittat karka'ot*, it unifies the Jewish People throughout the world with the unique power of an entire institution of *tzedek umishpat*, real social justice. Although the *prozbul* might, at first glance, seem to undermine this message, it actually strengthens it greatly.

As Rav Shaul Yisraeli concludes:

> One who walks in the way of the Torah, who observes this *mitzvah* ... will perform a whole social revolution that quietly and peacefully, in one fell swoop, voids the economic and social disparities that have occupied human society since time immemorial. With the conclusion of the *shemitta* year, the whole nation's course of work and creativity begins anew in a state where all people have virtually the same means at their disposal.

Chapter 28

Hakhel- A Spiritual Culmination for a New Physical Beginning

Making the Messages Last

We have already seen how the year of *shabbat ha'aretz*, with its unique treatment of agriculture and the year's produce, culminates with *shemittat kesafim*, the financial *shemitta*. As the final moment of *shevi'it* arrives and with its passing, the seventh year becomes the eighth; Rosh Hashana heralds the new year's arrival, and creditors release all their outstanding loans. Through this great act, which is not limited to the Land of Israel, the entire world gets a taste of *shemitta*'s goals. *Shemittat kesafim*'s financial implications last beyond the seventh year and ensure this year will be etched in one's memory. *Shemitta*'s lessons must live on through one's attitude and practices.

Furthermore, the agricultural effects of *shevi'it* endure as well. All fruit that blossomed during *shevi'it* have *kedushat shevi'it*, and one cannot harvest *sefichin* until there is ample time for them to grow after being planted in the eighth year.

In one of the final *mitzvot* in the Torah, commanded on Moshe Rabbeinu's final day on earth, we are introduced to the *mitzvah* of *Hakhel*, to be performed every seven years on the Sukkot holiday following *shevi'it*. This *mitzvah* aims to ensure that the aftereffects of *shemitta* not only include its *halachot*, but also its spiritual messages. It requires that every *shevi'it* conclude with an event that unifies the entire Jewish people around the Torah. This sets the stage for commencing the next agricultural cycle of six years with *shevi'it*'s goals in mind.

The Basics of *Hakhel*

The Torah describes *Hakhel* as a time when Jews of all ages, from all over, gather together in the *Beit HaMikdash* on the Sukkot holiday following *shevi'it*:

וַיְצַו מֹשֶׁה אוֹתָם לֵאמֹר מִקֵּץ שֶׁבַע שָׁנִים בְּמֹעֵד שְׁנַת הַשְּׁמִטָּה בְּחַג הַסֻּכּוֹת: בְּבוֹא כָל יִשְׂרָאֵל לֵרָאוֹת אֶת פְּנֵי ה' אֱלֹהֶיךָ בַּמָּקוֹם אֲשֶׁר יִבְחָר תִּקְרָא אֶת הַתּוֹרָה הַזֹּאת נֶגֶד כָּל יִשְׂרָאֵל בְּאָזְנֵיהֶם: הַקְהֵל אֶת הָעָם הָאֲנָשִׁים וְהַנָּשִׁים וְהַטַּף וְגֵרְךָ אֲשֶׁר בִּשְׁעָרֶיךָ לְמַעַן יִשְׁמְעוּ וּלְמַעַן יִלְמְדוּ וְיָרְאוּ אֶת ה' אֱלֹהֵיכֶם וְשָׁמְרוּ לַעֲשׂוֹת אֶת כָּל

דִּבְרֵי הַתּוֹרָה הַזֹּאת: וּבְנֵיהֶם אֲשֶׁר לֹא יָדְעוּ יִשְׁמְעוּ וְלָמְדוּ לְיִרְאָה אֶת ה' אֱלֹהֵיכֶם כָּל הַיָּמִים אֲשֶׁר אַתֶּם חַיִּים
עַל הָאֲדָמָה אֲשֶׁר אַתֶּם עֹבְרִים אֶת הַיַּרְדֵּן שָׁמָּה לְרִשְׁתָּהּ:

And Moshe commanded them, saying: At the end of every seven years, at the time of the year of release, on the festival of Sukkot, when all Israel comes to see the presence of the Lord your God in the place that He will choose, read this Torah before all of Israel to their ears. **Assemble** the entire nation: men, women, and children, and the strangers who dwell within your gates, in order that they hear, and in order that they learn to fear God their God and keep the words of this Torah. And their children, who do not know, will listen and will learn to fear the Lord your God, all the days that you live upon the land which you are crossing the Jordan to inherit. (*Devarim* 31:10-13)

The Torah designates the time for *Hakhel* "at the time of the *shemitta* year, the year of release," during the holiday of Sukkot. Immediately before the eighth year's rainy season, when planting will begin anew, all the Jews gather together for a spiritual experience that includes the reading of the Torah in the presence of every last Jew. The Torah delineates this event's goals as a learning experience that will also ingrain the fear of God in the entire nation.

It would seem that *Hakhel* serves both as a powerful conclusion to the *shemitta* year as well as a prelude to the challenges of returning to cultivating the land. It reminds us that the *shemitta* period is not only a year comprised of agricultural *halachot*, cancelation of loans, and economic refocusing; it is supposed to bring about a grand spiritual reawakening.[214]

The Rambam, based on the Talmud (*Sota* 41a), describes what occurred during the *Hakhel* experience:

It is a Biblical positive command to assemble all Israelites, men, women, and children, after the close of every sabbatical year, when they go up to make the pilgrimage, and recite to them sections from the Torah which will urge them to perform the precepts and encourage them to cling to the true religion, as it is written: "At the end of every seven years, the year set for remission, at the festival of Sukkot, when all Israel comes to appear before the Lord ... gather the people, men, women, and children, and the strangers within your towns"." (*Devarim* 31:10-12) (*Hilchot Chagiga* 3:1)

---

214 The timing of *Hakhel*, which occurs in the month of *Tishrei*, further reinforces the notion that *Hakhel* is both the end and the beginning of the *shemitta* cycles. Rav Amnon Bazak (http://etzion.org.il/en/pesach-and-sukkot-mishkan-and-mikdash) explains that there are really two calendars in the Torah, representing two different perspectives. The calendar that begins in Tishrei serves as the agricultural calendar, which begins at the onset of the agricultural year and ends with the conclusion of that year. Since the calendar in the Torah is based upon the lunar cycle, as opposed to the earth's revolution around the sun, we cannot point to a specific day as marking the onset of the year. Therefore, the Torah viewed the entire month of Tishrei as the period of transition from one agricultural year to the next. The essence of Sukkot is the occasion of *Chag HaAsif*, the festival celebrating the collection of one's harvested produce, when a person finally enjoys the results of his labor and toil throughout the year. By its nature, then, this festival symbolizes the end of the year. Correspondingly, during this period, people begin their preparations for the coming agricultural year, and we may thus view this month also as the beginning of the new year. The designation of this season as the beginning and end of the year is the most natural choice, as this season marks the beginning and end of the agricultural process. With this in mind, it is understandable that *shemitta* begins in Tishrei, the beginning of the agricultural cycle, while at the same time the beginning of the new cycle commences only after Sukkot. *Hakhel* marks the end the *shemitta* year and sets the stage for the upcoming year.

In the following *halacha*, the Rambam describes that this was performed on the first day of *Chol HaMoed* (the intermediate days of) Sukkot of the eighth year, about a month and a half after *shevi'it*'s conclusion. The entire nation would gather together in the *Mikdash*, and the king would publicly read sections of the Torah.[215]

The Rambam (summarizing the *Mishna, Sota* 7:8) details that beyond the learning, extensive efforts were invested in order to ensure that *Hakhel* was a significant experience:

> How did he read? Trumpets were blown throughout Jerusalem to assemble the people; and a high platform, made of wood, was brought and set up in the center of the Court of Women. The king went up and sat there so that his reading might be heard. All the Israelite pilgrims would gather around him. The *chazan* of the synagogue would take a *sefer Torah* and hand it to the head of the Temple. The head of the Temple would hand it to the deputy high priest, the deputy high priest to the high priest, and the high priest to the king to honor him by many persons' service. The king would receive it standing or sitting, as he pleased. He would open it and look in it, reciting the blessing used by anyone who reads the Torah in the synagogue. He would read the sections we have mentioned until he would come to the end. Then he would roll up the *sefer Torah* and recite a blessing after the reading, the way it is recited in the synagogue. (ibid. 3:4)

Echoes of Har Sinai

The very term "*Hakhel*" echoes the original transmission of the Torah from God to the Jewish People at Har Sinai. This connection is explicit in the term *Hakhel* itself. Regarding the giving of the Torah on Har Sinai, the Torah describes that Hashem commanded, "הַקְהֶל – Gather me the people together, and I will make them hear My words, that they may learn to fear Me all the days that they shall live upon the earth" (*Devarim* 4:10). Regarding *Hakhel* we are commanded, "הַקְהֵל –Gather the people together... that they may hear, and that they may learn..." (31:12). The *midrash* notes these similarities and concludes:

> The day of *Hakhel* is like the day on which the Torah was given. (*Midrash HaGadol, Parashat Vayelech*)

Shemitta's overall connection to Har Sinai culminates with a Har Sinai-like experience. The Torah even refers to the giving of the Torah on Har Sinai as יוֹם הַקָּהָל , the day of gathering, as the Revelation at Sinai took place before a complete gathering of *Am Yisrael*:

> וַיִּכְתֹּב עַל הַלֻּחֹת כַּמִּכְתָּב הָרִאשׁוֹן אֵת עֲשֶׂרֶת הַדְּבָרִים אֲשֶׁר דִּבֶּר ה' אֲלֵיכֶם בָּהָר מִתּוֹךְ הָאֵשׁ בְּיוֹם הַקָּהָל
> וַיִּתְּנֵם ה' אֵלָי:

---

215 The Rambam details the two lengthy selections from *Sefer Devarim* that were read: The first six chapters, until the conclusion of the *Shema* paragraph (6:9), followed by the section of והיה אם שמוע (*Devarim* ch. 11), and the 15 chapters from chapter 14 ("עשר תעשר") through the conclusion of the blessings and the curses in *Parashat Ki Tavo* (28:69)

> And He inscribed on the tablets, like the first writing, the Ten Commandments, which the Lord had spoken to you on the mountain, from the midst of the fire, **on the day of the assembly [hakahal]**, and the Lord gave them to me. (*Devarim* 10:4)

Defining Har Sinai by its role of gathering the nation is readily understandable, as the Har Sinai experience was defined by the unity it engendered. Rashi notes that the Torah goes out of its way to describe how Har Sinai brought a unique level of unity to the nation. The Torah distinguishes between the encampment throughout the sojourn in the desert, and the encampment around Sinai:

וַיִּסְעוּ מֵרְפִידִים וַיָּבֹאוּ מִדְבַּר סִינַי וַיַּחֲנוּ בַּמִּדְבָּר וַיִּחַן שָׁם יִשְׂרָאֵל נֶגֶד הָהָר:

> They journeyed from Rephidim, and they arrived in the desert of Sinai, and they encamped [**vayachanu**] in the desert, and Israel encamped [**vayichan**] there opposite the mountain. (*Shemot* 19: 1-2)

The singular וַיִּחַן regarding the encampment at Har Sinai, as opposed to the plural וַיַּחֲנוּ regarding the other encampments, leads Rashi to comment based on the *midrash*:

וַיִּחַן שָׁם יִשְׂרָאֵל כְּאִישׁ אֶחָד בְּלֵב אֶחָד, אֲבָל שְׁאָר כָּל הַחֲנִיּוֹת בְּתַרְעוֹמוֹת וּבְמַחֲלֹקֶת:

> "And Israel encamped there" – as one man and with one mind, but all their other encampments were made in a murmuring spirit and in a spirit of dissension. (Rashi, *Shemot* 19:2, citing *Mechilta d'Rabbi Yishmael* 19:2:10)

Rashi emphasizes that the unity of the nation at Har Sinai was unparalleled and was never to be repeated throughout their sojourn in the desert. It was this unity that allowed the nation to seal the covenant with Hashem with one voice, declaring נַעֲשֶׂה וְנִשְׁמָע, "we will do and we will listen" (*Shemot* 24:7).

The *mitzvah* of Hakhel aims to emulate the *Yom HaKahal* by ensuring that the entire nation is present and united "as one man with one heart." As we saw above, the Rambam writes that the Torah requires that every last Jew be attend the *Hakhel* experience: "It is a Biblical positive command to assemble all Israelites, men, women, and children…" (*Hilchot Chagiga* 3:1). Rabbi Shlomo Goren notes that the Rambam's language is somewhat unclear. On whom does the duty "to assemble" fall? Rabbi Goren explains that since *Hakhel* is a reenactment of the Revelation at Sinai — when the Jewish People ceased their tribal existence and became a nation — the command of *Hakhel* is for each Jew to "gather himself." The command is for every individual to assemble – not as an individual, but as an integral part of the nation.[216]

Rabbi Goren's explanation highlights that *Hakhel* places responsibility upon every individual to do his part in breaking down barriers and being open to the experience, uniting with one's brethren around *Har HaBayit*. If the nation is united at this event, then standing at *Har HaBayit* will serve as a true recreation of encamping around Har Sinai to receive the Torah as one nation with one heart.

The echo of Har Sinai can also be felt in the timing of both *Hakhel* and the Har Sinai

216 "Mitzvat Hakhel L'Or HaHalacha," in *Torat HaMoadim* (Tel Aviv: Tzioni, 1964), pp. 127-138.

experience. The Har Sinai experience occurred after seven weeks of seven days from the exodus from Egypt; *Hakhel* occurs on the seventh year of the *shevi'it* cycle in the seventh month (the month of *Tishrei*).

Transmission of the Torah

Notably, the original Revelation experience at Har Sinai entailed receiving the Torah directly from Hashem Himself. The people, however, were overcome by fear upon the encounter with Hashem, and they requested that Moshe Rabbenu serve as an intermediary for receiving the Torah (*Shemot* 20:16; *Devarim* 5: 3-7). In Moshe's review of the experience in *Parashat Va'etchanan*, he reminds the nation that the only reason there will be no future assemblies in which Hashem speaks directly to the nation is that this was the nation's request. The word of God will be transmitted through the Torah itself and through the Torah leaders who continue transmitting God's word through the *mesora* (tradition). Moshe reiterates this point in *Parashat Shoftim* in the context of the *mitzvah* to adhere to the words of a *navi* (prophet). After the nation requested at Har Sinai that they hear the commandments through Moshe and not through Hashem Himself, it became necessary for Hashem to communicate to the nation through prophets. Once again, in this context, the Torah refers to the Har Sinai experience as *Yom HaKahal*:

> כְּכֹל אֲשֶׁר שָׁאַלְתָּ מֵעִם ה' אֱלֹהֶיךָ בְּחֹרֵב בְּיוֹם הַקָּהָל לֵאמֹר לֹא אֹסֵף לִשְׁמֹעַ אֶת קוֹל ה' אֱלֹהָי וְאֶת הָאֵשׁ הַגְּדֹלָה הַזֹּאת לֹא אֶרְאֶה עוֹד וְלֹא אָמוּת: וַיֹּאמֶר ה' אֵלָי הֵיטִיבוּ אֲשֶׁר דִּבֵּרוּ: נָבִיא אָקִים לָהֶם מִקֶּרֶב אֲחֵיהֶם כָּמוֹךָ וְנָתַתִּי דְבָרַי בְּפִיו וְדִבֶּר אֲלֵיהֶם אֵת כָּל אֲשֶׁר אֲצַוֶּנּוּ:

> According to all that you asked of Hashem, your God, at Horev, on the **day of the assembly** [**hakahal**], saying, "Let me not continue to hear the voice of Hashem, my God, and let me no longer see this great fire, so that I will not die." And Hashem said to me, "They have done well in what they have spoken. I will set up a prophet for them from among their brothers like you, and I will put My words into his mouth, and he will speak to them all that I command him". (*Devarim* 18:16-18)

Since the nation cannot directly relate to the word of Hashem, the *Hakhel* of Har Sinai is replaced by the *Hakhel* of the leader who gives voice to the word of God. Moshe Rabbenu was the original spokesperson; after his death, the leaders of subsequent generations took on that role.

Indeed, our leaders continue to express the word of God even in the absence of prophecy. In the Rambam's introduction to his *Mishneh Torah*, he delineates the forty generations of *mesorah* Torah-transmission from Moshe Rabbenu through Rav Ashi, the arranger of the Babylonian Talmud. The Rambam refers to the first generation of Torah transmission as "מֹשֶׁה רַבֵּנוּ מִפִּי הַגְּבוּרָה, Moshe Rabbenu from the Almighty". Thus, "נִמְצָא שֶׁכֻּלָּם מֵה' אֱלֹקֵי יִשְׂרָאֵל–*It turns out that everyone received the Torah directly from Hashem, the God of Israel*."

While we perform *Hakhel* once every seven years, it recreates the first post Har Sinai *Hakhel* right before Moshe Rabbeinu's death. Immediately before the commandment of *Hakhel* every seven years, the Torah describes Moshe transmitting the Torah to his successor Yehoshua. Both descriptions appear in *Parashat Vayelech*, near the Torah's conclusion. The Torah scroll is virtually complete, and Moshe Rabbeinu transfers it to Yehoshua. This is the *Masoretic* tradition of teacher to student. On the final day of Moshe Rabbeinu's life, he informs the nation that Hashem will remain with them even after his passing; Yehoshua will lead the people both militarily and spiritually, as Hashem has commanded (*Devarim* 31:7-9). It is within this context that the *mitzvah* of *Hakhel* is taught. After detailing the *mitzvah*, the Torah returns to describe the transmission of the Torah and leadership from Moshe to Yehoshua. *Hakhel* thus emerges precisely at the critical juncture of Moshe tasking Yehoshua to take over the leadership role. *Hakhel* is not only a recreation of the past, but it is an insurance policy for continued *Masoretic* Torah transmission of the Torah.

Notably, the Torah doesn't explicitly state that the king reads the Torah during *Hakhel*, but only mentions an active reader and the assembled nation who listens and learns. The Bechor Shor and Chizkuni explain that the need for a king emerges from Moshe's directing his charge of the *mitzvah* to Yehoshua, who essentially became the king of Israel. Therefore, the obligation was forever incumbent on future kings.[217]

The Seforno explains that the passing of the Torah from one dignitary to another similarly parallels the transmission of the Torah scroll at the time of the original *mitzvah*: "Moshe inscribed this Torah and gave it to the *Kohanim*, the sons of Levi, who carried the ark of God's covenant, and to all the elders of Israel" (*Devarim* 31:9). The ceremonial handing over of the Torah from one leader to another is part of the *Hakhel* ceremony, as *Hakhel* itself is an outgrowth of that first transmission. Before that very first *Hakhel* in history, when Moshe handed the Torah to the *Kohanim* and elders, they were commanded by Moshe to transmit the Torah in their trust to the person destined to replace Moshe as leader of the nation – namely, the king. Indeed, the special status of the king as Moshe's successor during the *mitzvah* of *Hakhel* is almost explicit in the words of the Rambam: "The king is the agent who gives voice to God's words" (*Chagiga* 3:6) – in other words, the replacement for Moshe.

Thus, as we gather every seven years for *Hakhel*, we relive Har Sinai and impress upon ourselves the unbroken tradition we continually witness. The *Kohanim* handing the Torah to the king reminds us of the first and subsequent transmissions. The nation's leaders receive the Torah for safekeeping and ensure the king who leads the nation in place of Moshe is part of this transmission. The transmission of the physical Torah from one leader to another before it is read aloud and transferred to the next generation is a reminder of the role that the Masoretic leaders of the Torah play in ensuring the Torah and its oral teachings are transmitted accurately from generation to generation. Every individual hears the Torah from Hashem Himself, through His representatives accurately conveying His words and their eternal lessons.

The Rambam highlights this in explaining why it was so essential that everyone be in

---

217 Rav Binyamin Tabory (https://www.etzion.org.il/en/halakha/studies-halakha/philosophy-halakha/parashat-vayelekh-hak%E2%80%99hel-torah-reading-king) notes that from the Rambam's description of the *mitzvah*, it seems that it was not necessary for the king to be the one to read to the nation. He further notes that the *Yere'im* counts two separate *mitzvot* related to *Hakhel* – the gathering of the people (*mitzvah* 433) and the reading of the king (*mitzvah* 266), the latter being an obligation that applies to the king alone. According to this understanding, the *mitzvah* would not apply in the absence of the king.

attendance, even the young and the newly converted who didn't understand the language:

> Proselytes who did not know Hebrew were required to direct their hearts **and listen with utmost awe and reverence, as on the day the Torah was given at Sinai.** Even great scholars who knew the entire Torah were required to listen with utmost attention. If there was a person who could not hear, he had to direct his heart to this reading, which Scripture has instituted only for the purpose of strengthening the true faith. Each had to regard himself as if he had been charged with the Torah now for the first time, **and as though he had heard it from the mouth of the Almighty (*mi-pi ha-Gevura*), for the king was an ambassador proclaiming the words of God.** (*Hilchot Chagiga* 3:6)

While it is impossible to fully reenact the Har Sinai experience, the Rambam emphasizes that *Hakhel* is supposed to be accompanied by the same atmosphere as Har Sinai: "With reverence and awe".[218]

Hakhel is a reenactment of the giving of the Torah on Har Sinai, with the king serving the role that Moshe Rabbenu played in that event – transmitting the Torah heard ""*mi-pi ha-Gevura*"," from Hashem Himself, to the people. The purpose of the *Hakhel* event is to learn Torah and reconnect to the Har Sinai experience, which engenders fear of God. Thus, every member of the nation gathers for the event, including those who can't understand and the scholars who already understand.

The *midrash* explains that all souls – past, present, and future – were present at *Ma'amad Har Sinai*:

> Rabbi Yochanan said… All the souls which will ever be in existence were … present at the giving of the Torah, as it states: "For you that are present standing here today, and those who are not here" (*Devarim* 30:1). (*Midrash Tanchuma, Pekudei* 3)

Reenacting the Revelation allows the nation to re-experience the cataclysmic event that is indelibly imprinted in their soul, but requires experiential reminders.

Additional *Hakhel* Requirements

Based on this context, while *Hakhel* is performed every seven years in the aftermath of *shevi'it*, it is really a recreation of Moshe's transmitting the Torah to the next generation of Torah leaders. In fact, this transmission wasn't only performed by Moshe, but must be done whenever the Torah is transmitted to the next generation. Like Moshe Rabbenu his teacher, Yehoshua gathered the people and performed a *Hakhel* in his last days as a leader (*Yehoshua* ch. 24). There too, a transmission to the next leadership took place. As the *mishna* in *Avot* (*Avot* 1:1) teaches:

מֹשֶׁה קִבֵּל תּוֹרָה מִסִּינַי, וּמְסָרָהּ לִיהוֹשֻׁעַ, וִיהוֹשֻׁעַ לִזְקֵנִים, וּזְקֵנִים לִנְבִיאִים, וּנְבִיאִים מְסָרוּהָ לְאַנְשֵׁי כְנֶסֶת הַגְּדוֹלָה

Moses received the Torah at Sinai and transmitted it to Joshua, Joshua to the elders,

---

218 The Rambam here cites the description in *Yerushalmi Megilla* 4:1 regarding how Torah should be studied; see also *Berachot* 22a).

and the elders to the prophets, and the prophets to the Men of the Great Assembly.

Moshe transmitted to Yehoshua and Yehoshua transmitted the Torah to the *zekeinim*, and therefore, Yehoshua performed *Hakhel* at the end of his life.

Similarly, King Yoshiyahu arranged a *Hakhel* event when a Torah scroll was rediscovered during a restoration of the *Beit HaMikdash*:

> Then the king called together all the elders of Yehuda and Yerushalayim. He went up to the Temple of *Hashem* with the men of Yehuda, the people of Yerushalayim, the priests and the prophets - all the people from the least to the greatest. He read in their hearing all the words of the Book of the Covenant, which had been found in the Temple of *Hashem*. The king stood by the pillar and renewed the covenant in the presence of *Hashem* - to follow *Hashem* and keep His commands, regulations, and decrees with all his heart and all his soul, thus confirming the words of the covenant written in this book. Then all the people pledged themselves to the covenant. (*Melachim II* 23: 1-3)

A *Hakhel* also occurred in the time of Ezra, when the Jewish nation returned from Babylonian exile to *Eretz Yisrael*:

> So on the first day of the seventh month, Ezra the priest brought the Law before the assembly, which was made up of men and women and all who were able to understand. He read it aloud from daybreak till noon as he faced the square before the Water Gate in the presence of the men, women, and others who could understand. And all the people listened attentively to the Book of the Law. (*Nechemia* 8: 2-3)

Every new stage of Torah transmission and renewal of our covenant with Hashem requires *Hakhel*. At Har Sinai, the nation accepted the covenant upon themselves; every subsequent *Hakhel* is similarly about renewing the covenant with Hashem.

The Goalf os *Hakhel*- Hearing, Learning, and Experiencing

The *pesukim* regarding the *mitzvah* of *Hakhel* emphasize its goals:

> Gather the people together... that they may **hear**, and that they may **learn**, and fear the Lord your God, and **observe** to do all the words of this Torah. (*Devarim* 31:12)

Rav Soloveitchik (*Shiurim L'Zecher Abba Mari*, vol. II) notes that the terminology used to describe *Hakhel's* goals underscores two distinct forms of interacting with Torah – studying (which entails understanding the subject matter) and hearing (even when one does not fully comprehend the words they hear). Although the Torah places importance on the intellectual study of Torah, the words of Torah can penetrate the hearts of all those who hear them, even if they don't understand.

Although "hearing" is generally understood as a physical, mechanical act, it also refers to accepting and internalizing, as in the *pasuk*, "שְׁמַע יִשְׂרָאֵל, Hear O Israel" (*Devarim* 6:4; see Ibn Ezra there). Thus, beyond intellectual learning, the internalizing of listening and hearing is essential. Rav Aharon Lichtenstein notes that *Hakhel* teaches us that we must let the Torah words penetrate our personalities:

> Our learning must be accompanied by two kinds of emotion: passion and joy on the one hand, and fear, trepidation, and awe on the other. The concepts and principles which we learn must not only be understood, but also internalized. They must form our spiritual personality. The Torah we learn must also remain within us, just as the experiences of hearing the king read the Torah at *Hakhel* and of feasting in Jerusalem before God must be remembered in the years to come. (*The Experience of Hakhel*)

But beyond the learning and even hearing of the Torah, there is the Har Sinai experience. The Revelation at Har Sinai involved an experience of appreciating how the Torah connects us to Hashem Himself. It involved Hashem choosing the Jewish nation and forging a covenant with them through the Torah. Re-experiencing Har Sinai means reliving the nation's betrothal and marriage to Hashem, and the Torah's words as the constant connector for that experience.[219] Through *Hakhel*, we are supposed to remember that experience, connect to it, and bring it to bear on our Torah study.

What ensures that Torah learning doesn't become simply an intellectual enterprise devoid of spiritual context? The first step is to recognize Torah learning as central to the very existence of the Jewish people. The *Sefer HaChinuch* explains that this is the very purpose of *Hakhel*:

> It is from the roots of the commandment [that it is] because the entire essence of the people of Israel is the Torah; and through it are they separated from every nation and language, to be meritorious for eternal life, eternal pleasure that is not surpassed by anything among the creatures. Therefore, since their entire essence is in it, it is fitting that everyone should gather together at one point in time to hear its words, and for the voice to go out amongst the whole nation - men, women, and infants - to say, "What is the great gathering, that we have all been gathered together?" And the answer would be, "To hear the words of the Torah, which is our entire essence and glory and splendor." And they will come from this to tell of the great praise and the splendor of its value; and its yearning will enter all of their hearts. And with this yearning for it, they will learn to know God and merit good, and 'God will be happy with His creations' - like the matter that is written in explanation of this commandment "and in order that they will learn and fear the Lord." (*Sefer HaChinuch, mitzvah* 612)

Reconnecting to the experience of Har Sinai and seeing how the Torah connects us to Hashem is a fundamental necessity.

---

219 Rav Soloveitchik explains that our daily connection to Torah should entail both learning and an opportunity to reconnect to the Har Sinai experience. The *Birchot HaTorah*, the blessings recited before daily Torah study, reconnect us to those moments and remind us that the Torah wants to ensure that we not only connect to its teachings, but to its Teacher, Hashem, whom we refer to at the end of the blessings on the Torah as "*HaMelamed Torah l'amo Yisrael*," "the One who teaches Torah to His nation Israel."

Who Were Present for *Hakhel*?

As the Torah describes and the Rambam (cited earlier) highlights, *Hakhel* was for the entire nation, scholars and laypeople alike, new converts to the Jewish faith, children of all ages, and the learned. They all heard the exact words, but the Talmud citing a story derives from the *pesukim* varied goals for the diverse members of the population.

The Talmud tells the story of two Sages who visited Rabbi Yehoshua in the city of Peki'in. He asked what new thoughts were shared in the Beit Midrash and the two Sages deferring to Rabbi Yehoshua state that Rabbi Yehoshua is their teacher; nothing stated in the study hall should be of interest to him. Nevertheless, Rabbi Yehoshua states that it is impossible that nothing novel was shared in the Beit Midrash, and the sages, therefore, share with him a teaching regarding *Hakhel*. They note that R' Elazar ben Azaryah presided over Shabbat at the academy in Yavneh, and he taught the following thought regarding *Hakhel*:

> "הַקְהֵל אֶת הָעָם הָאֲנָשִׁים וְהַנָּשִׁים וְהַטַּף" אִם אֲנָשִׁים בָּאִים לִלְמוֹד נָשִׁים בָּאוֹת לִשְׁמוֹעַ טַף לָמָּה בָּאִין כְּדֵי לִיתֵּן שָׂכָר לִמְבִיאֵיהֶן.

[They said to him that Rabbi Elazar ben Azarya interpreted the following verse]: "Assemble the people, the men, and the women and the little ones" (*Devarim* 31:12). [This verse is puzzling]: If men come to learn, and women, [who might not understand], come [at least] to hear, **why do the little ones come? They come in order** for God to **give a reward to those who bring them**.

This little thought so greatly impresses Rabbi Yehoshua that he refers to it as a good pearl that was almost hidden from him by the Sages reticence:

> אָמַר לָהֶם מַרְגָּלִית טוֹבָה הָיְתָה בְּיֶדְכֶם וּבִקַּשְׁתֶּם לְאַבְּדָהּ מִמֶּנִּי?

[Rabbi Yehoshua] said to them: This **good pearl** [of wisdom] was in your hands, and you tried to conceal it from me?

At first glance, there doesn't seem to be any great novelty in this remark, and one can understand why the Sages might have thought it unnecessary to share with the great rabbinic leader Rabbi Yehoshua. But Rabbi Yehoshua's surprising response indicates that the Sages were unaware of how profound this teaching was. There was a need to bring little ones to *Hakhel* to reward those who bring them. Understanding the exact profundity involved depends on the age of the children who were brought.

The Educational Goals of *Hakhel* – An Experience of Children and Adults

Although all were present for *Hakhel*, not everyone understood the Torah. Some merely "heard" the Torah while others "learned". But what ages of children were in attendance? Logically, if one were to bring young toddlers even if they don't comprehend, they might be mesmerized by the experience. On the opposite end, if one would bring newborns, wouldn't they surely be noisy, and not only would they seemingly gain little from the event, they would also disturb the adults present.[220]

---

220 The *Ketav VeHakabbala* (*Devarim* 31) explains that the reason that the very young children were present was simply that they could not be left home alone. The Torah makes bringing them a *mitzvah* even though their parents

Notably, the Ramban (*Devarim* 31:12) maintains that the *pesukim* are not referring to infants, as they are too young to experience the moment at all and are liable to disturb others in attendance. Instead, he understands the Torah refers to children old enough to "hear and ask questions, and their fathers will educate them." Nevertheless, he notes that *Chazal* seemed to understand that even young children are brought in order to provide a reward for those who bring them.

The Maharsha (*Chagiga* 3a) explains that the *pesukim* actually refer to two different ages of children. A further *pasuk* refers to older children, "And their children, who do not know, will listen and will learn to fear the Lord your God" (31:13). Children who have reached the age of *chinuch* won't fully understand what they hear, but they should be present in order to learn the basics of *yirat Shamayim*. However, the very young children were brought to *Hakhel* for one purpose alone – "for God to give reward to those who bring them. Offhand, the Ramban's comment is rather understandable. Not only will the newborns and babies seemingly not gain from the experience, but they are liable to disturb all the others in attendance. Evidently, the attendance is significant even if no knowledge is gained. This is one of the sources of the Rambam that *Hakhel* is a re-experience of Har Sinai, as everyone is in attendance, even those who can't comprehend.

We recognize that experiences impact us, and if inculcated into our discussions, positive experiences can impact even those who were not yet born. This might be the meaning of the Talmud's comment: "Even fetuses in their mother's womb [during the Exodus] sang the Song [of the Sea]" (*Berachot* 50a), as they would benefit from this experience in the future due to their parents recalling and reliving the experience with them. This is an essential educational message for parents and anyone who takes on an educational role and guides the younger generations. The same way that *Hakhel* contains both learning and experiential elements, one must transmit to the next generation both knowledge and experience. That combination will impact the way in which lessons will be internalized.

Others (see Malbim, *Devarim* 31:1) note that specifically children who do not comprehend can more easily connect to the experience. An intellectual disadvantage can actually provide an advantage in the form of experiential Jewish education. Even the youngest of children stand to gain from simply being present. Children, no matter how young they are, are able to discern their surroundings. From the youngest of ages, they can benefit from the experience of being surrounded by *kedusha* and being part of a nation. During the reenactment of the Revelation at Har Sinai during *Hakhel*, every individual counts, as the goal is to renew the covenant that created the internal glue between the Giver of the Torah and the nation who received it.

Given the importance of exposing even the smallest children to the spiritual experience of *Hakhel*, why does Rabbi Elazar ben Azarya teach that these children are brought solely "to provide reward for those who bring them"? The Abarbanel explains that this reward refers to the extra tools gained by parents when they bring their children to experience *Hakhel*.

---

would have had to do so in any event! See also Rav Yaakov of Lisa, *Nachalat Yaakov*, and Rav Yosef Engel, *Gilyonei HaShas*, *Chagiga* 3a, citing a similar idea in the name of the Arizal.

Their ultimate reward is educational assistance in guiding their children to commit to religious observance and a deep emotional connection to Hashem and Judaism.

Once we recognize the educational benefits that children of all ages receive, often without realizing it themselves, we are faced with a dilemma. Why would Rabbi Eliezer explain the benefit for the children is merely "to provide reward for those who bring them" and not the educational and experiential benefits that bringing them provides?

A comment of the Abarbanel (*Devarim* 31) sheds light on this statement. He writes that *Hakhel* is an educational experience even for those children who are not yet born. Those present will share the experience with their future children as well, transmitting the knowledge and emotional experience they personally gained in attendance. This is not extra credit but extra tools for lightening the educational burden on the parent's shoulders. The ultimate reward is educational assistance towards guiding one's children to a life continuing the Har Sinai experience, commitment to religious observance and a richly deep emotional connection to Hashem and Judaism. The goals of *Hakhel* are not only for those present but also for all those in the future whom the mesora will be shared with.

At What Price? Taking Children to Shul and Other Spiritual Experiences

Hakhel also raises some significant educational questions. *Hakhel's* long-term educational benefits, even for young children, might come with a short term price tag. Adults watching the babies will probably find it more difficult to concentrate, and the children might even make noise that disturbs others. Nevertheless, the Torah tells us that every last Jew should be present for *Hakhel*. The powerful *kedusha* experience will impact even a suckling baby. Providing our children with *chinuch* opportunities is essential even before they fully intellectually benefit from them. But at what price to others, and possibly the children themselves? Should we be concerned that we will accustom children to attending for experiential reasons, even when they are too young to understand or even listen intently?

It is easy to understand how *Hakhel*, a once every seven-year experience that involves the entire Jewish population, is essential for children and adults. One might compare this to a large *siyum hashas* celebrated every seven and a half years. Even the youngest of children who can't comprehend can be overwhelmed by the awesomeness of the occasion. But what about daily or even weekly experiences? Does *Hakhel* serve as a basis for bringing children to the synagogue even when they are too young to comprehend or even follow along? Children consistently finding themselves bored with the experience might disturb and possibly even begin to see the synagogue as a playground. Should that be a concern?

Tosafot (Chagiga 3a, *Kdei*) learns from the requirement to bring children to *Hakhel* that the same should "serve as support for bringing children to the *Beit Knesset*".

One of the Rishonim, the Ohr Zarua (Vol. II Hilchot Shabbat, 48) adds that bringing children is not only for the parent's reward but also for the children's educational benefits. He cites the Mishna (Avot 2, 8) that describes Rav Yehoshua ben Chananya as "*ashrei yoladato,* praiseworthy is the one who gave birth to him", and the Yerushalmi (Yevamot 1:6) that explains that Rav Yehoshua's mother would bring the infant Rav Yehoshua to the Beit Midrash in order that his ears soak up the words of Torah long before he could understand them. The Ohr Zarua insinuates that beyond the parent's reward for educationally providing for their children, the children stand to gain immensely by connecting to the words of Torah even when completely lacking comprehension.

The Ohr Zarua's comments also provide great insight into Gemara's discussion surrounding this novel explanation of why the children were brought to Hakhel. We saw that the Sages heard this *derasha* from Rabbi Elazar ben Azaryah but didn't see it as noteworthy. Rav Yehoshua, however, recognized its profundity and referred to it as a great pearl that the Sages almost deprived him of by not sharing. Interestingly, Rav Yehoshua is the same individual described in *Masechet Avot* as praisworthy is his mother. His mother is credited with Rav Yehoshua's tremendous Torah stature, not for her intellectual teachings but for the experiential education she provided for the infant Rav Yehoshua. Rav Yehoshua's mother provided him with *kedusha* experiences that continued to impact him throughout his life. Who more than Rav Yehoshua could recognize the depth of Rav Eliezer ben Azaryah's teaching. The Torah wants every Jewish child, even the babies to experience *kedusha* through *Hakhel.*

But is this always proper?

The Rema (Shulchan Aruch O.C. 149) cites this ruling of the Ohr Zarua that one should bring young children to shul just as children attended Hakhel. However, the Mishna Berura (98,3) cites the *Shelah HaKadosh* that this is not always appropriate. He notes that young children who view shul as a playground act inappropriately by defiling the *shul's kedusha and disturbing* the adults. The worst part, he explains, is that the child actually gets miseducated to see shul as a place to do everything other than davening.

> In today's times, there are children who come to Shul who cause those who bring them to get punished, as they come to desecrate the holiness of the Shul, and play in it like they play in the streets. One kid laughs with another, another kid hits another, another sings, another cries, another shouts, another runs around and chases a friend. Some children even do their needs in Shul and are required to be cleaned and removed. At times, the father gives his child a Sefer and the child throws it on the floor, or tears it. To summarize, in conclusion these children disturb the worshipers and desecrate the name of Hashem. One who brings such children to Shul should not aspire to receive reward and is rather to worry of the punishment that is befitting him ... Furthermore, at times the parent begins playing with the child during his own prayer. The greatest evil of all this is that the child will grow up accustomed to his ill treatment of Davening and a Shul and continue to do so when older. Accordingly, one is not to bring very small children to Shul as he only loses out by doing so.

According to the Shelah, one must know their children. Those who will act improperly in shul will not bring reward, either practically or educationally to their parents. They will disturb others and be negatively impacted from the experience. The Mishna Berura, when citing the Shelah, notes that his words only apply to the young children, but one should certainly bring a child old enough to understand, making sure to guide them to act properly in shul.

The Mishna Berura repeats this idea in Hilchot Megilla (689:18), decrying bringing boisterous children to the Megilla reading. He notes that besides the disruption, there are no educational goals achieved when bringing loud children to shul. Interestingly, the *Chelkat Yaakov* (O.C. 234) differs and says regarding Megilla there is a special reason to bring children due to *Pirsumei Nissa*, publicizing the miracle. Even children who don't understand will be curious, and through their questions will begin to appreciate and understand Purim.[221]

What does this mean practically?

As the Mishna Berura notes from the Shelah, it is hard to imagine any short-term or long-term benefits for children who will misbehave in shul. Neverthelees, providing children with experiences that will have long-term positive effects even before they can fully comprehend them is essential. For quiet children, it might be bringing them to the Beit Midrash like Rav Yehoshua's mother. Those who enjoy shul can be brought weekly. Nevertheless, efforts should be extended for all children to gain from the shul experience, at least for more experiential events such as Megilla reading. This might require the parents to hear the Megilla at a different time so they can focus on their children when bringing them to the reading. It also might call for bringing children at the end of shul for Adon Olam or for as long as they can be awed before losing concentration and acting out. Creating *tefillat yeladim* options, allowing children to have their own tefilla uniquely catered to their needs, seems to provide a fantastic opportunity for age-appropriate intellectual appreciation and an opportunity for a greater experience. One thing is clear, *Hakhel* is a once in seven-year experience-focused event, and we should do our best to include our children in it.

Everyone Has a Part

It is notable that although the *pasuk* mentions that men, women, and children should attend *Hakhel*, and *Chazal* assign different goals to each group, it is clear from the Rambam's language that the primary distinction is between those who comprehend and those who do not.

> **Even great Sages who know** the entire Torah **are obligated to listen** with exceedingly great concentration. **One who is unable to hear should focus his attention** on this reading, for Scripture established it solely to strengthen true faith. He should see himself as if he was just now commanded regarding the Torah and heard it from the Almighty. (*Hilchot Chagiga* 3:6)

Hakhel concretizes the idea that every individual has his or her own portion in the Torah, some connecting intellectually and others experientially. The experience of Har Sinai is democratic; it is intended for everyone, independent of stature, previous knowledge, or

---

221 The Chelkat Yaakov doesn't advocate bringing children who will misbehave to shul, or even to Megilla, but adds that there is a clear benefit in all children attending the once a year Megilla readings, as they involve an experience of Pirsumei Nissa, and any curious child stands to gain.

intellectual capacity.[222]

Additionally, everyone needs to recognize that at times even the intellectually minded need experiences. Rav Yosef Dov HaLevi Solveitchik, the Rav zt" l, discusses the need to approach the Torah with childlike excitement alongside an intellectual pursuit of its wisdom.

In a eulogy for one of his revered teachers, Rav Chaim Heller zt" l, the Rav describes how truly great Jewish scholars posses not only intellectural maturity and creativity with "depth, scope and sharpness" of thought, but also the playfulness and innocence of a child, full of curiosity, enthusiasm and limitless faith. There he describes the "halakhic man-child":

> "The adult is too clever. Utility is his guiding light. The experience of God is unavailable to those approaching it with a businesslike attitude. Only the child can breach the boundaries that segregate the finite from the infinite. Only the child with his simple faith and fiery enthusiasm can make the miraculous leap into the bosom of God... When it came to faith, the giants of Torah, the geniuses of Israel, became little children, with all their ingenuousness, gracefulness, simplicity, their tremors of fear, their vivid experiences and their devotion to them... Whenever [Moshe] fell before God, he cried like a child. Who can fall before his father, raise his eyes to him alone, to seek consolation and salvation, if not the child! ... The mature, the adult, are not capable of the all-embracing and all-penetrating outpouring of the soul. The most sublime crown we can give a great man sparkles with the gems of childhood." (Divrei Hagut Ve-ha'arakha, pp.159-160; in English: Shiurei Harav, pp.63-64)

Rav Soloveitchik (*"Al Ahavat Ha-Torah U-Ge'ulat Nefesh Ha-Dor"*) describes a dialectic of *"gadlut ha-mochin"* and *"katnut ha-mochin"* that illustrates the two elements, intellectual and experiential, that are critical to the Jewish experience. Rav Aharon Lichtenstein has paraphrased the former as "the depth and force of a powerful mind mastering its environment and impacting upon it," and the latter as "the simplicity of the child ... the archetype of a helpless humble spirit groping towards his Father and finding solace in Him and through Him" ("The Rav at Jubilee: An Appreciation," *Tradition* 30:4 [Summer 1996], p. 50).[223] Although *gadlut ha-mochin* is the necessary starting point for a scholar, those who lack the "naive curiosity, natural enthusiasm, eagerness, and spiritual restlessness" of the child, as well as his sense of dependence and unlimited trust, cannot truly pray or have faith. In effect, they cannot approach God.

Rav Soloveitchik bemoans a young generation of *talmidei chachamim* who are intellectually proficient but experientially lacking:

> Therefore, I hereby announce that I am able to identify one of those responsible for

---

222 We might further add that just as one is never too young to take part in the Revelation experience, one is never too old to learn Torah. As the great Rabbi Akiva illustrated, one can begin learning at the age 40. My own grandfather, Leonard Scheinberg of blessed memory, learned to read Hebrew in his seventies and began learning *gemara* in his eighties. It is never too late to connect to Hashem through the mind as well as the heart.

223 See also the Rav's eulogy for Rav Chaim Heller, *Shiurei HaRav*, pp.63-64.

the present situation - and that is I myself. I have not fulfilled my obligation as a guide and teacher in Israel. I lacked the spiritual energies which a teacher and a rabbi needs, or I lacked the necessary will, and did not dedicate everything I had to my goal. While I have succeeded, to a great or small degree, as a teacher and guide in the area of *gadlut ha-mochin* - my students have received much Torah from me, and their intellectual stature has been strengthened and increased during the years they have spent around me - I have not seen much success in my efforts in the experiential area. I was not able to live together with them, to cleave to them and to transfer to them from the warmth of my soul. My words, it seems, have not kindled the divine flame in sensitive hearts. I have sinned as a disseminator of the Torah of the heart... Blame me for the mistake. (Translation based on Rav Lichtenstein, "The Rav at Jubilee," p. 55)

Hakhel seeks to produce both *gadlut hamochin* and *katnut hamochin*, the intellectual and the experiential. After a year of Torah study, on the brink of a return to backbreaking physical labor, the Torah reminds us that the intellectual attainments of the year must be concretized with the experiential power of the Har Sinai experience.

Inculcating Fear of God

The second stated goal of *Hakhel* is inculcating *yirat Hashem*, fear of God:

And that their children, who have not known anything, may hear, and learn to fear the Lord your God, all the days that you live in the land. (*Devarim* 31:13)

This was similarly the explicit goal of the overwhelming experience of *Matan Torah*. The Torah describes the thunder, lighting, trumpets, and smoke, all of which led to the trembling nation asking for a human intermediary to convey the word of Hashem. When Moshe Rabbeinu tried to calm their fears, he elucidated that one of the goals of the experience was to instill the fear of Hashem and thereby prevent sin:

וַיֹּאמֶר מֹשֶׁה אֶל הָעָם אַל תִּירָאוּ כִּי לְבַעֲבוּר נַסּוֹת אֶתְכֶם בָּא הָאֱלֹהִים וּבַעֲבוּר תִּהְיֶה יִרְאָתוֹ עַל פְּנֵיכֶם לְבִלְתִּי תֶחֱטָאוּ:

Moshe said to the people, "Do not be afraid, for God has come to test you, and that his fear may be before you, that you will not sin." (*Shemot* 20:17)

Similarly, in *Parashat Va'etchanan*, we are instructed to constantly remember the Revelation at Sinai, the goal of which was to instill *yirat Hashem*:

רַק הִשָּׁמֶר לְךָ וּשְׁמֹר נַפְשְׁךָ מְאֹד פֶּן תִּשְׁכַּח אֶת הַדְּבָרִים אֲשֶׁר רָאוּ עֵינֶיךָ וּפֶן יָסוּרוּ מִלְּבָבְךָ כֹּל יְמֵי חַיֶּיךָ וְהוֹדַעְתָּם לְבָנֶיךָ וְלִבְנֵי בָנֶיךָ: יוֹם אֲשֶׁר עָמַדְתָּ לִפְנֵי ה' אֱלֹהֶיךָ בְּחֹרֵב בֶּאֱמֹר ה' אֵלַי הַקְהֶל לִי אֶת הָעָם וְאַשְׁמִעֵם אֶת דְּבָרַי אֲשֶׁר יִלְמְדוּן לְיִרְאָה אֹתִי כָּל הַיָּמִים אֲשֶׁר הֵם חַיִּים עַל הָאֲדָמָה וְאֶת בְּנֵיהֶם יְלַמֵּדוּן:

But take utmost care and watch yourselves scrupulously, so that you do not forget the things that you saw with your own eyes and so that they do not fade from your heart as long as you live, and make them known to your children and your children's children: The day you stood before Hashem your God at Chorev, when Hashem said to me, "Gather Me the people that I may enable them to hear My words, such that they may learn to fear Me, all the days that they live on the earth, and that they may teach this message to their children." (*Devarim* 4:9-10)

The once-in-history experience of the Revelation at Sinai was meant to transmit fear of God that would last from one generation to the next. According to the Ramban (*Devarim* 4:9 and commentary on *Sefer HaMitzvot, mitzvot* omitted by the Rambam 2), there is a negative commandment not to forget the experience at Har Sinai and a corresponding affirmative obligation to transmit that experience to future generations.[224] Through remembering this experience, one should be overcome by the fear of God, and then to communicate this experience further:

> But, in my opinion, this verse is a negative commandment ... that you not forget the assembly at Mount Sinai or anything that your eyes saw there; the voices and the lightning, His glory and His greatness, and the words that you heard there out of the fire. And you shall teach all the things that your eyes saw at that great assembly to your sons and to your sons' sons forever. And He explains the reason, for God arranged for this assembly so that you would learn to fear Him all the days, and that you would teach your children for all generations. (Ramban, *Devarim* 4:9)[225]

Rav Aharon Lichtenstein (ibid.) points out that although there is a daily requirement to remember the Revelation at Sinai and to constantly remind ourselves of its significance, the message of *yira* is reinforced periodically through the event of *Hakhel*, which enables future generations to relive the Sinai experience. The "spectacle" of *Hakhel* provided the experiential aspects. The trumpets sounding on *Har HaBayit* echoed the trumpets that sounded at Har Sinai. The goal of both experiences was to instill *yirat Hashem*.

Torah Study, Humility, and the King of Israel

The element of transmitting the awesomeness of the experience of Sinai is critical, because Torah learning devoid of fear of God is worthless:

> Rabba bar Rav Huna said: Any person who has Torah in him but does not have fear of Heaven is like a treasurer to whom they gave keys to the inner doors of the treasury but they did not give keys to the outer door. With what key will he enter? ... Rav Yehuda said: The Holy One, Blessed be He, only created His world so that people would fear before Him, as it is stated: "And God has so made it that men should fear before Him" (*Kohelet* 3:14). (*Shabbat* 31a)

The relationship between *yirat Hashem* and Torah study is actually symbiotic. While *talmud Torah* without fear of God is worthless, Torah learning can help instill greater *yira*.

---

224 It is notable that in his commentary on the Torah, the Ramban emphasizes that there is a negative commandment not to forget the assembly at Mount Sinai and a positive commandment to teach about that assembly to the coming generations. In his strictures to the *Sefer HaMitzvot*, however, the Ramban includes both elements in the negative commandment: We must not forget the assembly at Sinai and we must not refrain from teaching about this assembly to our children and grandchildren.

225 The Ramban further notes that remembering Har Sinai is essential for imparting *emuna* (faith), as we are the only religion that claims a national revelation. Thus, the transmission of this message from generation to generation is a testament to its authenticity. The importance of national revelation plays a significant role in the *Kuzari* (Metzuda Edition, pp. 2-3, 96-9, 148-9). See Rabbi Dovid Gottlieb, *Living Up to the Truth* (1996), pp. 40–47, who explains the *Kuzari*'s argument. Remembering the Har Sinai experience is an important *mitzvah*, as it is not only to remind us that our Torah is God-given but also to reinject us with the *emuna* in the national revelation that our ancestors personally witnessed and experienced.

The Rambam describes (*Sefer Ha-Mitzvot, Asseh* 3-4) the path to a deeper relationship with God involves contemplating the Torah and appreciating its wisdom. Through learning God's Torah in its infinite wisdom, the individual is taken aback by his own insignificance. The experience involves not only intellectual comprehension, but inititates a fundamental change in self-perception. Fear of God leads to humility in the individual, who no longer views himself with a sense of self-importance.

Since the Torah connects us to Hashem, it also clarifies the sheer distance between humans and God and requires we all approach it with the necessary humility. Thus, Moshe Rabbenu was the only one fit to receive the Torah at Har Sinai. Humility, a direct outgrowth of *yirat Hashem*, was the very purpose of the event. In order for the giving of the Torah to have its desired effect, it would not be enough for the experience to be overwhelming; the one receiving it would need to embody the humility that stems from an awareness of the encounter. Furthermore, even the location where the Torah would be given imparts this lesson of humility; Har Sinai was chosen specifically because it was not a lofty mountain.[226]

The King's Role

We noted above that the king leads *Hakhel* as a "stand-in" for Moshe Rabbeinu in the reenactment of the Revelation at Sinai. Perhaps we can further suggest that it is due to the dual goals of *Hakhel* – to teach Torah and to inculcate fear of God – that it is specifically the king who is the "master of ceremonies" at that event.

Because of the king's extensive authority and the many honors bestowed upon him, he is at great risk of becoming haughty and of abusing his power as a result.[227] To mitigate this danger, the Torah instructs that a king should carry a Torah scroll with him at all times:

וְהָיְתָה עִמּוֹ וְקָרָא בוֹ כָּל יְמֵי חַיָּיו לְמַעַן יִלְמַד לְיִרְאָה אֶת ה' אֱלֹהָיו לִשְׁמֹר אֶת כָּל דִּבְרֵי הַתּוֹרָה הַזֹּאת וְאֶת הַחֻקִּים הָאֵלֶּה לַעֲשֹׂתָם: לְבִלְתִּי רוּם לְבָבוֹ מֵאֶחָיו וּלְבִלְתִּי סוּר מִן הַמִּצְוָה יָמִין וּשְׂמֹאול לְמַעַן יַאֲרִיךְ יָמִים עַל מַמְלַכְתּוֹ הוּא וּבָנָיו בְּקֶרֶב יִשְׂרָאֵל:

And it shall be with him, and he shall read therein all the days of his life; that he may learn to fear the Lord his God, to keep all the words of this law and these statutes, to do them, that his heart be not lifted up above his brethren, and that he turn not aside from the commandment, to the right hand, or to the left; to the end that he may prolong his days in his kingdom, he and his children, in the midst of Israel. (*Devarim* 17:19-20)

Although the king is the representative of the nation, deep down, he is like everyone else. He has his unique challenges and a heightened need to beware of arrogance, but the methodology for overcoming that challenge is through the Torah that belongs to all. In carrying the Torah scroll with him, the king is reminded that his crown is not the ultimate

---

226 This is alluded to by the strange phrasing of the *mishna* (*Avot* 1:1), משה קבל תורה מסיני, "Moshe received the Torah from Sinai." Why does the *mishna* seem to imply that Moshe received the Torah from the mountain itself? The *Tiferet Yisrael* explains: "This terminology indicates that Moshe was exceedingly humble, and through [his humility], he received the Torah, which is compared to water, as it always goes to the lowest point (*Ta'anit* 7a), and he therefore received the Torah from Sinai, the lowest of mountains, to indicate that only through humility, the foundation of all positive character traits, can one merit to receive the Torah."

227 See *Shmuel I* ch. 8, where Shmuel HaNavi notes these dangers.

crown; the crown of Torah reigns supreme, and that crown belongs to anyone who wishes to take it.[228] The king leads *Hakhel* to demonstrate that the Torah guides the entire Jewish People and engenders humility – even in the most powerful national figure.

Furthermore, *Halacha* distinguishes between a king, who is not entitled to waive his honor (see *Ketubot* 17a), and a Torah scholar who is. While one might explain the distinction is due to the intensity of the honor, Tosafot (*Shavuot* 32b) explains otherwise. Tosafot reason that the honor due to a Torah scholar really belongs to him, as the Torah he has learned becomes part of him, and therefore, he can decide to forfeit that honor. On the other hand, the honor given to a king is not for himself, but for the nation he represents. Honoring a human king provides a model for the nation to relate to the King of all Kings, Hashem. The fear of a human king is natural to everyone. Seeing him dressed in his royal garb at the top of the mountain while reading the Torah gives the nation a relatable example for what it means to fear the real King – God.

It is for these reasons that the king is chosen to perform the *Hakhel*. Not only is he the leader tasked by Moshe to give voice to God's words, but he is as an individual who constantly grappling with fear of God, while at the same time providing a model for the people of how to relate to God.

The Post-Shemitta *Hakhel*

With this understanding of *Hakhel* and its goals, we can better appreciate why Hakhel is performed on the Sukkot immediately following *shevi'it*.

Sukkot heralds the new *shevi'it* cycle as the nation will return to cultivating the land immediately after its conclusion. The Jewish nation descends from Avraham, who specifically chose a life of shepherding rather than agricultural acquisition. That time would only come as the nation would leave Egyptian bondage and forge a charitable society on holy soil. Indeed, the *mitzvah* of *yishuv Eretz Yisrael* would require physically building the land, but it would be done through the Torah's blueprint for a redeemed society.

Before the initial settlement of the land, at the end of his life, Moshe Rabbenu performs the initial Torah transmission and requires the nation to perform it anew every seven years. That *Hakhel* marked the transition from a miraculous desert existence, as a nation sustained by divine blessing and manna from the heavens had no need for agricultural involvement . During *shevi'it*, the Jewish nation essentially lives as they did in the desert.[229] Rather than working the land, they live by divine blessing. The overabundant yield of the sixth year is the double portion of "manna" that precedes the Shabbat. For a year, recognizing God's blessing from behind the scenes is far easier. What will happen as the nation returns to the fields? *Hakhel* reminds us of the importance of seeing Hashem's hand

---

228 The Rambam (*Hilchot Talmud Torah* 3:1) explains that of the three crowns that a Jew can wear, two are restricted; the crown of *Kehuna* (priesthood) is limited to Aharon's descendants, and the crown of Kingship is limited to the descendants of Dovid HaMelech. The crown of Torah, however, is open to all and is greater than the two others.

229 The basis of the idea emerged from a conversation with Rabbi David Silverberg.

in our agricultural success. Even when planting and harvesting in the land, it is the divine blessing that is the silent partner in our success.[230] Torah and its study are not impediments to financial success from agricultural development, but rather underlie the identity of our nation and are vital ingredients in bringing about the best of the Jewish farmers in *Eretz Yisrael*.

We reinforce these values every seven years following *shevi'it*, when we recreate the *Hakhel* concluding the nation's sojourn in the desert as a prelude to years of planting in the land of Israel. *Hakhel* ensures that the next six years of farming in the land will be guided by the Torah, a magnet for blessing, and it will remind us of the unbroken transmission from Moshe Rabbenu to the Torah leaders of subsequent generations.

Furthermore, during the entire year of *shevi'it*, socioeconomic divisions in society have been erased. Crops were *hefker* and free for all to take. Now, the people who had broken down those divisions are returning to work their lands. The distinctions between the wealthy and the poor will once again become pronounced, and individuals are liable to focus on what distinguished them from their neighbors. Before the new agricultural year begins, the Har Sinai experience of *Hakhel* reminds us that the connection to Torah requires humility. Even kingship does not accord one true honor; those with wealth alone should certainly focus on what binds us a nation, rather than what separates us.

Perhaps most importantly, one express purpose of the year of *shevi'it* is to have everyone fill the study halls of the *beit midrash*. During this year, the farmer's free time can be focused on learning Torah. *Shevi'it* is an entire year in which we reconnect to the Har Sinai experience.[231] After a year of Torah study and re-experiencing the intellectual connection to the Torah of Sinai, as the farmer returns to his fields, the Torah-centered event of *Hakhel* concretizes the lessons of *shevi'it* while preparing for six years to come. The primary focus is not the learning *per se*, but rather internalizing the fear of Hashem and living with the Har Sinai experience every day.

The deep connection between *shevi'it* and Sinai is highlighted by the *Ketav Sofer*, who goes so far as to state that *shevi'it*, like Sinai, is the foundation of all the *mitzvot*:

> "*BeHar Sinai*: What does the sabbatical year have to do with Mount Sinai?" In other words, it is indisputable that the Torah was given at Mount Sinai. Why, then, did He specify here "at Mount Sinai"? **Since this *mitzvah* is the basis and foundation of all commandments**, he writes here that it was proclaimed from Sinai and inclusive of all commandments.

---

230 Rabbi Dovid Zvi Hoffman (commentary on *Devarim*) explains that during the other years of the seven-year cycle, the Jews would come to Jerusalem at the close of the harvest season to offer prayers and sacrifices of thanksgiving for the produce of that year. After *shevi'it*, a year without a regular harvest or physical toil, the nation would nevertheless thank God for sustaining them as the Torah promised.

231 The Ibn Ezra (*Shemot* 24:7) points out that just as the weekly Shabbat serves as an oasis in time for spiritual solitude and Torah growth, *shevi'it* serves this purpose for an entire year. Similarly the Seforno (*Vayikra* 25:2-4) explains that the Torah refers to *shevi'it* as a year of "*shabbat laHashem*" because one's break from work can be dedicated to seeking God.

Although the laws of *shevi'it* do not apply during the six years of work, the Torah and its public reading are part and parcel of Jewish life. The more we recognize that Torah binds our entire nation and that what unifies us is far more than what divides us, the more we can enable every rendezvous we have with Torah to reinforce our national unity and responsibility for one another. *Hakhel's* lesson is eternal, as it combines with all encounters one has with the Torah over the next seven years.

The Weekly and Yearly *Hakhel* Experiences

Public reading of the Torah

The more we learn about *Hakhel* and its goals the more we recognize its importance. Recalling the experience at Har Sinai is a daily *mitzvah* but throughout the week we seek a communal *Hakhel* element as well. One of the goals of the communal *keriat haTorah* (public Torah readings), on Shabbat, festivals, and throughout the week is for a Hakhel-like experience. The Rambam explains that these readings were introduced to have the people re-experience "*shemiat haTorah*,": "So that the people would not have three days pass without hearing the Torah" (Rambam, Hilchot Teffila 12:1-2). Hearing the Torah is one of *Hakhel's* goals. Thus, for example, the gemara (Megilla 21a) derives from the description of *Ma'amad Har Sinai* that one should stand during the *keriat haTorah*. (Although the Shulchan Aruch [O.C. 146:4] rules that only the reader is required to stand, the Rema cites the view of the Maharam of Rotenberg that the entire congregation should stand during *keriat haTorah*.)[232]

Rav Soloveitchik (And From There You Shall Seek, pp. 139-140) expresses this idea clearly: "The purpose of reading the Torah aloud in the synagogue is not solely to teach the congregation, but also to arrange an encounter with God, as experienced by our ancestors at Mount Sinai. Every act of reading from the Torah is a new giving of the Torah, a revival of the wondrous stand at the foot of the flaming mountain…"

Concluding the Torah and *Simchat Torah*

It is not only the public reading of the Torah but even the schedule for doing so has its roots in *Hakhel*. We conclude the Torah every year on *Simchat Torah*, the same holiday where *Hakhel* was performed. Could there be any connection?

Our custom for public Torah reading is based upon Babylonian custom, which is followed

---

232 The *Zohar* (*Parashat Vayakhel*) describes at length how the Torah reading is supposed to resemble, and on some level reenact, the Revelation at Har Sinai:

When the Torah scroll is brought up to the table, all of the people must arrange themselves with dread, fear, trembling, and quaking. They must direct their hearts as if they were now standing on Mount Sinai to receive the Torah. They must listen and incline their ears, and they are not permitted to open their mouths and talk even about Torah matters, and certainly not about other matters… Only one person is permitted to read from the Torah scroll at a time, and all the others must silently listen to the words, so that they hear the words from his mouth as if they were receiving the Torah at that moment on Mount Sinai… All must be silent as one person reads, as it is written (*Shemot* 20:1): "And God spoke all these words, saying"… The one who reads from the Torah must direct his heart and will to these words, and he must understand that he is a messenger of the Holy One, blessed be He, in arranging these words to cause them to be heard by all the people, as he stands as if he were God…

today in all Jewish communities. It calls for completing the reading of the Torah once a year, by reading *Ve-Zot ha-Berakha* on *Simchat Torah* (Shemini Atzeret in Eretz Israel, and the second day of Shemini Atzeret outside Eretz Israel). Immediately, the new cycle begins with the reading of *Parashat Bereishit* on the first Shabbat after Sukkot.

The Babylonian custom seems to be focused on learning Torah, ensuring we learn the entire Torah every year, but the public setting involves a Har Sinai experience.

In fact, the obligation of *Shnayim Mikra V'Echad Targum*, reading the Torah twice and explaining it once, ensures that there is a public Torah reading for public Torah learning, a private one for individual learning, and a requirement that the Torah be explained and understood in at least one of those settings. The learning and studying Torah is an integral part of the cycle.

It is on this backdrop that we can understand how our yearly *Simchat Torah* seems to be an expression of *Hakhel*, where we gather together around the *Bimah* (the place the Torah is read) and surround it with an experiential celebration. *Simchat Torah's* focus is far less the learning, but the Har Sinai experience is paramount. Halachic works (see Mishna Berura 669) point out how it is improper to learn during the time of the *Hakafot*, as it is a time of experience, a community's *Hakhel* par-excellence.

The Ancient Eretz Yisrael Custom: *Simchat Torah* and *Hakhel*

The ancient Eretz Israel custom, on the other hand, was to complete the reading of the entire Torah once every three years. This appears in the Gemara in *Megila*:

> The people of the west [= Eretz Israel] complete the reading of the Torah once every three years. (*Megila* 29b)

In Eretz Israel the customary practice was to read *sedarim*, and not entire *parashot*; each Shabbat they would read one *seder*. Interestingly, although the Gemara in *Megila* mentions a three-year cycle other sources indicate three and a half years. The Marharshal in *Yam shel Shelomo* discusses the differences between Babylonian and Israel custom, noting that in Eretz Yisrael *Simchat Torah* was every three and a half years:

> The people of the east celebrate *Simchat Torah* every year on the festival of Sukkot, and in every province, and in every city, they read the same *parasha*. However, the people of Eretz Israel celebrate *Simchat Torah* **only every three and a half years.** And on the day that they complete the *parasha* that is read in this place it is not read in another place. (*Yam shel Shelomo*, end of *Bava Kama*)

This three-and-a-half-year cycle seems to emerge clearly as connected to the *Hakhel* experience in *Eretz Yisrael*. Much like the initial *Hakhel* experience in *Parashat Vayelech*, which was performed after concluding the Torah, our pubic Torah reading experiences *shnayim mikra*, two public Torah readings, every seven years, concluding at the *Hakhel* experience on Sukkot.

Hakhel was the initial *Simchat Torah*- in the presence of the entire Jewish nation, as the Torah is finished a second time during the seven-year *Shemitta* cycle, the nation rejoices as one, hearing the Torah as they initially did on Har Sinai.

What emerges from this understanding sheds light on the ancient *Eretz Yisrael* custom and explains why it is no longer practiced in Israel.[233]

The idea that our *Simchat Torah* is connected to *Hakhel* actually has a basis in the early commentaries. Abarbanel (*Devarim* 31:10) makes this assertion explaining that during the six years of the *Shemitta* cycle the High Priest, prophet, judge or leader of the people would read in public from the Torah and complete the first four of the books of the Torah. In the seventh year, the king would read from Devarim. He explains that from this the custom in our days was established on *Shmini Atzeret*, on the last day, we call it Simhat Torah, on that day we finish the Torah and the leader of the community gets up and finishes the Torah, reading himself. He reads the portion "*Ve'Zot haB'racha*" to resemble the act of the king in ancient times.

In fact, although our practice based on the Talmud Bavli is that *Hakhel* was observed on Chol HaMoed sukkot, the Talmud Yerushalmi differs, explaining it was performed "...at the conclusion of the last day of the Festival... ". This is exactly as the Abarbanel explains: *Hakhel* and Shemini Atzeret are one, and our current *Simchat Torah* is an attempt to re-experience it.

It should not surprise us at all that the Yerushalmi saw *Hakhel* as being the day of *Simchat Torah*- specifically the *yerushalmi* which observed the old *Eretz Yisrael* cycle of Torah reading most clearly equates the day of celebration of *Hakhel* with our *Simchat Torah*. Just as *Hakhel* concluded the *Shemitta* year and allowed the nation to begin the next cycle with its lessons inculcated, so too *Simchat Torah* concludes one Torah reading and begins the Torah again with its lessons that should accompany us throughout the year. *Simchat Torah* is clearly focused on experience far more than learning. In the absence of Hakhel, we need a unified acceptance and outpowering of love for the Torah every year. And this event cannot be only for adults, children must take center stage in this endeavor.

In other words, while we might see *Hakhel* as the end of our *Shemitta* cycle, in fact it is only the beginning. Much like our *Simchat Torah* is meant to celebrate the conclusion of the Torah, it begins it anew. As we conclude *Shemitta* with *Hakhel*, we embark on the next six years of planting with *Hakhel* in mind. It is the guiding light for our continued possession of Eretz Yisrael, as some might say עַם יִשְׂרָאֵל בְּאֶרֶץ יִשְׂרָאֵל עַל פִּי תּוֹרַת יִשְׂרָאֵל, *the nation of Israel in the land of Israel based on the Torah of Israel.*

הקהל

Hakhel in our Times

After learning about *Hakhel's* significance, it is surprising that we no longer perform the *mitzvah* as we did in

---

233 *Hakhel* was not merely a once every seven year experience, but there was a seven year cycle of Torah reading to ensure that the nation was constantly connected to *Hakhel* and Har Sinai. As noted above, the original enactment of public Torah reading was by Moshe Rabbeinu. As he finished the Torah and Parashat Vayelech describes the *Hakhel* ceremony amidst Moshe Rabbeinu's transmitting the Torah, Moshe Rabbeinu ensured that the palpable *Hakhel* experience be achieved every seven years in a more modest fashion through keriat HaTorah. Twice over seven years, shnayim mikra, and one targum of the experience that is concretized with *Hakhel*.

Temple times.[234] Rabbi Eliyahu David Rabinowitz-Teomim (known as the Aderet), the father-in-law of Rabbi Kook, asked why *Hakhel* is no longer practiced. He suggests that the Biblical *Hakhel* doesn't apply when *shemitta* is no longer Biblically mandated and the entire Jewish People wouldn't be present for the event.[235] Rabbi Shlomo David Kahane adds that *Hakhel* requires reading the Torah from a section of the Temple Mount where we are not permitted to traverse, and we lack a king to lead the reading.[236]

Nevertheless, although lacking an actual Biblical command, the Aderet wonders why there was never a formal Rabbinic requirement to perform *Hakhel*, at the very least, as a commemoration for Temple times, a *Zecher LeHakhel*?

The Aderet offers some reasons why a Zecher LeHakhel was never officially instituted, but still advises that we perform a *"zecher l'Hakhel,"* a rendition of a *Hakhel*-like experience akin to how it was practiced during *Mikdash* times.[237]

Like many *mitzvot* that are performed *Zecher LeMikdash*, the performance is not only meant to remember the glorious nature of the past, but entails yearning for the redemption. It aims to pave the way for the future, hopefully imminent, when the Mikdash will be rebuilt and *Hakhel* and so much more reinstated. The lack of a Biblical or even rabbinic obligation of *Hakhel* reminds us that despite all we have in the land, something is missing. Reconnecting to the observance and lessons of *Shevi'it*, the ticket to our return to the land, and concluding its messages through *Hakhel*, will hopefully help us speedily return to the Mikdash itself.

The Aderet's suggestion for a *Zecher leHakhel*, a symbolic observance of the *mitzvah* of *Hakhel* has, in fact, been instituted. Every *chol hamoed Sukkot* after the *Shemitta* year, the Israeli chief rabbinate organizes a *Hakhel* ceremony at the Kotel Plaza. At times, there are other *Hakhel* ceremonies as well, but clearly an event symbolizing unity around the Torah would seem to be ideal to have one ceremony attended to by Jews of all stripes.

With the unity and re-experience of Har Sinai, with a newfound connection to Torah and Jewish national unity, and concretized, inculcated Shevi'it values, the chance of celebrating *Hakhel* in the *Mikdash* itself seems attainable more than ever. As the Aderet expressed in his *tefilla* for a return of the Biblical *Hakhel* in the Mikdash:

> May He of Blessed Name grant us to merit to hear the reading of the *Hakhel* in our Temple, from the mouth of our Righteous Messiah, as the Priests and Levites engage in their service and all of Israel is assembled.

May it come speedily in our days.

---

234 See Rav Binyamin Tabory, https://www.etzion.org.il/en/halakha/studies-halakha/philosophy-halakha/parashat-vayelekh-hak%E2%80%99hel-torah-reading-king.

235 The Aderet wrote this in a pamphlet that was originally published anonymously in Warsaw over one hundred years ago, entitled *Zecher L'Mikdash* (A Remembrance of the Temple).

236 The Aderet rejects this latter reasoning, as it is unclear that a king is the only leader who can read the Torah.

237 The Aderet suggests that our observance of *keriat haTorah* and Simchat Torah may, in fact, be attempts at creating such a *zecher l'Mikdash*, as explained earlier.

Afterword

The Covid-19 pandemic that ravaged the world in 2020-2021 has had massive repercussions for society, and as of this writing, it continues to affect people around the world. Who could have imagined that lockdowns, masking, and social distancing would become part of our daily lives and that what we once considered necessities would become off-limits? Society has been turned upside down through anxiety, illness, death, unemployment, and loneliness, and the world economy has taken a massive beating. In some ways, there has been a *shemitta* of sorts, as society as we know it has grinded to a halt.

But while it is true that Covid-19 had some positive effects, including a temporary lapse in pollution and numerous social initiatives that brought out the best in people, how many of them will remain in the long term? As masks (hopefully) come off and the locks are opened, society still lacks a mechanism to ensure these values aren't short-lived.

Shemitta, in contrast, allows the world to take a time out, and *yovel* calls for a complete restart. In an agricultural society, *shemitta* not only calls for more limited agricultural production, but a year off, a rest period for the rich and poor alike. Preparation in the preceding years is an integral part of ensuring successful accommodation during *shevi'it*, but it also allows for a buildup. Coupled with the divine *beracha* of increased yield in the sixth year, there is an understanding that there will be a break, a year when the wheels of progress push towards another form of advancement – when the economy can be set aside for the sake of growth in realms other than business.

In the *Bein Adam LaMakom* arena, *shevi'it* affords a year to return to Har Sinai and learn Torah while being supported by the sixth year's blessing. *Shevi'it* is a year of harnessing and fortifying *emuna* and *bitachon*, trust and reliance on God. It illustrates that that land is His and that its agricultural beauty and yield are divine blessings.

In the realm of *Bein Adam LaChavero*, *shevi'it* provides the opportunity for dignified treatment of the poor, breaking down societal barriers as everyone shares, rather than gives and takes. *Shevi'it* envisions a redeemed economy and a unity whereby the nation becomes far greater than the sum of its parts.

The *Bein Adam LeAtzmo* lessons of *shevi'it* ensure a refocus on who we are and who we want to be. We can downgrade our materialistic needs and invest in our character and spiritual development.

Additionally, *shevi'it* provides the opportunity for strengthening our relationship with the land in general and our Land in particular. Its *Bein Adam LeArtzo* lessons include recognition that we live in God's world as His partners in helping the world achieve its purpose. The more we appreciate that God appointed us as His custodians of the land, the more we will consider if we are misusing the world He entrusted to us. And the more we recognize the uniqueness of our Land and that human efforts are not the primary cause of its agricultural success, the more we realize that Eretz Yisrael is uniquely suited for our nation to fulfill its destiny.

Shevi'it allows us to reflect on the Torah's perspective on the ideal economy, which rejects both pure capitalism and pure socialism. There is no doubt that much of what *shevi'it* has to teach us is very relevant for our contemporary world, in which the imbalance of wealth in our society is often extreme. Doing one's part to lessen the gaps both practically and attitudinally is an excellent way of connecting to *shevi'it*'s ideals.

The opportunity to once again fulfill the *mitzvot* of *shevi'it* is a realization of the Torah's promise in *Parashat Bechukotai*. *Shemitta* is so essential for our life in the Land that its nonobservance brought about our exile, but the land waited, remaining faithful and refusing to grow for anyone else. The modern agricultural revolution in Israel is a testament to the divine hand in history and the unique relationship between God, His Torah, His nation, and His land.

* * *

After learning about *shevi'it*, its centrality in the Torah, and its various themes, we are hopefully left with the inspiration to bring its messages to life. But how can we realize that goal?

As the Jews returned to the land and the land started to grow, *shemitta* observance once again became a reality – and a challenge. But over the years, this challenge has become the lot of an increasingly smaller population in the land. There is no doubt that *shemitta* will palpably affect the lives of farmers, but farmers no longer constitute the majority of society; only two-percent of the Israeli population currently work in agriculture. We live off the land, but we are not an agrarian society. For those who are lucky enough to own gardens in Eretz Yisrael, some of the agricultural *halachot* of *shevi'it* will be experienced, but with proper preparation, the impact will be minimal.

Most of us confront *shevi'it* as consumers – and at times, we may find its effect on our normal routine to be difficult. Some will be hard-pressed to find their favorite fruits or vegetables; others might wonder why some produce seems to be more expensive. Still, others will fret about whether it is proper to eat at the home of friends who either do or do not rely on the *heter mechira*. Many will be so worried about how to treat *kedushat shevi'it* produce that they will distance themselves from it as much as possible.

Throughout this work, we have presented the laws of *shevi'it* as prescriptions of something greater than simply the restrictions they outline. If we succeeded in conveying this message, the reader will focus his or her efforts on how to fulfill *shevi'it*, rather than how to avoid it. Understanding the necessity of *shevi'it* and its varied goals should inspire us to do our part in observing its laws and connecting to its goals.

As we discussed in section III, we should let the value system of *shevi'it* guide us regarding which produce to acquire throughout the year. The chance to eat produce with *kedushat shevi'it* is a dream shared by Moshe Rabbeinu and great Jewish leaders throughout the centuries. We have the opportunity! Let's take advantage of it. Consumers have the opportunity to assist their brethren by supporting Jewish farmers, especially those who observe *shemitta* fully. This can be done by contributing to Keren HaShevi'is to support farmers who let their fields lie fallow, joining an *Otzar Beit Din* service that delivers *shemitta* produce throughout Israel, and through additional endeavors.

The centrality of *shevi'it* has led some to search for ways in which even the non-agricultural sectors of society can experience the *mitzvot* of *shemitta*, with some even advocating buying land in order to fulfill the *mitzvah* of letting it lie fallow. This does not, however, provide a full experience of the *mitzvah*. After all, those who buy tiny plots of land and fail to cultivate them can hardly be described as a *giborei ko'ach*, as no particularly great dose of *emuna* or *bitachon* is necessary to do so.

Many recent initiatives have focused on inculcating *shemitta* values into other sectors as well. Debt-relief and debt-forgiveness ventures are an expansion of the values of *shemittat kesafim*. Rav Yoel Bin-Nun has called for an expansion of *shevi'it* to other sectors of the economy. There are business people who have adopted moderate forms of shemitta for their businesses.

Indeed, a year to stop, dedicate our time to learning, and focus on family, other people, and our spiritual lives seems like a dream. Even if we are unable to dedicate an entire year to the endeavor, whatever time we can commit to our loftier goals can be our "*shemitta* time" over the year. The more meaningful we make it, the better chance we will find much more "*shemitta* time," and its impact will become more and more pronounced.

These are all examples of attempting to translate the Torah's timeless values into a modern application for those not involved in agriculture. Still, they must be implemented in a way that retains *shemitta*'s lessons and does not aim to "update" them or supplant them. Rav Zev Weitman emphasizes that these goals, as lofty as they are, should not come at the expense of agricultural *shemitta*:

> There are those who initiate different ideas of extending the feelings of the *shemitta* year and inculcating its lesson to non-agricutural sectors, beyond the mission of helping ensure *shemitta* will be observed properly agriculturally. [This is done through] increasing acts of *tzedaka* and kindness, by recruiting volunteers to assist the needy, by relinquishing collection rights to certain debts, or by donating time to others. Some extend this even to efforts on behalf of safeguarding Hashem's inheritance, the special land we merit, *Eretz Yisrael*, for future generations through initiatives on behalf of protecting the environment and natural resources and the like, and they dedicate this year to ingraining the perspective of purifying our control of the environment, animal life, and nature, and developing a more modest approach to the use of the world and its resources.
>
> This is all good and beautiful and worthy of appreciation after we endeavor to realize *shemitta* as it is presented in the Torah, and on condition that these wonderful initiatives will supplement and add to the fulfillment of *shemitta* as presented in the Torah, with no intent to replace them. (*Shemitta Yisraelit*, June 6, 2021)

It seems to me that there is also another way to strengthen *shemitta* and its values. We have seen that *shemitta* observance is a significant factor in our exile and subsequent return to the land. The land is impacted by every Jew who steps foot on it, and even those who long to do so. Every Jew counts; indeed, the reinstatement of *yovel* (and the Biblical obligation of *shemitta*) depends on the nation as a whole living in the Land according to their ancestral plots. If *shemitta* is to succeed in connecting us to our land and strengthening our connection with Har Sinai and Torah study, its seems that one of the most tangible ways of connecting to *shevi'it* values is by strengthening Torah communities in Eretz Yisrael – especially those conducive to *olim* – by ensuring affordable housing and shared resources, as well as continuing to build up *Eretz Yisrael* physically and spiritually.

This is my personal initiative for *shemitta*, and I'm sure I'm not the only one who has these dreams. Like many aspects of *shemitta*, our strength lies in our unity around a shared mission.

A Parting Message

Throughout this book, we have quoted Rav Avraham Yitzchak HaKohen Kook's teachings regarding *shemitta* and related matters. More than many others, Rav Kook discussed the implications of *shemitta*'s return to the forefront at a time when the nation is returning to the land, but realities make the strict observance of its laws difficult. He firmly believed in the power of *shemitta* and *yovel* to cure society of many of its ills by providing a year in which to break out of everyday occupations and focus on spiritual needs, yet he also recognized that the ideal state has not yet been achieved. Indeed, perhaps it is achievable only in the Messianic Age.

In a powerful letter (dated 24 Sivan, 5675/1915), Rav Kook writes that we must anxiously await that moment when *shemitta* will be transformed, while at the same time recognizing the inner spiritual calling that *shemitta* exhibits even in our day:

> Let my master believe me that all these great and lofty things that were stated regarding the holiness of the seventh [year] in the present era were not stated specifically regarding fulfillment of particular deeds, for this holiness pertained even at such time as [the people of] Israel were not in the Land of Israel and the *mitzvah* of the seventh [year] was not fulfilled at all. Principally, it is a function of the gradual spread of holiness through the ages, with the light of the Messiah drawn from potential into reality as they come and go, so that the name of God, may His name be blessed, will be sanctified from one end of the earth to the other and all will form a single group to fulfill His will wholeheartedly. As for [the people of] Israel's preparing themselves with faith and anticipation of the salvation of the light of the Messiah and the full return of the holiness of the Land of Israel, at which point *shemitta* and *yovel* will return in full force, all of the spiritual reparations that are performed in the higher realms, at all levels, draw sustenance from this light. Thus whoever performs an action to broaden the borders of Israel so as to expedite the ingathering of Israel to the Land of Israel, which hastens the redemption — for the ingathering of exiles… precedes the coming of the Messiah, and the light of Israel becomes brighter little by little, as they of blessed memory said of the comparison to "the break of dawn" — he indeed rehabilitates the holiness of the supreme oneness of the principle of the seventh

[year], and there is no end to the holy, supreme delights that are thus multiplied, and they are influenced by the root of his soul and the soul of all Israel…

One who fears God ought to pursue both avenues, by endeavoring practically to bring to life all the aspects of the holiness of the seventh [year] — even in the present era, as much as is possible — and by endeavoring as well to expedite, with his deeds and influences, the rise of the horn of salvation and the revelation of the light of our righteous Messiah, so that these occur sooner, as the lights are operative in their plentiful holiness even if, God forbid, one's deeds are not effective in practice, because the spiritual power of a good intention regarding these holy and lofty things has no limit and no measure. …

We too feel especially privileged to partake of some of the *shemitta* realities that impact the lives of those who dwell in Israel, yet we long for the return of *yovel* and the day when all *shemitta* observance will be complete with the arrival of the Messiah. Until that day, may it speedily come, we hope that these lessons of *shemitta*, alongside the opportunities for practice, continue to grow, illuminating our perspective on *shemitta* and beyond.

I would be delighted to discuss further any ideas presented in this book.
I can be contacted at ravbinyamin@mizrachi.org.

Shabbat HaAretz Shalom